The Revolution That Failed

UNIVERSITY PRESS OF FLORIDA

Florida A&M University, Tallahassee
Florida Atlantic University, Boca Raton
Florida Gulf Coast University, Ft. Myers
Florida International University, Miami
Florida State University, Tallahassee
New College of Florida, Sarasota
University of Central Florida, Orlando
University of Florida, Gainesville
University of North Florida, Jacksonville
University of South Florida, Tampa
University of West Florida, Pensacola

THE
REVOLUTION
THAT
FAILED

Reconstruction in Natchitoches

Adam Fairclough

UNIVERSITY PRESS OF FLORIDA

Gainesville / Tallahassee / Tampa / Boca Raton

Pensacola / Orlando / Miami / Jacksonville / Ft. Myers / Sarasota

Library of Congress Cataloging-in-Publication Data
Names: Fairclough, Adam, author.
Title: The revolution that failed : reconstruction in Natchitoches / Adam Fairclough.
Description: Gainesville : University Press of Florida, 2018. | Includes
   bibliographical references and index.
Identifiers: LCCN 2017032241 | ISBN 9780813056623 (cloth : alk. paper)
Subjects: LCSH: Natchitoches Parish (La.)—History. | Louisiana—History.
Classification: LCC F377.N4 F35 2018 | DDC 976.3/65—dc23
LC record available at https://lccn.loc.gov/2017032241

The University Press of Florida is the scholarly publishing agency for the State University
System of Florida, comprising Florida A&M University, Florida Atlantic University,
Florida Gulf Coast University, Florida International University, Florida State University,
New College of Florida, University of Central Florida, University of Florida, University
of North Florida, University of South Florida, and University of West Florida.

University Press of Florida
15 Northwest 15th Street
Gainesville, FL 32611-2079
http://upress.ufl.edu

To the memory of
Professor W. A. "Bill" Speck, 1938–2017

CONTENTS

FIGURES

MAPS

ACKNOWLEDGMENTS

I have accumulated many debts during the long gestation of this book. First and foremost, I wish to thank the staffs of the Library of Congress Manuscripts Division, the Washington, D.C., branch of the National Archives, the New-York Historical Society, the Hill Memorial Library Special Collections at Louisiana State University, and the Amistad Research Center at Tulane University. They were all enormously helpful. I am especially indebted to Mary Linn Wernet, director of the Cammie G. Henry Research Center at Northwestern State University of Louisiana in Natchitoches.

Stepping into a controversial field, I was grateful for the encouragement of, among others, Lawrence N. Powell, Paul D. Escott, Michael W. Fitzgerald, J. Mills Thornton III, Michael A. Ross, Leslie Rowland, Michael Perman, Joseph G. Dawson III, and Scott Hovey. Elizabeth Shown Mills generously shared with me her unparalleled knowledge of Natchitoches Parish. Although my disagreements with Eric Foner are plain, all scholars of Reconstruction stand in debt to the superlative scholarship of *Reconstruction: America's Unfinished Revolution*.

The Nederlandse Organisatie voor Wetenschappelijk Onderzoek (NWO) gave a generous grant that not only financed the acquisition of microfilm and digital databases but also funded a Ph.D. student, Mark L. de Vries, and a postdoctoral researcher, David Ballantyne. Working alongside these young scholars was a stimulating experience that added immeasurably to the entire process of research and writing. NWO funding enabled me to devote all of 2013 to the manuscript. During that year I enjoyed an academic affiliation at George Washington University, thanks to the kindness of Eric Arnesen and William Becker.

My Americanist colleagues at Leiden University—Joke Kardux, Eduard van de Bilt, Giles Scott-Smith, and Damian Pargas—made a major contribution, albeit indirect, by providing a collegial environment that made my eleven years at the Institute for History thoroughly enjoyable and rewarding. The Raymond and Beverly Sackler Foundation enabled me to acquire books, periodicals, and microfilm, and Dr. Raymond Sackler took a personal interest in my work. My good friends Ellen Schrecker and the late Marvin Gettleman always provided a welcome for me in New York City, including wonderful cuisine and great conversation about history and politics.

Working with the University Press of Florida has been not merely painless but also enjoyable. Sian Hunter showed confidence in this book from the start and supervised the acquisitions process with speed and efficiency. Ali Sundook showed equal efficiency and helped to keep me on schedule. My copy editor, Jonathan Lawrence, meticulous in his attention to detail, was a pleasure to work with.

My wife, Mary Ellen Curtin, helped and encouraged me every step of the way. Without our ceaseless discussions of Reconstruction, the South, and the significance of race in American history generally, I doubt that this book would ever have been started, let alone completed. My debt to her is profound and ongoing. Thanks, too, to my daughter, Jennifer Fairclough, and my sister, Alison Gelfand, for showing interest and helping to keep me grounded. My son, Arthur, was a constant source of happiness throughout the writing of this book.

Finally, I wish to thank the staff of the Leiden University Medical Center, especially Professor G. P. M. Luyten and Dr. M. Marinkovic, for giving me a new lease on life.

I apologize in advance to anyone whose help I have inadvertently failed to acknowledge. Any factual errors are of course my own responsibility.

INTRODUCTION

To comprehend the spirit and condition of the South today, we must have
constantly in mind both its recent and remote history.

Albion W. Tourgee, *The Invisible Empire* (1880)

In 1867 Congress enfranchised black men in the former Confederacy with
the dual purpose of rendering justice to the freedpeople and making the
Union victory secure. By creating a new black electorate and by disfranchising numerous ex-Confederates, the Republican Party came to control
the state governments of the South. Over time, Republicans lost control
of most, and eventually all, of the southern states. Democratic electoral
victories, however, did not result from the normal swing of the electoral
pendulum but from campaigns based upon threats, intimidation, and
violence.

Congressional Reconstruction, often misnamed "Radical Reconstruction," ended decisively in 1877, when two Republican presidents, outgoing
president Grant and incoming president Hayes, allowed the Democratic
Party to forcibly seize power in Florida, South Carolina, and Louisiana.
Although the Democrats did not immediately disfranchise black voters—
they had pledged not to do so—they used fraud and violence to lock the
Republican Party out of state government. Democracy, in any meaningful
sense of that word, ended. Any semblance of justice and security for the
black population had to wait until the civil rights movement of the 1950s
and 1960s.

The Louisiana parish of Natchitoches (pronounced "Nack-a-tish") is an attractive setting for a study of Reconstruction. For one thing, it provides a
microcosm of Republican politics and government at the local level. Between 1868 and 1878 a coalition of ex-slaves, freeborn blacks, and former

Cane River Country

Map 1. Natchitoches Parish. Reproduced by permission of Louisiana State University Press.

Confederate soldiers governed the parish (county) in the name of the Republican Party. Sustained by black voters and intermittently protected by the U.S. Army, the Republican Party of Natchitoches Parish was the strongest in the Red River valley. Republican control of the state depended upon Natchitoches.

In the second place, the Natchitoches Republican Party was a homegrown political organization. Its most influential leader was a Baptist minister and former slave. The white Republicans were nearly all native Louisianans or residents of long standing: their southern credentials were impeccable. The only "carpetbaggers" in the party were a Freedmen's Bureau agent, who died in 1870, and a black immigrant from Canada. Republicans might have governed Natchitoches Parish indefinitely had they been allowed to vote freely. Time and again black voters spurned Democratic appeals to desert the party; in the face of threats and intimidation, they turned out to cast Republican ballots.

Third, the whites who did their level best to oust the Republicans from power refrained from violence. Throughout this study, Natchitoches Parish appears as an oasis of law and order surrounded by the most violent region of Louisiana. The Colfax massacre, the bloodiest incident of Reconstruction, took place in neighboring Grant Parish. In the adjacent parish of Red River, six white Republicans were murdered in cold blood. The Texas of John Wesley Hardin and his ilk lay close by. But for reasons to do with its peculiar history and culture, Natchitoches suffered relatively little political or racial violence. This is not another Reconstruction "horror story" that focuses upon bloodshed.

The following narrative combines a fine-grain community study with the "big picture" of Reconstruction. The story shifts between Natchitoches Parish, New Orleans (then the state capital), and Washington because the story makes no sense without local, state, and national perspectives. Running throughout is a question that is basic to an understanding of post–Civil War America: Why did Reconstruction fail, and why did it fail so badly?

The setting is the oldest European settlement in Louisiana. Natchitoches began life as French military post in 1714. By 1804, when France ceded control to the United States, it had grown into a community of about nine hundred free people, a slightly larger number of slaves, and a dozen or so *gens de couleur libre* (free blacks). Before it became part of the United States, virtually everyone in Natchitoches spoke French. The few non-French-speakers who settled in Natchitoches quickly learned the language. A relatively even gender balance enabled French-speaking whites to find marriage partners among other French speakers. This fact, and the frequency of second and third marriages, meant that most whites were closely related to each other, adding to the linguistic and cultural unity of the place.[1]

Between the Louisiana Purchase and the Civil War, the population of

Louisiana increased tenfold. Immigrants flocked to the state. New Orleans grew into the largest city in the South. The cultivation of sugar and cotton spread up and down the Mississippi River and its several tributaries. Natchitoches, previously the only European settlement in northern Louisiana with a vast hinterland, lost its isolation when white Americans and black slaves settled the rest of the Red River valley and the surrounding hill country. So vast was its original extent that Natchitoches gave birth to a dozen new parishes, including Winn, De Soto, Sabine, Bienville, Bossier, Claiborne, Webster, and Jackson. Even so, the population of the much-reduced Natchitoches had climbed to 16,699 by 1860, an increase of almost 14,000 over fifty years. After Rapides Parish, Natchitoches was the most populous in the Red River valley.[2]

The introduction of cotton cultivation transformed the local economy. In the eighteenth century Natchitoches had functioned as a fort, a trading post for neighboring Indians, and a center of tobacco production. It had served as the northern terminus of *el camino real*, the road linking Louisiana and Texas that ended in San Antonio. It had possessed strategic significance, marking the military frontier between French Louisiana and Spanish Mexico. By the early nineteenth century the Indian trade had ended, tobacco production had stopped, and Natchitoches had lost its military importance. However, as cotton culture spread westward as far as Texas, Natchitoches Parish quickly became a major center of production and transportation.

The town might have grown much larger but for an act of engineering and an act of nature. In 1838 Captain Henry Shreve, using specially designed steamboats, completed the task of clearing the "Great Raft," a massive logjam of ancient origin that had made the Red River unnavigable for about 160 miles. Natchitoches, north of which boats could not go, had served as the transfer point for all the cotton that came overland from Texas and was then shipped south to New Orleans. Now it lost most of that trade to the new town of Shreveport. Shortly afterward, in 1840, the Red River changed course, leaving Natchitoches with an oxbow lake that was picturesque but useless. The town's access to Red River was now a landing stage, Grand Ecore, four miles away. Natchitoches became, literally, a backwater. The railroad main line passed it by. Natchitoches prospered as a town that served the local cotton planters, but it could never compete with Shreveport, which by 1860 had surpassed it in population. Whereas Shreveport has grown into a substantial city, Natchitoches remains to this day a small town.

Cotton changed the population of Natchitoches. The bountiful economy attracted migrants and immigrants. Most of the Americans came from Louisiana and elsewhere in the South, but some came from points north. The immigrants came from England, Ireland, France, Belgium, Austria, and the German states. The non-white population also changed. While slaves continued to outnumber whites, the number of free blacks increased exponentially. In 1793, Pierre Metoyer, a Frenchman, freed his slave-concubine Marie-Thérèse Coincoin and several of their offspring. The descendants of Metoyer and Coincoin grew into a tightly knit "colony" of closely related families that farmed the flat, fertile area south of Natchitoches town, known as Isle Brevelle, that lay between Cane River and Old River. In 1860 these Creoles of color numbered 411 people and owned 379 slaves among them. Other acts of manumission swelled the total free black population to about a thousand, representing 5 percent of the parish's population. Natchitoches Parish was home to the largest group of free blacks in northern Louisiana by far. Along with St. Landry Parish, it had the largest free black population in the state outside New Orleans.[3]

Although denied the right to vote and hold public office, Louisiana's *gens de couleur libre* had considerably more freedom them free blacks in other slave states. They were also wealthier. The *gens de couleur libre* in Natchitoches Parish were not only exceptionally wealthy compared to free blacks elsewhere in the rural South; they were also better off, on average, than *whites* in Natchitoches Parish.

The *gens de couleur,* especially the inhabitants of Isle Brevelle, did not regard themselves as "black." The term *free black*, a modern construction, is a misnomer that reflects the current habit of applying the word *black* or *African American* to all Americans with some African ancestry. It reflects, too, modern distaste for such terms as *mulatto, quadroon*, and *octoroon*, words that once registered important distinctions not only of color but also of status. In legal terms, the *gens de couleur* constituted a third racial category. Socially, they regarded themselves as distinct from and superior to the "American" blacks. They called themselves "French" or "Creole." They owned slaves. Very light-complexioned, they generally married within their own group. They had good relations and extensive business dealings with the white Creoles.[4]

The large free black population testified to concubinage between masters and slaves. The practice had been relatively uncommon during the colonial era, because the small gender gap enabled white men to find white women as marriage partners. But in the nineteenth century several of the wealthiest cotton planters in Natchitoches Parish lived openly with slave women or free women of color. Marco Givanovich, an immigrant from Austria, formed a lifelong relationship with a slave with whom he fathered a large family. David H. Boullt, originally from Maryland, lived with a free woman of color, reputedly an octoroon, who bore him many racially mixed children. Neither man suffered any loss of social standing in the white community. The New Orleans practice of *plaçage,* whereby wealthy whites kept octoroon mistresses, reflected Louisiana's tolerance of interracial sex. Planters, governors, and businessmen fathered colored children and sometimes acknowledged them. "The mulattoes," wrote Marshall H. Twitchell, a native of Vermont who became the Republican leader of Red River Parish, "did not owe their existence to the white men nearest the social equal of the colored but, on the contrary, to the very highest in social and official life."[5]

The arrival of so many migrants and immigrants after 1804 challenged the French character of Louisiana. So did the influx of English-speaking slaves imported from Florida and other states. By 1860 English-speakers comprised 70 percent of the state's free population. Even in Natchitoches Parish, many newcomers never got beyond rudimentary French. The local newspapers began to print in English as well as French. As Louisiana's non-French-speaking population grew, anglophones sought to make English the official language of the state courts, a first step in supplanting French as the dominant language. The fact that most lawyers were English-speaking Americans added to the pressure to abandon French. The *Natchitoches Union*, edited by an immigrant from France, condemned such pressure, insisting that "no one has the right of suppressing the use of the French language in Louisiana."[6]

Although gradually eroded, French showed remarkable staying power. It remained the first language of the older white families even after they learned English. The free blacks of Isle Brevelle spoke French almost exclusively. A small but steady flow of immigrants from France augmented the French-speaking population. Upon the outbreak of the Civil War, francophone whites formed the Chasseurs à Pied, or Natchitoches Guards. Presenting a flag to the men of the unit, J. C. Janin extolled their identification with France: "All of us, whether the children of Louisiana by birth, or born on the soil of France, have the same blood running in our veins, the French blood. It was the civilizing genius of France which patiently conquered from barbarism the soil which now bears us."[7]

The houses in Natchitoches Parish made French-Creole culture visible to the eye. Many of the plantation homes and farmhouses followed a distinctive style of architecture. The town of Natchitoches looked very different from Alexandria, Shreveport, and Monroe, which were founded much later. Somewhat ironically—because it is so untypical—Natchitoches is a choice location for filmmakers who wish to evoke a timeless Old South. In 1870 Natchitoches was a long, narrow town, stretching about a mile along Cane River but reaching back from the river only two or three blocks.[8]

Religion also sustained French culture. Virtually all francophones, even if they rarely attended church, considered themselves Catholics. Indeed, the Catholic Church virtually monopolized religious life in Natchitoches. The town had no Protestant church of any description until 1843, when Episcopalians began holding Sunday services in a store. Construction on Trinity Episcopal Church started in 1857, but the building was only completed twenty years later.[9]

French-Catholic culture had a profound influence upon the enslaved population. Slaves of French-speaking masters became francophones and were recognized by the Catholic Church. Slaves received baptism from the parish priest, and whites often served as godparents. Slaves sometimes married in the church with the blessing of their masters. The importation of English-speaking slaves after 1804 created a culturally bifurcated slave population. Frederick Law Olmsted, who visited Natchitoches during his journey across the South in 1853–54, heard the slaves on one large plantation speaking English, French, and Spanish among themselves. By 1860 an indeterminate number of English-speaking slaves were holding their own religious services, which centered on preaching from the Bible. Slaves were powerfully attracted to the drama of full-immersion baptism, and after emancipation most of them formed Baptist congregations.[10]

The extent to which the Catholic Church mitigated the cruelest features of slavery is hard to assess. The law was one thing and the practice often another. Yet the latitude accorded to slaves in the colonial period, especially during Spanish rule (1766–1804), was considerable. Despite a harsh slave code, write two historians of colonial Natchitoches, many slaves owned horses, possessed weapons, grew their own foodstuffs, engaged in small-scale trading, and enjoyed considerable freedom of movement. During the American period, too, slaves in Natchitoches appeared to live under less harsh discipline than slaves elsewhere in the Red River valley. Olmsted's sketch from 1854 is revealing: "While returning to town, I met six negroes—

one of them a woman—riding on horseback. . . . Two negroes that I met, carried guns. During the day many negroes were in town, peddling eggs, nuts, brooms, and fowls." After emancipation, Natchitoches experienced far less white-on-black violence than adjacent parishes.[11]

Nevertheless, if Natchitoches managed to avoid the bloody excesses of Grant, Red River, Caddo, and Bossier Parishes, the course of Reconstruction there cannot be divorced from the surrounding violence. Although Natchitoches Democrats eschewed violence themselves, their chosen tactic, intimidation, hinged upon the *explicit threat* of violence. And that threat was omnipresent. The ubiquity of violence in Louisiana as a whole ensured that every encounter between a Republican and a Democrat carried lethal potential. "It is not a crime under the laws of Louisiana for a man to call another a 'damn liar,'" Milton J. Cunningham, a Democrat and a lawyer, explained. "And yet under the usages of society he would be justifiable in knocking a man down." During Congressional Reconstruction, old friends became enemies; family members stopped talking to each other; veterans of the same Confederate regiment disparaged each other's war record; newspaper editors vowed to shoot each other on sight. Democrats in Natchitoches, while eschewing outright violence, used first threats and then force to oust Republican officeholders. The peace of Natchitoches amounted to an armed truce maintained, from 1874 to 1877, by federal bayonets. Once the bluecoats departed, the doom of the Republican Party was sealed. Reconstruction ended as decisively in Natchitoches as it did in the rest of northern Louisiana and in much of the South.[12]

In 1878 local Democrats staged a coup d'état, destroying the Republican organization by expelling its leaders. Once it controlled the ballot boxes and counted the votes, the Democratic Party determined the outcome of every election regardless of how ballots were actually cast. In the 1890s, when many white voters rebelled against its oligarchical rule, the party almost lost power. After staving off this challenge through massive fraud, however, the Democratic Party disfranchised all black voters and many white ones as well. One-party Democratic rule in Louisiana, corrupt and authoritarian, endured six more decades.

The first chapter offers a general argument as to why Reconstruction failed, placing that experiment in the context of American and world history. The book then follows a straightforward narrative. Chapters 2 and 3 describe the experience of Natchitoches during the Civil War and the first two postwar years; they discuss the transition from contract labor to sharecropping and examine the role of the Freedmen's Bureau in that transition. Chapter 4 looks at how celebrations of the "Lost Cause" enabled former Confederates and slave owners to reconstruct a sense of racial and cultural superiority that helped them to resist Republican rule. Chapter 5 examines the formation of the Republican Party in Natchitoches Parish.

Chapters 6–11 relate the Republican Party's efforts to govern in the face of relentless and sometimes violent opposition from the Democratic Party. They show how Natchitoches Democrats, eschewing violence themselves but benefiting from the violence of others, attempted without success to suppress the Republican vote. The corruption and ineptitude of the Republican leadership in Louisiana is explored and contextualized.

Chapter 12 shows how Natchitoches became embroiled in the disputed presidential election of 1876–77, and chapter 13 relates how local Democrats ended Republican control once and for all by driving out the party's leaders. Chapters 14 and 15 recount the federal government's failed prosecution of the Democratic ringleaders and the inexorable decline of the Republican Party through 1898, when a new state constitution disfranchised black voters en masse. The final chapter examines the legacy of Reconstruction and what it meant for the twentieth-century civil rights movement.

1

RECONSTRUCTION IN HISTORY

That Reconstruction failed entirely to achieve the objects which it was intended to secure, is a fact so patent as to go without denial; whether any other feasible plan would have accomplished better results is, at the best, but an interesting historical question.

Albion W. Tourgee, *A Fool's Errand* (1880)

Grilled by a U.S. Senate committee investigating the 1878 congressional elections in Louisiana, and facing likely prosecution, Milton J. Cunningham cut a defiant figure as he testified inside the cavernous gray bulk of the "granite pile"—the New Orleans Custom House—on January 23, 1879. Described by the *New York Times* as a man "of fine appearance and a pleasant address," the thirty-seven-year-old lawyer, a future attorney general of Louisiana, headed the Democratic Party in Natchitoches Parish. Along with fifty other Democrats, he stood accused of violating the Fifteenth Amendment by denying blacks the right to vote. The previous year, the federal government alleged, Democrats in Natchitoches had stolen the congressional election by driving Republican leaders from the parish and intimidating black voters. The Republican Party was decapitated; having governed Natchitoches Parish for ten years, it did not field a ticket. Black voters, the most loyal of Republicans, were instructed to cast a Democratic ballot, or else. Many of them did so, receiving a badge that protected them from Democratic retaliation.[1]

Cunningham examined friendly witnesses himself and answered hostile questions with icy politeness. Yes, he and others had expelled the Republicans; yes, the Democratic Party had won the November 1878 elections without opposition. But the town of Natchitoches had been menaced by a "negro insurrection," he explained, and public order had demanded the removal of the men encouraging the mob. The Republican leaders had been

Figure 1. Slave cabins on Magnolia plantation, Natchitoches Parish, still being used as dwellings in 1940. Library of Congress Pictures and Photographs Division.

arrested and exiled not as Republicans but as demagogues who were whipping up a race war. He and other whites had acted as responsible citizens protecting their town, not as Democrats. Their actions had had nothing to do with politics. As for the intimidation of black voters, Cunningham added, there had been none. To be sure, several hundred blacks had voted the Democratic ticket, but they had done so of their own volition, having been freed from pressure to toe the Republican line. However implausible his claim of self-defense—the "negro insurrection" charge had been cut from whole cloth—there was no doubting Cunningham's hatred of his Republican accusers.[2]

One witness in particular caused the silky-tongued lawyer to vent his anger. Glaring across the room at a bearded, light-complexioned African American, Cunningham spat out the name "Blunt." This Republican leader, the most influential in Natchitoches, possessed no honor and no character. Alfred Raford Blunt, fumed Cunningham, was a liar, a thief, a coward, and a demagogue. He was a clergyman who lived in sin; a teacher who did no teaching; a politician who appointed rascals to fill the offices he controlled. "I have a great deal against Blunt," raged the Democrat. "He hates a white man worse than anyone I know." To Cunningham, Blunt personified the malignant, oppressive corruption of "Radical" Reconstruction and the intolerable humiliation of being bossed by a black man.[3]

Democrats hated Blunt because he was black and powerful. That a colored man, an ex-slave, represented Natchitoches Parish in the state senate drove them to distraction. Controlling the official patronage that flowed from the Republican state government, Blunt had a say in who was appointed to every position in the parish, from judge to inspector of weights and measures. "At the sound of his voice," wrote the editor of the *Natchitoches People's Vindicator*, "the gentle aspirant for official honors trembled in his boots." Even political enemies, ardent Democrats, had had to court the man's favor. No professional man, tradesman, or investor could transact business in Louisiana without greasing the wheels of government, and this meant seeking help from Blunt—"cringing to him," as Cunningham put it. Above all, Blunt's sway over black voters infuriated Democrats. With Blunt at the helm of his party, black voters had remained solidly Republican and, because they outnumbered the white electors, had exercised a decisive influence in local politics. Even after the Democratic Party "redeemed" Louisiana's state government from Republican control in 1877, Republicans held on to the key offices in Natchitoches Parish.[4]

Cunningham considered Blunt a rabble-rouser who "rules his party with a 'rod of iron.'" He and other Democrats alleged that the black minister kept Republican waverers in line by telling blacks to ostracize colored Democrats. Blunt avowed it no sin, detractors charged, if a woman left her husband for voting the Democratic ticket—he would consider their "marriage bonds dissolved." Every attempt by their party to win over black voters had failed because of Blunt. "As long as the scoundrel Blunt runs the negro churches, and with that influence, the women," wrote James H. Cosgrove, editor of the *People's Vindicator*, the Republican Party would continue to rule Natchitoches.[5]

To the frustration of Democratic candidates, Republican orators continually harked back to slavery, warning that a Democratic victory would return blacks to bondage. It was Blunt, averred district judge David Pierson, who "advised the people to draw the race line" by "talking about the blood trickling down their backs" during slavery times. "Blunt has made a good many incendiary remarks about white people to the colored people," complained Cunningham. "He appeals to their passions and . . . to their past conditions, in every way that man could to stir up bad feeling." Asked why he considered it legitimate for whites to vote as a bloc but not for blacks to do so, Cunningham stated that whites knew what was best for blacks and that blacks could not be trusted with political power. "The white people are bound to stand together, because if they do not the government will pass into the hands of the very worst class of people. . . . On the other hand, I don't think it necessary for the colored people to combine together against the whites. . . . Their objects are, I suppose, to be conserved and secured by acting with us."[6]

Blunt had been threatened many times over the years. Indeed, the *People's Vindicator* advocated the elimination of Republicans by means of "ropes and lamp-posts," and editor Cosgrove devoted his most vituperative attacks to this black political kingpin. In the summer of 1874, when the Democrats demanded that Republican officials resign or face a lynch mob, Blunt had taken to the woods in fear of his life. But he kept coming back. With a company of federal troops deploying in Natchitoches, the Republicans faced down Democratic threats and reclaimed their offices. The Republicans won again in 1876. If they could only remove Blunt, Democrats reasoned, the Republicans' stranglehold on Natchitoches could be broken. "In the interest of peace and order," advised the *Vindicator*, "we think he should be asked to emigrate."[7]

On September 21, 1878, a paramilitary squad of Democrats surrounded Blunt's house, winkled him out of the attic, marched him to the courthouse, and escorted him to the parish line. They then forced six other Republican leaders, two blacks and four whites, into exile. Never again did the Republican Party hold power in Natchitoches Parish. One hundred years would pass before Louisiana elected a Republican governor—after enough white voters, disgusted by the civil rights revolution, deserted a party that no longer stood for white supremacy.

To ask why white Democrats determined not only to defeat the Republican Party but also to destroy it is to ask why Congressional Reconstruction failed. That question lies at the heart of virtually every study of Reconstruction, including this one. There is no simple answer.

One thing is nevertheless clear. The copious testimony that black witnesses gave to congressional committees demonstrates that the former slaves who placed the Republican Party in power acted rationally and responsibly. Although illiterate and ignorant of the world, they knew that the party that had emancipated them, not the one that had led the South into a bloody last-ditch defense of slavery, best represented their interests. Nothing they did justified the charge, universally asserted by Democrats, that black suffrage was a failure because it produced bad government. "Negro suffrage failed," noted W. E. B. Du Bois in 1935, "because it was overthrown by brute force."[8]

It is equally clear that the white Republicans of the South, men to whom Democrats applied the insulting names of "carpetbagger" and "scalawag," were nothing like as venal and unprincipled as Democratic mud-slinging alleged. It was the simple act of joining the Republican Party, not their misdeeds, that caused Democrats to condemn them. A man who one day was a fine, upstanding member of the community, a "high-toned gentleman," was the next day a social outcast. The Democratic newspapers, complained U.S. District Judge Edward H. Durell, "calumniate me daily in the most outrageous and vile manner. There is no falsehood too gross for their columns." Democratic indictments of "carpetbaggers" and "scalawags" consisted of lies, distortions, and puerile abuse. It was their commitment to reestablishing white supremacy—which meant nullifying blacks' citizenship rights—that drove the Democrats' strategy and tactics.[9]

Embattled white Republicans regarded themselves as protectors of the freedpeople and defenders of the Constitution. "The large majority of the so-called 'scalawags and carpetbaggers,'" insisted a Texas Republican, "are as true and honorable men as ever lived in any age, or country, and a time will come when their heroism, the great sacrifices made by them, and their unfaltering devotion to the great principles of liberty and even handed justice for all, will be justly remembered and commemorated."[10]

Today's historians, although not uncritical of them, view the South's white Republicans in exactly this light. In the telling of James McPherson and Eric Foner, for example, the Civil War era was an uplifting story of emancipation achieved, democracy extended, and the promise of racial equality implanted in the Constitution. According to McPherson, the Civil War was not a needless war brought on by a blundering generation but a "battle cry of freedom" that vindicated America's role as "the last best hope of earth." The Union victory had a transcendent significance by ensuring the survival of democracy in a monarchical world. If the Confederacy had won, Great Britain would have remained an aristocratic oligarchy and the advance of democracy generally would have stalled. In Foner's estimation, Reconstruction represented a partial victory, or, put another way, a defeat that was only temporary. The fact that the Republican Party made a commitment to racial equality, however flawed, was of inestimable value to the freedpeople and their descendants. Black suffrage, even if curtailed after 1890, gave blacks a degree of political experience that former slaves in other societies never enjoyed. The postwar constitutional amendments, which were never repealed, provided the foundations for the modern rights movement.[11]

Stressing the anti-slavery fervor of the Republican Party as well as its commitment to equal rights, Foner and others portray Congressional Reconstruction as an idealistic project. By granting blacks full citizenship, writes Foner, Republicans attempted to "live up to the noble professions of their political creed—something few societies have ever done." An audacious experiment in interracial democracy, Reconstruction might perhaps have succeeded given better luck, and in any case chalked up notable achievements. In fact, since Foner first described Reconstruction as an "unfinished revolution" some thirty years ago, textbooks have been increasingly reluctant to label Reconstruction a failure at all. Now, Foner writes, "Scholars . . . view Reconstruction as a praiseworthy attempt to create an interracial democracy from the ashes of slavery and emphasize its accomplishments as much as its failings."[12]

This study takes a different view. It accepts the verdict of contemporaries like Henry C. Dibble and P. B. S. Pinchback that Reconstruction, judged by the expectations of its framers and the positive good it accomplished, was a disastrous failure. The congressional plan of Reconstruction assumed that the ex-rebel states, once blacks had been incorporated as citizens and voters, would quickly become self-governing. This proved to be an error. Louisiana's Republican Party and its sister parties in other southern states were from the very outset crippled by violence. Only military protection kept them in power. Given the fact that most whites were violently hostile, the chances of Reconstruction succeeding were slim at best.

Prospects for success were further reduced by the leaders of Louisiana's Republican Party, who committed a series of unforced errors that not only played into the hands of their political enemies but also alienated most of their Republican sympathizers in the North. The self-destructive behavior of these politicians resulted not so much from their individual failings as from a system of government in which patronage-driven political parties formed the administration. The cutthroat, anarchic two-party system, in which the spoils system reigned supreme, militated against political consensus and rendered the Republican Party incapable of offering honest, competent government. In this political context, the concept of "idealism" does little to explain the political dynamics if Reconstruction, and is in some ways misleading.

To criticize Louisiana's Republican leaders is not to assert a moral equivalence between the contending parties. In the post–Civil War South, the Republican Party, whatever its shortcomings, championed democracy and racial equality. The Democratic Party subverted democracy and never accepted blacks as full citizens. Whereas the Republican Party engaged in electoral shenanigans, Democrats committed murder. Nor were the Republicans of the South any more corrupt and petty-minded than the generality of politicians of their time, including the Democrats who replaced them. In fact, looking at today's rogues gallery of disgraced and incarcerated politicians—whether one takes Louisiana, New York, Illinois, or Washington, D.C.—the Republican politicians of the Reconstruction era were no more corrupt than those of our own time.

In the context of the postwar South, however, the normal rules of politics did not apply. And therein lay a problem. What might be acceptable in New York and Illinois—or in Louisiana before the Civil War—proved unworkable in a region that had been devastated by war, traumatized by defeat, humiliated by occupation, and subjected to a political and social revolution. Postwar Reconstruction demanded something more, something better, and something stronger, than "ordinary" politics. The Republican Party claimed the moral high ground, but Republican officeholders sank to the level of Louisiana politics. As agents of the victorious North, they set a terrible example. Even the northern Republicans, no angels, found their behavior embarrassing.

Stating that Louisiana's Republicans were typical politicians is not to deny them idealism. The concept of idealism, however, does little to illuminate the political dynamics of Reconstruction. In the first place, idealism is in the eye of the beholder. One person's idealist is another person's fanatic; the man who regards himself as a practical politician, others see as a sellout. The Democrats who resorted to intimidation and violence regarded themselves as honorable men who were acting from noble motives. In the second place, the wellsprings of political action are rarely clear-cut, and any attempt to isolate "idealism" as a discrete factor will fail. As Thomas J.

Durant told Henry C. Warmoth, one Republican to another, "In political matters and in the administration of party affairs, we are but little, if at all, concerned with men's motives, which are for the most part inscrutable. . . . [We] cannot modify our judgment of events and of results." Many of the self-described idealists of the Republican Party, the earliest supporters of black suffrage, were the first to turn against Congressional Reconstruction. The men who put loyalty to party above all else—the hard-bitten machine politicians—were slower to endorse black suffrage, but once committed they staunchly defended it.[13]

Treating Reconstruction as an idealistic project invites a more profound objection: it implies, and sometimes explicitly states, that the United States possessed an immanent commitment to freedom that somehow set it apart from the rest of the world. This belief that the United States differs from other nations in being based upon a shared political ideology (variously defined as Liberalism, the "American Dream," the "American Creed," and so on) is extraordinarily tenacious. Reconstruction, Foner contends, was a uniquely American project because freedom is "fundamental to Americans' sense of themselves" and "anchors the American sense of exceptional national identity." This notion of "American exceptionalism" is questionable. The belief that that the United States is more committed to freedom, democracy, and equality than New Zealand, Switzerland, Denmark, or any number of countries has no basis in fact. Even the alleged uniqueness of black suffrage is mistaken: after the Revolution of 1848 the Second French Republic not only abolished slavery in the French Antilles but also enfranchised male freedmen.[14]

The failure of Congressional Reconstruction contradicts the notion that the United States is a nation bound together by a set of written principles or core ideals. It underlines, instead, the centrality of racial hierarchy. Slavery formed part of the original design of the United States, and racial inequality, legally sanctioned, was embedded in every aspect of American society until the 1960s. When supposedly core principles are honored more in the breach than the observance, it seems misplaced to emphasize democratic ideals rather than, say, economic imperatives, racial ideologies, legal structures, and the distribution of power between and within social groups. The fact that universal suffrage and fair elections are still contested matters *today* suggests not consensus over democratic principles but rather the absence of consensus.[15]

The most serious shortcoming of an idealistic interpretation of Congressional Reconstruction is that it understates how badly the Republicans' attempt to remold the South failed. The Civil War abolished slavery only to condemn former slaves to another century of systematic oppression. Reconstruction tried to democratize the South but instead led to a new form of oligarchy based upon the suppression of black voting and a corrupt one-party system. As Paul Escott writes, "The white South was permitted to impose its will on African Americans with determination, consistency, and cruelty for one hundred years." The century of brutal, systematic oppression that blacks endured between the 1860s and the 1960s underlines the failure of Reconstruction to accomplish what it set out to do. That gap of one hundred years suggests that it was not the legacy of Reconstruction that facilitated the civil rights movement, but rather the radically transformed circumstances of the post-1945 world. To argue that Reconstruction provided the basis for the civil rights movement is to assume, in the words of C. Vann Woodward, "a space-time continuum that homogenizes time past with time present."[16]

Reconstruction's failure meant that the democratic potential of the American Civil War went unfulfilled. Certainly, liberal democrats everywhere cheered the triumph of the Union cause. But the growth of democracy was patchy, uncertain, and frequently reversed. Where democratic institutions took root and flourished, as in Switzerland, Finland, the Netherlands, the Scandinavian countries, the United Kingdom, and the British dominions, they owed their stability to distinctive cultures and histories rather than to the example of the United States as the "the last best hope of earth." Even in the United States, the triumph of democracy was less than clear-cut. The political system of 1900 was substantially *less* democratic than that of 1850. "The unfolding of freedom," Foner has suggested, is a universal theme of American history. Reconstruction's demise, however, contradicts such a narrative. "In no other civilized nation and modern land," noted Du Bois, "has so great a group of people, most of whom were able to read and write, been allowed so small a voice in their own government."[17]

Such arguments over the wider significance of the Civil War and Reconstruction might seem remote to the story of Natchitoches, Louisiana, a country parish "in the middle of nowhere." Yet they go the heart of this book's thesis, which is that Reconstruction, whatever else it achieved, came nowhere near to fulfilling its basic goal of producing a democratic South in which blacks could prosper as full and equal citizens.

In truth, the Republicans in Congress had set the southern party an impossible task. Congressional Reconstruction assumed that once the rebel states had been restored to home rule, the freedpeople would be able to advance and protect their interests on their own account. Blacks would cease to be "wards of the nation" in need of federal succor. The military occupation of the ex-Confederate states could end. The Freedmen's Bureau could be phased out. Radical proposals for land reform could be discarded because blacks would be able to prosper and acquire property through the operation of a free labor market. With blacks as voting citizens, the South would return to self-government and "politics as usual." Southern whites would adjust to the new political dispensation because equal citizenship and non-racial suffrage were written into the Constitution. However, in attempting to pacify and democratize the defeated Confederacy on the basis of black suffrage, and by assuming that the federal government could then stand back and leave the South to the cut and thrust of party politics, Congress handed the South's Republicans a poisoned chalice. Indeed, it placed them in peril of their lives.

Congressional Republicans knew that reforming the South by means of black suffrage was a political gamble, but they persuaded themselves that the Democratic Party, in time, would acquiesce in black suffrage. This was not a forlorn hope. In 1872 the Democratic national platform stated its opposition to "any reopening of the questions settled by the thirteenth, fourteenth, and fifteenth amendments." However, Democratic pledges to respect black rights were insincere. White southerners' culture of "honor" and their psychological and economic investment in racial supremacy allowed them to justify any means, up to and including murder, to undermine black suffrage. Moreover, they understood that the citizenship rights accorded blacks, although defined by the Constitution, depended upon state and local authorities far more than upon Washington. In attacking southern Republicans the Democratic Party carefully avoided violence against federal soldiers and never took defiance of the federal government to the level of open rebellion.

The peculiar relationship between government and politics also militated against the building of consensus. In Stephen Skowronek's phrase, the United States was a "state of courts and parties." The multiplicity of offices that were either elective or in the gift of politicians conformed in a rough-and-ready way to a definition of democracy as "government by the people." But the spoils system tended to make control of patronage the be-all and end-all of politics. It fueled incessant factionalism and made politics a zero-sum game in which there could only be winners and losers. The overlap between government and party hindered the emergence of a national consensus that might have accepted black suffrage as a legitimate part of the postwar constitutional settlement.[18]

With Congressional Reconstruction tied so closely to the political interests of the Republican Party it is hardly surprising that northern Democrats, and most white southerners, resisted. It proved impossible to place the amended Constitution above party politics because the Republicans, while committed to racially impartial suffrage, wielded the power of a thoroughly partisan national government to tip the electoral scales. The disfranchisement of many ex-Confederates, for example, helped the Republican Party to capture southern state governments, but at the cost of immense bitterness among the southern whites. As former Union general and veteran Republican politician Carl Schurz put it, disqualifying a quarter of a million former rebels was "not severe enough to terrify" but "just severe enough to exasperate." Military intervention had the same effect. Federal soldiers were far too few to guarantee order and police the ballot boxes, but they were sufficiently ubiquitous to fuel Democratic charges of "military occupation."[19]

Small-d democratic politics requires a degree of consensus; losers must accept electoral defeat without resorting to violence. Instead of security and stability, however, black suffrage, by displacing the South's former political rulers, prolonged the chaos of the postwar years. It failed to protect freedpeople from violence; it failed to give security to white Republicans. Most white southerners regarded black suffrage as a mortal threat to their economic interests, cultural identity, and "honor."

Thaddeus Stevens, the Radical Republican leader who died in August 1868, understood this. In order to break the power of the former "slaveocracy," he advocated a long period of direct rule from Washington, reducing the former Confederate states to "territories;" coupled with the breakup of large plantations and the allocation of land to the freedpeople. Others, too, regarded it as folly for Congress to enfranchise the former slaves and then, within a space of months, end military rule and restore the ex-Confederate states to political autonomy within the Union. To do so, warned Albion W. Tourgee, a North Carolina Republican, "would deliver the free men of the South, bound hand and foot, to their old-time, natural enemies." The restored state governments would quickly fall under the domination of ex-slaveholders and ex-Confederates who were unrelentingly hostile to the purpose of Congressional Reconstruction. The result, Tourgee predicted, would be anarchy and bloodshed, followed by the reduction of the freedpeople to a state of serfdom. There is no way of knowing, of course, if Stevens's prescription would have worked any better. It might have produced even *more* white opposition. Yet some have suggested, not without evidence, that ex-Confederates might have found even a lengthy period of military rule preferable to the immediate and wholesale enfranchisement of freedmen.[20]

The election of U. S. Grant in 1868 illustrated the short-term success of Congressional Reconstruction but pointed toward its long-term failure. Black suffrage helped to elect Grant president, a victory that dispelled Republican fears of a neo-Confederate revival. On the other hand, widespread terrorism in Louisiana and elsewhere exposed the fragility of the South's Republican state governments.

In the eyes of northern party supporters, the apparent defenselessness of southern Republicans in the face of Democratic-inspired violence weakened their claim to federal support. In an age that placed a high premium upon "honor" and "manhood," and in a political system that accorded state government an enormous reservoir of "police powers," it seemed incomprehensible, even contemptible, that Republican governments could only survive through federal protection. Attorney General Amos T. Akerman, although a resolute foe of the Ku Klux Klan, urged southern Republicans to fight their own battles: "A spirited, yes, a desperate contest with bad men is . . . the most expedient cause for the friends of the Government in the South. As long as these bad men believe you are unable to protect yourselves, they will cherish the purpose of injuring you, as soon as the hand of the Government shall be withdrawn."[21]

Such advice overlooked a fact of which southern Democrats were well aware: the inability of the black population to defend itself. White attackers enjoyed the advantages of surprise, mobility, military experience, ease of communication, and superior weaponry. Never sure when and where attacks would come, freedpeople could rarely organize an effective defense. Black army veterans were too few and far between to provide strong leadership or effective military training. When blacks did attempt armed resistance, the results were usually catastrophic. It took the Union four years to defeat the Confederate armies, John G. Lewis, a black leader from Natchitoches, reminded a congressional committee. How could poorly armed blacks with no experience of warfare withstand "these brilliant, gallant Southerners"?[22]

Although the violence of the Ku Klux Klan generated widespread sympathy for blacks' plight, the Republicans' constant harping on atrocity stories—"waving the bloody shirt"—also bred cynicism and contempt. It was a classic case of "blaming the victim." Yet blacks' weakness underlines the fact that democracy is not only an ideal but also a matter of power. In France it took repeated revolutions to establish a democratic republic. A century of working-class struggle preceded the attainment of universal manhood suffrage in Great Britain. Examples could be multiplied, but the point is simple: democracy must be wrested from those seeking to deny it. As Frederick Douglass put it, "Power concedes nothing without a demand. It never did and it never will." Ultimately, it took a hundred years of struggle by blacks to achieve even an approximation of equal suffrage. In 1867 Congress enfranchised former slaves not because of an irresistible demand from blacks themselves but because it was an expedient way to create a loyal element in the South that would both safeguard the Union and keep the federal government out of Democratic hands.

Having enacted black suffrage, the Republican Party made a serious effort to ensure free elections in the South and to protect blacks from violence. But practical and institutional restraints circumscribed its response to Democratic terrorism. The vastness of the South and its sparse, scattered population made policing a nightmare: the U.S. military could sustain Republican governments in state capitals but not guarantee order in the rural hinterland. Federal courts were few and far between. The jury system made convictions in federal court hard to secure, and, if obtained, the appeals process made them easy to overturn. Trial by military commissions was not an option.

The political restraints were equally limiting. Federal enforcement efforts strained the Republican Party's commitment to states' rights. Republican leaders jealously guarded their own power, which was rooted in state politics. They prized the system of federalism that made governors, U.S. senators, and Supreme Court justices coequals, in effect, of the president. Hence when the Republican Party created national rights, it expected the states to respect and enforce those rights. When states failed to do so, the federal government stepped in very much against its will. Continued military intervention dismayed northern Republicans and proved a political gift for the Democratic Party. Martial law was so politically unpopular that the federal government rarely invoked it. A Republican Supreme Court gutted the Enforcement Acts and drastically narrowed the definition of national citizenship. A Republican president, Grant, concluded that Congressional Reconstruction had failed.

General William T. Sherman had warned that state governments based upon black suffrage could never survive if an overwhelming majority of whites rejected them. "We cannot accomplish it by force," he wrote his brother, Senator John Sherman, "nor can we maintain an army large enough to hold them in subjugation." The general's opposition to universal suffrage and contempt for non-white races colored his opinion—he was an avowed white supremacist. Yet by 1872 many Republicans who once enthusiastically supported Congressional Reconstruction had reached a similar conclusion. The rise of the Ku Klux Klan necessitated the very thing they had hoped to avoid, constant military intervention by the federal government. The cure was worse than the disease, they argued. Nothing could be worse, warned Schurz, than the creation of a "monarchical police state."[23]

Ultimately, Congressional Reconstruction depended upon the consent— sullen acquiescence would have sufficed—of white southerners. Instead of consent, it met unrelenting opposition, ranging from a refusal to pay taxes to armed insurrection. Animated by a settled determination to subordinate the black population, the Democratic Party drew upon legal cunning, political skill, the pride of Confederate veterans in the "Lost Cause," and the military experience acquired during four years of warfare. They undermined the Republican state governments upon which the architects of Congressional Reconstruction had placed so much faith. The Republican governors of the South became prisoners in their own statehouses.

The problem was not so much that the federal government was weak: the Civil War had dispelled that notion, the North having created the most powerful army on earth. Rather, the North's political leaders rejected the option of centralizing government along the lines of Britain, France, or Prussia. Indeed, they never seriously considered it. In any case, centralizing power in the federal government, even if politically feasible, might not have affected the outcome. After all, racial discrimination in the form of colonialism flourished under Britain's parliamentary system and France's rule-from-Paris. The Belgians, the Germans, and the Dutch all treated dark-skinned colonials abysmally. Whatever the form of government, whites oppressed darker peoples. Placing human races in a hierarchy is something "educated moderns never do," notes Richard Dawkins, "but equivalent Victorians always did."[24]

Given the ubiquity and tenacity of racist thinking throughout the nineteenth century and well into the twentieth, Congressional Reconstruction seems anomalous, an outlier. But it was not only racist thinking that made it anomalous. As Gary Gerstle points out, until the "rights revolution" that began in the 1940s, the dominant view of the Constitution was that individual states enjoyed great latitude to exercise "police powers"—sometimes very oppressive ones—in virtually every area of public and private life. From the founding of the Republic to the middle of the twentieth century, "State governments were largely exempt from having to observe the federal Bill of Rights." Viewed in this context, Congressional Reconstruction, a short-lived extension of federal power, was the exception that proved this rule. Foner is correct in stating that the remarkable thing was not that it failed but that it was attempted at all. However, rather than testifying to America's exceptional democratic idealism, it is better interpreted as a panicky response by the Republican Party to a constitutional crisis provoked by President Andrew Johnson.[25]

2

THE COLLAPSE OF CONFEDERATE LOUISIANA

Great dissatisfaction prevailed in many sections, and generally among the mass our success [is] deemed almost a matter of indifference, and in many localities the advent of the enemy would be hailed as a relief.

Lieutenant Thomas E. Adams to General S. Cooper, C.S.A., January 29, 1864

On May 27, 1865, three paddle-wheel steamers carrying four thousand Union soldiers left New Orleans and headed up the Mississippi River. Escorted by gunboats, the steamers passed Baton Rouge, which Union forces had held on and off since 1862, and then turned westward along the Red River. The purpose of the expedition: to bring a vast area of Confederate-held territory under federal control. On June 3 it accepted the surrender of the Confederate garrison at Alexandria. Two days later the Union flotilla reached Grand Ecore, the landing post that served Natchitoches town. After setting up camp, men of the Twenty-First Iowa Infantry and Sixth Missouri Cavalry proceeded to Natchitoches, where they raised the Union flag atop city hall. Somber whites, some in Confederate uniforms, stood in knots on the raised sidewalks, making a low murmur as the soldiers marched by. Others watched the takeover through open windows.[1]

The Union occupation forces in the South had but a dim idea of the challenges that confronted them. They were taking charge of a bitterly divided white population, a ruined economy, and a collapsed social system. With the virtual demise of civil authority, outlaw bands thrived. The piecemeal disintegration of slavery through military action, writes David Brion Davis, "precluded careful planning and preparation" for the aftermath of emancipation. The army received little guidance from Washington. In March 1865 Congress created the Bureau of Refugees, Freedmen and Abandoned Lands in order to ease the transition from slavery to freedom. Beyond that, the federal gov-

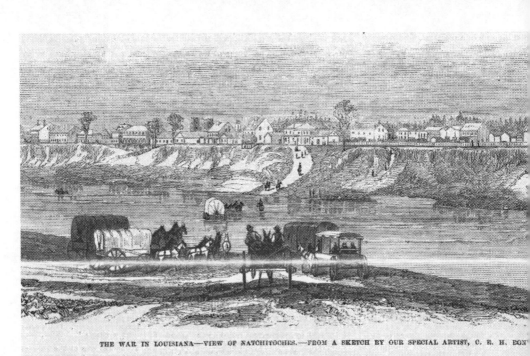

THE WAR IN LOUISIANA—VIEW OF NATCHITOCHES.—FROM A SKETCH BY OUR SPECIAL ARTIST, C. E. H. BON

Figure 2. The Union army comes to Natchitoches. *Frank Leslie's Illustrated Newspaper*, May 7, 1864. Library of Congress Pictures and Photographs Division.

ernment had no plan of Reconstruction because the president and Congress were at loggerheads.[2]

President Lincoln had worked on the assumption that popular support for the Confederacy was superficial and that lenient peace terms would encourage suppressed Union sentiment to come out into the open. Republicans in Congress, however, did not share Lincoln's optimism and wanted ex-rebels to pass a far stiffer test of loyalty before being allowed back into government. One loose grouping, known to history as the "Radicals," believed that blacks made up the only substantial loyal element in the South and should for that reason be enfranchised. But the whole question of loyalty was murky. How should it be defined?[3]

On the face of it, the collapse of popular support for the Confederacy boded well for a swift restoration of the Union on lenient terms. Large numbers of whites had abandoned the Confederate cause long before the surrender. Most of the thirty thousand Confederate soldiers who surrendered at Vicksburg on July 4, 1863, abandoned their units after receiving paroles from General U. S. Grant. One by one, they returned to their homes west of the Mississippi. "The men who had fought so long and bravely, and who had suffered so severely," one soldier recalled, "felt . . . as if they were exempt from all military duty, but privileged to go where they pleased, and do as they pleased, until exchanged." When the Confederate government instructed them to report again for duty, many refused to be forced back into military service. Ordered to reassemble near Natchitoches in January 1864, the Third Louisiana Regiment mustered only seventy-five men. Most remained absent without leave.[4]

How many whites felt a primary allegiance to the Union is hard to say. In Natchitoches Parish a majority of white voters had opposed secession, but most rallied to the Confederacy upon the outbreak of war. Whites served in the Second and Third Louisiana Infantry, the Second Louisiana Cavalry, and numerous other Confederate units. But support for the Confederacy was compulsory. The Confederate authorities remained firmly in control throughout the war except for a few days in April 1864 when a Union army under General Nathaniel P. Banks passed through. They cracked down hard on perceived disloyalty.

Even so, a stubborn few had refused to renounce their allegiance to the Union. Episcopalian priest Thomas S. Bacon, the first Protestant minister in Natchitoches, fled in May 1861 after continuing to offer prayers for the president of the United States. Samuel Parson, a Pennsylvania-born master carpenter with a French-born wife, spent eight months in the Natchitoches Parish jail for "high treason." Joseph Martin, a planter and justice of the peace, found himself under arrest after attending a secret conclave of anti-Confederates. A grand jury indicted Thomas W. Wall, an Irish-born physician, "for using language in private conversation with the intent to excite insubordination among the slaves." Released on $5,000 bond, Wall had the threat of prosecution hanging over his head until July 1865, when the U.S. Army ordered all such cases dismissed. John and Matthew Breedlove were small farmers who, after being jailed for disloyalty, escaped to federal lines and joined the Second Louisiana (Union) Cavalry.[5]

Some die-hard Unionists simply kept their views to themselves. Marco Givanovich, one of the wealthiest slaveholders in Natchitoches Parish, avoided persecution by sitting out the war on his four-thousand-acre plantation, confiding in no one but trusted friends. An immigrant from Dalmatia (then part of the Habsburg Empire, now part of Croatia), Givanovich cheered Union victories, refused to sell corn to the Confederacy, and sheltered a young man, Antoine Marinovich, who was evading conscription. "He told me many times that Jeff Davis ought to be hung," Marinovich recalled, "and that he himself would pull the rope."[6]

The arrival of the Union army in the spring of 1864 put silent Unionists to the test. Planter and physician Samuel O. Scruggs waved his hat and cheered the Yankee soldiers. After the Battle of Mansfield he tended to wounded federal prisoners with exceptional kindness. Upon learning that Scruggs had entertained Union officers at the dinner table, Confederate general Richard Taylor expelled the doctor from the field hospital. "Calling me a damned Yankee sympathizer," Scruggs related, he "threatened to have me shot." When Taylor ordered him to ready a team of horses for use by Confederate couriers, Scruggs had the animals taken to the swamp and turned loose. He then went into hiding. Fellow physician Edward R. Brownell, fearing for his life, fled Natchitoches Parish when the Union army retreated.[7]

Natchitoches also had many reluctant rebels who shed no tears for the Confederacy. Men who considered secession the height of folly, northerners and immigrants who had not wished to jeopardize their property and local standing, soldiers who served in the army under duress: these people had done enough to avoid persecution but had little enthusiasm for the rebel cause. "I was at first in favor of the Union," explained planter Emile Rost, "but public opinion was so strong I had to yield to it, and went along with the current." For a large but indeterminate group of outwardly loyal Confederates, the war could not end soon enough.[8]

The example of Rapides Parish, bordering Natchitoches to the south, suggests the shallowness of support for the Confederacy. After Banks's army seized Alexandria, fifty miles from Natchitoches, in March 1864, about fourteen hundred citizens took an oath of allegiance to the United States. These were men and women of all ages and conditions, from wealthy planters to illiterate laborers. Of course, their motives varied. Many believed that they could protect their property from being confiscated or plundered. Others wanted to sell cotton to the federal government. Some were simply hungry: a "loyal" citizen could more easily receive rations from the army. A few were coerced: the fiercely secessionist editor of the *Louisiana Democrat* took the oath as a condition of ending his house arrest. The many slaveholders who swore to abide by the Emancipation Proclamation had no intention of doing so. But among these fourteen hundred were a hard core of vehement anti-Confederates. Three hundred men voted in the

Free State elections organized by Banks, and five hundred men formed a company of scouts that joined the Union army.[9]

Dozens of people from Winn Parish, which bordered Natchitoches to the east, sought refuge within the Union lines. The previous September more than sixty Winn Parish whites had petitioned the commander of the federal garrison in Monroe to supply them with arms and ammunition and to give them a Union flag. "We hold no further allegiance to the Confederate States," they resolved, "except when overpowered and compelled by the sword." The parish became a virtual no-go area—the "Free State of Winn"—for Confederate officials.[10]

Confederate authorities applied "vigorous measures and some examples of severity" against paroled prisoners who failed to report for duty. The commander of the state militia in Alexandria was ordered to scour the country north of Red River for deserters and to shoot "on the spot" any found with arms. Companies of conscript hunters used bloodhounds—"negro dogs"—to track men down. If suspects ran away, their pursuers should "take possession of their horses, keep them in the swamps, and starve them out."[11]

Repression begot further resistance, fueling an escalating cycle of violence. Armed bands of Unionists, draft resisters, deserters, and free blacks—dubbed "jayhawkers"—hid out in the woods and swamps. Avoiding large Confederate patrols, they pounced on small ones. They robbed Confederate loyalists of horses and firearms and prevented Confederate officials from impressing livestock. One armed party, after capturing five hundred beeves earmarked for the Confederate army, declared that they intended "to starve out the Confederate forces and thus bring the war to a close." One Confederate related how, after flushing out a band of jayhawkers, they dealt with those they captured: "We walked them out of stinking distance and shot them."[12]

By 1864 large areas of central and northwestern Louisiana had become ungovernable. "The country between lower Little River and Red River is infested with recusant conscripts and jayhawkers," reported a Confederate officer. One estimate put their number at eight thousand. In St. Landry Parish, an anti-Confederate band led by Ozémé Carrière and Martin Guillory roamed at will. "These lawless bands are daily increasing in numbers," the Confederate conscription officer reported. "Not only are they collecting the discontented whites and the free negroes, but the slaves . . . are going to them every day." By 1864 the conflict resembled a guerrilla war: it was hard to suppress these bands, confessed General Taylor, when "the whole population . . . sympathizes with them." Taylor launched the desperate expedient of expelling the families of Union men to the federal lines, confiscating their property, and burning their homes.[13]

Even the most convinced Confederates began to doubt that the cause was worth the cost. Aside from suffering appalling human losses in battle, families found their property—foodstuffs, cotton, livestock, slaves—either confiscated by Union forces or impressed by the Confederate authorities. Against the confiscation or destruction of property by Yankees there was no redress. Compensation for impressed goods in valueless Confederate currency was little better, and many failed to receive any compensation at all.

Confederate forces repelled Banks's army at the Battles of Mansfield and Pleasant Hill, but the victory furnished little cause for celebration. Retreating through Natchitoches and back down the Red and Cane Rivers, Union forces left a trail of destruction. General Taylor described the wake of the Union army as he harried it back to Alexandria: "For many miles every dwelling-house, every negro cabin, every cotton-gin, every corn-crib, and even chicken-houses have been burned to the ground; every fence torn down and the fields torn up by the hoofs of horses and wheels of wagons." Despite orders to the contrary, Union soldiers in Alexandria plundered private homes with abandon. When the Union army finally evacuated Alexandria on May 14, a fire started by some soldiers turned into a conflagration that destroyed two-thirds of the town. "We left Alexandria," a Union marine recorded in his diary, "the front street being a mass of ruins."[14]

The timely arrival of Confederate cavalry hard on the heels of the Union army had saved the town of Natchitoches a similar fate, but in the surrounding countryside the destruction was enormous. "A desolate country," a Confederate private wrote in his diary. "Campti [and] Grand Ecore burned. . . . Fences gone. . . . Stores and persons robbed." Returning to his plantation below Natchitoches, a slave-owner found every building in ashes, only a few chicken coops left standing. "Our letters were scattered all over the plantation for the Yankees had been reading them." What little in the way of provisions the federal forces left untouched, wrote Governor Henry Watkins Allen, "our own pursuing troops generally appropriated. . . . Starvation literally stared this part of our population in the face." Civilians dreaded the plundering soldiers of General John G. Walker's Texas Division almost as much as they feared the Yankees.[15]

The Confederate policy of burning cotton upon the approach of the enemy compounded the misery. "It deprives our people of the means of subsistence at the very moment when we are leaving them to the mercy of the enemy," complained General Taylor. Rather than see their cotton torched, planters near the Union lines sold it to the enemy, a trade encouraged by the federal government and deplored (although often tolerated) by Confederate authorities. In order to stamp out this "contaminating trade," one rebel official recommended seizing the property of offenders even if these were "weeping girls" or "suffering widows." Small producers, who lacked the means and connections to transport their cotton away from the front line, were the hardest hit. Still worse off were town dwellers who had to purchase their foodstuffs. Two months after the retreat of Banks's army, the *Natchitoches Times*, noting the soaring cost of corn, butter, and apples, complained that the wives and children of Confederate soldiers were suffering "at the hands of the agriculturalists, on whom they are almost exclusively dependent for subsistence."[16]

The Confederate troops in northern Louisiana did not so much surrender as walk away. The never-say-die speeches of Governor Allen failed to move the rank-and-file of the army. While Allen and General Edmund Kirby Smith tried to rally support for an exodus to Mexico, the mass of soldiers voted with their feet. Confederate units melted away. "The whole country is filled with deserters," reported the commander of the Alexandria garrison on May 17. "The whole army and people, with scarce an individual exception, are determined to fight no more." The troops in Natchitoches were in "the same state of demoralization." On May 30 Kirby Smith bowed to the inevitable, confessing that "from one extremity of the department to the other, the troops, with unexampled unanimity of action, have dissolved all military organization . . . and scattered to their homes." Departing soldiers ransacked Confederate warehouses and public buildings. In Shreveport, wrote one soldier, "the streets [were] filled with goods, official papers, etc., scattered everywhere. It was awful, terrible beyond portrayal." Amid scenes of burning buildings and plundering mobs, the Confederacy's last stronghold collapsed.[17]

As the Confederacy collapsed, so did slavery. Although northern Louisiana lay deep behind Confederate lines, slaves ran away whenever Union forces came within striking distance. Early in the war Union commanders had regarded fugitive slaves, or "contrabands," as a useless encumbrance. By 1863, however, emancipation was a Union war aim, and military strategy demanded the liberation of slaves in Confederate-held territory. With the Confederate authorities commandeering slaves to work on fortifications and other military-related projects, the Union tried to create as many fugitives as possible. Liberating slaves deprived the Confederacy of military labor and added manpower to the Union army. The contending armies fought over the slave population just as modern armies might fight over, for example, oil. Union raiding parties, like Confederate ones, received orders to "bring in all horses and mules that they find," as well as "negroes without families, able-bodied, who will be of use to us as teamsters."[18]

In May 1863 a ten-day occupation of Alexandria by Banks's army attracted six thousand fugitives to the federal lines. "The arrival of the Yankees . . . turned the negroes crazy," wrote John H. Ransdell, owner of Elmwood Plantation. "All business was suspended and those that did not go with the army remained at home to do *much worse.*" The slaves ransacked the "big house" and took away the furniture. They ripped the portraits of the master and mistress out of their frames. They "forcibly put a Confederate soldier in the stocks . . . and abused him, very much." They commandeered wagons and slaughtered livestock. Eleven days after Banks left Rapides Parish, Ransdell reported that his slaves were finally getting back to work, but only after they all been whipped. [19]

Many planters, on the advice General Taylor, removed their best field hands to Texas. "Time dey ready for freedom in Louisiana," recalled Ella Washington seventy years later, "dey refugees us to Texas." Bill Homer described how he and other slaves walked from daylight to dusk, trudging along behind the wagons and singing "to the slow steps of the ox":

> Walk, walk, you nigger, walk!
> De road am dusty, de road am tough,
> Dust in the eye, dust in de tuft;
> Dust in de mouth, yous can't talk—
> Walk, you niggers, don't you balk.

Caravans of slaves and wagons sometimes stretched out for a mile or more.[20]

The long trek to Texas provided countless opportunities to abscond. "Six of M[onsieur] Cloutier's slaves have hidden that they may not go to Texas," a Natchitoches girl confided to her diary in March 1864. Private William H. Tunnard, who accompanied one of these Texas-bound caravans, recorded a "general stampede in camp" when a group of slaves made a break for it. "Chase and catch 11 negroes, two horses, 6 mules and ambulance. . . . Still missing 14 negroes, 7 mules and 3 horses." The cost of defending the Confederate heartland was getting steeper. In January 1864 an officer reported to the Confederate War Department that "the valley of Red River is deserted by emigration to Texas and crippled by wholesale impressment."[21]

Banks's return to Alexandria in 1864 and his advance up the Red River through Natchitoches as far as Mansfield, in De Soto Parish, created another wave of runaways. The appearance of black soldiers in Natchitoches was horrifying for whites, electrifying for blacks. One planter described the scene on April 6, as the Union army entered the town with drums beating and bands playing: "Several colored regiments came in; they were the ugliest and blackest set of negroes ever saw, but instead of having their natural color that day they were gray with dust. It is a terrible to think our own negroes are fighting their masters. . . . All of our negroes are gone with the exception of eleven." An Iowa soldier recalled that "as soon as the old drum began to beat they [the slaves] they would throw down the hoe and come trooping across the fields. . . . Some shouted, some prayed, while others danced to the music of their jubilant hearts." Such scenes left an indelible impression; many soldiers were profoundly moved. "One old auntie climbed the fence, spread out her hands toward heaven and shouted, 'Oh my, Oh my! I is so happy de Linkum sojers done come . . . an dey ain't got horns eider, bres de Lawd!'"[22]

As Banks's army passed by again, this time in retreat, "the blacks followed us in droves," wrote a Maine soldier. Most of them walked, "but thousands of them were mounted on mules which they had stolen, and thousands more . . . were piled in wagons." By the time the army approached Alexandria, two lines of ex-slaves, each one four deep, flanked the long Union column. Thousands of escaping slaves made their way to "contraband colonies" around New Orleans. There, the army commander employed them as laborers, contracted them to loyal planters, or compelled them to work on plantations that had been confiscated from rebel owners and leased to northern managers.[23]

Many of the fugitives joined colored regiments in the Union army. Of the 93,796 black soldiers who hailed from the South, the largest contingent, 24,502 men, came from Louisiana. Dozens of ex-slaves from Natchitoches Parish, including many from Marco Givanovich's plantation on Isle Brevelle, enlisted in Union regiments. They joined the Tenth U.S. Colored

Heavy Artillery and the Fourth U.S. Colored Cavalry. A few served in white regiments as cooks. The fact that Confederate soldiers fought black soldiers with particular ferocity—often shooting prisoners out of hand— did not appear to deter these volunteers.[24]

The war exposed the delusions of the master class regarding slave loyalty. "No dependence is to be placed on the negro," reported one planter. "They are the greatest hypocrites and liars that God ever made." The slaves whom masters had trusted most often turned out to be the instigators. Confederates and Unionists alike understood where the slaves' true loyalty lay. "The negroes are generally spies," a Confederate officer in Louisiana told President Jefferson Davis. Slaves provided succor for fugitive Unionists and furnished a stream of intelligence to the Union army. "I invariably had Negro guides," recalled General George Armstrong Custer, "and I never hesitated to place the most implicit confidence in them. They would sometimes ride or walk miles to give us information . . . such as the position of the enemy's forces, or of their [wagon] trains which we might desire to capture. They would count the guns and troops as they passed a certain point, and they would give us the number with remarkable accuracy." The *Official Records* are replete with such testimony.[25]

The advance-and-retreat of the opposing armies, however, taught many slaves to exercise caution. Slaves who greeted Union troops by behaving as if they were free risked savage reprisals if the soldiers in gray returned. "Several have been shot," reported John Ransdell at Elmwood Plantation after Banks's army retreated, "and probably more will have to be." Running away to the federal lines also proved risky, for the Union grip on southern Louisiana was tenuous. Confederate raiders made persistent efforts to break up the government-run plantations "and secure the negroes and teams for our own use." Even after Confederate resistance west of the Mississippi ended, the federal military presence in northern Louisiana was thin. In much of the countryside, where the vast majority of freedpeople lived, Union soldiers were rarely seen. The Freedmen's Bureau had yet to establish a presence. Battle-scarred, embittered ex-Confederate soldiers were returning home. Outlaws rendered the roads unsafe.[26]

In the presence of white southerners, therefore, blacks greeted emancipation with little outward jubilation. "After the surrender, missy reads de paper and tells us that we'uns is free," Bill Homer recalled as an old man, "but dat we'uns kin stay 'til we is 'justed to the change." That statement can stand for thousands like it. "Dere wasn't no celebration about it," remembered eighty-two-year-old Ella Washington.

Yet if newly freed slaves were outwardly reticent, they could not hide their feelings entirely. Witnessing the scene in Shreveport when people learned that the eastern armies had laid down their arms, one Confederate officer noted "the quiet but unsuppressable joy of the blacks." This man's own body servant, when informed that he was free, "uttered not a word and the only evidence that his emotions were stirred was the copious tears trickling down the old man's black and weather-beaten cheeks."[27]

For the *gens de couleur* of Isle Brevelle in Natchitoches Parish the Civil War was a disaster. The conflict had placed them in a classic bind. On the one hand, they might gain in status if a northern victory swept away distinctions based on color, for discrimination against free blacks had become increasingly severe in the 1850s. On the other hand, they had a direct financial stake in the maintenance of slavery. Moreover, the abolition of slavery would more likely reduce their status to that of ordinary blacks than raise it to that of whites. In any case, they had little option which side to support. Unlike the free blacks in New Orleans, who raised a Confederate regiment but then changed sides when Union forces captured the city, these *gens de couleur* lived a long way from the Union lines. Casting their lot with the Confederacy, they raised a cavalry squadron and a company of infantry, although the Confederate authorities declined to use them in battle. Governor Allen praised them as "good and loyal citizens in every respect."[28]

Little good did that loyalty do them. Their farms and plantations lay directly in the path of Banks's army. Confederates set fire to cotton barns before Banks's advance, and Union soldiers burned and plundered along the line of their own retreat. As they retired south from Grand Ecore, wrote one soldier, "our path was lighted by the fires of burning cotton." The non-white status of the *gens de couleur* did nothing to protect their property from the bluecoats; the fact that they were colored slaveholders may even have made some Union soldiers especially vengeful. Many of the farms and plantations on Isle Brevelle were devastated. The Creoles of color never recovered their former prosperity and declined into a state of genteel poverty. They retained a sense of separateness based on light complexion, Catholicism, the French language, and family ties. But their social isolation, no longer buttressed by wealth and slavery, now worked against them. When Congressional Reconstruction enfranchised the freedmen, the Creoles of color were ill-placed to exercise influence over the overwhelmingly Protestant, English-speaking, darker-complexioned former slaves.[29]

The five hundred other free blacks in Natchitoches Parish had much more to gain from the Union victory. Non-slaveholders, these free blacks greased the wheels of the local economy by doing many of the relatively humble but vital tasks that in the North would have been performed by whites. The U.S. census of 1860 listed their occupations. The men were blacksmiths, carpenters, cart drivers, stock minders, shoemakers, and laborers. The women were housewives, seamstresses, and "washer and ironers." Half a dozen women, all of them elderly (one of them a native of Cuba), were listed as midwives. This group of blacks proved well positioned to provide leadership to the freedpeople. Mainly literate, many of them moderately wealthy, they were accustomed to independence; they knew how to earn and dispose of money; they were confident in dealing with whites. Fifty-year-old farmer Richard Faulkner, born in South Carolina to parents who had bought their freedom, became the first black teacher in Natchitoches Parish. Charles Leroy, a thirty-two-year-old shoemaker who in 1860 owned real estate valued at $2,000, represented Natchitoches Parish in the constitutional convention of 1867.

One free black, Carroll Jones, needs a category of his own. Born in Tennessee and emancipated by his white father, Jones made a fortune before the Civil War as a planter, livestock trader, innkeeper, and breeder of race-horses (many of which he jockeyed himself). In 1860 he owned fifteen slaves. His Rapides Parish plantation, whose "big house" also functioned as a hotel, sat astride the path of the advancing and retreating armies during the 1864 Red River campaign. Its location on the road to Mansfield made it a convenient place for the Confederates to maintain a forage depot, as well as an attractive headquarters for the passing army commanders. By the time the campaign ended, Union soldiers had stripped the Jones plantation of food and livestock, as well as the contents of the house. After the war, the Southern Claims Commission flatly rejected Jones's application for compensation, describing him as "an active sympathizer with and aider and abettor of the rebellion." Like the colored Creoles of Isle Brevelle, Jones had backed the wrong horse. Unlike those Creoles, however, Jones managed to resurrect his fortune after the war, purchasing a twelve-hundred-acre estate in Natchitoches Parish in 1869 and acquiring more land in subsequent years. His fine Cane River mansion was such a prominent landmark that it saw regular service as a voter registration and polling place during the years of Republican rule.[30]

War weariness and widespread desertion prior to the Confederate surrender suggested that the Union might easily stamp its authority upon the demoralized and divided white population. In one sense, this turned out to be the case: even die-hard Confederates acknowledged defeat and had no stomach for resuming the fight.

Imposing federal authority, however, was no simple matter. For one thing, the war had produced such bitter divisions among whites that the occupying forces confronted a situation that, in large parts of the state, resembled anarchy. For another, it was far from clear what kind of obedience the president and Congress expected from ex-Confederates. When it came to war aims, the North was itself deeply divided. The Democratic Party favored the quick restoration of ex-Confederate states on lenient terms—the "Union as it was." The Republican Party favored some form of federal protection for freedpeople and wartime Unionists, as well as the exclusion of former Confederate leaders from political power. But Republicans had been unable to agree on peace terms before the war ended. Lincoln himself favored a quick reconstruction on magnanimous terms—"with malice toward none, with charity for all."

The most vexing question was that of black suffrage. Lincoln had tried to avoid the issue, but Republicans like Senator Charles Sumner and Chief Justice Salmon Chase kept pressing it. These men, and others, argued that the federal government should make black suffrage a condition for the restoration of self-government to the former Confederate states. But a majority of Lincoln's cabinet, and Lincoln himself, opposed any such condition. The opposition of Congress to Lincoln's own reconstruction policy left the question open.

Looming behind the question of black suffrage was a practical political consideration of vital importance to the Republican Party. A slave had counted as three-fifths of a white person when it came to calculating a state's representation in the House. If blacks were to be counted as full citizens, the South stood to gain at least a dozen congressmen. Senator John Sherman explained to his much more conservative brother, General William T. Sherman, why he and other Republican moderates worried about allowing ex-Confederates untrammeled power to govern restored southern states that enjoyed substantially increased representation in Congress:

Who shall exercise that political power? Shall the rebels do so? If yes, will they not in effect restore slavery? Will they not oppress the negroes? Is it not hard to turn these negroes over to the very men who endeavored to overthrow the Government? After all, how much more ignorant are the slaves than the uneducated white people down South? I answer you, that while I will not commit myself on these matters, I feel sorely troubled by them.

If most congressional Republicans were hesitant to advocate black suffrage, they were equally loath to reject it out of hand.[31]

In pressing Congress to recognize the Unionist government of Louisiana, which controlled barely a third of the state's territory, Lincoln had hoped to set the process of reconstruction in motion even before the war ended. Under his executive order of December 1863, former rebels had but to take an oath of allegiance to the United States to regain their civil and political rights. As the soon as these oath-takers reached or exceeded 10 percent of the number of votes cast in the 1860 presidential election, they would be permitted to form a state government. Lincoln excluded various categories of high-ranking Confederates from his offer of amnesty, but the exclusions affected relatively few people. Moreover, Lincoln reserved the right to grant amnesty on an individual basis, a right he intended to exercise liberally. Individuals taking the oath of allegiance, and the reestablished state government itself, must agree to "faithfully support" the Confiscation Acts and the Emancipation Proclamation. In other words, Lincoln made emancipation the sole condition, other than an oath of loyalty, of restoration. This was the basis upon which General Banks, after much prodding from Lincoln, organized elections in 1864 that led to the formation of a "free state" government in Louisiana.[32]

Before the constitutional convention met, Lincoln, prompted by a visit from Jean Baptiste Roudanez and Arnold Bertonneau, two free blacks from New Orleans, raised the matter of black suffrage with Michael Hahn, the state's Unionist governor. The president asked Hahn to consider "whether some of the colored people may not be let in—as, for instance, the very intelligent, and especially those who have fought gallantly in our ranks." But Lincoln did not press the matter. "This is only a suggestion," he emphasized, "not to the public but to you alone." His letter was not without effect: Hahn and Banks lobbied vigorously and ultimately successfully to prevent the new state constitution from explicitly restricting the franchise to white people.

But no blacks gained the right to vote: the constitution merely authorized the legislature, at some unspecified future date, to extend the franchise to those blacks "as by military service, by taxation to support the government, or by intellectual fitness, may be deemed entitled thereto."[33]

Lincoln's letter to Hahn was tentative and brief. The president had constitutional scruples about insisting upon black suffrage: defining the franchise had always been a prerogative of the states. Practical considerations were also important. Lincoln viewed his reconstruction policy as a means of undermining the Confederacy and winning the war. Ever the political realist, he knew how little political support black suffrage commanded and how much vehement opposition it would evoke. As Chief Justice Chase's own man in New Orleans, U.S. Treasury agent George Denison, patiently explained, "It is difficult if not impossible to make these Free State men, who comprise our legislature, take the same view of it as you do." And if Congress or the president were to make black suffrage a condition of Louisiana's restoration, Denison warned, the Union cause "will lose all white support, or nearly all." Banks made the same point to Lincoln in person on December 18, and Lincoln agreed. Former postmaster general Montgomery Blair, a Lincoln confidante, also attended the meeting. He opposed black suffrage in any shape or form.[34]

Advocates of black suffrage, however, appealed to Radicals in Washington to block Lincoln's plan. Congress should refuse admission to Louisiana's representatives, argued New Orleans lawyer and Unionist Thomas J. Durant. The Free State government lacked political legitimacy, he explained, because the elections had been organized by the U.S. military at a time when two-thirds of the state lay outside Union control. It was folly too, he believed, to adopt a new state constitution before the status of blacks and former Confederates had been defined in law, and that should only be done by Congress. "This is not a [legitimate] State Government," Durant wrote Massachusetts congressman George S. Boutwell.[35]

Officials of the Free State government itself, on the other hand, complained that the U.S. Army was undermining it. Governor Michael Hahn, writing to Lincoln, accused the military of treating the state authorities with contempt. The charge was well founded. According to General Stephen A. Hurlbut, Banks's successor, the state legislature was "entirely useless, very expensive, and liable to do serious harm." In reality, he pointed out, that portion of Louisiana that lay within Union lines was being governed by the military. An angry Lincoln reprimanded Hurlbut and ordered Banks—then in Washington lobbying Congress to recognize the Free State government—to return to Louisiana to reassert political control over the military.[36]

To Lincoln's surprise and disappointment, Congress refused to admit the delegation from Louisiana. They were "men of straw who represent nobody," charged Senator Ben Wade of Ohio. Sumner, using a repellent metaphor, described the Free State government as a "seven month child, begotten by the bayonet, in continuous conjunction with the spirit of caste." The Louisianans had not helped their cause when, on February 21, would-be congressman A. P. Field attacked Congressman William D. Kelley of Pennsylvania with a knife when he encountered the latter at the Willard Hotel.[37]

Nevertheless, Lincoln continued to support the Free State government. In a concession to the Radicals, he publicly expressed, for the first time, his own preference for qualified black suffrage. "I would myself prefer," he stated, "that [the franchise] were now conferred on the very intelligent, and on those who served our cause as soldiers." But he refused to make even limited black suffrage a condition for a state's readmission to the Union. Focused on securing the complete abolition of slavery, he argued that a restored Louisiana would provide one more vote to ratify the Thirteenth Amendment. The substance of Lincoln's last public address was not so much an argument *for* black suffrage as an appeal for Congress to recognize the Free State government of Louisiana *without* black suffrage.[38]

During the months after the surrender, Natchitoches Parish remained an island of relative tranquillity in a sea of anarchy and lawlessness. Within weeks, the town boasted two freedmen's schools. Agents of the Freedmen's Bureau felt safe; they described the parish as one of the quietest in the state. "Apparently the whites and blacks here live amicably together," wrote James Cromie, "no ill feeling whatever existing between them." An exaggeration, no doubt, but given the violent reputation of parishes like Winn, De Soto, and Caddo, an understandable one. Putting the "distress and humiliation" of 1865 behind it, the *Natchitoches Times* saw grounds for optimism as it welcomed the New Year. The town was repairing its streets and sidewalks; new bridges were being built. Above all, former Confederates could take pride in their bearing in the aftermath of defeat. "If the knee did bend, the mind, the wisdom, the fortitude, is yet unimpaired to do the bidding of the possessor." Meanwhile, politics took a back seat to economic survival.[39]

3

FREEDOM AND SURVIVAL

I feel quite out of spirits, and very much annoyed this morning. The *Gentlemen* of color find it too cold to work. I told them it was time to commence and either leave or go to work.

William Payne to Eliza Payne, January 10, 1870

The Civil War spared the town of Natchitoches but devastated the plantations. Charred remains of homes, cotton gins, corncribs, and hay barns littered the river valley. Not much cotton was planted in 1865, and the prospects for a crop in 1866 were uncertain. The levees, fallen into disrepair, would be hard put to contain the Red River in full flood. The "army worm," a caterpillar produced by a gray moth, had destroyed crops in Union-occupied Louisiana in 1864 and could appear further north at any time.[1]

With little cash and limited access to credit, whites resorted to barter. Specie virtually disappeared. Both the police jury and the Town of Natchitoches issued their own paper currency in the form of warrants, which they deemed valid for payment of taxes. This "parish paper" quickly depreciated to half its face value. Even so, many whites could not pay their taxes: by 1871 over $6,200 due the town remained uncollected. The parish treasury could no longer help indigent whites, and the parish authorities had no inclination to support blacks who could not fend for themselves.[2]

The economic situation of former slaveholders was dire. Before the war, they had provisioned their plantations by borrowing freely from New Orleans factors (supply merchants); using slave property as collateral, they could obtain easy credit. After emancipation, land values plummeted and planters found it hard to borrow. Their only collateral was land, which had little value without labor to cultivate it. Many were reduced to genteel poverty. In 1860, Hardy Bryan Jr. owned thirty-eight slaves, and his land and

Figure 3. Asbury Methodist Church, Natchitoches town (1879). Raford Blunt's First Baptist Church likely resembled this structure. Arthur Babb Sketchbook, Cammie G. Henry Research Center, Northwestern State University of Louisiana.

personal property was valued at $48,000. In 1866 he died insolvent and in debt to his workers for a year's wages.[3]

Pessimistic that free blacks could be efficient, trustworthy laborers, planters read their former slaves' embrace of freedom as arrogance and indolence. Unable to confine blacks to the plantation and to compel instant obedience, whites found the behavior of freedpeople unnerving. Coveting what had been denied them in slavery, freedpeople bred dogs, drank whiskey, and acquired firearms. A few managed to buy horses. "They come into town on Sabbath Days," complained one planter, "parading Colts, navy sixes, and large knives, and with an air of defiance to God, man and the law."[4]

Freedom came at a cost. Former masters, no longer responsible for the welfare of their ex-slaves, often refused to support the old, the sick, and the disabled. Illness among former slaves sharply increased, especially when freedpeople congregated in towns and army camps where they were especially vulnerable to smallpox and other contagious diseases. Freedmen's Bureau agent William Henderson found one freedman who was "dangerously ill and lying in the woods" on the Breda plantation. "There are a great number of such cases and . . . the civil authorities will take no action."[5]

Ironically, the fact that slavery remained intact until the end of the war insulated blacks in Natchitoches Parish from the worst effects of disease. It was the slaves liberated by Union armies who suffered the most: refugees thrown together in the thousands, with no regular nutrition, in unfamiliar environments where they lacked immunity to local pathogens. Both blacks and whites benefited from the geographic isolation of Natchitoches. The lack of both a railroad connection and direct access to Red River enabled the parish to impose effective quarantines, thereby escaping the yellow fever epidemics that ravaged New Orleans and Shreveport.[6]

Still, death from disease made orphans of many children. Other children were rendered homeless by parents who were unable or unwilling to look after them. Dozens of these minors were indentured to white employers until they reached adulthood. The indentures, which bureau agent Henderson co-signed, required employers to treat apprenticed children "kindly and humanely." But when parents sought to reclaim their children, some employers refused to give them up.[7]

The new free labor system left little room for sentiment. Both sides tried to drive a hard bargain. The freedpeople enjoyed a temporary advantage because emancipation created what planters referred to as a "scarcity of labor." It was not so much scarcity as such but rather the inability of planters to compel blacks to work the long hours, under the strict discipline, for the low wages that they, the employers, saw fit. Former slaves delayed entering into contracts until the last minute, set their own hours of work, quit if they were dissatisfied, and shopped around for the best terms. Women and children who had previously been part of the plantation's labor force did much less work in the fields. Domestic workers haggled over wages, queried instructions, and felt under no obligation to stay. "We have hired since the first of January, eight or ten cooks and as many wash-women," complained one white woman, "and we are still without any. . . . The last of the sable daughters that came to us to live, asked thirteen dollars per month, clothes, doctor's bills, and so on; we told her that was too much, and we would not give it."[8]

Former slaves compared notes about what white employers were offering and tried to "level up." Planters found themselves competing against each other, promising monthly wages of between six and seventeen dollars as well as supplying shelter, clothing, and rations. Some offered black workers a share of the crop as well; the lower the wage, the larger the share. The balance between supplies, wages, and share of the crop varied. Some workers received no cash wages at all but were promised one-half of the crop. Employers sometimes offered shares to "squads" of men rather than to household heads. Different employment arrangements could be found on the same plantation. Improvisation was the order of the day, and neither side felt satisfied. White employers and black workers each felt taken advantage of.[9]

Economic misfortunes deepened the mutual mistrust. In May 1866 levees along the Red River gave way, causing the bottomlands to be inundated. When cotton growers replanted bedraggled seedlings, millions of "army worms" gobbled up the plants. Throughout the state, reported the Freedmen's Bureau, planters cut their losses by dismissing laborers "on the slightest provocation" and then refusing to pay their wages "on the pretended ground of indolence, idleness, insolence, or something fully as trivial." Some also cheated laborers who had agreed to forgo a monthly cash wage, in whole or in part, in exchange for a share of the crop. The dismal cotton harvest meant that this "share wage" failed to cover the food and supplies that laborers had received on credit. Even if employers were scrupulously honest, laborers could still end up in debt to them for supplies.[10]

Still, planters' refusal or inability to pay their black workers did not necessarily indicate a lost crop. More often, it reflected the tangled skein of debt that had both planters and merchants fighting over what little cotton was harvested. Planters were indebted to provision merchants, and they often prioritized their own debts at the expense of paying their workers. Creditors sued planters and, gaining writs of sequestration from the courts, seized cotton and left laborers unpaid. The latter had little recourse other than to hire a lawyer or appeal to the Freedmen's Bureau. Intervention by bureau agents, backed up by the power to impound cotton in the possession of the planter or merchant, often did the trick. The sums involved were substantial. The freedmen employed by W. W. Breazeale, for example, were owed $4,581 for a year's work, and merchants were suing Breazeale for his entire crop. After bureau agent James Cromie threatened to seize the cotton, Breazeale settled with his hands. In Louisiana as a whole, wrote the bureau's commanding general, J. A. Mower, in September 1867, "thousands of freedmen were defrauded of their just due." Small wonder many black laborers felt cheated.[11]

The process of dividing the crop caused particular dissatisfaction. If employers collected the entire crop, ginned it and baled it, and only then paid their workers, how could the people who actually grew and picked the cotton be sure that they received their specified share? Blacks working on shares wanted to receive their portion immediately after the cotton had been picked. Some laborers refused to hand over what they had grown, especially when debt-pressed employers wished to market the first pickings, before waiting for the entire harvest. In East Feliciana Parish, reported a bureau agent, "the laborers refuse to divide the cotton that is now being baled, and insist on retaining the whole crop until the end of the year, before the division of the crop takes place." Disputes could turn deadly. In Natchitoches Parish, John Blackburn refused to hand over his crop to Thomas Freeman, his employer. Freeman shot Blackburn dead.[12]

By and large, planters in Natchitoches were less exploitative than employers in surrounding parishes. They were less cruel, less inclined to employ violence. They were ready to open schools on their properties. They were more willing to sign the standard contract drawn up by the Freedmen's Bureau. After the May 1866 floods, Cromie reported, they paid their laborers "squarely up to the 1st of June, and then offered them rations, clothing, medicinal attendance, and a share of the crop, for the balance of the year." Cromie forbade them to cut costs by dismissing workers. The laborers' share often depended upon the solvency and integrity of the employer. In the settlement of 1867, for example, which followed another year of flooding and poor harvests, the family of Isham Moore received $200 from planter William Payne.[13]

Yet Mary Bryan, writing in the *Natchitoches Times*, all but admitted that planters sometimes cheated. "Whatever immediate profit may be made by taking advantage of the weakness and ignorance of negroes, the practice will be found injurious in the long run." Some planters privately criticized the sharp practice of others. C. Plaisance, trustee for the estate of a deceased plantation owner, had expressly understood that "wages for laborers is first and advances by merchants next." Another trustee, however, had shipped the entire cotton crop to New Orleans merchants before disbursing wages. Plaisance urged Cromie to stop the merchants from spending the proceeds of the crop "and demand that it be held to pay the freedmen." A former employee of Dr. J. H. Cunningham asked a freedmen's school teacher to intercede for him. "He worked faithfully last year and should get something for it," the teacher wrote Cromie, "not only in making his crop . . . but also in building his gin."[14]

Cheating, however, was in the eye of the beholder. Planters generally scoffed at the notion that they owed their laborers money. They complained that they provided family rations but no longer commanded the labor of wives and older children. They pointed out that they supported the old, the sick, and the very young, all of them idle hands. G. S. Walmsley told Cromie that when Moses Woods, one of his workers, suddenly quit, he had to care for his sick wife and two small children. Then there was Mary Griffin, a mentally disturbed epileptic who wandered onto his place and refused to leave. Walmsley nursed her through a bout of smallpox, spending freely of his own money. "If I succeed in saving the poor woman's life and restoring her to usual health, I shall have done my duty." He billed the bureau for the medical expenses he had incurred.[15]

Planters also found it hard to accept that they could not extract a slave's work from a free person. When laborers set their own work pace and took breaks when they pleased, employers regarded them as indolent and careless. "When he is engaged at so much per month," a planter wrote the *Natchitoches Times*, "he spends the most time he can in concocting plans to do the least possible in the greatest length of time." When paid for every one hundred pounds of cotton picked, laborers left "the best part of the cotton . . . scattered by the wind, caught by the rain and trampled underfoot." Holding freedpeople to the letter of their contracts was impossible, this man went on. Any attempt to do so would simply scare off the workforce. Faced with a request to pay back wages to a former employee, Dr. J. W. Butler responded testily. "Ned has not worked more than one third of the time, was well cared for when sick, and left my premises without my consent." He did not owe Ned a cent, Butler told the Freedmen's Bureau; rather, it was Ned who owed money to him.[16]

Bureau agents advised freedmen not to contract with planters "who did not treat them fairly" in 1865 and 1866. Butler found it hard to retain his black workers; in 1867 he recruited a dozen Chinese immigrants. Harsh employers (many of whom had been cruel slaveholders) experienced similar problems. Former governor Thomas O. Moore, whose overseer had shot several slaves in 1863, dispatched labor agents to North Carolina and Delaware, presumably because local freedmen refused to work for him.[17]

Planters complained bitterly about laborers breaking their contracts by quitting mid-year, often leaving debts. Emile Rost told Cromie that he had advanced twenty dollars to a husband and wife, who then "left my place without any cause whatever." Gabriel Prudhomme claimed that he had lodged, fed, and furnished Alexander White and his wife with the understanding that they would work for him during 1867. But "under the pretext of taking a promenade on the Christmas holidays," Prudhomme complained, the couple had signed a contract with Emile Sompeyrac. Prudhomme pleaded with Cromie to bring back truant employees. "If these freedmen are at liberty to leave whenever their please . . . there will be no crop made." Planters often argued that fickleness, not bad treatment, prompted laborers to quit. "I dealt fairly with them," insisted the operator of Kenilworth plantation. "I have paid them every cent I owe them. . . . And yet they quit whenever they please."[18]

Freedpeople, for their part, felt no obligation to stay with an employer if they were dissatisfied and believed they could do better elsewhere. "They do not, of course, give the same amount of work as they did under the lash," a bureau agent noted, "nor can it be expected." In addition to setting their own work pace, freedmen objected to having their wives work in the fields. They disliked planters or overseers ordering their children about. Cromie advised planters that they stood a better chance of retaining laborers if they allowed freedmen's schools on their plantations; half a dozen did so.[19]

The "share wage" system, which applied to about two-thirds of the employment contracts for the year 1867, gave laborers a stronger incentive to remain on the plantation until the crops were in. But freedpeople signed these contracts reluctantly, suspicious of an arrangement that had left many penniless at the end of 1866. The 1867 settlement did little to allay their dissatisfaction. Many freedmen saw little cash at the end of the year, reported bureau agent Charles Miller, "and some are indebted largely to their employers." On one plantation, where flooding destroyed the entire cotton crop, the employer owed his hands $1,200, which he was unable to pay. Miller seized the corn crop, 300 bushels, to ensure that the freedmen at least had something to eat. The bureau offered loans to planters who could not feed their hands. David H. Boullt Jr., whose two plantations housed seventy freedpeople, received 2,192 pounds of corn and 1,200 pounds of meat. Freedpeople supplemented their diet by raising hogs, chickens, and vegetables. Even so, hunger stalked the parish. Early in 1868 Miller distributed 3,165 rations to people who were destitute, many of them whites.[20]

Small wonder black farmers wished for something better. "All have a great wish to become landholders," reported Cromie, "but have not the means to carry it out." But they still clung to the belief that the federal government would allocate them freehold homesteads. This expectation was no idle fantasy. The bureau held many abandoned and confiscated plantations, and Congress had authorized that agency to assign forty acres to "every male citizen, whether refugee of freedman." A bill introduced by Senator Lyman Trumbull in January 1866 to extend the bureau's life proposed reserving three million acres of public land for the freedpeople.[21]

President Andrew Johnson, however, vigorously opposed the transfer of land to ex-slaves. In September 1865 he ordered the Freedmen's Bureau to return all abandoned and confiscated properties to their previous owners once the latter had received pardons from the president. Former slaves who had already received land were dispossessed. Johnson vetoed Trumbull's bill. The result, wrote General Oliver O. Howard, was "a complete reversal of the Government's generous provision for the late slaves." But freedpeople refused to accept that the government had reneged on its promise. They continued to hope for "forty acres and a mule," and the Republican Party's growing opposition to Johnson, which eventuated in Congressional Reconstruction, fed that hope.[22]

On May 29, 1865, Johnson issued a Proclamation of Amnesty and Reconstruction that offered a general pardon to all former rebels who took the oath of allegiance except for high-ranking Confederate politicians, civilian officials, and military officers. Former rebels who owned taxable property worth at least $20,000 were also excluded. Johnson appointed a provisional governor whom he instructed to arrange the election of constitutional conventions on the basis of white suffrage. If the conventions condemned secession, repudiated Confederate war debts, and ratified the Thirteenth Amendment, states would be permitted hold elections and regain the right of self-government within the Union. "Clemency will be liberally extended," Johnson promised, to ex-rebels who, excluded from the general amnesty, applied to the president for individual pardons. These conditions were about as lenient as anyone could have reasonably expected. Proclamations covering other occupied states quickly followed.[23]

Some Radical Republicans were alarmed by the terms of these proclamations and the speed with which Johnson issued them. During the first months of his presidency, however, Johnson basked in the goodwill of the northern public. Appearing to stand above partisan politics, he was all things to all men. His tough talk of punishing traitors heartened Republicans, who had opposed what they regarded as Lincoln's excessive leniency. Republicans who were repelled by the apparent vindictiveness of the Radicals acclaimed Johnson as the heir to Lincoln's magnanimous policy. War Democrats and southern Unionists saw him as one of their own. The honeymoon could not last, but the universal desire for peace, the fluidity of the political scene, and the desire of most Republicans for a rapid demobilization of the army in the South enabled Johnson to press ahead. Congress, moreover, seemed happy to leave Reconstruction in the president's hands until it reassembled in December. Johnson was no enthusiast for black suffrage, but for the moment he obfuscated, as did many leading Republicans.[24]

Johnson's hostility to the Freedmen's Bureau and his low opinion of blacks eventually alienated Republican moderates like John Sherman and Lyman Trumbull. A pro-slavery Democrat who had refused to support the Confederacy, Johnson accepted emancipation but had never regarded slavery as oppressive to the slaves. He considered the freedpeople lazy. He denied that they required any protection beyond that already provided by the civil authorities. He sympathized with white southerners' complaints about black soldiers. In private, Johnson appeared bitterly hostile to blacks. Although he concealed the full extent of his racial prejudice, Johnson's antipathy to the freedpeople, together with his expansive view of states' rights, set him on a collision course with the Republican-controlled Congress. The clash vastly complicated the process of Reconstruction and, in hindsight, undercut Republican efforts to reform the South on the basis of equal citizenship.[25]

Southern Unionists and northern visitors believed that Johnson's proclamation of May 29 made ex-Confederates dangerously cocky. Before it, the defeated rebels had been so despondent and apprehensive that they would have accepted virtually any peace terms dictated by the North, including black suffrage. After it, they believed that they could not only quickly regain political power in their states but also treat the ex-slaves as a subordinate caste. By dispelling their fear of punishment and by implying that they could ignore Congress, Johnson encouraged white southerners to treat the Republican Party with contempt. It was only in the summer of 1865 that former rebels became defiant.[26]

The truth, however, was vastly more complicated. If there had ever been a moment when ex-Confederates would have acquiesced to stringent peace terms, that moment was brief—just five or six weeks, counting from the surrender of General Joseph E. Johnston's army on April 26. Johnson issued his proclamation only days after the Confederate armies in the trans-Mississippi theater formally capitulated and when Union forces had yet to occupy most of Louisiana and nearly all of Texas. Moreover, surrendering Confederates expected recognition from the North that they had fought honorably and well. Accepting the verdict of battle was one thing, confessing to guilt and accepting anything that the conquerors might dish out quite another.[27]

The first edition of the *Natchitoches Times*, published only two days after the surrender of the local Confederate garrison, was no exercise in sackcloth and ashes. True, the *Times* advised readers that further resistance would be futile. But it advised the conquerors to "treat our people with the respect due to a fallen enemy," for it would be folly to "pursue us with a spirit of rank animosity." The South's "valiant deeds" and the "gallantry" of the Confederate armies "have made it entitled to magnanimous and mild treatment." These were not words of penitence and resignation.[28]

Even if Lincoln had lived, the federal government would have been in no position to impose stringent terms immediately after the surrender, because the president and Congress were at loggerheads. Congress had refused to recognize the Free State government of Louisiana but failed to pass the alternative plan of reconstruction proposed by Radical congressman James M. Ashley. Most congressional Republicans were not prepared to insist upon black suffrage. Neither Lincoln nor Congress had given much thought to the role of the army in the postwar South. Lincoln's assumption, widely shared among Republicans, seems to have been that no lengthy military occupation would be necessary.[29]

Lincoln's terms for postwar reconstruction, therefore, would in all likelihood have resembled those of Johnson. Johnson's proclamation of May 29 was modeled on a draft that Lincoln had discussed in cabinet on the day he died. Like Johnson, Lincoln wanted maximum feasible leniency and wished to maintain executive control over reconstruction for as long as possible. Like Johnson, he had opposed making black suffrage an unconditional requirement. He apparently failed to anticipate the kind of aggressive obstinacy that ex-Confederates displayed in the summer and fall of 1865. The ex-rebels would yield to federal authority, Lincoln told Secretary of the Navy Gideon Welles, because they were "were too badly beaten" and "too exhausted" to resist.[30]

Lincoln was mistaken. The example of Louisiana showed that many ex-Confederates were boldly confident *before* the surrender and that Lincoln himself had inadvertently encouraged this truculent attitude. His Louisiana policy had fostered the impression among former Confederates that they would not only be quickly pardoned but also become the dominant political voice in the postwar South. This, at least, is how Governor James Madison Wells interpreted Lincoln's policy. In March 1865, after stepping into the governor's office when the Free State legislature selected Michael Hahn as U.S. senator, Wells began appointing former Confederates and pro-slavery Unionists to positions that had been held by men who identified with the Republican Party. Distracted by other war-related matters, Lincoln did not intervene. Indeed, until his dying day he pressed Congress to recognize the government headed by Wells.[31]

Still, a Lincoln administration that survived through 1865 would almost certainly have changed tack on reconstruction. Publicly and privately, Lincoln emphasized his flexibility. He did not wish to bind himself to any single policy. Congress could recognize the Free State government of Louisiana, he argued, without setting a cast-iron precedent; other rebel states could be treated differently. He expected to cooperate with congressional Republicans in formulating a new policy should they reject that government. In the words of John W. Burgess, a Unionist from Tennessee and one of the founders of political science in the United States, Lincoln consistently displayed a "cautious habit of leaving open a way of escape out of any position when necessity or prudence might require its abandonment." Confronted by southern defiance, he would have acted very differently from Johnson.[32]

Had Lincoln discovered the full extent of Wells's pro-Confederate appointments policy, he almost certainly would have forced the governor to backtrack. His reassignment of General Banks to command the Department of the Gulf in April 1865 implied as much. Returning to New Orleans, Banks replaced the mayor with his own man and dismissed several more of

Wells's appointees. He also instructed the chief of police to ensure that "the men composing the force should be of known loyalty"—a factor of special importance given that ex-Confederate soldiers were flooding into New Orleans. The governor had been dismissing loyal Unionists, Banks wrote President Johnson, replacing them with "the worst of rebels and secessionists."[33]

With Johnson ensconced in the White House, however, a political difficulty that might have been squared within the Republican Party turned into a political deadlock, followed by a constitutional crisis. Having served bravely and loyally as Lincoln's wartime governor of Tennessee, Johnson was elected vice president in1864 on a "Union" ticket when the Republican Party renamed itself in a bid for Democratic support. Johnson did not regard the Republican Party as his natural political home and felt little obligation to it. He loathed Radicals like Thaddeus Stevens and Charles Sumner. He believed that the franchise should be restricted, not widened, and he found the idea of black suffrage repugnant. Privately, he laid plans to run for president in 1868 at the head of a new political party composed of northern Democrats, southern Democrats, conservative Unionists, and conservative Republicans.

It took many months for the Republican Party to coalesce in opposition to Johnson. Apart from a small group of Radicals, Republicans were disposed to accord the new president time to see how ex-Confederates responded to generosity. They were inclined in any case to afford the executive ample leeway. Moreover, having been accustomed to dealing with the pragmatic, flexible Lincoln, they assumed that Johnson's policy, which initially resembled that of Lincoln, was an experiment, subject to modification in the light of circumstances. They expected, too, that the president would consult with Republican leaders, especially when Congress reconvened in December. Wary of repudiating Johnson lest he defect to the Democrats, Republican moderates believed they could influence him. Johnson encouraged this belief by being less than forthright about his intentions.[34]

When he met Governor Wells, however, Johnson made his sympathies quite clear. Wells found the president entirely at one with his policy of appointing former Confederates. Heeding Wells's entreaties, Johnson dismissed Banks and allowed the governor to reinstate his own men. "Tell the boys," Wells wrote his wife, "that they shall not again be troubled with further Yankee adventurism." Once in a position to make appointments throughout the state, Wells informed Johnson, he favored "men of reso-

lution and intelligence who had seen military service in the rebel ranks."
On June 10, just four days after Union troops occupied Shreveport, Wells
authorized the parishes of the former Confederate heartland to elect their
own officials.[35]

People excluded from the terms of Johnson's Proclamation of Amnesty
and Reconstruction quickly gained individual pardons. Planter and secessionist Lewis Texada, for example, had signed the oath of allegiance during
the Union occupation of Alexandria in March 1864, but he subsequently
served in the Confederate army. Johnson's proclamation specifically excluded people who had taken the oath and repudiated it. But when Texada
applied for a presidential pardon, with an endorsement from Wells, Johnson signed it straightaway.[36]

With Confederate soldiers still stacking their arms and signing paroles,
Wells assailed the Republican Party as "unscrupulous," "obnoxious," and
bent upon "our utter humiliation." The "radical abolition party," he warned,
sought to enfranchise the ex-slaves in order to "prevent the return of power
to the Conservatives of the South" and hand the government to "political
adventurers" from the North. Setting himself squarely against black suffrage, he warned that former slaves, if given the right to vote, would nine
times out of ten "support their former masters." But if the Republican Party
ever enfranchised blacks over the objections of the ex-rebels, he added,
no Union man could remain in Louisiana "otherwise than on sufferance."
It was a sinister non sequitur—If their former masters would control the
black vote, wherein lay the danger of black suffrage?—but the implication
was clear: former Confederates would drive Unionists from the state—even
kill them—should blacks be permitted to vote. Never once did Johnson
rebuke Wells or attempt to restrain him.[37]

The Union army was slow to sense the political danger. "You hardly yet
realize how completely this country has been devastated and how completely humbled the man of the South is," General William T. Sherman
wrote his brother, U.S. senator John Sherman. General Philip Sheridan,
headquartered in New Orleans, acknowledged a "spirit of bitterness and
discord" among ex-Confederates but played down its significance. "Bitterness is all that is left for these people." Sheridan, the Commander of
the Gulf, expressed the complacent view held by many in the North that
the South's antebellum elite would never recover. Northern settlers, he predicted, would "at no very distant period" control the economy and politics
of Louisiana. "There will be an almost total transfer of landed property, the

North will own every Steamboat, every large mercantile establishment and everything which requires capital to carry it on."[38]

But the former ruling class, already halfway restored to power, was determined to prevent that from happening. The word "carpetbagger" had yet to be coined. Yet even before the final Confederate capitulation, Governor Wells had stoked local resentment against federal officeholders—men "from the Eastern States, who are neither identified with us by feeling, family ties, residence, or the ownership of property." These were the very men, of course, who formed the nucleus of Louisiana's embryonic Republican Party, whose current position and future preferment rested upon the disfranchisement of ex-Confederates and/or black suffrage. "As a rule," Wells told President Johnson, "they are insolent, overbearing and rapacious."[39]

Wells urged Johnson to end military "interference in civil matters." Federal troops and martial law were no longer necessary, he insisted; the white South was "honestly disposed to submit to the law of the land." The Union soldiers who remained were doing more harm than good, he complained. The black soldiers who comprised most of the occupation forces were arrogant and overbearing, and their presence encouraged freedpeople to break their contracts, quit the plantations, rob and steal, and congregate in the towns in a state of idleness. "Their very presence demoralizes the negroes for all purposes of useful industry," Wells asserted. He and some of the interim governors appointed by Johnson implored the president to remove all black troops and authorize the formation of state militias. They claimed that whites could be trusted to maintain order and do justice to blacks, without federal interference.[40]

Anxious to see crops planted and harvested, the Freedmen's Bureau tried to make black laborers stay on the plantations. But when Thomas W. Conway, head of the Freedmen's Bureau in Louisiana, ruled that blacks should have the right to seek their own employers, Wells was apoplectic. "The effect of this order," he wrote Johnson, "will be to utterly demoralize the negroes . . . to say nothing of the dangerous and revengeful spirit that idleness and want may engender in the breasts of the negroes toward the whites." He appealed to Johnson as a former slaveholder and fellow white southerner: "Your knowledge of the race Mr. President must surely convince you that if left to idleness, they will not work." Conway, he added, was "a radical negro suffrage man."[41]

Whites presented their desire to reestablish control over the black labor force in terms of crime control, and the two issues became entangled. There was certainly a need to suppress outlawry. Many of the guerrilla gangs that originated in opposition to the Confederacy made a seamless transition to outright banditry after the surrender. Army officers sometimes allowed former Confederates to form "vigilance committees" for the purpose of hunting down "robbers, thieves, and jayhawkers." Such committees, however, quickly became instruments to oppress freedpeople. When the newly constituted civil authorities began to organize local militia companies, it became apparent that these militias bore a close resemblance to the antebellum slave patrols.[42]

From every corner of Louisiana, and from every state in the former Confederacy, whites justified strong measures by citing the threat of organized violence by the freedmen, which threat the presence of black soldiers, they claimed, was exacerbating. "The colored troops manifest great malignity towards the white population," petitioners from Shreveport complained to the general in charge of Louisiana, E. R. S. Canby, and "are instigating the former slaves of the country to deeds of insurrection and Massacre." As 1865 drew to a close, rumors abounded that blacks would rise up during the Christmas holidays, murder the whites, and seize their lands. In Caddo and Bossier Parishes, to the north of Natchitoches, militia companies scoured the plantations in search of firearms in the hands of freedmen. Forcibly entering black homes, they confiscated any weapons they discovered.[43]

The state elections in the autumn of 1865 confirmed that Louisiana, if left to its own devices, would be governed by former Confederates. True, the Democratic Party endorsed Wells, the state's most prominent wartime Unionist, but in all the other races, where Democrats ran their own candidates, ex-Confederates trounced former Unionists. The Democratic platform, moreover, opposed the notion of extending any legal or political rights to ex-slaves. It not only affirmed "this to be a government of the white people . . . for the exclusive political benefit of the white race," but also denied that blacks could ever become citizens of the United States. To reinforce the point, Democrats declared that "there can, in no event, nor under any circumstances be any equality between the white and other races." The platform accepted the abolition of slavery but wanted former slaveholders to receive financial compensation.[44]

Louisiana's white electorate expected the new state legislature to adopt stiff regulations to make blacks return to the plantations and stay there— what the *Louisiana Democrat* called "laws enforcing the obligations of contract, apprenticing minors, punishing vagrancy etc." When the legislature met in November 1865, it duly seized the opportunity. Black household heads were required to sign contracts with an employer during the first ten days of January and to stay with that employer for the duration of the contract. Leaving the plantation without permission incurred a fine of two dollars a day. Should a laborer fall sick, he lost pay; in cases of "feigned sickness" he paid a fine as well. An employee who refused to work could be "forced to labor on roads, levees, and other public works." Workers could be fined or docked pay for poor work and breaches of discipline, including "impudence, swearing, or indecent language." Blacks classified as "vagrants" could be hired out to planters, or compelled to labor on public works, for a year. Blacks living on plantations were prohibited from carrying firearms. Municipalities like Opelousas barred blacks from living in town, except as servants, and prohibited trading, preaching, or holding any kind of meeting without permission.[45]

The Republican Party condemned these "Black Codes" as thinly disguised efforts to reintroduce slavery. But Francis Preston Blair Sr., a founding member of the Republican Party and a close adviser to Andrew Johnson, urged the president to accept them. It was only to be expected, Blair argued, that southern whites would "mass and discipline and arm the militia and make laws to keep down the negroes." Without white supremacy America would become "a nation of bastards." Johnson needed little persuasion. The admission of black testimony in southern courtrooms, he believed, was all the proof required to demonstrate that blacks were equal in the eyes of the law. Black suffrage, he warned, far from protecting ex-slaves, as a growing number of Republicans contended, would inaugurate a "war of the races" that would result in the "Negro race" being exterminated. Inundated by complaints from white southerners, Johnson badgered his generals about the conduct of black soldiers and pressed for their removal.[46]

The army insisted that black regiments exhibited good discipline. "In the majority of cases of collision between whites and negro soldiers," General George H. Thomas wrote Johnson, "the white man has attempted to bully the negro, for it is exceedingly repugnant to the Southerners to have negro soldiers in their midst and some are so foolish as to vent their anger upon the negro because he is a soldier." In any case, the army had no option but to deploy black regiments for occupation duty in the former Confederacy.[47]

Local commanders dismissed charges that the freedmen threatened whites' safety. "There is not the slightest danger of a negro insurrection," Colonel F. M. Crandall wrote from Shreveport. Called upon to investigate an allegation that blacks were engaged in "an armed conspiracy . . . to destroy the white population," Captain James Harrison discovered a figment of fevered imagination. Blacks acquired weapons, he concluded, as an expression of freedom rather than "from any desire to do harm." Commending blacks for "their uniform courtesy and politeness towards the whites," Harrison noted that "they invariably lift their hats in passing."[48]

Union commanders concluded that militias composed of former slaveholders and Confederate veterans had no other purpose than to curb black freedom. The commander in northwestern Louisiana reported that "frequent and flagrant outrages committed by the militia . . . are driving the negroes to desperation, and if an insurrection does take place, of which I see no prospect, it will brought about by the whites denying to them the right to life, liberty and property." Under pressure from the army, the militias disbanded. They reappeared over the coming years in various shadowy guises: the Ku Klux Klan, the Knights of the White Camelia, the White League, and the "298."[49]

Army officers believed that blacks needed protection, not whites. "The treatment of colored people in some instances beggars description," wrote an officer stationed at Port Hudson. "Only yesterday a colored man came into the Fort most cruelly beaten by two white men. . . . The man was mangled and bruised and his strength almost exhausted from the effect of the beating, simply because he was about to remove his personal property from their plantation." From Natchitoches, Freedmen's Bureau agent James Cromie reported that two blacks had been murdered, and lamented the "inability of the civil authorities to arrest the perpetrators."[50]

Some degree of white-black violence was to be expected. Emancipation created for whites "strange and hitherto repugnant relations," a southern politician explained. The law now restrained them "from exercising accustomed rights by prohibiting and punishing them as wrongs." Former slaves and ex-masters "have not only to learn new lessons . . . but to unlearn old ones." The new situation demanded "almost superhuman wisdom and virtue." Andrew Johnson pointed out that violence followed "in the wake of all great civil commotions and revolutions" and noted that parallel situations in history had produced far worse carnage. Former Confederate general Richard Taylor accused Republicans of grossly exaggerating "southern outrages." From 1865 onward, he wrote tongue in cheek, "the entire white race of the South devoted itself to the killing of negroes."[51]

But Republicans did not exaggerate. Stabbings and shootings nearly always originated in attempts by blacks to defend their freedom, confirmed presidential assistant Benjamin C. Truman after an eight-month tour of the South. "Nowhere are there any negroes so ignorant of the great change that has taken place to submit to the lash," he told Johnson. Freedmen resisted working in gangs, took time off when it suited them, quit their employer if dissatisfied, withdrew their wives and children from the fields, and refused to make contracts in the expectation of receiving government land. They argued with their former masters, presuming to bargain with them as equals. As one bureau agent noted, "They are very jealous of their new rights." Accustomed to complete mastery, whites reacted with fury when they encountered this kind of behavior. "When freedmen did not act exactly to suit the employer," claimed Thomas Conway, "a resort to violence is the first thought."[52]

The Civil War added another element to whites' propensity for violence. That conflict had cheapened human life, especially black lives. Most whites of military age were hardened veterans; they had all seen friends, comrades, and relatives killed; many had inflicted death on others. Raised in a culture of honor that bred personal violence, they were even more likely to reach for the gun having lived through the war. Whites were well aware, moreover, that the slaves, for all their outward loyalty, had done all within their limited power to undermine the Confederacy. Confederate soldiers had routinely shot black prisoners in cold blood, often with the tacit or explicit approval of their officers. General Taylor tried to discourage the practice—not from moral objections but from the calculation that it would discourage black soldiers from deserting. With the freedmen celebrating the Confederacy's downfall, many ex-soldiers, in the words of Benjamin Truman, "vented their wrath upon the head of the unoffending negro." Now standing outside the protection of their former masters, blacks were acutely vulnerable to violence from former masters, embittered Confederate veterans, and outlaw bands.[53]

A study of homicides in postwar Louisiana confirms the evidence scattered throughout congressional investigations and army reports on "outrages against freedmen." The Pelican State was an extraordinarily violent place during Reconstruction, and in most cases of homicide the perpetrator was white and the victim black. The Red River valley had an exceptionally high homicide rate. Its six parishes contained only 13 percent of Louisiana's rural population but accounted for half of all murders.

The significance of these crimes was not so much their raw number but rather the absence of punishment. When blacks were the victims, white perpetrators invariably got away scot-free. After listing seventy cases of blacks killed by whites and over two hundred cases of blacks being wounded by whippings, stabbings, beatings, and shootings, the Freedmen's Bureau noted that "In no instance . . . has a white man been punished for killing or ill treating a freedman."[54]

Whites' refusal to concede civil equality to former slaves reflected a nonchalant attitude toward violence against blacks. The constitutional conventions of 1865 had permitted courts to consider the testimony of blacks, but not when whites were the defendants. It was with the greatest reluctance, and only after much prodding by Andrew Johnson, that some state legislatures amended their laws to place blacks and whites on an equal footing.[55]

The depth of whites' repugnance to the idea of civil equality can be gauged by the example of Kentucky, which was never subject to either Presidential of Congressional Reconstruction and hence under no pressure to enact even a facade of legal equality. The prewar and soon-to-be-postwar governor, John Helm, reported that the Kentucky legislature would "not consent that a negro shall be viewed as a witness between two white men as litigants." Moreover, the legislature "would not and will not change" the law mandating the death penalty when a black man attacked a white women but imprisonment when a white man committed the same crime. The rationale for this discrimination, he explained, was that whites were prepared to grant blacks only those rights "as our manhood would allow."[56]

Army officers reported that blacks could never obtain justice in the state courts. From Rapides Parish, Lieutenant Colonel Orrin McFadden advised that juries, consisting exclusively of white men, automatically sided with white defendants. McFadden quickly learned to mistrust anything that whites said in respect of blacks. "The facility with which the best people of this Parish misinform anything pertaining to 'niggers' is quite astonishing." A report from Caldwell Parish, detailing a travesty of justice in a case involving the murder of freedmen, concluded with the observation: "I have not yet seen a case in this District . . . decided in favor of a black man." Many cases never came to trial because jailors and sheriffs allowed accused men to escape. The willingness of many whites to provide false alibis, perjure themselves, intimidate black witnesses, and discount black testimony made the Civil Rights Act, passed by Congress in April 1866 over Johnson's veto, ineffective throughout much of Louisiana and the South.[57]

In short, the Black Codes might be a dead letter, but their spirit permeated the administration of justice. The civil authorities "embrace every possible opportunity to put freedmen in jail for the most frivolous offences," extorting fines and pocketing the proceeds, one bureau agent reported. A notice in the *Louisiana Democrat* showed the kind of thing he meant: "The Mayor [of Alexandria] has fined several of the darkie tribe for having a little dance, without paying license and for kicking up a fuss generally." Conversely, if blacks attempted to assert their rights in disputes over wages, property, and the division of crops, the law remained beyond their reach. Any freedman wishing to sue his employer, the Bienville Parish agent explained, "must first be able to give security for loss in case his suit should go against him, which not more than one in a hundred can do."[58]

With Congress powerless to stay Johnson's hand until it assembled in December 1865, the agents of the Freedmen's Bureau, backed up by a thin force of federal soldiers, constituted the only barrier between the freedpeople, who wished to make decisions for themselves, and a vengeful white population bent on keeping them on the plantations.

The most crucial issue turned on the definition and punishment of vagrancy. Strict enforcement of draconian vagrancy laws would severely restrict blacks' freedom of movement, as well as greatly enhance the power of the employer over his laborers. Thomas Conway's July 1865 ruling that freedmen were at liberty to choose new employers tilted the balance toward black laborers. When Johnson replaced Conway with a conservative, J. Scott Fullerton, the latter tilted the balance back again by abolishing the bureau's tribunals, insisting that the negotiation of contracts was a private matter, and acquiescing in the state's sweeping definition of vagrancy.[59]

By refusing to recognize the South's state governments, Congress weighed in on the side of the freedpeople. General Absalom Baird, who replaced Fullerton after a scant three months, instructed his officers to oppose any effort to use the vagrancy laws "as an engine of oppression, or as a means of coercing the negro into making bargains which they regard as unfair." A man should not be classed as a vagrant, Baird explained, "because he refuses to work on a cotton plantation or because he refuses to work for such wages as the planter wishes to give him." Because it seemed likely that

Congress would legislate to protect black freedom, the Freedmen's Bureau questioned the whole notion of separate laws for blacks. Its model contract between laborers and employers emphasized that "no restraints or disabilities shall be imposed upon the freedmen that are not imposed upon white men." The vagrancy laws, Baird insisted, "shall be applied to black men only as they are to whites."[60]

Although not quite an independent political force, and by no means united behind the Republican Party, the army enjoyed enormous prestige. It was not about to relinquish all power to the state governments of the South, especially when their legal status remained in dispute. With the backing of Congress and Secretary of War Edwin Stanton, the army attempted to protect the free people. When the police in New Orleans took to arresting as vagrants "all colored laborers who were found on the streets . . . and not employed just at the moment the police saw them," the army freed them. When policemen interfered with black religious services, General Canby ordered them to desist.[61]

In August the army appointed a provost marshal general for Louisiana to investigate complaints from freedmen and their employers and "give such redress as may be necessary." The army had already prohibited the use of whipping and corporal punishment in general. In October, by order of General Canby, employers were forbidden to appoint overseers on their plantations. In December, as the state legislature enacted stringent laws regulating contracts and punishing vagrancy, the Freedmen's Bureau issued its own model contract, which specified "good and wholesome rations, comfortable clothing and quarters, medical attention and just treatment, and opportunity for the instruction of children." No other contracts would be deemed binding by the bureau.[62]

The army thus prevented the civil authorities, or at least hindered them, from implementing the Black Codes. Although political pressure from the Johnson administration compelled the army to turn over most cases to the civil courts, bureau agents continued to adjudicate complaints of assault and battery, denial of wages, and breach of contract, dispensing a rough justice that struck a balance between white employers and black employees. Agents exerted pressure on landlords to treat their employees fairly. As an agent informed one planter, "cussing and harsh treatment towards the freedmen will not be tolerated." When whites attempted to bind children to apprenticeships over the protests of their guardians, agents intervened to stop them. As 1865 drew to a close, President Johnson declared that "restoration" had been accomplished and that military rule had ceased. The Republican Party, disturbed by the South's reaction to Johnson's leniency, believed that Congress should legislate to protect the freedpeople and that the army must remain active as an occupation force.[63]

Any new policy, however, would run smack against southern white resistance. Johnson had encouraged ex-Confederate recalcitrance first by inadvertence and then by design. The North had "lost the physical advantages of a large occupation army," writes an authority on counterinsurgency, "and the psychological advantages of having just won victory on the battlefield." In truth, however, the Republican Party had been utterly unprepared in 1865 to exploit those advantages in a way that might have ensured substantial freedom to the former slaves.[64]

The residents of Natchitoches had as much at stake in the postwar settlement as anyone. With more plantations and more black laborers than any other parish in Louisiana, the survival of the white planters as the dominant social class—and that class included doctors, lawyers, merchants, and small farmers—turned on the question of who would govern. The *Natchitoches Times* made no secret of its view that stringent laws were needed "to force this lazy race to work," advocating a system of "peonage" to supplant slavery. The ability of blacks to prosper as free people therefore hinged upon the degree to which Congress would protect them by checking the power of the white minority. Even if Congress intervened, however—even if it legislated black suffrage—the prospects for reconstructing the South were dim. Judging by Natchitoches, ex-Confederates were uncowed and unapologetic. Far from repudiating the Confederacy as a catastrophic mistake, they celebrated it as a noble "lost cause."[65]

4

THE LOST CAUSE AND THE POLITICS OF LOYALTY

An attempt to guarantee and protect a revived State government, con-
structed in whole or in preponderating part from the very element against
whose hostility and violence it is to be protected, is simply absurd. There
must be a test by which to separate the opposing elements, so as to build
only from the sound.

Abraham Lincoln, Annual Message to Congress, December 8, 1863

The question of loyalty bedeviled Reconstruction. Republicans and Democrats defined loyalty in radically different terms. To Republicans, Confederates had committed treason; they wanted ex-rebels to show penitence and
to repudiate the men who had led the Confederacy. Former Confederates
insisted that they had acted honorably and, while accepting the verdict of
the battlefield, saw no reason to humble themselves. Republicans were appalled that southern whites took pride in their war records; former Confederates saw no contradiction between taking an oath of allegiance to the
United States and commemorating the "Lost Cause" of the Confederacy.
Instead of bridging this divide, Congressional Reconstruction reinforced
it. The Republican Party stigmatized southern Democrats as unrepentant
rebels; southern Democrats branded every white Republican a traitor to
his race.

The *Natchitoches Semi-Weekly Times*, edited by Louis Dupleix, a French
immigrant, and Mary Edwards Bryan, a poet and aspiring novelist, was a
politically moderate newspaper. But when it declared its preferences for
the spring 1866 local elections, it endorsed candidates who had served in
the Confederate army. The candidate for clerk of court, the *Times* pointed
out, had "lost his arm in Virginia"; the man running for sheriff had "lost
the use of an arm, by wounds received in battle"; the aspirant to the office of
recorder had "lost his right arm in the Battle of Mine Run." These wounded

Figure 4. Mary Edwards Bryan (1839–1913), coeditor of the *Natchitoches Times*, poet, and author. Courtesy of Albert Sydney Johnson.

soldiers had gallantly served "the cause once dear to all of us" and deserved to be rewarded. The only protest that the *Times*' picks elicited was a complaint that they stacked the deck against candidates "fortunate enough to return from the conflict of arms with sound limbs." Whether maimed or unwounded, the letter writer argued, all "noble Confederates" should receive equal consideration.[1]

White voters' preference for Confederate veterans appalled the Republican Party. In the state elections held in the fall of 1865, white Louisianans chose men who had been officers in the Confederate army or members of the Confederate government. The collapse of the Confederacy, far from prompting recriminations over the disastrous experiment in secession, ushered in a wave of nostalgia for the Lost Cause. Many of these successful candidates, their rank excluding them from the terms of Johnson's general amnesty, had not received individual pardons and were therefore ineligible to hold office.

The Lost Cause took its name from the eponymous history of the Confederacy published by Richmond, Virginia, newspaper editor Edward A. Pollard in 1866. It reflected a very human desire to honor the Confederate fallen and to salvage a measure of self-respect in the face of defeat and occupation. Nearly one adult white male in five had perished in fighting for the Confederacy—three times the proportion among northern men of military age. Of those soldiers who survived, half had suffered wounds. Many had lost limbs or were otherwise disfigured. The wives, mothers, and daughters of these men salved their grief by tending soldiers' graves and raising money to build Confederate cemeteries. The literary-inclined paid tribute to the "martyrs of the South" in poetry and prose.

The Lost Cause also furnished a basis for the reconstruction of southern white identity. It challenged a widespread conviction in the Republican Party that the defeated South was a tabula rasa upon which the North could inscribe its own values. It not only deified the Confederacy but also romanticized slavery, nurturing an accompanying myth of the Old South. It helped white southerners create what Robert J. Norrell has called "white ethnic nationalism," replacing the pro-slavery ideology of the antebellum South with a more inclusive creed of white supremacy.[2]

The Confederacy became an object of veneration even before the last rifles were stacked and the last flags furled. Writing to Andrew Johnson from Mississippi, after the surrender of Lee and Johnston but before that of Kirby Smith, a Connecticut-born schoolteacher noted the mood of the paroled Confederate soldiers: "They say 'that they had a clear *casus belli*, that they were acknowledged as belligerents, that they fought gloriously in a good cause, that they are not traitors but defeated patriots and merit the sympathy and respect of the world.'"[3]

Pollard's *Lost Cause* appeared in 1866; it was an instant best-seller. A French-language edition for Louisiana, *La cause perdue*, quickly followed. In the same year, Baton Rouge native William H. Tunnard published *A Southern Record: A History of the Third Regiment Louisiana Infantry*, the first of many histories of Confederate units. "Our revered dead shall live ever fresh and green in our memories," wrote Tunnard, "while the living are united in those indissoluble bonds which bind brave spirits to each other, cemented by . . . a stern defence of cherished principles."[4]

In *Recollections of Henry Watkins Allen*, also published in 1866, novelist and planter Sarah A. Dorsey set out all the key themes of the Lost Cause. The South had fought in defense of the "fundamental principles of

Republican liberty." The Confederacy had conducted itself gallantly and with honor, enduring the "fiercest vicissitudes of any war ever waged by any peoples." Despite "unparalleled suffering" and "gallant resistance," the Confederate armies had been overpowered by superior numbers. Southerners accepted defeat but refused to be humiliated. Like all apologists for the Confederacy, Dorsey played down slavery as a cause of secession while in no wise regretting the South's "peculiar institution." Slavery was "the normal condition of the African race," she affirmed, in her one mention of the word.[5]

The pages of the *Natchitoches Times* laid bare an aspect of the Lost Cause that was, perhaps, fundamental: the need to reconstitute southern whites' sense of "honor." Emancipation not only abolished a system of labor but also destroyed an institution that had molded the values and mores of a society. Slavery had been central to white southerners' sense of self-esteem, fostering the master's slaveholder's self-image as a benevolent patriarch and bountiful aristocrat. It had encouraged an extreme form of individualism that persuaded non-slaveholders, too, that they were far superior to blacks and were the political and even the social equals of the big planters. White men had bolstered their aristocratic pretensions by denying "honor" to the women they protected and the slaves they commanded. Long after "honor" had declined in significance elsewhere, the concept flourished in the South. It reinforced white southerners' reputation for being arrogant, pugnacious, and ultrasensitive. It had fed the delusion that "one southerner can whip half a dozen Yankees."

Defeat challenged "southern honor" at its core. The South's white men had proved unable to fulfill their patriarchal role as defenders of hearth and home; they had left their womenfolk exposed and defenseless. The slaveholders had been unable to count on the loyalty and gratitude of their slaves, who had sided with the Yankee invaders. The South's white population, instead of displaying unbreakable unity, had been riven with division. The Confederacy's best and brightest had shown incompetence of the highest order. Yankee soldiers had demonstrated just as much courage and prowess as the Confederates. Even despised blacks had shown that they could fight with bravery and distinction. The insistence of former Confederates that they were defeated but not humiliated revealed, in fact, the depth of their humiliation. That black soldiers constituted the bulk of the Union occupation forces rubbed salt into the wounds. "There is no humiliation more degrading and galling to the southern mind," a white Mississippian complained to President Johnson, "than to be completely under the control of sabers and bayonets in the hands of negroes."[6]

The Lost Cause provided a rallying point, psychological and political, for former slaveholders and for white southerners in general. Far from apologizing or acknowledging guilt, ex-Confederates demanded respect for their manliness. "They are sorry the war ever began," a Mississippi man wrote Senator Lyman Trumbull, "but only because they were unsuccessful." Former Confederates explicitly linked the Lost Cause—even before it was named that—with the restoration of home rule and the maintenance of white supremacy. Trumpeting the "gallant and skillful soldiership" of Confederate veterans, the *Natchitoches Times* proclaimed its vehement opposition to "Radical schemes." The South must not allow itself to be "trampled upon and used by factious demagogues and tyrants."[7]

Mary Bryan filled the *Times'* pages with poetry and fiction that celebrated the Confederacy and romanticized the Old South. Like the thousands of women who founded local Confederate Memorial Associations, she was eulogizing Confederate heroism long before the United Daughters of the Confederacy began erecting statues of Confederate soldiers. Union commanders "forbid us to build monuments over our dead," the *Times* lamented, but the more they tried to suppress the building of monuments to the Confederate fallen, "the more will we honor and cherish their memories" and "teach our children the history of their great deeds."[8]

The Lost Cause looked forward as well as backward. Bryan's pieces mocked southern patriarchy and called upon whites to emulate Yankee ingenuity. In "Captain Jenkins Wooing" she satirized a politician, "the big man of his section," who ardently supported secession but declared that "he could do his country more service by remaining to care for helpless women and innocent children." When he could no longer avoid being conscripted through feigning illness, "Captain" Jenkins contrived to join the state militia, his duties consisting of "lying around headquarters, with unlimited furlough and plentiful rations of Louisiana rum." Finally sent into action, he was sent scampering toward the rear by the first shot from a gunboat, a cowardly flight that he dignified as "masterly retreat." On the one hand, this sketch criticized the politicians who had precipitated the proverbial "rich man's war and poor man's fight." On the other hand, it lamented the lack of manhood that had sapped the Confederacy's strength.[9]

When it came to southern men, in fact, Bryan could be scathing. Far from being chivalric protectors of hearth and home, many of them, she wrote, were quite useless. The burden of supporting families often fell upon women, like it or not, because their husbands were "indolent, intemperate, spendthrift . . . disabled or sickly." Yet the education of girls taught them to be "silly husband-hunters" who exhibited "flower-like delicacy" and a "halo of loveliness." At present, she complained, school-teaching was the only form of paid work deemed acceptable for "the higher class of women." Women should have more opportunities to work outside the home, Bryan argued—not only because it was right, but also the shortage of men would leave many widows and single women without husbands. Women should not, in any case, be defined solely by marriage. "Self-asserting and self-sufficient" women who chose to remain single should be respected for their independence, not ridiculed as old maids. Moreover, if marriage were treated as an option freely chosen rather than an unavoidable obligation, there would be "fewer shrewish wives and disenchanted husbands and unhappy children."[10]

Mary Bryan was hardly typical; she may well have been the only woman in the South to list her occupation as "authoress" in the census of 1870. Yet her writings illustrate how the Lost Cause could accommodate forward-looking and unconventional views. Even in the matter of race, Bryan looked to the future, not the past. She never questioned the rightness of slavery, but regarded any effort to circumvent emancipation through oppressive laws as futile. Planters should act with "scrupulous fidelity," she insisted, in fulfilling their contracts with black laborers. Lost Cause thinking, however, looked forward to a new form of white supremacy, not to racial equality. "I hold that the African and the Caucasian are two widely separated species of the genus man," wrote Bryan, "as the Cur and the Newfoundland are different species of the Canine race; the eagle and the barnyard fowl distinct species of the genus bird."[11]

Paradoxically, it was by renouncing any desire to restore slavery that Lost Cause writers could idealize the Old South. In *The Dream of Life: A Romance of the Late War*, serialized by the *Semi-Weekly Times* in 1866, "Stannie Lee" (Laura S. Webb) sketched the slave plantation as a place of harmony and contentment, peopled by happy-go-lucky "darkies" and kind, caring masters. In lamenting its passing, Lee had Aunt Dinah rebuke her husband, "a large surly looking negro man," for failing to appreciate the blessings of slavery:

I wish Mr. Lincum would let us all lone . . . and stop dis big fuss bout freeing the niggers. Ise free nuff now, and I done seen nuff dese free niggers dat's got nuffin but rags to wear, and nuffin to eat but de chickens dat dey steal off other folks hen roofs. I tell you I don't believe in dis freedom no way. . . . You is always preaching about de freedom dat is coming . . . but dis nigger nebber wants to see the day come when she has to leave de old place, and de white folks dat she was raised wid from a child.

Bryan expressed identical sentiments. "Where are the beaming smiles and the hearty tones of days gone by?" she wondered.[12]

The Lost Cause quickly acquired a political dimension. "Southerners, you have lost that Confederacy, but you still have its honor to sustain," a woman wrote to the *Natchitoches Times*. "You have to battle against being reduced to vassalage, by the Radicals of the North, who are exerting every nerve to lower and degrade the chivalry of the South. But Southerners, if you *resolve* to be unconquered by them, you may laugh their efforts to scorn. They have triumphed . . . over you in the field, but they have not lowered your proud spirit yet." Bryan asked readers if "all this heroic sacrifice and high endeavor" had been in vain. She then answered her own question: Whites could salvage something from the ruins by defeating Republican plans to impose "Austrian despotism." A good dose of hot air and wishful thinking informed such pieces, yet they also reflected a clear-sighted recognition that the postwar settlement was very much up for grabs and that ex-Confederates could exert a decisive influence.[13]

In *The Lost Cause Regained* (1868), a sequel to his 1866 bestseller, E. A. Pollard elaborated on an argument that had been going the rounds ever since the surrender. Although slavery was gone, he contended, white southerners could still reestablish their racial supremacy, thereby preserving both the honor and the substance of the Confederacy. If blacks could be consigned to a position of "specific, permanent, irrevocable inferiority," then "the true and logical expression of that 'Lost Cause'" would be accomplished. The Lost Cause thus became intertwined with the politics of Reconstruction.[14]

However much it offended northern Republicans, it was hardly surprising that ex-Confederates lamented their defeat and nurtured the memory of the short-lived Confederate States of America. Lost Cause myths are common in modern history. Defeated nationalists—Poles, Irish, Greeks,

Serbs—have often cultivated heroic representations of failed struggles. Nor was it remarkable that many Confederate veterans felt a powerful sense of comradeship and viewed their careers as soldiers with pride. This, too, is a common phenomenon after wars. "Around the returned soldier of the South gathers the same circle of admiring friends that we see around the millions of hearth-stones in our own section," reported Benjamin C. Truman in April 1866, having toured the South at the request of President Johnson. "The rank and file of the disbanded Southern army . . . are the back-bone and sinew of the South."[15]

The South's celebration of the Confederacy, however, differed from other Lost Cause myths. Usually, such myths sustain the hope of ultimate victory and the establishment of national independence. But nostalgia for the Confederacy had nothing to do with sustaining territorial nationalism. Virtually all former Confederates agreed that their defeat was final and that any attempt to reverse it would be folly. In the common parlance of the time, they "accepted the situation"; there could never be an independent southern nation. In that sense, therefore, ex-Confederate protestations of loyalty were sincere, and Republican fears that the Lost Cause expressed Confederate revanchism were misplaced. Tellingly, the commanders of the Union army, whatever their political persuasion, rarely worried about the prospect of another rebellion. The very thinness of the postwar military occupation attested to that fact.

The second difference was this: the Lost Cause flourished in the postwar South because the national government allowed it to do so. Such myths are normally cultivated either clandestinely or in exile; they are not tolerated by the victorious power. In most civil wars, notoriously, the winning side not only inflicts bloody reprisals but also seeks to extirpate every symbol of the opposing cause. Victors do not normally accord respect to the vanquished, let alone allow the defeated side to openly celebrate its military leaders. After the restoration of England's monarchy in 1660, men who had condemned Charles I to death suffered gruesome executions; the body of Oliver Cromwell was disinterred and desecrated. The Nationalists' destruction of the Spanish Republic in 1939 ushered in a wave of reprisals. "Without pity," writes Paul D. Escott, Franco's dictatorship "executed fifty thousand soon after the war ended, [and] imprisoned hundreds of thousands." Franco permitted no monuments to the Republic's fallen soldiers and statesmen. Such examples of civil war's vindictive aftermath could be endlessly multiplied.[16]

Nothing remotely resembling this kind of repression took place after the defeat of the Confederacy. True, local commanders tried to prohibit the flaunting of Confederate symbols and discourage the open expression of "disloyal" opinions. They decreed that Confederate uniforms could be worn, but only if shorn of military insignia. They banned the display of Confederate flags. They refused to countenance military-style funerals for Confederate generals. They sometimes suppressed newspapers deemed to be disloyal. Yet these efforts were sporadic and halfhearted, and quickly ceased to be significant. There was never any effort to impose general press censorship.

Unionists and Republicans blamed Andrew Johnson's excessive leniency for emboldening ex-Confederates and encouraging the cult of the Lost Cause. Because of Johnson, they argued, ex-Confederates lost any fear that they might be punished, fueling their arrogance and encouraging them to cast off any restraint in expressing their opinions. Certainly, Johnson weakened all attempts to hold former Confederates to account or to place them on probation. By promiscuously issuing individual pardons instead of making amnesty conditional on good behavior, he surrendered an important means of influencing the ex-Confederate leaders. When General Grant asked local army commanders to monitor newspapers for "disloyal sentiments" with a view to suppressing the worst offenders, Johnson pressured Grant to revoke his order. When military commissions issued death sentences against men convicted of murdering Union soldiers or black people, Johnson commuted them, overriding the protests of Judge Advocate Joseph Holt that justice should be carried out.[17]

At the same time, however, it is hard to see how a harsh or repressive policy could have been implemented. Powerful cultural and institutional factors militated against press censorship, imprisonment without trial, and military courts. Such curbs on civil liberties had been controversial in wartime; to maintain them in peacetime against the opposition of the Democratic Party, and a portion of the Republican Party as well, would have been extraordinarily difficult. Besides that, there was little stomach in the Republican Party for a punitive peace. Lincoln's magnanimity is legendary; he famously stated that rather than punish Jefferson Davis he would prefer to see the Confederate president escape into exile "unbeknown to me." Less well known is the fact that Thaddeus Stevens, usually depicted as the most bloodthirsty of the Radicals, had no desire to see former Confederate leaders—not even Davis—executed. Abolitionists Wendell Phillips and Horace Greeley felt the same way.[18]

The commanders of the U.S. Army also opposed singling out the military leaders of the Confederacy for punitive treatment. Grant's surrender terms at Appomattox, which permitted Confederate officers to retain their horses and sidearms and allowed rank-and-file soldiers to return home after the simple act of signing a parole, fully accorded with Lincoln's desire for leniency. The solemnity with which the Army of the Potomac witnessed the stacking of Confederate arms indicated deep respect for the valor of the soldiers they had defeated. William Sherman, despite his reputation for harsh treatment of Confederate civilians, was the soul of magnanimity in victory. Indeed, his proposed terms of surrender for the Confederate army under General Joseph Johnston were so mild that the Johnson administration overruled them. Sherman, like Grant, fostered the idea that former Confederates should be viewed as valiant soldiers rather than heinous traitors.[19]

With some in the North clamoring for Robert E. Lee to be tried for treason, Grant protected his former adversary from arrest. He also prevented General George Pickett from being put on trial for having ordered the execution of twenty-two Union prisoners in Kinston, North Carolina, in 1864. Philip Sheridan—like Sherman, a byword for cruelty in the eyes of ex-Confederates—agreed with Sherman and Grant that a punitive policy would be unwise. Although he disliked the Lost Cause and acknowledged the bitterness expressed by many white southerners, he considered them of little consequence. The former Confederates had "no power of resistance left," he advised President Johnson. "We can well afford to be lenient to this last annoyance, impotent ill feeling." Through their chivalrous treatment of the capitulating rebel armies and resolute opposition to criminalizing the ex-Confederate commanders, the Union's three senior generals inadvertently fostered the emergence of the Lost Cause.[20]

Well before the year was out, ex-Confederates had ample reason to conclude that they would escape punishment. After an interview with Johnson, one journalist guessed that "Davis is more likely to be paroled during the next year than tried, and if he is ever hanged, he must do it himself." He added, "The President is clearly averse to confiscation, and that question is practically settled." It was hardly surprising, then, that ex-rebels failed to display the penitence that Republicans expected. "None of these men seem to think that it necessary to make the slightest apology for the past," noted one of the provisional governors appointed by President Johnson.[21]

Former Confederates put forward any number of reasons for refusing to acknowledge guilt. They did not consider themselves traitors: they had honestly believed that the Constitution permitted a state to secede. They had opposed secession, but felt that loyalty to their state overrode loyalty to the Union. Once war had commenced, they had had no choice but to support the Confederacy. They had not volunteered to serve in the Confederate army, but had been conscripted. They were guilty of no crimes; they had simply failed: the war had been decided by might, not right. To repudiate secession or confess to wrongdoing would be dishonest and dishonorable. They had sworn allegiance to the United States in good faith and had no intention of taking up arms again.

Above all, ex-Confederates took pride in their war service. The following exchange between lawyer-politician Thomas C. Ellis and his congressional interlocutor perfectly captures the stubborn pride that exasperated Republicans.

Q: Were you in the rebel army?
A: I say this in no feeling of resentment towards you or the government of the United States; but you must allow me to preserve my own self-respect by denying in toto the term "rebel." I was captain in the Confederate army, in the 16th Louisiana regiment. I was endeavoring to do my duty. . . . Under the same circumstances I would do so again. . . . Allow me, at the same time, to state that . . . I never desired to see [the Union] sundered. . . . I was an earnest opponent of secession.
Q: Are you not conscious of a feeling of repentance?
A: Only that I might perhaps have been a better soldier.

The reply of Thomas Macon, the chairman of Louisiana's Democratic Central Committee, illustrated how pride shaded into arrogance. Yes, he admitted, he did feel repentance, but only in the sense that "I dislike to undertake anything in which I do not succeed." As much as Republicans deplored this lack of penitence, northern Democrats tended to sympathize with it.[22]

So did President Johnson. He did not wish the South to come back into the Union "eviscerated of its manhood," he told one reporter. Johnson's association of penitence with castration was telling. For many ex-Confederates, defeat represented more than a failed bid for nationhood; it struck at the very core of their identity as men in a patriarchal society in which "honor" was everything. They regarded any acknowledgment of guilt as an unbearable act of self-abasement. "Having fought for four years for the maintenance of certain truths, to abjure them is enough," thundered the

Louisiana Democrat in December 1865. "To do so *cheerfully* would be to evince a want of manliness." Writing to President Johnson in a tone of militant self-righteousness, former colonel Alcibiades De Blanc, a lawyer-politician from St. Martinville who had been wounded at Gettysburg, argued that "if our only crime be our failure," then the North must "extend a generous hand to the vanquished and respect the greatest and most respectable misfortune of the nineteenth century."[23]

Benjamin Truman, reporting to President Johnson on the mood of the South, dismissed this kind of bombast as "simply the returning wave that followed the depression of defeat." That ex-Confederates would overnight become Union-loving patriots was hardly likely, he argued. That they should harbor pride in their war service and express bitter feelings toward their conquerors was predictable. To most ex-Confederates loyalty consisted in giving up the goal of southern nationhood, acknowledging that secession was to all practical purposes a dead doctrine, and accepting the abolition of slavery as irreversible. The cult of the Lost Cause, in their eyes, in no wise contradicted their profession of allegiance to the United States. They did they not construe the election of prominent former Confederates as evidence of a continuing commitment to secession.[24]

To wartime Unionists and northern Republicans, ex-Confederates' professions of loyalty rang hollow. They argued that celebration of the Lost Cause and bitterness toward the North violated the spirit, if not the letter, of the oath of allegiance. After all, the oath pledged the swearer not only to "bear true and faithful Allegiance and Loyalty" to the government and Constitution of the United States, but to do so "without any mental reservation or evasion whatsoever." Yet no sooner had former Confederates taken the oath and regained their civil rights than they elected former Confederates. In the words of General Sheridan, white southerners showed an "unmistakable desire to glorify rebellion." Writing from Rapides Parish shortly after the surrender, a returning Unionist found "the influential men of the Parish as hot rebels as they were during the rebellion. They may, by mouth, profess Union sentiments, but their hearts are filled with hatred."[25]

The notion that oath-swearing could produce the kind of inner loyalty that Republicans seemed to expect was, in hindsight, unrealistic. The war had revealed that large numbers of southern civilians were willing to take the oath of allegiance while maintaining inward loyalty to the Confederacy— exactly the sort of mental reservation that the postwar oath obliged then to forswear. Eminent Confederate divines had condemned this kind of false swearing, but the reality of occupation meant that people who refused to take the oath were liable to swinging penalties. Non-swearers were liable to loss of employment, loss of civil rights, disfranchisement, ejection from the pulpit, house arrest, imprisonment, confiscation of property, and banishment to the Confederate lines under pain of death if they returned. Most therefore took the oath and justified their decision to swear falsely by arguing that they had no choice.[26]

The oath of allegiance had thus been debased by wartime practice. Union commanders recognized that many took the oath "fraudulently and treacherously." As General Banks told Secretary of War Stanton after the Red River campaign, "the word loyalty has only a constrained application" to the hundred of white people who took the oath of allegiance in Alexandria. "Their loyalty is in effect a submission to power." The day after Lee's surrender, General John Pope warned Lincoln not to place too much credence in loyalty oaths. "The events of this war have conclusively shown that oaths of allegiance are of little use in determining any man's loyalty."[27]

It seems strange, therefore, that the Republican Party placed so much emphasis upon loyalty oaths after the war—especially when it dismissed the oaths sworn under Johnson's Proclamation of Amnesty and Reconstruction as evidence of true loyalty. During the war, the oath taker was choosing sides and incurring risk. After the war, as one historian put it, "there was no longer a choice of sides, and . . . universal swearing as an instrument of government became practically worthless."[28]

Moreover, while the element of coercion that existed during the war had diminished, the notion that oath takers were swearing loyalty of their "own free will" hardly described the situation. Without taking the oath, ex-Confederates could not enjoy civil rights or regain confiscated property; they could not vote, hold office, or serve on juries; they could be excluded from a variety of professions. Many ex-Confederates struggled with their conscience, trying to reconcile the oath with their sense of personal honor. If all but a few ended up "swallowing the dog," as the saying went, they often did so feeling anger, resentment, and shame. As one plantation mistress put it, apostrophizing the "Yankee nation" in her private journal, "You have sullied the purity of our integrity. You have made us say with the lip what we do not intend to fulfill with our *acts*, made us promise what we will not pay, and for all this we hate you."[29]

French newspaperman Georges Clemenceau surmised that oath taking was an old Anglo-Saxon tradition: "For anything or nothing, a man has to raise his hand and kiss the Bible." But the more often he was required to swear, the greater the cynicism of the oath taker, for "familiarity breeds contempt." Democratic congressman S. S. Cox condemned loyalty oaths as wholly ineffective. "The history of political oaths," he concluded, "is a history of oath-breaking. They were as cheap as those proverbial of the dicer or the custom-house."[30]

Loyalty oaths thus encouraged downright dishonesty. High-ranking civilian and military officials of the C.S.A., excluded from Johnson's general amnesty, were required to make individual applications, and many sought to minimize their support for the Confederacy by engaging in casuistry, logic-chopping, and deception. Just as Germans after 1945 played down their support for the Nazi regime, and Frenchmen conveniently forgot their collaboration with German occupiers, former Confederates tried to disassociate themselves from the failed regime. They portrayed themselves as Unionists at heart who had opposed secession and war. "There was a large majority who opposed this fight," a Louisianan wrote Johnson, a "large conservative element who opposed the war." This statement, of course, embraced a host of active Confederates, many of whom, it is true, had voted against secession before following their states out of the Union. One applicant for pardon, having fought as a captain in the Confederate army and served in the Confederate Congress, claimed to have been "a Union man" who "never voluntarily abandoned" his U.S. citizenship.[31]

For Jesuitical reasoning and self-deception, few applications for pardon surpassed that of Alexander H. Stephens, the former vice president of the Confederacy, who languished in federal custody at Fortress Warren in Boston Harbor.

> Much is said in the papers about "loyalty" and "disloyalty," "Union men" and "traitors." What is meant by "loyalty" as thus commonly used, I do not exactly comprehend. No one ever lived with stronger feelings of devotion to the Constitution of the United States and the Union as myself. I regarded it as the best system of government on earth. . . . My effort was to rescue and save the Constitution.

He had opposed secession "to the utmost of my ability," Stephens wrote Johnson. "The war was inaugurated against my judgment. It was conducted on our side against my judgment." As for slavery, he had "never owned one [slave] that I would have held a day without his or her free will and consent."

He added that his famous "cornerstone speech"—at his inauguration as vice president of the C.S.A., Stephens described slavery as the cornerstone of the Confederate government—had been misunderstood. The speech had merely restated the beliefs and principles of the Founding Fathers that slavery was "the normal condition of the African among European races."

In fact, Stephens had argued the exact *opposite* in 1861: that the Founding Fathers had considered slavery "wrong in principle, socially, morally and politically," and had hoped that "the institution would be evanescent and pass away," whereas the Confederacy recognized slavery as a positive good that would endure indefinitely.[32]

The readiness of ex-Confederates to take the oath of allegiance and their willingness to falsify the record also revealed an aspect of "southern honor" that northern Republicans proved slow to recognize. The lie outright was regarded as perfectly acceptable, and in no way at odds with "honor," when it came to upholding white supremacy. Just as an army depends upon a soldier's automatic obedience to his superior, slavery had demanded automatic obedience by the slave to the master. Under the laws and conventions of slavery, a black person did not contradict the word of a white; black testimony was inadmissible in southern courtrooms in cases involving white people. Racial solidarity among whites trumped truth.

For many whites, therefore, taking the oath of allegiance was a distasteful means to an honorable end: the preservation of their self-perceived status as a superior race. Only by taking the oath could they hope to regain their political rights in order to fight northern control of state politics and, above all, black suffrage. The wording of the oath and the sincerity of the swearer became minor considerations, if not entirely irrelevant. As "IVA," a frequent contributor to the *Natchitoches Times*, put it: "Yes, go forward and seek pardons, if pardons are necessary to get Southern men in good positions to guard our homes from Yankeeism and African equality. You go not as the menial, seeking pardon for a crime committed, but as the brave man demands his rights at the bar of justice."[33]

Those who took the oath in this spirit did not, of course, admit to false swearing. But the conversion of Governor Madison Wells to the Republican Party prompted this revealing, if maliciously motivated, observation from the *Louisiana Democrat*: "Since the surrender, time and again has [Wells] told and advised our people to take the amnesty oath, that it was nothing, but on the contrary it was just the thing to place us all in a position to outvote the d—n Yankees and drive them from the country."[34]

Wartime southern Unionists cried foul. Having expected to rule the roost after the Union victory, or at least receive some kind of political reward, ex-Union men found themselves political pariahs. After suffering persecution from Confederate authorities during the war, they saw their persecutors flaunt their Confederate credentials and confidently prepare to reassume political power. "In accepting the amnesty," one ex-Unionist wrote Senator Trumbull, former Confederates "mean simply to transfer the contest from the field of arms to that of politics." Unless the federal government stepped in to help them, the politically inexperienced and numerically small band of wartime Unionists would be outmatched and overpowered.[35]

In Natchitoches as in the rest of Louisiana, white voters elected men who had worn the gray. The same pattern manifested itself in Alabama, Mississippi, Georgia, the Carolinas, and other ex-Confederate states. Even in Kentucky, which had never joined the Confederacy, Confederate veterans trounced former Unionists.

The results dismayed President Johnson and shocked the Republican Party. Yet they might have been expected. Outside North Carolina and Tennessee, Unionists had comprised a small minority of the Confederacy's white population. True, widespread dissent had eroded the Confederacy from within. But many of these dissenters had been deserters, conscription evaders, and war-weary people who had simply lost faith in victory. Many now welcomed the opportunity to be reconciled to their communities. Even staunch Unionists felt the pull of conformity, reported the post commander at Baton Rouge; they feared they would "lose office, or caste, if they do not hate Yankees." Other former Unionists felt betrayed by the emancipation of their slaves without compensation—not a few slaveholders had believed that the South could better protect slavery by staying *within* the Union. The growing influence of the Radicals within the Republican Party and the increasing likelihood of black suffrage completed their disillusionment. In Kentucky, which had supplied far more soldiers for the Union armies than for Confederate ones, Democrats carried the state with substantial support from wartime Unionists.[36]

The dwindling band of former Unionists who styled themselves "Loyalists" lacked confidence and prestige. They elicited none of the admiration that former Confederate officers commanded. Those "who had the courage and manhood to imperil their lives in battle," one governor wrote President Johnson, "were more deserving than their compeers, who had meanly skulked from danger and kept out of the war." As the *Louisiana Democrat* argued with insolent logic, "it was obvious to all that if the 'rebels' were allowed to vote, they would bestow the honorable offices in their gift upon those . . . who were recently denominated 'disloyal.'" Only the mass disfranchisement of former Confederates, it pointed out, could have kept political control of the southern states from ex-rebels. Wholesale disfranchisement, however, ran counter not only to the liberal policy of Andrew Johnson but also to that of his predecessor, Abraham Lincoln.[37]

But it was not so much Lost Cause rhetoric and the election of former Confederates that persuaded the Republican Party to repudiate Johnson's policy of "restoration." Rather, it was the conviction that the restored state governments could not be trusted to protect the lives of southern Loyalists, northern immigrants, and blacks. By the end of 1865 the Republican Party had come to the conclusion that "home rule" was putting at risk the very groups most closely identified with the Union.

Southern newspapers openly abused ex-Unionists. Alexandria's *Louisiana Democrat* urged voters to shun candidates who had "turned their hand against their own State in the hour of danger." The results of the first gubernatorial election after the war illustrated this enduring bitterness. Although Madison Wells, Louisiana's most prominent wartime Unionist, carried the state in the face of a divided Democratic Party, he did so only because the Democratic Party decided to place him at the head of its own ticket. The rest of the Democratic ticket, which was easily elected, consisted of former Confederates. A Conservative Unionist Party, which also endorsed Wells, mustered barely five thousand votes, a quarter of the Democratic total, for its own ticket.[38]

The Democrats' endorsement of Wells was purely expedient. In his home parish of Rapides, Wells was so unpopular that white voters opted for former Confederate governor Henry Watkins Allen, then living in Mexico in self-imposed exile and ineligible to hold office. E. R. Biossat, the *Democrat's* editor, still smarting from his imprisonment during Banks's occupation of Alexandria in 1864, praised this result. "Jayhawkers" like Wells, who touted their wartime opposition to the Confederacy, were "depraved beyond all measure."[39]

It quickly became clear that the former Confederates who led the Democratic Party had no intention of sharing political power with former Unionists. Convinced that Johnson was on their side, and that he planned to abandon the Republican Party, they became increasingly brazen in their

scorning wartime Unionists. A New Orleans man wrote Illinois congressman Elihu Washburne:

> It is declared treason against the heroic South to be a Union man.
> They call us negro worshippers blue bellied Yanks, and what else. . . .
> "Don't you see [they say], they pardon us all; they dare not hang Jeff
> Davis it would make 1,000 Booths. Look at Mississippi, South Caro-
> lina, the minute we elect our late leaders, they are pardoned. . . . John-
> son is a Southerner and is with us."

Former Unionists and army officers complained of threats, malicious prosecutions, and physical assaults. Writing from Donaldsonville, Ascension
Parish, Union veteran Joseph P. Newsham reported "unjust and diaboli-
cal" persecutions. Ex-Confederates seemed determined to "drive out of the
parish and state every loyal man." If military protection were withdrawn,
warned New Orleans lawyer A. P. Field, "hundreds will be compelled
to leave here." Army post commanders in Alexandria and Baton Rouge
claimed that former Unionists were too scared to express their opinions.
In northwestern Louisiana, reported one officer, loyal men "sacrifice . . . all
social and political relations with their former friends and neighbors."[40]

We should be cautious in accepting at face value the allegations of southern Loyalists. They had a vested interest in exaggerating their plight. Moreover, where Unionists had dominated during the war—West Virginia, Missouri, eastern Tennessee, western North Carolina—the boot was on the
other foot, with former Confederates the victims rather than the perpetrators. Then again, some former "jayhawkers" who presented themselves as
persecuted Unionists were little more than bandits. Union commanders had
not inquired too closely into the character or conduct of the men who composed the partisan units that harassed Confederate loyalists. After the war,
some of these men simply carried on plundering and killing. Thus "Guillory's Independent Scouts" became the "Guillory gang," which, according
to historian Gilles Vandal, "terrorized St. Landry and other surrounding
parishes . . . and was responsible for no less than a dozen murders."[41]

In Natchitoches, former Unionists suffered relatively little public con-
demnation. The editorial tone of the *Natchitoches Semi-Weekly Times* was
restrained. "I know of no instance wherein a Union man merely because he
was a Union man, has ever been in jeopardy in this community," declared
Republican sympathizer Charles A. Bullard, a Massachusetts-born lawyer
long resident in Natchitoches.[42]

Nevertheless, the mounting hostility toward former Unionists and northern immigrants was palpable. President Johnson's assertion that blacks needed no federal protection, expressed in his vetoes of the Freedmen's Bureau Bill and the Civil Rights Bill, and his proclamation, issued in April, stating that the war was officially over, emboldened ex-Confederates. The latter gambled that Johnson, in alliance with the northern Democrats, could frustrate Republican proposals to impose further conditions on the South. The president "sides with the South, and its position," opined the *Natchitoches Semi-Weekly Times*, "and will undoubtedly be sustained by the whole Union."[43]

Madison Wells and his ally Hugh Kennedy discovered that their policy of conciliating former Confederates had backfired: the Democrats were determined to ditch them at the earliest opportunity. Having vetoed several acts of the legislature only to see his vetoes overridden, Wells complained to Johnson that "nine-tenths [of the] members" were behaving like "unrepentant rebels." Kennedy, the mayor of New Orleans, told Johnson that the very people whom he and Wells "had taken unusual pains to commend for your clemency" had paraded their Confederate war records and, once in office, had turned against them. In the first postwar mayoral election, in 1866, the winning candidate, John T. Monroe, was a former Confederate who, as mayor when Union forces captured the city in 1862, had refused to swear an oath of allegiance and, after a spell in prison, had been expelled from the Union lines. At the time of his election he did not qualify for office, being excluded from Johnson's general amnesty. Wells and Kennedy implored Johnson to disbar him. Instead, the president confirmed Monroe in office by granting a special pardon.[44]

Southern Loyalists looked to black suffrage as the only way to bolster their position; tension between wartime enemies escalated sharply. On the streets of New Orleans, recalled Thomas Conway, former head of the Freedmen's Bureau in Louisiana, former Unionists became "the objects of sneers and curses by men wearing gray coats." The post commander in Alexandria noted a distinct change for the worse, claiming that Union men were "living in extreme jeopardy of their lives." In St. Landry Parish, the Freedmen's Bureau agent reported, Loyalists were afraid to talk to him. "They beg me not to come in plain day, as their life is in danger if they are suspected."[45]

The aggressive self-confidence of ex-Confederates made even Union soldiers feel vulnerable. In the rural areas, especially in northern Louisiana, whites not only expressed open contempt for the bluecoats but also threatened them. "Officers are subjected to constant insult on Steamboats! In Hotels!! Everywhere!!!" reported an incredulous officer after a tour of inspection. The commander of a small detachment in Lake Providence made a pathetic admission of impotence. "My situation here is an embarrassing one, with not force sufficient to protect myself from insult, or my men from abuse." One soldier, dispatched to the post office on an errand, had been kicked and beaten. "I have not the power to protect myself from these outrages, they outnumber me, and are as well if not better armed." Officers of the Freedmen's Bureau often feared venturing into the countryside. "My life is threatened for . . . investigating the cruelties inflicted upon the colored people," the Bienville Parish agent reported. "I am not safe travelling alone." The agent assigned to Caddo, Bossier, and De Soto Parishes was "nearly powerless in 7/8 of the territory he is set over." Another agent described Franklin Parish as too dangerous to visit.[46]

As the political breach between President Johnson and Congress widened, the status of the ex-Confederate states remained in a kind of constitutional limbo, with two systems of law operating in parallel and often in conflict. On the one hand, the civil authorities continued to act as if "restoration" were complete, as Johnson insisted; they opposed any further role for the army in the administration of justice. On the other hand, the army refused to allow the civil authorities a free hand. Soldiers were still needed to protect Union men, General Sheridan reported, and "there would be a great deal of trouble" if the freedmen were left "under the exclusive control of the white people." Sheridan ordered General Canby, his subordinate in Louisiana, to provide semi-monthly reports on "the treatment of the freedmen" and on "the actions and feelings of the people toward the Government and Union citizens." He told Canby to pay particular attention to the Red River valley, where "the condition of affairs is not creditable." The adjutant general supported Sheridan by confirming that Johnson's proclamation that the insurrection was over did not end martial law or abolish the authority of the Freedmen's Bureau. However, he advised Sheridan not to convene military tribunals if justice could be obtained through the civilian courts. It was a confusing situation that mirrored the political confusion in Washington.[47]

The New Orleans riot of July 30, 1866, did much to end that confusion, in a terrible way. When members of the 1864 constitutional convention gathered at the Mechanics' Institute to consider black suffrage, a white mob broke into the building and attacked those inside. The attack was premeditated.

> As during the war, when it was desired to announce that the Yankees were coming, the bells of the city were rung. Immediately work ceased in saw mills and shops, and Mayor Monroe's police, the firemen with their iron wrenches, bands of ex-Confederate soldiers and the rabble generally, ran into the streets and rushed pell-mell for the convention hall. Whites and blacks inside and outside the building were attacked, clubbed and shot. The wounded, pleading for mercy, were cruelly beaten with brickbats.[48]

The attack left 48 people dead and 146 wounded. The vast majority of the victims were blacks, but they also included white Loyalists, among them former governor Michael Hahn (wounded) and the most prominent white advocate of black suffrage, A. P. Dostie (killed). Given the meeting's dubious authority—few thought it possessed any legal standing to amend the state constitution—many delegates had anticipated arrest. Given the bitter white hostility to black suffrage and the charged political atmosphere, some had anticipated violence and stayed away.

What nobody had predicted was that the police would aid and abet the rioters, leading to what General Sheridan called "an absolute massacre." After the convention members in the Mechanics' Institute hall had raised a white flag, wrote political scientist John W. Burgess, policemen "rushed into the building . . . [and] fired their revolvers upon the persons present indiscriminately and with terrible effect." Jean-Charles Houzeau, the Belgian editor of the *New Orleans Tribune,* saw policemen stopping horse-drawn streetcars and killing black passengers. Of course, each party blamed the other and milked the incident for political effect. But the facts of the riot supported the Republicans' claim that, as Burgess put it, "the public authorities of the reconstructed 'State' of Louisiana not only would not extend the equal protection of the laws to all persons, but would themselves deprive persons even of life without due process of law."[49]

The response to the riot on the part of the southern press—described by historian Dan Carter as "a barrage of self-congratulatory editorials" praising the rioters—reinforced the Republicans' determination to restart the process of Reconstruction. Ascribing the violence to "an unprovoked attack" by a "negro mob" on "unoffending white men," the *Louisiana Democrat* claimed that the riot "was got up by the Radicals" in order to influence the congressional elections. "The people of New Orleans have . . . done their duty well and manfully." Even the more moderate *Natchitoches Semi-Weekly Times* justified the rioters, pinning all the blame on "a party of broken down politicians, and disappointed, and demented fanatics, who are attempting to overthrow the government." President Johnson not only failed to condemn the rioters and express sympathy for the victims but also, in Burgess's words, went to the "imprudent extreme of almost making an excuse or a quasi-excuse for the riot."[50]

Shortly before the New Orleans riot took place, Sheridan had noted that organizations of Confederate veterans carried the potential for violence. The stated purpose of the Hays Brigade Relief Society, for example, was to help widows, orphans, and wounded veterans, as well as to commemorate the Confederate fallen. But in the event of a riot, the general warned, federal soldiers might find themselves fighting not just a mob but a military organization. Sheridan's fears were not misplaced. According to a historian of the riot, the society "served as a nucleus for a strike force that could respond quickly when called upon." Former Confederate brigadier general Harry Hays, now sheriff of Orleans Parish, enrolled two hundred members of his former unit as special deputies, in which capacity many participated in the violent attacks of July 30, 1866.[51]

The New Orleans riot laid bare the political dimensions of the Lost Cause. Confederate identity no longer sustained Confederate nationalism, but it united ex-Confederates in their efforts to oppose black suffrage and to isolate and discredit any whites who supported it. It kept alive wartime hatred of Unionists, labeling them traitors and jayhawkers. Although a multifaceted cultural phenomenon, the Lost Cause functioned as a political weapon to be wielded against Louisiana's nascent Republican Party.

In the spring of 1867, having secured a decisive victory in the 1866 congressional elections, the Republican Party declared the existing state governments unconstitutional. Overriding vetoes by President Johnson, Congress ordered the election of constitutional conventions in the former Confederate states. It charged the army with compiling a new registry of voters, one that included black males and excluded leading ex-Confederates. The Republican Party was about to transfer political power from the former masters to their former slaves.

5

ORGANIZING THE REPUBLICAN PARTY

Sunday, we had a novel exhibition. About seventy-five freedmen passed through our town, in procession, two by two. At the head of the column was a Baptist preacher, singing with some others and their followers, just newly baptized in the Cane River, accompanied by a crowd of other freedmen, anxious probably to witness the ceremony. The order was perfect. . . . The procession reached the church and after some fervent prayers . . . they retired to their business.

Natchitoches Semi-Weekly Times, October 10, 1866

When the Republican Party began to enroll black voters in the spring of 1867, the unnamed preacher observed by the *Times*, Alfred Raford Blunt, was set to become the most influential black leader in Natchitoches Parish. Throughout the South, preachers like Blunt, most of them Baptists and former slaves, stood at the front and center of black communities. Many were not only preachers but also teachers and politicians. As a Democratic witness explained to a congressional committee, the freedpeople "mix up in their churches, religion, school, and politics."[1]

The wearing of many hats was typical of black leaders who came to the fore after emancipation. A man who could memorize the scriptures and then learned to read as well as recite them, quickly acquired influence among former slaves. Such a man became the fount of political knowledge by reading aloud newspapers and political tracts. The whites who organized the Republican Party noticed him; they treated him as a spokesman and nominated him for office. Such a man, however rudimentary his letters, could teach school, magnifying his influence. If he honed his speaking skills and "received the call to preach," this schoolteacher could cement his position as a community leader by founding a church. His church building then doubled as a schoolhouse and Republican meeting place.

Figure 5. Black members of the 1867–1868 constitutional convention. Charles Leroy of Natchitoches Parish is depicted above extract from Bill of Rights (*farthest left*). Library of Congress Pictures and Photographs Division.

It helped to possess personal magnetism. Indeed, the Baptist faith of the ex-slaves demanded it. Beholden to no bishop or church hierarchy, Baptist ministers answered to God and to the members of their own congregation. To a large extent they appointed themselves by attracting a core of loyal followers. Although the church deacons could remove them, rivals and malcontents usually found it easier to quit the church and found another than to dislodge the sitting minister.

White missionaries complained that black ministers, especially Baptists, were ignorant, leather-lunged demagogues who mangled the scriptures and indulged in cheap rhetorical tricks to whip up emotion. But white ministers from the North, and even black ministers from the North, could rarely compete with these ex-slave preachers. The latter spoke the language of the folk because they sprang from the same soil. Cooperating with northern white Baptists but resisting dictation, black Baptist churches embodied a rough kind of democracy. They nurtured indigenous leadership and cultivated racial pride; they allowed ex-slaves, most of whom lived on scattered farms, to maintain a sense of community. The founding of black Baptist churches in Natchitoches Parish carried an extra significance. Many former slaves were not only rejecting the Catholic faith of their former white masters but also the leadership of the Creoles of color, those light-complexioned blacks, also Catholics, who had been free before the war, many of whom had owned slaves.[2]

"Brother Blunt," as his church members called him, rose from the obscurity of slavery with amazing rapidity. By the summer of 1867 he was the most prominent freedman in Natchitoches Parish. He mastered the alphabet, founded a church, organized a school, and ascended the political ladder to serve as a state senator and, for the better part of thirty years, chairman of the Natchitoches Parish Republican Party. As a teacher, preacher, Republican, and Mason, he had a hand in all the institutions that underpinned the black community.

What were his antecedents? In testimony before congressional committees in 1875 and 1879, Blunt disclosed that he had lived on a plantation of "137 colored hands" at a place "above Natchitoches." He also related that he had moved to Natchitoches from Thompsonville, Georgia, in 1853, when he was about sixteen years old.[3]

Here, however, the stenographer who recorded Blunt's testimony inadvertently planted a false trail. Walker County, Georgia, the location of Thompsonville, had no white Blunts or Blounts, no large slaveholders, and very few slaves. Situated in the hills of northern Georgia, cotton did not grow there. If, however, we substitute "Thomasville" for "Thompsonville" we find ourselves hundreds of miles to the south, close to Florida, in the heart of the Black Belt. Thomas County, Georgia, was an area of large cotton plantations and many slaves. Moreover, one Thomas County slaveholder *did* move to Natchitoches Parish in 1853. This was none other than Hardy Bryan, the father-in-law of Mary E. Bryan, coeditor of the *Natchitoches Semi-Weekly Times*. Bryan's newly acquired Louisiana plantation, Kenilworth, lay near the village of Campti and was home to well over a hundred slaves. It therefore fits Blunt's description of a place "above Natchitoches" with "137 colored hands."[4]

The slave manifest of the *Chipola*, which sailed from the northern Florida port of Apalachicola to New Orleans in March 1853, confirms Blunt's provenance. The slaves on board, signed for upon arrival by Hardy Bryan, included a fifteen-year-old boy called Raford, described as five foot one and light rather than black. Years later, recollecting when he first arrived in Louisiana, Blunt cited not only the year, 1853, but also the month, March. He was one of fifty-six slaves that Hardy Bryan shipped to New Orleans that year. When Bryan died in 1859, Blunt passed to Maria, his widow.[5]

Although many former slaves kept the family names of their ex-masters, Blunt did not. Why he chose "Blunt" is impossible to say. There were no other Blunts/Blounts, either black or white, in Natchitoches Parish. How he acquired his middle name "Raford," which he used in preference to "Alfred," is also unknown. It was so out-of-the ordinary that it has caused endless trouble to census enumerators, stenographers, and historians, who have called him Ranford, Radford, Buford, Ruford, Raphael, Rayford, and Raeford. The fact that most people knew him as "Rafe" fed the confusion.[6]

"Upon being freed," Blunt recalled, "I went out as a woodchopper and sold wood to steamboats." Chopping wood may have been a skill he learned in slavery, for masters had often relied upon slaves to supply wood for fuel, sometimes paying them for such work when undertaken in the slaves' "own time." A skilled woodchopper could earn substantial amounts of money. Blunt soon became a familiar face in Natchitoches. William M. Levy, who served on General Richard Taylor's staff in the Civil War and after the war became a lawyer and Democratic congressman, testified that he first noticed Blunt as early as 1865.[7]

Baptist ministers like Blunt had, in many cases, first started to preach on the slave plantations. Although direct evidence is lacking in Blunt's case, popular memories of nearby Evergreen Baptist Church illustrate how slaves formed religious communities and, as freedpeople, maintained and developed them.

Oral tradition held that the slaves on a plantation in St. Maurice (then in Winn Parish, later part of Natchitoches Parish) held nightly prayer meetings, in secret, posting guards to warn of approaching whites. When their master discovered what was going on, he prohibited the meetings but arranged for a white minister to preach to the slaves on Sunday. When satisfied that he could supervise the prayer meetings himself, the master dispensed with the white preacher and permitted a slave, "Parson Taylor," to conduct the services. Taylor, although illiterate, "was blessed with a powerful memory," and when the master read passages from the Bible, the slave learned them by heart. From about 1848 until emancipation, Taylor officiated at the Sunday prayer meetings under the master's increasingly lenient eye. In 1866 two Baptist missionaries from New Orleans, both white men, helped Taylor to organize a constituted church, the fifteen-member congregation meeting under an oak tree.[8]

Those same missionaries, Rev. William M. Moody and Rev. Isaac T. Langston, organized First Baptist Church of Natchitoches, and Blunt, who in 1866 began to "exhort," became its first regular minister. The congregation made do with improvised meeting places, but in 1868 Blunt acquired a parcel of land from Theophile Bossier, a former sheriff and member of a prominent planting family. There, on New Second Street, near the historic heart of Natchitoches, First Baptist Church erected a permanent building. The church was aptly named. It was literally the first Baptist church, black or white, in the area. It soon had about five hundred members.[9]

In 1870 his fellow Baptists elected Blunt to the presidency of the Twelfth District Baptist Association, which soon embraced about fifty black churches, over half of them in Natchitoches Parish. As was often the case, no clear line separated the finances of the church and those of the minister. Both Blunt and First Baptist prospered. The minister acquired a fine two-story home on Second Street, another house, several town lots, and 120 acres of land outside town. He told a Senate committee in 1875 that his net worth exceeded $7,000.[10]

In 1867 Blunt was already making a name in the Republican Party and coming to the attention of local whites. In June he was one of eighteen signatories to a public letter addressed to Governor Benjamin Flanders. The following month he addressed the first Independence Day barbecue-rally of the Natchitoches Parish Republican Party. Years later one of his political enemies, James H. Cosgrove, editor of the *Natchitoches People's Vindicator*, recalled that speech. "He advocated the taking by force of the lands of the whites by the negroes, as they had by their labor made it, and were for that reason entitled to it." Cosgrove may not have reported Blunt's words accurately, but he certainly remembered their power.[11]

The process of organizing the Republican Party began with the recruitment of blacks into ward clubs. A piece in the *Christian Recorder* vividly described the dramatic effect when, on a Saturday evening in April 1867, a large group of freedpeople marched into Natchitoches to enroll. Spotting a cloud of dust hanging over a road into town, whites rushed home, bolted doors, closed shutters, and drew curtains. "The niggers are coming to take the town," one of them explained. Shortly afterward about one hundred freedmen, many carrying clubs and sticks, arrived at the office of the Natchitoches Parish Republican Party. There, on a "tattered and torn" American flag, they were sworn in as members. The white officers of the party, pleased by the turnout but alarmed that the blacks had armed themselves, "told them not to come that way anymore." The freedmen dispersed quietly and went back to their plantations.[12]

Over three or four Saturday evenings, the Republican Party enrolled about eighteen hundred members, perhaps one-fifth of them whites. Three hundred of them braved driving rain and muddy roads to attend a meeting on May 18 that elected officers, endorsed resolutions, and nominated two delegates to the proposed constitutional convention: Charles Leroy (black) and Cyrus W. Stauffer (white).

The *Times* provided a snapshot of the nascent Republican Party by publishing the names of the men, about ninety in number, who were designated vice presidents. Blacks accounted for about three-quarters of them. They included farm laborers like Henry Brown and Isaac Moody, artisans such as shoemaker Shedrick Brown and painter Andrew Carter, and a sprinkling of small businessmen such as saloonkeeper Charles Dupré and boardinghouse keeper Albert Blanchard. Many of the blacks, including Dupré, Charles Leroy, and John B. Vienne, were freeborn mulattoes. One black minister, Rev. Ebenezer Hayward, came to the meeting. With support from the Freedmen's Aid Society of the Methodist Episcopal Church, North, Hayward had organized the first black church in Natchitoches. Like so many black preachers, he doubled as a teacher; his church building served as a schoolhouse. However, Hayward, unlike Blunt, did not play a prominent role in the Republican Party.

The white Republicans included wartime Unionists and reluctant Confederates. At least three of the Unionists, Joseph Martin, Samuel Parsons, and Matthew Breedlove, had been imprisoned by the Confederate authorities. Robert B. Jones, a planter from Catahoula Parish, had fled to the Union lines in New Orleans, where, shortly before the surrender, Governor Wells appointed him to the state supreme court. Some of the whites had been born in other countries. Merchants Victor Durand and Jacob Israel were natives of France. Saloonkeeper Theodore Schuman, farmer John Neuman, and bookbinder George Rehn hailed from Germany. Dry goods merchant Edward Phillips and painter George Monroe had emigrated from England. Laborer John Conner came from Ireland. Other whites, like carpenter Fred Hubley, had long resided in Louisiana but had been born in the North. Charles A. Bullard, the seventy-year-old lawyer who chaired the meeting, was a native of Massachusetts. Most of the others hailed from elsewhere in the South.[13]

It might be thought that the presence of so many "foreigners"—a term applied at that time to both immigrants from overseas and migrants from other states—made these Republicans atypical. But they were not as different from their white political opponents as might appear. Although white settlement in Natchitoches can be traced back to the beginning of the eighteenth century, the bulk of the 1860 white population was of more recent origin. With the booming cotton-based economy offering wonderful opportunities for white people to prosper, Natchitoches Parish had attracted newcomers from across the South and from England, Ireland, France, Belgium, Italy, Austria, and the German states. Although a few white Republicans came from humble backgrounds—in 1860 they were printers, carpenters, shoemakers, and farm laborers—many prominent Democrats had sprung from similar soil. Most of the white Republicans were artisans and small businessmen, with a sprinkling of former slaveholders.

One group of whites conspicuously absent from this first meeting of the local Republican Party was the old slaveholding elite. Not one of the forty-one planters in Natchitoches Parish who in 1860 had owned more than fifty slaves, together accounting for 38 percent of the local slave population, attended. There were no Prudhommes, Dranguets, Breazeales, Hertzogs, Sompeyracs, or Cloutiers—the slaveholding families, interrelated through marriage, that had comprised the local aristocracy. From the start, this class regarded the Republican Party with suspicion if not hostility and contempt. The former slaveholders who joined the Republican Party had each owned between eight and fourteen slaves: men like Charles Bullard, Joseph Martin, Madrid P. Blackstone, and Joseph Ezernack. Only Robert B. Jones, formerly of Catahoula Parish, had owned more than fifty. Marco Givanovich, who had been one of the largest slaveholders in Natchitoches Parish, was sympathetic to the Republican Party but was never actively involved in its affairs.[14]

Very few former Confederates joined the party at its inception. The only one elected to office, Navile A. Robinson, a struggling lawyer and former shoemaker, had served the Confederacy reluctantly. David H. Boullt, a dentist and former slaveholder who owned one of the finest plantation houses in Louisiana, St. Maurice, joined the party in Winn Parish; boundary changes later placed him in Natchitoches, where he became a mainstay of the party. Boullt's common-law marriage to a colored servant had harmed his antebellum social standing not one whit. His unofficial marriage produced a large family, including three sons who, classified as "white," served in the Confederate army. Jules J. Bossier, another former Confederate, was the son of a merchant. He belonged to one of the oldest and best-known families in the area.

Apart from Blunt, two other blacks, Henry Raby and John G. Lewis, joined the party's inner councils. Together, these men formed a triumvirate that held together into the 1890s. The provenance of Raby, who served in the lower house of the state legislature from 1871 to 1878, is obscure. He achieved the rare distinction of never testifying before a congressional committee, and nearly always escaping the notice of census enumerators. We know virtually nothing about his background other than the fact, which he disclosed in a court case, that he arrived in Natchitoches in 1857. Whether he moved to Natchitoches as a slave or of his own volition as a free man is not known. The one time that a census enumerator managed to corner him yielded the information that in 1870 he was a thirty-two-year-old carpenter, married with no children. His occupation and his designation as "mulatto" suggest that he had been a free person of color. But Raby failed to show up in any of the prewar census returns.[15]

Of the remarkable John Gideon Lewis we know far more. Born in Canada in 1849, Lewis arrived in Natchitoches in 1866, first entering the United

States in New Orleans. Apart from a few years spent in the Crescent City after Democrats expelled him in 1878, he spent the rest of his life in Natchitoches. When he died in 1931, he had served as grand master of the Louisiana Lodge of the Prince Hall Masons for almost thirty years.

Why would a lad of sixteen years move from Toronto to Natchitoches after the Civil War? One explanation, albeit speculative, is that the Prince Hall Masons provided a pathway from Ontario, Lewis's birthplace, to New Orleans, his initial destination in 1866. Black Masons from Cincinnati, where his parents lived until moving to Canada, had taken Prince Hall Masonry to both Canada and New Orleans before the Civil War. Moreover, several Ohio Masons who migrated to Canada in the 1850s, including Richard H. Gleaves and Rev. Thomas W. Stringer, moved to the southern states to take part in Reconstruction. They taught in freedmen's schools, organized Masonic lodges, and took part in Republican politics. Lewis may well have been part of this movement.[16]

The connection between the Prince Hall Masons in Cincinnati, Ontario, and New Orleans was a strong one. Martin R. Delany, the noted black abolitionist, helped organize the first grand lodge of the Prince Hall Masons west of the Alleghenies, Corinthian Lodge No. 17, in Cincinnati, Ohio. In 1849 the Cincinnati Masons, along with two other lodges, formed the Grand Lodge of Ohio, through which Prince Hall Masonry spread to other states, including Louisiana. Between 1849 and 1861 the Grand Lodge of Ohio chartered twenty-two new lodges, the first of which, Richmond Lodge No. 4, opened in New Orleans in 1850—"the first Masonic light south of Mason and Dixon's line." Thomas W. Stringer, an elder in the American Methodist Episcopal (AME) Church, organized it. Two other New Orleans lodges, also chartered from Ohio, were organized in 1854 and 1857. In 1863, after the Union occupation of New Orleans, the Eureka Grand Lodge of Louisiana came into being. It too, was affiliated with the Grand Lodge of Ohio. One of the founders and early Grand Masters, Oscar J. Dunn, became the most influential black Republican in the state.[17]

Joseph Collins Lewis, John's father, was probably a Mason: his religion and class were typical of black Masons then. In 1840, Lewis, a free man of color born in Kentucky in 1799, was living in Cincinnati, earning a living as a barber. Barbering was one of the most profitable and secure occupations open to black men at that time. "Throughout Ohio, barbering [was] a trade relegated exclusively to blacks," and Cincinnati's growing population provided plenty of customers. Joseph Lewis married a woman from

Virginia, and shortly after the birth of their first child in 1842, the family migrated to Canada.[18]

John Lewis's father trod a path followed by thousands of free blacks and fugitive slaves who migrated from Ohio to Upper Canada. The reason for this exodus was simple: Canada offered blacks a freer, more secure life. Ohio, by contrast, was decidedly inhospitable. With the state squarely committed to enforcing the Fugitive Slave Act of 1793, runaways stood at constant risk of being captured and reenslaved. As for free blacks, the state made every effort to make life difficult for them and to emphasize their inferior status. The Black Laws barred blacks from the state militia, denied them the right to vote, excluded them from public schools, prevented them from sitting on juries, and discounted their testimony in court cases involving whites. In the labor market, discrimination against blacks by employers and trade guilds was the norm. In Cincinnati, blacks were at the receiving end of mob violence. A race riot in 1829, fueled by hate-filled Irish immigrants, prompted about half the city's blacks—a thousand people—to leave for Upper Canada.[19]

In 1842 Joseph Lewis concluded that he had to get out. In September 1841 another riot had convulsed Cincinnati, "the most destructive and . . . violent in the city's history." This time blacks mounted an armed defense that prevented whites from doing their worst. Nevertheless, black lives were lost and black neighborhoods suffered massive property damage. Adding insult to injury, the state legislature roundly rejected abolitionist-inspired proposals to abolish or soften the Black Laws. In short, the Lewis family had ample reason to exchange Cincinnati for Toronto.

The bare facts about John G. Lewis's early years in Toronto are contained in his entry in the 1861 census of Canada. He was then the second youngest of Joseph Lewis's seven surviving children, who ranged in age from nineteen to seven. The children lived with their father, now a widower, in a two-story frame house, which suggests that Joseph Lewis, who still plied his trade as a barber, earned a good income. Joseph listed his religion as Baptist, and John hewed to the faith of his father.

We can infer something about Lewis's background from what historians know about Toronto's black community. Black Canadians comprised about a thousand of the city's forty-five thousand people, forming a tightly knit community with a "strong infrastructure to support new black immigrants." Black American immigrants found Toronto a hospitable place. They encountered little difficulty in finding regular employment and by the standards of the time were relatively well off. Moreover, at a time when other towns placed black children in segregated schools or failed to educate them at all, Toronto's public schools neither excluded blacks nor segregated them. The city's medical school accepted blacks, and the Toronto Normal School trained both black and white teachers. Blacks organized their own churches: Baptist, Colored Wesleyan, AME. Home to Canada's most prominent anti-slavery campaigners, Toronto gave John Lewis a sound education and, in all likelihood, a sense of mission.[20]

Whatever it was that prompted Lewis to quit Toronto for Natchitoches, by way of New Orleans, he evidently knew what he was doing. Migration is rarely a leap into the totally unknown: individuals usually move to a new country when they have some kind of personal contact at their destination. The connection between the Grand Lodge of Ohio, the lodges in New Orleans, and the lodges in Ontario suggests that the Prince Hall Masons provided just such a contact for Lewis when he arrived in New Orleans as an immigrant from Canada.

Although much of this is conjecture, one fact stands out. In 1870 the U.S. census located Lewis in the same residence as Toussaint L'Ouverture Delany, the son of Martin Delany, the black abolitionist and Mason who chartered the first Prince Hall lodge in Ohio. Like his Masonic brothers Thomas Stringer and Richard Gleaves, the elder Delany spent part of the 1850s in Ontario and, like them, moved to the South after the Civil War. In 1861 Toussaint was living in Upper Canada, like John Lewis. He served in the Fifty-Fourth Massachusetts Colored Infantry and in 1870 was listed as a schoolteacher. Could mere coincidence have placed Delany and Lewis in such close proximity to each other in, of all places, Natchitoches? The fact that Lewis named one his sons "L'Ouverture" strengthens the suggestion that a Masonic network linked Ohio, Ontario, New Orleans, and Natchitoches. The Masons in New Orleans may have suggested to Lewis that, if he wished to teach freedpeople, Natchitoches would be fertile territory. There might well have been a Mason there to welcome him, the most likely candidate being freeborn Charles Leroy, who boarded both Lewis and Delaney.[21]

The Freedmen's Bureau was using Leroy's home as a temporary schoolhouse, but Lewis was too young to be considered for a teaching position. In the meantime he helped Leroy build a grocery store, later buying and operating the business himself. His partnership with Leroy introduced him to Alice, one of Leroy's four daughters, whom he married in 1873. It also connected him to the inner circle of the Republican Party. His youth notwithstanding, Lewis made himself indispensable. Fully literate, with exemplary penmanship, Lewis's administrative and writing skills complemented Raford Blunt's talents as an orator and charismatic leader.[22]

Lewis's political career was linked to that of Blunt: they rose and fell together. Social and personal connections strengthened the bond. Lewis was a founder member of Blunt's church, and Blunt headed the Masonic lodge organized by Lewis. The two men became brothers-in-law. By 1870, the year Natchitoches Parish elected Blunt to the Louisiana House of Representatives, Lewis was serving as secretary, and then president, of the local Republican Party. From that year on he was a permanent fixture on the parish executive committee and was Raford Blunt's righthand man. After being naturalized as a U.S. citizen in 1872, at age twenty-one, he ran for public office, serving on the Natchitoches Parish Police Jury. In 1876 he was elected to the state legislature.[23]

A small circle of Unionists from New Orleans helped to organize the Republican Party in Natchitoches. Cyrus W. Stauffer had enlisted in the Confederate army but switched sides after the fall of New Orleans, leaving the Union army with the rank of captain. He was a seasoned Republican by the standards of the time. In 1864 he served as a delegate to the constitutional convention. There, with the backing of Governor Michael Hahn, General Nathaniel P. Banks, and, indirectly, President Lincoln, he prevented the adoption of a suffrage clause that would have explicitly restricted the franchise to white men. In 1865 Governor Wells appointed Stauffer registrar of voters for Orleans Parish. The following year he attended the meeting at the Mechanics' Institute that occasioned the New Orleans riot, barely escaping with his life. Stauffer moved to Natchitoches in the autumn of 1866 and opened a variety store on Washington Street. In 1867 Sheridan appointed him to the parish's three-man board of registration. Stauffer and his business partner, John S. Jones, and two of the latter's brothers, Richard and Robert, helped set up the local Republican Party. Stauffer was a natural choice as one of the party's two candidates for the constitutional convention that was scheduled for the autumn of 1867.[24]

Before these men could make their mark, however, they vanished from the scene. On June 3, 1867, John Jones shot and mortally wounded Cyrus Stauffer. The business partners had fallen out, and Jones's two brothers had threatened to kill Stauffer on sight. Stauffer was about to have the Joneses bound over to keep the peace when Richard and Robert Jones assaulted him. John Jones then shot Stauffer with a double-barreled shotgun. The murder was flagrant, and Sheriff John C. Hughes immediately went after the three brothers. Hughes apprehended Richard and Robert Jones, but John Jones escaped, shooting and wounding the sheriff. Two days later, Richard and Robert attempted to break out of Natchitoches Parish jail with the aid of an outside accomplice. The plan failed, and Robert—who had recently served as an associate justice on the Louisiana Supreme Court—was wounded in the attempt. The local Republican Party petitioned General Sheridan to have the prisoners transferred under military escort to New Orleans, citing the inadequacy of the parish jail and the likely difficulty of convincing a local all-white jury that killing a Republican constituted a crime. Confined in New Orleans, the two brothers contracted cholera and died a few weeks later. The law caught up with the third brother, John Jones, in (inevitably) Jonesville, Texas.[25]

The Jones-Stauffer affair offers a tempting metaphor for the political fratricide that soon engulfed the Louisiana Republican Party. But we are unlikely to get to the bottom of the quarrel that eliminated four wartime Unionists who had seen a bright future for themselves in a Republican-controlled Natchitoches. On its face, the affray had no political significance. It was nevertheless symptomatic of the personal violence that was part of Reconstruction's background music. Republicans killed Republicans, and Democrats slayed Democrats, over money, women, politics, and "honor." Barely a week after the Stauffer murder, A. J. Fletcher, justice of the peace for the Thirteenth Ward, a white Democrat, was working in the fields when another Democrat, Henry Adcock, felled him with a blast from a double-barreled shotgun.[26]

Natchitoches Republicans chose Major William H. Hiestand, late of the Union army, to replace Stauffer as the parish's white delegate to the constitutional convention. Hiestand's father, Ezra, was a prominent Unionist in New Orleans, a lawyer and a judge. Like Stauffer, the elder Hiestand served in the 1864 constitutional convention and had lived through the New Orleans riot. At the outbreak of the Civil War, William Hiestand enlisted in the Confederate cavalry, but in 1863 he joined a Louisiana regiment of the Union army. After the war he served as an agent of the Freedman's Bureau in Hallettsville, Lavaca County, Texas. Resigning from the army in the spring of 1867, he moved to Natchitoches as a collector for the Internal Revenue Service, an appointment he probably secured through the influence of his father. Once in Natchitoches he began re-cruiting blacks to the Republican banner.[27]

The Reconstruction Acts passed by Congress in 1867 charged the U.S. Army with supervising the registration of a new electorate, to be composed of adult males without consideration of "race, color, or previous condition . . . except such as may be disfranchised for participation in the rebellion." General Sheridan, commanding the Fifth Military District, which embraced Louisiana and Texas, embraced his duties with gusto. Determined to enroll as many voters as consistent with the law, he prescribed liberal hours and an ample period of time for registration, twice extending the deadline. Exercising tight control of the whole process, he required local registrars to take the "iron-clad oath" and placed the three-man boards under former army officers. "This gives me a check on each board by having a good and tried man as chairman of each," he told Grant. "Then in addition I have the boards supervised by intelligent army officers."[28]

THE PARISHES OF
LOUISIANA 1877–1900

(1) Acadia Parish detached from St. Landry, 1888
(2) Part of St. Martin Parish

Map 2. Louisiana's parishes. Reproduced by permission of Louisiana State University Press.

Sheridan removed any sitting official whom he deemed obstructive or incompetent. He ousted the state attorney general, the superintendent of education, and Governor Wells himself, whom he denounced as a "political trickster." Mayors, judges, sheriffs, and police jurors found themselves out of office. Sheridan purged the New Orleans police force and insisted that half its members should be Union veterans. He abolished the state levee board and appointed his own. All registrars and election officials, he warned, "will be subject to trial by military commission for fraud, or unlawful and improper conduct." As he explained to U. S. Grant, "Nothing will answer here but a bold and strong course."[29]

The Natchitoches Parish board of registration began its work on May 6, 1867, at the courthouse. "We never saw such a number of colored men on our streets," the *Semi-Weekly Times* reported. "It was a perfect *furore* among them." The *Times* worried that registration was stripping the plantations of their workforce, but it drew comfort from the fact that incessant rain was preventing much work being done anyway. Beginning on May 20 the board set to work outside the town, sitting at ten different locations and enrolling voters every day, including Sundays. It selected locations where blacks would feel comfortable. The men who welcomed the registrars onto their plantations, Joseph Martin and Marco Givanovich, were former Unionists. In town the board enrolled voters not only at the city hall but also at the grocery store of John Lewis. By early June the board of registrars had enrolled 1,356 black voters and 187 whites.[30]

The small number of white voters in Natchitoches and elsewhere in Louisiana raises the question of how many white applicants were rejected on account of their Confederate records. Critics of Congressional Reconstruction, including President Johnson, suspected that the army discouraged white applicants, and disfranchised too many of them, so as to create black majorities that would serve Republican interests. Certainly, Sheridan and the other generals enjoyed considerable leeway when it came to deciding who should be disfranchised. The Reconstruction Acts were vague about which former Confederates should lose their right to vote, and individual commanders interpreted them as they saw fit. Sheridan pleaded for guidance as to who was ineligible to register, and Grant passed on his request to the president and cabinet. Pending a ruling by the attorney general, however, Grant told Sheridan to use his own judgment.

Sheridan's staff drew up a "memoranda of disqualifications" that instructed registrars to disfranchise not only those senior military officers and civilian officials specified in the not-yet-ratified Fourteenth Amendment but also all manner of small fry down to auctioneers, coroners, street commissioners, policemen, prison warders, sextons of cemeteries, and "inspectors of tobacco, flour, beef, and pork." Sheridan ordered that these guidelines, and the set of questions that registrars could ask of applicants, should remain confidential—presumably because their publication would enable applicants to rehearse untruthful answers. Registrars should err on the side of stringency, Sheridan added, excluding "every person about whose right to vote there may be a doubt."[31]

Former Confederates were stunned by the sweeping character of the disqualifications. "My God how rigidly they construe the military law," a friend of Natchitoches lawyer Chichester Chaplin complained from neighboring Sabine Parish. "Every police juror, commissioner of election, notary, constable, Returning officer—and even a clerk of election 17 years old, who took no oath—is excluded—every man who ever had any position on God's earth, nearly everybody out here has held something. Are they doing this in Natchitoches?"[32]

The much-anticipated ruling by U.S. Attorney General Henry Stanberry, issued on May 24, tried to restrict the scope of disfranchisement by exempting conscripts, militia officers, and minor state and city officials. More important, it opened up a giant loophole by insisting that registrars lacked the right to challenge or investigate an applicant's qualifications: they must take a man at his word or else prosecute him for perjury in the state courts.

Sheridan was appalled. "To adopt Mr. Stanberry's opinion," he complained, "would defeat the purpose of Congress." Its effects, he told Grant, could already be seen in a palpable increase in "defiant opposition to all acts of the military commander." Grant told Sheridan not to worry; the attorney general's opinion was just that, an opinion. "Enforce your own construction of the military bill." By now the Johnson administration commanded so little authority that the army could virtually ignore Stanberry's ruling. Congress, to place the matter beyond doubt, explicitly authorized registrars to investigate applicants and, if they had any suspicions, to reject them without any recourse to judicial proceedings.[33]

Sheridan denied that the registration boards turned down large numbers of white applicants. Taxed as to why the new electorate consisted largely of black voters, he explained that whites did not wish to register alongside blacks and were "waiting until the colored get through." But many whites failed to apply at all, he added, as a protest against Congressional Reconstruction. Anxious to complete the registration by the end of June, he warned that further extensions would provide more opportunities for disqualified whites to engage in "perjury and fraud." At the behest of Andrew Johnson, however, and advised by Grant to obey the president, Sheridan kept the registrars at work until the end of July so as to give whites ample opportunity to apply. Urged on by local newspapers to register— "we should use every proper and legal means in our power in coming to elections," the *Natchitoches Semi-Weekly Times* editorialized—thousands did so. Many white applicants, thanks to the wide publicity accorded the attorney general's opinion, belatedly realized that service in the Confederate army did not automatically disqualify them. The total registration increased by a whopping 40,000. By the time registration closed, the new electorate consisted of 84,436 blacks and 45,218 whites.[34]

This lopsided black majority cannot possibly be explained by the disfranchisement of former Confederates. Even by the most generous estimate, the number of people ineligible to register cannot have exceeded 10,000. The army reported that only 2,169 applicants had been rejected—a mere 52 in Natchitoches Parish. The white shortfall can only be attributed to a widespread failure by whites to apply. As Joe Gray Taylor put it, "apathy, preoccupation with making a living . . . and racism which rejected the indignity of standing in line with Negroes" dissuaded about half the eligible whites from applying. The vote in the September 27–28 election on the holding of a constitutional convention reinforces the impression that whites were deliberately abstaining from a political process they looked upon as abhorrent. Whereas 75,083 people voted for a convention, a figure approximating the number of black voters, the vote against amounted to barely 4,000. The army estimated that 50,480 registered voters failed to cast a ballot, of whom the great majority were whites. In Natchitoches Parish, 913 electors did not turn out to vote.[35]

The Freedman's Bureau looked with mixed feelings upon blacks' enthusiasm for politics. General Robert C. Buchanan, who took a decidedly dim view of the freedpeople, complained that politics "materially interferes with their real interests" and that blacks were "spending their money on political clubs, instead of supporting schools." Some agents tried actively to discourage political activity. In St. Landry Parish, for example, the local agent interrupted a meeting of the Republican Club in Opelousas and berated those present for neglecting their crops. Pointedly turning his head to the white officers of the club, he told the audience that "These men want office and the Almighty dollar; the moment they get your votes they will not look at you." The army officer accompanying him chastised the blacks for holding a meeting on the Sabbath—something that, he claimed, would never be tolerated in the North. This was an extreme example, no doubt, and both officers landed themselves in hot water, but it was not an isolated incident. The agent in Lafourche Parish was dismissed after he had three leading Republicans jailed for "such discourse, conversation, sign, and action, calculated to bring about a riot and insurrection."[36]

Even agents who were generally sympathetic to the freedpeople deplored the way politics interrupted work routines, which they saw undermining their own efforts to inculcate good work habits and promote harmony between ex-slaves and former masters. One officer complained about a Republican recruiter in Lafourche "whose influence is bad upon the negroes," explaining that "he has been known to go on a plantation during working hours and induce all hands to leave and come to the registration office, telling them it was their last chance before they were reduced again to slavery." In Winn Parish, Delos White reported, "the freedmen are meddling with politics, and instead of remaining at home on Saturdays and working their own pieces of land, they come into town and go to the club meetings." The hitherto industrious freedmen of Natchitoches Parish, James Cromie complained, were being misled by demagogues who gave them "extraordinary ideas to their self-importance." Cromie decried the manner in which a few white leaders of the Natchitoches Republican Party appeared to control the black voters: marshaling them in ranks, marching them to the polls, and confiscating any opposition ballots they spotted. "There was no chance given to the Freedmen in this Parish to exercise their right as Freedmen."[37]

Yet only a few months later both Cromie and White had resigned from the army and joined the local Republican Party. They belonged to a large contingent of Freedmen's Bureau agents and other army officers who jumped into Louisiana politics. Perhaps the criticisms of black political activity contained in their official reports had been pro forma, reflecting what they perceived to be the attitude of their superior officers. They were certainly aware of Andrew Johnson's hostility to the Freedmen's Bureau, and may have sought to protect themselves by leaving a paper trail of conservative sentiments. As Johnson's authority waned, however, the bureau relaxed its unofficial self-denying ordinance regarding political activity. "It is the duty of all Officers and Agents of the Bureau," a June 1867 circular stressed, to teach the freedmen "concerning their rights and responsibilities as citizens." Agents could attend political meetings and instruct the freedmen "that they may vote intelligently." They could thus forge links with local Republican organizations and prepare the ground for political careers. Many of them also invested in plantations.[38]

It became an article of faith among Democrats that white Republican politicians manipulated ignorant and gullible freedmen by promising them "forty acres and a mule," a notion perpetuated in popular culture by the immensely successful films *Birth of a Nation* (1915) and *Gone with the Wind* (1939). There is no doubt that the freedpeople earnestly desired to acquire land of their own. Nor is there any question that they remained stubbornly optimistic that the federal government would furnish them with small plots and plow teams. Every year, as the time for entering into new labor contracts approached, agents of the Freedmen's Bureau reported blacks' reluctance to commit themselves because they believed that *this year* their hope of land would come true. Moreover, any number of bureau agents referred to Republican politicians encouraging this belief during the September 1867 canvass. Cromie, for example, explicitly stated that candidates in Natchitoches Parish "went so far as to promise [the freedmen] a number of acres of land, the Government to furnish them with seed to cultivate it for the incoming year."[39]

It is extraordinarily difficult, however, to find direct evidence that Republican candidates uttered such promises. When pressed by congressional committees as to whether they had actually heard Republican candidates promise "forty acres and a mule," Democratic witnesses confessed that their information was secondhand. Black witnesses, moreover, denied having been misled. One described how the Republican candidate in Morehouse Parish, Frank Morey, a former Freedmen's Bureau agent, disabused blacks of the idea that the plantations would be divided among the freedmen:

He said, "I have heard that some of you have got it into your heads that you are going to get horses and mules and land from the government. There is no such thing as that. The government cannot give them to white folks, and how can you black folks expect it? But if you be honest and careful and save your money, you will be able, after a while, to buy a piece of land, and have your chickens and turkeys and hogs."

The freedmen, this man affirmed, never expected "anything more than they work by their own hands."[40]

By the time that the first elections were held under the new constitution, in the spring of 1868, Thaddeus Stevens's proposal for confiscating the estates of ex-rebel planters and allocating this land, along with government-owned lands in the South, to the freedmen was dead. Even the limited land redistribution authorized by the Freedmen's Bureau Act of 1865 had failed to materialize. For Republican candidates to have promised the freedmen "forty acres and a mule" would indeed have been dishonest.

Yet it is scarcely credible that the Republican Party did not excite black voters by holding out the prospect of land. After all, "free land," along with "free labor" and "free men," had been one of the central planks of the party in 1860, and the Homestead Act of 1862 authorized the government to grant 160-acre plots in the West to settlers who were prepared to occupy and cultivate them. The Southern Homestead Act, passed in June 1866, opened up forty-six million acres of public lands in five States, including Louisiana, for settlement in lots of forty and eighty acres (depending upon the proximity to railroads and waterways) for a filing fee of two dollars. That Republican candidates failed to tout this act is inconceivable. In 1867, moreover, the land question was still a live issue. The platform of the Louisiana Republican Party included a proposal for homesteads, and candidates in the September canvass could tell voters that the constitutional convention, due to assemble in November, would take up the land question. In the event, the convention gave land reform short shrift, rejecting proposals to grant homesteads "on the most liberal terms practical." Nevertheless, writes historian Charles Oubre, "as long as the convention remained in session freedmen apparently anticipated a division of land."[41]

Regardless of whether Republican candidates promised "forty acres and a mule," blacks' overwhelming support for the party of Lincoln was scarcely evidence of gullibility. The state government elected by white voters in 1865 had spurned blacks as would-be citizens, rejected them as would-be voters, and belittled their desire to be educated. Left to their own devices, the state courts had failed to accord blacks legal protection—white violence against them went unpunished—while the state legislatures had restricted their mobility and otherwise circumscribed their freedom. Virtually all the help, protection, and sympathy that blacks received had come from the North: from the U.S. Army, the Freedmen's

Bureau, the freedmen's aid societies, and Congress. All these institutions were controlled by or closely associated with the Republican Party. No wonder blacks in the South regarded the Republican Party as their salvation. "I understood that it was to give every man an equal chance," one black voter told a congressional committee. "We unlearned men could understand that."[42]

The Louisiana 1868 Constitution, drafted by a convention in which African Americans comprised a majority of the delegates, gave blacks virtually all that they desired, at least on paper. Adopting as its first article the preamble of the Declaration of Independence—but modifying it to state that "all men are created *free* and equal"—the constitution expunged every legal distinction between blacks, whether freeborn or former slaves, and whites. It accorded state citizenship to every resident of Louisiana of a year's standing and stated that all citizens enjoyed the same "civil, political and public rights and privileges." Those rights included equal access to public conveyances (railroads, streetcars, steamboats) and public accommodations (hotels, theaters, restaurants). The constitution enfranchised all male citizens over twenty-one years of age, "except those disfranchised" for supporting the Confederacy. Public schools were to be established in every parish, and children between the ages of six and twenty-one had the right to attend them "without distinction of race, color, or previous condition." Every legislator and state officer must swear an oath that he accepted the "civil and political equality of all men" and pledge never to "attempt to deprive [any person] of any political and civil right" on the basis of race or color.[43]

On July 4, 1868, the Natchitoches Parish Republican Party held the second of its annual Independence Day rallies. About three thousand blacks flooded into town from the surrounding plantations. They marched in serried ranks from the courthouse to a picnic spot called Fourth of July Springs. There, while feasting on barbecue, they listened to speeches from party leaders W. H. Hiestand, J. J. Bossier, James Parker, and Naville Robinson.

Raford Blunt, the only black speaker, riveted the overwhelmingly black crowd. No report of his words survives; indeed, texts of Blunt's sermons and political speeches are entirely lacking. But we do know that he was a powerful speaker. The best evidence of that can be found in the testimony of his political enemies. The *Natchitoches Spectator* complained that his "agitating harangues" were "calculated to arouse the prejudices and passions of the blacks." Blunt "could arouse the negroes easier than any other leader could," stated Milton J. Cunningham. He "can exert great influence . . . over the colored people," Congressman William Levy agreed. Others likened Blunt to a medieval pontiff. One Democrat's description of Blunt as "bishop of all the [Baptist] churches up there," while technically inaccurate, correctly gauged his influence. For the next ten years, Blunt's popularity would help to sustain black political unity in Natchitoches Parish.[44]

6

LOUISIANA DEMOCRATS AND THE 1868 ELECTIONS

Q. Was the election in Natchitoches very peaceable and quiet?
A. It was more like a funeral than like an election.

N. A. Robinson, Republican, testimony
to House Subcommittee on Elections in Louisiana, 1869

Northern Republicans hoped that black ballots would obviate the need for federal bayonets. By amending the U.S. Constitution they made citizenship national and equal. They saw no need to build permanent national institutions to protect the new citizens thus created. Congress rejected proposals to support public schools. It phased out the Freedmen's Bureau. It declined to allot land to freedpeople. It reduced the number of military posts in the South. Thaddeus Stevens warned that it would be folly to impose black suffrage and then quickly concede home rule to ex-Confederate states. But fellow Radical Charles Sumner contended that the vote would provide blacks (and white Loyalists) with an effective means of protection. "The right of suffrage once given can never be taken away," he exulted. "It will be immortal."[1]

It proved to be a delusion. Ever since the surrender, southern newspapers had warned of racial strife, sometimes predicting the extermination of the black race, should black suffrage come to pass. During the winter of 1867–68 the anti-Republican press—nearly all of Louisiana's newspapers—ridiculed the constitutional convention. The *Natchitoches Spectator* labeled it the "black-and-tan convention," the "un-Constitutional State Convention," the "So-Called State Convention," and the "monkey show." It called the resulting constitution a "long string of balderdash." It predicted that such a government could never last, for "no one supposes for a moment that the highly intelligent and free Caucasian can, or will, live under an abortive government foisted upon them by an irresponsible and unprincipled conclave of ignorant negroes, and their white equals." And this was

Figure 6. David Pierson (1837–1900), a leader of the Natchitoches Democratic Party. Courtesy of Pierson Marshall.

from a relatively moderate paper. Alexandria's *Louisiana Democrat* simply repeated the word "nigger" ad nauseam.[2]

Congressional Republicans assumed that much of this opposition was bluster and would soon abate once the Republican Party assumed power. They drew encouragement from statements by ex-Confederates such as P. G. T. Beauregard and James Longstreet, respected former generals and Louisiana residents, urging whites to accept black suffrage as a fait accompli. But the most revered symbol of the Confederacy, General Robert E. Lee, declined Longstreet's request to make a similar statement. Like most whites, he refused to be reconciled to black suffrage and all that it entailed and implied. He remained silent but sullen.[3]

The rejectionist rhetoric of newspapers and displaced politicians encouraged a resort to violence. Sometimes the call to arms was all but explicit. In *The Lost Cause Regained* (1868), a sequel to his best-selling *The Lost Cause*, Edward A. Pollard sketched the following scenario:

The South is incapable of the *grand duello* of the past, but not incapable of the fierce and desultory rebellion of mobile columns and raids; incapable of a war of calculation, but not incapable of a war of vengeance. She may repeat on a much larger scale the Fenianism of Ireland, and may even take a lesson from the few Indian tribes which have sufficed to hold a year's campaign against the military power of the United States. Such vengeful rebellions, spread over the whole space of the country . . . have sometimes, as we are assured by history, been more difficult to quell than regular wars. . . . Let Congress beware of too much experiment on the temper of the South, for a rebellion may yet be kindled there.[4]

This was incitement masquerading as prophecy.

The Republican Party's vulnerability to violence became evident in the state elections of April 1868. Natchitoches had a peaceful election, but the same could not be said of adjacent parishes. Two weeks before the polls opened, the *Natchitoches Spectator* reported that "a procession of the Ku Klux Klan was seen in Montgomery [Winn Parish] on the night of the 21st [of March]." In De Soto Parish more than two hundred white residents joined the Knights of the White Camelia (KWC), another secret organization. The Democrats carried the election. In Caddo Parish, where Democrats also triumphed, a Republican candidate reported that "no man of our party could go into the country to hold a political meeting without running the risk of being bushwhacked and assassinated." From Homer in Claiborne Parish, home to another Democratic win, William R. Meador complained that "the colored people . . . were kept from the poles by the reble [*sic*] element." Three weeks later, Meador, a free man of color, Union army veteran, and delegate to the constitutional convention, was ambushed outside his home and shot dead. Another ambush felled Franklin St. Clair, a Republican candidate in Ouchita Parish and "one of the best educated colored men in the community." Ten days after the election, Republican governor-elect Henry Clay Warmoth received a death threat from the Ku Klux Klan.[5]

Congressional Republicans had plenty of evidence at hand suggesting that black suffrage, if accompanied by the rapid termination of military rule, would expose black and white Republicans to violent reprisals. A steady flow of reports and letters from Freedmen's Bureau officials, army commanders, northern migrants, and former wartime Unionists warned that the removal of troops would embolden ex-Confederates to further acts of aggression.

Yet at the very time when they were most needed, the federal government thinned out its military presence in the South still further. On July 13, 1868, as soon as the Republican-dominated state legislature had ratified the Fourteenth Amendment, General Robert Buchanan announced that his military authority had ended and that the civil authorities now assumed all responsibility for governing Louisiana. The circumstances of the handover could hardly have been more inauspicious. "Without organized police or militia forces, without arms and without money, and without even authority of law to organize and arm a militia," the secretary of war reported, the new state governments of the South were helpless. No sooner had Buchanan passed the baton to Governor Warmoth than he and his successor, General Winfield Scott Hancock, wired Washington with requests for reinforcements. They noted that the political situation had become more tense, not less. The presidential election campaign, they warned, threatened to raise violence to a new level.[6]

Warmoth sent agents North to procure arms and ammunition. But Congress, in suppressing the neo-Confederate militias that resembled the old slave patrols, had enacted a blanket prohibition on the organization of state militias. It had not considered that the new Republican governments might need militias to protect themselves. Warmoth's emissaries had to ask President Johnson to send more soldiers. Johnson needled his visitors by observing that Warmoth had insisted on his civilian government assuming power at the earliest opportunity, but now, having got his wish, Warmoth wanted the military back again. Point-scoring aside, Johnson had identified the weakness of the newly elected Republican administrations. As historian William A. Dunning noted some decades later, "The actual working of the reconstructed governments during the first few weeks of their existence . . . suggested, if it had not clearly revealed, the inability of those governments to stand alone."[7]

When the Natchitoches Council of the KWC met to consider what action it should take to prevent a Republican victory in the 1868 election, virtually every "respectable" white man in Natchitoches Parish—planters, lawyers, doctors, merchants—attended the conclave. Among the options they considered: threatening to discharge blacks who voted Republican; burning down the office of the *Red River News*, the local Republican newspaper; and assassinating selected "Radical" leaders.[8]

Alcibiades De Blanc of St. Martin Parish, a planter, lawyer, and colonel in the Confederate army, founded the Knights of the White Camelia in May 1867. He devised an elaborate initiation ceremony that swore initiates to "maintain and defend the social and political superiority of the white race on this continent." Knights must "vote for none other than white men" and do everything in their power to "restrain the black or African race to the condition of social and political inferiority for which God has destined it." Failure to do so could lead only to the "eternal degradation" of the white race, because interracial marriages, the inevitable product of black suffrage, would birth a "degenerate and bastard offspring."[9]

After lying dormant for about a year, the KWC took wings. Spreading from southern to northern Louisiana, it enrolled whites en masse. In New Orleans, seventeen thousand men reportedly joined the secret order. In many of the rural parishes the KWC embraced the entire Democratic-Conservative leadership, and then some.[10] William H. Tunnard, author of the regimental history *A Southern Record* and an occasional newspaper contributor, brought a copy of the KWC ritual from Baton Rouge, where his family lived, to Natchitoches, where he now resided. J. Ernest Breda (like Tunnard, a future Republican) inducted "every white man in the parish" into the organization.[11]

The reasons for the explosive growth of the KWC were simple. The Republican victory in April had revealed the futility of Democratic-Conservative efforts to win black votes. In the summer of 1868, when Republican officials elected in April took office, thousands of native whites lost positions, income, and status. The national Democratic Party's nomination of Horatio Seymour and Frank P. Blair offered this displaced ruling class the hope of ousting the Republican upstarts. The Democratic platform condemned Congressional Reconstruction as a "flagrant usurpation of power." Blair, a former Union general and erstwhile Republican, opined that Seymour, if elected president, should simply declare the Reconstruction Acts "null and void" and order the army to "disperse the carpet-bag governments." Denouncing black suffrage, he vowed to defend "our race" from being "trodden underfoot by an inferior and semi-barbaric race." If the Democrats could only elect Seymour, they might destroy Congressional Reconstruction in one fell swoop. Even if Seymour lost, Democrats could elect Louisiana's congressmen and begin to undermine Republican control of the state.[12]

During the two months leading up to the election, the Republican Party lost control over much of Louisiana. In about half the rural parishes a surge of violence intimidated black voters and paralyzed Republican leaders. In Bossier, St. Landry, and St. Bernard Parishes, whites perpetrated massacres that killed about three hundred blacks. Elsewhere, terrorists assassinated individual Republicans. On September 3 Valentine Chase, a Republican judge in St. Mary Parish, wrote a friend that local Democrats "openly avow their intention to murder all the newly elected State and parish officers, or drive them from the State." Six weeks later Chase was gunned down in a hotel in Franklin, the parish seat, where he was lodging. Republican sheriff Henry Pope, a Union veteran, died in the same attack. In St. Helena Parish, John Kemp, the black coroner, was shot dead by masked horsemen. In Caddo Parish, Robert Gray, a black justice of the peace, was murdered on Shreveport's busiest street. The head of the Freedmen's Bureau in Louisiana, General Edward Hatch, listed 297 politically related deaths during September and October. His report did not claim to be comprehensive. Other estimates ranged from five hundred to a thousand.[13]

Hundreds of Republican leaders fled the countryside for the relative safety of New Orleans. Even in the city, however, Democratic threats proved unnerving. George M. Wickliffe, the state auditor, betrayed the strain when he wrote to General Lovell Rousseau a few days before the election to plead for a bodyguard. "It is utterly impossible for me to perform the duties of my office without military protection against men determined to assassinate me." Rousseau gave him one. In New Orleans, Democrats took over the city, appointing a police force composed of 500 white men that completely overawed the Republican force, which consisted of 230 blacks and 130 whites. Republicans found the atmosphere so menacing that Warmoth advised blacks to stay home on election day. Only ten blacks cast ballots.[14]

When the votes were counted it became apparent that the Republican vote had collapsed in over half of Louisiana's forty-eight parishes. In April more than 66,000 people had endorsed the state constitution and supported Republican candidates. In November, Grant received only 33,000 votes. In a dozen parishes the murder or exile of Republican organizers had prevented the party from distributing ballot papers. Seymour carried Louisiana for the Democratic Party in a landslide.

The Knights of the White Camelia forswore "forcible means" and claimed to act purely in self-defense. Historians have treated this assertion with skepticism, rejecting the notion of a nonviolent KWC and a violent Ku Klux Klan. "Basically," Joe Gray Taylor concluded, "all of these were terrorist organizations." Moreover, the KWC's definition of "defensive" covered a multitude of sins, including preemptive attacks to head off the alleged danger from black insurrections. For many, the very fact of black suffrage constituted an assault on the white race.[15]

Yet in Natchitoches Parish the KWC decided to do nothing. To be sure, there was plenty of fire-eating rhetoric in the run-up to the election. Some wanted to follow the example of Rapides Parish, where KWC members twice wrecked the offices of the *Rapides Tribune* and where a committee of planters vowed "not to rent, lease, or give any portion of their lands to freedmen, reserving, however, the right to settle known conservative freedmen, who are to be under the eye and direction of the planters." Amid much wild talk of blacks plotting to seize Natchitoches, massacre the whites, and burn down the town, there were even proposals to assassinate Republican leaders.[16]

Calmer counsels prevailed. David Pierson, a young lawyer from Bienville Parish who had settled in Natchitoches in 1866 and served as district attorney during presidential Reconstruction, dismissed the danger of a black insurrection and opposed calls for violence. Raford Blunt described him as a "very quiet, clear-headed man." Then, as on future occasions, Pierson opposed violence. He also rejected the idea of pressuring laborers and sharecroppers to vote Democratic by threatening to discharge them. "There were some young hot-heads in favor of including this in the Democratic program," recalled J. M. Scanland, who published and edited the *Natchitoches Spectator*, "but this was opposed by myself and Colonel [Ross E.] Burke, and was rejected." The KWC subsequently disbanded.[17]

The only violent incidents to mar the peace in Natchitoches Parish were perpetrated by Ku Klux Klan members from De Soto Parish. A few days before the election, Richard Faulkner, a member of the Natchitoches Parish Police Jury representing Ward Five, went to collect ballot papers from the office of the *Red River News*. The paper's editor, former Freedmen's Bureau agent James Cromie, asked if Faulkner could also get ballot papers out to Republican voters in De Soto, where white Republicans from Natchitoches feared to tread. Faulkner, a farmer and freedmen's school teacher, left with both sets of ballot papers. He found a courier, a young man named Anderson, to take the De Soto Parish ballots to Mansfield, the parish seat.

Spotting Anderson on his horse, a Klan party waylaid the messenger, hanged him until he was half-dead, stole the ballot papers, and forced him to name the man who had sent him on his mission. The whites then broke into Faulkner's house and demanded the ballots for Ward Five. Blindfolded and beaten, Faulkner divulged that he had already distributed most of the ballot papers to officers of the local Republican club, naming Alfred Hazen, who lived nearby, as one of them. The Klan members repaired to Hazen's house and murdered him—perhaps because the elderly black man recognized someone among the party of whites.[18]

What happened next was typical of how Klansmen got away with murder. Freedman's Bureau agent E. H. Hosmer and General N. B. McLaughlin of the Fourth U.S. Cavalry gathered the names of at least half a dozen whites suspected of Hazen's killing and persuaded one informant, who had been at home with Hazen at the time, to swear an affidavit identifying a man called Jim Louis. But when the local justice of the peace examined Louis, he called no black witnesses and failed to question the man providing Louis's alibi. The justice of the peace, Clinton Berry, a white planter who had defeated Faulkner by two votes in the April election, released Louis. "The whites will give no information," a frustrated Hosmer reported, "and the Negroes are afraid to."[19]

In Ward Five, a thinly populated "hill ward" where whites predominated, only about forty out of the two hundred registered black voters cast ballots. The Klan party had ordered Richard Faulkner to vote the Democratic ticket and to report that fact to his landlord. Faulkner, who suspected that the landlord knew all about the Klan attack, explained that his registration certificate had been stolen and that he would not be voting at all. The Klan also told him to quit the police jury, and Faulkner agreed. But he did not resign. "I was in a tight place," he later explained, "and I would say anything under the circumstances."[20]

Democrats in Natchitoches Parish pretended to deprecate Hazen's murder, and their regret may have been genuine. As always, however, professions of regret came hedged with qualifications that took away with one hand what had been offered by the other. The *Natchitoches Times* described Hazen as "industrious and honest" but added that he was "fanatical in religion and politics." The paper commented that Hazen's death could "perhaps . . . be justly charged to his zeal as a Radical." The qualification "perhaps" hardly disguised the fact that the paper offered what amounted to an excuse for murder. This was already standard practice in the Democratic press. As one politician put it: "First they murder a Republican, and then, after he is dead and gone, they assassinate his character."[21]

In the thickly populated wards of the bottomlands, where most of the freedpeople lived, the Republican vote held up nicely. The Republican Party carried Natchitoches Parish by 1,945 votes to 1,375. In Natchitoches town, the Democrat-controlled city council had appointed special policemen, blacks and whites, to patrol the streets. "On the day of the election there was the most perfect order and tranquility, to the agreeable disappointment of many," related Aaron H. Pierson, a Democrat. The Republicans, although always keen to advertise thuggish behavior on the part of their political opponents, conceded that they had little cause for complaint. "I never doubted that we could have had a fair election in the parish of Natchitoches," James Cromie admitted. If it had not been for Hazen's murder "we could have had a fair election all through."[22]

The contrast between the strong Republican showing in Natchitoches and the collapse of the party elsewhere in the Red River valley could scarcely be starker. In the seven parishes that abutted Natchitoches, only in Rapides did blacks register something approaching their strength, enabling the Republican Party to carry the election there by about three hundred votes. In the other six parishes, the combined Republican vote totaled less than fifty. Grant received two votes in Sabine, one each in Bienville, Bossier, and Caddo, and none in De Soto. Most of the white Republicans in those parishes fled; the brave souls who remained cautioned blacks that if they attempted to vote they would be risking their lives. Natchitoches Republicans made a desultory attempt to canvass Winn Parish, where Grant received forty-five votes, but steered clear of the others. "I did not care about getting killed," explained M. P. Blackstone.[23]

Two of the worst instances of Reconstruction-era violence, the Colfax massacre of 1873 and the Coushatta murders of 1874, occurred within an easy day's ride of Natchitoches town. Natchitoches Parish itself, however, was spared that kind of politically inspired violence. Subjected to repeated congressional investigations, Democratic leaders protested that no political murders had occurred in their parish with the single exception of Alfred Hazen. These leaders had nothing against employing ostracism and intimidation. In 1874 they used the threat of a lynch mob to force the resignation of

Republican officials. Nevertheless, their larger point was valid: Natchitoches Parish was a far less violent place than the rest of the Red River valley.[24]

Everyone noted the contrast. "Natchitoches Parish has the honor of being the most quiet parish in the State by all itinerants," reported the *Christian Recorder*. Agents of the Freedmen's Bureau reported that "the different races seem to get along agreeably together" and that "the feeling between black and white is remarkably good." The fact that these agents felt safe in Natchitoches no doubt colored their views. But the contrast with the rest of the Red River valley could also be seen in other ways. When blacks in Caddo, Bossier, De Soto, and Bienville Parishes were too frightened to go to the polls, blacks in Natchitoches time and again carried their parish for the Republican Party. When white hostility made the founding of freedmen's schools in other parishes difficult, dangerous, and sometimes impossible, planters in Natchitoches Parish welcomed schools onto their properties. Whites seemed "well disposed to have the children of freedmen educated," reported bureau agent Charles Miller.[25]

Why did local Democrats reject political violence? The age of the white settlement, its tightly knit upper class, and its Anglo-French culture all distinguished Natchitoches from the rest of the Red River valley. Natchitoches lacked the raw frontier character of more recently settled parishes such as "Bloody" Caddo, where, according to one estimate, more than five hundred people were murdered between 1868 and 1875. During the same period Natchitoches Parish, with a larger population, recorded fewer than fifty murders. Whereas Caddo Parish shared the lawless culture of nearby Texas, the white elite in Natchitoches, dominated by a small number of French-speaking families who were interrelated through marriage, tried to protect their parish from the desperadoes who infested the Texas-Louisiana border and preyed on the freedpeople. The large population of freeborn blacks, many of whom had close ties to white planters and were, like them, Roman Catholics, also discouraged white aggression.[26]

French Catholic culture alone, however, cannot account for the pacific record of Natchitoches Parish. St. Landry Parish was also French-speaking and Catholic, and it had as many *gens de couleur libres* as Natchitoches. Yet in September and October 1868 white men in St. Landry, thousands strong, violently suppressed the Republican Party, smashing its printing press, whipping its white editor, and over a two-week period killing an unquantified number of blacks (estimates of the dead ranged between 59 and 400).[27]

One key difference between St. Landry Parish and Natchitoches Parish was the history of vigilante violence in the former. In 1859 affluent whites in the French-speaking parishes of southern Louisiana had formed local vigilance committees for the ostensible purpose of bringing outlaws to justice. Victims were variously flogged, banished, shot, and hanged. Like the later Ku Klux Klan, the vigilance committees targeted "persons deemed socially or politically unacceptable by the local gentry." In St. Landry, the vigilantes targeted prosperous free people of color, many of whom fled the parish, some of them settling in Mexico and Haiti.[28]

Nothing comparable had happened in Natchitoches Parish before the war: no vigilance committees, no aggression against the *gens de couleur*. Whites there had not regarded the free people as much of a threat. The *gens de couleur* of Isle Brevelle formed a compact, self-contained, and relatively isolated community. In their daily lives these colored Creoles got on well with their white Creole neighbors, but they had limited contact with the "American" whites. During the Civil War, the *gens de couleur* of Natchitoches Parish had displayed steadfast loyalty to the Confederacy, whereas many in war-ravaged St. Landry Parish had, when given the opportunity, resisted the Confederacy, some by joining the jayhawker band of Ozémé Carrière.[29] After the war, the freeborn blacks of Isle Brevelle played a relatively small role in politics. In St. Landry, *gens de couleur* dominated the early leadership of the Republican Party.

Demographics also distinguished Natchitoches and St. Landry Parishes. Whites in St. Landry Parish outnumbered blacks, but the sheer size of the black majority in Natchitoches Parish may have inhibited whites from employing violence. Although intimations of black uprisings were a staple of Democratic propaganda, there is little doubt that whites in Natchitoches felt vulnerable. It was not so much a black insurrection that worried them; rather, they feared economic ruin should blacks fail to harvest their cotton. White landlords were just as dependent upon black laborers as they had been when slaveholders, but now their employees could refuse to sign contracts and quit the plantation if they were dissatisfied.

Republican orators continually reminded blacks, and not so subtly warned whites, that crops would wither in the field if blacks withdrew their labor. An employer who beat his employees, dismissed them for political reasons, or refused to permit a freedman's school on his property might find himself working in the fields alone. Even as slaveholders, many masters knew that the carrot could be more effective than the stick. Now that the stick had been removed, maintaining the goodwill and cooperation of the workforce became more important than ever. The *Natchitoches Semi-Weekly Times*, aware that some planters took advantage of their laborers' ignorance in order to cheat them, urged employers to "carry out their promises to the letter" so that the freedmen would "labor hard and diligently." The same kind of enlightened self-interest persuaded many planters to allow freedmen's schools on their property.[30]

Abstention from violence also served a strategic political purpose. From the moment that Congress enfranchised the ex-slaves, anti-Republicans differed over how best to destroy the new order. Some diehards refused even to acknowledge the reality of Congressional Reconstruction. In a petition to the military authorities, fifteen citizens of Natchitoches Parish protested that the commissioners of election had denied them the right to vote on spurious grounds: that they had not registered under the "partisan legislation of a Radical Congress, in violation of the Constitution and laws bequeathed us by our fathers." They had already taken an oath of amnesty, they explained, and had been "fully restored to all their rights of citizenship" by President Johnson. District Judge W. B. Lewis was another refusenik. Dismissing a jury venire that contained blacks, he ruled the Reconstruction Acts unconstitutional and declared that Louisiana had been restored to the Union with all the powers of a state. These protests were, of course, futile. In the case of Judge Lewis, they were the fulminations of a dying man.[31]

For most whites it was now a question of dealing with unpleasant reality. A debate ensued over the relative merits of a "straight-out" policy of condemning black suffrage and appealing solely to white voters, and a more nuanced policy of accepting black suffrage as a fait accompli, and seeking to win over enough black voters to create an anti-Republican majority. Discussions over the use of coercive methods were central to that debate. "Straight-out" Democrats tended to believe that violence and intimidation could pay short-term dividends, felling the Republican Party with a single blow. Advocates of abstention from violence preferred a longer-term strategy, banking on the inherent instability of the Republican coalition and waning interest among northern Republicans.

Louis Dupleix and Mary E. Bryan, coeditors of the *Natchitoches Semi-Weekly Times*, consistently preached caution. For the moment, they argued, white southerners could do nothing to stop the "Radical Juggernaut." Calls

by northern Democrats for open resistance would, if followed, only produce "more blood-shed and further impoverishment and demoralization
of an already nearly ruined country." Violence was self-defeating because it
promoted Republican unity and provided a pretext for federal intervention.
The New Orleans riot provided a cautionary object lesson, argued Bryan.
Whites must be "patient and prudent, and afford no pretext for the employment of armed interference."[32]

Others believed that if the Democratic Party made overtures to black
voters, they might split the Republican vote. Amid all the racist satires and
white supremacist rhetoric that appeared in the Natchitoches newspapers,
some called for the acceptance of blacks as citizens and voters. A "prudent
and conciliatory course," one contributor to the Times advised, would make
black voters "an element of strength rather than an element of weakness."
An "esteemed friend" argued that black suffrage was "as much a fixed fact
as the abolition of slavery" and that propertied whites should act accordingly—much as they had come to terms with the extension of the franchise
to poor whites in the 1830s and 1840s. Whites should not delude themselves
that blacks were incapable of intellectual improvement, he added, for "there
are too many proofs to the contrary." Even Bryan, who regarded blacks and
whites as "widely separated species," urged her readers to "throw aside the
prejudices of the past" and strive to elevate the race "now firmly established
as citizens." (She had difficulty following her own advice: a letter from a colored teacher elicited a withering commentary in which Bryan highlighted
the writer's grammatical errors and spelling mistakes.)[33]

The Times sometimes presented blacks in a positive light. William H.
Tunnard, writing from Baton Rouge, described black soldiers there as "well
behaved." His description of a river baptism was vivid without being con-
descending. A piece titled "Pass Him Around" praised Ebenezer Hayward,
a black minister and schoolteacher, for his "powerful influence over the
Freedmen here." Complaints about black indolence yielded to admissions
that "freedmen are diligently and faithfully at work." Even the execution of
a black man for the murder of his child elicited a grudging tribute: "Never
have we witnessed such resolution, composure and calmness."[34]

From the start of Congressional Reconstruction, Democratic leaders in
Natchitoches looked to win over black voters. William M. Levy and William H. Jack spoke at one of the first meetings of the Natchitoches Parish
Republican Party, sitting on the platform alongside their political opponents. A year later, Levy and another Democrat, Ross E. Burke, popped up

at a freedpeople's barbecue and addressed the solidly Republican gathering in a "mild, conciliatory, and advisable manner." The *Natchitoches Spectator*, whose editor, J. M. Scanland, was an ardent Democrat, praised the freedmen for their "peaceful and orderly manner," as well as for the "excellent dinner" they prepared. The Natchitoches Democratic Conservative Club, organized in May 1868, voted to admit black members and set about wooing them. Levy, the club's president, again took the lead. Speaking at a Democratic barbecue put on for freedmen, he advised blacks that their "success or prosperity in life depended . . . upon that of the Southern people." Two freedmen, King Johnson and Elijah Berry, spoke at Democratic ward clubs in an effort to drum up black support. Throughout the summer, the *Spectator* touted the number of blacks joining the Democratic Party.[35]

All this effort availed the Democrats naught. Republican candidates romped home in November. "The Democratic Party [in Natchitoches Parish] expected to do much better than they did," admitted E. R. Biossat. "They were awfully deceived as to the result of that election." Posing as the freedpeople's "friends," all they offered blacks were lectures on morality and an updated version of paternalism. Asked if blacks were treated "kindly" at Democratic barbecues, one freedman responded, "Yes . . . but just in the same way you treat a dog kindly if you want that dog to come home with you."[36]

As one of the first historians of Louisiana Reconstruction pointed out, Democrats appealed to black voters "for the purpose of securing white supremacy." Blacks were well aware that the Democrats had vowed to destroy Congressional Reconstruction. Quizzed about his knowledge of the Democratic platform, Richard Faulkner replied that all he knew and needed to know was contained in Frank P. Blair's widely publicized letter to Missouri Democrat James O. Broadhead. "I remember one passage very well, which was (to put it in a common way) that if they licked, there would be no more voting for Mr. Nigger; he said it was a white man's country." Blacks attending Democratic barbecues had no intention of voting Democratic. As Faulkner put it, "they feed you with the corn and choke you with the cob."[37]

Nevertheless, some Democrats in Natchitoches Parish never relinquished the hope that they might attract enough black votes to win. The Republican Party would make such a hash of governing, they believed, that appeals to black voters would in the long term pay off. They remained hopeful, too, that their personal contacts with individual blacks could be translated into political support. A skeptical Democrat noted that William H. Jack, a lawyer, "is sanguine enough to suppose that every Negro he ever defended is a firm personal and political friend."[38]

The short-term results of the election seemed to bear out the arguments of Democrats who opposed violence. Grant was easily elected despite losing both Louisiana and Georgia. Of more immediate concern to Louisiana Democrats was the loss of congressional seats they thought they had won. In the district of which Natchitoches Parish formed a part, the fourth, Congress awarded the seat to Republican candidate and Union veteran Joseph Newsham. It concluded that Alexandria lawyer Michael P. Ryan's voluntary support for the Confederacy made him ineligible to take office because it violated the "iron-clad" loyalty oath required of congressmen. Ryan's principal offense, in reality, was to be a Democrat. His support for the Confederacy had been minimal—just enough to avoid being arrested or expelled. Even Madison Wells attested to his Unionism. But the evidence of Democratic thuggery exposed by the congressional investigation gave the Republican Party all it needed to justify Ryan's exclusion.[39]

The Louisiana hearings were but a curtain-raiser for a sweeping congressional investigation of the Ku Klux Klan that yielded fourteen volumes of compelling and often horrific testimony. All this evidence—and congressional committees amassed much more—provided grist for the Republican mill. After the Fifteenth Amendment was added to the U.S. Constitution in 1870, forbidding states to deny the suffrage on the grounds of "race, color or previous condition or servitude," Congress passed two enforcement acts with the aim of protecting Republican voters against Democratic violence and intimidation.

The Louisiana legislature passed stringent prophylactic measures of its own. In 1869–70 it approved a package of bills designed to fortify the Republican Party and provide a quick and effective response to Democratic aggression. One set up a Metropolitan Police District, combining the police forces of Orleans, Jefferson, and St. Bernard Parishes, placing it under a five-man board appointed by the governor. Governor Warmoth could deploy the "Metropolitans" wherever he wished. Another act created a state militia consisting of five thousand men, half black and half white. Warmoth appointed former Confederate general James Longstreet, Robert E. Lee's longest-serving corps commander, to lead it. An act empowering the governor to appoint a chief constable in every parish, with deputy constables in each ward, might have strengthened Republican control had the legislature actually funded the measure.

Another set of laws centralized the supervision of elections. Voters were to be enrolled by parish supervisors appointed by the governor, each assisted by three commissioners of election. A state registrar, also appointed by Warmoth, oversaw the process and served as the registrar of voters in New Orleans. Stringent regulations governed conduct during polling day. They prohibited the carrying of firearms by ordinary citizens, placed local law enforcement officers under the direct control of the governor, and forbade judicial interference with the state-appointed election officials. A State Returning Board, likewise controlled by the governor, was empowered to scrutinize the count and reject any returns that had, in its judgment, been tainted by fraud, intimidation, or violence.[40]

The Republicans further bolstered their position by manipulating elections, carving out new parishes, and creating a vast array of patronage jobs. The legislature empowered Warmoth to appoint people to vacant offices, and then it set about creating a plenitude of such positions. Apart from disqualifying numerous officials because of their Confederate pasts, the legislature created new political units to be administered by Warmoth's appointees until elections took place—elections that were often deliberately delayed. When the legislature passed a new city charter for New Orleans, for example, Warmoth appointed the mayor, the council, and all the other officials. When the legislature created the new parishes of Iberia, Grant, Tangipahoa, Richland, Cameron, and Red River, Warmoth filled all the offices with his own men. The result, as Lawrence Powell has demonstrated, was a steep increase in the number of local officials who owed their position to the governor. According to Powell, Warmoth made at least sixteen hundred appointments, and he sometimes required these men to give him undated letters of resignation as a guarantee of their loyalty.[41]

The printing of official business gave the Republican Party another source of political patronage. Republican newspapers were paid to publish the proceedings of the legislature and other state business. Republican-controlled police juries paid them to publish parish business. These contracts sustained a network of Republican newspapers, most of which could not have survived without them. When, for example, James Cromie purchased the *Natchitoches Spectator* and renamed it the *Red River News*, he did all the public printing of both the parish and the state.[42]

The Republican Party also controlled a host of federal positions: jobs in the Internal Revenue Service, federal courts, federal land offices, post offices, and, above all, the New Orleans Custom House, which, according to Ted Tunnell, "employed 63 per cent of all the customs service personnel in the former Confederate states." Federal patronage accounted for perhaps six hundred jobs, most of them in New Orleans, all of them filled by loyal Republicans. On paper, at least, the party had created a formidable state apparatus and a powerful political machine. The elections of 1870—"quiet, orderly, and reasonably honest"—delivered a solid Republican majority.[43]

The long-term implications of the fall 1870 elections, however, were ominous for the Republican Party. The Republican vote remained static; the party was still failing to win substantial white support. There was little sign that former Confederates were reconciled to black suffrage. The overwhelming majority bitterly opposed Congressional Reconstruction and detested a Republican regime elected by black voters. Moreover, the five thousand or so native whites who adhered to the Republican Party found themselves saddled with the insulting term "scalawag" and ostracized by (former) friends, colleagues, comrades, and even family members.

The congressional inquiry into the contested elections in Louisiana documented the vehemence with which Democratic leaders opposed the participation of blacks in politics. Witness after witness, from the chairman of the Democratic State Central Committee down, condemned black suffrage and black officeholding, and proudly affirmed his belief in white supremacy. Few were as extreme as E. R. Biossat, publisher of the *Louisiana Democrat*, who told his interlocutor that "the colored people were certainly a thousand times better off in slavery than they are now." But the testimony of E. B. Bolton, a white teacher from Union Parish, was typical. Blacks were neither qualified nor capable of voting intelligently, he explained. Besides, he added, "I, for one, do not wish to be put upon an equality with the negroes, because I regard them as an inferior race and so created." Pressed as to whether he might change his opinion should blacks so improve their condition as to attain equality "in fact," this witness rejected the suggestion as absurd. "That is supposing a thing which I do not believe ever will exist."[44]

Forced to deal with black politicians in the Republican-controlled legislature, Democratic lawmakers suffered agonies of mortification. Shreveport Democrat John C. Moncure recorded such feelings in a letter to his wife:

I am brought in contact hourly almost with aspiring, ambitious and disgusting Negroes of every shade of color and crammed to overflowing with manifest consciousness of their importance. There are some forty odd of these animals in human shape in the house some of them with native smartness enough to make them troublesome and all together presenting a spectacle which every respectable man must look upon with humiliation and the gloomiest forbodings for the future.[45]

Moncure, it should be added, was the most influential and respected Democrat in the lower house.

Democratic witnesses offered an unapologetic defense of the preelection violence in Bossier, St. Landry, and St. Bernard Parishes. While some regretted these "riots," none condemned them outright. Instead, they praised the restraint of the whites for not killing more blacks than they did. "The truth of it is this," stated a young planter from St. Bernard Parish, "that in all of those riots, you have seen but three, four, or five men killed, whereas we could have killed thousands." Others emphasized that killing in "hot blood" could not be equated with cold-blooded murder. "I do not consider a man responsible for excesses committed under excitement," explained a St. Landry Parish planter. This "hot blood" argument comported with white conceptions about the character of the race to which they belonged. There was something in the blood of the Anglo-Saxon that made him terrible when roused to fury, especially when insulted or provoked. His drive to dominate inferior races was a law of nature, wrote General Richard Taylor. "Doubtless there were many acts of violence. When ignorant Negroes, instigated by pestilential emissaries, went beyond endurance, the whites killed them, and this was to be expected. The breed to which these whites belong has for eight centuries been the master of the earth wherever it has planted its feet."[46]

The ultimate justification for such violence was that whites were acting in self-defense. "What was done was done in self-protection," claimed Thomas Macon, chairman of the Democratic State Central Committee. Challenged to produce evidence of black aggression, witnesses explained that their actions had been preventative—"it would have been an unwise policy to have waited until they would have burned us out." When pressed, however, Democrats defined black aggression in the widest possible terms, citing any and every example of assertive behavior by blacks. Leaving the plantation without the employer's permission, attending mass meetings and listening to "radical" speakers, carrying guns and drinking whiskey—all were deemed threatening.[47]

The mass of Democratic testimony suggested that many whites had yet to accept the consequences of emancipation, let alone black suffrage. They treated blacks' refusal to exhibit deference as an intolerable insult. Sometimes they complained about specific behavior. "For instance, when passing by the homes of white men," explained one, "colored men would kiss their hands to the family." The same witness took offense in hearing blacks openly proclaim "that the bottom rail was now on top." For the most part, however, whites pointed to blacks' general demeanor: "There was a disposition not to be careful or respectful . . . [and] to regard the whites as their natural enemies, which was indicated by a want of courtesy, and a disregard of civility."[48]

As long as their opponents remained divided as to strategy, the Republican Party benefited from low Democratic turnouts. It could also use the state constitution's disfranchisement clause to weaken the Democrats. However, after the legislature amended the constitution to restore political rights to ex-Confederates—an act of reconciliation that did little to appease the objects of the amnesty—the Republican Party could no longer use past disloyalty to disqualify political opponents. With the population roughly balanced between blacks and whites, Republicans faced the real possibility that a reenergized and reunited Democratic Party could win a state election.

Much more was at stake, moreover, than the mere winning or losing of an election, important as that was in terms of who benefited from the thousands of patronage jobs. Louisiana's 1868 Constitution required all public officers to swear that they "accept the civil and political equality of all men, and agree not to attempt to deprive any person . . . on account of race, color, and previous condition of any political or civil rights." The Republican Party's promiscuous insistence upon oaths, however, had long since emptied such declarations of any real force. Few southern Republicans believed that Democrats, given the opportunity, would hesitate to violate their oath of office. If the Democratic Party came to power, the Republican Party risked political extinction, and blacks faced the reduction of their newfound freedom. In concrete terms, the Democrats might withdraw public funding from black schools, pass laws favoring landlords over employees, curtail black suffrage, and exclude blacks from juries. They could reenact the Black Codes in all but name.

Not all Democrats or Republicans viewed the political situation in such stark terms. In every southern state, including Louisiana, some men in both parties envisaged a moderate alternative that would somehow unite white conservatives, "respectable" white Republicans, and a sizable number of black voters. But Civil War loyalties and racial polarization remained stubbornly resistant to such appeals. Most voters continued to view politics as a zero-sum game. Hence the temptation for the Democratic Party to offset the small Republican majority by means of intimidation, and the corresponding temptation for the Republican Party to use its control of elections to cheat. Both made the establishment of a stable two-party system extremely difficult. Moreover, advocates of "reform" parties, like Governor Warmoth, often turned out to be no more committed to free and fair elections than the parties they criticized. The prospects for what we now call "democratic consolidation" remained bleak.

7

REPUBLICANS IN POWER

Q. Did he charge Myers with corruption?

A. Yes, he charged him with corruption. In fact they will charge
    anybody with corruption to get rid of him, me or anybody else.

Raford Blunt to House Select Committee on the Condition of the South, 1875

The Natchitoches Parish Republican Party rested upon a base of about
twenty-one hundred black voters, the vast majority of them recently emancipated slaves. That base displayed remarkable solidity between 1867 and
1876, making the party the strongest in the Red River valley and a bastion
of Republican power in the state.

Its overwhelming black support, however, was the Republican Party's
Achilles' heel. The party had little appeal to former slaveholders and appeared equally unpopular with the poorer whites of the hill wards. Only
forty-two white voters favored the new state constitution. This extreme racial polarization boded ill for the party's future survival. "Reconstruction's
opponents," writes Eric Foner, "viewed the new [Republican] regimes as
alien impositions, and their black constituency as not entitled to a permanent role in the body politic." That seemed to hold true for Natchitoches
Parish.[1]

Its exclusively black constituency clouded the party's prospects in another respect. The Republican Party had instigated a political revolution in
the South, but it was not a revolutionary party. It was the party of property,
middle-class respectability, and, increasingly, big business. It championed
universal suffrage in idealistic terms, but the party's actions in the North,
where in states like New York Republicans employed subtle means to dis-
criminate against immigrant voters if it suited them, belied its rhetoric.
During the constitutional crisis of 1866–68, black suffrage had appeared
essential to preserving the Union. But in the same way that they looked

Figure 7. David H. Boullt Sr. (1813–1879), Republican tax collector. Courtesy of Michael Ram.

askance at the poverty-stricken Irish, many Republicans harbored doubts about penniless, illiterate former slaves. They wanted the freedmen to become honest, thrifty, industrious laborers. They did not want them to act as a discontented proletariat that responded to radical, even revolutionary, appeals.[2]

It was thus vital for the southern wing of the party to attract substantial numbers of white voters, especially former slaveholders, in order to gain political legitimacy. Only in this way could the Republican Party persuade Democrats to acquiesce in black suffrage and overcome its own doubts about black political participation. "Capital and intelligence must rule," insisted former Ohio governor Jacob D. Cox to Congressman James A. Garfield. The party must appeal to "thinking and influential white native Southerners, the intelligent, well-to-do, controlling class." Garfield, like Cox a former Union general, had had to swallow his own doubts in order to back Congressional Reconstruction. "It goes against the grain of my feelings to favor negro suffrage," he admitted in 1865, "for I never could get in love with [the] creatures."[3]

Northern Republicans therefore had no qualms about the fact that whites dominated the southern party's leadership and filled the most important posts. In Natchitoches Parish whites took all the judicial positions and most of the other parish offices. John Osborn of Rapides Parish, who in 1860 had owned 108 slaves, was elected district judge. Irish-born James Cromie, until recently assistant commissioner of the Freedman's Bureau for Natchitoches, Rapides, and Sabine Parishes, was elected clerk of the district court. Twenty-four-year-old Navile A. Robinson, a former Confederate soldier, filled the office of district attorney. William H. Hiestand, formerly of New Orleans and late of the Freedmen's Bureau, became parish judge. Staunch Unionist Samuel Parsons took on the powerful, dangerous job of sheriff. B. B. Moore, a native of Georgia, occupied the tax assessor's office. Only the election of Charles Dupré as coroner prevented whites from monopolizing the parish offices.[4]

Nevertheless, blacks received more than token recognition. The party selected Charles Leroy, a freeborn mulatto, as one of the parish's two representatives in the lower house. The eleven-member police jury, the principal governing body of the parish, included four black members: Henry Dallas, a small farmer; Emile Silvie, a carpenter; Richard L. Faulkner, a small farmer and freedmen's school teacher; and John B. Vienne, another carpenter. These men held influential positions. As historian Ted Tunnell put it, "the police jury's decisions affected schools, levees, taxes, roads, and law enforcement. On a day-to-day-basis, the police jury was more important in the lives of people than the state legislature in New Orleans." As for law enforcement, Felix Mezière, a freeborn mulatto, served as justice of the peace for the Fourth Ward, and blacks comprised at least five of the eleven ward-based constables. Three blacks served on the six-man town council.[5]

The *gens de couleur* of Isle Brevelle, many of whom possessed education and business experience, provided few political leaders and played a relatively small role in the Republican Party. Many had owned slaves or been members of slave-owning families. Catholic in religion and very light in complexion, this tightly knit community of francophones had little in common with the mass of darker freedpeople, most of whom joined Protestant churches and spoke English.

Blacks who spoke only French or who spoke English poorly found themselves at a disadvantage under the Republican regime. The Republican Party conducted its business entirely in English, and the state government made no secret of its hostility to the French language. Before 1868, the proceedings of the state legislature were published in both English and French, each language enjoying equal prominence. Beginning in 1868, they were printed in English alone. The 1868 Constitution forbade the use of any language other than English in the state courts. It required the public schools to conduct lessons in English. Three years later, Raford Blunt introduced a bill in the legislature requiring all parish announcements, advertisements, judicial proceedings, and minutes to be published in English and English alone. These measures made public life more difficult for colored Creoles. That may well have been their purpose.[6]

The new governing class can best be characterized as middle class and lower middle class. The native whites included a laborer, a shoemaker, a clerk, a carpenter, a saloonkeeper, a liquor dealer, a printer, and a dry goods merchant. A few had owned slaves, but with the exception of John Osborn, the district judge who resided in Rapides Parish, none had been a large slaveholder. Marco Givanovich, the largest slaveholder in Natchitoches Parish, sympathized with the Republican Party but eschewed politics. Some officeholders had been wartime Unionists, others had fought for the Confederacy. Four Republican officials were recent arrivals from the North: two former agents of the Freedmen's Bureau and two freedmen's school teachers. Many of the African American officials had been free men of color, but a former slave sat on the police jury, and three freedmen on the town council. The black constables were also ex-slaves.[7]

The number of black officeholders in Natchitoches Parish was never proportionate to the number of black voters. The same was true across the state, and the disparity quickly became a sore point among black Republicans. P. B. S. Pinchback, the state's most influential black leader after the death of Oscar J. Dunn in 1871, accused the party's white leaders of exploiting black voters' inexperience and loyalty in order to secure the lion's share of the offices for themselves. Year in and year out, he charged, black voters marched in unbroken ranks to support overwhelmingly white tickets, only to be short-changed. "In the army they might be soldiers but not officers," complained Pinchback, "and in politics they might be voters but not office-holders." Congress's refusal to seat him as a U.S. senator undoubtedly embittered Pinchback, but he had every reason to be bitter. Moreover, his general complaint was not without substance, especially when it came to higher positions. "If a colored man aspired to office," he recalled, "he was told it was 'too soon—it would injure the party at the North and embarrass our friends in Congress.'"[8]

The overrepresentation of whites, however, did not simply reflect greed for office or disguised racial prejudice. Two other factors came into play. The first had to do with political strategy. It was more important for the Republican Party to attract white voters, the bulk of whom were hostile, than to attract black voters, whose support could be counted upon. The Republicans had to be ready, therefore, to offer patronage positions to disaffected Democrats and Whigs-at-heart. The second consideration had to do with class. Poor and working-class voters are *always* underrepresented in political parties; or, to put it another way, the wealthy and well educated—and, in American politics, lawyers—are always overrepresented. In short, the Republican Party should be judged in comparison with the other parties of the day. And by this standard, its inclusion of blacks, former slaves, and whites of relatively humble means was remarkable.

Yet the revolutionary nature of black suffrage meant that the Republican Party was on trial. Many Republicans admitted that the freedpeople were unprepared for political responsibility. Blacks had to prove themselves as moral, upright citizens. Their loyalty to the Union had earned them immense goodwill among northern Republicans, and for the moment they enjoyed the benefit of the doubt. But unless southern Republicans governed effectively, that goodwill would rapidly dissipate, and a failure to attract white support might well be interpreted as de facto evidence of black incompetence.

How well did the Republican Party serve its constituents? From the start, Democrats worked to discredit black suffrage, and the whole principle of racial equality, by charging southern Republican governments with corruption, extravagance, and oppression. These charges were copiously documented in congressional investigations and court records. The first academic histories of Reconstruction, published in the early twentieth century, endorsed and embellished them. Over the past fifty years, however, historians have demonstrated that Democratic allegations were grossly exaggerated and, in many cases, downright false.

One achievement of Republican government in Natchitoches Parish is easy to overlook: the freedom it gave blacks to move, meet, and organize. In many other parishes, fear hung over the black population and never dissipated. In Natchitoches Parish, fear was intermittent—confined mostly to the election campaign of 1874—and blacks showed little sign of being intimidated. In the town of Natchitoches they shared the streets and sidewalks with whites and patronized bars and coffee houses. Wesley Sheppard's saloon on Horn Street was a favorite meeting place.

In parades through Natchitoches, blacks asserted their right to use public spaces. "The archetypal black response to the jubilee of Reconstruction," writes Geraldine McTigue, "was the procession (political or impulsive) through a village whooping, hollering and riding at full gallop." Whites deplored such displays. "Like a Knight of old," the *Vindicator* recalled in 1875, Raford Blunt used to "cavort through this city . . . with a hundred or more negroes at his heels mounted on plug ponies and armed with guns and pistols, who, with whoops and yells, rendered it dangerous to walk about much." Blunt's recollection was rather different. "We have had a peaceable parish," he told a congressional committee. Blacks and whites had got along "about as well as they can anywhere else in this State or in the South." To blacks in repressive parishes like Winn, De Soto, and Sabine, Natchitoches was a haven.[9]

Political mobilization emboldened blacks. When they held political meetings in the outlying wards, they posted armed guards. They marched to the polling places en masse, in ranks, like a column of soldiers. Freedman's Bureau agent James Cromie advised blacks not to bring firearms to public meetings, but many did so anyway.[10]

The recruitment of blacks as voters undermined efforts by white employers to confine blacks to the plantation during the year-long contract and to strictly supervise their working week. Contracts typically specified that workers should start work by sunrise and labor for ten hours a day, Sunday excepted; they should obey orders and show respect, take proper care of tools and equipment, and remain on the plantation unless granted permission to leave. Infractions were punishable by loss of wages or dismissal.[11]

By the spring of 1867, however, employers were finding it impossible to stop laborers from quitting during the term of the contract. In March, for example, a parish constable arrested Frank Vienne and delivered him to the plantation because he had "left without permission." Vienne absconded again. In the same month, Marco Givanovich complained to bureau agent Cromie that a female employee, Françoise Hall, had "left my place without cause" and moved to a plantation in Rapides Parish. "My dear Major," he wrote, "every freedman in my neighborhood looks to this case which is: Are the freedmen after they had signed a contract at liberty to leave without any cause whatever, the place of their employer?"[12]

Planters tried to maintain a united front in order to control wages and conditions of work, but so acute was the demand for labor that many broke ranks. Employers who found themselves shorthanded were quite willing to take on workers who had quit other plantations. "Under the pretext of taking a promenade on the Christmas holidays," complained Gabriel Prudhomme, two of his employees had signed a contract with Emile Sompeyrac. Having reported previous cases to the provost marshal to no effect, Prudhomme pleaded with James Cromie to "have justice done." But attempts to enforce anti-enticement laws—of dubious legality given the passage of the 1866 Civil Rights Act—proved unavailing. "I dealt fairly with them," another planter grumbled. "I have paid them every cent I owe them. . . . And yet they quit whenever they please."[13]

Freedpeople also left plantations to attend political meetings. In fact, the complaints of white employers constitute the best evidence we have for the liberating effect of political participation. "Please come or send some person to straiten [sic] out matters on my place," a Natchitoches Parish planter wrote Cromie. "My freedmen are growing perfectly uncontrollable." Complaints multiplied in the run-up to the election of the constitutional convention in September 1867. Employers reported that "freedmen are neglecting their duties and disobeying orders," behavior they attributed to "doctrines preached by some leaders of the Republican Club at this place." When planters ordered freedmen to stay at work, they often met with flat refusals:

> They left their places without leave, and when you spoke to them about it, they said they had the right to do as they pleased; servants left their houses where they had engaged to work, and went off. . . . All of those immediately under my control . . . left in a body to attend a political meeting.

During political campaigns, one Freedmen's Bureau agent confirmed, blacks "will not work nor can they be compelled."[14]

Efforts to make laborers work when, where, and how their employers directed became increasingly futile. When working under the "master's eye," the *Shreveport Southwestern* noted, blacks had maintained fences and farm buildings. Now, it complained, they regarded "every lick struck aside from the farming routine . . . as so much labor expended by them without any return." When William Payne assigned his hands their tasks one January morning, he was met with a flat refusal. "The *Gentlemen* of color find it too cold to work," he wrote his daughter.[15]

The extension of the franchise to freedmen indirectly encouraged the emergence of family sharecropping. "Working on shares"—being paid with a share of the crop than with a money wage—was already widely established, but employers had generally contracted with teams of men, or "squads," rather than with individual families. This "squad system" became increasingly burdensome, however, as blacks asserted their independence from white supervision. Moreover, more black workers were changing their employers, and they usually moved as families. With plantation workforces becoming increasingly mixed—they were less likely to be the same group of people who had worked together as slaves—the formation of "squads" became correspondingly difficult. Even if black laborers knew each other, many disliked the squad system because they felt that if other members of the team did not pull their weight—economists call this the "free rider" problem—they did not receive their just share. Resentment of "free riders" diminished if squads consisted of close kin. It was then but a small step to having a single household as the squad, with the advantage for employers that, if they contracted with individual families, women and children were more likely to work in the fields.[16]

It is not clear when the cultivation of separate plots by individual families became the predominant form of sharecropping, but by 1870 the transition was well under way. "Many of our planters," observed Mary Bryan, "are willing to cut up their large farms into small ones. . . . Many have already scattered little settlements about over their plantations, and these neat little framed buildings are occupied by negroes." Although a few black farmers rented land for cash, perhaps nine-tenths worked for a landlord and received between one-third and one-half of the crop for their labor.[17]

The most enduring Republican achievement was the establishment of public schools. The state government elected by white voters in 1865 made no effort to establish schools for blacks. On the contrary, it explicitly opposed them. But the Freedmen's Bureau, working with northern-based freedmen's aid societies and missionary associations, established numerous schools for blacks: in 1866 Natchitoches Parish boasted fourteen of them. A 5 percent tax on employers, however, proved impossible to collect after floods destroyed most of the 1866 cotton crop. Agent Charles Miller then instituted a subscription scheme whereby black parents paid a monthly tuition fee. But he had little confidence in this expedient "because the freedmen have not the means to pay teachers." The complete destruction of the 1867 crop by caterpillars gave freedpeople even less disposable income, and the number of schools plummeted. When black teacher P. W. Holmes closed his school in the fall of 1868 he was owed $491 in back pay. During the hiatus between the termination of the Freedmen's Bureau and the Republicans' assumption of power, schools outside Natchitoches all but disappeared. The restoration to their original owners of buildings requisitioned by the army added a further difficulty by reducing the number of schoolhouses.[18]

The 1868 Constitution obliged every parish to establish "at least one free public school" to be open to children between the ages of six and twenty-one, "without distinction of race, color, or previous condition." Thomas W. Conway, former head of the Freedmen's Bureau in Louisiana, served as the first Republican state superintendent of education; former Union general James McCleery supervised public schools in the Fourth Congressional District, which included Natchitoches. In 1870 the police jury of Natchitoches Parish appointed two school boards, one for the town and one for the parish. With a combined budget of about $4,500, two-thirds raised from local taxes and one-third from state taxes, they immediately set about securing teachers. By 1871 three city schools and eight country schools had enrolled 431 pupils, about 10 percent of the educables in the parish. A year later, fifteen schools, all of the standard one-teacher variety, catered to about 860 blacks and 200 whites.[19]

The white teachers who had taught in the Freedmen's Bureau schools were quickly succeeded by blacks. Raford Blunt, president of both town and parish school boards, taught a school in his newly built First Baptist Church. Pennsylvania native Toussaint L'Ouverture Delany taught another school in town. Ohio-born William H. Redmond taught in a third town school. Redmond and Delaney had both served in the Fifty-Fourth Massachusetts Infantry Regiment and likely moved to Natchitoches together. On Redmond's recommendation, the board appointed George W. Green of St. Louis to open a school in the village of Campti in 1871. Green had been born into slavery, but his father purchased his freedom. He probably acquired the rudiments of an education during the Civil War, perhaps even earlier. The five black churches in St. Louis had been maintaining Sunday schools since before the war, notwithstanding intermittent enforcement of an 1847 state law prohibiting the education of blacks. Freedmen's schools were operating in the city from 1863 on.[20]

The number of schools fluctuated from year to year, and teachers came and went. John G. Lewis and George Green, however, taught school for decades, their careers long outlasting the demise of Republican rule. Both of them, not coincidentally, were active in the Twelfth District Baptist Association, of which Blunt was president. Denominationalism strongly influenced the appointment of public school teachers. Schools were often held in black churches, mostly Baptist churches, whose ministers did not want teachers of a different denomination. Black preachers regarded today's schoolchildren as tomorrow's congregation.

Teaching offered blacks one of the very few well-paid jobs open to them. Numerous ex-Confederates had been employed in the earliest freedmen's schools, but most of them taught out of necessity rather than conviction and had been unpopular with black parents. The shift to black teachers, strongly promoted by Baptist ministers like Blunt, was driven in part by a desire to claim these positions, which paid between fifty and one hundred dollars a month, and in part by a determination to develop black leadership.

Schools became an integral if unofficial part of the Republican Party organization. In a complaint to Cromie before the November 1868 elections, Thomas Hunter reported that the school he had allowed on his plantation was being used for Republican meetings and that its teacher, Mary Casey, had denied its use to local Democrats. Hunter added that Casey had "made herself particularly obnoxious to his neighbors and himself by creating dissatisfaction among the laborers."[21]

The Republican school boards, Democrats complained, used teaching appointments as a form of political patronage. The charge was in large part correct. For example, one of the few white teachers appointed to teach black children, Vermont native S. van Deusen (or Duzen), led a Republican club in the Third Ward and served as justice of the peace. Given the fact that Republicans maintained public schools in the face of indifference and hostility from the Democratic Party, it would have been hard to find a black teacher who was not also a Republican. Still, the school board's appointment policy, while obviously partisan, did not favor incompetence. Henry C. Myers, who succeeded Blunt as board president upon the latter's election to the state legislature, looked beyond Natchitoches Parish to find qualified teachers.[22]

The most questionable appointment was that of Blunt himself. The problem was not so much his competence as his absenteeism. Democrats put it about that he was illiterate, a charge that first appeared in the *New York Times* in 1874 and has been recycled by historians ever since. The charge was false: Blunt could certainly read and write. However, his political activities took up so much time that he had recourse to paying a substitute. Offered twenty-five dollars, Redmond refused, insisting upon a better-paying position. Blunt then paid a young woman from Virginia, Lucy Davis, half his salary. He retained the other half, fifty dollars a month, for doing in effect nothing. On the Louisiana scale of corrupt practices, this barely registered. Nevertheless, it reflected no credit on the Natchitoches Parish School Board or on Blunt himself.[23]

Republican government had profound consequences for the criminal justice system. Freed from the master's arbitrary authority and no longer subject to the constant oversight of slave patrols, blacks became subject to a criminal code that, on paper, applied equally to all. From 1869 to 1878 white Republicans more often than not held the positions of sheriff, coroner, parish judge, district judge, and district attorney. Blacks served in the office of ward constable, justice of the peace, and clerk of court. They also served on grand juries and trial juries, often comprising a majority on the panels. Almost by definition, the administration of justice became more impartial.[24]

This new legal system proved woefully deficient, however, when it came to punishing whites who inflicted deadly violence upon blacks, whether the perpetrators were individuals, lynch mobs, or Democratic paramilitaries. With one or two exceptions, Natchitoches Parish remained free of these kinds of racist and politically motivated homicides. The infrequency of lynching and political murder, however, had more to do with the cultural characteristics of Natchitoches Parish than with the efficiency of Republican law enforcement. When it came to "ordinary" murders—ones in which no racial or political motivation could be discerned—the criminal justice system remained much as it had been before the Civil War: grossly inadequate.

It had always been extraordinarily difficult to bring murderers to justice, and it remained so during the years of Republican political control. The abundance of forest and swamp, the proximity of Texas, and the reluctance of many sheriffs to risk life and limb made the apprehension of dangerous criminals difficult. Often the killer was never identified. If a defendant were arrested, he might escape from the ludicrously porous parish jail. If he ever faced a jury, he would most likely be acquitted. Killers were especially difficult to punish when they belonged to criminal gangs. In neighboring Winn Parish, for example, a gang led by John West and Lawson Kimble intimidated the civil authorities and defied the military authorities. These "desperadoes, murderers, robbers, and horse thieves" took refuge in Texas whenever it suited them. In May 1870 whites in Winn Parish formed a committee of self-styled "Regulators" that that took the law into its own hands, tracking down and killing at least eighteen men. Natchitoches Parish, however, remained free of organized banditry and never resorted to vigilance committees. The solitary case of vigilante "justice" more nearly resembled a lynching. It occurred in October 1876, when a group of masked men gained access to the parish jail and killed Anderson Douglass, a black man accused of larceny.[25]

The relatively low murder rate in Natchitoches Parish appeared to have little connection with the deterrent effect of likely punishment. Most homicides arose out of a "personal quarrel" or "personal difficulty," and they rarely resulted in prosecution unless presenting a clear-cut case of cold-blooded murder committed in clear sight of several witnesses. Of the forty-one homicides recorded in Natchitoches Parish between 1871 and 1874, only three resulted in a trial and only one in a conviction. Killers, white and black, usually walked free.[26]

Democrats complained long and loud that Republican-controlled courts punished property thefts by blacks too leniently or not at all. They charged that Republican judges held court infrequently and that jurors were reluctant to indict and eager to acquit. "It is a notorious fact," asserted the *People's Vindicator*, "that a negro hog, cow or chicken thief cannot be convicted." Of the two hundred defendants brought before the criminal court over a period of eight years, the paper went on, three-quarters were clearly guilty on the evidence, but juries "acquitted all they could."[27]

The truth about this alleged tsunami of theft is hard to assess. For many freedpeople, as some sympathetic whites noted, straitened circumstances made theft a matter of survival. Before emancipation, moreover, petty theft had been common—stealing from the master was part of slavery's "moral economy," a custom that slaves scarcely considered a crime. There is no reason to assume that this lax attitude to theft ended with emancipation, especially when so many freedmen believed that their former masters were swindling them. "The negroes are doing very well," wrote Mary Bryan in

1871, "setting aside a characteristic difficulty of distinguishing between *meum* and *teum*, especially in the matter of pigs and poultry."[28]

Still, Freedmen's Bureau officials generally praised the freedpeople for their honesty, often contrasting it favorably with the dishonesty they saw among many whites. Cromie reported "but a few complaints of theft" among freedpeople. It doubtless helped that the corn crop was abundant and that many families could supplement their diet by raising hogs, chicken, and vegetables, selling any surplus at the market. Employers encouraged such enterprise. They also permitted hands "to cut wood and sell it, charging nothing for the teams." A strong laborer could earn one hundred dollars a month at such work.[29]

This is not to say that the postwar rise in property theft was a figment of Democratic propaganda: it was real and substantial. But according to Gilles Vandal's exhaustive study, blacks were *less* likely to commit property crimes than whites were. Moreover, white defendants "were more often charged with violent and aggravated property crimes."[30]

Black jurors may have entertained a more lenient attitude toward the theft of food and livestock than white jurors did. Yet their presence on juries acted as a check against the kind of arbitrary justice that had prevailed before Congressional Reconstruction, when courts automatically discounted black testimony if it conflicted with the word of a white person. A recent study of neighboring De Soto Parish by Mark de Vries contradicts the notion that Republican courts, with their mixed juries, were less likely to convict blacks than whites. It should also be noted that Democratic lawyers, often the same people who complained about the difficulty of securing convictions, were quite willing to represent black defendants and seek acquittals. Louisiana's "culture of acquittal" was nothing new. Law enforcement may have been lax, but it did not deteriorate under the Republican regime.[31]

What did Republican political control do for black laborers, the bedrock of the party's support? During the transition years 1867 and 1868, when the U.S. Army implemented Congressional Reconstruction, the Freedmen's Bureau had shielded freedpeople from hunger and homelessness after caterpillars destroyed almost the entire cotton crop. It obliged employers to provide rations and living quarters, prohibiting them from evicting any laborers before the end of the year. It also tried to prevent them from cheating their laborers. "In no case will planters be permitted to ship the freedmen's share of the crop," General Joseph A. Mower decreed, "until good and sufficient bond is filled with the office of the Bureau agent." Moreover, if civil courts failed to protect the freedmen from being cheated, bureau agents had the authority to seize "a sufficient portion of the crop . . . to cover the amount justly due the freemen." In Natchitoches Parish, Charles Miller did just that.[32]

But two crop failures left many planters virtually penniless and often themselves indebted to merchants, who then refused to advance them more credit. "Thousands of plantations are mortgaged for the debts of their owners," the Freedmen's Bureau reported, "farming implements, movables etc. having been seized and sold." In 1868 the bureau adopted a scheme to advance planters food and supplies against that year's crop. By August, thirty-seven planters in Natchitoches Parish had signed up. E. L. Pierson, for example, a Confederate veteran who employed twelve hands with five children between them, received eight hundred pounds of cornmeal and four hundred of pork. Before the rations arrived, Pierson's employees were "very much dissatisfied and almost refused to work."[33]

After the bureau agents departed at the end of 1868, black laborers had to rely upon the Republican state legislature and Republican courts to protect their interests. Legislation, however, was intermittent and ineffectual. At its very first session, the legislature prohibited the dismissal of employees for political reasons but rejected a bill to restrict a landlord's freedom to exclude visitors from the plantation. Homestead exemption laws failed to prevent the seizure of a laborer's personal property. Republican courts defined the sharecropper as a wage laborer and the landlord his employer. Only after the landlord had ginned, baled, and sold the crop, and then deducted what the employee owed for provisions, did the cropper receive his share. Typical contracts prohibited laborers from removing any cotton, corn, or livestock "until the supplies are paid for."[34]

Sharecroppers had few possessions they could call their own, making homestead exemption laws of little help. If a laborer failed to clear his debt to the landlord, the latter could secure judgments against the laborer's property. So could the merchant who advanced his supplies. Contracts required laborers to sign away their right to "any relief whatever from stay, homestead, or exemption laws." Horses, mules and any other personal possessions were liable to seizure. Contracts also stipulated that laborers receive no compensation for any improvements they made to the property. Such improvements (as was the case in Ireland before 1870) belonged to the landlord.[35]

In extracting what they could from sharecroppers, landlords exploited the law and their access to the courts to the fullest extent. Indeed, it was much more common for landlords to sue laborers than vice versa. Few blacks had the money to engage in litigation, and as Henry Adams, a black Republican of De Soto Parish, put it, "the one that's got the money will gain the suit." Many landlords took advantage of their laborers' illiteracy, innumeracy, and ignorance of the law. "Being without experience in doing any business," Martin Flood reported from Caddo Parish, the freedmen were "entirely at the mercy of the Planters at the end of the year in the final settlement." Blunt claimed that planters in Natchitoches Parish presented their laborers with a "piece of paper" instead of the actual receipt from the New Orleans commission merchant, enabling them to pocket still more of the proceeds from the sale of the baled cotton. Laborers found it hard to fathom how, in the event of a good crop, they might see no cash at all after the landlord deducted the cost of provisions supplied on credit.[36]

Hence, although the Republican legislature made laborers' wages a first privilege on the crop, such protection was more apparent than real. Merchants who supplied sharecroppers on credit or supplied them indirectly by furnishing the landlord sought to cover their loans by insisting on a "lien" on the laborer's crop. An 1874 law made the merchant's lien binding on the sharecropper while subordinating it to the landlord's lien. Thus the claims of both landlord and merchant had to be satisfied before the sharecropper received a penny. With goods bought on credit incurring from 20 to 100 percent interest, the cropper's share was often, as Blunt noted, "gobbled up" by the merchant. The annual settlement left sharecroppers with little disposable income—less than five dollars in cash per family member per year.[37]

The law, moreover, was not self-executing, and while resorting to law was not always futile, it was invariably expensive and complicated. In 1868, for example, Louis Dupleix, the lessor of a 640-acre plantation, sued the lessee, Victor Durand, for nonpayment of a debt. When Dupleix gained a writ of seizure from William H. Hiestand, the Republican parish judge, the black laborers refused to pick the cotton, figuring that they stood to receive nothing if the crop went to satisfy Durand's debt to Dupleix. Of the three bales that were already ginned, the hands received nothing; the rest of the standing crop was trampled by cows. But there was still the matter of the corn crop, over which Dupleix, Durand, and the black laborers had contending claims. Durand had contracted with Lewis Haines to work seventy-five acres on half shares; Haines had hired seven laborers to assist him on the basis of receiving one-third of Haines's share in lieu of wages. Having paid Haines forty barrels of corn and each of the seven other hands five barrels each, Durand then demanded that Haines repay him ninety barrels: twenty-five advanced to make the crop and the rest allegedly for corn taken from the fields before gathering. But Dupleix had also taken corn from the field before the harvest, and Haines claimed that his fifty-fifty settlement with Durand had not taken those seven barrels into account. With the corn crop covered by the writ of seizure obtained by Dupleix, Haines and his team hired a lawyer to intervene in the suit, demanding half of the entire crop irrespective of Dupleix's and Durand's claims.[38]

Before the phasing out of the Freedmen's Bureau, an agent might have satisfied the laborer's claim by ordering the corn crop to be seized, dispensing justice that was both quick and free. Now, however, the sharecroppers had to engage a lawyer and take the case to the district court, where, luckily for them, a sympathetic Republican judge, John Osborn, decreed that Haines and his fellow workers should receive forty barrels of corn. Before his order, the keeper appointed by Sheriff Sam Parsons under the writ of seizure had refused to allow the hands to dispose of their corn, permitting them to draw only a bushel every fortnight, enough to provide themselves with bread but not enough to sell.[39]

Employers may have cheated less frequently than blacks believed. A cropper's share of the proceeds could well fall below what he owed the country merchant who advanced him food and supplies. When the price of cotton dipped below ten cents a pound, few sharecroppers realized a profit, and many were mired in debt. Not a few sharecroppers rid themselves of debt by quitting before the settlement and seeking a new employer in a different parish. This kind of movement, however, had the effect of *increasing* indebtedness overall as merchants raised their interest rates to offset anticipated defaults.

Whether their wages were depressed by market forces or dishonest planters, black laborers felt deeply aggrieved, and this feeling may well have accounted for much of what the landlords regarded as theft. For example, contracts required sharecroppers to hand over their entire crop to the landlord: they had to trust the latter to divide the proceeds equitably. But they could never approve a situation in which they had no proprietary right in the crop they were growing. When debt-strapped planters wanted to sell the first cotton picked, some sharecroppers refused to hand over any part of the crop until the entire harvest was in. Others sold seed cotton—cotton that had been picked but not ginned and baled by the landlord—for cash to country merchants. Planters regarded such transactions, which invariably took place at night, as theft. They proposed making it a criminal offense to buy and sell seed cotton under cover of darkness. When the legislature balked at outlawing the trade, planters in some parishes had the stores of offending merchants torched. Sharecroppers had an entirely different view of the trade in seed cotton. "If I had helped to make a crop then I ought to have a right to take my share of it."[40]

The confusion between tenant and sharecropper fueled this resentment. Tenants, who paid the landlord a fixed annual rent in cash or cotton, owned the crop they grew and could dispose of it as they wished. "They make the crop and divide it," explained Blunt. "They are masters of the situation." Sharecroppers wanted the same freedom, an aspiration encouraged by the fact that common parlance often referred to them as "tenants." But in the most productive cotton lands, including Natchitoches Parish, few planters rented land to blacks. Sharecroppers had to accept the bitter truth that the law gave them little security and that the landlord was a controlling presence.[41]

Overall, the Republican Party neglected the interests of sharecroppers. Even when the legislature tried to protect them, the law often made no difference. Democratic police juries, for example, compelled blacks to perform labor service by maintaining roads and bridges if they were unable to pay a poll tax, ignoring an act that forbade such compulsion. In Natchitoches Parish, Republican control mitigated the most oppressive features of sharecropping. Blacks suffered little violence or physical maltreatment, and landlords proved receptive to the location of public schools on their plantations. When the police jury conscripted blacks for road duty, white Republican leader Ernest Breda told them that they had no obligation to perform such work. The laborers quit.[42]

Republican officials in Natchitoches faced a barrage of accusations, investigations, and lawsuits over parish finances. Citizen lawsuits, ostensibly designed to expose corruption and maladministration, conformed to a Democratic strategy of using the courts to harass, divide, and discredit the Republican Party while at the same time inflaming white taxpayers. In a sense, the Democrats acted on the theory that if you throw enough mud, some of it will stick. Their calculation proved correct.[43]

Yet Republican officeholders laid themselves open to attack. They indulged in "honest graft," engaged in inside trading, and in one case embezzled public funds. They governed with as much probity, and lack thereof, as the political standards of the time permitted. But herein lay a fundamental weakness of Congressional Reconstruction: it relied upon routine politics in a highly abnormal political environment. Run-of-the-mill ethics might be good enough for New York or Chicago, but they were inappropriate to the postwar South.

In 1871 Natchitoches Democrats, posing as outraged taxpayers, alleged that members of the Republican "ring" enriched themselves through padded expenses and outright embezzlement. They formed a committee, headed by R. M. Kearney, a nominal Republican, to examine the books of the police jury. Although the committee found no evidence of financial malfeasance, three actions of the police jury provided it with ammunition. The first was the creation of an "immigration bureau," the second a contract to make maps of the parish, and the third the grant of a franchise to maintain a bridge and toll road between the town of Natchitoches and the landing stage on the Red River at Grand Ecore. The police jury proposed to pay for the immigration bureau and the maps by issuing warrants, "parish paper," to the tune of $8,000 and $5,000. The operators of the toll road were to receive $1,500 in warrants to spend on repairs, and in return would pay the parish 5 percent of gross receipts.

All three actions were insider deals, and typical of the times. There was no question of competitive bidding: the contracts went to Republican officials and their friends. The franchise to operate the toll road, for example, was awarded to Charles Leroy, Henry C. Myers, Louis Dupleix (editor of the *Natchitoches Semi-Weekly Times* and now a Republican), and two others. In order to avoid the appearance of blatant partisanship, the Republicans included one or two Democrats as beneficiaries. The Democrats camouflaged their own partisan purpose by finding litigants who were not aspirants to political office and by associating Republican attorney R. M. Kearney with lawyers David Pierson and William H. Jack, two leading Democrats. By employing these outside attorneys, the Democrats saddled the parish with a $3,000 "Kearney tax."

In three separate but connected lawsuits, petitioners called the immigration bureau, the map contract, and the toll road franchise illegal, fraudulent, and "oppressive to . . . the taxpayers of Natchitoches." District judge John Osborn, a Republican, agreed. In June 1872 he canceled the contracts and forbade the police jury from incurring any further debt through the issue of bonds, warrants, and other forms of "parish paper."[44]

The contracts of 1871 were voided before anyone could benefit financially; most of the warrants were destroyed before they were issued, let alone presented for payment. Nevertheless, the Democratic Party never ceased to advertise them as egregious acts of Republican plundering. And the tale grew bigger in the telling. Paying $5,000 for a map, for example, appeared absurdly exorbitant. Left unmentioned was the fact that mapping the parish required making *forty* separate maps, as well as taking extensive field notes.[45]

Still, the issuing by the police jury of "warrants" and "certificates of indebtedness" provided a lucrative form of speculation for Republican insiders. In an economy starved of cash and easy credit, state and parish governments resorted to issuing paper money that was not backed by specie. Public school teachers and jurors, for example, were paid in warrants, not cash. These bonds, warrants, and certificates were, in effect, IOUs whose value fluctuated with the market. Although they quickly lost value, they could be used in payment of parish taxes. By speculating in this depreciated paper currency—for example, buying warrants for fifty cents on the dollar and selling them for seventy-five—Republican officials could make a tidy profit. Holders of bonds could also go to the district court to demand the payment of interest. In 1869 the police jury levied a 1 percent "special tax" to pay such judgment creditors; in 1870 it levied another 2 percent tax. Both taxes had to be paid in U.S. currency. Between 1870 and 1873 the courts issued judgments against the parish amounting to $147,000 dollars, of which $95,000 was collected in hard cash.[46]

Such figures appeared to sustain Democratic charges of Republican profligacy. But there was more to them than met the eye. Much of this "parish paper" had been issued before 1869 by Democratic-controlled police juries in the form of warrants and interest-bearing bonds. Moreover, many of the judgment creditors who sued the parish for payment were Democrats. Republican judge Henry C. Myers claimed that of the $108,000 in "parish paper" that police juries had issued between 1867 and 1874, Democrats had bought up $70,000. And he asserted that of the ninety judgments obtained in court against the parish, eighty-eight of the creditors were Democrats. The account books of Republican Parish tax collector David H. Boullt, produced in court, bore this out. In short, Democrats were buying heavily discounted paper and suing, successfully, for the payment of interest. When whites complained about the special taxes imposed to fund those claims, the same judgment creditors were the loudest in their protestations.[47]

Republican control of Natchitoches town proved less secure than that of the parish: the population was about evenly divided between black and whites, with the latter enjoying a slight edge in voters. Political control swung back and forth between the Republican Party and its white opponents, who in town politics eschewed the Democratic label and campaigned as a "reform" or "people's" ticket. Republicans elected the mayor and town council in 1868, but two years later a disputed election, eventually decided by the district judge, brought the Democrats to power. Prominent in the new administration were two men, both Confederate veterans, who later became deadly enemies: E. L. Pierson, the mayor, and J. H. Cosgrove, the tax collector and chief of police.[48]

Although Natchitoches was a small town, control of the council offered numerous perks and offices, from town constable to inspector of weights and measures. Moreover, a city charter granted by the state legislature in 1872 expanded the powers of the council and made it independent of the parish police jury. Many of the offices in the gift of the council were part-time, but they still paid something: city attorney, secretary and treasurer, collector of taxes and licenses, physician, and so on. The city had its own school board, with the power to appoint teachers. Acting as a magistrate, the mayor had the authority to "examine, try and sentence persons for violation of city ordinances."[49]

Chronic indebtedness, however, hampered the city's ability to effect improvements. Lack of U.S. currency had forced the city to issue its own paper money ("warrants") to the tune of $37,000 between 1867 and 1873. When Republicans retook control after the first elections held under the new city charter, they inherited a debt of $6,000 in the form of outstanding warrants, a sum approximately equal to the amount of unpaid taxes dating back to 1867. The job of assessor and collector of city taxes was therefore of paramount importance. The new Republican tax collector, the northern-educated schoolteacher and Union veteran William H. Redmond, seemed qualified for the post, and during his first year in office he collected nearly $15,000 in taxes and license fees. But he only turned in $10,652. Upon discovery of the shortfall, Redmond fled. In the election held in May 1874, J. D. De Vargas, a Republican, won the office of mayor, but all the Republican candidates for the six-man city council lost.[50]

Redmond's defalcation was a serious blot on the Republican Party's record in government. But it was an isolated case. Judged in toto, that record was neither exemplary nor disgraceful. It was reasonably competent and secured solid benefits for freedpeople. But Republican officeholders, as typical nineteenth-century politicians, also helped themselves. "Money, and there was precious little of it, was the glue that held political coalitions together," argues historian Richard H. Kilbourne. Republicans attempted "to fund spoils by helping themselves to what was in the public purse, both at the state and local levels." Speculating in government-issued warrants amounted to a cheap, easy, and legal way to do that. Supporters of both parties played this game, but speculation and insider dealing both profited and hurt politically those who held the reins of power. Forewarned when delinquent taxes would be collected, Republican warrant holders "would present their documents within a few hours after the money was received at the treasury." At the state level, moreover, Republicans, many of them recently settled northerners, were in a position to enrich themselves on a much grander scale. In exploiting that opportunity such men inflicted incalculable political damage on Congressional Reconstruction.[51]

8

UNPRINCIPLED POLITICS

Patronage is a powerful engine in political affairs.

Republican governor Henry C. Warmoth, 1871

The Republican Party legitimized its claim to power on the basis of its loyalty to the Union. As a political tactic, "loyalty" paid off, at least in the short term. From the start, however, the use of loyalty for personal and party advantage challenged principle and stoked cynicism. Former Unionists disparaged each other's loyalty when they competed for public office. The Republican Party characterized former Confederates as disloyal, but exempted those who became Republicans. Warring Republican factions had no compunction about striking political deals with "disloyal" Democrats.

The behavior of the first two postwar governors, J. Madison Wells and Henry C. Warmoth, illustrated how personal ambition and hunger for office, not loyalty or lack thereof, determined political behavior. Wells had risked his life by refusing to support the Confederacy, eventually fleeing from Rapides Parish "as the guerillas and murderers who infest Red River had ordered him to be shot at sight." Yet in 1865 this gallant Unionist abandoned his Republican sponsors when, realizing that Lincoln and Johnson wanted a swift return to home rule, he calculated that his political future lay with the former Confederates. A year later, when Democrats rejected his political overtures, he switched again, supporting the Republicans' call for black suffrage, a policy he had previously denounced. General Sheridan compared Wells's shiftiness to "the marks left in the dust by the movement of a snake." Wells's Republican successor, Henry Clay Warmoth, proved equally sinuous. He also abandoned his party and allied with the Democrats. He, too, returned to the Republican fold when the alliance failed. As historian Lawrence Powell puts it, Warmoth "played politics like a riverboat gambler."[1]

Figure 8. Henry Clay Warmoth (1842–1931), Republican governor, 1868–73. Library of Congress Pictures and Photographs Division.

Such behavior made the Republican Party a poor advertisement for the alleged superiority of northern values and institutions. High ideals and low politics made a bad mix. Confronted by a political challenge of staggering complexity, and menaced by a campaign of violence fomented by the Democratic Party, Louisiana's Republicans required unity, integrity, and clarity of purpose. They exhibited none of those qualities. Within three years of assuming power the state party was knee-deep in scandal and convulsed by internal warfare. Instead of providing the shining example of Republican government that Lincoln and Banks had hoped it would, Louisiana's Republican Party became the exemplar of political chicanery and financial dishonesty. By 1872, writes Powell, the party was "completely discredited in the eyes of northern public opinion."[2]

According to one view, the native northerners who dominated the party's leadership, the so-called carpetbaggers, were dragged down to the level of

Louisiana politics. In a state notorious for corruption and crooked elections, these Yankees "went native." Warmoth placed the blame on the people who offered bribes rather than the politicians who took them. Elected officials, he explained, "are as good as the people they represent. Why, damn it, everybody is demoralizing down here. Corruption is the fashion." George W. Carter, his political ally turned enemy, offered a similar explanation: "There seems to be something in the climate here that affects both parties."[3]

These self-serving explanations were too kind. The northern arrivals took to Louisiana politics like ducks to water. They needed no tutoring in the dark arts of manipulating elections, fighting over patronage, padding expense claims, taking bribes, and insider dealing. Such practices were part and parcel of the political culture of the time—just as common in New York, Ohio, Indiana, and Illinois as in Louisiana. Louisiana's Republicans should not, of course, be faulted for sharing that political culture. But the postwar South needed fair elections, honest and efficient government, and cooperation between victors and vanquished. The Republican Party had portrayed northern civilization as not only materially superior to that of the South but also morally superior. The actions of Republican politicians belied that claim. "But one purpose seems to influence their conduct," one Democrat wrote his wife. "It is to make all the money they can, from the governor down to the very pages in the House."[4]

No sooner had it assumed power than the Louisiana Republican Party showed signs of overreaching. Its majority in the state legislature fell short of the two-thirds that would render it invulnerable. Republican leaders therefore considered how they might eliminate the required number of Democrats to make their control cast-iron. The new constitution had restored the franchise to all ex-Confederates except

> those who held office, civil or military, for one year or more, under the . . . "Confederate States of America"; those who registered themselves as enemies of the United States; those who acted as leaders of guerilla bands during the late rebellion; those who, in the advocacy of treason, wrote or published newspaper articles preached sermons during the late rebellion; and those who voted for and signed an ordinance of secession in any State.

These sweeping exclusions applied to many if not most of the politicians, military officers, editors, and ministers who had supported the Confederacy.[5]

When the legislature met on June 29, however, Lieutenant Governor Oscar J. Dunn, president of the senate, and Robert H. Isabelle, chairman of the house, proposed that all members should take the even stricter "iron-clad oath," which required the oath taker to swear that he had never voluntarily aided the Confederacy. The effect of this proposal would have been to exclude nearly all of the Democratic legislators, few of whom could have truthfully sworn never to have rendered aid to the Confederacy. The "voluntary" character of such aid, however, could be hard to define. As one reluctant Confederate put it, "It was almost impossible for a man to live in the South without contributing in some way to the rebel cause." Democrats reacted with fury, thousands of whites menacing the Mechanics' Institute, where the legislature sat. "The excitement was so bitter," reported General Buchanan, "that there was an imminent danger of a bloody riot." Determined to avoid a repetition of 1866, Buchanan sent the entire police force, as well as two companies of soldiers, to protect the legislature.[6]

The Republicans decided not to impose the "iron-clad oath." But they found other means to attain the desired two-thirds majority. "This is easily accomplished," former governor Michael Hahn advised Warmoth. "The ousting of about five Democrats in each house, and admitting in their stead their Republican opponents who will contest their election will do the business." One by one, the legislature seated Republican challengers. In their defense, Republicans could claim, accurately, that numerous Democrats had won election by means of fraud, intimidation, and violence.[7]

Yet such manipulations betrayed a political ruthlessness that further alienated them from the majority of whites. As a Baton Rouge lawyer, former slaveholder, and ex-Confederate officer complained to Warmoth, "whether justly or unjustly, it will be regarded as an evidence of the determination of the dominant party to possess themselves of every office, State, Parish and municipal, by any and all means in their power. Surely scarcely anything would more directly tend to exasperate and alarm."[8]

The temptation to use "loyalty" as a political weapon proved too great for the Republican Party to resist. In deciding whether a man could hold office, a politician's actual record in the Civil War became secondary to his party affiliation. The 1868 Constitution disfranchised certain classes of former Confederates but specifically exempted those who had, before 1868, "favored the execution of the . . . Reconstruction Acts of Congress." This at least ended the squalid finger-pointing in which ex-Confederates seeking office had tried to discredit rivals by informing on their war records. But it implied that a former Confederate could only be considered loyal if he supported the Republican Party.

In a penetrating discussion of Civil War–era loyalty oaths, Harold Hyman saw a clear parallel with the abuse of loyalty oaths during the McCarthy years (he published his study in 1954). Loyalty oaths had little to do with being loyal, he argued; they were political weapons pure and simple. Hyman noted the blatant inconsistency with which the Republican Party applied the "iron-clad oath." In judging the credentials of elected members, Congress placed partisan advantage before evidence of actual past loyalty. Republicans stigmatized Democrats as disloyal and characterized themselves, whatever their actual record, as loyal. The Republicans' approach to "loyalty" bred cynicism about oaths and oath-taking and made the concept of loyalty meaningless. It further embittered former Confederates who, having accepted defeat and emancipation, and having taken Lincoln's or Johnson's oath of amnesty, believed that they had done more than enough to qualify as "loyal."[9]

Adding insult to injury, the 1868 Constitution required a public mea culpa from excluded former Confederates who applied for their political disabilities to be lifted. The applicant for amnesty must write and sign a statement "setting forth that he acknowledges the late rebellion to have been morally and politically wrong, and that he regrets any aid and comfort he may have given it." The penitent must then file his confession with the secretary of state, who would publish it in the official journal.[10]

It did not help the Republican cause that most of the men attempting to govern in Louisiana were political neophytes and newcomers. Governor Warmoth was only twenty-six years old when he took office; the constitutional convention had lowered the qualifying age from thirty-five to accommodate him. Although a wily tactician, Warmoth lacked the political judgment that is honed by rising through the party ranks and having close contact with voters. President Grant once called him "the shrewdest, sharpest, boldest, ablest, and most conscienceless young man that he ever knew." Although often criticized for being a poor judge of character, in this case Grant was spot-on. The last adjective in Grant's list of superlatives pinpointed Warmoth's weakness: he was a political freebooter with little regard for either principle or party loyalty.[11]

Many of the other recently settled northern whites who dominated the party leadership fit the "carpetbagger" stereotype: men who had no interest in putting down roots in the communities they ostensibly represented and whose desire for office trumped all else. As Henry C. Dibble, whom Warmoth appointed to the state bench in 1870, explained to a congressional committee, "I was ambitious to rise at the bar . . . and [of] obtaining position in society. . . . I went into politics with the deliberate purpose of getting a foothold, and I have remained in politics from that day to this for the purpose of sustaining that foothold." Only the frankness of Dibble's public admission was exceptional. In private, many cheerfully acknowledged that their interest in public office was pecuniary. George A. Sheridan, appointed by Warmoth to serve as registrar of voters in Carroll Parish, resigned his post when nominated the Republican candidate for sheriff. "As the position is worth from seven to ten thousand dollars a year, my patriotism will not allow me to decline." Sheridan then wangled the plum appointment of collector of taxes for New Orleans; pocketing 5 percent of all receipts, he earned at least $30,000 a year, a sum that even Warmoth considered "entirely too much."[12]

The desire to use public office for financial gain made these men no different from the generality of politicians. Indeed, it was axiomatic in Louisiana (and still is) that men go into politics to benefit themselves, their families, and their friends. Public office not only paid well but also offered ample opportunity for extracurricular profit; a politician who did not leave office substantially richer was commonly regarded as stupid. But these politicians were newcomers who came from the ranks of the northern conquerors. They had used their positions as army officers, Freedmen's Bureau agents, and voter registrars to vault into public office. They owed their election to the fact that the Republican Party had "gerrymandered" the electorate and eliminated the opposition. Every office they occupied was a position denied to a former Confederate—but only if that former Confederate were a Democrat.

This was exactly the political problem that Lincoln had hoped to avoid: a takeover of southern politics by "a parcel of northern men." Some of the former Freedmen's Bureau agents and other army veterans who got elected to the Louisiana legislature had virtually no connection with their districts. Having satisfied the residence requirement of ten days, the time it took to qualify as a registered voter, they rarely set foot in them again. Charles W. Lowell, for example, represented Caddo Parish but never returned there after the April 1868 election. The same applied to J. J. Walsh, who represented De Soto Parish, and to his successor, Mortimer Carr. The latter, adding injury to insult, gained his election by deceiving black voters. Carr persuaded a popular black candidate, George Washington, to stand down in his favor, but he retained Washington's name on the ballot paper. "Some men would vote for George Washington who would not vote for me," he told a congressional committee, "and we did not want to lose the whole ticket on that account."[13]

The leaders of Louisiana's Republican Party quickly became enervated by factionalism. By 1871 Governor Warmoth, who controlled the state patronage, warred for control of the party against the politicians who held federal patronage jobs in the New Orleans Custom House. By 1872 the fight between the Warmoth and Custom House factions had become so acute that Congress dispatched a committee to New Orleans to conduct hearings on the "political troubles in Louisiana." Each faction hoped to utilize the hearings to discredit the other. In that they succeeded, but in so doing they revealed a culture of greed and cynicism that was far removed from the idealistic arguments for Congressional Reconstruction.[14]

The hearings shone a light on the get-rich-quick attitude that animated Louisiana's elected representatives. Republican witnesses admitted, to a man, that the state legislature was corrupt. No one confessed to taking bribes himself, but a parade of legislators testified to having been offered bribes and to seeing or hearing of others being offered bribes. The promoters of the Chattanooga railroad bought off opposition by purchasing votes, testified former house speaker Charles Lowell. "I have seen money paid right on the floor of the house," confirmed former secretary of state George E. Bovee. "After the passage of the Chattanooga Railroad Bill, I saw a man with his hands full of money, paying it out." The Levee Company gained a state charter the same way. "You cannot pass anything without . . . money," Judge Dibble told the congressional committee. "All these governments in the South are corrupt." Legislators on both sides "have bought and sold themselves," testified Carter, former house speaker and leader of the anti-Warmoth faction. Congressman J. Hale Sypher urged voters to "hurl from power the thieves and corruptionists whose misrule has ruined and dishonored the State." He could only have been referring to his own party. Or perhaps to himself. "How about the new Levee Bill," Sypher wrote Warmoth six months before giving that testimony. "I want to be among the beneficiaries of that measure."[15]

Republican politicians appeared to distinguish between accepting bribes (not illegal but never to be admitted), stealing public money (illegal), and insider dealing (potentially embarrassing but otherwise acceptable). The passage of bills to benefit companies in which legislators had a financial stake was normal practice. Republicans of every stripe and faction incorporated companies that gained legislative charters and/or received shares in these concerns. Lowell voted for the Ship Island Canal Bill and "had a sort of interest in being a subscriber to the stock." The incorporators of the Crescent City Gas Company included half a dozen state legislators and the tax collector of New Orleans. Carr, another former house speaker, took out one thousand shares in the company. P. F. Herwig, a legislator allied to the Custom House faction, admitted telling the promoters of the Levee Company "that after the bill was passed I would have no objection to buying some of the stock" on the same generous terms that the incorporators enjoyed.[16]

As the quarrel between the Warmoth and Custom House factions deepened, legislators received mouth-watering inducements to change sides. The contest to succeed the deceased Oscar Dunn as lieutenant governor generated a flurry of bribe offers and counteroffers. One senator changed his vote to P. B. S. Pinchback for the promise of $35,000; another declined to change his vote to T. V. Coupland, a Democrat backed by the Custom House faction, for a much lesser sum. "I can hold $5,000 ready to place in your hand if you change your vote to our man," read the offer. The offering and taking of bribes was so commonplace that it did nothing to disqualify a man from office. After turning down $50,000 to sign one bill, Warmoth proposed to appoint John A. Walsh, the man proffering the bribe, to the position of state registrar of voters.[17]

That the Louisiana Republican Party suffered from factionalism was unsurprising. Faction fights were endemic to both political parties, partly because there was never enough patronage to go around. The scale and intensity of the infighting that afflicted Louisiana's Republicans, however, testified to the shallowness of the party's roots and the absence of any overriding sense of purpose. Faced with an existential threat from the Democratic Party, Republicans engaged in political fratricide.

Republican leaders appeared oblivious to the mortal danger they faced. Stephen B. Packard, a native of Maine and former captain in the U.S. Army, now the federal marshal in New Orleans, denied that blacks faced "any apparent hostility . . . at all." Indiana-born Union veteran Dibble, now a state judge, believed that "the masses of the [white] people have accepted the situation and are becoming measurably free from prejudice toward the blacks." Others displayed similar insouciance. Lulled into a false sense of security by the election of U. S. Grant, resident in New Orleans and enjoying the fleshpots thereof, rarely venturing into Louisiana's rural hinterland, Republican politicians proceeded to enrich themselves. They then set about attacking each other. Republicans in the state legislature made war upon Warmoth. Republicans threatened, arrested, and even killed other Republicans. Opposing factions tried to enlist the aid of the Democrats in order to destroy each other. Governor Warmoth split his own party, abandoned it, and then made an electoral pact with the Democrats. By the time of the 1872 elections, the Republican Party had created political chaos and rendered the prospect of a free vote and a fair count nil.[18]

W. E. B. Du Bois likened Louisiana politics after 1870 as a "Chinese puzzle. . . . a witches' cauldron of political chicanery." But the spectacular fragmentation of the Louisiana Republican Party can be simply summarized. By 1870 Governor Warmoth's hold on the black vote, and hence his prospect of reelection, was shaky. The governor had vetoed a civil rights bill and failed to appoint many blacks to office. Skeptical about blacks' capacity to govern, and hostile to efforts by the Creoles of color to legislate every aspect of racial equality, Warmoth tried to shore up his position by pursuing the votes of native whites. Instead of consistently rewarding his Republican supporters, he used state patronage to appoint white conservatives, many of them Democrats and former Confederates. Every state job that went to a Democrat, however, created numerous disappointed Republicans.[19]

The main spokesman for Louisiana's blacks until his death in November 1871, Lieutenant Governor Oscar J. Dunn, denounced Warmoth's appointments policy and charged the governor with denying blacks, who comprised about 95 percent of Republican voters, their just reward. As Warmoth put it, Dunn "felt some distrust of me and my fidelity to his race." Widely respected as a man of integrity who, almost alone among Republican leaders, bore no taint of corruption, Dunn allied with the Custom House faction in order to reverse Warmoth's policies and combat his increasingly authoritarian methods.[20]

The Republican faction based in the Custom House had its own reasons for distrusting Warmoth and allying with Dunn. It strenuously resisted Warmoth's efforts to gain control of the federal patronage. It strongly opposed the governor's evident intention of forging a coalition with southern white conservatives. It feared that Warmoth would manipulate the tough election laws in order to put his own placemen in the state legislature—as indeed he did in the November 1870 elections.

When the Custom House faction and the Dunn forces gained control of the State Central Committee, they packed the forthcoming Republican convention with their own supporters and proceeded to clip the governor's wings. Warmoth fought back by organizing his own delegation. Finding his opponents in possession of the convention hall, the Custom House itself—on the roof of which the army, at the request of Stephen B. Packard, had sited two Gatling guns—he took his delegates to another building. There, at Turner Hall, Warmoth presided over a rival convention. For the next year or so, the Republican Party was split down the middle. Each side accused the other of "bolting"; each claimed to be the legitimate Republican organization of Louisiana.

The internecine warfare affected every parish in the state. In Natchitoches, the Republican Party barely had time to settle into power before it found itself wracked by the schism that was splitting the party at the state level. The quarrel forced local Republicans to choose sides in a frantic struggle to retain jobs, position, and patronage. Here as elsewhere, the intra-party feud pitted Republicans who depended upon Warmoth's patronage against those who held federal positions. In country parishes like Natchitoches, this gave Warmoth a decided edge, for federal offices were few and far between, state positions numerous. Moreover, the feudalistic patronage chain meant that if the two house members from Natchitoches, Raford Blunt and Henry Raby, wished to retain any influence over appointments within their parish—all of which required the governor's signature—they could not afford to alienate Warmoth.

When Warmoth organized his rival convention in August 1871, Blunt and Raby were among the 118 delegates who followed him to Turner Hall. Natchitoches Parish judge Henry C. Myers and police jury member M. P. Blackstone, the registrar of voters in 1870, also sided with Warmoth. So did John G. Lewis, the secretary of the local party. Claiming to be the legitimate officers of the Republican Party, these men praised Warmoth in lavish terms and condemned the Custom House faction as "bolters and disorganizers."[21]

Former Union soldier Lucius H. Burdick led the local opposition to Warmoth. As collector of internal revenue and then register of public lands, Burdick was the senior federal official in Natchitoches. He also published the *Red River News*. Charles Leroy also joined the anti-Warmoth camp, as did William H. Tunnard and Virgil A. Barron, former Confederate soldiers and recent Republican converts. District Attorney N. A. Robinson, removed by Warmoth but reinstated by the Louisiana Supreme Court, allied with those opposing the governor.[22]

The split within the Natchitoches Republican Party soon became public knowledge. In May 1871, Oscar Dunn, acting as governor while Warmoth was temporarily absent from Louisiana, canceled a number of printing contracts and awarded several new ones. He gave the contract for official printing in Natchitoches Parish to Burdick's *Red River News*. This anti-Warmoth maneuver prompted Blunt to publicly disavow any connection with the *News* and to establish a rival paper, *The Republican*. The following month, in a spat over Burdick's authority as a federal tax collector, Judge Myers jailed Burdick for contempt of court. Burdick thereupon had Myers arrested on a charge of obstructing a federal officer. This tempest in a teapot quickly blew over, but it was symptomatic of the clash between state and federal officials. Before long the pro- and anti-Warmoth factions were organizing rival parades and mass meetings.[23]

If the Republican Party had deliberately set out to demonstrate the truth of the carpetbagger stereotype, it could hardly have done a better job. In their eagerness to discredit the opposing faction, Republican witnesses described their political rivals in language that could have passed for Democratic election propaganda. Oscar Dunn, who died unexpectedly before the congressional hearings opened, labeled Warmoth "the prototype and prince of the tribe of carpetbaggers," a class of men "who came . . . with a single axiomatic maxim as the basis of their lives, which they always, with the pertinacity of the sleuth hound, follow: 'Put money in thy purse.'" Pinchback, Dunn's successor as lieutenant governor, was no less scathing. An on-again, off-again ally of Warmoth, Pinchback complained that the northerners "out-Herod Herod in their love for the negro until they get an office, and then they grow colder toward their benefactors than any Southern man." A tough political survivor but also a deeply sensitive man, he noted that his carpetbagger colleagues readily accepted his hospitality "but rarely extend theirs."[24]

During the hearings themselves, Republicans assailed other Republicans as rootless freebooters. As Carter put it, "There is a class of white Republicans in the State who are mere adventurers, having no permanent interest in the community." Carter himself, a Texan whom Warmoth appointed to a judgeship in newly created Cameron Parish, was a prime example of just such an adventurer. B. F. Joubert of New Orleans, a Creole of color, assailed northerners "who come here to fill their pockets . . . [and] just want to use the Negro for their own benefit." He cited the example of General A. L. Lee, a friend of Warmoth and a legislator from St. Bernard Parish. When Warmoth awarded the state printing to the *New Orleans Republican,* Lee, the proprietor, made a handsome profit, as did Warmoth himself, who owned stock in the paper. By 1870 Lee had quit Louisiana politics and returned to New York.[25]

Completing their self-portrait of the Republican as carpetbagger, rival factionalists accused their opponents of being creatures of patronage, political puppets rather than authentic representatives. The Custom House faction charged Warmoth with exploiting his power to appoint voter registrars in order to have his favorites elected to the legislature. The "supervisors of election" enjoyed so much discretion in registering voters and arranging the polls that they could, in effect, elect themselves. Many of these Warmoth legislators lived in New Orleans, having no real connection with the districts they purported to represent. As Lowell rather colorfully put it, "a good many of them did not live anywhere. I know some of them who had been cavorting all over the State, from one parish to another, for the last three years." In loving detail, the Custom House faction described how Warmoth's "bolters" all owed their positions to the governor. The governor happily admitted to appointing men who would support him; why would he appoint personal enemies?[26]

The Custom House faction displayed no sense of irony in characterizing the Warmoth faction as placemen. It was a classic case of the pot calling the kettle black. The Custom House faction was aptly named. As Warmoth delighted in telling the congressional committee, the delegates at the "regular" Republican convention of 1871 had included "eleven internal revenue collectors and assessors, three post-masters and mail-agents, three United States marshals or deputy marshals . . . eighteen employees of the Custom House, [and] one collector." Some of these men sat in the legislature for districts they rarely if ever saw. While ostensibly representing Caddo Parish, Lowell also served as the postmaster of New Orleans. In Caddo Parish itself he was invisible.[27]

An undercurrent of violence pervaded the congressional testimony. The Carter faction had the army deploy Gatling guns on the roof of the Custom

House; it issued double-barreled shotguns to the federal employees inside. Carter's sergeants at arms shot and killed Walter R. Wheyland, a legislator and former Freedman's Bureau agent who was loyal to Warmoth, when they tried to arrest him. The Warmoth faction played by the same thuggish rules. The governor deployed the state militia to occupy the Mechanics' Institute (the statehouse). He used toughs, some of them off-duty policemen, to disrupt club meetings of the Custom House faction, while uniformed police officers stood by and did nothing. He even employed Lucien Adams, a "free-lancing plug-ugly" notorious for his role in the 1866 New Orleans riot, as one of his enforcers. Warmoth ally Dibble—a state judge, no less—described this known killer as "an old and very respectable citizen." No wonder virtually all politicians went about armed. "I carried a revolver on my person," Mortimer Carr admitted, "and I guess you would if you lived in Louisiana."[28]

Many contended that Louisiana was in a league of its own with regard to corruption. Northern visitors often left Louisiana reeling from the cynical double-dealing they witnessed. "I have been in what seemed a different world from ours—a world in which the modes of thought and action are, in many respects, un-American and un-Republican," wrote Congressman and future president James A. Garfield. Even the hard-bitten Massachusetts politico Benjamin F. Butler found himself shaking his head over the absence of any kind of moral compass in the Pelican State. As he wryly noted, "they do things differently here."[29]

The horrified reactions to the New Orleans hearings bring to mind Captain Renault's professed shock that gambling was going on in Rick's bar in *Casablanca*. The greed of Louisiana's Republican officials, although egregious, was typical of postwar politics throughout the nation. Politicians in New York, Illinois, California, and elsewhere also accepted bribes from railroad companies and enriched themselves through insider deals. And patronage was the glue that held the political parties together, the motive power that kept the electoral system going.

What seemed to distinguish Louisiana was less the scale of corruption than the brutal honesty with which politicians plied their trade. The assumption that politicians used public office for private gain was universal. Republican stalwart Aaron B. Levissee once told a congressional committee that he had rejected a bribe because the offer was far too low. He demanded ten times as much "with the view of putting myself beyond temptation as regards my political virtue," reasoning that the briber would not be able to come up with such a stratospheric sum. Sensing the committee's incredulity, he admitted that "you might think it strange that a man should be talking of political virtue in regard to Louisiana politics." In short, it can be argued that the Republicans in Louisiana were different in degree, not in kind, from any other set of politicians, and that the Democrats who preceded and succeeded them were equally dishonest. One might even conclude that the problem was not so much that the Louisiana's Republicans were corrupt but that they were inefficiently corrupt. Lacking discipline, they fell out among themselves and got caught in the spotlight.[30]

Yet these mitigating factors, if such they were, did nothing to diminish the political damage that the Republicans inflicted upon themselves and, in so doing, upon their black constituents. The Republican Party had framed Congressional Reconstruction in idealistic terms. The values and practices of the North—democracy, liberty, public education, Yankee ingenuity, free labor, and honest toil—would transform a corrupt, lazy, benighted South. The record of the Louisiana Republicans in office belied this vision and undermined the party's claim to moral superiority. The avarice of the Republican leaders and their grubby, violent fights over patronage made it impossible to present Congressional Reconstruction as an idealistic project.

The hearings on "political troubles in Louisiana" confirmed what some leading northern Republicans already suspected: that the main function of "carpet-bag government" was the enrichment of white politicians. Men like Senator Carl Schurz of Missouri and New York Tribune editor Horace Greeley, both of whom once earnestly supported black suffrage, now denounced the Republican state governments of the South. They blasted them for gerrymandering, manipulating the registration rolls, and calling upon federal soldiers to sustain them in power. Above all, they attacked the northern-born politicians who led the party in the South for operating, to quote Schurz, "a revolting system of plunder." Such critics had little sympathy for the argument that politicians in the North were just as greedy. To Schurz, that simply illustrated that the entire political system had become corrupt. The only thing holding the parties together, he argued, was "the mere possession of power and office for its own sake." To Greeley, stealing by "carpetbaggers" was far more damaging than similar thievery in the North. "The South was already impoverished—was bankrupt—without money, without thrift, almost without food; and these went there robbing and swindling when there was very little to steal."[31]

The interests of the freedpeople were shoved aside in the contest for patronage and profit. To be sure, blacks were adequately represented in the state legislature, numerically at least, and participated in all the intra-party quarrels. But the main protagonists were white politicians who put personal profit and tactical advantage ahead of the interests of the freedpeople and their own party's chances of survival.

The political warfare between Warmoth and the Custom House faction offered blacks no good choices. On paper, the latter stood firm on the issues of civil rights and patronage for loyal Republicans. In practice, however, blacks' share of the federal patronage was minuscule. Moreover, in allying with the Custom House faction Oscar Dunn assented to a tactical alliance with Democratic legislators who, by their own admission, were exploiting their opponents' divisions in order to weaken the Republican Party. Black support for Warmoth had a certain logic, given the fact that far more blacks held state positions than federal ones. However, Warmoth struck his own deal with the Democrats, with similarly damaging results for the Republican Party, and his black appointments were few and far between. Warmoth even boasted that "a majority of the persons appointed . . . by me to office have been Democrats or conservatives." In short, whichever side they chose, blacks would be complicit in weakening the Republican Party and damaging their own interests. Pinchback recognized the danger of blacks being drawn into a lose-lose situation. "We are between the hawk of Republican demagogism and the buzzards of Democratic prejudices." Attempting to steer an independent course, Pinchback formed his own Republican state organization.[32]

Democrats recognized that they might profit by siding with one Republican faction against the other; but which one? Upon this question, they could not agree. Most at first backed Warmoth in return for the chairmanship of certain committees and control over state patronage in their parishes. As the fight between the two Republican factions intensified, however, Democrats sensed an opportunity to engineer a repeal of the election laws, and perhaps even replace Warmoth as governor. A majority of the Democratic legislators switched their support to the Custom House faction led by Carter.

To William M. Levy and P. A. Morse, Democrats of Natchitoches Parish, this tactical alliance with the Custom House faction was the height of folly. Writing to Warmoth confidante Thomas J. Semmes, an attorney and former Confederate senator, they argued that the impeachment and removal of Warmoth, which the Custom House faction could only accomplish with Democratic votes, would make Dunn governor and unite the Republicans under the leadership of the "Radical party." To avoid such a "supremely disastrous" outcome, Democrats ought to swallow their misgivings about Warmoth and throw their weight *against* the Custom House faction. Levy and Morse sensed, correctly, that Warmoth's estrangement from President Grant, who sided with the Custom House faction, would make him amenable to a de facto alliance with the Democratic Party. Such an alliance, they emphasized, would need to be tacit, not overt. "We do not expect, nor do we wish, Governor Warmoth to throw himself into the embraces of the Democratic Party. Such an alliance would ruin him so far as any power to benefit our people is concerned." All that Democrats needed to do was to fight the common enemy: the "ultra-Radicals" of the Custom House faction.[33]

This advice, coming from such a source, carried weight. Peabody Atkinson Morse and William Mallory Levy were pillars of the legal and political establishment of Natchitoches. The former had practiced law there since the 1830s, the latter since 1852. Each had served in the state legislature. Both had impeccable Confederate war records.[34]

For most Democrats, however, the idea of allying with Warmoth was abhorrent. "They said that they could not trust him," recounted one advocate of cooperation. "That was the reply I always got when I attempted to moderate their hostility to him." Some Democrats refused to countenance any form of political rapprochement with Republicans, whatever the faction. They considered it futile; they deemed it a betrayal of political principle; they doubted that many black voters could be won over to the conservative cause. Given the confused political situation, Democrats found it exceedingly difficult to chart any course of action. "They are in a terribly chaotic condition," a Ouachita Parish Democrat informed Warmoth, "and their public opinion is unformed."[35]

During the spring and summer of 1872 the Democrats and Warmoth drew closer together. Members in both parties believed that the time was ripe to found a third political party that would repudiate the corruption and radicalism of the one and the racism and reactionary conservatism of the other. An initiative by a group of New Orleanians prompted the formation of a Reform Party. At the national level, disenchanted Republicans founded the Liberal Party with a view to nominating a candidate who could defeat President Grant, whose administration they condemned irredeemably corrupt. Warmoth's break with Grant was by now irrevocable, and he placed himself at the head of the Liberal Party in Louisiana. In May he led a delegation to a national convention in Cincinnati where the Liberal Republicans nominated Horace Greeley for president. The national Democratic Party endorsed Greeley. With Warmoth openly opposing Grant, more and more Democrats in Louisiana were persuaded that a Liberal-Reform-Democratic alliance offered the *only* prospect of defeating the Republicans.[36]

Warmoth still retained some black support. The one-hundred-man delegation that he took to the Liberal Republican convention included thirty blacks, among them Raford Blunt and Henry Raby from Natchitoches. Although Greeley's candidacy held little attraction for blacks, many were prepared to support a Liberal state ticket headed by Warmoth while at the same time voting for Grant. But, as one newspaper noted, "the political kaleidoscope in Louisiana changes almost every day."[37]

A set of resolutions adopted by the "colored Republicans" of Natchitoches Parish in June 1872 reflected the confused situation. The meeting endorsed Grant for president, praised Warmoth as "an able man and a true Republican," disavowed any interest in the Liberal and Reform movements, and supported Pinchback's efforts to reconcile the Republican factions. Yet Raby, Blunt, and Myers were still associated with the Liberals, and at the traditional Fourth of July Republican barbecue eight hundred freedmen declared for Greeley and Warmoth. Reporting the meeting to Warmoth, Morse predicted that "we can carry the Parish by a large majority." In truth, black voters were sitting on the fence, waiting to see what a Liberal-Democrat electoral pact would offer and, above all, waiting to see which way Pinchback—"the smartest black man in the State"—would turn.[38]

In August 1872 Liberals and Democrats finally agreed to a "fusion" ticket. Its terms, however, drove most of Warmoth's Republican supporters, including the wavering Pinchback, back to the "regular" party, now firmly controlled by the Custom House faction. While nominating several Liberals lower down the ticket, including a black candidate for secretary of state, the Democrats insisted on retaining John McEnery as their candidate for governor. Everything about McEnery offended moderates, who had hoped to create a genuine political alternative—a "new departure"—that could attract voters from both parties and both races. A planter from Ouachita Parish, which had an evil reputation for violence against blacks and Republicans, McEnery has the reputation of an extreme "Last Ditch" Democrat.

He and other members of the McEnery family had insulted and threatened local Republicans, including Judge T. J. Ludeling.[39]

McEnery's selection, Warmoth recalled, "produced a stampede among the colored voters." Pinchback reconciled with the Custom House faction, taking Blunt, Raby, and Myers with him. The "fusion" ticket also drove most of the Liberals back into the regular Republican camp. Rather than acting as "an instrument of reconciliation and reform," one of them wrote Warmoth, the Liberal-Democratic alliance had become "an instrument for our political annihilation." Thomas C. Durant, watching the campaign unfold from his law office in New York, was dumbfounded. "I can scarcely believe that *you* would consent to an arrangement which does not preclude . . . a new Bourbon domination." Others, however, despaired that the Democrats, in writing off the black vote, had ensured the election of the regular Republican ticket.[40]

Despite his misgivings, Warmoth endorsed McEnery. Indeed, the Fusionists were counting on the governor. With black voters arrayed against them, they realized that their only real chance of victory hinged upon Warmoth's control over the election machinery. The governor appointed the supervisors of election and could, with a good political wind behind him, control the Returning Board. In other words, Warmoth's men would register the voters, site the polling places, count the ballots, and ratify the returns. As Warmoth sardonically recalled many years later, the Democrats "were not nearly so boisterous in their denunciations of the existing registration and election laws as they had been before the fusion." Indeed, they were relying upon the governor to wield the election laws in their favor. In return, they promised to send Warmoth to the U.S. Senate. The governor now proceeded to apply, on a much larger scale, the electoral magic he had first used in 1870.[41]

Natchitoches Parish furnished a classic example of how the election laws enacted by the Republicans were now wielded against them. The process began with Warmoth's appointment of E. L. Pierson, the young protégé and law partner of William M. Levy, as supervisor of registration. Like many of the Warmoth supervisors, Pierson was himself a candidate for office, in his case the state legislature. The fact that supervisors were also candidates had the intended effect, according to state registrar of voters B. F. Blanchard, of "stimulating them to extra exertions to cause themselves to be returned, and thus contribute to the general success of the entire fusion ticket."[42]

Pierson did everything he could to maximize the registration of whites and minimize that of blacks. Required to begin registering voters on September 2, he did not start until September 17. Blacks had trouble finding out where and when he would be taking applications; whites always knew. When blacks tried to register in Cloutierville, Pierson "pretended to be out of [application] blanks." When they went to Pierson's office at the courthouse in Natchitoches, they found it closed at odd hours. It was a testimony to the strength of the Natchitoches Republican Party that 1,833 blacks succeeded in registering despite Pierson's non-cooperation. That gave the Republicans a potential majority of 300.[43]

In order to overcome that Republican majority, Pierson hindered blacks on the way to the polls. He turned election day for Republican voters into a game of "hunt the ballot box." Instead of the usual twelve polling places, three in town and one in every other ward, Pierson set up only four. He gave no advance notice as to their location other than identifying the ward, one of which was thirty miles long. He ensured that the four ballot boxes were hidden from black voters, although whites had no difficulty finding them. In Ward Five, for example, voting had traditionally taken place at Beulah church. But when blacks showed up at the church they found no ballot box, only a knot of Democrats gathered around the building giving whispered directions to white voters. William H. Redmond and Edward Ezernack, Republicans serving as U.S. election supervisors, followed some white voters along a path through the woods, taking about one hundred Republicans with them. They arrived at a field, about three miles from Beulah church. The ballot box was in an old, abandoned hay barn.[44]

Blacks had no problem finding the one polling place in Natchitoches, but they did have trouble voting. Whites were allowed to vote first on the grounds that they were "special policemen," a badge to that effect being passed from one man to another. When blacks finally reached the ballot box, the election commissioners engaged in a slowdown, poring over the voter lists and using up valuable time. After five or ten minutes they might allow the voter to cast a ballot or, more likely, tell him that the number on his certificate of registration did not match the number against his name on the list, or that he was not registered at all. An atmosphere of intimidation hung over the proceedings. Whites, many of them carrying open arms, crowded the polling place. The state supervisors of election barred John Lewis from the polling place; they refused to let him witness the count. Despite serving as a U.S. supervisor—a federal election observer—Lewis did not persist. Pierson had threatened to cane anyone who filed a complaint, and he was known to be volatile.[45]

Through such methods Pierson delivered a Fusion vote of 1,250 while keeping the Republican tally down to 550. The Fusion Party carried the Fourth Congressional District—which in 1870 had recorded 10,000 Republican and 5,500 Democratic votes—by 3,000. The white vote had almost doubled. The Republican vote, in contrast, declined from 10,000 to 7,500, with the largest loss occurring in the strongest Republican parish, Natchitoches. According to Warmoth's election officials, the Fusion ticket carried the state by between 7,000 and 10,000 votes.[46]

The Fusionists knew that the Republicans would contest the result. In Natchitoches Parish the latter gathered affidavits from 1,206 blacks who claimed to be registered voters denied the right to cast ballots. Moreover, all the parish officers, with the exception of Pierson, were Republicans, and they would surely resist yielding their positions when the results of the election were in dispute. Fearful—almost frantic—lest the "glorious victory" slip away, William Levy implored Warmoth to quickly ratify the results so as to present local Republicans with a fait accompli.

> Blount and his whole party including Myers, Boultt etc . . . are terribly disappointed and embittered on account of their defeat and will make every effort to thwart us in our victory. Send up at once by Pierson or by some other perfectly safe hand the Commissions for all our Parish officers, including Parish Judge. They rely upon holding over under contestations which they think will prevent you from issuing Commissions until decided. It is therefore all important that the Commissions should be dated before any action of contest is served.

The Fusionists elected to the state legislature, Levy added, would support Warmoth for U.S. senator.[47]

The chances of a quick resolution, however, were nil. The Republican Party did indeed raise holy hell, and it had the federal judiciary and the Grant administration on its side. Warmoth tried with might and main to promulgate the results. He packed the Returning Board, and when that ploy was enjoined by state judge Dibble he appointed a different board, only to have that one enjoined by U.S. Circuit Court Judge Edward H. Durrell. With Durrell's blessing, U.S. Marshal Stephen B. Packard, a Republican stalwart, occupied the statehouse with a contingent of federal soldiers. A Returning Board appointed by the Republican Party, which Durrell declared to be the legal one, announced that Grant had carried the state and that Republican candidate William P. Kellogg was the rightfully elected governor. This board had no returns in its possession. Nevertheless, it set aside the result in Natchitoches Parish as "an organized fraud." Counting the 1,206 Republican affidavits as actual votes, it decided that the Republican ticket had won. President Grant recognized Kellogg as the legally elected governor.[48]

That did not of course end the matter. As one historian has noted, "the election . . . was so shot through with fraud that no one ever had any idea who had actually won."[49] In effect, the Fusionists stole the election, and the Republicans stole it back. The Fusionists, however, had no doubt that they had won. True, the election would hardly pass muster by the standards of today's "monitory democracy." But few American elections, even today, could. Judged by Tammany Hall standards, it was par for the course. Moreover, if the Fusionists had bent the rules, they had played by the bendable rules laid down by the Republican Party itself. In Natchitoches and other parishes, the Fusionists refused to go quietly. Far from strengthening Louisiana's fledgling democracy, the election of 1872 ushered in four years of anarchy. In the parishes of northern Louisiana, white Republicans found themselves under siege.

9

THE NATCHITOCHES "SCALAWAGS"

Discountenance any person who meets them as gentlemen upon the streets, shut your doors and your houses to them, let them be outcasts to every feeling of mercy you may have.

Natchitoches People's Vindicator, October 10, 1874

On May 12, 1872, shortly after joining the Republican Party, Ernest Breda sat on a pile of lumber in front of the family-owned drugstore on Front Street, chatting with friends in the spring afternoon. A few yards away, standing outside Jim Allen's coffee house, an intoxicated Democrat named John Cosgrove bellowed, "Kiss my arse!" Cosgrove obligingly explained to Breda that the insult was directed at him.

Breda was a Confederate veteran, a lawyer, and member of a wealthy Natchitoches family; he could not ignore this public indignity. Honor demanded that, first, he must offer Cosgrove the opportunity to take it back. "What did you say?" asked Breda, cupping his ear in his hand. "I told you to kiss my arse!" Cosgrove replied. Inviting Cosgrove to repeat the insult twice more, Breda riposted, "If I did that, I would have to kiss you under your nose." It was now Cosgrove's turn to ask "What did you say?" Breda twice repeated his suggestion that Cosgrove was talking through his backside.

The confrontation escalated. "Watch me make him take it back," Cosgrove told a knot of white men standing outside the coffee house. He walked over to Breda, grabbed him by the collar, and shouted, "*What did you mean?*" Breda threw the question back at Cosgrove: "What did *you* mean?" "*I mean what I say,*" each man insisted. Cosgrove then drew a knife from his pocket and held it over Breda's head: "God damn you, take it back or I will make you take it back." Knowing Cosgrove to be a violent drunk, Breda took back what he had said. "You damned son of a bitch," Cosgrove snarled, turning him loose, "you can go in your store and get

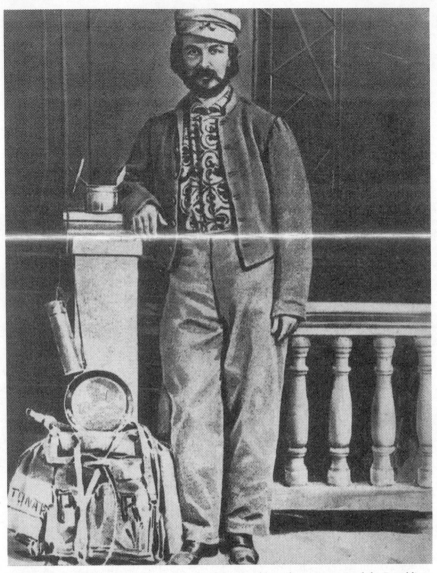

Figure 9. William H. Tunnard (1837–1916), Confederate soldier who in 1870 joined the Republican Party. Courtesy of Cammie G. Henry Research Center, Northwestern State University of Louisiana.

a pistol and shoot me if you like." Breda retreated behind the counter of the pharmacy while Cosgrove cursed him and dared him to come out and fight. Ross E. Burke, a local merchant and prominent Democrat, tried to calm Cosgrove and led him away from the Breda drugstore. Back at Allen's coffee shop, Cosgrove carried on drinking. "My friends always told me not to carry a pistol," he announced, "because if I did, I would have done killed the sons of bitches." Several men left the coffee shop in order to get away from him.

Four hours later, when Ernest Breda and his brother Philippe stepped into the street after locking up the drugstore, they found their way blocked by John Cosgrove and his brother James. Ernest Breda and John Cosgrove locked arms and tussled, calling each other "damned scoundrels." The melée ended when Breda took out a knife and drove it into Cosgrove's chest. Although the wound was serious, Cosgrove recovered. Breda was arrested and tried, but he escaped conviction. "I struck a blow to save my life," he later recalled, "for my liberty."[1]

Breda's fiancée, Elcey Hertzog, pleaded with Ernest to "Give up all these political ideals, [and] leave the Radicals." His friends had abandoned him, she pointed out, and he was surrounded by enemies. Breda declined her advice, remaining loyal to the Republican Party for the rest of his life. It was not a commitment taken lightly. The white Republicans of Natchitoches Parish found themselves socially isolated. Their political allegiance brought life-threatening, and sometimes life-extinguishing, consequences.[2]

By 1872 former Confederates had displaced ex-Unionists as the dominant white leaders in the Natchitoches Parish Republican Party. Ex-rebels joined the party at different times and for different reasons, but they all had one thing in common: a desire for public office, federal or state, appointive or elective. The earliest party switchers, Henry C. Myers and Jules J. Bossier, both held positions in the local federal land office, Myers managing the feat of being appointed by Andrew Johnson and retaining his position under Grant. Both had been well connected socially. Bossier, the son of a merchant, belonged to one of the oldest, best-known families in Natchitoches. Myers, another merchant's son, was a lawyer.[3]

William Tunnard and Louis Dupleix, both of them journalists, had an obvious incentive to join the Republican Party after the *Natchitoches Times*, which Dupleix published and Tunnard edited, lost the state printing contract to the *Red River News*, the paper founded by Freedmen's Bureau agent James Cromie. In 1870 Tunnard left the *Times* and became editor of the *News*. Dupleix, a native of France, who in 1864 had fled Natchitoches when the Union army entered the town, received an appointment as register of the local U.S. Land Office in 1872. C. J. C. Puckette, who bought the *Times* from Dupleix but had to close the paper in 1873, accepted an appointment from Governor Kellogg as parish tax collector.[4]

Given the fact that Natchitoches was overstocked with lawyers, the decision of young, struggling attorneys to join the Republican Party is not hard to explain, especially if they lacked the social connections that would enable them to partner with someone older and more experienced. N. A. Robinson, a boot- and shoemaker, joined in 1868 and four years later was elected district attorney. Ernest Breda, by contrast, came from a wealthy and socially prominent family. In 1860 his father, a physician, had owned a plantation with twenty-one slaves, a pharmacy in the center of town, and numerous city lots. Ernest served as district attorney and parish judge; his brother Philippe, like their father a doctor and pharmacist, served as the parish coroner. Madrid P. Blackstone, who joined the Republican Party at its inception, had been a small slaveholder. He served as president of the police jury and was elected to the state legislature. A combination of ambition and idealism, in unknowable proportions, influenced all these men. When pressed by a congressional committee to explain why he had become a Republican, Blackstone simply responded, "Because I believed it to be just and correct," adding, "My principles have undergone a very considerable change."[5]

The Union veterans who dominated Louisiana's Republican Party hoped that the accession of former Confederates would make their party less objectionable to the mass of southern whites. They hoped, too, that by displaying magnanimity toward ex-rebels they could draw more whites to the party. The year 1870 was to be one of reconciliation. When the house debated a senate resolution to donate $5,000 toward the reburial of Confederate dead, numerous Republican legislators spoke out in favor. A counterproposal to donate the money to the National Cemetery at Gettysburg, a resting place for Union dead, received little support. Former Freedman's Bureau agent Frank Morey summed up the prevailing sentiment when he urged fellow Republicans to "pour oil on the wounds," "stretch out the olive branch," and "bury the hatchet." In the same spirit, the legislature passed a constitutional amendment, approved in the following election, removing the political disabilities imposed by the 1868 Constitution.[6]

But the proffered olive branch did little to soften the overwhelming hostility of white Louisianans toward Republican politicians. Neither Confederate war records nor previous social standing insulated native white Republicans from ostracism and the threat of violence. Family members, former friends, and old comrades snubbed them. On the steamboat to New Orleans, Ernest Breda wrote Elcey, men he had known for years "acted as if they do not know me, and I did the same thing to them." Breda pretended not to care—"enough of the contemptible things for they are not worth mentioning"—but such incidents hurt.[7]

In 1868 Democrats came up with an epithet to describe southern white Republicans: "scalawag." The word implied that Republicans native to southern soil were turncoats who, for the sake of office, betrayed their families, their communities, and their race. They were men without honor. In Democratic eyes, the white Republicans of Natchitoches fell into this category. Abuse became an unavoidable part of the scalawags' lot. In the Democratic press they saw themselves described as traitors, Judases, and negro-lovers. In the streets they heard insults that were unprintable.

In testimony to congressional committees, Democrats insisted that they only applied the word "scalawag" to men of bad character. In Natchitoches, explained David Pierson, "there were republicans who were not molested, but were indorsed [by conservative whites]." Republicans were assailed because of their misconduct in office, he added, not because of their party affiliation. But Republicans could only escape ostracism and abuse if, in effect, they acted like Democrats. A man who voted for U. S. Grant but stayed out of state and local politics might be tolerated. But committed Republicans were a different matter. When Lieutenant Colonel Henry A. Morrow asked Democrats "why it was that this man or that was ostracized, the answer was . . . not on account of his political views at all, but because he is a rascal." Republicans were "rascals" because they associated with blacks on something like equal terms. James Cosgrove, who launched the *Natchitoches People's Vindicator* in 1874, denied "most emphatically" that "we ostracize a man because he is a republican," but added that "we cannot be expected to associate with a set of blackguards, liars, and thieves, as all the southern radicals are."[8]

Politics demands a thick skin, but public insults could not always be shrugged off as partisan boilerplate. Southern conceptions of honor gave personal abuse greater force than it carried in the North. Native white Republicans knew that how they responded to insults affected their reputation in the eyes of family, friends, and community. "Honor, not conscience, shame, not guilt, were the psychological underpinnings of Southern culture," argued Bertram Wyatt-Brown. A man who allowed public insult to stand unchallenged would be deemed a coward, his reputation destroyed. "The stigma had to be dealt with, or the labels would haunt the bearer forever."[9]

A willingness to employ violence in reply to threats and insults might discourage actual physical attacks. As Henry C. Dibble noted, "carpetbaggers" like himself generally disdained dueling, resorting to violence only in self-defense. "Scalawags," by contrast, "were able to maintain a certain restraint upon their enemies by accepting at all times the duello." When the *People's Vindicator* singled out Ernest Breda for lacerating abuse, Breda insisted on a published apology from the editor, James Cosgrove, the brother of the man he had stabbed in self-defense. "I hope I will not be forced to measures I would not be forced to resort to," he wrote Cosgrove, "but I am determined to suffer no insult to be added to injury."[10]

The maintenance of "honor," however, became increasingly risky. Insults were constant, threats never-ending: where to draw the line? To have answered every Democratic insult, one Republican explained, "would have resulted in our total destruction." Moreover, if a man challenged his traducers he would face them alone. Honor pertained to the individual, not the group. No man could defend another's honor, writes William Fitzhugh Brundage, "for to do so was to imply that the slighted individual was unable or unwilling to defend his own honor and therefore was undeserving of community esteem in the first place." If a "scalawag" defended his honor, he could not count on fellow Republicans' coming to his aid. Restraint and civility were essential survival tactics.[11]

During the first four years of Republican government, Democratic leaders also pursued a policy of civility and restraint. Dominated by lawyers like David Pierson and William M. Levy, the local Democratic Party rejected violence. It tried to restrain "hot-heads" like John and James Cosgrove. It made repeated overtures to black voters. In 1870 it nominated black candidates for the offices of sheriff, coroner, and state legislator. "The Democratic party of Natchitoches Parish," the *Times* declared, "has accepted in good faith the incorporation of the colored population into our political system." In 1872 local Democrats endorsed the "Fusion" strategy that made them allies of Governor Warmoth and the Liberal Republican Party. The editor of the *Times*, C. J. C. Puckette, himself a candidate for the state senate, enthusiastically backed the strategy.[12]

With the results of the 1872 state elections in dispute, Puckette sat for three months in the "Fusion" legislature at Odd Fellows Hall trying to stitch together a compromise that would save at least some of the legislators. One proposition would have recognized William P. Kellogg as governor in exchange for the Republican legislature seating eight senators and sixteen representatives from Odd Fellows Hall. But Republican senators rejected the proposal, as did the Democratic delegation from New Orleans. President Grant threw his weight behind Kellogg, the Republican claimant for the governor's office, and federal soldiers dispersed the "Fusion" legislature. The Republican legislature then passed an act requiring all officials to hold commissions from Governor Kellogg. Any claimant lacking such a commission would be subject to criminal penalties if he attempted to act in an official capacity. "It looked as if all our hopes for compromise were gone," Puckette told *Times* readers.[13]

Natchitoches Democrats still hoped to salvage some of their local ticket. A civil tone, then, pervaded Milton Cunningham's letter to Ernest Breda regarding their parties' conflicting claims to office. "We have repeatedly given each other verbal assurances of mutual good feelings," Cunningham reminded his rival for the position of district attorney. After protracted negotiations the two parties agreed to a divide the parish offices. The compromise confirmed Breda as district attorney and Henry Myers as parish judge but ratified the election of Democrat Ross E. Burke as sheriff. A Democrat also gained the office of parish recorder. The agreement awarded three positions on the police jury to Democrats and two to Republicans, with each party appointing one city constable. Accepting the Republican parish judge was a bitter pill for the Democrats. "We tried our best to get rid of Myers," explained David Pierson, but "we had to do that or have no relief whatever."[14]

The contrast between the amicable settlement of the disputed election in Natchitoches Parish and the mayhem that resulted in neighboring Grant Parish could scarcely be greater. Grant Parish Republicans defended their claims to office by occupying and fortifying the courthouse in Colfax. Armed Democrats, many of them Confederate veterans, laid siege to the building and on April 13 mounted a military-style attack. When the black defenders of the courthouse fled the burning building, the Democrats took them into captivity and then shot them in cold blood. The precise number of dead will never be known. The first state officials to arrive after the massacre counted sixty-five bodies. Two weeks later the *Louisiana Democrat* conceded that eighty-one blacks had been killed. Three white attackers lost their lives.[15]

So large was the death toll, and so plausible the stories of a massacre, that even "last-ditch" Democrats realized that the events in Colfax would prove politically damaging. The *Louisiana Democrat* struggled to explain why so many blacks had died after giving themselves up. It painted a lurid picture of a marauding black militia that had threatened to massacre white men and rape white women. "The whites of Grant were driven in pure self-defense to act the part they did." That these white men had shot black prisoners in cold blood, however, was impossible to refute. The *Democrat* therefore depicted the blacks as savages and claimed that they had fired upon a white flag of truce. The barbarous nature of the blacks and their act of treachery thus excluded them from the normal laws of war. "In a war of races under such circumstances *there can be no quarter.*"[16]

The men who perpetrated the Colfax massacre included Democrats from Grant, Rapides, Winn, and Catahoula Parishes. Whites in Natchitoches Parish, it seems, did not join the attacking force. Whether Natchitoches Democrats stayed away because they apprehended violence and wished to avoid it, or simply because their help was not needed, is impossible to say. The outcome of the Colfax affair, however, was exactly what Democratic leaders in Natchitoches feared: a massacre that inflamed public opinion in the North and triggered the return of U.S. soldiers.

Yet the Colfax massacre proved calamitous for Louisiana's Republican Party. The state authorities stood exposed as impotent and incompetent. Governor Kellogg's vacillation over the disputed offices had exacerbated the conflict, and when the Grant Parish Democrats organized a private militia, Kellogg did nothing. The Republican-controlled state government, despite having a militia of its own, could ensure neither law nor order. When blacks organized their own armed defense, they suffered a crippling defeat.

Louisiana's white Republicans tried to explain the ease with which whites overpowered blacks. The freedpeople were "naturally timorous," wrote one, "for they have been raised under the whip [and are] for the most part ignorant of drill, and devoid of military organization." Opposing them were "the sons of their old masters, many of whom have not yet forgotten that discipline . . . which they learned in the school of rebellion." Even when they enjoyed a numerical advantage, blacks with shotguns were no match for Confederate veterans armed with the latest repeating rifles. Any show of resistance by blacks, Kellogg wrote U.S. Attorney General George H. Williams, ended with "ten, twenty, or fifty negroes killed, and perhaps one white man wounded."[17]

The bloodily effective use of violence by whites at Colfax underscored the dangerous isolation of white Republicans outside the safety of Natchitoches Parish. On the day of the massacre, Elcey Hertzog pleaded with her fiancé to quit politics. Breda's vulnerability became frighteningly apparent when, as district attorney, he arrived in Colfax on July 24 to attend the new term of the Grant Parish court. No sooner had parish judge R. C. Register opened court than about seventy white men armed with knives and revolvers forced it to close. Two weeks earlier, a Grant Parish grand jury had on Breda's direction indicted about 140 whites for their involvement in the Colfax massacre. These armed men, who included many of those under indictment, threatened to kill anyone attempting to make arrests in connection with that affair. Register and Breda left Grant Parish and vowed not to return unless U.S. soldiers accompanied them. "I left Colfax at sunset to save my life," Breda informed Attorney General Williams, "for I knew . . . that it would have been taken."[18]

The Colfax massacre emboldened whites in northern Louisiana to defy the state authorities and scorn the federal government. They not only issued death threats but also carried them out. In Franklin Parish, reported the Republican tax collector, W. H. McCoy, a white militia had threatened to kill all the Kellogg appointees. These men dismissed the threat of federal intervention, McCoy added. "They have gone so far as to say . . . we will be killed before the troops reach Winnsboro." Six months later a party of white men ambushed and shot dead the district judge, Thomas S. Crawford, and the district attorney, Arthur H. Harris, as they journeyed on horseback to hold court in Winnsboro.[19]

Intimidation and violence rendered the writ of the state government unenforceable, and the hesitant response of the Grant administration to the Colfax massacre gave Republicans little comfort. Some became so discouraged that they threatened to throw in the towel. Writing to the U.S. attorney general, Ernest Breda pointed out that while he and other Republicans were risking their lives by trying to hold court in Grant Parish, U.S. soldiers were standing idle in camp outside Pineville, a mere thirty miles from Colfax. "We cannot give our lives," he wrote, "for we would not be noticed any more than the unfortunate murdered of April 13th." Incredulous that the federal government had failed to make a single arrest, Breda suggested that abandoning the prosecution altogether might be preferable to the continuing uncertainty. That, at least, might persuade local white to allow Republican officials to carry out their normal duties. William B. Phillips, a former Confederate soldier who had served as Grant Parish's first Republican judge, declared that if the perpetrators of the Colfax massacre escaped punishment, "it would show sound sense and wise generalship to discontinue the fight." A few more bloody affrays like Colfax, he argued, would annihilate the rank and file of the Republican Party.[20]

U.S. Attorney J. R. Beckwith shared the frustration of Breda and Phillips. Determined to bring the Colfax murderers to book, he convened a grand jury in New Orleans that returned indictments against ninety-eight individuals. Washington's tepid response, however, gave him little encouragement. Attorney General Williams rejected Beckwith's request for cavalry and denied him the funds to mount a detachment of infantry. Beckwith himself, Williams unhelpfully suggested, might procure the horses from his own resources. In reply, Beckwith pointed out the obvious: without a mounted posse, "the prosecution might as well be abandoned. As most of the accused will secret themselves in piney woods . . . and defy arrest." It took months for Beckwith to organize an expedition in pursuit of the suspects. The state authorities acquired and refitted a gunboat, but they lacked money to buy fuel and pay the pilots. Finally, in October, the *Ozark* transported a party of mounted militiamen up the Red River and back.[21]

During October and November, a militia unit led by U.S. Deputy Marshal Thomas DeKlyne arrested seven of the Colfax suspects. The vast majority of the whites involved in the Colfax massacre, including their leader, Christopher Columbus Nash, evaded capture. Nevertheless, Attorney General Williams believed that the conviction of a few ringleaders "would have all the desired effect to vindicate the law and induce the future observance of it by the people." Nine of the ninety-eight named defendants eventually stood trial in New Orleans.[22]

The outcome of *United States v. Cruikshank* was an unmitigated disaster for the Republican Party and the Grant administration. Two trials, lasting from February 25 to June 10, led to all nine defendants being acquitted of murder. Six of them escaped conviction entirely. The majority-white jury did find three of the defendants guilty of conspiring to violate the black victims' civil rights, a federal crime that carried a maximum sentence of ten years. But on June 27, Justice Joseph P. Bradley of the U.S. Supreme Court, acting in his capacity as a circuit court judge, overturned the guilty verdicts and dismissed the indictments. The trial judge, William B. Woods, dissented from Bradley's opinion, thus providing grounds for an appeal. Many months later, however, the Supreme Court unanimously dismissed the prosecution case. The Colfax defendants had got away with cold-blooded murder.

In overturning the Colfax verdicts, the Supreme Court interpreted the Fourteenth and Fifteenth Amendments narrowly. The Fifteenth Amendment prohibited any state from denying the vote on the grounds of "race, color, or previous condition of servitude." But the Court reasoned that the prosecution had failed to establish a racial motive behind the Colfax murders, making the Fifteenth Amendment inapplicable. According to the justices, what happened at Colfax fell into the category of ordinary murder, and that was a state crime that belonged in a state court. Unless prosecutors could prove that white people conspired with conscious racial intent to deprive blacks of a federal right, the Enforcement Act of 1870 could not be invoked. The Court declared, further, that the safeguards afforded by the Fourteenth Amendment—that a state must not "deprive any person of life, liberty, or property, without due process of law"—did not authorize the federal government to directly protect life, liberty, and property. It was the primary responsibility of the states to ensure those rights. The federal government could only intervene if a state failed to do so, and only if a racial motive could be demonstrated. The only distinctly federal rights, "privileges or immunities of citizens of the United States," consisted of a few mostly irrelevant matters like the right to petition Congress. The Bill of Rights contained in the Constitution prohibited the national government from *abridging* certain rights; it did not empower that government to *protect* them.[23]

The Court's cramped definition of national citizenship contradicted the notion of a powerful federal government that directly protected the civil and political rights of its citizens. In one sense, it reflected the original conservatism, in the constitutional sense, of Congressional Reconstruction. In strengthening federal power, Congress had had no intention of creating a centralized, "consolidated" government along European lines. It refused to make suffrage a national right; it declined to support public schools. Above all, it clung to the view that states were indestructible political entities. Congressional Republicans had assumed that the states, not the federal government, would have primary responsibility for implementing black suffrage and equal citizenship. That is why Congress imposed only a brief military occupation and restored the ex-Confederate states to self-government as quickly as possible. Only the unanticipated violence of the white opposition had compelled the federal government to repeatedly intervene in the South. Such interventions, however, raised the unwelcome prospect of an almost indefinite extension of federal power. Emphasizing the limited authority of the national government and the duty of the states to enforce legal equality, the Court reflected the ideas of the moderate Republicans who had shaped Congressional Reconstruction.

In placing the burden of enforcement on the states, however, the Court demanded the impossible. The State of Louisiana had been unable to prosecute the Colfax killers because, as Ernest Breda explained, the district court had been unable to function in the absence of a military guard. It was the very weakness of the state governments that forced southern Republicans to seek protection from Washington. Republican officials "who have only a Kellogg commission for authority and no U.S. troops to protect them" were not only powerless, Breda wrote the attorney general, but also in danger of their lives.[24]

Reducing federal power, then, did nothing to increase state power. On the contrary: it further weakened the authority of Republican state governments. The attorney general instructed James Beckwith to begin no further criminal proceedings under the Enforcement Act until the Supreme Court had decided *Cruikshank*. Increasingly contemptuous of federal authority, the Democratic Party stepped up its efforts to defy, destabilize, and destroy the Kellogg administration. Some Democrats felt that they now enjoyed carte blanche to engage in acts of violence and intimidation. Many, including some of the most influential leaders, believed that the time had come for an open rebellion against the Republican regime.

The violence at Colfax persuaded both political parties in Natchitoches to conclude the negotiations over disputed parish offices. But the division of offices, while ending the governmental paralysis, did not terminate the political warfare. With a controlling voice on the police jury, local Democrats renewed their efforts to expose profligate spending and shady financial dealings by Republican officials.

In July 1873, P. A. Simmons, the Democratic president of the police jury, and Charles Leroy, the Republican parish treasurer, filed suit in district court against David H. Boullt Sr., the tax collector. Boullt, the suit alleged, had illegally profited from his office by speculating in parish warrants, which bore interest at 8 percent of their face value. The trial, presided over by district judge John J. Osborn, a Republican, revealed that Boullt had profited through speculation in a number of ways. One was by receiving taxes in U.S. currency and turning in depreciated warrants. Another was by trading in these warrants, acting "at once [as] 'bull' and 'bear' of the market." Yet another was by accumulating warrants himself and then applying to the parish court for the payment of interest. An act of the legislature permitted holders of parish debt to seek judgments in the state courts to make police juries pay up. The parish then had to impose special taxes to satisfy the claims of such "judgment creditors." Seeking to disguise his own involvement in this speculation, Boullt had William M. Levy, a Democratic attorney, sue the parish in his, Levy's, name. The two men then shared the proceeds. The suit by Simmons and Leroy complained, in addition, that much of this "parish paper" had been illegally issued and was therefore worthless. The plaintiffs claimed that Boullt owed the parish $67,000.[25]

The inclusion of Charles Leroy as one of the two plaintiffs was a major coup for the Democrats. Leroy had served as a delegate to the constitutional convention in 1867–68 and was one of the first Republicans to be elected to the state legislature. Why he joined the suit is unclear. He may have been disappointed that the party failed to renominate him as its candidate for the state legislature or reward him with a postmastership. In any case, when the time came for Boullt to settle his accounts, Leroy asked him to swear that he had not speculated in the funds of the parish, a condition of his office. That oath had never been asked before, probably because other Republican officials also speculated in "parish paper." Like all tax collectors, Boullt received a hefty commission on the revenues he gathered. And like many officials similarly situated, he regarded profiting from the buying and selling of parish warrants as a perk of his job. Boullt declined to so swear the required oath.[26]

When the case went to trial in September 1873, an all-black jury decided against Boullt and ordered him to pay $40,000 into the parish treasury. The final disposition of the case proved no great victory for the Democrats, however, for in March 1874 the Louisiana Supreme Court reduced the judgment against Boullt from $40,000 to $1,890. The trial, moreover, disclosed the embarrassing fact that the tax collector's partner in speculation was William Levy, one of the most influential Democrats in Natchitoches Parish.[27]

Yet the response of the state legislature to Boullt's prosecution suggested that the Democrats were on to something. In creating a new judicial district, the seventeenth, which included Natchitoches Parish but excluded Rapides Parish, the legislature ensured that no further cases from Natchitoches would go to district judge John Osborn. An honest Republican, Osborn had ruled that the police jury acted illegally in issuing paper warrants that added to the parish debt. He had also presided over the trial that found David H. Boullt a delinquent to the parish treasury. In short, Osborn was a thorn in the side of the Natchitoches Parish Republican Party. In 1874, therefore, Governor Kellogg appointed Henry Myers as the new district judge and named David H. Boullt Jr., the son of the tax collector, to the position of parish judge that Myers vacated. Any lawsuits against Republican officials in Natchitoches would henceforth be tried in Myers's court. It appeared that the legislature had created the Seventeenth Judicial District so that the "ring" which governed Natchitoches Parish would be protected by one its members—a man who had himself been charged with financial impropriety.

The legislature also redistricted parish wards, a move that stopped the police jury from pressing its investigations. The redistricting enabled governor Kellogg to replace the "Simmons Police Jury," whose membership formed part of the 1873 compromise, with a new one appointed by himself. Whereas the old police jury contained three Democrats and two Republicans, the new one consisted of five Republicans. Democrats complained that the terms of the 1873 compromise had been violated. They further charged that three members of the new police jury were illiterate blacks who would simply do the bidding of Myers and Boullt.[28]

These political maneuvers—one historian described such ploys as "defensive Machiavellianism"—did the Natchitoches Republicans little good. As Democrats dug deeper into the parish finances they stumbled across something much more serious than Boullt Sr.'s shady dealings in parish paper. In July 1874 a Democrat-sponsored Tax Reform Association examined the books of William H. Redmond, the assessor and collector of city taxes, and discovered a shortfall of $4,338. Taking office in July 1873, Redmond failed to hand in all that he collected. Shortly thereafter he absconded, only to be captured by Sheriff Burke and locked in the parish jail. The mayor and city council prosecuted Redmond for the defalcation.

Redmond's dishonesty cost the Republican Party dearly. It not only confirmed Democratic allegations of Republican stealing but also exacted a heavy financial penalty on Redmond's Republican colleagues. State law required tax collectors to furnish a bond as a guarantee of financial probity. Lacking the assets to cover the required amount, Redmond had arranged for Raford Blunt, Henry Raby, J. J. Bossier, John G. Lewis, and David H. Boullt Sr. to act as guarantors. The state supreme court ruled that these men owed the City of Natchitoches $3,000, the amount of Redmond's bond. The debt dogged them for years, even after death. When Bossier died in 1875, the City made a claim against his estate, even though it amounted to less than $500. The burden of paying Redmond's bond then fell upon Boullt, Blunt, Raby, and Lewis. It took Blunt, Raby, and Lewis until 1882 to clear the debt (Boullt died in 1879), which accrued 5 percent annual interest.[29]

Released from jail after six months, Redmond assailed his former Republican colleagues in an open letter to the citizens of Natchitoches. "By not understanding the office, and leaving my business in the hands of bad designing men," he claimed, "I came out a defaulter." The real culprit, he insisted, was parish tax collector David H. Boullt Sr., whose excessive and illegal demands had angered blacks. In 1872, Redmond explained, he had signed a petition calling for Boullt's removal, a document that contained fifteen hundred other signatures or marks. However, Blunt, Myers, and Raby refused to forward the petition to the governor, and Boullt marked Redmond down as an enemy.[30]

Redmond's letter was a gift for Natchitoches Democrats. The scandal could not have come at a better time. High taxation and corruption had been long a staple of Democratic propaganda—the formation of taxpayers associations was an old tactic. But the Tax Reform Association that emerged from a mass meeting at Firemen's Hall on June 13, 1874, was more potent than its 1871 predecessor. For one thing, it enjoyed the support of a newspaper, the *People's Vindicator*, whose first issue coincided with the new movement. The *Vindicator*'s tone was very different from that of the *Natchitoches Times*, whose editor, Louis Dupleix, advocated accommodation with Republicans. The *Vindicator* denounced compromise as betrayal and called for a "white man's party." The paper's bloodthirsty rhetoric—"ropes and lamp-posts are the only arguments"—alarmed Republican officials.

Ominously, the Tax Reform Association shadowed the rise of the White League. Organized during the spring and summer of 1874, the White League proposed that racial solidarity should be the Democratic Party's organizing strategy, and white supremacy its overriding objective. At a state convention in Baton Rouge, Democrats resolved that "the radical party" had so "inflamed the passions and prejudices of the negroes, as a race, against the whites" that "it [is] necessary for the white people to unite and act together in self-defense and for the preservation of white civilization."[31]

Denouncing Governor Kellogg as a usurper, the White League made plans to forcibly overthrow his administration. In New Orleans the league organized a militia, equipping it with weapons purchased in the North and clandestinely shipped South. This formidable force, which possessed the numbers and fighting power of a Confederate division (which in effect it was), planned an armed insurrection to install John McEnery as governor.

In Natchitoches Parish the White League introduced a new tactic: "bull-dozing." It offered Republican officials a choice: resign or face a lynch mob. At its June 13 meeting, the Tax Reform Association demanded that four members of the police jury step down on the grounds that they were "either corrupt or incompetent." As was standard practice by now, the Democrats masked their aggressive intentions by seeding false rumors of insurrection. "300 stands of arms have been passing through Cloutierville for this city to equip the negroes," the *Vindicator* reported. At a Republican meeting in Campti, the paper charged, black minister and schoolteacher George W. Green had urged blacks to "apply the torch and lay in ashes every building from one extreme of the parish to another" if whites resisted "negro rule."[32]

Republican leaders denied advocating violence. At the party's Fourth of July barbecue they rejected the demand for resignations and denounced former partisans like Sam Parsons and Lucius Burdick who had thrown in with the Democrats. However, hundreds of armed whites had converged on Natchitoches for a meeting of the Tax Reform Association, and they posted guards on all the roads leading into town. Stopped by sentries on his way home, Louis Dupleix rushed back to the Republican meeting and reported that the White League had taken over Natchitoches. The Republican leaders reversed themselves. Within forty-eight hours the four police jurors, three blacks and a white, had resigned.[33]

It was a clear victory for Natchitoches Democrats, but a modest one. Although some Democrats argued for a total boycott of the Republican state government, calmer heads realized that without functioning state courts, all business would grind to a halt. The Tax Reform Association therefore delegated Milton Cunningham and David Pierson to travel to New Orleans to present Governor Kellogg with a list of replacement police jurors who would be acceptable to the Democratic Party. Kellogg approved two of the Democratic nominees but also, at the behest of the Raford Blunt, Henry Myers, and E. L. Pierson—in New Orleans on a similar mission—appointed two Republicans. One of them, Alfred Woodward, a black man, declined to serve (probably out of fear), leaving the police jury evenly divided between the parties.[34]

Having drawn blood, the Tax Reform Association took aim at the tax collector, David Boullt Sr.; the district judge, Henry Myers; the parish judge, David Boullt Jr.; and the parish attorney, Jules J. Bossier. Every one of these officials was a "scalawag," and all had served in the Confederate army. But the editor of the *People's Vindicator* belittled their war records and showered them with abuse. James Cosgrove's treatment of Myers was typical. He described the man who had once been his friend as a "slanderous, crooked-necked, scurfy scalawag; liar, thief, coward; contemptible citizen, undutiful son, heartless father; a failure as a lawyer, as a soldier a deserter, a legal abortion as a judge." The organization of the White League, with the *Vindicator* as its mouthpiece, made Cosgrove's editorials tantamount to incitement to murder. And it made the Tax Reform Association far more menacing than its innocuous name implied. Indeed, most Republicans regarded the Tax Reform Association and the White League as one and the same.[35]

Raford Blunt had no doubt that his life was in danger. When he returned from New Orleans on July 21 after his meeting with Kellogg, a group of blacks hailed the *Bart Able* before the steamboat reached Grand Ecore, bidding Blunt disembark. The mounted guards, suspecting a plot to assassinate their leader, escorted him home.[36]

Later that day, as Republicans met at the courthouse to nominate candidates for the autumn elections, the Tax Reform Association's "Committee of Seventy" gathered across the street at Fireman's Hall. Looking through the window into the building opposite, Blunt fancied he saw men carrying weapons. As the Republican meeting broke up, Marshall Twitchell, the "carpetbagger" from Red River Parish and a candidate for state senator, encountered Cunningham on the steps of the courthouse, and the two men began to argue. Calling Cunningham hotheaded and impulsive, Twitchell denounced the White League as a political movement aimed at ousting every Republican, regardless of ability or character. Cunningham insisted that the Tax Reform Association was a popular uprising against corrupt and profligate government. He warned that the "People's Party" would carry the forthcoming elections "peaceably if we can, but forcibly if we must." Republicans like Twitchell, he added, must quit politics.[37]

The Republican meeting failed to nominate candidates for the positions of district judge and district attorney. Myers and Breda held these positions by appointment from Governor Kellogg, and they argued that according to the four-year cycle of judicial elections the posts would not be contested until 1876. But this seems to have been a face-saving excuse. Cunningham, convinced that the Republican-controlled State Returning Board had cheated him out of the district attorneyship, personally confronted the Republican leaders and warned them to leave the positions vacant. "We did not nominate these officers . . . in consequence of the threats," Blunt admitted. Later that evening Cunningham visited Blunt at his home to demand the resignations of Myers, Bossier, and the two Boullts.[38]

Democrats denied that the Tax Reform Association was a front for the White League. "We had no White League, no armed organization, and no drilling," David Pierson told a congressional committee. The Committee of Seventy decided against organizing a White League, he explained, because they believed that the Tax Reform Association would more effectively accomplish their object. True, the People's Vindicator carried regular notices of White League meetings. But without the support of the Committee of Seventy, Pierson emphasized, the White League never got off the ground.[39]

In truth, the "Tax Reform Association" was a flag of convenience that enabled Natchitoches Democrats to distance themselves from the vehemently racist White League while simultaneously drawing upon that organization's considerable manpower and fearsome reputation. Natchitoches Democrats had close ties to White League organizations in the surrounding parishes. David Pierson's brother Joseph headed the White League in Red River Parish. The People's Vindicator made no effort to distinguish between the Tax Reform Association and the White League, indicating that they were two sides of the same coin.[40]

It was nonetheless characteristic of Democratic leaders in Natchitoches that they eschewed the White League label. This was partly out of deference to "old-line Democrats"—men like Dick Sinnott, the captain of the Bart Able, and Joseph Henry, a planter known for his fair dealing—who opposed casting the Democratic Party as a "white man's party." Such men would, however, join a Tax Reform Association. The innocuous name also enabled senior Democrats to describe the association as a nonpolitical, biracial movement that enjoyed broad popular support. They could point out that its Committee of Seventy included blacks like Charles Leroy and Richard Faulkner, both of them former Republican officials; wartime Unionists such as Sam Parsons, the first Republican sheriff of Natchitoches Parish; and other whites who had once identified with the Republican Party and sometimes still did. Moreover, in permitting a couple of Republicans to remain in office, Democrats bolstered their claim that the Tax Reform Association opposed corruption and high taxes, not the Republican Party per se.[41]

Whether or not taxation was truly oppressive is another matter. Foner and others have questioned the oft-told tale of planters losing their land to "carpetbaggers" through inability to pay crushing taxes, arguing that most of the property seized by sheriffs and put up for auction was eventually redeemed by the owners when the latter coughed up. In Mississippi, for example, officials issued writs of seizure against six million acres for non-payment of taxes; however, all but 5 percent of that land "eventually found its way back to the owner." The implication is that former slaveholders, as a class, did not suffer unduly from high taxation and, as Jonathan Wiener has argued with regard to Alabama, managed to keep their holdings largely intact. Criticism of Republican taxation, moreover, reflected a widely held view that white taxpayers were subsidizing public services that principally benefited non-taxpaying blacks—a view that also considered the freedpeople as something less than full citizens.[42]

Still, escalating tax rates, however unavoidable given the need to repair wartime damage and fund public schools, inflicted real hardship upon many whites. Debt-strapped planters struggled to find the cash to pay their tax demands. Small landowners fared even worse. Before the war, taxes on slaves and luxury items had placed the main burden of taxation upon the wealthy. Now it fell upon all landowners, with small farmers contributing a much larger share of the whole. The economic depression triggered by the Panic of 1873 worsened their predicament. "For landowners," writes Mark Summers, "the Republican governments' taxes . . . now fell with a crushing burden." Even as tax rates fell, plummeting cotton and land prices meant that incomes fell faster. Many delinquent taxpayers "lost their livings and their property went under the sheriff's hammer."[43]

That Democratic anger over taxation was real, not feigned, is evident from a letter that William H. Jack addressed to the U.S. attorney general.

Under our multiplied misfortunes it is absolutely impossible for the people to pay their taxes and the consequences will be that in a very short time, the greater part of the lands of this Parish will be sold and bought by the State or by the few speculators who are the authors of this onerous and outrageous parochial taxation, as has been the case with thousands of acres already sold, and the present Land Owners will be literally set adrift upon the world.

Jack enclosed a demand for unpaid taxes signed by David Boullt Sr. He owed $143.86, about $2,870 in today's prices.[44]

Economic hard times intensified Democrats' anger in less obvious ways. Planters who combined agriculture with the practice of law, a common breed, found themselves increasingly dependent upon their profession when raising cotton ceased to be profitable. With more lawyers competing for fewer clients, the temptation to seek economic security through public office increased. More than ever, Democrats condemned those men who switched parties in order to gain office as opportunists and race traitors. The business slump also illustrated the old adage that the devil makes work for idle hands. Enforced leisure meant more time to cultivate hatreds, to stew in bitterness, and to attend political meetings. To people who, in the words of one reporter, "have nothing to do or do nothing but drink mint juleps and talk politics," the White League offered a welcome diversion.[45]

The mass meeting held by the Tax Reform Association on July 27 attracted so many armed White Leaguers (estimates varied between eight hundred and thirteen hundred) that the gathering moved out of the courthouse and into the street. The meeting charged a committee of seventeen to call upon the Republican officials and demand their resignation. The delegation found that Myers and David Boullt Jr. had fled Natchitoches three days earlier and that Bossier had already sent a letter of resignation to Governor Kellogg. It then visited David Boullt Sr. who, confronted by a demand for his resignation, readily complied. The fact that each member of the committee "gave his personal pledge that no violence would be offered him . . . by the people" showed all too clearly what the alternative would have been. Had Boullt refused to resign, David Pierson admitted, "it would have been almost impossible to have controlled the populace, or to have controlled the mass-meeting then assembled."[46]

There was nothing subtle about "bulldozing." Nevertheless, it was a more discriminating tactic than the generalized anti-Republican violence of the Knights of the White Camelia and the Ku Klux Klan. As Henry C. Dibble, the Republican assistant attorney general, noted, the White League "fell under the leadership of the more discreet and better-thinking men, whose influence was sufficient to check, in great degree, further instances of outrages on the blacks." "Bulldozing" targeted the white leaders of the Republican Party, without whom, the White League calculated, blacks would be disorganized, demoralized, and politically ineffective. In addition, by focusing on corruption and misgovernment, the White League exploited one of the dominating issues in national politics, and one well designed to exacerbate divisions within the Republican Party.[47]

It was in keeping with the Natchitoches way of doing things that senior Democrats avoided violence. Their preference for non-lethal methods reflected political pragmatism but was also, perhaps, sincerely felt. It was the proud boast of Natchitoches Democrats that only one political murder, the 1868 slaying of Alfred Hazen, had marred the good name of the parish. These planters, lawyers, doctors, and merchants believed that violence not only damaged the Democratic cause and risked federal intervention but also threatened the tranquillity for which Natchitoches Parish was renowned. When, for example, a company of White Leaguers accompanied the committee of seventeen to the residence of David Boullt Sr., its commander, W. E. Russell, kept the men under strict discipline. This ex-Confederate officer, who had served as a captain in the Third Louisiana Infantry, answered offers to "hang that God-damned scoundrel" with a stern, "This must be stopped. We must have no difficulty here today." Democratic leaders had a holy horror of the ruffians who traversed the Texas-Louisiana border and gave Shreveport a grim reputation for mayhem and murder.[48]

Still, although Republican leaders in Natchitoches escaped bodily harm, the formation of the White League/Tax Reform Association made them acutely conscious of their vulnerability. The insults and social ostracism that the Natchitoches "scalawags" had always endured escalated sharply. And now they were accompanied by open threats. According to Henry Myers, white Republicans had been accustomed to being snubbed socially by local Democrats, but they had been able to transact business with political foes in a reasonably civil manner; they had not felt in danger of their lives. But the mass meetings of the Tax Reform Association, the armed patrols of the White League, and the threats of the *Vindicator* frightened them. Myers, after fleeing Natchitoches on July 23—a journey that took him by carriage to Coushatta, steamer to Shreveport, and railway to Little Rock, Memphis, and New Orleans—was too scared to return. "Gentlemen who belonged to the Democratic Party," he reported, "told me in New Orleans that it was not safe . . . to go back, and I thought I would take their advice." David Boullt Sr. agreed to quit politics for good. "The opposition to me here is so great," he explained, "that I am determined to take no further part in public matters."[49]

"Bulldozing" spread like wildfire. White Leaguers compelled the resignation of Republican officials in parish after parish. The threat of being mobbed persuaded even the stoutest to flee or step down. The result was the virtual collapse of the Republican Party north of Red River and, with it, another paralysis of civil government.[50]

One of the most shocking instances of domestic terrorism took place not far from Natchitoches Parish. In Coushatta, the seat of Red River Parish, White Leaguers took six Republican officials into custody, and after the men left for Shreveport under mounted guard, ostensibly for their own protection, a large party of assassins overwhelmed the small escort and murdered its prisoners. All six victims were white men, four of them northerners. Responsibility for the "Coushatta massacre" has never been clearly established, but there was obviously collusion between the White League leaders in Red River Parish and the men who murdered the Republican prisoners. According to Mary Bryan, "Most of the young men and not a few of the older owners of the large cotton plantations near Coushatta were implicated."[51]

Although nobody from Natchitoches Parish appears to have been involved in the murders, the "bulldozing" in Natchitoches had inspired Democrats in Red River to form a White League in the first place. Leaders of the Tax Reform Association, including James Cosgrove and William Jack, spoke at a White League rally in Coushatta on August 6 and urged all present to compel the Republican officials to resign. Cosgrove's *Vindicator* disseminated reports that Republican leaders in Red River Parish were organizing a black insurrection, a wholly manufactured threat that provided the league with a pretext for "bulldozing." The hundreds of White Leaguers who descended upon Coushatta included many men from Natchitoches. In testimony to congressional committees, Democratic leaders deprecated the "Coushatta massacre." White League–supporting newspapers, however, justified it. "The men who were killed met a just and fearful doom," wrote Cosgrove, "and their deaths should serve as a warning to the white demons who strut in our midst."[52]

The Coushatta affair ramped up the pressure on local Republicans. E. L. Pierson, who declared his Republican allegiance at the Fourth of July barbecue, experienced a harrowing journey back to Natchitoches after Governor Kellogg appointed him parish judge in place of the "bulldozed" David Boullt Jr. Upon arriving in Alexandria by steamboat on August 25, Pierson and his traveling companion, Raford Blunt, called at a stable to hire a carriage. While negotiating with the stable-keeper the two men encountered John R. Williams, formerly one of the largest slaveholders in Rapides

Parish. A violent man who the previous year had assaulted a U.S. deputy marshal, Williams cursed Blunt as a "damned radical leader son of a bitch" and warned that "in a few days there will be a damned big priest's funeral in Natchitoches." He then smacked Pierson with the back of his hand and instructed the stable-keeper to "get him out of this town in damned short order." To Blunt's surprise, Pierson, who "was very fiery, and always stood up for himself," let the insult pass (an act of restraint that came back to haunt him). Completing the journey under cover of darkness, Pierson arrived in Natchitoches to be warned that "under no consideration must I attempt to hold court or exercise the functions of my office."[53]

In the absence of any legal government, some whites in Natchitoches Parish turned to lynch law. On August 22 a group of men pursued and killed Charles Bell, a freedman who started a shooting affray after a game of cards in Wesley Sheppard's saloon turned ugly. Amid the subsequent excitement, whites formed mounted patrols on the grounds of self-defense: blacks were "collecting on the hill" and planning to commence a "war of the races." Although David Pierson dismissed fears of black insurrection as the "wildest rumors," the patrols made Republican leaders take extraordinary precautions. Raford Blunt convinced himself that one such patrol, led by a known killer named Samuel "Curley-headed" Hynes, was "scouring Cane River hunting for me." Two days after arriving back in Natchitoches, Blunt went into hiding, taking cover in woods about seven miles from town.[54]

Thoroughly frightened, and scared that his hiding place had been discovered, Blunt decided to seek political protection from the Democrat he trusted most, David Pierson. First writing a letter, and then meeting Pierson and other Democrats in person, Blunt promised to quit politics if his life were spared. The Democrats demanded that Blunt resign from the state senate, step down from the school board, and "quiet the tone" of the *Natchitoches Republican*. Pierson later testified that Blunt's fright "was entirely unfounded" and that his life had never been in danger, but William A. Ponder was so hostile to Blunt—accusing the Republican of "endeavoring to arm and equip the negroes to fight against the white people"—that he, Pierson, had to intervene on Blunt's behalf. Not for the first time, Pierson's coolness may have saved his life. After mollifying Ponder, Pierson pledged to maintain the peace and see that blacks were not subjected to violence during the election campaign. According to Blunt, Pierson was as good as his word: "I do not know of any colored man being disturbed in the parish of Natchitoches."[55]

Democrats like David Pierson may well have calculated that their party would be better off with Blunt alive than with Blunt dead. They knew that he was the only Republican leader who had sufficient political influence to call black people to arms. They recognized that should they sanction Blunt's murder, blacks would seek vengeance. They were all too aware, moreover, that their own economic survival depended upon the cooperation of black laborers. Blunt was not afraid to remind them of that fact. "Said I, 'Remember that you have good crops, and the merchants have got their money out on the crops.'" Still, Blunt took precautions. He regularly left his house at nightfall to stay with friends. "I did not sleep in my house any night during September."[56]

The Democratic Party had moved beyond the limits of electoral politics and entered the realm of insurrection. "It is a political revolution," Pierson told Blunt. "Nobody must stand in the way of this movement." John McEnery, who was stumping northern Louisiana on behalf of the Democrats, breathed fire. The defeated candidate from 1872, who regarded himself as the rightful governor, urged listeners to drive Republicans from office or else hang them. "We shall carry the next election, if we have to ride saddle-deep in blood to do it."[57]

10

THE WHITE LEAGUE INSURRECTION

The Louisiana question has staggered the best minds in the country.

Lieutenant Henry A. Morrow to House Select Committee
on the Condition of the South, January 1875

In 1874 the Republican Party still controlled state governments in Florida, Alabama, South Carolina, Mississippi, Louisiana, Texas, and Arkansas. But Republicans in those states were uncomfortably aware that public opinion in the North had become increasingly hostile to them. Northern voters could not understand why the federal government had repeated recourse to military intervention in order to prop up state governments in the South, especially when Republicans were continually fighting among themselves. President Grant declined a request for troops by Mississippi's governor, Adelbert Ames, enabling whites in Vicksburg to seize the city government through force. He also refrained from using troops to sustain Republican governments in Texas and Arkansas, allowing the Democratic Parry to reclaim both states.

The deep economic depression triggered by the failure of the Jay Cooke & Company banking firm in September 1873 added to Republican woes. It would be too much to argue that, absent hard times, Congressional Reconstruction would have endured. The Republican Party had already lost control of Georgia, Virginia, Tennessee, and North Carolina; the Colfax massacre had already occurred; Republicans in Louisiana, Arkansas, Florida, and Texas were already badly splintered. Nevertheless, the Panic of 1873 hurt the cause of southern Republicans. Northern Republicans, in line for a drubbing in the 1874 congressional elections, became convinced that Reconstruction had become an electoral liability. More generally, as Mark Summers has written, "for most Americans the depression . . . created a final breaking point with the importance of Civil War issues."[1]

It was with a deep sense of foreboding, therefore, that Louisiana's Republi-

Figure 10. White League intimidation depressed the Republican vote in parts of the Red River valley, but in Natchitoches Parish blacks voted in force. *Harper's Weekly*, October 31, 1874. Library of Congress Pictures and Photographs Division.

cans entered the 1874 political campaign. The only way for the Democrats to carry the state, Governor Kellogg wrote U.S. Attorney General George Williams, "lies in the intimidation of the colored man in the heavily Republican parishes along the Red River." The Democrats were planning a violent campaign, Kellogg warned Grant, because they calculated that the North had lost its appetite for intervention in southern politics. Moreover, the decision of Justice Bradley in the *Cruikshank* case, throwing out the three Colfax convictions, convinced whites that the Enforcement Acts could not be enforced and that they had nothing more to fear from the federal courts. The Democrats' renunciation of violence, Kellogg explained, was patently insincere. "In the most distant parishes of the state," he noted, "turbulence and lawlessness are chronic, much violence prevails, and much more is anticipated before [the] election." Now the Democrats were organizing paramilitary White Leagues with a view to staging a coup d'état. "If Louisiana goes, Mississippi will inevitably follow," Kellogg predicted, "and . . . all the reconstruction acts of Congress will be so much waste paper." The governor asked for federal troops to be stationed at strategic points throughout the state.[2]

The governor's panicky letters did not exaggerate. The ink was scarcely dry on the page when Kellogg received news of the Coushatta massacre. A telegram dispatched by state attorney general A. P. Field conveyed the impact of that event: "Unless protected by military force every white republican in Louisiana will be either murdered or driven from the state before November." Democratic newspapers now brazenly advocated the violent overthrow of the Kellogg government. Grant's palpable reluctance to use troops, the *New Orleans Bulletin* editorialized, meant that "every carpetbag governor must . . . sustain himself with worthless negro militia against the disbanded confederate army." With one big push the Democrats could tip the Kellogg administration over, predicted John McEnery: "The people need have no fear of troops, for Kellogg cannot get them."[3]

The White Leagues drew their power from mass meetings, in which more moderate Democrats found themselves shouted down. "I would draw no white or black line," wrote David F. Boyd, the president of Louisiana State University. "Individually, most of our leading men think that way, but when they get together in a body or convention with no one bold enough to express his real views, the White League mania rises to a *white heat.*" Since the debacle of Fusion in 1872, Democrats who favored some kind of accommodation with the Republican Party had lost influence. During the summer of 1873 a New Orleans–based "Unification Movement," headed by former Confederate general P. G. T. Beauregard and businessman Isaac Marks, preached interracial harmony and promised to respect blacks' civil and political rights. Rejected by Democrats and Republicans alike, it quickly collapsed. The bitterness engendered by Grant's installation of Kellogg cannot be overstated. Henry C. Warmoth told the governor to his face that "we would overthrow him with force if we could." In northern Louisiana, Democrats condemned the very notion of common political action on the basis of racial equality.

"We abhor it in every fiber of our being," railed the *Ouchita Telegraph*. Republican politicians, both whites and blacks, saw the Unification movement as a threat to their positions and did their best to undermine it.[4]

By August 1874 it was an open secret that Democrats in New Orleans were plotting a coup d'état. "Things here are very quiet," reported Republican Jack Wharton, "but I fear that is the calm before the storm. The White League[s] are eight thousand strong in this City and all armed." Wharton overestimated the numbers, but a leading Democrat privately disclosed that the leagues had "2,200 white men armed and enrolled." They could wield the fighting power of two Confederate brigades.[5]

On September 14 the White League militias launched an insurrection against the "illegal" Kellogg government. After a street battle that left thirty-two participants dead, the thirty-five hundred men of the state militia and the Metropolitan Police fled the field. The White League seized control of New Orleans, installed John McEnery as governor, and recognized all the other candidates who had been "counted out" by the Returning Board in 1872. Kellogg took refuge in the Custom House.[6]

"The Battle of Liberty Place," as it became known in Democratic folklore, caused jubilation among Democrats throughout the state. When news of the coup reached Natchitoches, Democrats lit bonfires and, after a celebratory mass meeting, "quietly installed all the McEnery officers." Denouncing Kellogg as a usurper and depicting Republican rule as a nightmare of tyranny and corruption, the Democrats claimed to represent all people of "property, intelligence and honesty." In ousting Republican officials, they explained, they had acted as patriotic Americans in the tradition of 1776. Throughout northern Louisiana, Democrats assumed the reins of government and Republican authority collapsed.[7]

By engaging in insurrection the Democratic Party dared the Grant administration to intervene. It calculated that if Grant believed that only a full-scale military occupation could keep the Republican Party in power, he would tolerate a Democratic victory. "We intend to carry the State . . . in November next," vowed the *People's Vindicator*, "or she will be a military territory."[8]

But the Democrats overplayed their hand. Northern Republicans were not yet ready to abandon Louisiana in the face of brazen, organized Democratic violence. On September 15 Grant issued a proclamation calling upon the insurgents to disperse. He instructed General W. H. Emory to restore Governor Kellogg to office. After the White League in New Orleans yielded to federal authority, Emory dispatched soldiers to the interior, explaining that "nearly every parish in the State, following the example of New Orleans, is more or less in a state of insurrection."

After prodding from Kellogg, who persuaded Attorney General Williams to intercede with Secretary of War William W. Belknap, Emory agreed to oust the McEnery officials throughout northern Louisiana and install the Kellogg ones in their place. He ordered Major Lewis Merrill of the Seventh Cavalry, a foe of the Ku Klux Klan who had battled the secret order in South Carolina, to take charge of federal troops in the Red River valley and restore order. Merrill dispatched a company under the command of Lieutenant Donald McIntosh to accompany U.S. Deputy Marshal J. B. Stockton to Coushatta and Natchitoches. Stockton carried a sheaf of arrest warrants relating to the Coushatta murders.[9]

On October 19, 1874, McIntosh's soldiers rode into Natchitoches. The cavalrymen spotted James H. Cosgrove riding in a buggy and promptly arrested him. The editor was drunk and belligerent. Cursing the soldiers, he took a cud of tobacco from his mouth and flung it in Stockton's face. "With admiral forbearance," McIntosh reported, "the marshal did nothing." All in all, the posse arrested twenty-five men: eighteen in and around Coushatta, seven in Natchitoches Parish. McIntosh kept the prisoners under close guard and allowed visits only from family members. He denied them "the use of all malt and spirituous liquors."[10]

The arrests failed, however, to bring the Coushatta murderers to justice. Stockton apprehended only a fraction of the suspects on his list, the remainder having fled or gone into hiding. "I found it impossible to employ any one, white or black, to act as a guide," McIntosh complained, "and the reason given was that they afraid they would be killed." After a few days he gave up the search. Moreover, the men Stockton arrested in Natchitoches Parish turned out to have had no involvement in the Coushatta massacre, and after five weeks in custody they were released without charge. Even with actual perpetrators in the dock, U.S. Attorney J. R. Beckwith had never entertained much hope of obtaining convictions. Since Bradley's decision in *Cruikshank*, he told Attorney General Williams, it had become impossible to prosecute political violence. "A large portion of the whites in this state will consider any attempt to punish the crime as remorseless persecution."[11]

Restoring Republicans to office also proved difficult. The arrests, far from cowing local Democrats, infuriated them. David Pierson, chairman of the Natchitoches Parish Democratic Party, protested that the men in custody were all innocent, and alleged that the arrests were designed to "deprive our people of their influence and votes in the approaching election." Cosgrove presented himself as "living evidence of the attempt to muzzle the freedom of the press in the so-called State of Louisiana." The story of his arrest grew in the telling. Years later, an aging Democrat had Cosgrove throwing the tobacco cud at Lieutenant McIntosh, "the man who in those days under open insult would not challenge and fight." The Natchitoches prisoners posed as martyrs, even though Deputy Marshal Stockton released them from jail and permitted them to board at a friend's house. "We are under no restraints," reported one, "except not to go onto the streets." They even voted on election day.[12]

Stockton pleaded for a company of infantry to be posted to Natchitoches. Otherwise, he feared, the White League would not only remain in power but also exact revenge. "These people swear as soon as I go away with the Cavalry they intend to kill all the leading white and black republicans in the Parish." By the time of the election, three troops of cavalry and five companies of infantry had been posted to northern Louisiana.[13]

In the 1874 campaign, in contrast to previous elections, the Democratic Party made little effort to attract black support. On the contrary, it went out of its way to insult black voters. References to blacks in the *People's Vindicator* dripped with contempt. Democrats had appealed to the freedmen in every way they knew how, Cosgrove explained, only to have their overtures rejected. Further appeals were futile, he went on, because "the negro" was "a creature without reason" who, "guided by his prejudices only," had become the political tool of "very bad colored men." Their ignorance made blacks incapable of exercising the functions of office, Cosgrove trumpeted. "We insist that the white race alone is . . . fitted to govern."[14]

The danger of this strategy, of course, lay in the fact that it was bound to assist the Republicans in patching up divisions and shoring up black support. Democrats faced electoral defeat if the Republican Party were to turn out its full vote. Some Democrats, doubting the wisdom of deliberately alienating black voters, insisted on using the party label of their choice— People's Party, Conservative Party, Conservative Democratic Party, and so on—and moderated the Democratic platform to include the statement, "The rights of all men, under the Constitution and laws of the land, must be respected and preserved inviolate, irrespective of race, color, or previous condition." But blacks were scarcely likely to believe such promises when the party making them advocated government by whites alone. And the argument advanced by some Democrats that their party was *more* likely to win black support when it did *not* appeal to black voters could scarcely be taken seriously.[15] Some Democrats were sufficiently worried about the political risks of "drawing the color line" that they made overtures to Republicans. In the sugar parishes of southern Louisiana, where many planters blamed the White League for disrupting the smooth running of their plantations, Democrats openly bid for black support. In Terrebonne Parish, for example, Democrats negotiated an electoral pact with Republicans whereby the two parties agreed to divide the offices.[16]

In northern Louisiana, however, Democrats rejected compromise. The Democratic Party had tried it before, the *Vindicator* stated, and the party had always "come out of the canvass worse beaten than ever." Cosgrove condemned any tactic that diluted white unity. "Every man who votes a split-ticket," he wrote, "is not only an enemy to our citizens, but a traitorous foe to his own race and civilization."[17]

Yet even if Democrats were to poll a solid white vote, black men outnumbered white men by a wide margin in Natchitoches Parish. The only

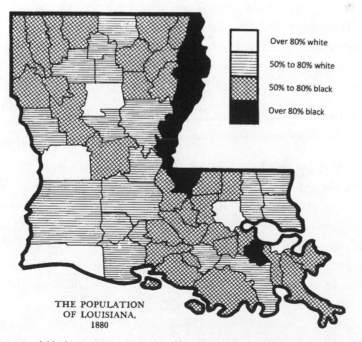

Over 80% white

50% to 80% white

50% to 80% black

Over 80% black

THE POPULATION
OF LOUISIANA,
1880

Map 3. Louisiana's black population. Reproduced by permission of Louisiana State University Press.

way for the Democrats to win, therefore, was by depressing the black vote through intimidation and/or fraud. As Cosgrove explained to two skeptical Democrats on board the steamboat *Bart Able*, their party "had tried . . . to work upon the negro in every way, upon his passions, and on his desire for gain, and in previous campaigns they had been uniformly unsuccessful." In this campaign, he went on, "they proposed to work upon the negro's fears."[18]

The presence of soldiers enabled the Republicans to organize a campaign. But a strange and subdued campaign it was. "The white voters of each parish north of Red River constituted an armed conspiracy," wrote Shreveport Republican Aaron B. Levissee, "with the . . . purpose of carrying the election at all costs—by threats, intimidation, and fraud if possible and by violence if necessary." In Caddo and De Soto Parishes, employers threatened blacks with dismissal if they voted the Republican ticket. Threats of assassination were so open and general that Republican leaders feared canvassing outside the towns. At the few meetings they held in the country districts, armed whites jeered Republican speakers and promised dire punishment to any blacks who voted "radical." Bienville and Sabine Parishes were regarded as so dangerous that the Republican Party did not even contest them.[19]

Natchitoches Parish remained the solid Republican bastion in the Red River valley. The large black majority, strong Republican leadership, and parish Democratic Party that was averse to violence fortified blacks' resolve to stand up and be counted. Yet even here Republicans felt menaced. Every public meeting threatened to turn into a violent brawl. On October 24, for example, a Republican rally outside the parish courthouse drew seven or eight hundred blacks to hear speeches by Ernest Breda, E. L. Pierson, and John G. Lewis. The meeting was remarkable not only for its size but also for the fact that David Pierson accepted an invitation to address the crowd. As Raford Blunt recalled, "that was the first time that I had ever seen the republicans and the democrats on the same stump for a long time." But the meeting turned ugly after a white man aimed his pistol at Lewis. The ensuing commotion attracted hundreds of bellicose Democrats, and soldiers had to intervene. "Both parties appeared to be generally armed," reported Lieutenant McIntosh, "and many were drunk." The officer asked the crowd to disperse and had his men clear the streets. His actions had, McIntosh believed, averted a "general and bloody collision."[20]

The loss or absence of crucial leaders stunted the Republican campaign. Blunt had been frightened into silence. So had David Boullt Sr. Henry Myers was in New Orleans, afraid to return to Natchitoches. Madrid P. Black-stone, a mainstay of the party since its inception in 1867, was dead, killed by another Republican in an accidental shooting. Blacks in the country were afraid to attend meetings or even ride from one plantation to another. The few Republicans who actively campaigned rarely ventured outside town. Even in town, they feared assassination. E. L. Pierson, a candidate for the state legislature, claimed that his brother-in-law, a staunch Democrat, begged him to quit the Republican Party lest he end up with a knife in his back. This constituted a friendly warning. Not so friendly were the insults and threats he encountered on the streets. Sheriff Ross Burke, a Democrat, advised him to stay away from crowds, "or I would be killed."[21]

Natchitoches Republicans also suffered from the fact that despite the presence of an army post Democrats still exercised de facto control of the city and parish governments, and used that power to influence the elections. The Democrat-controlled police jury located the polling places. Dr. J. H. Cunningham, the father of Milton J. Cunningham, overawed the Republican supervisor of registration, P. W. Holmes, a mild-mannered Baptist minister and former slave, and acted as de facto registrar. Anxious to avoid the charge of intimidation and keen to avoid violence, Democrats sought to maximize white registration and depress black registration. When Kellogg appointed white Republican Edward Ezernack in Holmes's place, two armed Democrats warned Ezernack not to take up the position. The young printer, who worked for the *Natchitoches Republican,* heeded their advice. It testifies to the resilience of the local Republican Party that so many blacks succeeded in registering.[22]

Democrats challenged numerous black voters when they tried to cast ballots on November 2. In Ward 4, Republicans claimed that 177 blacks were turned away because the names on their certificates of registration did not correspond exactly with the names recorded in the registration books. A man named "Battiste," for example, was rejected because the name in the book was "Baptiste." In the town of Natchitoches more than one hundred "special policemen," all of them Democrats and all of them armed, patrolled the streets. Mayor I. F. De Vargas, who appointed these men, was a nominal Republican, but the Democrats allowed him to stay in office because he could be bullied.[23]

According to the official returns, compiled under the eyes of Democratic election commissioners, the Republican Party failed to carry Natchitoches Parish by about sixty votes. In the senate district that comprised Natchitoches, De Soto, Bienville, and Sabine Parishes, Democrat J. B. Elam beat Marshall H. Twitchell by more than six hundred votes. In the Fourth Congressional District, which embraced the entire Red River valley, the returns put Democrat William M. Levy comfortably ahead of his Republican rival, George L. Smith. But the razor-thin Democratic majority in Natchitoches Parish itself had only been obtained because Democratic election commissioners persuaded the Republican supervisor of registration, the easily swayed Rev. Holmes, to exclude Ward 9 from the count on the grounds that returns had been improperly compiled. The election for parish judge was so close that the first count put Ernest Breda ahead by a single vote, while a recount gave C. L. Dranguet, a Democrat, a four-vote advantage.[24]

The atmosphere in Natchitoches remained charged. The day after the election, E. L. Pierson sought refuge in the courthouse after a man in the street fired three shots at him. Friends implored him to stay indoors and not be caught outside after dark. Pierson holed up in his house, "a perfect arsenal," for several days. He left Natchitoches in the middle of the night and in the company of Ernest Breda made his way to New Orleans. "They slunk away through the back of town," jeered the *People's Vindicator*, "slunk through Bayou Pierre swamp, slunk up to Coushatta, and slunk aboard the steamboat *Royal George*."[25]

Writing to his wife from New Orleans, Ernest Breda cast his trip in a rather different light:

> Pierson and I were the heroes of northwestern Louisiana, and our daring trip was the comment and theme of conversation for several days . . . among the leading men of our Party. . . . I have made many acquaintances and have met with . . . expressions of assurance as to my future career in the Judiciary. It is true that we are beset by enemies and surrounded by dangerous elements, but it gladdens and strengthens one's heart to meet men . . . of like opinions who have the fortitude to think like free men and the courage to battle for their rights.

Deputy Marshal Stockton assured Breda that "all will be well in the end" and that both Breda and Pierson would be confirmed by the Returning Board.[26]

The vote on November 2, therefore, decided nothing, for everyone expected the Republican Party to challenge the results in the Red River valley. "The negro vote cannot be brought out in the parishes," predicted Jack Wharton, "and if they expect to succeed it must be through the Returning Board." Unless the board revised the official returns, the Democratic

Party stood to gain a large majority in the state house of representatives. The Democrats, for their part, vowed to stand by the official returns. A stream of candidates, elected and defeated, Republicans and Democrats, made their way to New Orleans in the hope of swaying the members of the board.[27]

The Returning Board lost little time in changing the result in Natchitoches Parish. Simply including the poll from Ward 9, which Democrats had contested, gave the Republican candidates a majority of twenty-two votes. The board also found it easy to throw out the results in Bienville Parish on the grounds of intimidation. The White League had frightened black voters throughout the state, the board explained, nowhere more so than in the parishes of the Red River valley, where the election "was almost a farce."[28]

Yet however valid the charge of intimidation, the Returning Board could not resist cherry-picking the results. In order to elect Marshall Twitchell to the state senate it needed to further depress the Democratic total in the four-parish senatorial district. It therefore increased the Republican majority in Natchitoches Parish by rejecting the returns from Wards 5 and 6 on the grounds that a "perfect reign of terror" had prevented 328 blacks from voting. It threw out the entire vote of Winn Parish because the supervisor of registration had failed to sign the required oath of office and had refused to vacate his post when Kellogg appointed a successor. In one of the most bizarre stories arising out of this bizarre election, the returns from De Soto Parish went missing. The registrar of voters for De Soto, former Freedmen's Bureau agent E. N. Bean, later claimed that one of Twitchell's political allies, E. W. Dewees, had with Kellogg's connivance used a combination of threats and bribes to induce him to "lose" the returns. They somehow ended up in the possession of "a noted courtesan of New Orleans," who offered to sell them to the Returning Board for cash. The board refused to consider her proposition. It also refused to accept a second set of returns from the clerk of court on the grounds that they had not been certified by Bean.

The result of all this fine-tuning was to ensure the election of Twitchell to the state senate and to bring about the reelection of Antoine Dubuclet as state treasurer. Finalizing the results on December 24, the board declared that fifty-three Republicans and fifty-three Democrats had been elected to the state house; it left five disputed seats to be decided by the house itself.[29]

The White League had threatened dire consequences in the event of a false count by the Returning Board: "Give us a fair election or we will make

Louisiana a *hell*." After the failed putsch of September 14, Democrats pinned their hopes on electing a majority of the lower house of the state legislature. Hence they received the board's announcements with predictable outrage. The canvass of 1874 looked set to reproduce the chaos of the 1872 contest, when two rival legislatures had made Louisiana ungovernable. Whites in the Red River valley were vehement that they would never recognize the existing state government, reported Lieutenant Henry A. Morrow. He warned that when the state legislature assembled on January 4 there would be "a terrible scene of disorder, and perhaps bloodshed," unless the United States afforded military protection. U.S. Attorney Beckwith called the atmosphere in New Orleans "volcanic." General Emory agreed. "This community is in a very sensitive condition; the least disturbance—crack of a pistol—produces an alarm."[30]

Two incidents after Christmas, resulting in two deaths, underlined the dangers attending Louisiana politics. On December 26, former governor Warmoth encountered D. C. Byerly, the assistant editor of the *New Orleans Bulletin*, the mouthpiece of the White League. Warmoth was embroiled in a bitter, name-calling dispute with the newspaper's editor, E. L. Jewell, and had reluctantly accepted the latter's demand for "satisfaction." Before the duel could take place, however, Byerly, Jewell's second, assaulted Warmoth in the street, beating him over the head with a cane. Warmoth reached for a pocketknife and stabbed his assailant, inflicting wounds that turned out to be mortal. Five days later Fabius McKay Dunn, a black Republican serving as an assistant U.S. appraiser, was shot and killed while walking in the city. Nobody was apprehended, and the motive remained a mystery. However, prominent white Republican Hugh J. Campbell charged that the intended victim was Blunt, Dunn's companion, and that the assassin's bullet had found the wrong target.[31]

Kellogg asked President Grant to deploy troops in and around the statehouse. Grant declined. Let Kellogg do his duty, he replied, "without apprehension of danger." Washington would only consider military intervention *after* trouble broke out and *if* the state authorities proved inadequate. Grant nevertheless ordered his most trusted general, Philip H. Sheridan, to proceed to Louisiana to "ascertain the true condition of affairs."[32]

On the very day that Sheridan arrived in New Orleans, January 4, 1875, Democratic members of the lower house staged a parliamentary coup de main. Aided by supporters who had surreptitiously entered the building to suddenly identify themselves as "sergeants-at-arms," Democrats seized the speaker's chair, stopped Republicans from leaving the chamber, and swiftly awarded the five disputed seats to Democrats. The following day, soldiers under the command of Colonel P. Regis de Trobriand entered the chamber, deposed the Democratic speaker, and declared the five disputed seats vacant.[33]

De Trobriand's action restored Republican control of the lower house, keeping the entire state government in Republican hands. But it also underlined the critical weakness of the Kellogg administration. The street battle of September 14, when the White League routed the combined forces of the state militia and the Metropolitan Police, had demonstrated Kellogg's dependence upon "federal bayonets" and driven the governor into hiding. His assurances that he could maintain his government without federal aid had been exposed as baseless.[34]

By the end of 1874, Michael Perman has argued, "the Republican Party in Louisiana was effectively demolished." An overstatement, perhaps. Nevertheless, the White League had exposed the party's utter dependence upon Grant's protection. In the Red River valley, reported Major Lewis Merrill, "the State government has no power outside the United States Army, which is here to sustain it—no power at all." Republican officials in the Red River valley had reason to be afraid: Democratic threats were "very seriously made," Merrill believed. The three Republican legislators from Caddo Parish could hardly be blamed for staying in New Orleans: "Beyond doubt [they] could not safely return here now." In Natchitoches Parish the White League continued to hold regular meetings. "We recognize no one holding a commission of appointment from Kellogg," insisted the *Vindicator*. Local Democrats proposed setting up "boards of arbitration" to replace the absent Republican parish judge, Ernest Breda.[35]

The *Vindicator* and the even more extreme *Shreveport Times* warned Republican candidates who had been elected through the machinations of the Returning Board not to claim their offices. "If George L. Smith is counted in over W. M. Levy, or if Twitchell is counted in over Elam, let Smith and Twitchell be killed," wrote *Times* editor Albert H. Leonard. Slightly less explicit but hardly less threatening was Cosgrove's warning in the *Vindicator*: "There is but one way to meet these scoundrels, and that is short and quick. Ropes and lamp-posts are the only arguments." Even by the standards of their own violent rhetoric, the two editors outdid themselves.[36]

Writing from Natchitoches in his native tongue, Dr. Jean Philippe Breda relayed the threats to Ernest. All the Democrats were *enragé*, he warned his son. The French-born doctor, a pillar of the Natchitoches community, advised Ernest to take extraordinary precautions should he return. "You will probably be watched. Guard against being ambushed." Ernest planned his return in the utmost secrecy. Suspecting that local Democrats might be intercepting the mails, he addressed his letters to a third party, who then personally delivered them. He promised his wife that he would soon be back in Natchitoches. Grant, he explained, would order the army "to recognize and protect the officers holding Kellogg commissions and none other." Breda instructed his wife to breathe no word about his imminent arrival. "I will turn up all right, when you will least expect it."[37]

But it was an open question as to whether Republican officials from the country parishes would ever be able to carry out their public duties. As long as an army post remained in Natchitoches, they could not be "bull-dozed." But Democrats believed that as soon as the soldiers departed they could topple the Republican government "with the tip of a stick." In the meantime, they stepped up their campaign of psychological intimidation, every threat and insult proclaiming that "scalawags" were cowards and men without honor. White Republicans learned to ignore the threats and swallow the insults. Better to lose face than to lose one's life.

General Sheridan proposed to confront the White League head-on. "Human life has been held too cheaply in this State for many years," he wired Secretary of War Belknap from New Orleans. Since 1866, he elaborated, nearly thirty-five hundred people had been killed or wounded, "a great majority of whom were colored men," but no one had been arrested, tried, or convicted for these crimes. Fully twelve hundred Republicans, he added, had been slain "on account of their political sentiments." The White League had cowed the citizenry, intimidated the state authorities, and "even went so far as to say that the United States troops here only remained upon their sufferance."

The general who had laid waste to the Shenandoah Valley and chased Lee's army to Appomattox wanted to crack down hard. If Congress or the president could declare the White Leaguers banditti, he telegraphed Belknap, "they could be tried before a military commission." Summary punishment of the ringleaders would restore order and act as powerful deterrent against political violence. Such a course, moreover, would relieve the federal government of the necessity to take any further action: Sheridan himself would deal with the problem.[38]

Such an iron-fisted policy might well have had the tonic effect that Sheridan claimed it would. Thus far, state and federal courts had failed to bring white perpetrators to book. The men who carried out the Colfax massacre, the leaders of the September 14 insurrection, and the perpetrators of the Coushatta murders had all gone, in Grant's pithy phrase, "unwhipped of justice." To assert that the state courts had failed to punish a single political murder would not be literally true. One of the men who killed Sam Watson, the only black voter in Caddo Parish to cast a ballot for Grant in 1868, served five years in the state penitentiary. But this lonely counterexample was the exception that proved the rule. As for the federal courts, whites felt virtually invulnerable after Justice Bradley's overturning of the Colfax convictions (a decision affirmed by the U.S. Supreme Court). When it came to slaying black and white Republicans, Democrats could get away with murder, and they knew it.[39]

A return to martial law, however, was the last thing the Republican Party contemplated. Congress had designed Reconstruction so as to *avoid* the necessity of employing troops to enforce law and order. It had assumed that the reconstructed states would be self-governing and self-sustaining. The rise of the Ku Klux Klan compelled Congress to pass the Enforcement Acts, but these laws were intended to create a secure political environment that would obviate the need for repeated federal interventions. This they had failed to do. Political instability persisted wherever a state government remained in Republican hands. Grant's continued use of the army to sustain Republican rule in the South became increasingly unpopular in the North. The Democrats' capture of the House of Representatives in the November 1874 elections convinced Republican elders that each federal intervention in the South further damaged the party's standing in the North.

Sheridan's so-called banditti telegrams provoked a political furor. The Democratic Party cried military tyranny, and some Republicans echoed it. "The policy he has proposed is so appalling," thundered Senator Carl Schurz, "that every American who loves his liberty stands aghast." Condemning Louisiana's carpetbaggers as "adventurers and bloodsuckers" who had made black voters "the tools of their rapacity," Schurz deplored Grant's use of force to keep such men in power. Better to allow the Democrats to take office, he argued, than to undermine the Constitution through repeated resort to military force: "I prefer the conservative government of Virginia to the Republican government of Louisiana." Asserting that Republicans as well as Democrats tried to intimidate voters, Schurz belittled the outcry over political murders as "convenient partisan stage-thunder." In the end, he argued, republics like the United States must simply put up with periodic disturbances, even violent ones. "The citizens . . . have to pay some price for the great boon of their liberty."[40]

Although most Republicans in Congress remained loyal to the administration (Schurz had been opposing Grant since 1870), the army's purge of the Louisiana legislature and Sheridan's bombastic statements regarding the White League made them inwardly cringe. "I am shocked and saddened beyond measure at the use of U.S. troops . . . in Louisiana," Ohio congressman James A. Garfield, a quintessential moderate, confided to his diary. "This is the darkest day for the Republican party I have ever seen since the war." Vice President Schuyler Colfax told Garfield that, in his estimation, "Grant is more unpopular than Andrew Johnson was."[41]

Initially sympathetic to Sheridan's call for a hard-line policy, Grant backtracked in the face of public opposition and dissent within his own cabinet. In a special message to the Senate on January 13, 1875, he refuted Schurz's suggestion that "southern outrages" were simply partisan propaganda. Politics in Louisiana, he noted, was still characterized by "lawlessness, turbulence, and bloodshed." Nevertheless, while convinced that "summary modes of procedure" would "soon put an end to troubles and disorders in that State," Grant acknowledged that Sheridan's proposal for military commissions could not be adopted. Instead, Grant asked Congress to suggest a solution. Kellogg, too, had proposed congressional intervention to bring about some kind of compromise that would end, at least in the short-term, Democratic attempts to forcibly seize power.[42]

Congress had failed to take action before and was reluctant to do anything now. In 1873 a Senate committee had thoroughly investigated the disputed election of 1872. Concluding that neither Kellogg nor McEnery could claim to have been honestly elected, it recommended that Congress provide for a fresh, federally supervised state election. A bill to that effect failed by two votes. In 1875 Congress considered the proposal once again, but another debate led to further inaction. Louisiana Republicans lobbied against the measure, fearing that a new election would "result disastrously" for the party.[43]

If leaving Kellogg in place appeared the least bad option, northern Republicans embraced it without enthusiasm. Congressional Republicans detested the White League, but they had little sympathy for their Louisiana clients. Backing the Louisiana party meant supporting "worthless reprobates," lamented a member of Grant's cabinet. It was a choice, complained James Garfield, of choosing between "a reckless and careless set of scamps . . . on the one hand, and the armed negro-hating band of murderers on the other." The Senate's refusal to seat P. B. S. Pinchback, elected by the Republican state legislature, reflected persistent doubts about the legitimacy of the Kellogg government. The most Congress would do was send a committee to New Orleans to investigate the latest disputed election.[44]

The White League had failed to hold on to power, but it had established its physical and psychological dominance over the Republican Party. "We have reestablished our claim to manhood," exulted a Democrat from Shreveport. "We have broken the back of the party spirit of the Robbers—they no longer boast and strut—they are greatly cowards." In a culture that placed great emphasis upon "manhood," the ignominious showing of the state forces on September 14 struck many northern Republicans as shameful. The White League had not merely defeated the state militia; it had destroyed it. After Kellogg abandoned the statehouse and hid in the Custom House, the men of the militia ignored his order to fight on. Instead, writes James Hogue, "they deserted individually and *en masse.*" Southern Republicans' repeated appeals for federal protection evoked irritation and disdain. As early as 1871, Attorney General Amos T. Akerman, although a resolute foe of the Ku Klux Klan, had urged them to fight their own battles and "fearlessly defy the bad men who are threatening them with injury."

> A spirited, yes, a desperate contest with bad men is, in my judgment, the most expedient course for the friends of the Government in the South. . . . If you take the position that the country is as much yours as theirs . . . and that you are determined to live in it, and enjoy all your rights; or to die in it, bravely asserting your rights, you will teach them that you have a strength of your own; and this, in the end, will mean more than the temporary exertion of the power of the U.S. Government.

By 1874 Kellogg's impotence struck many as pathetic. "It is contemptible to call every day for troops, almost for police duty too," complained H. N. Frisbie, a former Union officer who had bought a plantation in Rapides Parish. "Is liberty and republicanism so poor that none will fight for them?"[45]

Blacks' inability to mount any effective resistance to the White League engendered similar feelings of contempt. Why was it, northern whites asked, that in violent confrontations blacks always lost, even when they constituted the majority of the population? Southern Republicans repeatedly offered reasons. Blacks coveted firearms, M. A. Southworth told a committee of Congress, but few had the means to buy them, and even fewer acquired "what we would call a good gun." Moreover, between 1865 and 1867 whites had "very generally disarmed blacks," even former Union soldiers. When the Republican Party took over the state government in 1868 blacks again acquired guns, but whereas whites were equipping themselves with repeating rifles and revolvers, blacks could generally afford only shotguns and obsolete muzzle-loading pistols.[46]

Whites not only outgunned blacks; they also outmaneuvered and overawed them. P. B. S. Pinchback, testifying before the Republican National Convention, tried to explain the obvious:

> The whites, as a class, are wealthy and intelligent, armed with the most improved weapons, skilled in the use of them—as the North has had occasion to know—possessed of every avenue of communication and transportation—the telegraph wires, railroads, and steamboats, all being at their disposal—in a few hours they can concentrate a large armed force. On the other hand, the colored as a class are poor. Without experience, unarmed, no channels of communication or transportation open to them, naturally docile and peaceable, utterly without organization, they scatter at the first appearance of danger.

How could the country be surprised at blacks' refusal to fight back, asked Pinchback. "Under like circumstances what people would fight?"[47]

Yet the more blacks suffered from assassination, lynching, and "bulldozing," the more the charge of cowardice clung to them. A U.S. senator once asked John G. Lewis if he did not feel "a little ashamed" that blacks, despite being a large majority, "cannot stand up against a few bad and violent men." Lewis pointed out that it had taken the North four years to defeat the "brilliant, gallant Southerners" of the Confederacy. The whites not only had superior weaponry but also superior organization, which extended to Grant, Red River, Winn, Sabine, and De Soto Parishes. Moreover, whites were always the aggressors: choosing the time and place of their attacks, they enjoyed the advantage of surprise. If blacks responded with retaliatory violence, the entire back community suffered. The mere rumor of a black insurrection could trigger "frightful and bloody retribution." At Colfax, the blacks who mounted an armed self-defense were slaughtered. "It was suicidal for the negro to fight against the white man," Lewis told the senator.[48]

Such explanations, however, failed to stop a spreading cynicism among whites in the North, and southern Republicans knew it. Dismissed as partisan boilerplate—"waving the bloody shirt"—Republican complaints of Democratic atrocities evoked skepticism rather than sympathy. Even such a stalwart defender of Reconstruction as Oliver P. Morton concluded that the Republican Party had lost the battle for public opinion. "The painful truth is that the political murders in the South have ceased to be shocking, and are readily justified by energetic talk about carpet-baggers, scalawags and Radical thieves." The *New York Tribune*, which had long since turned against Republican rule in the South, advised Congress that the "rotten carcass in Louisiana is past saving. Throw it overboard."[49]

11

THE POLITICS OF MURDER

What would you think of the negro called out of his cabin at night by masked men, lassoed, dragged along the road till dead, and then hung to a tree? Another shot, but not killed, and then coal oil poured over him, and then burnt to death! For what? Nobody seems to know. Such things have been done in this parish recently.

David F. Boyd to fellow Democrat Charles Venable, August 8, 1876

Two widely read accounts of Louisiana's alleged suffering under Republican government reflected badly upon the Republicans of Natchitoches Parish. The anonymous author of "On Horseback through Louisiana," published in the *New York Times* in October 1874, cited the parish as an egregious example of misgovernment and corruption. With David Boullt Sr. playing the part of "Boss Tweed," Republican leaders had formed a "ring" that emptied the parish treasury, piled up the parish debt, and pocketed the taxes of property holders. The writer claimed that Raford Blunt could "neither read nor write," which would have been scandalous if true. (It was not true, but the assertion that Blunt was an illiterate schoolteacher has been recycled by historians for 120 years.) Six months later, Charles Nordhoff, a reporter for the *New York Herald*, described how whites in Natchitoches Parish had driven out "a corrupt judge and a thieving tax-collector." Republican misrule gave Natchitoches "an especially evil reputation" and made it "the most unruly [parish] in the State."[1]

The Louisiana situation "appears to be the mill-stone that threatens to sink our party out of sight," fretted Ohio congressman James Garfield. A report submitted on January 15, 1875, by the House Select Committee on the Condition of the South proposed to jettison that millstone. The three congressmen who took evidence in New Orleans, a subcommittee of the

Figure 11. James H. Cosgrove (1842–1914), editor of the *Natchitoches People's Vindicator*. Courtesy of Cammie G. Henry Research Center, Northwestern State University of Louisiana.

whole, portrayed the Louisiana Republicans as unworthy of support. Their
report dismissed the "wrongs to colored citizens for political offenses" as
unproven allegations. If any intimidation had occurred, the committee
concluded, it had been directed by *Republicans* against "blacks who sought
to act with the conservative party." The report placed the White League in
the best possible light. Justifiably, conservative whites "regard themselves as
defrauded out of the election of 1872, and yet more out of this last election,"
and considered the Kellogg administration as "to the last degree destructive
and corrupt." With Democrats on their best behavior, the report asserted,
the 1874 election had been "free, full, fair, and peaceable," rendering the actions of the Returning Board "arbitrary, unjust, and illegal."[2]

That two Republicans joined a lone Democrat in expressing such sympathy with violent opponents of the Republican Party was unprecedented.
Former Confederate colonel John S. Mosby, now a Republican, opined to

Grant that the midterm elections of 1874, which delivered the House of Representatives to the Democratic Party, offered an explanation:. "Many Republicans who have been frightened by the Democratic victories have... made use of Louisiana as 'a plank on a ship wreck' on which to cross over to the Democrats."[3]

Equally striking was the report's hostility to the two main constituencies of Louisiana's Republican Party: black voters and white officeholders. "Throughout the rural districts of the State the negroes . . . had come to filching and stealing fruit, vegetables, and poultry," the report asserted, and Republican officials had looked the other way. In many parishes, it added, the sum total of the white Republican vote consisted of Republican officeholders, who in some cases belonged to a single family. In Natchitoches Parish, it noted, "there are seven of the Boullts in office."[4]

These conclusions were so embarrassing to the Grant administration that George F. Hoar, the Massachusetts congressman who chaired the Select Committee, repaired to New Orleans to convene another set of hearings. Hoar and two other Republicans then issued a second report that laid out in detail the record of Democratic-inspired violence and intimidation. It alluded to, among other incidents, the "bulldozing" of Henry Myers and the attempt to silence Raford Blunt. The 1874 election had been "neither full, free, nor fair," their report concluded. The Democrats owed their victory to the fact that blacks "were prevented from voting at all or coerced into voting the white man's ticket." The three Republicans urged the Democratic Party to recognize the Kellogg administration.[5]

The second report may have done something to offset the first, but it suffered from the fact that only three of the seven committee members, and only three of the five Republicans, signed it. Moreover, it provided plenty of ammunition to conservative whites. Implicitly questioning the wisdom of black suffrage, it argued that slavery had failed to teach blacks "the virtues of frugality, of honesty, [and] of respect for justice" and that "these masses of illiterate voters" were the instruments of demagogic politicians. As for the Republican Party's record in government, the report had this to say: "There has been great maladministration; public funds have been wasted, public credit impaired, and taxation is heavy." Like the first one, the second report castigated the Returning Board for acting illegally. Some of the Republicans seated by the board, it argued, should be replaced by Democrats.[6]

Underlying the minority report, and informing a great deal of Republican reaction to the Louisiana imbroglio, was weariness with federal intervention and the belief that a state government had to rest upon consent. If half the population withheld that consent, no action taken in Washington could confer political legitimacy upon such a government. Hoar and his colleagues implied that right might have to yield to might:

> The remedy . . . lies out of the range of our powers. This great move-
> ment of the public mind in great States is not to be dealt with as if it
> were a street riot. You cannot change great currents of public senti-
> ment or the habits of thought and feeling of great bodies of men by
> act of Congress. In a republic, you cannot long or permanently check
> their manifestation by the exercise of national power.

The Republican Party was close to doing what many modern governments do when faced with irrepressible terrorist or guerrilla-type movements: sit down with the enemy and negotiate. Rejecting the mailed fist proffered by General Sheridan, it offered a kid-gloved hand. It appeased Democratic wrath by offering concessions.[7]

Desperate to shore up his authority, Kellogg asked the Select Committee on the Condition of the South to "propose a plan for the immediate and final settlement of our political difficulties." The Hoar Committee proved willing. Democrats who had been denied their seats by the Returning Board agreed to abide by the committee's verdict. Congressman William B. Wheeler of New York offered to act as an intermediary.[8]

Reassured by an invigorated army presence in the Red River valley, Ernest Breda, E. L. Pierson, and Raford Blunt returned to Natchitoches. But it was hardly a rapturous homecoming. Their testimony to the Hoar Committee had preceded them. The Republican witnesses had related hair-raising tales of threats and attempted assassinations; they depicted the local Democratic Party as an arm of the White League. Democrats had chosen the calm and conciliatory David Pierson to rebut their testimony. However, from his editorial chair in Natchitoches, James Cosgrove flayed the Republican wit-nesses as liars, crooks, ingrates, cowards, and traitors. Blunt, the "saddle-colored senator," was a "cowardly wretch" who had "begged like a dog" for his life to be spared. Myers and company had "turned against their own race, and taken most lovingly to the negroes." Cosgrove told his readers to "despise them because they are hypocrites; to shun them because they are thieves; [and] to hate them because they are traitors."[9]

Cosgrove concentrated his fire upon E. L. Pierson. Marshall Twitchell, the Republican boss of Red River Parish and a conspicuously brave man himself, considered Pierson "the boldest Republican leader in Natchitoches, and the only one they have not succeeded in driving out." But Cosgrove treated him as a rank opportunist, pointing out that Pierson's conversion to the Republican Party had been immediately rewarded with high office. Pierson's allegations against William M. Levy, his former law partner and now a Democratic member of Congress, compounded the offense. When Pierson and Levy dissolved their law partnership, the two parted on bitter terms. In his testimony before the Hoar Committee, Pierson made the sensational allegation that Levy had "offered money to persons to take my life." Cosgrove came out with all guns blazing:

> Does he not remember that to Colonel Levy he owes his miserable existence? . . . He is a liar, a thief, a forger, and a deserter. . . . In no capacity has he acted but that he has betrayed; an apostate to a thousand creeds and a Judas to them all; as a boy a pilferer and a story-teller; as a soldier a deserter and a forgerer; as a citizen a thief and unreliable; as a lawyer he embezzled monies collected for his clients; as a politician a cheat and a swindler; and as a witness before a Committee of Congress, a most unmitigated liar and slanderer.

In a humiliating climb-down, Pierson reappeared before the Hoar Committee and retracted his allegation against Levy.[10]

During the next few months, Cosgrove blew hot and cold, as Democrats fell to quarreling again over the merits of seeking an accommodation with the Republican Party, this time through the "Wheeler Compromise." Many rebelled at the thought of abandoning their efforts to unseat Kellogg. But as long as Grant backed him, the Republican governor was immovable. Moreover, a compromise brokered by Wheeler would seat some of the Democrats who claimed victory in 1874 at the expense of Republicans "counted in" by the Returning Board. The prospect of gaining by gift what they had failed to obtain by force proved too tempting to pass up.

Leading the pro-compromise Democrats was none other than Albert Leonard, fire-eating editor of the *Shreveport Times* and the most influential White League spokesman in northwestern Louisiana. Explaining his volte-face at a public meeting in Shreveport, Leonard reasoned that open resistance had failed and that any further resort to force would be "actual madness." A visit to Washington convinced him that Grant would never abandon Kellogg and that Congress would provide no relief in the form of a new election. Democrats therefore had everything to gain and nothing to lose by accepting Wheeler's terms, which proposed seating sixty-three Democrats and forty-seven Republicans in the lower house. Democratic senators in Washington urged the Louisiana party to accept the compromise, telling Leonard that the terms were the best that could be had. By April 17 both parties had ratified the Wheeler Compromise. Presenting the result as a personal triumph, Leonard hastened to add that he remained a "staunch, unrelenting Democrat." Privately, however, he saw his political future with the Republican Party.[11]

Cosgrove was stunned by Leonard's apostasy. But when party leaders agreed to back the compromise and tamp down political violence, he reluctantly fell into line. "We are now called upon to yield obedience to a government, however odious, we have not the means or power to subvert," he wrote through gritted teeth. "It is our duty to support the Kellogg government in all acts which we consider . . . to the benefit of our people.[12]

The Wheeler Compromise saved Kellogg's skin and enabled Republican officials to return to their posts. But it was a hollow victory. The White League had crippled the Republican Party. It had routed the state militia and humiliated the governor. Kellogg had then offered the Democrats representation on an electoral advisory committee. General Emory considered this unwise: "It may ease matters for the time, but it looks like a recognition of the legal rights of insurgent parties." The Wheeler Compromise represented a further concession. Northern Republicans "rid themselves temporarily of a political embarrassment" by giving the Democrats "nearly all they claimed," thought Shreveport Republican A. B. Levissee. It was "the beginning of the end of Republican domination in Louisiana."[13]

The compromise left untouched the underlying problem that threatened the destruction of Louisiana's Republican Party: the intimidation, beating, and killing of black voters. Ostensibly "under the protection of a great and benevolent government," blacks were more vulnerable than ever, Levissee told Attorney General Williams. From Shreveport to Natchitoches, whites were redoubling their effort to "terrorize the blacks and to annihilate all opposition." If federal laws were speedily and vigorously enforced, the situation might change for the better. But the nearest federal court was in New Orleans, Levissee pointed out, seven hundred miles and a week's journey away. Such distance defeated "every attempt to bring . . . violators to justice, and they will thus go unpunished."[14]

In dispatches to Washington, General Sheridan identified the scale of the problem. When his estimate of thirty-five hundred victims of political violence elicited Democratic guffaws, he compiled a parish-by-parish toll of dead and wounded, paying particular attention to the Red River valley. Major George A. Forsyth, sent to Shreveport to gather information, promised to "substantiate all you said about this part of the country and give names and places." At first, however, Forsyth ran into a wall of silence. "The blacks dare not say what they know," he reported. "They feared the vengeance of the whites and were painfully aware that the State and National government had failed to protect them." Forsyth recruited three informants, two black and one white, to gather information via "the old underground grapevine telegraph."

Henry Adams, a freedman, Union veteran, laborer, and "faith doctor," proved especially effective as an underground telegraph operator. Working as an army scout for fifty dollars a month, Adams spent March through June collecting evidence. "A very dangerous business," he recalled. "We daren't let nobody know what we was up to." He eventually submitted a list of 683 blacks who had been killed or wounded by whites, most of the violence taking place in Bossier, Caddo, Webster, Sabine, and De Soto Parishes. "When the evidence is finally given to the country," Forsyth predicted, "you will see such a burst of indignation as is rarely witnessed." However, although the Hoar Committee accepted Sheridan's revised figure of 2,141 political murders between 1866 and 1875, no gulf of national indignation followed. Rather, the tally of victims—list upon list upon list—provoked derision.[15]

Democrats had perfected a series of responses to the charge of violence which, if sometimes contradictory, were well rehearsed. The first was to concede Louisiana's penchant for personal violence but to deny that it was in any way politically or racially motivated. "I think our people are more liable to sudden freaks of passion," stated Bishop J. P. B. Wilmer of the Episcopal Church, but acts of violence "are not confined to one side or the other." The great majority of homicides, Nordhoff asserted, "were of blacks by blacks, instigated by whisky and jealousy." Illinois congressman Samuel S. Marshall dismissed Republican charges that political murders were commonplace as "atrocious slanders." According to the Louisiana correspondent of the *New York Times*, "the stories of negroes being shot down in the fields and in their huts on the plantations are absolutely false."

A second line of defense was to pin the blame for white-on-black violence upon idlers, gamblers, and other lowlifes—men frequenting brothels and barrooms who, according to the stereotype, descended from the despised class of slave traders and overseers. After committing their alcohol-fueled acts of random violence, these ruffians avoided arrest by leaving the state. "There has never been a time, before the war or now, when homicides could not be committed and men make their escape across the Texas line," explained a Caddo Parish Democrat. T. W. Abney, the leader of the White League in Red River Parish, disavowed any responsibility for the Coushatta killings by claiming that a party of unknown Texans had committed the crime.[16]

Democrats also invoked the necessity for lynch law. Lax administration of justice, they argued, had given free rein to black criminals. "In many parishes little or no stock is raised, no poultry, not even vegetables, so unsparing is the spirit of depredation," claimed Bishop Wilmer. Ten years of attacks upon their property had driven white planters to desperate measures. "It is the impossibility of obtaining justice . . . that has made the actions of the white men so bloody," agreed a sympathetic reporter. "If these men who steal cattle are brought to trial, they are at once acquitted by a stupid Judge, who can neither read nor write," and by jurors who were "mere blocks of ebony, knowing nothing [and] caring for nothing." Was it surprising that whites dealt with cattle thieves by dispensing summary justice? Whites also resorted to lynching in cases of sexual assault, and for this they made no apology. If "a colored man commits a rape upon a white women; and if that colored man is shot down by some friend of the woman," Shreveport lawyer John C. Moncure told the Hoar Committee, "it makes no serious impression upon anybody." The hanging of Hamp Henderson, accused of raping Coralie Lacour of Grant Parish, met with "the approbation of the civilized world," another Democrat told the committee.[17]

Rape also furnished a justification for the Colfax massacre and the "bulldozing" in Coushatta. Democrats depicted blacks as naturally placid and submissive, but dangerous when inflamed by demagogues. Robert A. Hunter of Rapides Parish told the Hoar Committee that "the Negroes were in arms, in large numbers, in Colfax; that the women and children were fleeing from the country; that the open threats of the Negroes were to kill the white men and violate the white women." According to Bishop Wilmer, blacks "openly proclaimed" their intention "to sack and burn the towns of Natchitoches, Alexandria and Pineville." Whites in Red River Parish had armed themselves to defend Coushatta after learning that the black population planned an attack on the town. Even "the most pusillanimous coward," proclaimed the *Coushatta Times*, would "defend the lives and chastity of our women" against "black demons, whose atrocity, when in power, knows no bounds." Congressman Marshall of the Hoar Committee endorsed this line of argument. "One successful rising . . . by the negroes would endanger the lives of the entire white people of the Red River region," he wrote. So great was the danger that whites were obliged to stamp hard on any sign of insurrection.[18]

Barefaced denial constituted another response. Quizzed by the Hoar Committee, Democratic witnesses professed ignorance of any political murders. "I don't know of a single one, sir," John Moncure told the incredulous chairman. Knowing the reputation of "Bloody Caddo" parish, Hoar pressed the witness about the shooting of Justice of the Peace Robert Gray and the murder of James Watson, the only person to cast a Grant ballot in 1868. Moncure disclaimed any memory of the first and denied that the second had ever happened. Watson, he told Hoar, was alive and well and living in Shreveport. When Hoar asked sarcastically if Watson were exhibited in a museum as a curiosity, Moncure shot back, "If we were to put all the curiosities of that sort in a museum it would have to be a very large affair, and it would be very well filled."[19]

Natchitoches Parish was the Democrats' prime exhibit in the debate over political murders. Over and over again, local Democrats insisted that no political murders had taken place within the parish. Statistics in hand, David Pierson told the Hoar Committee that of the forty-one homicides that had taken place since 1867, twenty-six were intra-racial, with the numbers evenly divided between black and white. Only three blacks had been killed by whites, and only four whites by blacks. Recycled by Nordhoff in *The Cotton States in the Spring and Summer of 1875*, Pierson's figures reinforced northern skepticism about Republican atrocity stories. "At least nine-tenths of these stories are without any just foundation," concluded Marshall.[20]

In the U.S. Senate, Democrats ridiculed Oliver P. Morton's claim that the Democratic Party of Louisiana aimed "to seize the State government . . . by murder, by terrorism." T. M. Norwood of Georgia satirized Morton's speech as "Bloody Shirt" propaganda:

The Senate has been entertained, not to say charmed, by the sheet-iron thunder which has constituted the staple production of the Senator from Indiana for the last six years. . . . He has rung the changes in a gamut of two notes, which are murder and fraud, with their appropriate variations, consisting of assassination, killing, butchery, manslaughter, and infanticide . . . I pray the Senator to vary the performance. . . . [E]ven the cry of murder, when the audience knows it is only it is only part of the play, loses its charm.

Many alleged "southern outrages," Democrats asserted, were deliberately provoked, or "got up," by the Republican Party in order to justify the deployment of troops at election time.[21]

While Senator L. Q. C. Lamar of Mississippi took the high ground of constitutional principle, calling the Thirteenth, Fourteenth, and Fifteenth Amendments "sacred and inviolable," John S. Hager of California appealed to white racial prejudice. Lauding "the noble godlike Caucasian of North America," the senator dismissed blacks as "unchanged and unimproved" and asked rhetorically, "Who ever heard of an African negro state that has emerged from barbarism and risen to any position among civilized nations?" In Haiti, Hager continued, blacks were characterized by "degeneracy and decay"; in Jamaica they were reverting to "primitive barbarism." Warning that miscegenation would drag down "the Caucasian Adam" to the debased level of the "ignoble hybrid Mexican," he invoked the growing hostility of white Californians toward the Chinese in their midst. If blacks could vote, he asked, why not enfranchise the Chinese, who were, after all, "superior as a race to the negro?" This was not, needless to say, an appeal for Chinese suffrage, which, if ever enacted, would hand political power to "Chinese coolies and prostitutes." Hager did not bother to dispute Sheridan's and Morton's statistics. "A thousand homicides, murders if you will, will not justify unlawful assaults upon the life of the nation." An extreme statement, but no different, apart from its lack of subtlety, from what Carl Schurz, a Republican, had already said in support of states' rights.[22]

Sheridan's call for tough action against the White League thus proved fruitless. Furthermore, the Democrats' acceptance of the Wheeler Compromise persuaded the new department commander, General Christopher C. Augur, that the number of troops in Louisiana could be safely reduced from about two thousand to less than one thousand. During the summer months—yellow fever season—Augur moved most of these soldiers out of the state.[23]

The political calm was deceptive. The Democrats' eschewal of political violence was a temporary expedient, not a principled commitment. Army officers in the Red River valley, acutely aware that they were surrounded by an armed and hostile white population, became increasingly reluctant to heed Republican requests for assistance. In Natchitoches, in October 1874, Lieutenant Donald McIntosh refused to depose Democrats who had taken over the sheriff's office, parish judgeship, and other positions. If he had tried to install Republicans, he explained, "I should now be swinging from a tree with a rope around my neck." Even the pugnacious Major Lewis Merrill worried that "my little force might prove a tempting morsel" for whites "to try and swallow." After the furious reaction to Sheridan's banditti telegrams and the failure of Congress to do anything other than endorse the Wheeler Compromise, local commanders had little stomach for galloping to the rescue of embattled Republicans. Increasingly passive, they invariably responded when it was too late—*after* Republican officials had been "bulldozed" and black voters murdered.[24]

Blacks in the Red River valley felt bereft. In 1872 the *Weekly Louisianan*, the organ of P. B. S. Pinchback, had condemned the efforts by the American Colonization Society (ACS) to promote black emigration to Liberia. Now that blacks had equal rights, the paper argued, the notion that blacks could only gain freedom by leaving the country no longer applied. The ACS was "pander[ing] to the prejudice of caste" when it contended that free blacks and whites could never live in peace. After the Colfax massacre and the White League uprising, however, blacks in northwestern Louisiana were at their wit's end. Emigration may have been a counsel of despair, but blacks were losing hope that Congressional Reconstruction would ever deliver what it promised.[25]

Pathetic petitions arrived at the White House. They beseeched Grant to help blacks leave Louisiana and settle in a territory set aside specifically for them. "It is impossible Mr. President for we colored people to live in the condition that we now stand in," stated a petition dated September 26, 1874. "We look to you and you alone. To give us aid in this cause." The petitioners, who declined to attach their names, explained that because local whites checked the mails they felt compelled to carry their letters many miles "before we can be shore that they will go through to the Post Office to you."[26]

In May 1875 a petition signed by almost two thousand blacks in Caddo Parish complained that the Wheeler Compromise had merely given the Democratic Party "more power to steal from us and to whip us, and to kill us, and to run us off our places, and take the colored people crops from them." The petitioners asked "to be colonized," understanding the word "colony" to mean a self-governing territory, a nation in effect. They pointed out that England, France, Spain, Prussia, Russia, Mexico, "and all other nations are colonized to themselves." Answering the objection that blacks, as slaves brought to America, could hardly found a country of their own, they cited the book of Exodus. "The children of Israel . . . were under bondage for 430 years. We was under bondage 474 years. [T]hey got the land where the milk and honey flows and we can get it too."[27]

Loosely coordinated and secretive, the colonization movement gained coherence through the growing network of black Baptist churches. By 1875 these little churches crisscrossed the Red River valley and had banded together in the Twelfth District Baptist Association, founded in 1870 and led by Raford Blunt. John G. Lewis, educated in Canada and far more literate than his fellow Baptists, served as the association's recording secretary. Blunt and Lewis became increasingly sympathetic to the colonization movement. During that 1874 campaign, Blunt told the Hoar Committee, he had called upon blacks to emigrate. "Said I, 'I have . . . no further use for this country. I am more in favor of colonization now than any man that ever lived. Nothing else will suit the colored people of this country now than to be separated from the white men.'" That appeal, he recalled, had evoked a chorus of approving shouts and applause.[28]

In July 1875 Blunt chaired a mass meeting in Natchitoches to discuss emigration. The meeting resolved that in the absence of government protection against the White League, "we, each one of us, do solemnly pledge to settle up our business the coming fall, and be ready to leave the Parish of Natchitoches by the 1st of January 1876." It is probable that these resolutions were more a negotiating tactic than a fixed intention to emigrate. Blunt had often proclaimed that planters would be ruined if blacks ceased to cultivate and harvest their crops. Nevertheless, pro-emigration sentiment was real and it was growing. The availability of land in Kansas and elsewhere made emigration much more attractive and realistic when it meant *migration* to a northern state rather than *emigration* to Liberia.[29]

More a cease-fire than a peace treaty, the Wheeler Compromise ended, for the time being, Democratic attempts to seize power by force. But for Republicans in Natchitoches Parish, the atmosphere remained menacing. Cosgrove's fulminations in the *People's Vindicator* may have been hot air, but they were unsettling. If Blunt attempted to parade black Republicans through Natchitoches, thundered the *Vindicator,* "someone will be hurt and we are pretty well satisfied it will be Senator Blunt." Cosgrove stopped short of explicitly calling for Blunt to be lynched, but his meaning was not hard to discern. "Blunt lives here on sufferance . . . [and] if he thinks he can go on his old way . . . he will certainly come in contact with the white people."

Within weeks, Cosgrove abandoned his support for compromise. Once again he advocated no reconciliation with the Republican Party—a "weak, puling, puking policy"—and condemned Democrats of the "moderate, cringing, cowardly class" who advocated breaking down the color line. Cosgrove called for "war to the knife" against Republicans. "We are for a clean white man's platform in 1876."[30]

Other whites, however, welcomed the political truce and hoped to profit thereby. As in the past, periods of détente encouraged party switching, and the Republicans continued to attract white recruits. In 1875, C. J. C. Puckette, former editor of the *Natchitoches Times*, accepted an appointment from Kellogg as tax collector for the parish. Assigning motive to party switchers is difficult and probably irrelevant. As Lawrence Powell has argued, economic and idealistic motives were inseparable. Grant's intervention in support of Kellogg undoubtedly caused some Democrats to recalculate the political odds and conclude that their best chance of obtaining office now lay with the Republican Party. Puckette had been elected to the state senate on the 1872 Fusion ticket but had been denied his seat by the Returning Board. Describing himself as a Liberal, he had refused to support the Democrats' "white line" strategy. "The true feature of this campaign should have been reform," he explained, "not social ostracism." He sided with Albert Leonard in backing the Wheeler Compromise and pressed Kellogg, successfully, to recognize Milton J. Cunningham's election as district attorney.[31]

Puckette scarcely had time to settle into his office before falling foul of James Cosgrove. As one of his first acts as tax collector, Puckette refused to accept parish warrants, or "scrip," that had been issued by the Democrat-controlled police jury. Democrats who had previously blasted Republican police juries for issuing "worthless, spurious and illegal warrants" now demanded interest on the warrants they held. "Loud profusions of patriotism are often employed to hide selfish motives," Puckette wrote, and he referred to Cosgrove by name. Cosgrove denounced Puckette, and shortly afterward the latter was "assaulted and beaten by a set of ultra-democrats." Puckette accused the editor of instigating the attack, while Cosgrove dismissed the incident as a personal rencontre that Republicans misrepresented as a Democratic "outrage." Cosgrove had a penchant for turning the political into the personal, and before the year was out another rencontre left a man dead.[32]

The decision of P. A. Simmons to join the Republicans was more of surprise than Puckette's. A planter and ex-Confederate soldier, and formerly a prominent Democrat, Simmons had presided over the "compromise" police jury of 1873, where he had used his position to sue David Boullt Sr. and make it "very unpleasant for the [Republican] combination." He had a violent reputation—in 1869 he had shot John C. Trichel, a white man, over a "purely personal difficulty." William H. Jack described Simmons as "the most violent, extreme, and unrestrainable man we had in the whole party." David Pierson recalled being castigated by Simmons for refusing to sanction violence against Republican leaders. According to Pierson, Simmons had Raford Blunt specifically in mind.[33]

Simmons deserted his party when the Democrats backed the incumbent mayor of Natchitoches, J. F. De Vargas, a Republican, in the city election of May 1875. The Tax Reform Association had left De Vargas in office because he had proved pliable. When he stood for reelection as the sole Republican on a "People's Ticket," the Democrats saw no advantage in replacing him. The disappointed Simmons then ran as an independent Democrat on an "Opposition Ticket" in which all the other candidates were Republicans, two of them blacks. Thus a Republican headed the Democratic ticket and a Democrat the Republican ticket: a classic example of how ambition and tactics trumped loyalty to party. After being soundly defeated in the election—whites made up most of the voters in town—Simmons transferred his allegiance to the Republicans. Governor Kellogg then appointed him mayor and appointed the other defeated candidates to the city council.[34]

Kellogg's action was a textbook example of what Powell has called the "defensive Machiavellianism" practiced by Louisiana Republicans. The Machiavellian tactic in this case was electoral gerrymandering. In April 1875, at the behest of E. L. Pierson, the state legislature amended the city charter of 1872, moving the election from odd years to even years. The act authorized the governor to replace the current elected council, as of May 1, with an appointed one. This appointed mayor and council would serve until the next election, in November 1876. The intention was plain: to oust a Democratic city council and install a Republican one.[35]

The De Vargas council, however, refused to yield office. Simmons then sued De Vargas, and the suit wound its way through the state courts, leaving Democrats in de facto control of the city council. In July, William Jack and David Pierson, representing De Vargas and the Democrats, filed for a change of venue, arguing that the defendants "do not expect to obtain a fair and impartial trial . . . in this parish." They wanted the trial to take place in majority-white Winn Parish instead of majority-black Natchitoches Parish. District judge C. C. Chaplin, although a Republican, granted the change of venue. The trial jury drawn by district judge H. B. Taliaferro, consisting of nine whites and three blacks, dismissed Simmons's suit, leaving De Vargas and the Democrats in office. Simmons appealed, and on the last day of 1875 the state supreme court ruled that he was entitled to the office of mayor. However, the court rejected the claims of the Republican councilmen on a technicality.[36]

Surrounded by a Democratic council, Simmons found himself powerless. The council refused to hand over official papers. When Simmons appointed J. B. Plaisance as city marshal, the current marshal, Leon Greneaux, who owed his position to De Vargas, ripped off his badge. Plaisance never put the badge on again. "The feeling was so hard against Simmons," he explained, "that I might get into a fight with someone." Simmons found that practically the only function that the city council allowed him to fulfill was arranging the burial of parish paupers. If he had tried to assert his authority, be believed, "I would have been killed."[37]

Democrats refused, as well, to surrender control of the police jury. They had narrowly won in November 1874, beating the Republican ticket by about 1,500 votes to 1,450. When the Returning Board declared a Republican majority and reversed this result, the Democratic police jury declined to step down. After Kellogg issued commissions to the Republican candidates, Natchitoches Parish had *two* police juries, one headed by William Payne, Democrat, the other by Joseph Ezernack, Republican. The Republican Party had taken care this time not to nominate any illiterates, selecting freeborn Carroll Jones as its only black candidate. The *People's Vindicator* was reduced to claiming Jones was illiterate and that Joseph Ezernack, a printer by trade, "is unable to read" and "can only write his name mechanically." The dispute provided yet more work for the town's lawyers, who, although nearly all Democrats, were quite willing to pocket fees from Republicans. As the case dragged its way through the courts, parish business ground to a halt. When the Payne police jury assigned blacks to road duty, for example, Ernest Breda persuaded the gang to quit. Only in October 1875, six months after Kellogg appointed the Ezernack police jury, did the Democrats give way.[38]

To the endless frustration of James Cosgrove, the word "reform" cropped up with maddening frequency. Governor Kellogg adopted a policy of reducing public expenditure and scaling down the state debt. Party switchers like Puckette and E. L. Pierson explained that they had joined the Republicans in order to eliminate corruption. The Wheeler Compromise itself had called for a special session of the legislature for the purpose of enacting "reform" measures. Albert Leonard, the strongest advocate of the compromise, proposed to combine the "Whig, Conservative and Liberal elements" of the white vote, which now sided reluctantly with the Democrats, into a new political party committed to reform.[39]

In taking up the cause of "reform," however, Republicans gained a handful of Democratic defectors without any significant accession of white voters. By the end of 1875 the Democratic Party had turned against the Wheeler Compromise, and in February 1876 the lower house impeached Kellogg, ending the spirit of compromise once and for all. Although the impeachment vote was futile—Republicans still controlled the state senate—it dispelled the illusion that "reform" might provide the basis for continuing cooperation.

By repeating the mantra of "reform," moreover, Republicans conceded the validity of Democratic criticisms. In Natchitoches Parish, Puckette told the Hoar Committee, "they have had a very bad government." He pointed to exorbitant taxation and the way members of the Boullt family held many of the offices. Assistant Attorney General Henry C. Dibble judged taxation in Natchitoches Parish to be "out of all reasonable bounds" and in actual violation of state law. E. L. Pierson charged that Henry Myers had made off with $10,000 of the parish's public school fund. Republican professions of "reform," however, were unconvincing. Too many of those decrying high taxes and corruption were implicated in the very abuses they now proposed to tackle. Late party switchers like Pierson and Puckette could be dismissed as office-hungry opportunists.[40]

Nevertheless, Cosgrove recognized that "reform" rhetoric threatened his beloved "white line" strategy. Proposals for a "reform party," renewed talk of attracting black votes, and high-profile defections from the Democratic ranks all threatened the white unity he believed essential if the Republicans were to be ousted. "It is useless to imagine that success is in breaking up the 'color line,'" he wrote. "This 'harmonious union' is but the dream of the visionary or the hope of the spoil-hunter." With unfailing regularity, the *Vindicator* abused, threatened, and denounced white Republicans and wavering Democrats.[41]

Whites who felt the sting of Cosgrove's insults had to be careful how they responded. If offended Republicans stood upon their honor every time Cosgrove insulted them, they would soon find themselves in a "personal difficulty" with all that that implied. "Scalawags" like Breda learned to put up with Cosgrove's invective lest they be goaded into brawling or dueling. Survival demanded a thick skin, a level head, and the wisdom to back down.[42]

E. L. Pierson was an impetuous, combative man who alarmed senior figures in both parties by his readiness to pursue a quarrel rather than walk away. Barely two weeks after taking his seat in the state legislature, he got into a shouting match with the chairman. When the latter ordered him to sit down, Pierson bristled: "I would like to see you try it. I will give you a chance after we get out." In Natchitoches, some Democrats worried that Pierson's caustic articles in the *Republican* and the sarcastic replies of William Jack in the *Vindicator* might escalate into a violent quarrel. They appealed to Pierson and Jack to stop writing "cutting and satirical articles" about each other. Invited to step back without loss of face, both men seized the opportunity. "I had no intention of wounding the feelings or impugning the motives of Mr. Jack," wrote Pierson. Jack affirmed his willingness "to resume the friendly feelings that have hitherto existed between us."[43]

Cosgrove was another matter. If the *Republican* published any more "allusions which we consider personal," he vowed, the writer would be "dealt with." His failure to mention Pierson by name softened the threat. Nevertheless, other Republican leaders, wary of being drawn into the controversy, made it clear that Pierson's quarrels were his own, not theirs. "If he offered insult, I am not responsible for it," Ernest Breda assured Cosgrove. "I have nothing in common with him and know nothing of his affairs."[44]

In November 1875, having resumed the editorship of the *Republican*, Pierson entered into a war of words with Cosgrove. The loss of the *Republican*'s files means that only Cosgrove's ripostes survive. Cosgrove appeared to relish the confrontation, and he ratcheted it up. Branding Pierson a liar and a coward, he claimed possession of damaging facts with which he could destroy Pierson's reputation. "Does he desire the opinion of fifty leading merchants and planters, of him, published?" Friends implored Pierson to walk away from the quarrel. Instead, he published a "card" denouncing Cosgrove and demanding the right of "satisfaction."[45]

Cosgrove guaranteed a violent denouement when he devoted the December 4 edition of the *Vindicator* to an assault upon Pierson's character. According to Cosgrove, Pierson had twice deserted when serving as a Confederate soldier in the Second Louisiana Infantry. Caught both times, he had been tried by two courts-martial and sentenced to death on each occasion. Only the intercession of Jefferson Davis had saved him from the first firing squad. He evaded the second by escaping.

On the same page, the *Vindicator* published the "card" that Cosgrove had held back. Signed by forty-one individuals and several law firms, the statement condemned Pierson as unworthy of "the confidence and respect of any decent man in the community."

Adding insult to injury, Cosgrove brushed aside Pierson's challenge to a duel. Referring to an incident recounted by Blunt before the Hoar Committee, Cosgrove recalled that Pierson had "had his jaws publicly slapped on the public streets of Alexandria" and had suffered the insult "without resenting it." Cosgrove would accept no challenge from Pierson "until he wipes out this disgrace." Only "gentlemen," he explained, had the right to demand satisfaction, and Pierson did not qualify. Pierson vowed to shoot Cosgrove on sight.[46]

On Christmas morning, on an errand to buy children's toys, the two editors came across each other in front of Weinberg's store. Cosgrove removed his hat and slapped Pierson's face with it, "saying he had a difficulty to settle with him." When Pierson drew his gun, Cosgrove revealed that he was unarmed. "Then go and arm yourself," Pierson replied. Cosgrove went into the store and borrowed a pistol. Pierson shot at him three times without effect, and when his gun misfired he rushed out of the store, Cosgrove in pursuit, firing as he ran. As the chase unfolded, several onlookers joined in, firing at either Pierson or Cosgrove. Pierson fell when a bullet pierced one of his lungs. A black woman carried him home, and he died within the hour. Cosgrove was arrested but never prosecuted. The multi-party shootout made it impossible to establish whether Cosgrove had inflicted the fatal wound. If the case had gone to trial, any jury would have returned a verdict of "justifiable homicide."[47]

The Democratic press attributed Pierson's death to a personal quarrel between two newspaper editors, a common enough occurrence in the South. As John Hope Franklin long ago pointed out, southern editors made a habit of fighting and occasionally killing each other. Sometimes they dueled, but "if the offense were grave enough and the aggravated person impulsive enough, the latter might well storm into the editor's office or meet him on the streets and start shooting." Moreover, white men in Louisiana understood that if a challenge were spurned with further insults, the punctilious code duello could be dispensed with. "If any man insults me," explained one Louisianan, "I will call that man out, and if he refuses to come out, I will shoot him on sight."[48]

Although Democrats insisted that Pierson's death carried no political significance, this did not stop them from dancing on his grave. Pierson had served the Confederacy, explained the *New Orleans Democrat*, but his affiliation with the Republican Party had brought upon his head the odium of the "more respectable people." His end was to be regretted, the newspaper conceded, but Louisiana was none the worse for it. The *Shreveport Times*, as always, did not mince words: "Pierson had no friends here and his death is looked upon as a blessing to the community."[49]

In Natchitoches Parish itself, Pierson's death saddened friend and foe alike. Two of his political adversaries, David Pierson and Milton Cunningham, acted as pallbearers. "He was followed to his tomb by old and young, rich and poor, white and colored," reported the *New Orleans Republican*.[50]

When questioned by a congressional committee, Philippe Breda, the Republican coroner of Natchitoches Parish, rejected the contention that the Pierson-Cosgrove feud was personal rather than political. "It is very difficult to draw the line between what is politics and what is not politics in the killing," he told a congressman. Obviously, he acknowledged, the conflict had a personal element, but "the reason for it" had been politics. "I believe Pierson was killed in a difficulty which originated in politics." Cosgrove, he added, had instigated the quarrel. But Republicans had to let the matter drop. This was not good "Bloody Shirt material." The fact that Pierson had fired first made it impossible to present the affair as a political assassination.[51]

Pierson's death reinforced a siege mentality among the white Republicans of Natchitoches. Ernest Breda placed an order with a New Orleans gun shop for two Winchester rifles and six boxes of ammunition. Anyone who attacked the Breda family home would face five men, each armed with a small pistol, a large pistol, and a repeating rifle. The Breda brothers, Ernest and Philippe, never traveled unarmed. In 1876 Marie Cora Breda and Mathilde Coralie Breda, the younger sisters of Ernest and Philippe, married northern-born soldiers stationed at the Natchitoches army post. Their choice of marriage partner underlined the Breda family's isolation from the white community.[52]

After being locked up for two months, James Cosgrove emerged from jail unrepentant and hopping mad. "I have made enemies, bitter and personal," he declared, "but they are of a class I am proud to construe as such, and for them I leave my lasting, undying contempt." Indeed, his slaying of Pierson seemed only to increase Cosgrove's belligerence. He threatened the *Republican*'s new editor, William Tunnard, with "a lesson he will not be apt to forget . . . if he even hints at untruths concerning us." He promised to fight Ernest Breda, whom he declared a "scoundrel and a blackguard," at a moment's notice. "When he desires a display of his vaunted courage, he can find the time, place, and the opponent at any season."[53]

The army still maintained a company-strength post at Natchitoches. Its presence reassured Republican officeholders, and as long as the soldiers stayed, Cosgrove's threats in the *People's Vindicator* were so much hot air— as long as Republicans ignored them and declined to enter into any "personal difficulty." Still, both the soldiers and the threats begged the question of when, if ever, Republicans would *not* need military protection. The Democratic Party in Natchitoches Parish repressed political violence. But it demonstrated in 1874 that it could, at a moment's notice, force Republican officials to resign. Without the soldiers, Republicans could not hold office. When the soldiers departed, they could again be "bulldozed." As one Democrat, a lawyer, told a Republican, "Don't you know that those bayonets will soon be withdrawn, and that the white people of Louisiana will clean the State of the last radical office-holder?"[54]

The army's presence was thin, fewer than a thousand soldiers at the start of 1876. Throughout much of northern Louisiana, and in some southern parishes as well, the black population remained as vulnerable as ever to "bulldozers" and "regulators." In October 1875 four Republican officials fled East Feliciana Parish after whites accused them of planning an armed insurrection. One of them, John Gair, was murdered while in the custody of a sheriff's posse that had arrested him in Baton Rouge. As soon as the returning posse crossed the parish line, a party of sixty white men overpowered the guards, tied Gair to a tree, and shot him to ribbons. Gair's sister-in-law, Babe Matthews, was hanged that night from a tree outside the courthouse at Clinton, the parish seat, allegedly for poisoning her white employer at Gair's instigation. Another refugee, Sheriff Henry Smith, returned to the parish only to be shot inside the courthouse while a trial was under way. In West Feliciana Parish, Democrats demanded the resignations of the sheriff, the parish judge, the tax collector, the state senator, and four black members of the police jury. Under the pretext of exposing yet another plot to murder white people, a party of "regulators" apprehended black Republican Gilbert Carter and shot him dead.[55]

White Republicans also suffered. In May 1876 an assassin killed George King, the tax collector of Red River Parish, and caused his companion, state senator Marshall Twitchell, to lose two bullet-shattered arms. Units of the Seventh Cavalry had recently left for Dakota Territory, and without them infantry found the pursuit and capture of mounted terrorists impossible. The Republican sheriff organized a posse but declined to lead it himself. The *Louisiana Democrat* called it a "personal affair, of no political significance." A congressional subcommittee consisting of two senators agreed. Twitchell was not a victim of politically motivated violence, they concluded, because the parish had been quiet for two years, there was no intimidation, and "no one was in danger for his political views." Twitchell brought his fate upon his own head, they implied, through his "mismanagement" of parish affairs, including "gross frauds" in building contracts and "malpractices" in the public schools. Answering the senators' questions from his sick bed, Twitchell wondered if *he* were on trial for not having died. The fact that a Republican senator cosigned the report provided further evidence that northern sympathy for southern "carpetbaggers" had evaporated.[56]

The army's failure to suppress political violence reflected inadequate numbers and lack of mounted troops. But it also indicated reluctance on the part of officers with Democratic sympathies. In the Felicianas, for example, white "regulators" flogged and lynched blacks suspected of stealing seed cotton and livestock, and burned the stores of merchants suspected of trading in stolen produce. These bands also broke up interracial marriages by threatening the white men and whipping the black women. Blacks deemed to be dangerous were pursued and killed. "There seems to have been no disposition on the part of the whites to place the investigation of such matters in the hands of proper authorities, even when all possibility of bloodshed might have been avoided by doing so," an army officer reported. The local commander, Captain G. M. Bascom, made no effort to curb this vigilantism; instead, he condoned and even assisted it.[57]

Democrats in Louisiana smelled blood. The furor over the army's intervention in January 1875, exacerbated by Sheridan's banditti telegrams, weakened Grant's resolve to continue propping up ailing Republican governments in the South. Edwards Pierrepont, the newly appointed attorney general, was even more reluctant to further intervene. When Governor Adelbert Ames of Mississippi, in the run-up to the 1875 state election, requested federal assistance to help counter Democratic violence, Pierrepont replied that he ought to do more for himself before asking for U.S. soldiers. Suggesting that southern Republicans lacked backbone, he unhelpfully suggested that they should "Let the country see that the citizens of Mississippi . . . have the courage and manhood to fight for their rights." Grant appeared resigned to the loss of Louisiana in 1876. Referring to southern Republicans as "dead weight," he declared that they would "have to take care of themselves." He would do all within his power to make the presidential vote as free and as fair as possible. As soon as the voting was over, however, he intended to stop using troops to police southern elections.[58]

12

THE ELECTION OF 1876

Inertia of conscience in Louisiana politicians is a fact to be taken with us
whenever we are dealing with their political actions.

Congressman Ben F. Butler, *Investigation of Alleged Electoral Frauds*, 1879

In 1876 the question was not whether the Democratic Party would oust the
last three Republican state governments in the South, but when and how.
Eight years of Congressional Reconstruction had revealed not so much the
weakness of the federal government but the weakness of the political will
to maintain black suffrage.

Washington was perfectly capable of acting forcefully when it so desired.
The military was in the process of conquering the western Indian tribes, a
struggle whose outcome (despite the embarrassment of Little Big Horn)
was not in doubt. In 1877 President Rutherford B. Hayes employed troops
to help defeat the great railroad strike. But when it came to using soldiers to
prop up "carpetbag" governments, the president and the Congress had had
enough. Grant's own exasperation was evident when he openly complained
that "the whole public are tired out by these annual autumnal outbreaks in
the South, and there is so much unwholesome lying done by the press and
the people in regard to the causes and extent of these breaches of the peace,
that the great majority now are ready to condemn any interference on the
part of the government."[1]

Beyond the matter of political will lay the question of efficacy. Federal
power could subdue Indians and break strikes, but it could not police the
entire South, or even those parts of it most disturbed by Democratic terrorism. How could a government suppress terrorists if the terrorists commanded the sympathy of the population whence they sprang? It could not
disarm or coerce millions of white southerners. A policy of repression, had
it been adopted, might have turned the South into the kind of "bleeding

ulcer" that defeated the French in Spain, or produced the kind of "dirty war" that colonial powers waged. "To win that sort of war you must be ruthless," noted a British general during the Irish Troubles. "Oliver Cromwell, or the Germans, would have settled it in a very short time. Nowadays, public opinion precludes such methods; the nation would never allow it, and the politicians would lose their jobs if they sanctioned it." Even if troops had been used in a relatively benign way, as in 1865–68, policing the ex-Confederacy would have required at least one soldier for every fifty inhabitants—180,000 instead of the 3,327 that remained there in 1875.[2]

If using the army to maintain peace was both politically and practically unworkable, prosecuting perpetrators of violence had become almost impossible. After the Supreme Court's *Cruikshank* decision, handed down on March 25, 1876, the federal government maintained that it could neither protect Republicans from threatened violence nor punish their assassins. As Secretary of War Alphonso Taft explained to one anxious Republican, "Murder . . . is a crime against the peace and dignity of the State within whose boundaries it is committed . . . and it is within the cognizance and jurisdiction of the State alone to punish it." Should the state authorities fail in their duty, Taft added, a man could always resort to self-defense. Beyond that, he unhelpfully suggested, "I see no other way to escape except by emigration."[3]

Confident that victory was within sight, senior Democrats urged their party to proceed cautiously. The failure of the White League revolt demonstrated that President Grant was unpredictable and stubborn. Military intervention in the event of a Democratic power grab, especially if violent, was by no means out of the question. Hence the Democratic Party in Louisiana, as Michael Perman notes, "was preoccupied not with the problem of how to arouse its white constituents, but rather with how best to restrain them."[4]

Democrats also considered whether to make any effort to attract black voters. "Bitter-enders" like James Cosgrove considered any further quest for black support futile. Others, however, especially in southern Louisiana's sugar parishes, believed it folly to write off the black vote and hand it to the Republican Party on a plate. Bad economic times, blacks' dissatisfaction with their share of party patronage, and never-ending allegations of official malfeasance convinced them that the Republican Party's electoral base was vulnerable. In many parishes, Democrats needed only a fraction of the black vote to secure victory. Statewide, too, the races were so evenly

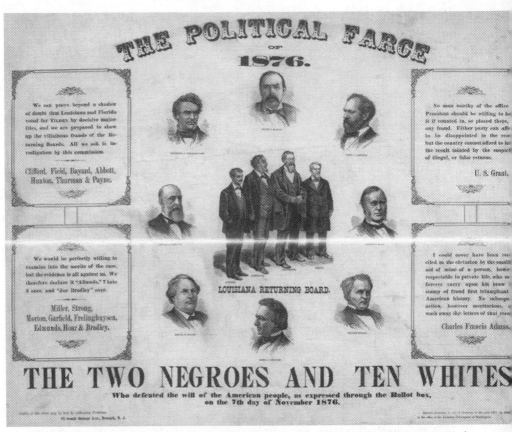

Figure 12. Democrats won the 1876 election through violence and intimidation. Republicans countered by having the Returning Board adjust the results. Library of Congress Pictures and Photographs Division.

balanced that a relatively small shift in the black vote might elect a Democratic governor and give Louisiana's electoral vote to Samuel Tilden, the Democratic presidential candidate.

The Democratic platform of 1876, therefore, was a far cry from the White League–inspired platform of 1874. Instead of placing race first and foremost, it declared "administrative and political reform to be the paramount issue." Instead of calling for white unity, it appealed to "fellow citizens of every former political affiliation, white and colored." The party pledged itself to a "fair and peaceable election" and decried any attempt to intimidate black voters who wished to quit the Republican Party. The platform reassured blacks and northern Republicans that they considered the Civil War amendments to be binding and final. It pledged to protect "every citizen" in the exercise of his constitutional rights, "whatever be his race, color, or previous condition."

The selection of Francis T. Nicholls as the gubernatorial candidate underlined this message of moderation and racial harmony. A West Point graduate, former U.S. Army officer, and Confederate brigadier general who had lost an arm and a leg in the war, Nicholls lived in Ascension Parish, where he practiced law. The fact that he hailed from a southern Louisiana sugar parish, where relations between blacks and whites were usually less tense and violent than in the northern Louisiana cotton parishes, made him appear far less threatening to blacks than had John McEnery, the Democratic candidate in 1872. Accepting the nomination, Nicholls, who had held no political office before and was not identified with any Democratic faction, went out of his way to portray himself as a friend to blacks. "I will unflinchingly protect them in all their rights," he promised.[5]

In circulars to party workers, state campaign chairman Isaac W. Patton admonished Democrats to scrupulously refrain from any acts of intimidation and violence. "We knew that under the law any pretext would be sought for the purpose of throwing out polls in the parishes by the returning officers," he explained, "and we knew that every instance of violence would be readily seized upon for the purpose of excluding votes." Democratic leaders sometimes physically restrained white hecklers who became too belligerent at Republican meetings. Patton instructed Democratic campaign workers to gather affidavits from black voters swearing that they had voted the Democrat of their own free will. He also told them to secure official letters, signed by the parish clerk of court, confirming that the poll had been free and fair.[6]

Intimidation and violence nonetheless remained integral to the Democratic strategy. "You cannot convince a negro's reason," Patton told party workers, "but you can impress him by positive statements continually made." Speakers should tell blacks that a Democratic victory was a foregone conclusion, "as we have the means of carrying the election and intend to use them." Democrats should form ward clubs, whose members should assemble on horseback in order to "impress the negroes with a sense of your united strength." Patton instructed Democrats to attend all Republican mass meetings. Read between the lines, this seemingly innocuous campaign circular constituted an invitation to overawe blacks. Whether following Patton's advice or acting upon their own initiative, Democrats organized mounted patrols that called themselves "rifle clubs" or "home guards." Democrats on horseback, weapons prominently displayed, showed up at Republican rallies, interrupting and insulting the speakers.[7]

Democrats targeted five black-majority parishes for White League tactics. By 1875 the Democratic Party had learned to use violence and intimidation *before* polling day, ensuring that nothing untoward happened on election day itself. In Ouchita Parish "rifle clubs" killed several black Republicans and broke up Republican meetings. On August 30 an assassin shot and killed Dr. B. F. Dinkgrave, a white Republican, in broad daylight. Two days later the Republican sheriff fled the parish. Democrats claimed that Dinkgrave was the victim of a personal vendetta that had nothing to do with politics. This was now the standard Democratic response to the murder of Republican leaders. It had the great advantage of being impossible to disprove: when the murderers got away, as they invariably did, motive could never be positively established.[8]

In the Felicianas and other "bulldozed" parishes, hundreds of blacks, thousands even, joined Democratic clubs out of fear. Those who refused to join voluntarily, admitted one Democrat, "had to be worked on." In West Feliciana Parish blacks were so intimidated that Republican leaders decided to sit out the election, declining to nominate any candidates.

Democrats who engaged in bulldozing had the tacit approval of the state party. The bulldozers of Ouchita and the Felicianas were not young tearaways who refused to toe the party line. They were doctors, lawyers, and planters, including former governor Robert C. Wickliffe: men who comprised the Democratic leadership in their parishes and were intimately involved in the state campaign. Although Nicholls repeatedly denounced violence and intimidation, the state party sanctioned selective bulldozing because it had nothing to lose. If Democrats carried these black-majority parishes with the aid of coerced black votes, they aided the state ticket. If the Returning Board rejected those parishes on the grounds of intimidation, it would have to exclude more potential black votes than actual white ones. Either way, the Democratic Party gained.[9]

In Natchitoches Parish the Democrats relied almost entirely upon persuasion. Through gritted teeth, James Cosgrove endorsed the "peace policy" agreed upon by the state party: downplay white supremacy, abjure violence, and reassure blacks that they could safely vote Democrat. "We do not desire to murder or maltreat any colored man," asserted the *People's Vindicator*, "but will, on the contrary, protect them from violence." Disclaiming any nostalgia for slavery, the paper proclaimed that "the battle for the equality of man on the broad principles of the Declaration of Independence has ended in victory."[10]

The Democratic state campaign committee recruited a team of speakers, including several ex-Republicans, to appeal to black voters. Its prize catches were three former officeholders from Grant Parish: William B. Phillips, William Ward, and Eli H. Flowers. Phillips, a native of Alabama and a Confederate veteran, had joined the Republican Party in 1867 and served briefly as parish judge. In 1871 he had witnessed his friend and fellow Republican, Delos W. White, shot dead and his body consumed in the flames of his house. An opposing Republican faction deposed him and then indicted him for murder. Phillips fled to New Orleans.[11]

William Ward, the second Democratic convert, was a black Union veteran who had been commissioned by General James Longstreet to organize a Grant Parish unit of the state militia. So aggressive was his leadership, and so ill-disciplined his men, that Longstreet disbanded the unit and had Ward arrested and dismissed. But Ward continued to operate the unit as a kind of unofficial posse. In 1874, while in the Grant Parish courthouse, he engaged in a shoot-out with a white Republican named Charles Morse, suffering three bullet wounds. The following year he got himself expelled from the state legislature when, in the chamber of the lower house, he waved a pistol while intoxicated. Nevertheless, to many blacks Ward remained an inspiring leader.[12]

The third newly minted Democrat, Eli Flowers, was doggedly loyal to Ward and rarely left his side. A native of Pennsylvania and also a Union veteran, Flowers had taught public schools in several parishes, but in 1876 he was stranded in New Orleans. Without employment, the three refugees from Grant Parish agreed to campaign for the Democratic Party in return for two hundred dollars a month plus expenses. Joining them in Natchitoches was a fourth speaker, Jerry Hall, a freeborn mulatto who had sat in the constitutional convention and served a single term in the state legislature. In 1876 he was keeping a saloon in New Orleans. Hall spent the better part of a month in Natchitoches. He had lived there once and "was acquainted with the people up there."[13]

Democratic speakers appealed to blacks' economic interests by telling them they were worse off in 1876 than four years earlier. They depicted the Natchitoches "scalawags" as cruel slaveholders and rabid Klansmen who had embraced the Republican Party to gain "fat offices, fine homes, and plenty of money." Although the issue of corruption rarely stirred black audiences, Democrats shrewdly emphasized the theft of school funds in various parishes and linked such thefts with the inadequacy of the public schools. Republican leaders promised blacks the earth but gave them crumbs. "You and your children may starve, you may go in rags, they would not loan you a dollar, and you know it." The collapse of the Freedmen's Savings Bank and the closure of its branches in New Orleans and Shreveport gave the Democrats more ammunition. As historian Joe Gray Taylor put it, "some $300,000 in savings belonging to Louisiana blacks vanished into thin air."[14]

Above all, Democratic speakers appealed to blacks' yearning for peace and quiet, pointing out "the utter incapacity of the Republican party to protect our people." Should Nicholls carry the state, blacks in Louisiana would enjoy peace and security. Elect Democrats, they promised, and bulldozing, political violence, and vigilantism would end. It was ironic, to say the least, that Democrats blamed Republicans for failing to curb the violence of Democrats. However, the fact that violent men consistently evaded punishment enabled Democratic speakers to plausibly claim that the Republican Party was more interested in making political capital from outrages—cynically "waving the bloody shirt"—than in ending them.[15]

Local Democrats tried to exert personal influence on their sharecroppers, tenants, laborers, clients, and domestic servants. In the tradition of slaveholder paternalism, they depicted themselves as the true friends and protectors of black people. "Was it not the white Democrat who gave him food, who nursed him in ill-health, to whom he comes when in want of bread or clothing?" Democrats, not Republicans, gave blacks employment, medical care, and legal assistance. "When they had domestic troubles or were in distress they invariably applied to their old masters, to the Democrats." Such arguments had failed to sway blacks in the past. This time, Democrats hoped, black voters would pay more attention if the message were repeated by Phillips, Ward, Flowers, and Hall. Planters invited speakers onto their plantations. By election day about five hundred blacks had enrolled in Democratic clubs—enough voters, if they stayed true to their word, to carry Natchitoches Parish for the Democratic Party. "Let every white man pledge himself to vote a colored man," urged the *Vindicator*.[16]

Given the raucous scenes that attended its state convention, which opened in New Orleans on July 28 and lasted a week, the Republican Party entered the campaign in reasonably good shape. Despite "shouting, fisticuffs, and one shooting," the convention smoothed over factional rivalries and agreed upon a ticket headed by Stephen B. Packard, the chief U.S. marshal and head of the Custom House faction. In rejecting Warmoth's bid for the gubernatorial nomination and selecting Packard, the quintessential machine politician, the party obviously considered it pointless to appeal to white voters. Maximizing black registration and turnout was the overwhelming priority. The party instructed supervisors of registration, all of them appointed by Governor Kellogg, to "register and vote the full strength of the Republican party in your parish." Supervisors were expected to equal the registration of 1874. If they could achieve that, and also ensure a 95 percent turnout among black voters, they would receive "ample and generous recognition" from the "next State administration."[17]

Much was riding on the contest in Natchitoches Parish, which boasted the strongest Republican organization in the Red River valley. On July 26 the local party formed a campaign committee that elected state legislator Henry R. Raby president and *Natchitoches Republican* editor William H. Tunnard secretary. Subcommittees, each consisting of two whites and a black, organized Republican clubs in the respective wards. These arrangements recognized the primacy of black support while at the same time ensuring that whites played a dominant leadership role. It could hardly be otherwise: of the one hundred or so members listed by the committee, about four-fifths could not sign their names. In September the *Vindicator* charged that Henry Myers was opening public schools "all over the parish" in order to boost the Republican campaign. Given that schoolteachers were also active Republicans, having the schools in session certainly did not hurt. Republican clubs signed up more than a thousand members. After a visit to the campaign headquarters in New Orleans, Raby reported that "this parish headed the list for favors."[18]

Brigadier General Francis T. Nicholls, C.S.A., fought "to keep you in slavery," John G. Lewis reminded a Republican mass meeting at Carroll Jones's place in Ward 11. "Can you vote for him?" Eliciting a chorus of "No! No!," Lewis, a native of Canada but now a U.S. citizen and candidate for the state legislature, worked the crowd. "Say it louder so that they can hear you in Natchitoches." "No! No!" With the audience warmed up, Raford Blunt took the platform. If the Democrats came to power, he warned, blacks would lose their right to vote and their right to sit on juries. Their churches and schools would be closed. Blacks must stay loyal to the Republican Party. "If any colored man join the Democratic party, leave him alone. If he asks you for a piece of bread, give it to him, but leave him alone."[19]

The Republican candidate for governor experienced some nasty moments before reaching Natchitoches. Packard's canvass took him through bulldozed parishes, where he and other Republican speakers were insulted and threatened. In Clinton, East Feliciana Parish, hundreds of Democrats attended the Republican rally and repeatedly interrupted the speakers. "A man drew a revolver and said I was a damned liar," recalled J. P. Harris. Packard struggled to make himself heard about the din. When it was Jack Wharton's turn, a heckler called him "a damn dirty joker" and told him to shut up. The only black speaker, James Lewis, was threatened by Dr. James W. Sanders, who took exception to Lewis's discussion of miscegenation. Referring to his own light complexion—he was the son of a white planter and a slave woman—Lewis pointed out that whites, not blacks, had fathered a race of mulattoes. Blacks had no wish to intrude upon whites, he added, but they asked whites not to "intrude themselves upon our families hereafter, as they used to do before the war, unbidden." The well-lubricated doctor called Lewis a liar and demanded that he take it back—"that I must not tell those niggers anything of that kind." Lewis retracted the statement. Henri Burch, a black senator from Baton Rouge, was so unnerved that he declined to mount the speaker's platform and sought refuge at the local army post.[20]

It was a relief to reach Natchitoches, where blacks turned out in their thousands to hear Packard. Milton Cunningham, chairman of the Democratic campaign committee and candidate for district attorney, spoke from the platform at Packard's invitation.

A single instance of intimidation, and a minor one at that, marred the campaign in Natchitoches. A few days before the election the Republican candidates addressed a meeting at Campti. Four or five white Democrats, armed and mounted, hovered at the edge of the meeting and waited for an opportunity to disrupt it. When Blunt started to speak, one of the white men called him a liar and told him to hush up. The man who interrupted, Samuel "Curly-Headed" Hynes, was known to Blunt—and generally known in Natchitoches Parish—as someone who had killed a white man and got away with it. He and Blunt "got into a right smart row." After repeated interruptions, Blunt broke up the meeting. Had he continued, one witness believed, "both sides would have went at it."[21]

The day before the election, Ernest Breda requested the commander of the Natchitoches army post, Captain Charles Albert, to station soldiers at certain polling places. Democrats assured the captain that soldiers would not be needed, pledging their honor to "keep the peace in every respect." Albert declined Breda's request.[22]

Polling day, November 7, 1876, was the most closely monitored election in Louisiana's history, before or since. General Christopher Augur stationed soldiers in New Orleans, Natchitoches, and two dozen other country parishes. In New Orleans itself soldiers and police kept order, and the Department of Justice paid for 840 federal marshals, six at each polling place, to watch the balloting and the count. About twenty-eight hundred temporary marshals served in the country parishes. Election day passed off peacefully. The returns from Natchitoches were mailed to New Orleans in three packages. They contained no protests about the conduct of the election. Indeed, Republicans across the state filed few complaints.[23]

The Republican Party easily carried Natchitoches Parish. The Democrats' strong showing in De Soto and Sabine, however, deprived Blunt of his senate seat and enabled David Pierson to edge past Breda in the contest for district judge. The statewide vote, moreover, showed a majority of several thousand for Nicholls. If Nicholls carried Louisiana, then so did Samuel Tilden, the Democratic presidential candidate, giving him enough Electoral College votes to beat Rutherford Hayes. In South Carolina and Florida, too, Democrats claimed victory. Congressional Reconstruction appeared to be all but over.[24]

But the vote was close enough to give the Republican Party grounds for hope. Tilden fell one vote short of the necessary majority in the Electoral College, and the results in Louisiana, South Carolina, and Florida had yet to be confirmed. Republicans controlled the election machinery in all three states, and "returning boards" could adjust the results. At the Fifth Avenue Hotel in New York, members of the Republican National Committee fired off three identical telegrams: "Hayes is elected if we have carried South Carolina, Florida, and Louisiana. Can you hold your state? Answer immediately." National committee chairman Zachariah Chandler went one step further. "Hayes has 185 votes," he declared, "and is elected." The message to Republican leaders in Louisiana could not have been clearer: the Returning Board was to transform a Democratic majority into a Republican one.[25]

Northern Republicans proposed to elect Hayes by depriving Tilden of all three disputed southern states. This cheered Louisiana's Republican Party.

If the Returning Board declared a majority for Hayes, then that same majority would surely elect Packard. If Louisiana's electoral votes proved decisive, then the incoming national administration would surely reward its Louisiana supporters by recognizing Packard's claim to office.

But Republican politicians in Louisiana underestimated just how obnoxious they had become in the eyes of northern Republicans. The latter were quite prepared to pocket Louisiana's Electoral College votes while letting Nicholls, the Democrat, take over the statehouse. President Grant was no longer willing to use troops to prop up southern Republicans. He wanted the election to mark the end of military interference for partisan purposes. The army ordered all post commanders in the country parishes to break up their camps and reassemble their men in New Orleans. Four days after the election, the soldiers left Natchitoches, never to return.[26]

Also taking the steamboat to New Orleans were Ernest Breda, Raford Blunt, David Pierson, and Ross E. Burke, who would present the parties' respective claims to the Returning Board. Cosgrove jeered that "hitherto 'bold and outspoken Republicans' took flight" the moment the troops departed. The editor's jibe got under Breda's skin. "The *Vindicator* says we ran off," he wrote his wife. "Why did it not say that Dave Pierson and the Democrats ran off also?" After years of being on the receiving end of Cosgrove's abuse, Breda was still sensitive to any imputation of cowardice.[27]

All eyes now turned to New Orleans when the Returning Board opened its proceedings on November 17. Its challenge: to convert a Democratic majority of eight thousand into a Republican majority that would carry the state for Packard and Hayes and, at the same time, help as many local candidates as possible. The national committee of each party dispatched high-powered delegations to New Orleans, "visiting statesmen," to witness the board's deliberations and, if possible, influence its decisions.

Few people had expected the result in Natchitoches Parish to be contentious. It registered a clear Republican majority. The Republican registrar of voters filed no protest. No Republican complained that he had been prevented from casting a ballot. The deputy clerk of court certified that the election had been free of violence and intimidation. "Whatever may be said about the fairness of the election in other sections of the State," David Pierson wrote his father, "I know it was honest and fair on the part of the Democrats *here.*"

William Tunnard, the Republican clerk of court, was therefore astonished when, on November 25, seven days after the Returning Board began deliberating, local Democrats demanded the set of returns that had been lodged in the parish courthouse, under lock and key, as a safeguard against fraud. After mildly protesting, Tunnard complied. Cunningham boarded a steamboat for New Orleans, taking the documents with him. "I do not exactly know what is wanted of them," a puzzled Tunnard wrote Breda. "Is there any contest in our parish?"[28]

Breda knew exactly what was at stake in the returns from Natchitoches and adjacent parishes. He was at that moment in the New Orleans Custom House, drafting protests and affidavits with which to challenge parish results before the Returning Board. That Natchitoches Parish became a bone of contention, despite the absence of Democratic bulldozing, reflected the razor-thin margin between the two parties at both the state and the national level. The narrowness of the election made every vote potentially decisive. As the Republican Party saw victory slipping away, it scrambled for extra votes, challenging the results in more and more parishes, including Natchitoches. When the Returning Board opened the Natchitoches results on November 21, the Democrats entered a protest. Then, when it became apparent that the size of the Republican vote in Natchitoches might prove critical to securing Louisiana for Hayes, the Republicans filed protests of their own. Once again, the Republican Party had to fall back upon creative counting in order to offset Democratic bulldozing.[29]

The Returning Board maintained a facade of impartiality. Its president, James Madison Wells, maintained that he and his three colleagues scrutinized the returns on a parish-by-parish basis without ever considering how their decision on each one would affect Republican candidates, be the latter Hayes, Packard, or a humble state legislator. This was pure fiction. The Returning Board, as well as U.S. senator John Sherman of Ohio and the other Republican "visiting statesmen," calculated precisely how many Democratic votes needed to be rejected in order to deliver Louisiana to Hayes and put Packard in the statehouse. The board even tried to accommodate the claims of local Republican candidates as far as it plausibly could. In short, the Returning Board was set on achieving certain results and adjusted the figures accordingly.[30]

The board's commitment to maintaining Republican power was obvious from the start. It was evident from its mode of procedure and from private comments by its members. For example, the law establishing the five-man Returning Board required that both parties be represented, but the four sitting members, all of them Republicans, rejected the Democratic nominee for the vacant fifth seat. Although Nicholls had promised to treat blacks fairly, one of its members confided, the Democratic Party could not be trusted: he regarded it as his "moral duty to keep the Democratic party out of power." In a letter to U.S. senator J. R. West of Louisiana, Wells made plain where he felt his own duty lay. "Not with my consent shall this oppressed people be governed by [Grant's] paroled prisoners, aided by the white-livered cowards of the North."[31]

The board faced a difficulty, however. The law required parish registrars to include any protests about the conduct of the elections—fraud, intimidation, violence—in their official returns. Hardly any of them did so. Wells therefore made up the rules as he went along.

His key decision was to accept post-election protests and affidavits. Having made this concession to members of his own party, he could not deny it to the Democrats. But the fact that Republicans, not Democrats, sought to alter the results gave the former a head start when it came to bringing witnesses to New Orleans. Democrats anticipated that some parish returns would be challenged, but they could not be sure of others until the challenge actually came. While the Democrats were kept guessing, U.S. Marshal J. R. G. Pitkin dispatched members of the Metropolitan Police—"sturdy, hard-fighting men"—to serve subpoenas upon Republican witnesses across Louisiana. When the witnesses arrived in New Orleans they proceeded directly to the Custom House, where a team of Republican officials, including Breda, drafted affidavits attesting to intimidation and violence. In several cases, Republican officials intercepted the returns at the post office before they had been delivered to the Returning Board; they then opened the packages and inserted the affidavits.[32]

The absence of protests in the original returns did not, of course, indicate that the elections had been free and fair. Registrars in the bulldozed parishes feared Democratic reprisals if they protested. They feared for their lives. As D. A. Weber, the registrar of West Feliciana Parish, put it, "My head is a damned sight more important to me than Packard's being governor." Only in the safety of New Orleans could men like Weber be persuaded to sign protests. The promise of a federal patronage appointment helped. A larger problem, however, was that the Democratic Party had taken pains to ensure that election day itself passed peacefully, compelling Republican affidavits to delve into violence and intimidation during the months, and even years, before November 7, 1876.[33]

The Returning Board had ample reason to reject the votes of the five bulldozed parishes. The evidence of intimidation supplied by Republican registrars and by other witnesses summoned to New Orleans was irrefutable. Collated by the Republican "visiting statesmen" and summarized in a report by Senator Sherman that was rushed into print on December 6, it demonstrated that "violent and terrible means" had converted a Republican majority of almost 4,000 in 1874 into a Democratic majority of 4,495 in 1876. The oral testimony of Eliza Pinkston, a black woman from Ouchita Parish, was especially shocking. Exhibiting wounds on her body that had not yet healed, she recounted how local Democrats had murdered her husband, killed her babe in arms, and then raped, beaten, shot, and stabbed her. Even the visiting northern Democrats found themselves shaken: "I see before me a woman who has been foully dealt with," stated Governor John Palmer of Illinois. "Certainly, it is horrible."[34]

It soon became clear, however, that throwing out the ballots of these five parishes would still leave a small majority for Nicholls and Tilden. The Republican Party therefore extended its protests to the parishes of Grant, De Soto, St. Tammany, Bienville, Lafayette, and Webster, and the Returning Board rejected additional heavily Democratic polls. This gave Packard a slim majority. But the Returning Board confronted a further difficulty. The Republican vote for Hayes trailed the Republican vote for Packard. Rejecting Democratic ballots in these nine parishes might ensure Packard's election, but it might not elect all eight Hayes electors—and the Republican candidate needed all eight if he were to stand any chance of becoming president.[35]

The problem became apparent on November 23, when the Returning Board opened the Natchitoches returns to discover that five of the Republican presidential electors fell several hundred votes short of the other three, which put five Democratic electors ahead. In other parishes, too, some of the Republican electors ran significantly behind others. Given the high level of partisan voting—the Republican vote for state and local candidates was notably consistent—these results defied common sense.[36]

It turned out that in several parishes, Republican election officials had tallied the votes for only three of the eight presidential electors. The error stemmed from confusion about the workings of the U.S. Electoral College. The two "at large" electors corresponded to Louisiana's two senators, the other six to the state's six congressmen. Misunderstanding arose because ballot papers printed the name of a specific congressional district against each of these six electors, feeding the impression that voters could only choose *one* of the six—the one listed against their own congressional district. In reality, the vote for these electors was tallied statewide, not as six separate contests, and voters normally endorsed all eight of their party's electors. In other parishes, the Republican Party had, through sheer incompetence, left five of the its presidential electors off the ballot paper. Democratic ballots sometimes made the same mistake, but less often.[37]

Natchitoches Democrats were already aware of the discrepancy in the Republican vote for presidential electors and gave early notice that they intended challenging any attempt by the Returning Board to correct it by "adding" votes. The fortuitous appearance on November 24 of a letter from John Lewis, the U.S. supervisor for Ward 11, heightened their suspicion that the board intended to do just that. In counting the votes in Ward 11, Lewis explained, "I thought it was only necessary to canvass the electoral vote for the electors at large and for the fourth congressional district." After learning of his error, he had gone back to count the votes for all eight. Ward 11 was heavily Republican, and Lewis's correction credited the five trailing Democratic electors with 173 votes and the five trailing Republicans with 542. It meant that the Republican Party carried Natchitoches Parish for Hayes.[38]

Democrats smelled a rat. Did Lewis's letter accompany the official returns from Natchitoches, or was it added later? Wells insisted, with a show of indignation, that the letter had simply been "overlooked." But Lewis's report bore no date, and Democrats were understandably reluctant to accept the uncorroborated word of the Returning Board. Moreover, although Lewis's statement implied that the ballot paper in Ward 11 had listed all eight presidential electors, Democrats wanted proof. The point could only be settled by examining the ballots themselves, which were back at the courthouse in Natchitoches. Somewhat reluctantly, the Returning Board agreed that the Democrats could send for these returns. Hence the demand on Tunnard to hand over the documents to Cunningham.[39]

Democratic objections proved unavailing. The Returning Board accepted Lewis's rectification and took similar action when the same mistake occurred elsewhere. The board thereby increased the Republican Party's statewide vote by more than two thousand.

This was still not enough, however, to create clear majorities for all eight Republican presidential electors. When Republican leaders woke up to this unsettling fact, they protested the results in yet more parishes on the grounds of violence and intimidation, and the Returning Board, having exhausted the possibility of adding Republican votes, rejected more Democratic ones. All told, the board ended up rejecting 15,600 votes in twenty-three parishes, of which 13,200 were votes for Tilden. On December 3, after the board had gone into secret session, U.S. Marshal Pitkin telegraphed Senator West, in code, the reassuring words of J. Madison Wells: "Board will return Hayes, sure. Have no fear."[40]

The legerdemain of the Returning Board did not end there. The board tinkered further with the returns in order to elect a number of local politicians, among them Blunt and Breda. On December 2, Assistant Attorney General Henry Dibble presented the board with affidavits signed by Blunt, Breda, and half a dozen others alleging that "the colored Republicans were generally intimidated" in Natchitoches Parish, especially in Wards 5 and 6. Their statements referenced the bulldozing of 1874, the death of E. L. Pierson, the editorials of the *Vindicator*, threats by landlords to discharge laborers who voted Republican, and the rumors—and openly expressed warnings—that any Republican "counted in" by the Returning Board would not be able to live. While long on history, the affidavits were short on evidence of intimidation or violence during the election. Blunt's referred to the Republican meeting at Campti that was disrupted by S. M. Hyams. Only two of the affidavits were by black voters from Wards 5 and 6.[41]

In sworn statements of their own, David Pierson and other Democrats insisted that the election in Natchitoches had been entirely free of intimidation on their part. Wards 5 and 6, they argued, were sparsely populated, mostly white "hill wards" where many of the black farmers owned their own land and, if they voted Democrat, did so of their own free will. The only threats during the election, they added, emanated from black Republicans seeking to pressure other blacks from voting the Democratic ticket. The Returning Board was unmoved: it declared that Blunt and Breda had both been elected. All told, the board boosted the Republican majority in Natchitoches Parish by more than five hundred votes.[42]

Pierson, who lost out to Breda, surmised that the only reason the board rejected the polls in Wards 5 and 6 was that, even after throwing out half the polls in De Soto Parish, turning a Democratic majority of 400 into a Republican one of 500, the Democratic candidates in the four-parish district still ran about 150 votes ahead. "It required the throwing out of votes here to elect a [Republican] senator and [Republican] district judge." It was a reasonable assumption to make. What Pierson failed to note, but others did, was that by certifying Blunt and two other senatorial candidates who had been outvoted, the Returning Board made it possible for the state legislature to elect William P. Kellogg, the outgoing governor, to the U.S. Senate.[43]

The returning boards of Louisiana, Florida, and South Carolina duly delivered the required Republican majorities, and Hayes attained the magic number of 185 electoral votes. But he could not become president unless Congress accepted those votes, and this it declined to do. Outraged Democrats, claiming that Tilden was the legitimate president-elect, refused to accept the result, and they used their control of the House or Representatives to block the counting of the electoral votes. Hayes sat in political limbo.

Louisiana Democrats pinned their hopes on a Tilden victory, for the fate of the state and national tickets seemed inextricably linked. Agents representing Tilden considered various schemes to bribe Wells and, after these plans fell through, to "buy" one of the Republican presidential electors. The Hayes campaign, too, sought to reward Wells financially for voting the right way. A combination of indecision and insufficient funds defeated both parties' efforts.[44]

With the presidential election still in play, Democrats had no intention of recognizing the decisions of the Returning Board. In Natchitoches, Tunnard readied the paperwork for the next session of the district court. But after the board returned Breda as district judge, the local bar association branded him a "shameless usurper" and boycotted the court.[45]

On January 8, when Packard succeeded Kellogg as governor, Nicholls also took the governor's oath, in front of a vast crowd in Lafayette Square. Nicholls immediately organized a legislature and reactivated the White League. The following day, the White League, claiming to be the state militia, took control of New Orleans. Packard had scarcely taken his seat in the executive chair when the Democratic militia occupied the arsenals, the police stations, and the supreme court, forcibly ejecting the Republican judges. "The whole aspect of affairs changed just as quickly as you would shift the scenes in a theater," recalled Kellogg.[46]

As in 1873 and 1875, Louisiana had two governors, each claiming to be lawfully elected, and two legislatures, each claiming exclusive legitimacy. But while Nicholls commanded the streets and public buildings of New Orleans, Packard controlled only the St. Louis Hotel (the statehouse), which was still ringed by U.S. soldiers whom Grant had placed there to protect the Returning Board. Beyond the ring of bluecoats, a crowd of several thousand Democrats menaced the seat of Republican power.

Republican leaders possessed no force, other than the lightly armed Metropolitan Police, to oppose the Nicholls militia. The latter reportedly possessed fifteen thousand stands of arms, including seventeen hundred rifles and two howitzers stolen from the state armory. Anticipating the Democratic coup, Kellogg, the outgoing governor, had pleaded with Washington to recognize and protect the incoming Packard administration. Grant's frosty reply—"I am constrained to decline your request"—must have chilled him. He could not recognize either of the rival governments, the president explained, while two congressional committees were investigating the election and trying to decide which one had legal standing. Republicans in Louisiana were "always in trouble," he complained, "and always wanting the U.S. to send troops."[47]

Governor Packard's frantic telegrams requesting military assistance evoked the same dusty response. The federal government would remain neutral; the army would be employed only in the event of insurrectionary violence. General Augur, the federal commander in New Orleans, did nothing to restrain the Democrats from taking over the city—even after they forcibly ejected the three judges of the supreme court—because they did so without bloodshed. Nicholls ordered the crowds around the statehouse to disperse. On January 14 Grant ordered both sides to adhere to the status quo. He warned the Democrats not to install Democratic officials in the country parishes if it meant forcibly removing Republican ones. Grant again referred to ongoing congressional investigations as a reason for his neutrality.[48]

Congress launched multiple investigations (seven in all) into the disputed election. In the end, however, the overlapping hearings and reports did little to determine the outcome, because the House and Senate committees arrived at diametrically opposite conclusions. The principal House committee, chaired by Democrat William R. Morrison of Illinois, rebutted Republican charges of bulldozing, denounced the Returning Board as fraudulent and corrupt, and pronounced the vote for Nicholls and Tilden a fair one. The main Senate investigation, led by Timothy O. Howe of Wisconsin, a Republican, unearthed copious evidence of intimidation and outright violence in the five bulldozed parishes and twelve others. Endorsing the work of the Returning Board, it argued that only "very great intimidation" could explain the Democratic majority. Clearly, a divided Congress would never agree on the respective claims of Packard and Nicholls, especially as any decision about the governors would also decide—many assumed—the fates of Hayes and Tilden.[49]

Privately, Grant believed that the party's leaders in Louisiana had forfeited their right to govern. He considered them incompetent, fractious, and corrupt. "They had no interests there," he told Secretary of State Hamilton Fish, "but had simply gone there to hold office." He regarded the Returning Board as an embarrassment, "an outrageous contrivance," whose record had been tainted with fraud. He doubted that Packard could be sustained, Grant told James Garfield, and predicted that the Republican claimant would be "driven from the state as soon as the electoral count is decided." Garfield was shocked, as he failed to see how Packard could be abandoned without undermining Hayes's claim to Louisiana's Electoral College vote. Either way, he told his diary, "This seems to be a bad outlook for our friends in Louisiana."[50]

13

THE COMPROMISE OF 1877

Senator Sherman said that the country was tired of Louisiana matters,
and I thought so myself.

Agnes Jenks, Republican witness, to the House Select Committee
on Alleged Electoral Frauds in the Presidential Election of 1876

The contrast between the disputed presidential election of 1876 and that of 2000 vividly illustrates the decay of political parties and the declining prestige of Congress in the late twentieth century. For all their faults, the parties of the Reconstruction era effectively mobilized public opinion, and the House of Representatives, the most democratic element in the Constitution, insisted on having the final say in determining the outcome. Congress went over the election with a fine-tooth comb, producing a documentary record of unparalleled detail. The notion of permitting the unelected judges of the Supreme Court to preempt Congress was unthinkable. The process, although thoroughly partisan, involved negotiation between the two parties that involved concessions by both sides.

The outcome, however, was not so much a genuine "compromise" as the ratification of a fait accompli—the Republicans' abandonment of military intervention and acquiescence in the Democrats' ouster of three Republican governors.

As the dispute over the presidential election raged on into 1877, Democratic leaders in Louisiana explored the possibility of winning control of the state government with or without a Democratic president. In mid-January, encouraged by Grant's status quo order, Francis Nicholls dispatched his close adviser E. A. Burke to Washington to negotiate directly with the president. Louisiana's three Democratic congressmen—E. John Ellis, Randall L. Gibson, and William M. Levy (whose district embraced Natchitoches)—joined in the talks. "Our first effort was to secure non-intervention," Burke stated later, "and then, if possible, to secure recognition."

Figure 13. Inauguration of Francis T. Nicholls, Democratic claimant to the governorship, January 8, 1877. Public domain.

It was a delicate assignment. Although Grant displayed little sympathy for Packard, recognition of Nicholls was out of the question as long as the presidential election remained undecided. The president also made it plain that any further resort to force by the Democrats—any violation of the status quo—would ruin their chances and compel him to recognize Packard.[1]

The status quo, however, left Nicholls in control of New Orleans and enabled him to consolidate his position. Nicholls appreciated his advantage and aimed to exploit it. "Packard has no power," he wired his agents in Washington. "The putting of my government into full operation . . . requires no effort, and is a mere matter of *accretion*." Burke instructed Nicholls to do nothing to provoke or unsettle Grant: the Democrats must play a waiting game. In Natchitoches and other country parishes, Democratic claimants sat by in frustration as Republicans clung to office. The political cease-fire produced a tense calm but paralyzed local government.[2]

For Democrats in Natchitoches it was more important than ever to portray themselves as orderly and law-abiding. The death of local merchant Alex Garza at the hands of Texas outlaws enabled them to underline that reputation to the congressional subcommittee that arrived in town in the closing days of 1876. Five desperadoes, led by "Scabby Face Bill" Horton, had ridden into Natchitoches on November 27 with the proclaimed intention of killing "niggers and damned Radicals." They "raised perfect hell in the streets," wrote one witness, "whipping one Negro and telling him, 'You d——d son of a B—— go home or I will kill you.' Shooting their guns all along Front Street." A liquored-up Horton entered J. P. Breda's drugstore and tried to pick a fight with Philippe Breda, who refused to take the bait. Breda was convinced that someone had offered Horton money to kill him and his brother.[3]

Democrats ridiculed Breda's assertion, telling the visiting subcommittee that Horton's raid had nothing to do with politics. They were probably correct. Breda's claim that his name was on Horton's hit list prompted one skeptical congressman to note that he, Breda, was very much alive. In fact, Horton and his men seem to have been equal opportunity outlaws. In the words of William Tunnard, the Republican clerk of court, the gang "attacked citizens promiscuously, broke up bar rooms, insulted ladies, and ended up by shooting and mortally wounding a negro from Sabine Parish." When the outlaws returned on Christmas Day, Horton found great sport in "indiscriminate firing at any and every Negro he met." Spotting a black man fleeing down Second Street, four prominent Democrats left the Merchants' Club, where they had been dining, and stepped into the street to challenge Horton. "We are all friends here," they remonstrated, "and we must have no fighting." Horton replied with bullets, one of them killing Alex Garza, another wounding J. P. Johnson. Horton then escaped on horseback. A citizens' posse tracked him down and killed him.[4]

The Horton raids showed the Democrats of Natchitoches in the best possible light. White Democrats had intervened to protect a black man, and one of them paid with his life. Democrats could also mock the Republican sheriff and the Republican chief of police for their impotence in the face of a handful of Texan desperadoes. "The radical officials . . . cowered in their homes like craven curs," the *Vindicator* sneered. The Horton affair underlined a Democratic narrative that portrayed Natchitoches Democrats as law-abiding people who deplored political violence. When the congressional subcommittee arrived in town shortly after the raid, Democrats produced black witnesses from Wards 5 and 6 who testified that they had voted the Democratic ticket of their own volition. The Republicans, by contrast, could not find a single black witness to sustain their charge of intimidation. The fact that two white Republicans testified to the election having been free and fair—one of them repudiating the affidavit he had signed in New Orleans—spoke for itself.[5]

Democratic leaders recognized the need for absolute party discipline. They must follow the lead of Nicholls, who in turn followed the advice of Burke, who was in almost daily contact with President Grant. And Burke warned them that national politics trumped local politics, that Grant "will crush you to save Hayes, if necessary."

Natchitoches Democrats therefore backed down when Grant insisted that David Pierson refrain from acting as district judge as long as the status quo remained in effect. Nicholls had commissioned Pierson on January 11, and Pierson took the oath of office on January 20. But Republicans resisted. When Pierson issued an arrest warrant, Virgil A. Barron, the sheriff, and Phillipe Breda, the coroner, refused to execute it. When he appointed a constable, the police jury refused to recognize him. Ernest Breda's protest that *he* was the legally elected district judge found its way to the White House. In the case of disputed offices, Grant ruled, neither contestant may take office: the incumbent, in this case retiring Republican C. C. Chaplin, should remain in post. Pierson reluctantly gave way. "Under the status quo orders and the urgent request of Gov. Nicholls I could not act as a judge," he wrote his father, "so that I am literally doing nothing."[6]

Ernest Breda was equally unhappy. Arguing that Kellogg had already commissioned him district judge when Grant issued his status quo order, he instructed Sheriff Barron to ignore any orders issued by Chaplin, the holdover judge. Writing from New Orleans, where he sat in the Packard legislature as a state senator, Raford Blunt sent Breda encouraging words. "Rest assured that you will win this battle. Stand firm and the victory is ours." In the meantime, the district court ceased to function and judicial business piled up.[7]

The political uncertainty kept both sides guessing. Republicans clung to the belief that Grant would come to their rescue. Democrats told themselves that the passage of the Election Bill, which created a fifteen-man electoral commission to determine the result, gave Tilden an even chance of being confirmed as president—after all, the bill had passed the House with two-thirds of Republicans voting against it.

Democrats also took heart from a House investigation into the Returning Board, whose star witness, James H. Maddox, claimed that J. Madison Wells had tried to extort a bribe from the Republican Party in return for delivering Louisiana to Hayes. "The evidence of Maddox," Natchitoches attorney Thomas Chaplin wrote a friend, "will be sufficient to . . . so completely disgust honest Republicans north (if there be any) that they will be ashamed to contend for the electoral vote of Louisiana." But to Republicans in Louisiana who were fighting for their political and even physical lives, the ends justified the means. As Jack Wharton put it, "I do not consider it bribery if I give a man $100 to keep him from blowing my brains out." Besides, the investigation reflected equally badly upon the Democrats when it turned out that the Tilden campaign had also tried to bribe Wells. "I would not give a cast-off button for the patriotic motives of either side," E. H. Durell, U.S. judge for the Eastern District of Louisiana, wrote a fellow Republican.[8]

An early decision by the Electoral Commission not to "go behind the returns"—that is, not to question how the returning boards arrived at their results—weakened the Democrats' hand. The commission's award of all Florida's electoral votes to Hayes, with the eight Republicans outvoting the seven Democrats, suggested that Tilden's cause might be hopeless. When the commission took up the Louisiana case, former Supreme Court justice John A. Campbell held forth for two hours in defense of Tilden's claim. His performance left James Garfield unimpressed: "I doubt that any Louisiana man is competent to discuss this question wisely." On February 17 the commission allocated Louisiana's electoral votes to Hayes. "A day of the most nervous strain and anxiety I have ever passed since [the Battle of] Chickamauga," a relieved Garfield noted in his dairy. Ten days later the commission disposed of South Carolina's votes in the same way.[9]

With the increasing likelihood that Hayes would be inaugurated president, Republicans in Natchitoches fully expected the Union cavalry to ride to their rescue. When Edward Ezernack complained to Packard that Nicholls had violated the status quo by commissioning C. F. Dranguet as mayor, Packard told him not to worry. "In a few days the Louisiana case will be finally and favorably settled. Better wait till then." Writing from New Orleans, where he served in the Packard legislature, John G. Lewis was even more optimistic. "You will have soldiers in a short time," he assured Ernest Breda. "Blunt will succeed in this, and Packard as soon as recognized will organize militia all over the state—the tables are fast turning in our favor." Packard would be recognized by Hayes, wrote former governor Kellogg, "if not by Grant before he goes out of office." After all, he explained, Louisiana's electoral votes had become the "corner-stone" of Hayes's victory.[10]

Were politics governed by logic and consistency, events would have conformed to Kellogg's prediction. But in the national councils of the Republican Party self-interest ruled. Republican Party managers and Louisiana Democrats were warming to the possibility of separating the White House from the statehouse. "Even should Tilden fail," wrote David Pierson, "I yet have hopes that Nicholls will hold as Governor of this State, and we would scarcely feel the National Government if we had our own." Writing from New Orleans, Thomas Chaplin reported that Nicholls was in full control of the city and would not be dislodged. "Those parties who suppose that Grant or anyone else will ever again send troops to Natchitoches to protect them," he added, "are woefully mistaken."[11]

The moment he learned that the Electoral Commission had placed Louisiana in the Hayes column, Burke concluded that the Republican would be president. But he felt confident that Nicholls would become undisputed governor of Louisiana. Frequent visits to the White House convinced him that Grant had no sympathy for Packard and was ready to abandon military intervention. For those with eyes to see, the writing on the wall was plain. Immediately after the election, the army had withdrawn its soldiers from the South's interior. All the post commanders in Louisiana's country parishes had struck camp and reassembled their men in New Orleans. For the first time since 1874, Natchitoches lacked a U.S. military presence.[12]

Burke understood, of course, that Grant, in the interests of the Republican Party, would not repudiate Packard before Hayes took office; he would leave that decision to his successor. Maintaining the status quo, meanwhile, enabled the president to keep Democrats worried, exerting pressure on them to end a last-ditch effort to filibuster the counting of the electoral vote. Nevertheless, everything Grant said and did (and refrained from doing) convinced Burke that, as he wired Nicholls, "your chances of final recognition have never been better."[13]

A meeting on February 20 between Grant, Burke, and Louisiana's Democratic congressmen marked a turning point. A month earlier, Grant had struck them as a "grim, silent man" who appeared unyielding. Seeing him on an almost daily basis, however, E. John Ellis observed a "gradual process of 'thawing out' . . . and his ultimate transition into, I will not exactly say our friend, but our adviser."

Grant's policy of non-recognition had already benefited Nicholls and hurt Packard. Now the president began actively to assist Nicholls. When Burke and Ellis told Grant that Nicholls wanted to appoint tax collectors but did not wish to breach the status quo order, the president laughed and responded with a joke. An Irishman who had forsworn drink, he related, visited a drugstore for some medicine. When the pharmacist suggested that alcohol would make the medicine more effective, the man said no. "I am a strict member of the temperance society, but if you'll put a little whisky in it unbeknownst to me, it'll be all right.'" Grant's anecdote required no explanation. Burke and his confederates wired Nicholls that he could now "prudently and peacefully . . . complete [the] organization of your government." In the meantime, the Louisianans were meeting Senator Stanley Matthews, Hayes's brother-in-law, and other Ohio Republicans with a view to extracting a commitment that Hayes would recognize Nicholls by withdrawing the troops. Republican rule in Louisiana was doomed.[14]

The desperate telegrams that Packard and his allies kept sending to Washington merely underlined the impotence and inconstancy of Louisiana's Republican leaders. As early as December 14, U.S. Marshal and party organizer J. R. G. Pitkin warned the Department of Justice that the Nicholls legislature would try to undermine the Packard legislature by offering Republicans financial inducements to change houses. "Some of these Republicans may exhibit, as in the past, less patriotism than greed." Packard's government, starved of tax revenue, had no money to pay its legislators; Nicholls could furnish travel expenses and a per diem. Other Republicans simply concluded that the Packard administration was a sinking ship, and clambered aboard Nicholls's lifeboat.[15]

L. G. Barron, one of the first Republicans to join the Nicholls legislature, represented Natchitoches Parish in the lower house. He was the brother of Virgil Barron, the Republican sheriff, and his departure cracked the unity of the Natchitoches delegation and became the first of many. Nicholls worried that Grant might disapprove his efforts to encourage Republican defections, but the president registered no objection provided he managed them "without display." Very soon, within days of Packard's inauguration, the Republican legislature lost its quorum and could pass no bills. It carried on legislating nonetheless, its deliberations increasingly detached from reality.[16]

Faced with another existential threat, the Louisiana Republican Party once again exhibited the self-destructive factionalism that had torn it apart in 1871 and 1872. Henry C. Warmoth and P. B. S. Pinchback, political rivals and occasional collaborators, had both coveted the gubernatorial nomination, and both nurtured the ambition to be U.S. senator. When Packard won the nomination, Warmoth and Pinchback refused to take any part in the campaign. After the Returning Board declared Packard the victor, they had no interest in sustaining him as governor. Instead, they schemed to deny the senatorship to Kellogg, and to promote their own cause, by breaking the quorum in the state legislature. Each man tried to induce four Republican senators to absent themselves. Pinchback bribed the quartet to do his bidding. When the Packard legislature elected Kellogg anyway, despite the absence of a quorum, Pinchback joined the Nicholls legislature and took two of the bribed senators with him.[17]

Blunt and other black legislators, having nominated Pinchback for the senatorship, denounced him as an ingrate and traitor. Pinchback was unrepentant. In a classic case of the pot calling the kettle black, he denounced the Packard legislature as the most corrupt body "on the face of God's earth." Warmoth, Pinchback's on-again, off-again ally, his senatorial ambitions again thwarted, took solace in schadenfreude. "I was a witness to the disintegration of the Packard Legislature and finally had the satisfaction to see Kellogg and Packard overthrown."[18]

Under pressure from what he called "rabid Republicans," Grant did not rule out recognizing Packard. However, the latter's dispatches helped to make up his mind. At the end of January, Packard informed Attorney General Alphonso Taft that he could not collect taxes, the state stood on the edge of bankruptcy, business in New Orleans was at a standstill, and "[we are] almost without support—at least from the white element of the population." Given the fact that the Republican Party had controlled the state for nine years, this was a most damaging admission. Nothing Grant heard from Packard's partisans contradicted it. "The feeling here is still . . . most bitter against everything *Republican*," wrote a railroad official from New Orleans. "This I say is universal amongst all classes, whether Business Men, Men of no business, and both sexes of whites. It is carried into their schools, churches, [and] the social circle." The Republican Party had as little white support in 1877 as it had in 1867. The stark reality was that if Packard, like Kellogg, depended upon black support alone, his administration was doomed.[19]

U.S. Marshal Pitkin later asserted that recognition by Grant would have enabled Packard to raise a militia, allowing him to protect his government and dispense with federal troops. The claim strains credulity. Packard's efforts to organize a militia smacked of desperation. "I only had 250 muskets," he admitted. "That was my entire equipment of arms after the 9th of January." Had the army loaned him twenty-five hundred rifles, he believed, he could have found a man for every gun and stood his ground. But a larger, better-trained, and fully armed state militia had crumbled before the White League in 1874; how could the force Packard proposed to recruit fare any better? Such a hastily organized militia, composed of black men "unused to war," would be no match for Nicholls's Confederate veterans. Republican stalwart Henry C. Dibble stated the painful truth: even if the five thousand men of the Metropolitan Police doubled as a militia, they would lose badly in an armed confrontation with the White League. New Orleans was occupied by an "insurgent army," he told the attorney general, and only the federal government could put it down.[20]

Despite his public stance of scrupulous neutrality, Grant had decided that Louisiana would be better off if Nicholls became governor. On February 26 he told Burke as much. Nicholls commanded the confidence of "the most influential elements of the State," he admitted, while "the Packard government cannot exist without the support of troops." He even committed himself to removing the troops from the statehouse as soon as Congress completed the count of the electoral vote and Hayes's election was secured. Burke triumphantly wired Nicholls news of this breakthrough.[21]

Burke, Levy, Ellis, and Gibson had succeeded in not only neutralizing Grant but also enlisting his sympathy. But they worried that Hayes, who declined to make himself a party to any negotiations or agreement, might still sustain Packard if subjected to sufficient pressure from Republican stalwarts. They therefore organized another filibuster movement in the House in order to, in the words of historian Paul Haworth, "scare the Republicans, and particularly the friends of Hayes, into giving assurances."[22]

The Speaker of the House, a Democrat, had already ruled that the count should go ahead; the filibusters could only delay Hayes's election, not prevent it. Burke later confessed that the Louisianans were playing a "bluff game." Still, as C. Vann Woodward noted, the bluff appeared sufficiently credible to make the Republicans "lose nerve and become panicky." At a meeting at Wormley House hotel on February 26, Ohio Republicans gave Burke and company the assurances they wanted. John Sherman raised the question of how blacks and former Republican officeholders would be treated under a Democratic administration. Burke assuaged his concerns by having the Nicholls legislature adopt resolutions promising to safeguard the civil and political rights of blacks, to give blacks equal advantages in public education, and to persecute no one for past political conduct.[23]

The next day, Senator Matthews relayed the bad news to Packard. "The Nicholls government is the government which should stand," he wired. It would be "out of the question," he added, to maintain Packard's government "by force of Federal arms." On March 1, when Packard sent another plea for recognition, Grant's private secretary, C. C. Sniffen, advised him to start packing his bags. The president, stated Sniffen, "does not believe public opinion will longer support the maintenance of state government in Louisiana by the use of the military and that he must concur in this manifest feeling."[24]

Hayes punctiliously denied that he was party to any political bargain. Nevertheless, his "Ohio friends" assured Burke that they were thoroughly familiar with Hayes's views. Hayes, in fact, was already convinced that military intervention must end. He therefore authorized the Republican negotiators to indicate that his policy would be to give "the people" of Louisiana "the right to control their own affairs in their own way." This definition of "the people" implicitly excluded blacks. It proved satisfactory to Burke and the Democratic Louisiana congressmen. William Levy of Natchitoches, speaking from the floor of the House, pronounced himself satisfied with the assurances of prominent Republicans "high in the confidence of Mr. Hayes." The filibuster ended, and on March 2 Congress completed the electoral count. Hayes took the presidential oath two days later.[25]

Removing the troops, however, proved no simple matter. Hayes had to establish that he was his own man and that he had made no "corrupt bargain." He also had to assuage Republican critics of his "conciliation" policy. He must, above all, avoid the appearance of betraying Louisiana's Republican officials. As historian Brooks Simpson put it, "The question was not whether to withdraw federal support, but how." Hayes therefore continued the status quo while he pondered his alternatives. Visiting New Orleans, David Pierson received instructions from Nicholls to conduct no official business until the status of his administration had been resolved.[26]

Packard's refusal to go quietly added a further complication. Spurning Hayes's invitation to abdicate, he continued to press for federal recognition. He also made a strenuous effort to dissuade members of the Packard legislature from going over to the Nicholls legislature. Offered financial inducements from both sides, Republican legislators "swung like a pendulum." In the meantime, the Nicholls administration further entrenched itself, seizing the tax collectors' offices in New Orleans and frustrating Packard's attempt to organize a state militia by imprisoning the men he sent out as recruiting officers. In mid-March, Pierson assumed the functions of district judge in Natchitoches. After a perfunctory show of resistance, Ernest Breda yielded his claim to the office.[27]

Discussing "Louisiana troubles" on March 20, Hayes's cabinet firmly rejected any intervention to save Packard. Instead, they agreed to send a five-man commission to New Orleans (the McVeigh Commission) in order to dismantle Packard's government and consolidate that of Nicholls. In framing the commissioners' instructions, Secretary of State William Evarts did not openly avow that purpose. Instead, he charged the commissioners with settling the Packard-Nicholls dispute "without involving the element of military power." He suggested that "a single legislature would remove this difficulty." The condition and the suggestion pointed toward recognition of Nicholls.[28]

Democrats understood the politics of the McVeigh Commission perfectly well: Hayes was attempting to "wipe out the Packard government" while letting it down gently. In other words, its mission was to secure a Republican surrender rather than a repeat of the 1875 Wheeler Compromise. Significantly, Evarts did *not* instruct the commissioners to assess the respective legal claims of Packard and Nicholls. As Hayes confided to his diary, he accepted Evarts's opinion that the federal government should never again use military force to settle contested elections. "If this leads to the overthrow of the *de jure* govt. in a State, the *de facto* govt. must be recognized."[29]

Louisiana Republicans were quickly disabused of the idea that the McVeigh Commission had come to adjudicate between Packard and Nicholls. During their two weeks in New Orleans, Hayes's emissaries employed "cajolery, persuasion, and threats" to induce Republican legislators to desert Packard. They also used money, persuading the Nicholls legislature to vote back pay for Republican legislators and members of the Metropolitan Police. Large contributions from the New Orleans Cotton Exchange and the Louisiana Lottery facilitated these above-board inducements; they also funded under-the-table bribes. Rejecting a last-minute plea from a delegation of the Packard legislature, the northern Republicans were brutally clear. "The troops are going to be removed next Tuesday," McVeigh told them, and if they resisted the inevitable, the Democrats "will hang every one of you to the lamp-post." The following day only ten legislators stood firm for Packard. On April 20 Marshall Twitchell and two other Republicans urged him to throw in the towel. When he abdicated on April 25, Packard recalled, "I was without a legislature." By then the president had instructed the army to stop guarding the statehouse.[30]

On paper, the Republicans of Louisiana were down but not out. The Nicholls legislature contained only a slim Democratic majority. Republicans held office in many parishes across the state. True, Republican candidates "counted in" by the Returning Board fell by the wayside. Three senators, including Raford Blunt, lost their seats, and Ernest Breda gave up his claim to the district judgeship. But in Natchitoches Parish, Republicans still held the offices of sheriff, coroner, parish judge, and clerk of court. Republicans controlled the police jury, and three Republicans represented the parish in the lower house of the state legislature. With Hayes in the White House, the Republican Party controlled all the federal patronage. In short, the party appeared well placed to make a comeback and recapture the state government.

In reality, however, the Republican Party had been so gravely weakened that its chances of recovering state power were slim. It was not a matter of arithmetic: blacks still outnumbered whites, and the Republicans could theoretically carry the state again. But this was no mere swing of the electoral pendulum. The Democratic Party sought to end Republican government once and for all, not simply take a turn in power. The notion that it would permit a free and fair election was fanciful. Democrats had employed violence and intimidation; Republicans had countered with fraud and military coercion. Small-d democratic politics had never stabilized or gained legitimacy. Having captured state power, it was inconceivable that Democrats would not exploit their advantage to ensure that Republicans never again controlled the statehouse. As for Republican political power in the country parishes, it remained to be seen if Democrats would accept on the local level what they deemed intolerable at the state level.[31]

Louisiana Republicans would have a hard time recovering, regardless of what the Democrats did. Loss of the state government and its accompanying patronage crippled the party organization. Republican newspapers lost the state printing contract, and without that subsidy most went under. When the Nicholls legislature awarded the contract to Cosgrove's *People's Vindicator*, the *Natchitoches Republican* ceased publication.[32]

Many Republican "carpetbaggers" left Louisiana for good. These men were professional politicians who depended upon a salary from the state. They could seek positions with the federal government, but the Custom House in New Orleans remained the principal source of federal employment, and with a couple of thousand displaced Republicans seeking relief even in low-level jobs, many party leaders sought out fresh fields. Stephen Packard, Hugh J. Campbell, Henry C. Dibble, George A. Sheridan, and J. R. West all departed.[33]

The Hayes administration tried to find government positions for as many jobless Republicans as it could. In seeking to broaden the party's appeal to native southern whites, however, it further weakened the party organization. Encouraging the exodus of "carpetbaggers," Hayes gave preference to native-born Louisianans, thus depriving the party of its most assiduous leaders and organizers, who were also the people who enjoyed the closest ties to the northern wing of the party. At the same time, the fact that so many leading Republicans quit the South upon losing office only reinforced the image of a political party dominated by rootless "carpetbaggers." Some professed to be happy to leave Louisiana, where, as Hugh Campbell wrote President Hayes, "it was a mistake for any of us to go."[34]

In their eagerness to conciliate conservative whites, Hayes and other advocates of a new southern policy engaged in a kind of mea culpa which implied that the Democrats had been correct all along in denouncing "carpetbag government." Its dependence upon black votes had rendered southern Republicanism "incapable of self-support," asserted outgoing U.S. senator J. R. West. "Corruption, venality and almost barbarism . . . have rendered it an absolute farce in the conduct of republican institutions." Former congressman J. H. Sypher denounced a policy that had treated black voters like "children to be held up and supported with bayonets." The *New Orleans Republican* jumped on the anti-carpetbagger bandwagon. Patronage jobs had too often gone to "nomadic and irresponsible incumbents," some of whom had "sold themselves openly for a price." Such men did not care where they held a position: "a salary in one place will be the same as in another."[35]

"Scalawags" who had labored in the Republican vineyards, often at risk of their lives, might have welcomed Hayes's patronage policy, but many were profoundly aggrieved. U.S. Marshal Pitkin, for example, who had re-organized the state Republican Party in 1875–76, was asked to resign in favor of Colonel Jack Wharton, a friend of ex-governor and inveterate in-triguer Henry C. Warmoth. Pitkin refused to go quietly, forcing Hayes to dismiss him. "I could not thank Hayes for swindling Louisiana Republicans after profiting by their labors," he explained. Blaming his dismissal on War-moth and outgoing congressman George A. Sheridan, Warmoth's political ally, Pitkin denounced both men: "They represent no holier passion in poli-tics than greed."[36]

Pitkin's blast can be seen as a simple case of sour grapes or, at most, a reflection of the factionalism that made patronage such a divisive issue. In courting (yet again) the so-called Henry Clay Whigs of the South, Hayes had only so much patronage to dispense. A single appointment generated several complaints from the displaced and the disappointed. A man dis-missed became a political enemy. As Republican John E. Leet told a con-gressional committee—provoking general mirth—"I lost confidence in [Governor Kellogg] when I was removed." It was almost obligatory to bite the hand that stopped feeding.[37]

The appointment of Albert H. Leonard as U.S. attorney for Louisiana was a different matter altogether. At least Jack Wharton had been a long-time Republican. Not so Leonard, who only joined the party in 1875 and had been the leader of the White League in Shreveport. As editor of the *Shreveport Times,* Leonard had run editorials calling for the killing of lead-ing Republicans. Republican veterans were appalled. What had converted this Saul, E. H. Durell wrote a friend, who "produced threats and denun-ciations against the Christian Radicals, myself included," into a saint-like Paul?[38]

The man he replaced, James R. Beckwith, had battled political violence for years and had prosecuted the Colfax cases. He had also investigated corruption in the Treasury Department, which he suspected may actually have been the proximate cause of his dismissal. Although Beckwith "bowed out gracefully," his dismissal dented his loyalty to the Republican Party. In 1879, back in private practice, he faced Leonard in federal court as the at-torney for Democratic "bulldozers"—the very kind he had previously tried to put behind bars. Replacing him with Leonard turned out to be a costly decision.[39]

For many Republican Party workers and displaced officials, securing their own financial future became the number one priority. Warmoth, referring to the Republican "visiting statesmen," stated the matter with his customary cynicism, advising one party worker that "these fellows have come down here . . . to steal the State, and they are going to steal it, and you can make your calculations accordingly."[40]

Even before all the returns had come in, some election officials were calculating how they could profit financially from their ability to influence the result. Madison Wells tried, and failed, to secure large sums of cash from both parties. In the end he and the other three members of the Returning Board (as well as numerous friends and family members) received lucrative federal patronage jobs. A. B. Levissee, one of the Republican presidential electors, turned down a bribe of $40,000 to cast his vote for Tilden, but only because he considered the bribe too small. "That was a small consideration for such a big thing," he told the Democratic emissary, suggesting $200,000 as a more fitting sum. The Democrats fell short, and Levissee ended up accepting a patronage position in Washington, D.C. He had never intended selling his electoral vote, he later claimed; he had only asked for $200,000 because he knew the Democrats could never come up with such a total. "I did it with the view of putting myself beyond temptation as regards my political virtue."[41]

The most egregious example of this "every man for himself" mentality may have been James E. Anderson, a Pennsylvania-born journalist who had served as registrar of voters in East Feliciana Parish. Upon realizing that the election might turn upon his willingness, or unwillingness, to sign a post-election protest, Anderson traded with both parties, seeking cash from the Democrats and employment from the Republicans. Persuaded to sign a protest but unhappy with his lowly position in the Custom House, he tried to secure a consulate in a warm foreign clime. His trump card, he believed, was a threat to reveal that he had falsified his election protest at the request of Senator John Sherman, who, he alleged, had given him a written guarantee that Anderson would be "provided for." The claim was false. The "Sherman letter" was a forgery, and even the forged document went missing. Nevertheless, several "scalawags" from the Felicianas joined Anderson's plot, and the blackmailers engaged in extraordinary, not to say farcical, antics in pursuit of their quarry. "The story seemed like a dime novel," admitted one Republican. The intrigue failed, but not before a Democrat-controlled congressional committee exposed, yet again, the seamy side of the Republican Party. As one of Anderson's co-conspirators aptly commented, "To be notorious in Louisiana politics was the most unfortunate thing that could happen to any young man."[42]

Whatever the Republicans' internal problems, the greatest threat to its revival remained the Democratic Party. The Democratic majority in the state legislature refrained from moving too quickly and too aggressively to restrict black rights. They did, as was to be expected, tilt the election laws in their favor. The Returning Board, now composed of four Democrats and one Republican, was barred from investigating the "truth or fallacy" of the official returns. Another law combined the position of registrar of voters with that of tax assessor (appointed by the governor). The same law required registrars to be bona fide residents of the parish and made them ineligible for elective office. Command over the appointment of voter registrars gave the governor's party a huge advantage; Warmoth and Kellogg had both exploited it to the full, and it was hardly to be expected that Nicholls would do otherwise. Requirements that registrars provide separate ballot boxes for the election of ward and parish officers and that voters cast ballots in the wards where they resided potentially hampered Republican turnout, but they were no more onerous than similar regulations across the country.[43]

The legislature weakened Republican power at the local level by increasing the membership of police juries from five to ten and by authorizing the governor to appoint five additional jurors "in such country parishes as he may see fit." In Natchitoches Parish, where Republicans had nominated and elected only three candidates, Nicholls packed the police jury to create a Democratic majority. In appointing a school board for the parish he included four blacks, all of them Democrats, and the committee appointed by the board to examine teachers consisted of William H. Jack, James H. Cosgrove, and Charles F. Dranguet, Democrats all. Act No. 44 was rather more ominous: it gave "certain discretionary powers to the district judge" in the selection of jurors. If Republicans had engaged in what Lawrence Powell calls "defensive Machiavellianism," Democrats now practiced an offensive version of the same tactics.[44]

With Democrats controlling the state government, the level of political violence in the state as a whole dropped sharply. But in the "bulldozed" parishes, political assassinations continued. Republicans who had testified before congressional committees were marked men; those who had fled to New Orleans returned home at their peril. Staring poverty in the face and fearing Democratic retaliation, landing a patronage job was not merely an economic necessity but a matter of physical survival.

Don A. Weber, a French-speaking "scalawag" who had served as registrar of voters in West Feliciana Parish, feared that by signing a protest in New Orleans he may also have signed his own death warrant. Nevertheless, he returned to his family home in St. Francisville. Pleading for Packard's recognition on the eve of Hayes's inauguration, he asked if it were just that "after our services to the nation we should be left in the hands of Nicholls and his murderers." Cooped up in his house and wary of appearing on the streets, Weber resolved to stay put, "even if it should cost me my life." Three days after writing those words, he tumbled to the ground after a hidden assassin shot him dead. He had been walking past the parish courthouse in broad daylight in the middle of the afternoon. Three months later, John Laws, a black Republican and former state legislator, returned to East Feliciana and met a similar fate. He was relaxing on his front porch beside his mother when the band of assassins caught him.[45]

Although Nicholls condemned Weber's murder and offered a $5,000 reward for information about his killer, many Democrats made light of it. The *West Feliciana Sentinel* disclaimed any political significance to the killing, explaining that the victim "had made himself obnoxious to a number of our citizens." Weber's offense, it seemed, had been to write a newspaper article in which he published the names of prominent Democrats who had defaulted on their taxes, along with a promise to name more. Local attorney William Leake stated that Weber was the author of his own fate: "If he had written such an article about me I would have shot him down in the street." Such affairs, the lawyer added, "are personal, not political." As for Laws, Democrats insisted that his death resulted from a family feud—"a murder of the ordinary class."[46]

Some Democrats scarcely bothered to offer excuses. Once the Packard government had fallen, James Cosgrove lost no time in repudiating the policy of conciliation that he had reluctantly supported during the 1876 campaign. Deploring the governor's opposition to political violence, the choleric editor ridiculed the notion that Nicholls could "don a policeman's uniform and skip out to arrest every man who kills another in Louisiana." Weber and Laws had had no business returning to the Felicianas, he wrote; to expect local whites not to exact revenge was to "argue against nature." Unless such "scoundrels" kept out of the country parishes, there would be "plenty more" assassinations.[47]

Bulldozing continued to exact a toll on Republican officials. Former parish judge John S. Dula, about to take up his appointment as postmaster of West Feliciana Parish, found a crude "coffin," six inches in length, on his doorstep, accompanied by a note that read, "You damned nigger Republican, get in this or get out." Leading Democrats denied that white people had anything to do with the threat, attributing it to a family feud. "This affair is purely personal." Dula resigned the $900-a-year postmastership, never having served a day in the job. Democrats also deterred Sam Chapman, appointed postmaster of East Feliciana, from taking up his position. Playing a game of "good cop/bad cop," they said that they themselves had no objection to him, but his testimony to the U.S. Senate committee chaired by Timothy O. Howe, a Republican, had made Chapman "very obnoxious to the white people of the parish." Pledging to do what they could to protect him, they warned that nothing would be able to stop a determined lynch mob. In any case, "an ignorant field hand was not a fit personage to take charge of the post office."[48]

In a report to Grant's attorney general written shortly after the 1876 election, J. R. G. Pitkin conceded, in essence, that the Republican Party's project of democratizing the South had failed. Black solidarity, he argued, was a defensive reflex against white violence and contempt. The freedpeople understood that self-protection favored harmony with the white population, but the latter "denounce every white man that extends a generous hand across the color line." Finding themselves in a state of siege politically, blacks had been forced to "find refuge in their own numbers and to station in the offices, like so many sentry boxes, stewards who should not be indifferent to their needs." With black voters standing en masse against them:

> The whites are compelled to court them by bribes or menaces, or to *drag* them across the color line in order to rifle them out of their ballots, to get them at all, and then they thrust them back with a scoff at their race. . . . To the intelligence of the blacks no appeal is made whatever. . . . A crude civilization, which holds that white men have a private pocket constitution of their own, . . . recognizes no civil and political equals who are not whites, and no laws as of binding force which are not enacted by whites.

One hundred years later, historian Michael Les Benedict agreed that "it was irrelevant to speak in terms of democracy in discussing Louisiana."[49]

The Republican Party's most glaring failure was its inability to enforce the law. In a violent region where most men went about armed, a tradition of private justice persisted, and state borders were political but not physical barriers, the Republican regime never established its claim to a "monopoly of violence." Confronted by widespread, persistent terrorism, its task may well have been impossible given limited support from the president and Congress and outright obstruction on the part of the Supreme Court.

Yet the Kellogg administration's response had been inadequate and misguided. By 1875, with the state militia shattered and the Colfax prosecutions derailed, it had virtually abandoned any effort to suppress political violence. Instead, Kellogg tried to appease the "bulldozers" by appointing them to public positions. Whatever the morality of this tactic, it would have been politically justified had it succeeded. After all, many governments in many situations have denounced terrorism and vowed never to give in to it, only to make political accommodations with terrorists. In Kellogg's case, however, such deals failed to establish the legitimacy of the state government and failed to strengthen the Republican Party. Instead, they undermined both.

The most egregious example, perhaps, was Kellogg's appointment of Colonel Frank Powers as the tax collector of East Feliciana Parish. Powers had headed the "regulators" who terrorized the black population in 1875 and 1876. "I want to get into office," he told a fellow Democrat. "I want to be in a position where I can make money." Local Republicans recommended Powers's appointment on the grounds that once bought off in this way, he would order the "regulators" to disband and "they would perhaps let us alone." Only Powers had the influence to stop the outrages, they told Kellogg. But it was an expensive way of buying "peace." As tax collector, Powers made a handsome salary and took a tidy percentage of the revenue he collected, but he brought no other whites into the party with him. In fact, he had no interest in the Republican Party other than as a stepping-stone to office. Moreover, appeasing individuals could only possibly work as a temporary, occasional expedient. As one Republican put it, his party "did not have an office for every bull-dozer. There were more bull-dozers than officers."[50]

The appointment of men like Powers represented a tacit acknowledgement that a Republican governor and a Republican sheriff were incapable of enforcing the law. Republican officials had made virtually no attempt to prosecute the "regulators" or "bulldozers" who committed murder. The identities of the men who lynched John Gair in October 1875, for example, were public knowledge; many of these men openly admitted to the deed; eyewitnesses described its commission. Yet the lynchers escaped prosecution. Well before Republican administration ended in Louisiana, the open commission of lynching had become commonplace.

The condition of the Republican Party in Natchitoches was not as dire, but bulldozing had taken its toll. By forcing the resignation of four police jurors in 1874, Democrats had asserted a practical power of veto over nominations, forcing the Republican Party to restrict its candidates to men who were literate. They had compelled the resignations of Henry Myers as district judge and David Boullt Sr. as tax collector, and they had made those resignations stick. When one leading bulldozer, P. A. Simmons, joined the Republican Party, Governor Kellogg immediately appointed him to public office. Meanwhile, most of the old Unionists who had joined the party at the time of its formation had gone over to the Democrats.

President Hayes knew full well that he had helped to extinguish Republican governments in Louisiana and South Carolina without providing for "safety and prosperity for the colored people." The previous policy, he argued, was politically untenable, and he had had no choice but to abandon it. He hoped nevertheless that his policy of conciliation would make blacks less vulnerable. If the party in the South recruited enough native whites and removed the issue of "black domination," then political allegiances might cease pivoting on the color line. Moreover, Nicholls and the state legislature had pledged to faithfully observe the Civil War amendments and to guarantee the rights of black citizens.[51]

Was the "Compromise of 1877" a betrayal of the South's Republicans and an abandonment of the black population? Yes and no. Like the negotiators who tried to extricate America from Vietnam while securing guarantees for the pro-American Saigon government, the national Republican Party had a very weak hand.

The parallel with Vietnam is instructive. As long as American troops propped up the pro-American Saigon government, North Vietnam and its South Vietnamese allies could not "win." But the United States, recognizing that its efforts to control the interior were futile and that public opinion had turned against the war, acknowledged that it could not win either. In extricating itself from the quagmire, America tried to negotiate a peace that would ensure the survival of the Saigon government. But Nixon's prior commitment to withdrawing U.S. troops anyway—"Vietnamization"—undercut America's negotiating position. Tacitly recognizing that the Saigon government would not survive unaided, the United States signed a peace treaty that meant, at best, a "decent interval" between U.S. withdrawal and North Vietnam's takeover of South Vietnam.

Politically, the South proved to be the Republican Party's Vietnam. As long as federal troops occupied the state capitals and propped up Republican governors, the Democrats could not "win." But the Republican Party, unable to police the rural hinterlands, and recognizing that public opinion had turned against military intervention, concluded that it had to abandon Reconstruction. It tried to protect southern Republicans by securing guarantees from the Democratic Party, but the decision of Grant and Hayes to end military intervention come what may rendered such promises of dubious value.

Just as Richard Nixon and Henry Kissinger privately admitted that the Saigon government was doomed, Republican leaders predicted that the withdrawal of military protection would lead to the "destruction of the Republican party in the South." Only "time would tell," Hayes admitted, if Democrats would honor their pledges. But Democrats regarded those pledges as cynically as North Vietnam regarded the Paris Peace Accords of 1973. In Vietnam, the "decent interval" lasted a scant two years. In Louisiana, there was no "decent interval" at all.

14

ENDGAME IN NATCHITOCHES

Today I am an exile from my home, father, mother, brothers, sisters, my
adored wife and darling children, my God, my all, my very life, for having
desired to be free, and desiring, dared to say it.

Ernest Breda to Elcey Breda, May 14, 1879

John G. Lewis placed little credence in Democratic pledges of good behavior: "Blacks have long since learned that Democratic promises are the
cheapest and most worthless things we have in Louisiana." Nevertheless,
on April 25, 1877, in one of his first actions upon joining the Nicholls legislature, he nominated David Pierson for the U.S. Senate. Pierson was not a
candidate; Lewis's speech was simply a conciliatory gesture, a bid to bury
the political hatchet. Republicans had little choice but to hope for the best.
Black members of the state legislature formed a caucus, with Lewis its secretary, "in order that we may be able to control such legislation we deem
proper."[1]

Governor Nicholls took some steps to make good his promise of a conciliatory policy. Reassuring blacks that they were not "proscribed," he appointed "a number of them to small offices, sandwiching them on Boards
between white men where . . . they were powerless to do harm." He named
P. B. S. Pinchback to the State Board of Education. He appointed blacks to
parish school boards and other minor offices.[2]

But from the start of his administration, Nicholls recalled, "there were
men around me trying to injure me and to break down my influence." Many
Democrats who had backed him in 1876–77 reverted to the White League
policy as soon as the moderate candidate had served his purpose. Labeled
"Bourbons," these Democrats wished to extinguish black political influence
entirely or, failing that, so to reduce it that blacks could no longer elect men
of their own race. Especially influential in the majority-black cotton parishes,

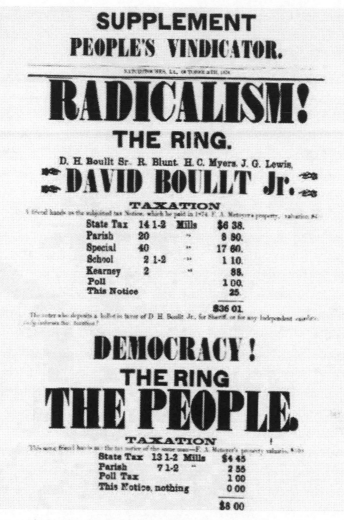

Figure 14. The *Natchitoches People's Vindicator* denounces the only non-Democratic candidate in the 1878 election. Library of Congress, Chronicling America.

the rural Bourbons found powerful allies in Treasurer E. A. Burke, Lieutenant Governor Louis Wiltz, and *New Orleans Daily Democrat* editor H. J. Hearsey. The Bourbons enjoyed the backing and financial support of Charles T. Howard, who represented the Louisiana Lottery Company, a corrupting political influence that Nicholls strove, without success, to eliminate.[3]

It quickly became apparent that many Democrats had no intention of abiding by the pledges made by Nicholls and the state legislature to refrain from political persecution. In Natchitoches the new district attorney, W. P. Hall, instructed a grand jury to indict Ernest Breda, Henry C. Myers, Carroll Jones, and two other Republicans. The charges ranged from bribery to embezzlement. This represented a relatively mild form of retaliation, and when a trial jury acquitted Breda, it stopped. More serious was the indictment by a criminal court in New Orleans of all four members of the old Returning Board. Thomas C. Anderson, the first to be tried, was swiftly convicted and received two years at hard labor. "My dear Sir, you see our helpless and desperate condition," wrote Madison Wells, the next in line to be tried, to Treasury Secretary John Sherman.[4]

Sherman was outraged by the prosecutions. Having investigated the bulldozing in East and West Feliciana Parishes, he knew only too well how vulnerable Republicans were to intimidation and murder, and in helping to negotiate an end to military intervention in 1877 he had insisted on written guarantees from Louisiana's Democratic Party regarding the rights of blacks and Republicans. Now, he complained to President Hayes, Democrats were engaging in a "shameless abuse of judicial process to gratify partisan hate and prejudice in utter disregard of fairness and justice." The federal government had little basis for intervening in what was, ostensibly, a criminal case that fell under the jurisdiction of the state courts. But the Hayes administration, prodded by Sherman, used its influence to have the prosecutions dropped. The state supreme court reversed Anderson's conviction, and no further trials took place. Still, the prosecution reflected badly on Nicholls's ability to implement his policy. It showed, too, that judges were taking advantages of their discretionary powers regarding jury selection. The jury panel included no blacks "nor a single person of known Republican principles," noted Assistant U.S. Attorney George S. Lacey. Agreeing that "the jury was packed to convict," Sherman drew the conclusion that "this spirit of conciliation is not mutual, and cannot be successful."[5]

The spirit of conciliation was wholly absent from Cosgrove's *Vindicator*. Condemning the retention of even a few Republican officials, Cosgrove argued that any pledges to protect blacks' political rights extended to voting only, not to the "further appointment of the ignorant and corrupt." Lest there be any doubt about his meaning, Cosgrove spelled it out: "We emphatically deny the right of the negro to hold office. . . . He is not fitted by education or association to rule the white race."[6]

To a self-confessed "Last Ditch Bourbon Democrat" like Cosgrove, the 1876 election underlined the futility of appealing for black votes. Despite abstaining from coercion, supporting free and fair elections, and courting black voters, Democrats had failed to break down Republican solidarity. Having recruited several hundred black men into Democratic clubs, Cosgrove persuaded himself that his party might actually carry the parish. When polling day came, however, blacks had returned to their Republican allegiance—if, indeed, they had ever truly abandoned it. "Let it be remembered that five hundred Negro voters went back upon their promise on election day," the editor fumed. "Not one third that belonged to our [Democratic] club voted the ticket, which alone defeated us."[7]

Planters and other white employers watched in impotent fury as their employees, who had led them to believe they would vote for Nicholls and Tilden, cast Republican ballots. The fact that employers failed to influence blacks by means of economic pressure stoked their anger. Threats to discharge sharecroppers remained idle. Where, after all, were landlords to find laborers outside the solid mass of black Republican voters? Occasionally, however, a white Democrat retaliated against a vulnerable employee, usually a house servant. Even then, Democrats maintained that such dismissals were not "political." William H. Jack, who fired his servant Joseph Mosely after the latter failed to vote the Democratic ticket, explained that "I turned him off for lying more than anything else." By the same reasoning, Cosgrove attributed Republican solidarity to "treachery and duplicity in [the Negro's] character."[8]

More specifically, Cosgrove blamed that "malignant, bloody-shirt, natural-born liar," Raford Blunt. On the eve of the election, he charged, Blunt had warned blacks that a Democratic victory would return the freedpeople to slavery. From the pulpit of his church, Blunt had threatened that Republican bolters would be ostracized and that even their wives would leave them. On election day itself, Cosgrove noted with disgust, black women, encouraged by Blunt, had stood by the polls and shouted, "Niggers, fight for your color." Blunt himself had called out, "Men, vote with your race." The result: would-be Democrats were tricked and intimidated into staying in the Republican fold.[9]

As an explanation for black loyalty to the Republican Party this analysis fell short. Understandably, Democrats found the "return to slavery" allegation infuriating. But their own contention that emancipation was an unplanned by-product of the Civil War for which the Republicans deserved no credit convinced few black voters. What Democrats refused to admit, or were incapable of grasping, was that "slavery" functioned as a metaphor for black voters, not a literal prediction. "The colored people are remarkably bright in politics," noted J. P. Harris, a native white Republican. "There are few who believe they could be put back in slavery; but they think, for instance, that Democratic ascendancy would restrict their right to vote; they would be taken off juries, and not sufficiently recognized in the partition of offices."[10]

That black ministers wielded tremendous political influence is beyond doubt. Democratic organizers marveled at the hold these preachers appeared to have over their congregations. More perceptive Democrats understood that men like Blunt derived their authority from the character of the black Baptist church, which was rooted in the community in a way that equivalent white churches were not. The pressure to maintain Republican solidarity ran both ways: ministers who refused to actively campaign for the party's candidates could find themselves without a church, "turned out" by an angry congregation. W. W. Washburn of Morehouse Parish observed that this kind of community solidarity made it very difficult to persuade individual voters to abandon the Republican Party. "They are generally divided into societies or churches, and unless you can convert the whole community it is almost impossible to get them to join the Democratic party."[11]

Black ministers certainly encouraged their flocks to shun black Democrats. But white Democrats vastly overstated the amount of intimidation involved. Political campaigns in the nineteenth century were rough affairs in which all parties sought to exert whatever pressure they could in order to influence voters. Open voting, the spoils system, and the "militarized" character of election campaigns made moral and economic pressure potent factors. In antebellum times, the Democrats and the Know-Nothings (American Party) had employed gangs, "plug-uglies," and police officers in order to intimidate opposition voters. New York and New Orleans were both notorious for their thuggish brand of machine politics. In the Reconstruction South, Democrats employed threats, social ostracism, dismissal, eviction, whippings, and murder.[12]

Republican intimidation was small beer by comparison. It consisted mainly of insults and social ostracism. "You cannot go to any balls or dances or churches," complained one black Democrat. "You have to keep away from them." But personal violence was rare. Jerry Hall, one of the black speakers who canvassed Natchitoches Parish for the Democratic Party in 1876, saw no violence against black Democrats: "I have known them to be jeered at." William Ward, another black Democrat, testified that Democrat-leaning freedmen feared being expelled from their churches and being abandoned by their wives. "I don't know if you can call that intimidation," he added. Ward, a hardbitten survivor of the political wars in Grant Parish, knew the difference between social pressure and physical violence.[13]

Black voters who bucked Republican solidarity and cast Democratic ballots of their own free will—fewer than the Democrats claimed but more than the Republicans admitted—stood somewhat apart from the mass of laborers, domestic servants, and sharecroppers who filled the Baptist churches. In Natchitoches Parish they included men like Daniel Bell, who kept a saloon; George Duncan, a freeborn barber; Alfred Henry, who owned a small farm; Frank Breward, who was "raised by old General Bossier"; and Herbert Sharp, who "waited on gentlemen up town." None complained of intimidation. When asked who had told him to vote Democrat, another black witness, Isaac Smith, replied, "I told myself." Then there were the former Republican leaders R. L. Faulkner and Charles Leroy, both literate and freeborn, who had associated with the Democrats since 1874.[14]

Yet however inadequate his explanation for black solidarity, Cosgrove correctly identified the problem facing the Democratic Party: it could never attract a substantial share of the black vote in a free and fair election. "As long as the scoundrel Blunt runs the Negro churches, and with that influence, the women, this parish will have a color line political fight." In short, Democrats had tried, but consistently failed, to break the attachment of black voters to the Republican Party. The question facing Louisiana Democrats, now that they controlled the state government, was how to treat black voters and how to handle the machinery of elections. Should they suppress the black vote entirely, or manipulate it through various combinations of fraud, bribery, and coercion?[15]

As the 1878 elections approached, the *Vindicator* invoked the "Spirit of 1874" to urge a solid white front to put the Natchitoches Parish Republican Party out of business. The Democratic Party must consign the Republicans to "death and eternal oblivion," ensuring that "no more Blunt or Boullts or Barrons or Bredas will ever strut officially through the parish." As in 1874, Cosgrove promised that whites would carry the parish come what may: black voters "had better come with us or stand aside." If Republican leaders failed to retire to private life, he threatened, whites might "invoke summary justice to rid the community of their evil presence."[16]

Republicans had read such threats many times before and were not about to turn tail now. John Lewis advised Ernest Breda to be on his guard for cheating now that Democrats controlled the election machinery. "It would be wise to have one of our number follow up the register and keep a record of all those who are registered . . . in order that we may have proof sufficient to tackle any fraud." Lewis assured Breda that he had the ear of Governor Nicholls and would try to have him appoint former sheriff Virgil A. Barron the quarantine officer for Natchitoches Parish (yellow fever was again ravaging the Mississippi Valley). Barron received the appointment. Nicholls also named other Natchitoches Republicans to minor offices. Neither Lewis nor Breda had any inkling of what was to come.[17]

On the morning of September 21 about 150 men, women, and children gathered at Lewis's former grocery store, then serving as the town's quarantine station, to begin organizing the Republican campaign. Virgil Barron, president of the First Ward Club (dubbed the "mother club"), called the meeting to order. Speakers outlined registration procedures and explained recent ward changes. The officers arranged to hold a second meeting, four hours later, to nominate candidates. The morning meeting lasted about an hour and ended at noon. One Republican, however, had decided not to attend after he spotted more than a dozen white men gather in front of Marshall H. Carver's store on Front Street, "all of them armed with guns."[18]

After leaving the meeting, Ernest and Philippe Breda encountered twenty white men on horseback barring the road into the center of town. None were disguised; all were prominent citizens. Approaching the roadblock, their horses almost touching the knees of the Democrats, Ernest asked by whose authority they were being stopped. "Damn you, you'll find out soon enough," replied one. "Seize the bridles and stop them," shouted another. "If another one attempts to pass, drop him in his tracks." Speaking in French, Ernest told his companions to ride back the way they came. The two brothers and their brother-in-law, H. L. Briggs, bolted. Skirting the center of town, they followed a cow trail through the woods back to the Breda plantation. Later that day messengers arrived with news that Raford Blunt had been taken into captivity.[19]

Blunt had left the meeting on horseback and reached his home on New Second Street without let or hindrance. Along the route, however, blacks shouted warnings that whites were bent on killing him. After letting in eight men, members of First Baptist Church who offered to protect him, he bolted the front door. He handed out three double-barreled shotguns to his bodyguards. Grabbing a Winchester rifle and two pistols, he climbed up to the attic and lowered the trapdoor. He instructed his wife, Alice, not to allow anyone else into the house.[20]

The Natchitoches Parish Democratic Party had opened its own meeting, in the courthouse, just as the Republicans were ending theirs. Spooked by planted rumors that a Republican mob planned to march on their convention and "bring on a fight," the Democrats immediately recessed, fetched weapons, and repaired en masse to the quarantine station. Finding the Republican meeting already over, Milton J. Cunningham, acting as the Democrats' "captain," ordered a squad of men to find Blunt and arrest him. The party soon reached Blunt's house (Natchitoches is a very small town), but Alice refused to let them inside. When Cunningham ordered the door broken down, some of the men objected. They did not wish to be party to a lynching. Besides, they knew that several armed black men were inside.[21]

Leaving Sam Raines in charge of the siege, Cunningham returned to the courthouse to consult Democratic bigwigs. The informal committee agreed that Blunt should be arrested and that he would be offered safe conduct if he surrendered. Cunningham, who hated Blunt with a passion, declined to convey the offer. The committee delegated two men whom they thought Blunt might trust to take the message. One of the envoys peered through a window and exclaimed, "God damn it, there's fourteen negroes in here." The other, former Republican judge C. C. Chaplin, pleaded with Mrs. Blunt "for humanity's sake" to open the door. Meeting another refusal, Raines's men forced their way inside. Chaplin took Mrs. Blunt's keys, and the men opened all the cupboards and closets. They even looked in the water cistern. Blunt's hiding place eluded them.

A frustrated Cunningham ordered his men to clear everyone out of the house, including the women. Alice became, in Cunningham's words, "violent, bitter, and defiant." One man pointed a pistol at her, she recalled, "and said if I did not hush up he would shoot my head off." Far from quieting down, Mrs. Blunt, who was pregnant, began to shriek: "Shoot, shoot! Why don't you shoot me? Kill him! Go in and kill him!" Worried that he was losing control of the situation—a large crowd of blacks and whites witnessed all of this—Cunningham instructed his men to take Blunt's wife and daughter to the courthouse.

Raines's squad finally discovered the trapdoor and opened it. "Come down, by God, and make a speech," one of them shouted. According to Blunt, the barrel of a Winchester rifle appeared through the trap, whereupon he stepped on the barrel "and snatched it from his hands." He only agreed to come down, he claimed, when the whites agreed to guarantee his safety. The only reason he allowed himself to be taken alive, he added, was his fear that a shoot-out would endanger the women in the house.[22]

Raines and his men painted Blunt's surrender in less heroic hues. "For God's sake don't kill me," Blunt pleaded, "and I'll leave the parish and never come back." Raines told him they had no intention of killing him, and after taking Blunt outside he instructed the hundred or so white onlookers that he wanted no lynching. "Gentlemen, I have promised this man that he shall not be hurt, and I hope that you will respect my promise." Blunt claimed that he showed Raines the Masonic distress signal, and believed that the secret sign may have saved his life. Raines testified that he saw no such signal. According to Cunningham, Blunt proffered a hand and "begged me to protect him."[23]

There is no dispute about what happened next. Pinioned between two white men, Blunt was marched off to the courthouse and placed under guard. Badly frightened, he shouted through the window, pleading for assistance to anyone who walked by.[24]

Worried how blacks might react to news of Blunt's arrest, Democrats distributed a handbill under the signature of Mayor C. F. Dranguet calling upon "all citizens capable of bearing arms" to report to Lacoste Hall on Front Street at six in the evening. "Our lives and property must be protected at all hazards," read the flyer. "M. J. Cunningham is appointed chief of police." Squads of armed, mounted Democrats patrolled the streets and roads that evening and the following two days.[25]

In the past, fear of black retaliation had inhibited Democrats from eliminating Blunt. They now feared that his arrest would anger the black population and might lead to a rescue attempt by blacks under arms. News traveled fast, and now that some blacks possessed horses the plantation grapevine was more effective than ever. A white farmer "saw negroes all that evening in great commotion riding to and fro." By late afternoon, as day turned to dusk, black men gathered outside town, perhaps 150 strong, with whatever weapons they could procure. Rehearsing military-style maneuvers, they debated whether they should cross the "dirt bridge" across the Cane River—a kind of earthen dike—that led into town. Charles Porter, one of the white men guarding the bridge, "heard negroes making speeches and applauding," and then "singing war songs and making threats." Gabriel

Goldstein, a young man whom Blunt regarded as an adopted son, told Porter that "there would be hell to pay that night—they were going to have Blunt or burn the town."

The seriousness of the threat, however, can be gauged from the fact that Cunningham posted a mere four men on the dirt bridge, a major point of ingress into town. The blacks who threatened to force their way across the bridge were equipped with shotguns, muskets, and axes. It took only one exchange of gunfire, which produced no fatalities, for the blacks to retreat. Deputy Sheriff John Hartman, dispatched to "disperse a mob of negroes" somewhere else, found a dozen blacks "standing there talking." Only "one or two had guns." The Democrats felt sufficiently secure to reconvene their nominating convention at nine in the evening and complete their official business before midnight. G. W. Lucky could not recall "any apprehension of trouble." The next morning, weaponless, he rode the thirty miles home without encountering any armed blacks. Charles Payne, who chaired the Democratic convention, found it hard to credit reports that blacks were mobilizing to attack the courthouse. In all his years living in Natchitoches, he "had never heard of a negro attack before."[26]

But Cunningham was taking no chances. He sent messengers to Colfax and Coushatta requesting assistance. He kept patrols in motion throughout the night. And he demanded that Blunt, his prisoner, instruct any blacks still under arms to go home. Blunt demurred, disclaiming any ability to control anyone from his place of confinement. When Cunningham insisted, he offered to go to the dirt bridge in person. Cunningham squelched that proposition and ordered him to send a messenger. Two young men, separately, rode out to the bridge and urged the crowd to disperse. Cunningham did not trust their assurances. Blunt asked his wife to convey the message again. With a white man escorting her, Alice Blunt arrived at the dirt bridge to find that most of the crowd had already left. About thirty remained, and they told her that they were going to the courthouse to demand Blunt's release. Mrs. Blunt implored them not to, warning that the Democrats would kill her husband rather than release him. The men drifted away, and Mrs. Blunt went home. Recognizing her in the dark, William Jack told her in no uncertain terms that Blunt must "stick to his church and quit politics."[27]

Sometime after midnight, six guards escorted Blunt to his house, where he packed his saddlebags and mounted his horse. Raines, the squad's leader, made sure he collected no weapons and then led the party out of town.

After about a mile, Raines asked if Blunt would leave the parish and desist from politics. "Mr. Raines, you will not hear from me," Blunt promised. The party then let their prisoner loose and departed. Convinced that an ambush had been set for him, Blunt left the road and took to the woods, where he laid low, deciding not to travel during the day. Cunningham adamantly denied that he ever ordered Blunt to be exiled, claiming that the offer to leave Natchitoches originated from Blunt himself, who exhibited "abject, pitiful cowardice." Regardless of Blunt's state of mind at the time, Cunningham's denial was false. "We ordered him '*out of the parish never to return,*'" reported Cosgrove in the *Vindicator*.[28]

On the morning of September 22, a Sunday, the committee of Democrats decided that *all* leading Republicans should leave the parish "for the peace and quiet of the community." The list included Virgil Barron, Henry Raby, the Breda brothers, and John Lewis. The committee entrusted the plan to Cunningham and requested that he be "as mild about it as practicable."[29]

Lewis had eluded the previous day's dragnet by hiding in the back yard of his father-in-law's house in weeds "rank enough to hide a good-sized man." The house lay directly opposite the quarantine station, and the Democrats, having failed to bag Blunt or the Bredas, went there at once. Posting guards at the front and back doors, they searched the house room by room. "He is in there; get him out, by God," shouted William Levy. "He is playing 'possum.'" Another Democrat, Beverly Tucker, rode about the weeds on his pony but soon gave up: "He is not in there." Lewis remained hidden for a couple of hours and then sought refuge in the house of a friend, Valcour Merrity.

Pondering his situation, Lewis decided to appeal to David Pierson, whom he regarded as a fair-minded Democrat. He asked Merrity to find Pierson and deliver a note, which read, basically, "What shall I do?" Merrity located Pierson in a coffeehouse and waited outside for him. Pierson had kept himself at arm's length from the events of the day and did not wish to become involved. However, he asked a friend, Joseph P. Johnson, the registrar of voters, to go and talk with Lewis. Merrity took Johnson to the meeting-place and let out a whistle to summon Lewis. "Well, Mr. Johnson?" Lewis began. "What do you gentlemen want that I should do?" Johnson advised him to go to the courthouse, give himself up, "and stand your chances with Blunt." While he pondered Johnson's suggestion, Lewis heard firing from the skirmish on the dirt bridge. When he heard that Blunt had been taken from the courthouse by a party of white men, he made up his mind. Rather than give himself up, he hid in woods outside town. The following afternoon he received word that Blunt was also hiding out. The brothers-in-law arranged to meet after dark at a point thirteen miles below town. They rode together to Alexandria, where they took a steamboat to New Orleans. The city was in the throes of a yellow fever epidemic, and Blunt quickly fell sick.[30]

Cunningham delegated the task of inducing the Breda brothers to leave Natchitoches to Mayor Dranguet, their uncle. Dranguet had scarcely spoken to the Bredas since 1874, but he played upon their concern for his sister, their mother. He also played good cop to Cunningham's bad cop, telling his nephews that he had "interceded nearly the whole night to prevent them from coming . . . and disturbing the family." Unless they left within two hours, however, they would be facing "250 or 300 men armed to the teeth, infuriated, and many of them inebriated." Ernest said they would consider the ultimatum but wanted a guarantee that his extended family would be safe. Dranguet left and returned with two other members of the Democratic committee, who pledged that nobody would disturb the family as long as the Bredas exiled themselves. Ernest and Philippe took their rifles and pistols and secluded themselves in the woods on the extensive Breda property.

For the next few weeks the brothers laid low, keeping in touch with their family while trying to create the impression that that they had left the parish. But nobody had seen them leave—all the crossroads and ferries were guarded—and the Democrats suspected that the family was hiding them. On October 25, Dranguet warned one of the Breda sisters that the Democrats intended to search the house and scour the woods, with bloodhounds if necessary. "For God's sake, if the boys are here, tell them not to remain." Shortly after midnight on October 31, Ernest and Philippe left on horseback, arriving in Shreveport twenty-four hours later.[31]

Virgil Barron had also evaded capture on September 21, taking refuge with his brother who lived thirty miles away. Returning to Natchitoches nine days later, he was summoned to see Cunningham, who asked him why he was back in Natchitoches when he had been ordered to leave. After consulting other Democrats, Cunningham confirmed the order: they would make no exception for Barron. The Democrats intended to carry the election, he explained; the government was theirs; they had been beaten out of it long enough; they could endure it no longer; they would brook no opposition; "they wanted no leaders of the [Republican] party about." To soften the blow a little, Cunningham added that if Barron stayed with his brother and made himself as unobtrusive as possible, the committee would consider allowing him home after the election. Barron was not reassured: "I left and went to Shreveport."[32]

Henry Raby had eluded arrest by staying away from his house. However, trapped in Natchitoches and afraid to go home, he decided to surrender to Cunningham, who confined him in the courthouse. Several hours later, Cunningham ordered him to leave the parish forthwith, following a specified route. "Mr. Cunningham said that he had never killed anybody," Raby testified, "but if I returned to the parish he would kill me himself." Cunningham denied making any such threat, presenting himself instead as magnanimous protector. "I told him as far as I was concerned that I would do anything I could to make it as easy as possible for him, because I didn't regard Raby as bad a man as some of the others." Raby started out on the assigned route, but as soon as he found himself in open countryside he hid in a ditch for the rest of the night and most of the following day. After darkness fell, "I gradually made my way out of the parish."[33]

The Democrats allowed a few Republican officials to remain in post, including parish judge P. A. Simmons, Sheriff D. H. Boullt Jr., and Justice of the Peace J. R. Hornsby. They considered these men small fry. Leaving them in place enabled Democrats to claim that they did not oppose Republicans per se, only crooks and incendiaries.[34]

But the Democrats had no intention of allowing the Republican Party to mount a campaign. Hornsby discovered this to his cost when a committee of Democrats asked him to pledge in writing to stop "indulging in incendiary talk and exciting the negroes." Hornsby, a former slave overseer and Confederate veteran, refused. In that case, the committee told him, three of their number would be back on October 9 to make sure he left the parish. Before the triumvirate returned, Hornsby got into a dispute with a neighbor that involved threatening language and the brandishing of weapons. "The next thing I knew," he testified, "there was a bill of indictment against me for assault with intent to murder." Hornsby fled to New Orleans. On December 10 the police arrested him as a fugitive from justice on a warrant from Natchitoches.[35]

The Democratic leadership was top-heavy with lawyers—Cunningham, Levy, Jack, Pierson—and they anticipated that the coup of September 21 would lead to federal prosecutions under the Enforcement Acts. Any prosecutor, however, would need to establish a racially motivated conspiracy to deny blacks federal rights. It was therefore essential for the Democrats to present their actions as defensive, spontaneous, apolitical, and free from racial bias. It was important, too, to get that story into print as soon as possible, so that the Democrats retained the initiative and the Republicans would be forced to respond.

This is where James Cosgrove came in. The editor lost no time in "spinning" the story. Taking advantage of the telegraph, he sent dispatches to the *New Orleans Daily Democrat* and the *New York Times* in which he described how blacks, harangued by Blunt and the Bredas, had become dangerous, reckless, defiant, and threatening. Citizens had "dispersed the mob" in self-defense. They had then saved the town from destruction by foiling an armed attack by hundreds of blacks. Within two days, the Democrats had got this version of events into the public domain. Their story that blacks planned to attack the Democratic convention was the one that stuck.[36]

It took the Republican Party far longer to present its own version of events. For one thing, it proved difficult for the state party, based in New Orleans, to establish what exactly had happened. The Republican leaders in Natchitoches had, in effect, disappeared. While Cosgrove was disseminating Democratic propaganda, the Bredas were hiding in the woods, Blunt and Lewis were en route to New Orleans, and Raby and Barron were in seclusion. It was only when Blunt and Lewis reached New Orleans that the state executive committee could piece the story together and publish it in the *Republican*. Blunt's own account did not appear in print until October 5.[37]

The Natchitoches Democrats could not have timed their coup better. New Orleans and Natchitoches were both in quarantine on account of the yellow fever epidemic. Nobody could move in or out of Natchitoches; the only communication was by letter and telegram. When a Republican delegation visited Governor Nicholls on September 26, reminding him of Democratic pledges to safeguard blacks' rights, the governor batted away their complaints by stating that "he had not been officially informed of any disturbances." Instead of bringing him facts, Nicholls added, the Republicans brought unsubstantiated allegations. Was it not a "little singular," he asked, that the Republicans in Natchitoches should have arranged to meet when and where they did "unless it was desired to bring about an issue?" Nicholls saw no reason to act on the matter.[38]

Republicans in Natchitoches faced an additional obstacle in getting their story to the outside world: they did not trust the mails, convinced that their correspondence was being intercepted. "No Republican can receive anything by this P[ost] Office," Elcey Breda wrote U.S. Marshal Jack

Wharton, "the postmistress being the sister-in-law and willing tool of Cosgrove." Whether true or not, the suspicion made Republicans extremely cautious about what they committed to paper. To ensure that their letters got through, they had friends mail additional copies. To make sure they received letters, they asked correspondents to address them to other people.[39]

Elcey Breda's letter to Wharton was the first eyewitness information the U.S. Department of Justice received from Natchitoches. Ernest's wife branded Cosgrove's account a "fabrication from beginning to end." The Democrats had driven out the Breda brothers, she wrote, because they wanted a free hand to illegally manipulate the voter registration rolls. Appealing to Wharton as a "Christian gentleman with human principles and feelings," she begged him to "alleviate our sufferings and relieve us from our murderous assailants." Wharton forwarded the letter to U.S. Attorney General Charles S. Devens, who urged federal officials in Louisiana to act promptly and vigorously. U.S. Attorney Albert H. Leonard engaged four men as special agents, instructing them to locate witnesses in Natchitoches and three other parishes. It was not until mid-October, however, when the quarantine was finally lifted, that the detectives could get down to work.[40]

The federal response was much too slow to help the Republican Party in Louisiana. On November 5 it suffered a crushing defeat. The party's statewide vote fell from 51 percent to 36 percent, and in northern Louisiana it virtually collapsed. In Natchitoches Parish the entire Democratic ticket was elected virtually unopposed. Sheriff David H. Boullt Jr. ran for reelection as an Independent, but he received fewer than 100 votes; his opponent received 2,682. The Democrats increased their majority in the state legislature from slightly over one-half to more than three-quarters. Democrats were elected to all six seats in Congress. The Republican Party was all but dead, crowed the *New Orleans Daily Democrat*. "North of Red River it cannot poll a thousand votes, and it exists today only in a few parishes of Southern Louisiana."[41]

Bourbon editors taxed their powers of imagination to explain these results, which they had of course anticipated. The *Daily Democrat*, edited by Cosgrove's political ally H. J. Hearsey, professed astonishment and confusion—"it was scarcely possible to fully understand the greatness of our triumph." Cosgrove himself painted a fanciful portrait of joyful blacks embracing the Democratic Party in scenes that evoked heart-warming memories of slave times. "We were carried back to those happy days when we coon-hunted with Ike and Steve, or listened in the kitchen to Uncle John's stories of ghosts and goblins, while snugly seated in our old loving 'mammy's' lap." No longer estranged from each other, he wrote, blacks and whites were "united forever."[42]

Blacks remembered the day differently. "I voted the Democratic ticket," recounted John B. Vienne, "because I was in a manner forced to do it." A party of Democrats visited his home and told his wife that "if I did not vote I would have to take the consequences." Valcour Merrity tried to avoid voting by hiding, but his wife received a visitation from the same men with the same message. "I went out after that and voted." The Democratic candidate for coroner told Joe Reid that if he did not vote "he would not guarantee my life." After voting, blacks received a pink ribbon that read, "Voted the Democratic Ticket of 1878." Democratic poll watchers explained that the ribbon would protect them for the next two years.[43]

Shedrick Brown's experience of voting presented a sobering reflection on the failure of the local Republican Party to retain its support, let alone increase it, among whites. Charles Bullard handed him the ballot paper, William Tunnard gave him the badge, and Theodore Schuman ordered him to put the badge on. All three white men were former Republicans. Bullard and Schuman had been Unionists who joined the party at its inception. Bullard was the first to quit. Schuman, elected mayor of Natchitoches in 1868 on the Republican ticket, switched parties two years later. Former Confederate Tunnard, elected clerk of court on the Republican ticket in 1876, decided to join the Democrat Party shortly before the 1878 election.[44]

Across the South, Democrats utilized threats, violence, and fraud to decimate the Republican Party. The most flagrant illegalities took place in Louisiana and South Carolina. There could be no clearer evidence that the conciliatory policy of President Hayes and his supporters had failed. The optimistic belief that ditching the "carpetbaggers" and abandoning military intervention would attract educated, propertied, and politically moderate white southerners (the much discussed "Henry Clay Whigs") had been found wanting. The Republican Party recoiled in horror at the election results. Hayes himself was appalled. "By state legislation," he confided to his diary, "by frauds, by intimidation, and by violence of the most atrocious character, colored citizens have been deprived of the right of suffrage." He publicly admitted that conciliation had failed and promised "determined and vigorous action" to punish malefactors under the Enforcement Acts.[45]

The Republican Party responded on two fronts. The Department of Justice, acting through U.S. Attorney Leonard and U.S. Marshal Wharton, pressed ahead with its investigation with a view to prosecuting Democratic ringleaders. Answering criticism that he was paying his special agents too much, Wharton pointed out to Devens that "the mission of the detectives is one of great hazard, requiring courage as well as other special qualities." On December 1, Leonard sent Devens his report: the Democrats had launched a "reign of terror" that in Natchitoches, Caddo, Ouchita, and Tensas Parishes had wiped out Republican majorities. He empaneled a federal grand jury and summoned witnesses. Shortly before Christmas the grand jury issued indictments against 120 people, half of them from Natchitoches.[46]

Opening a second front, the U.S. Senate—still controlled by the Republican Party, but only until the new Congress convened—appointed a five-man committee, chaired by Henry M. Teller of Colorado, to hold hearings into the elections in Louisiana and South Carolina. The committee began its work on January 7 in the Custom House building in New Orleans, the scene of so many congressional investigations. The witnesses who had testified before the grand jury told their stories all over again, this time in public.

The testimony of Milton Cunningham, the principal Democratic witness, spoke volumes about the changed political climate. Unlike the emollient David Pierson, the Democrats' main witness before the Hoar Committee in 1875 and the Morrison Committee in 1876, Cunningham was combative, contemptuous, angry, and threatening. "I don't intend to hurt them," he said about the Breda brothers, "but if anybody wants to do it I am not going to interfere, that is certain." He described J. R. Hornsby as a "miserable sot [who] lives with a negro wife in a wretched hovel." He reserved his sharpest barbs for Blunt, whose "prejudices against the whites were so strong, that he was the most dangerous man." Using words like "coward," "demagogue," and "incendiary," Cunningham attacked Blunt's character in every way he could. However, when he charged Blunt with abandoning his wife to cohabit with Rachel Williams, he walked into a trap. The following day he was presented with a marriage certificate that Blunt and Williams had long ago obtained from the Freedmen's Bureau. "I know that you would not willfully do him an injustice," needled the counsel for the Republicans.[47]

In October the Breda brothers had considered unobtrusively returning to their home in Natchitoches. But Cosgrove somehow got wind of their intentions. "They must not return," warned the *Vindicator*. "If they do they will be dealt with." Their father, Dr. J. P. Breda, asked two senior Democrats—W. W. Breazeale and J. H. Cunningham—to intercede on behalf of his exiled sons.[48]

He did not receive much encouragement. Cunningham reminded Breda that his sons had been ordered never to return, that only the Democratic "advisory committee" could take decisions, and that any initiative must come from Mayor Dranguet, the head of the committee. Breda immediately sought out Dranguet (his brother-in-law and the boys' uncle) and asked him to present the committee with a written request that his sons be allowed to return. Dranguet agreed to submit the document, and he helped Breda père, who normally wrote in French, to couch it in suitably respectful English. On November 26 Breda received the committee's reply: his sons may return, but only if they signed a groveling mea culpa and pledged to "abstain in future from all efforts or acts of incendiarism, and to conduct themselves at all times and on such a manner as to secure the approbation of the good citizens of Natchitoches."[49]

The Bredas treated this abject confession with contempt. If they signed it, they would be taking a vow of silence; they would have to lie or stonewall before the Teller Committee; they would be unable to act as prosecution witnesses in a federal trial. They refused to sign. Since reading Cosgrove's death threat in the *Vindicator*, Ernest wrote his wife:

> I have been employing my whole time procuring and forwarding facts and evidence for the prosecution and punishment of the scoundrels. Commencing with Nicholls, whom I hold as the chief and prime [culprit] and down to the loathsome Levy, Pierson, Jack, Carver, Cosgrove *et sui generis*. . . . [If] we must be ruined, I am determined that they shall not enjoy it or gloat over their success. . . . If they wish that we suffer persecution, they should have prepared to suffer also, for they must, will and shall.

Ernest and Philippe Breda were the first to testify before the Teller Committee.[50]

All Republican witnesses from northern Louisiana placed themselves in danger. Two blacks who had been subpoenaed to give evidence about Caddo Parish left Shreveport but failed to arrive in New Orleans. A party of armed white men took them off a steamboat, and they were never heard of again. "I have little doubt they have been killed," Leonard wrote Devens. After giving their testimony to the Teller Committee, Ernest and Philippe Breda received a letter from their father warning them not to return to Natchitoches, because "you would be in danger of assassination." Their younger brother, Emile, underlined the danger: "The democrats swear that if you, Philippe, Blunt, Lewis, Raby, Barron or any others who testified against them ever return to Natchitoches, that he will be killed at sight."[51]

On January 29, after the Teller Committee departed for South Carolina, federal marshals arrested thirty-two Democrats in Natchitoches Parish. More arrests followed, bringing the total from Natchitoches to forty-eight. All told, including the defendants from Tensas and Caddo Parishes, the number of arrestees exceeded two hundred. Justice Department officials questioned the wisdom of prosecuting so many people. But Leonard had the bit between his teeth. Every guilty party should be put on trial, he advised Washington, regardless of number. "Unless the laws be enforced to [their] fullest extent it will soon be impossible to have anything like protection for property and life in Louisiana."[52]

Leonard acknowledged the enormity of his task. The defendants, he predicted, would use delaying tactics, present perjured testimony, and attempt to pack and bribe the jury. They had the advantage of being prominent and respected citizens: judges, lawyers, large planters, well-known merchants, and high state officials—"the leaders of society." They could command the best lawyers in New Orleans, "whose sympathies are with the accused." It was nonetheless a shock to learn that the defendants had retained James R. Beckwith, Leonard's predecessor, to lead their five-man defense team. Leonard, the former White League leader, and Beckwith, the former foe of the White League, had swapped hats. To call this reversal of roles ironic would be to miss the point: the desire for office and income was a major determinant of political behavior and often trumped principle or ideology.[53]

To help him oppose this formidable array of legal talent, Leonard hired none other than Ernest Breda, who would also testify as a prosecution witness. The defense attorneys outnumbered them five to two. Upon the verdict in this trial hinged the future of the Republican Party in Natchitoches Parish.

15

THE SLOW DEATH OF THE REPUBLICAN PARTY

I have never been in a community where there appeared to be so little
regard paid to truth, principle and honesty, nor where there was so much
intrigue, double dealing, and dishonesty generally.

George C. Tichnor to Senator John Sherman, 1888

"The balmy air and cloudless sky yesterday gave the last touches to the
scene of hilarity in our city," reported the *New Orleans Daily Picayune* on
February 26, 1879. "Never did a more beautiful day and happier crowd
unite to welcome the Man who Laughs." Rex, the self-proclaimed King of
Carnival, had assumed the character of Richard Coeur de Lion, and his
krewe presented a pageant of the history of the world. In the recent past
Carnival floats had satirized Republican politicians. Not this year. There
was no longer any need. After all, the state had been "redeemed" in 1877,
and the last Republican strongholds in northern Louisiana eliminated the
following year. New Orleans, relieved that another epidemic of yellow fever
had subsided, partied in a nonpolitical way.[1]

The trial of forty-eight Natchitoches Democrats in *U.S. v. Cunningham*,
presided over by Judges Edward C. Billings and William W. Woods, began
the day before Mardi Gras and resumed the day after. The fine weather,
however, soon turned cold, and the trial was accompanied by coughs and
sneezes. "Seldom if ever before," noted the *New Orleans Daily Democrat*,
"have we met with so many gentlemen suffering from colds. A short, rapid
skirmishing fire of coughs would start on the outposts of the crowd and
then firing by battalions would commence. As was shown from the short,
sharp cough to the deep artillery roar, every caliber of nose was represented." The trial attracted a fair amount of interest and was faithfully covered by Democratic newspapers. But it evoked a sense of déjà vu and, eventually, of boredom. After the failure of the Colfax prosecutions, Democrats

Figure 15. John G. Lewis Sr. with wife, Victoria, sons Scott (*standing left*), Lambert L'Ouverture (*standing right*), and John G. Lewis Jr. (*foreground*), and daughters (*left to right*) Ruth, Beulah, Vinita, Clara, and Beatrice. Amistad Research Center, Tulane University.

felt little anxiety. "There is no doubt of an acquittal," wrote one of those indicted, on March 5. "I think we will all get off on Saturday."[2]

The difficulty of the prosecution case was obvious from the start. The indictment charged the Democrats with a conspiracy to prevent the election of Republicans to parish office and to prevent Raford Blunt and other Republican leaders from "advocating and supporting" J. Madison Wells, the Republican candidate for Congress in the Fourth Congressional District. U.S. Attorney Albert Leonard had to demonstrate intent, prior planning, and the continuous operation of the alleged conspiracy from September 21 until November 5, the day of the elections. This would be hard enough, and the reference to Wells made it harder. The legal logic behind invoking Wells was simple: although there was considerable uncertainty as to the constitutionality of the Enforcement Acts, the power of Congress to regulate federal elections was relatively clear-cut. However, it would not be easy to link the congressional election to what happened on September 21. Wells's candidacy was the last thing on the mind of either the bulldozers or the bulldozed.[3]

Leonard's evidence of conspiracy was twofold. First, he tied the Democrats' actions on September 21 to their membership in a secret society called the "298," which had been organized in Natchitoches during the summer of 1878. The 298 had originated in the Florida Parishes years earlier. Its character remains opaque. Alabama historian Walter L. Fleming, writing in 1915, likened it to the Ku Klux Klan. But hard information about the organization is scarce. When taxed by Leonard, Democratic witnesses described it as a social and benevolent organization akin to the freemasons, with no political agenda and no military or quasi-military character. M. J. Cunningham, the "grand commander" of the Natchitoches lodge, depicted it as innocuous. "We have a great deal of fun. There is no harm in it. . . . It is not a dangerous organization." Other Democratic witnesses characterized it in the same way. Although Blunt, Lewis, and other Republicans described the 298 as the successor to the White League—"no one but a white man and a Democrat is allowed to join it," claimed Philippe Breda—Leonard produced no evidence to prove its involvement in the affair of September 21.[4]

Leonard's second argument was equally weak. Like the Republican witnesses, he cited editorials in the *People's Vindicator* as evidence of a Democratic scheme to carry the elections by fraud, violence, and intimidation. But newspaper editorials had never carried much weight in trials under the Enforcement Acts. Editors could claim protection under the First Amendment and, if pressed, explain away their fire-breathing prose as poetic license. Moreover, as the former editor of the *Shreveport Times*, Leonard was singularly ill-placed to cite newspaper editorials as evidence. James Beckwith, in his summation, made the obvious point: "It is unfair to ascribe to a whole community the sentiments of a newspaper, or to indict a people for the utterances of a journal. How would it have looked had all Shreveport been indicted for the offense committed by the district attorney when he was publishing an extreme partisan newspaper and advocating the assassination of Republican candidates and officers?" Inexplicably, the Teller Committee failed to call James Cosgrove as a witness, and Leonard did not examine him.[5]

The Democrats' defense was simple and consistent: they had arrested Blunt and exiled other Republican leaders in order to protect the peace and safety of Natchitoches. There was no plot or conspiracy, no prior planning; the delegates to the Democratic convention had gone to the court-house unarmed. They only created a quasi-military organization when they heard that the Republicans intended to break up the Democratic convention. They only decided to arrest Blunt when they received reports that blacks were preparing to attack the town. Blunt himself offered to leave Natchitoches Parish. The Democratic "advisory committee" only decided to arrest and exile the other Republican leaders on September 22, and with the same purpose in mind: to stop then making incendiary speeches that invited blacks to embark on a rampage. There had been no intention to harm them or send them into permanent exile. The Democrats had acted as honest citizens, not partisans, and the prospect of reaping an electoral dividend never entered their minds.[6]

The main prosecution witnesses repeated the testimony they had given to the Teller Committee. C. C. Chaplin, formerly a Republican district judge but now in the Democratic camp, described them as bitter. "Breda was very severe on Dranguet, Lewis on Levy, and Blunt on all." In selecting his own witnesses, however, Beckwith ensured that the aggressive M. J. Cunningham, the lead defendant, restrained his temper, stuck to the script, and took a back seat, leaving others to provide most of the defense's testimony.[7]

Beckwith reserved to himself the task of attacking Blunt's character. The black leader exercised enormous influence over his people and was potentially dangerous, Beckwith asserted, and that made him "a man to be watched." Blunt's own testimony showed that the decision to arrest him was justified "in the interest of peace and public safety." Beckwith rebutted the notion that Blunt had been exiled in order to prevent him from advocating the election of Wells to Congress. The Republican meeting on September 21 was merely a ward meeting, he pointed out, and Wells's candidacy was not even discussed. Besides, he added, "advocacy" covered only the act of voting, and blacks *had* voted on September 21. The Republicans had simply failed to distribute a ticket. Exploiting every inconsistency in their testimony, Beckwith accused Blunt of lying and challenged the veracity of "possum" Lewis and "vixenish" Miss Blunt. The *Picayune* described Beckwith's summing up as "intense, withering, direct, fearless, thorough, and pitiless." It showed why both prosecution and defense had competed for his services.[8]

Instructing the jury on March 6, Judge Woods, a Republican, the same man who had presided over the Colfax trials, defined "conspiracy" in wide terms. Conspiracies rarely produce direct evidence, he pointed out. It was quite legitimate to infer the existence of a conspiracy from circumstantial evidence alone: "It is not necessary to prove any direct concert or even any meeting of the conspirators." Intent, he added, could be inferred from deeds. He added that those who took part in those deeds, even if they had no hand in planning them and did not expressly assent to them, were also part of the conspiracy. "By knowingly and tacitly falling in with it . . . they are just as guilty as if they had agreed in writing at the outset to engage in the unlawful combination." Appealing to the jurors to "lay aside all partisan prejudice and feeling," Woods implored them to show the "courage and manhood" to bring in a verdict of guilty if they considered the evidence sufficient.[9]

The jury consisted of eleven white men and one black man. Beckwith used peremptory challenges to exclude several blacks, and Leonard invoked the federal juror's "test oath" to exclude a number of former Confederates. Half of the whites were natives of New Orleans. Three northern-born men had served in the Union forces. The sole black juror was the only one to have gone to war for the Confederacy, albeit as the servant of a Confederate officer (which may explain why Beckwith declined to challenge him). It was about as fair a selection as the prosecution could reasonably hope for. Nevertheless, as he watched the jurors' faces, Chaplin became "fully convinced that their minds are already made up for acquittal." The jury deliberated late into the night of March 6 and all morning on March 7. It was rumored that two of the jurors were holding out for the conviction of at least some of the accused. At 12:45 p.m. on March 7 the jury trooped back to the courtroom. The foreman, William Arms, a native of New York who had lived in New Orleans since 1853, delivered the verdict: "Not guilty, as to all."[10]

Minutes later, members of the Orleans Artillery, a state militia unit, wheeled a cannon onto the levee and fired a fifty-gun salute. "It seemed that the entire population was vomited from home and business upon the streets," the *Daily Democrat* reported. "Cheers rent the air, hands were grasped, and joy beamed from every face." At five in the afternoon, in a Lafayette Square packed with spectators, a battery of the Washington Artillery fired a one-hundred-gun salute. The following day, a Saturday, thousands turned out to watch the freed prisoners, led by militiamen "with bands playing and colors flying," walk from City Hotel to the foot of Canal Street, where they boarded the *Bart Able*. As the steamboat headed upriver, a band playing on its roof, thousands more cheering spectators lined the nine miles of levee from Canal Street to Carrollton, and "every tug, ferry boat and steamer saluted with bell and whistle." At each landing on the Mississippi and Red Rivers, more cheering crowds and blaring bands greeted the *Bart Able*.

The acquitted prisoners arrived in Natchitoches to be hailed as conquering heroes. At a reception in Lacoste's Hall, Cecile Hertzog, on behalf of the "Ladies of Natchitoches," presented Cosgrove with a hand-sewn banner with the words "Welcome to Our Patriots" on one side and, on the other, "September 21, 1878." Ida Buard draped a floral wreath on Cunningham's shoulders.[11]

The expelled Republicans had no happy homecoming. J. P. Breda, writing from Natchitoches, told Ernest and Philippe that their plantation risked losing its harvest if it failed to pay its black laborers. The aging doctor was working in the fields himself, rarely quitting before dark. He warned his sons that "the bandits who call themselves the people say that they will never allow you to set foot again in the Parish." James J. Davis, Ernest and Philippe's brother-in-law, reported that members of the 298 had taken an oath "to murder the leading Republicans on sight."[12]

For blacks who had testified, the outlook was worse. Ambrose Wallace arrived back in Natchitoches but immediately turned around when friends and relatives, "entreating him with tears to get away," reported that armed white men were visiting the homes of black witnesses. The latter would only be allowed to return if they pledged to vote the Democratic ticket for the rest of their lives. "Most of them choose to linger in New Orleans and starve," reported the *New York Times*.[13]

The Hayes administration recognized the acquittal of the Natchitoches prisoners for what it was: a disaster for the federal effort to ensure free and fair elections in the South. Attorney General Devens complained that Leonard had mishandled the case by putting so many people on trial at the same time, "thus arraying against him the combined influence of the defendants." Leonard complained that a Democratic-controlled jury commission had packed the jury venire with "pronounced Democrats, many of them well known for their pronounced partisanship." The truth, however, was much simpler: the Enforcement Acts had become impossible to enforce. The government, the *New York Times* noted, "has spent $40,000 to discover that it cannot vindicate a statute." In the South, it concluded, "elections are arranged to suit the local leaders, with no disquietude as to the consequences from the courts." The Natchitoches trial was not the last of its kind. The Department of Justice continued to initiate prosecutions under the Enforcement Acts until Congress repealed that legislation in 1894. But the number of prosecutions plummeted and acquittals usually followed, except in minor cases where defendants faced fines rather than jail terms. After the Natchitoches verdict, Leonard dropped the Caddo and Tensas Parish cases.[14]

In an open letter signed by leading Democrats congratulating the Natchitoches defendants, one name was conspicuously absent: that of Governor Francis T. Nicholls. Having pledged to protect black rights, Nicholls was embarrassed by Democrats' use of violence. After visiting Tensas Parish, he condemned the attempted assassination of black politician Alfred Fairfax as "utterly wrong—in my opinion without justification." Yet no action followed. He could only use persuasion, Nicholls confessed, as his powers were "extremely limited." Any prosecutions must come from the local authorities, and he had no idea what steps they were taking to punish the culprits. Nicholls made no mention of Natchitoches, perhaps because what happened there seemed relatively minor compared with the events in Caddo and Tensas Parishes, which left several blacks dead. Republicans now knew for certain what they had already suspected. As Blunt put it during a mass meeting in Lafayette Square, "if [Nicholls] held the law and the prophets in one hand and a big iron poker in the other, he could not, if he wanted, quash the bulldozers."[15]

The bulldozing in northern Louisiana in 1878 was the logical sequel to the "redemption" of the state in 1877. If Democrats found Republican rule at the state level intolerable, why would they put up with it at the parish level, where it was more visible and intrusive? "What 'national statesmen' insisted on as a 'necessity' in the government of the State," commented the New York Times, "local politicians insisted was equally a necessity in the government of its parishes." Noting the absence of violence in Natchitoches, the Times paid a back-handed compliment to M. J. Cunningham, "a gentleman of fine appearance and a pleasant address," who ensured that "no more physical force was used than was absolutely necessary. "As bulldozers went, better "the clean-shirted and kid-gloved variety." But though their methods varied locally, Democrats of every stripe, at least in northern Louisiana, were equally determined to crush the Republican Party. "This is a white man's country," opined the Colfax Chronicle, "and will be from this time until the end of the world."[16]

Exiled black Republicans in New Orleans called for a "convention of colored citizens" with the aim of encouraging blacks to leave Louisiana. Fourteen people from Natchitoches Parish signed the call, including Raford Blunt, John G. Lewis, Henry Raby, and Ambrose Wallace. In words that bore the stamp of Lewis, the chairman, the convention resolved that "life, liberty, and happiness [are] sweeter in a cold climate than murder, rapine, and oppression in the South."[17]

For the first time, blacks left Louisiana in large numbers. They had grievances enough, but a message of hope may have influenced the timing. On January 16, 1879, Senator William Windom of Minnesota urged Congress to help blacks leave "states and congressional districts where they are not allowed to freely and peacefully exercise their constitutional rights" so that they could settle in more welcoming states or territories. From Madison Parish and other majority-black cotton parishes along the Mississippi River, families took the steamboat to St. Louis, whence they could strike out overland for Kansas. Caddo, Bossier, and other parishes in northwestern Louisiana fed the migrant stream. To raise money for their passage, reported the New Orleans Daily Democrat, "they have sold their horses, mules, wagons and implements." Such was the scale and suddenness of the out-migration that it generated nationwide interest. Newspapers dubbed the phenomenon an "Exodus" caused by "Kansas Fever." According to one estimate, fifteen thousand blacks had left Louisiana and Mississippi by the end of March, and "the movement is going on with renewed energy."[18]

The exodus was not really an organized movement, although some emigrants may well have been influenced by semi-clandestine networks of the kind put together by Henry Adams, an ex-Union soldier, "faith doctor," and laborer from Caddo Parish. In 1874 Adams got up a petition that asked President Grant to set aside a territory for blacks or, failing that, help them emigrate to Liberia. The intention was less actually to emigrate than to persuade Washington that it should protect blacks from violence and intimidation. His "colonization committee" met in secret, and during the White League revolt, Adams recalled, "we were scared to hold meetings." Nevertheless, Adams, who was constantly on the move, expanded his network in Caddo to adjacent parishes. In September 1877, after "we lost all hope," he organized a mass meeting in Shreveport that in the name of the National Colored Colonization Society submitted another appeal for federal protection, this time to President Hayes. Three days after the acquittal of the Natchitoches prisoners, Adams, stranded in New Orleans, petitioned Hayes to "give us employment of some kind . . . for we cannot go home; yet, our families are there in want in north Louisiana." None of these letters received a reply.[19]

At the "Colored Convention" that met in New Orleans on April 17–21, about two hundred men gathered at the First Free Mission Baptist Church to decide upon a policy regarding emigration. The participants endorsed the exodus and appointed a "committee on emigration and relief" to negotiate discounted steamboat fares and ensure that blacks received food, shelter, and medical assistance upon their arrival in St. Louis. The convention concluded with a stirring rendition of "John Brown's Body."[20]

The New Orleans convention, like similar meetings that took place across the South in the spring and summer of 1879, had little influence over the migration. For one thing, most of the men who attended were either from New Orleans or were bulldozed officeholders. The conclave attracted virtually no farmers or laborers from the country parishes. "It was emphatically a mass meeting," P. B. S. Pinchback snarkily noted, "ran and controlled almost wholly by small-fry politicians."[21]

Second, the meeting revealed considerable tension between the politicians, who had hitherto discouraged emigration, and the clergymen, who now wanted to support it. Blunt, for example, denounced politicians who had "led the colored people to the slaughter-pen and then deserted them." It was time, he argued, for black ministers to assert their leadership. When someone put it to Blunt that he was both a politician and a preacher, he riposted (not entirely accurately) that he was "no politician . . . and never solicited a vote in my life." And in a barbed comment aimed at Pinchback he added that "I never sold out, like some others did, to the other side." His remarks captured the sentiment of the meeting. "One hundred . . . brogans pounded the floor," noted one reporter, "and cries of 'Go on' were heard."[22]

But Pinchback, still the most influential black politician in Louisiana, remained skeptical. At the start of the convention he argued that blacks "should stay and protect themselves" rather than emigrate. The three-day meeting did nothing to persuade him otherwise. It had urged blacks to emigrate, he complained, "without making one practical suggestion as to the manner in which they should go, where they should go, and what they should do when they went." The convention could have been more productive of results, he added, had it devoted less time to speech-making and more to raising money. Pinchback nevertheless hoped that by holding out the threat of emigration he might persuade whites to address the "hunger and oppression" that drove blacks to leave.[23]

Similarly, bulldozed politicians like Blunt were less interested in promoting emigration than in using "Kansas Fever" as a bargaining chip. Having no desire to personally lead an exodus to Kansas—wishing, in fact, to return to Natchitoches—Blunt saw the convention as a means of influencing the white Democrats who had expelled him. Planters worried that laborers would leave, because they knew that emigration often took the form of Baptists emigrating in a body at the urging of their preacher. They also worried that black laborers, angry over Blunt's expulsion, were sullen and recalcitrant. "Colored men over whom Blunt has hitherto exercised a vast influence," the *Vindicator* noted, "have gone so far as to say that they will only work as they choose and have in a few instances refused to work at all." After Blunt's forced departure, one visitor reported, "the negroes were very much excited and had entirely abandoned the crops." From Natchitoches to Monett Ferry, "the fields were white, and yet there were no hands picking the cotton." Blacks were holding nightly meetings, reported a merchant, where they discussed how to retaliate if Blunt were not allowed to return. According to an unnamed Republican quoted by the *Daily Democrat*, whites in Natchitoches were so alarmed by the exodus that they would shortly allow Blunt, Lewis, and the Breda brothers to return, "in hopes that their presence would induce the colored people to hold out awhile longer."[24]

The Natchitoches Republicans were determined to return to their homes and families. But the when and the how remained uncertain. The Hayes administration renounced use of the military to restore bulldozed politicians, but it could at least offer victims of bulldozing a safety net in the form of federal jobs. The New Orleans Custom House, controlled by the former commander of the Metropolitan Police, A. S. Badger, provided employment for, among others, Pinchback, Blunt, Lewis, and Raby. These positions, writes historian Justin A. Nystrom, "allowed them to continue their political activism shielded from the threat of economic reprisal." Moreover, federal patronage might enable at least some exiled leaders to return to their communities. Federal positions outside New Orleans were few in number, but they did exist.[25]

Ernest Breda was the first to go back. "I plan to return no matter what," he wrote Elcey in April, "and I want to be prepared for anything I might encounter." To this end he asked his wife to do some discreet intelligence-gathering. He instructed her not to rely on blacks for information ("they exaggerate and contradict each other") but rather to ascertain from "responsible people" how whites would view his sudden reappearance, and whether, according to them, he need fear physical assault or assassination.

Breda cautioned her not to tell anyone about his intention to return. By 1880 both Ernest and Philippe were back in Natchitoches, living with their extended family on the Breda plantation. They appear to have encountered little hostility. Indeed, Cosgrove chastised unnamed Democrats for accompanying the Breda brothers on "drinking sprees."[26]

In June 1880, U.S. census enumerators placed Raford Blunt in a boardinghouse in New Orleans, and his wife, toddler, and baby in Natchitoches. By 1882, however, he was back in Natchitoches serving as registrar of the U.S. Land Office. He resumed the ministry of First Baptist Church and went back to teaching school. In June 1884, as a thousand spectators waited in front of the courthouse, Blunt ascended the scaffold as the "spiritual advisor" of a man about to be hanged, a service he repeated for another condemned man in December.[27]

John Lewis was the last to return. During his four-plus years as an employee of the Custom House, he involved himself in a variety of projects. He helped organize a volunteer black militia company when a society of white Union veterans refused to accept black members. He explored the possibility of settling blacks in California to work on fruit farms. Lewis's real passion, however, was the Prince Hall Masons. With the consolidation in 1878 of two rival state organizations, black Masonry in Louisiana entered a time of steady growth. A member of Parsons Lodge in New Orleans and an officer of the statewide Eureka Grand Lodge, Lewis helped organize new lodges in Baton Rouge, Natchitoches, Shreveport, and elsewhere. By the time he installed Raford Blunt as Worshipful Master of Corinthian Lodge No. 19, in 1884, Lewis was back in Natchitoches, where, like Blunt, he signed a teaching contract with the school board.[28]

Why did the Democrats who had expelled them allow Lewis, Blunt, Raby, and the Breda brothers not only to return to Natchitoches but also reorganize the local Republican Party? It is quite likely that they wished to appease their black employees and restore a sense of calm after the political turmoil of 1878–79. That calm, moreover, reflected a distinct change in how blacks behaved toward white people. In Natchitoches, blacks had not been apt to show deference. When they encountered whites on the sidewalks coming in the opposite direction, for example, they felt no obligation to yield the right of way by stepping aside. Now things were different. Blacks spoke about a "take to the road" law that compelled them to step into the street to allow white people to pass by. No such law could be found in the statute book, but blacks found it politic to accept this assertion of white privilege.[29]

Black legislators, a shrinking band, were also taught lessons in deference. In 1880 the state senate suspended four Republican members for signing a memorial to the U.S. Senate that backed the claim of William P. Kellogg in a disputed election case. The document, Democrats complained, spoke of the Louisiana legislature in "contemptuous" language. After framing a "suitable apology," the men were "discharged from the custody of the Sergeant-at-arms" and allowed to resume their places.[30]

Democrats in Natchitoches could afford to be magnanimous because the Republican Party posed no threat locally. Once Democrats possessed all the parish and district offices, they could, aided by a Democratic governor, "win" every election. They no longer needed to engage in intimidation and bulldozing: they controlled the registration of voters, the location of the polling places, the casting of ballots, and the counting of votes. This last, of course, was the most important. Even as black registration in Louisiana rose—black voters still outnumbered white ones—the Republican vote declined. In 1880 the party polled 524 votes in Natchitoches Parish against a Democratic total of 1,609. This would be the pattern for the next sixteen years. In the cotton parishes of northern Louisiana, Democrats implemented the so-called Ouchita Plan of simply counting enough Republican ballots as Democratic ones to ensure a comfortable margin of victory.[31]

Republicans in Natchitoches came to regard political campaigns as futile. They argued over whether to nominate a local Republican ticket at all. With no hope of winning, might it not be better to support to disaffected Democrats who were standing as Independents? "Under the present election law," H. P. Mezière told the Republican Parish Executive Committee in 1884, "there was but little hope of Republican success in this State, much less in this Parish." Blunt agreed, labeling it "folly" to put up a local Republican ticket. "It would be for the best to vote our State ticket and let the parish ticket go by default." Ernest Breda, however, could not stomach the thought of giving local Democrats a free ride, and advocated supporting "anything that was an Opposition to the Regular Democratic nominees." Agreement proved impossible, and Edward Ezernack urged members to "heal what was wrong in our own side first." The party appointed a committee of three to ask the Democratic registrar of voters for "higher recognition [of Republicans] at the Ballot Box." Such requests did nothing, however, to enhance Republican prospects, because Democratic officials ignored them. In every election, the latter manipulated the results—a process known as "ballot box stuffing"—to guarantee Republican defeat. The election of a Democratic president, Grover Cleveland, brought the wholesale ejection of Republicans from federal jobs.[32]

The election of 1888 confirmed the obvious: the state's Democrats, no matter how bitter their own internal divisions, would not permit the election of a Republican as governor. The Democratic convention had revealed a fissure between two factions. One consisted of the southern Louisiana sugar parishes and the predominantly "white" parishes of northern Louisiana; the other was made up of "Ring"-controlled New Orleans and the majority-black parishes of northern Louisiana, whose white delegates owed their election to the suppressed Republican vote. The party finally settled on the reform-minded Francis T. Nicholls over incumbent governor Samuel McEnery, a Bourbon. This was just the sort of tactical opportunity for which Republicans had been waiting. Moreover, the attachment of many sugar planters to the party enhanced Republican prospects, for the sugar growers could not survive without heavy duties on imported sugar, and they needed a Republican to replace Grover Cleveland in the White House to safeguard the high tariff. With a strong state ticket headed by Henry Clay Warmoth, the Republicans believed they were in with a chance, especially when outgoing governor McEnery promised "an honest and fair election," a pledge he repeated to Warmoth in person.

It was not to be. The Bourbon wing of the party had never forgiven Nicholls for his 1879 report on the Tensas Parish troubles. Nicholls himself, however, having condemned the Bourbons for ballot-box stuffing, realized that an "honest and fair election" might elect Warmoth. His advisers, therefore, dispatched Natchitoches Democrat Dick Sinnott, captain of the steamboat *Bart Able*, to offer an olive branch to McEnery and the Bourbons. "Gentlemen, if you think it necessary for the election of General Nicholls to manipulate the ballot boxes, go and do it," stated Nicholls's campaign manager, future U.S. Supreme Court justice Edward D. White. "But don't let me know anything about it." Over dinner at Moreaus's restaurant in New Orleans, the Nicholls and McEnery forces agreed to steal the election by depressing the Republican vote in northern Louisiana. Faced with a credible challenge from Warmoth, whose election would imperil their control of the ballot boxes, the Bourbons decided that Nicholls was the lesser of two evils.

Stumping for Nicholls in Natchitoches, McEnery made one of the bloodthirsty speeches for which he and his brother had made themselves notorious in the campaigns of 1874 and 1876. A Warmoth victory would lead to the "Africanization of the State," he warned, "and before I will consent to such a calamity I will wrap the State in revolution." McEnery instructed registrars of voters to turn in "a large Democratic majority in the Parishes north of Red River." This they did. In twenty-seven northern Louisiana parishes, Democratic election officers recorded 59,220 votes for Nicholls and only 2,959 for Warmoth. In Natchitoches Parish they placed only 6 percent of the ballots in Warmoth's column. Yet while the Republican vote slumped to 251, the Democratic vote, padded with black ballots, swelled to 3,373. Republican representation in the state legislature dwindled to four senators and twelve representatives.[33]

Benjamin Harrison's victory over Grover Cleveland at least gave Louisiana Republicans access to federal patronage. But as the party's share of state and local offices evaporated, quarrels over federal jobs came to define party factions and, increasingly, the content of politics itself. Writing to John Lewis from New Orleans, top Mason C. F. Ladd bemoaned the futility of it all. "Politically we are all torn to pieces. The Bosses all divided. Some went with the Ring Democrats and some with the Citizens Party, and to make the thing worse the Ring counted out both the Citizens ticket and the Republican state ticket also." Ladd characterized the fault line within the Republican Party as pitting Pinchback, Louis A. Martinet, and other "outs" against Kellogg, Badger, and the "ins." The divide reflected the long-standing tension between black and white Republicans, and, recalling the politics of the Warmoth years, the factional enmity sometimes erupted into fisticuffs and knife fights.[34]

Blunt had no prospect of being elected to political office again, but he remained on the Republican state committee and retained some influence in the disposal of federal patronage. Importuned by Republicans and Democrats alike to recommend them, he found himself accused of trading influence for money. In 1889 he defended himself to the parish executive committee. "He stated that he had been offered money by L. G. Barron to have him appointed marshal for the northern district of Louisiana." Another office-seeker offered him half his earnings as receiver of public money if Blunt endorsed his application for the post. He refused both offers. The most serious allegation, which he also denied, was that "he had got money to go to Washington to work in the interests of the Democrats."[35]

When it came to campaigning, however, Blunt was pessimistic about nominating a local Republican ticket. Although perennial chairman of the

Natchitoches Parish Republican Party, he often found himself in a minority on the executive committee, sometimes a minority of one. "As so much talk and confusion had arose . . . he had nothing to say," stated the record of one meeting. After the local election in April 1884, he worried that the Democratic-controlled school board would refuse to renew his teaching contract because he had participated in the campaign.

With each succeeding election, the Natchitoches Republicans grew increasingly timid. In 1889, for example, Ernest Breda argued against organizing a campaign committee lest it "bring on trouble." The Democrats, he explained, were once again agitating the race question. Given the Hobson's choice of voting the Democratic ticket or not voting at all, most blacks saw no point in voting. In 1892 and 1894, noted the *Louisiana Populist*, the elections in Natchitoches Parish "were practically the voice of the white people" because blacks had mostly stayed away from the polls.[36]

In southern Louisiana, blacks continued to vote and enjoy some political representation; Republicans and Democrats even ran "mixed tickets" in some parishes. Yet this habit of bargaining with the opposing party for local concessions led to the next logical step: offering votes for sale. In 1892, for example, Democrats in Ascension Parish ran up a debt of $3,100 in buying black voters; planters were assessed $100 to $400 a head to clear it. Given the drift of the Republican Party, blacks could hardly be blamed for taking Democratic money. An "inducement" of ten to twelve dollars represented almost a month's wages on a sugar plantation. Both "mixed tickets" and vote-buying had the effect of further demoralizing the Republican Party.[37]

That party, increasingly dominated by commercial and industrial interests, had little to offer blacks. Indeed, the rise of class consciousness among black workers showed that Republican planters could be just as brutal as Democratic ones. A strike by sugar workers in 1887 prompted Lafourche Parish planter Taylor Beattie, the party's gubernatorial candidate in 1880, to raise a vigilante force and call upon Democratic governor McEnery to deploy the state militia. The strike, waged under the banner of the Knights of Labor, was suppressed with great brutality. Although "sick with the horror of it," wrote planter Mary Pugh, she considered the violence necessary "to settle the question of who is going to rule the nigger or the White man? for the next fifty years." C. F. Ladd, grand master of the Prince Hall Masons, reported that a "reign of terror" had prevented him from setting foot in St.

Mary, Lafourche, and Terrebonne Parishes. Nearly all the Masons there had joined the strike, and they fled to New Orleans to save their lives.[38]

The national Republican Party, dismayed by the declining Republican vote in the South, still pursued the will-o'-the-wisp of winning over white voters. In various southern states Republicans formed "lily-white," or "National" organizations that challenged the "regulars," who remained committed to "black-and-tan" electoral tickets. In Louisiana, stated Congressman H. Dudley Coleman, National Republicans aimed to "build up . . . a Representative White Man's Party" that would give blacks "a fair proportion of the patronage, according to qualifications." What this entailed, in effect, was a drastic reduction in the number of black officeholders. President Harrison reassured a delegation of white southerners that he would never appoint blacks to positions involving "personal contact with and official authority over white citizens."

Veterans of Reconstruction regarded the "lily-white" strategy as futile. Appointing or electing former Democrats did nothing to increase the Republican vote, even among their friends and relatives. As Kellogg put it, "The whites will all stand together, that's all there is to that." Kellogg warned that denying patronage to blacks would kill the party, and he protested against the unfairness of it. Blacks only wanted the "laborers places in the court-house—they want to lift the mail bags and drive the wagons. . . . When competent they want a fair proportion of places like inspectors and clerks."[39]

If whites stood together on the race issue, however, they were falling out over economic questions. The first sign of political division came in 1878, when the Greenback-Labor Party found a sympathetic hearing among many whites in northern Louisiana's hill country, including some in Natchitoches Parish. During the 1880s, dissatisfaction with Bourbon rule mounted. White farmers formed local clubs and then, in 1887, a statewide organization called the Louisiana Farmers Union. Black farmers joined lodges under the banner of the Colored Farmers Alliance, which originated in Texas. In Natchitoches, Blunt and others founded the Farmers and Laborers Mutual Union "to carry on a general cooperative business, to purchase lands, homes, and to establish stores and exchanges." Relations between the white and black farmers' organizations were tentative. But the leaders of both emphasized how the two groups of farmers shared common economic interests.[40]

The formation of the People's Party (Populists) in 1891 provided white voters with a credible alternative to the Democratic Party—one that was not, like the Republican Party, tainted. The Populists fared poorly in Louisiana in the elections of 1892, but the onset of a deep financial depression, the "Panic of 1893," turned the trickle of Democratic defectors into a flood. Winn Parish, during the Civil War a stronghold of Unionism, was the most fervently Populist parish in the state. Natchitoches, where party leader Hardy Brian published the *Louisiana Populist*, was not far behind. The Populists recruited not only farmers hurt by falling prices but also doctors, lawyers, planters, and small businessmen—anyone who was dissatisfied with Louisiana's Bourbons and the Cleveland administration. These people believed in white supremacy, but they had become tired of, and cynical about, Democratic warnings of "Negro domination."[41]

Here was the strategic opportunity that Republicans had long awaited: a split in the Democratic Party that would make black votes decisive. By allying with the Populists against their common enemy, the Bourbons, Republicans could once again exercise influence in state politics. A Populist-Republican electoral alliance might elect a governor, a legislative majority, and a host of parish and district offices. In North Carolina a "fusion" ticket swept the state in 1894, ousting the Democrats from power. Blacks immediately benefited in terms of more elected officials, a substantial share of state patronage, and fairer elections. In Louisiana, Populists were also open to cooperating with blacks, and in the state elections of 1896 they agreed upon a joint ticket with the Republican Party.[42]

The Populist-Republican alliance, however, was shaky from the start. Populists could only benefit from fusion if Republican votes were counted fairly. When Democrats continued to stuff ballot boxes with black votes, more and more Populists concluded that only the elimination of this manipulated black electorate could deprive the Democrats of their contrived majorities. For the moment they rejected Democratic proposals for suffrage reform, suspecting—correctly, as it turned out—that measures ostensibly designed to disfranchise only blacks would also ensnare many whites. Instead, Populists in Natchitoches offered the Democrats a combined party primary in which only whites would be permitted to vote—both parties would agree not to "vote Negroes." The Democrats rejected the proposal precisely because the Populists stood to gain from such an arrangement. Although demanding "a free ballot and a fair count," Populists preferred to see blacks not voting at all rather than be "voted by" the Democratic Party.

When Democrats in Richland, Red River, and De Soto Parishes marched blacks to the polls, Populists cried foul.[43]

There was another reason why the Populists were halfhearted, at best, in bidding for black votes. Faced with the biggest threat to their control of state government since 1877, the Democratic Party attacked them for betraying the white race. A Populist-Republican victory, warned the *Natchitoches Enterprise*, would revive the "negro domination" of Reconstruction days. Populists ridiculed this argument. "The wild shrieks of the *Enterprise* . . . fall upon deaf ears in the hills of North Louisiana," averred the *Louisiana Populist*. "These brave people have no fear of the negro controlling them." But this insouciance masked anxiety that Democratic attacks were hitting home. Instead of offering a principled defense of black voting, Populists equivocated. They opposed black officeholding. They considered it best if blacks "voluntarily stay away from the polls." They had "proven their sincerity for white rule by offering the Democracy a white primary." In appealing to white supremacy, however, Populists were fighting on ground of the Democrats' own choosing. Economics was the Populist Party's drawing card. The race issue put it on the defensive.[44]

Even the Republican Party was incapable of mounting a robust defense of equal rights. The sugar planters who joined the party in 1894 had no interest in the old issues of Reconstruction. Attracted to the Republican Party because of its high-tariff policy, they organized themselves into the National Republicans, a faction that opposed black officeholding in principle. The Fusion ticket negotiated by the Nationals and the Populists in 1896, and reluctantly endorsed by the Regulars included no blacks and was headed by wealthy sugar planter John N. Pharr. Campaigning to be governor, Pharr seemed uncomfortable, even embarrassed, to be seeking black votes. Speaking before a largely black crowd in Natchitoches—three thousand people turned out to hear him—he made his position clear. "This will be a white man's government," he stated, because "the white man is your superior." Blacks should refrain from office-seeking and, if they voted, "to vote always on the advice of some honest, trustworthy white friends." Blacks should stay away from the polls, he added, if local whites opposed blacks voting.[45]

"I was afraid of the negro vote," admitted Samuel J. Henry, chairman of the Populist Party in Natchitoches Parish. If Populists bid for it, Democrats accused them of "massing the negro and voting them in hordes." If they ignored it, Fusionists would be giving the Democrats carte blanche to stuff the ballot boxes. Encountering Phanor Breazeale, a prominent Democrat, on Front Street, Henry suggested that both parties should renounce the black vote and agree that only white men cast ballots. After all, he explained, "Mr. Breazeale was accusing the Populists of wanting the colored votes, and I was accusing the Democratic party of wanting the colored votes, and we were, of course, both denying that our party wanted the negro." Local Democrats rejected Henry's proposition. Whatever their public position regarding black voting, they controlled the electoral machinery and would, if necessary, count black ballots as Democratic ones. According to Henry, Breazeale told him that "the Democrats expected to beat our Senatorial ticket by voting 2,000 negroes in De Soto [Parish]."[46]

Voting and "being voted" were, of course, entirely different propositions. The scope for black political action had become so circumscribed that by 1896 only St. John the Baptist Parish "had not completely suppressed its Negro and Republican elements in local affairs." Throughout much of Louisiana, blacks had ceased to campaign as Republicans. In Natchitoches, a report that Blunt and Lewis were about to organize a Republican campaign sparked vicious, threatening editorials in the *Natchitoches Enterprise*. Blunt, who supported the Fusion ticket, wrote an abject letter to the *Enterprise* disclaiming any intention of "organizing negroes against whites." He went further. "I am not in political accord with J. G. Lewis," he stated. "I am an old man, and I desire to pass out the remainder of my days in peace and good will to all men." It was a far cry from the proud, defiant Blunt of the 1870s, when he had been the most powerful politician in Natchitoches.[47]

Lewis made no such published disclaimer, prompting the *Louisiana Populist* to speculate that he was working for the Democrats. The newspaper alleged that Lewis had attached himself to the Kellogg faction of the "Regular" Republicans, which was so hostile to the lily-white "Nationals" that it was cooperating with Murphy J. Foster, the incumbent Democratic governor campaigning for reelection. The charge was not as outlandish as it might seem. Throughout the South one could find black Republican leaders who threw their support to Democratic candidates in exchange for specific concessions. The practice of running "mixed tickets" for local offices was well established. The advantage for Republicans was obvious: they inoculated themselves against Democratic violence and stood to gain something as opposed to nothing. In Natchitoches Parish, however, the Republican Party nominated no candidates of its own. "Judging by the past," Ernest

Breda told the parish executive committee, "we are certain that we cannot obtain a free vote and fair count or honest return of our votes."[48]

Even for a state notorious for electoral skullduggery, the blatant dishonesty of the 1896 election stood out. In Plaquemines Parish, recounted former governor Warmoth, Democrats "surrounded the court-house with 100 armed men and . . . stuffed the returns with 1,500 votes that were never polled, and laughed at us." The official returns had Foster trouncing Pharr by 116,116 votes to 87,968. But almost 17,000 of Foster's votes came from the seven largest "black" parishes, which included only 4,093 white males. Pharr easily carried the predominantly "white" parishes, including all those north of Red River, and he attracted a respectable vote in New Orleans. The Fusionists claimed a 20,000 majority statewide.[49]

On the day of the poll Natchitoches was bristling with armed partisans. About five hundred Populists—"the wild and woolly variety," according to the *Natchitoches Enterprise*—assembled at the Breda plantation, determined to ensure that the Board of Supervisors counted the votes fairly. Late in the morning about 140 armed Democrats gathered in front of the courthouse so that the board could cheat without interference. At noon, Democratic leaders telegraphed Governor Foster to send a state militia unit to the city. Foster complied. When the soldiers eventually arrived, complete with Gatling gun, the danger of a violent clash had passed. The Board of Supervisors counted all the votes cast in four wards where, according to the *Louisiana Populist*, "the Democrats voted the negro." But election officials rejected the poll in Ward 3, the one ward where Populists "voted the negro," which resulted in the election of two Democrats to the state senate and one to the state house. John Tetts, Populist candidate for the state legislature, squeaked in by three votes. Praising the board's action, the *Enterprise* explained that the Fusionists had tried to "defeat the will of the white people of the parish by a lot of illegal negro votes." Fusionists carried the parish for Pharr, but Democrats won most of the parish offices.[50]

The gubernatorial election of April 21, 1896, confirmed the thorough corruption of democratic politics in Louisiana and marked the end of black political participation. The Populists had made fair elections a central plank of their platform, but the chances of ensuring an honest count were slimmer than ever. In 1890 Senator Henry Cabot Lodge of Massachusetts had introduced a bill to strengthen federal supervision of elections. Its rejection by the Republican-controlled Senate marked "the end of an era," writes Michael Perman. As one senator privately admitted, "the interest of the

Republicans of the United States in an honest ballot, in maintaining the rights of citizenship, and in holding sacred the pledge of Abraham Lincoln's proclamation to the colored men is dead." In 1894 Congress, now controlled by Democrats, repealed all the federal election laws, including the Enforcement Acts. Republicans fought hard against repeal but accepted it with resignation. To the South's "lily-white" Republicans, who had opposed the Lodge Bill, repeal was a blessing. Even black Republicans had grown weary of the fight. Younger black spokesmen especially—men like W. E. B. Du Bois, Booker T. Washington, and J. C. Price—thought the Lodge Bill ill-considered.[51]

With the threat of federal intervention removed, Louisiana's Democrats had less reason than ever to respect black voting rights. Impervious to Populist charges of electoral fraud, the Returning Board declined to "go behind the returns," simply accepting the figures submitted by local Democratic election officials. The Democratic-controlled legislature rejected the Fusionists' demand for an investigation. Instead, exploiting Fusionists' anger over ballot-box stuffing, the Democrats proceeded to eliminate the black vote entirely. An apparently innocuous law mandating use of the "Australian" (secret) ballot caused turnout to plummet. The number of votes cast in the presidential election in November was less than half that cast in the state elections in April. A second law, also seemingly harmless, required all voters to register anew after January 1, 1897. Only 87,000 succeeded in doing so; how many attempted is unknown. White registration declined from 125,407 to 74,133; black registration fell from 128,150 to 12,902.

The registration law had its intended effect: it enabled the Democratic Party to secure an overwhelming majority in the constitutional convention of 1898, which had been called to emulate the examples of Mississippi and South Carolina in ending universal male suffrage. In addition to the disfranchising effects of the secret ballot and registration laws, the demoralization of the Fusionists after their defeat in 1896 contributed to an abysmally low turnout of about forty-four thousand voters—only one-fifth of the number who had voted less than two years earlier. The Populist-Republican alliance disintegrated in bitterness, confusion, and mutual recrimination. The new state constitution erected further barriers to black voting, including a poll tax and a literacy test. A solitary Populist and a lone Republican had "constituted the entire opposition" in the constitutional convention.[52]

By 1900 black registration had fallen to 5,320. In 1906 only 1,201 black voters remained on the rolls, and a law passed that year permitted the Democratic Party to exclude them from the only election that mattered, the Democratic primaries. Although the new electorate was virtually lily-white, far fewer white men registered and voted. Some whites found themselves disfranchised; others stopped voting because they considered it futile.[53]

In Natchitoches, the all-powerful Democratic Party flexed its muscles by humiliating John Lewis. When the McKinley administration appointed Lewis to the plum post of registrar of the Land Office, the *Natchitoches Enterprise* threatened dire consequences should he accept it. Lewis declined the position, insisting he had never sought it. Ernest Breda was appointed in his stead. The *Enterprise* pronounced Breda a worthy choice. With the base of the Republican Party obliterated and white supremacy enshrined in law and custom, Democrats could tolerate the occasional Republican officeholder as long as he was white.[54]

Booker T. Washington, the preeminent black leader of the time, regarded black powerlessness as a fact of life that simply had to be reckoned with. "The Negro is like any other weak people," he wrote his friend Charles W. Chesnutt. "No one can give him strength which he does not intrinsically possess, and I fear . . . the Negro will have to continue to take his medicine until he gains material, mental, moral and political strength enough to enable him to change his present condition." It was a bitter lesson, but the conclusion was unavoidable. Deserted by the Republican Party, oppressed by the Democratic Party, abandoned by the Supreme Court, and disdained by the mass of whites both North and South, many blacks found Washington's assessment coldly realistic.[55]

On June 19, 1902, a graduate of Tuskegee Institute took Washington's message of self-help and moral improvement to a celebration and barbecue attended by about a thousand people in Natchitoches Parish. John Lewis spoke on the significance of "Juneteenth," the date in 1865 when the U.S. Army proclaimed the abolition of slavery in Texas. Raford Blunt preached a non-political sermon. Another Baptist minister, Benjamin Perrow, closed the meeting "with an appeal to the colored people to educate their children, to get prosperity, and to live friendly with the white people." The *Natchitoches Enterprise* nodded its approval.[56]

16

RECONSTRUCTION'S LEGACY
AND THE CIVIL RIGHTS MOVEMENT

One hundred years later the Negro still is not free. One hundred years later
the life of the Negro is still badly crippled by the manacles of segregation
and the chains of discrimination. One hundred years later the Negro lives on
a lonely island of poverty in the midst of a vast ocean of material prosperity.

Martin Luther King Jr., August 28, 1963

Raford Blunt died on March 19, 1905, at age sixty-seven. He left six minor
children, his third wife, Florence Varner, having died the previous year.
His estate was appraised at $2,897; his personal effects included a piano, an
organ, and one hundred books.[1]

Shortly afterward, the members of First Baptist Church fell to quarreling.
Four days after Christmas, a fire destroyed the church building. Amid charges
and counter-charges over who had set the fire, the congregation split into two
factions, each side claiming possession of the church's property and taking
its case to court. The schism proved permanent: Natchitoches boasts two
black churches named First Baptist, each claiming descent from the church
that Blunt founded in 1869. First Baptist Church North Street displays a bell
from the original church, the only object to survive the conflagration. First
Baptist Church Amulet Street displays a cornerstone bearing the name Rev.
W. M. Moody and the date 1867. In hearing the case, the district judge could
not help but pay tribute to the strength of Blunt's leadership, praising him as
"the master builder, not only of churches, but of character as well."[2]

If whites remembered Blunt the political leader, they pretended not to.
After disfranchisement the Natchitoches newspapers rarely referred to any
blacks by name, except when the court reports listed criminals. Editors and
politicians did, however, evoke the horrors of "carpet-bag rule" whenever

Figure 16. The "Uncle Jack" statue (1927) symbolized the subordinate position of blacks after they lost the right to vote. Now located in the LSU Rural Life Museum, Baton Rouge. Author's photograph.

they sought to discredit an opponent or a policy. Local congressman James B. Aswell, elected in 1912, became a master of the technique. National prohibition, he warned, would "endanger the southern people again with negro rule through the police power of the federal government." The election of John M. Parker as governor, he thundered, would allow black women into the voting booths. Although the Louisiana Republican Party was dead if not buried, the *Natchitoches Enterprise* found Parker, a mild progressive, guilty by association with Theodore Roosevelt, who stood for "the social and political equality of the nigger."[3]

In 1899 the *Enterprise* had personally threatened John G. Lewis. In 1922 it did so again, but without deigning to mention him by name.

> In this city and parish it is of common report that a few negro politicians, and some of them of the old reconstruction period, who were run away from here, and who have returned under promise that they would not mix or meddle with political affairs, are undertaking to dictate the appointment of our postmaster and other federal officials.
>
> This is a white man's country . . . [and] this state stands for white supremacy. . . . The powers at Washington had better understand where such a policy will lead; these are the things which produced the Ku Klux Klan and kindred organizations.

Lewis, the only surviving black Republican leader from Reconstruction, could hardly mistake the reference to himself.[4]

From a refusal to mention black Reconstruction leaders by name, it was but a short step to fabricating Uncle Tom in bronze. Twenty years after Blunt's death a white businessman conceived the idea of commissioning a statue, to be placed in a prominent position in town, so that the white people of Natchitoches could express their gratitude to the black population. Jackson L. Bryan, a planter and banker in his fifties, remembered the traumatic election of 1896 and would have known something of Blunt's history. What he proposed, however, was not a monument to an actual person but, rather, a statue that portrayed a timeless "darky"—an idealized "old-timer" that represented white people's image of what a black man should be: loyal, polite, and subservient. Bryan's cousin was skeptical. He predicted that whites would be hostile. Bryan should expect comments like, "Well now, it's damn funny that the only statue we have in town is erected to a nigger; we are having enough trouble keeping them in their place, and trying to get work out of them. I don't think this statue is going to help any." Bryan nevertheless persisted. Spending $4,300 of his own money—well over $50,000 in today's prices—he commissioned Baltimore artist Hans Schuler, one of the foremost sculptors in the land, to produce the larger-than-life statue.[5]

Unveiled in 1927, Schuler's statue depicted an elderly black man, shoulders stooped, doffing his hat. "His kindly, wrinkled features, gnarled hands and big feet show him to be a genuine type," wrote one admirer. "He seems ready to tell an Uncle Remus story to any of the wondering white children who come to play in the grass nearby." A plaque on the statue's base contained the following dedication: "Erected by the City of Natchitoches in Grateful Recognition of the Arduous and Faithful Service of the Good Darkies of Louisiana."[6]

Monuments praising "Faithful Slaves" and "Good and Loyal Servants" can be found scattered throughout the South. Some refer to individuals and are located in cemeteries. The Cunningham family plot in Natchitoches, for example, includes the grave of Mary Pitcher (1847–1913), "Our Mammy, who was the most faithful human being that ever lived." Others referred to slaves in general and explicitly commemorated the "Lost Cause." An obelisk in Fort Mill, South Carolina, praised "the faithful slaves who, loyal to a sacred trust, toiled for the support of the Army [and] with matchless devotion and with sterling fidelity guarded our defenseless homes, women, and children, during the struggle for the principles of our Confederate States of America."[7] Similar sentiments adorned some of the Soldier monuments that the United Daughters of the Confederacy, founded in 1895, assiduously promoted. Friezes upon the Confederate Memorial in Arlington National Cemetery, unveiled in 1914, included a tearful "Black Mammy" clutching a white infant as his father marched off to war.[8]

"Uncle Jack," the name conferred upon Hans Schuler's statue by Natchitoches residents, fitted into neither of these categories. Neither "slave" nor "servant" appears in the inscription. In proposing and funding it, moreover, Jackson Bryan had no neo-Confederate agenda to push. The monument seems to have been a sincere tribute by a southern white man, albeit a paternalistic one, to the former slaves he had known in childhood.

Despite its ambiguity, the "Uncle Jack" statue is of a piece with the monuments that praised faithful slaves. Everyone assumed that the "Good Darky" was either a slave or a servant who had once been a slave. In the description of S. M. Byrd, a local college teacher, "The old negro looks as if he had just shuffled into the square and recognized some of his white folks." Relations between the races in Natchitoches Parish had always been pleasant, Byrd went on, "not only in slavery days but also down to the present." Moreover, although the statue's inscription made no reference to the Confederacy, the words "arduous and faithful service" recalled a well-known phrase in Lee's much-quoted farewell address to the Army of Northern Virginia.

By 1927 almost all of the actors in the political struggles of Reconstruction had passed from the scene. Among the Democrats, William Levy died in 1882, David Pierson in 1900, William H. Jack in 1912, James Cosgrove in

1914, and M. J. Cunningham in 1916. Most of the men who lived beyond "Redemption" prospered politically. Governor Nicholls appointed Levy to the state supreme court; during his second term he made Jack superintendent of public instruction. Pierson, elected district judge in 1876, held that office for sixteen consecutive years. Cunningham served in both houses of the state legislature and was twice elected attorney general. He became a footnote to history in 1896 when he represented Louisiana in the case of *Plessy v. Ferguson.* The constitutional convention of 1879 awarded Cosgrove the state printing contract; the following year Natchitoches elected him to the legislature.

A brilliant newspaper editor, whose take-no-prisoners style had emboldened Democrats and frightened Republicans, Cosgrove ended his days a lonely and dejected man. Never a natural politician, he dabbled in planting but always returned to his first love, journalism. As he grew older and assumed the identity of "General Jim," his writing focused more and more on his days as a Confederate soldier and foe of Radicalism. But after his last venture, *Cosgrove's Weekly*, published in Shreveport, failed, he sank into poverty. "I can get no work," he wrote a friend, "nor sell stories. Everything is syndicated now and Southern reminiscences are not wanted."

> Here I am among strangers . . . broke flat, living on the charity of a Confederate's daughter, who keeps a laborer's boarding-house, clothes going to rags . . . and a fit object for the grave. I brood over the inhumanity of the thing, and it nearly makes me crazy. Sometimes I think of just going back to Natchitoches and throw myself on them. I'll say, "You owe me a funeral! Keep me until it comes!"

Fixated on past glories, he died of cancer shortly afterward.[9]

William Tunnard, the journalist whom Cosgrove had mercilessly abused in the pages of the *Vindicator*, quit the Republican Party in 1878. The two men reconciled and became friends and occasional business partners. After moving to Shreveport around 1890, Tunnard pursued his vocation as a newspaper editor. As with Cosgrove, the passage of years made him increasingly nostalgic over the Lost Cause. As grand commander of the Louisiana division of the United Confederate Veterans, he reached the impressive rank of major general—not bad for a private in the Commissary Department of the Third Louisiana Infantry. He died in 1916.[10]

Black legislator Henry Raby returned to Natchitoches in 1884, after losing his job in the New Orleans Custom House upon the election of Grover

Cleveland. He died ten years later. Of the prominent white Republicans, Madrid P. Blackstone was killed in an accidental shooting in 1874. Jules J. Bossier succumbed to disease in 1875, still a young man. David H. Boullt Sr. died in New Orleans in 1879. Henry C. Myers left Natchitoches in 1875 after being indicted for embezzling school funds. When Myers returned to face trial in 1878, the district attorney dropped the prosecution, but Myers had already settled in New Orleans and chose to remain there. He died a few years later.[11]

Philippe and Ernest Breda lived until, respectively, 1911 and 1914, still Republicans. Their graves can be found in a small family plot near the old Breda plantation, although only Ernest's can be identified. According to a local legend, the Catholic Church refused them burial rites because they had been "Scalawags." The story is almost certainly false; at the time of their deaths, both men were respected members of Natchitoches white society. The youngest of the three Breda brothers, Emile, survived until 1936 and was buried in the Catholic cemetery. A teenager during Reconstruction, he later served two four-year stints as the town's postmaster under Republican administrations. By the 1930s the Breda plantation had been sold for development, allowing the City of Natchitoches to expand northward. The largely black neighborhood built on the land is to this day known as "Breda Town."[12]

John G. Lewis died in 1931 at the age of eighty, a loyal Republican to the last. He had served as a public school teacher for fifty years. For much of that time his wife, Virginia, and sister, Martha Sompeyrac, taught in the same school. Lewis had also climbed the ladder of the Masonic hierarchy, attaining the uppermost rung in 1903. From the exalted position of grand master of the Most Worshipful Eureka Grand Lodge, he presided over Louisiana's black Masons for a record (at that time) twenty-eight years. Lewis was "well known as a Mason," noted his obituary in the Natchitoches Times, "and as a pioneer negro educator." The obituary was perfunctory, to say the least. It said nothing about Lewis's importance during Reconstruction—he had, after all, served as a state legislator—and it even misspelled his name. In death, however, Lewis triumphed over his political enemies, symbolically at least. His white marble mausoleum sits in the middle of American Cemetery, near the burial places of David Pierson and Milton J. Cunningham, the most eye-catching and impressive tomb in the entire graveyard.[13]

Shorn of its black electorate, Louisiana's Republican Party survived after 1898 as a "patronage and national convention delegation party." The state party continued to select black delegates to the Republican National Convention, and when those delegates died their sons sometimes replaced them. John G. Lewis Jr., for example, served as a delegate to every Republican national convention from 1928 to 1940. Unlike his father, however, he operated in a party that was increasingly white. Although Louisiana's "lily-whites" never managed to eliminate blacks from the party entirely, by 1928 they dominated it. Outside New Orleans, blacks received no federal patronage. During the long presidency of Franklin D. Roosevelt, the Republican Party did not even have patronage jobs to dispose of. Every four years, Republican state delegations from the South, some of which included blacks, participated in the selection of the presidential candidate. Given the fact that they represented no actual voters, southern delegates wielded disproportionate influence and often sold their support for cash, which presidential hopefuls had no qualms about paying.[14]

As a vehicle for defending the interests of black Louisianans, the Republican Party had become irrelevant long before the Constitution of 1898 wiped out its electoral base. Its most striking failure, in the economic sphere, was its inability to advance black landownership. The Southern Homestead Act, passed in 1866, entitled both blacks and whites to apply for eighty acres of public land, of which six million acres lay within Louisiana. But defects in the law, widespread corruption, political opposition, and administrative incompetence of staggering proportions saw to it that few blacks even applied. The U.S. Land Office in Natchitoches did not open for applications until 1871, and not many blacks gained government land and managed to keep it. Blacks who acquired land usually had to buy it, and, outside the sparsely populated hill parishes, where land was cheap but less productive, few could afford to do so. Of the 2,476 black farmers in Natchitoches Parish in 1900, only 381 owned their farms, about 15 percent of the total. This was the same proportion that obtained for Louisiana as a whole, and Louisiana had one of the lowest rates of black landownership in the South. Most black cultivators remained lifelong sharecroppers.[15]

The position of those sharecroppers deteriorated inexorably after Reconstruction. Laws enacted by Democratic legislatures, as well as extra-legal coercion, reduced blacks' bargaining power vis-à-vis employers. A long-term decline in cotton prices made it increasingly difficult to clear end-of-year debts and accumulate savings. The pressure to plant more cotton to offset lower prices led to a decline in food production. About one-third of black-run farms in the cotton belt did not grow enough corn to be self-sufficient. Such farmers relied upon expensive food items purchased at plantation stores on credit. In Louisiana's sugar parishes a drastic leveling down took place after the failed strike of 1887. "Sugar workers became a rural proletariat," writes John C. Rodrigue, "living within a larger South characterized by a deplorable lack of educational opportunities, economic underdevelopment, and discrimination in all forms of life." Joe Gray Taylor concluded that blacks in the cotton and sugar parishes may have been worse off in 1900 "insofar as food, clothing, and shelter were concerned" than they had been as slaves.[16]

Higher cotton prices between 1900 and 1920 boosted the incomes of both white and black farm operators, but the upward trend went into reverse after in 1920. Conditions on the plantations deteriorated. On some, reported Clinton Clark, an organizer employed by the left-wing Louisiana Farmers Union (LFU), sharecroppers risked a whipping if they left the property without permission, and the planter or "riding boss" forbade laborers to converse with each other while they hoed or picked cotton. An official of the LFU characterized Natchitoches Parish as "reactionary— planter-dominated, anti-union, [and] anti-Negro," where whites "take law in their own hands."[17]

As cotton parishes went, in fact, Natchitoches was far from the worst. For one thing, farmers could supplement their diet through hunting and, especially, fishing, there being an abundance of lakes, bayous, and rivers. For another, Natchitoches remained averse to racial violence. In Caddo, Bossier, and other northern Louisiana parishes, whites lynched blacks frequently, publicly, with impunity, and well into the twentieth century. Records attribute a single lynching to Natchitoches Parish, which took place near the village of Victoria in 1902. Blacks who committed violence against whites received trials, occasionally the semblance of a fair one. In 1897, for example, an all-white jury acquitted a black defendant of murdering a white man. In 1940, when planters decided to suppress the LFU, they had Clark arrested and expelled from the parish. That was the Natchitoches way of doing things.[18]

By the time of John G. Lewis Sr.'s death, lynching was in decline throughout the South. Judged by every other metric, however, the position of black southerners vis-à-vis whites had scarcely improved since Reconstruction and in some areas had deteriorated. Blacks suffered disproportionately from Depression-induced retrenchment. Between 1930 and 1935 the average salary of black teachers fell from 40 percent of the white average to

32 percent; per capita spending on black schoolchildren, compared with spending on white schoolchildren, dropped from 22 percent to 17 percent. The New Deal's agricultural programs did little for black sharecroppers, many of whom were pushed off the land by their employers. In 1930 there were 74,000 black farm operators in Louisiana; in 1940 there were 10,000 fewer. As if the miniscule black electorate could get any smaller, it did: from 2,000 voters in 1928 to 800 in 1940.[19]

During Lewis's long tenure, blacks in Louisiana made little headway in organizing opposition to white supremacy. It was not from want of trying. Blacks in the village of Clarence, in Natchitoches Parish, obtained one of the earliest NAACP charters in the South. Shreveport boasted a branch of the NAACP in 1914, New Orleans in 1915. By 1930 the NAACP had chartered nine branches in Louisiana, including Baton Rouge, Alexandria, and Monroe. However, an effort to weld the branches into a statewide organization came to nothing. Intimidation by whites ensured that most were only sporadically active or entirely dormant.

During the decades of white supremacy, when open protest seemed futile or downright suicidal, blacks focused on a slower, safer strategy of institution-building. Slower, because progress was measured in decades rather than years; safer, because churches, schools, colleges, and private businesses did not challenge racial segregation and appeared outwardly nonpolitical. Labor unions were more risky, but by the 1930s, in New Orleans at least, they too had become part of blacks' organizational infrastructure. In the 1940s these institutions provided the building blocks for a bigger, stronger NAACP. In the 1950s and 1960s they furnished a base for the civil rights movement.

The Prince Hall Masons provide an impressive, remarkable instance of long-term institution-building. John G. Lewis Sr., barred from politics, spent fifty years building a network of Masonic lodges. In 1931 his son Scott succeeded him as grand master of the state organization, Eureka Grand Lodge. When Scott died ten years later, Lewis's youngest son, John G. Lewis Jr., took over the position, serving as grand master until his own death in 1979. The elder Lewis thus founded a dynasty that endured for seventy-three years, from the presidency of Theodore Roosevelt to that of Jimmy Carter. Longevity in itself has no particular historical significance. In this case, however, the Masonic organization headed by the Lewis family played a significant role in the civil rights movement.

Primarily a fraternal organization, the Masons always had a political dimension. During Reconstruction they furnished numerous Republican leaders, including Oscar Dunn, James Lewis, J. Henri Burch, and Raford Blunt. But the reach of the order was limited. For one thing, its steep membership fees and expensive regalia helped restrict the membership to about five hundred men (leaving plenty of opportunity for less elitist fraternities such as the Elks and the Odd Fellows to attract members). In addition, it had little presence outside New Orleans. The Shreveport lodge, the only one in northern Louisiana, folded during a yellow fever epidemic in 1873.

During his exile in New Orleans after 1878, John G. Lewis, a member of Parsons Lodge No. 5 and deputy grand master of Eureka Grand Lodge, extended the organization. He organized new lodges in Baton Rouge, Alexandria, and Monroe. Returning to Natchitoches in 1884, he established Corinthian Lodge No. 19 and installed Raford Blunt as worshipful master.[20]

Shortly thereafter, Lewis and Blunt had a falling out. Whether the rift had its origin in politics and spilled over into Masonic affairs or whether it began as a quarrel between two Masons and carried over into politics is unclear. It may simply have reflected a rivalry between an ambitious, younger man who no longer felt beholden to a political mentor who no longer commanded political power. In 1889 the Grand Lodge threatened both men with expulsion for "conduct unbecoming Masons." By 1893 Natchitoches boasted two lodges, one headed by Blunt and the other, Dawn of Light No. 22, by Lewis. The breach between Blunt and Lewis never healed.[21]

After his election as grand master, Lewis ran the Grand Lodge from Natchitoches. The location facilitated his goal of setting up new lodges north of Alexandria and ending the dominance of New Orleans. Between 1902 and 1906 the number of lodges increased from 67 to 116. In 1910 Lewis established the Dawn of Light Printing Company, which published a Masonic magazine, *The Plumb Line*. The Lewis family prospered, acquiring a 470-acre plantation that they rented to blacks farmers.

With the NAACP struggling to gain a foothold in Louisiana, the network of Masonic lodges provided an alternative means of organization. The lodges furnished a channel of communication, secret and secure, between the black ministers and professionals who made up the core membership. They also provided succor in moments of danger. When Clinton Clark arrived in Natchitoches in 1938 to organize sharecroppers, he received encouragement from Scott Lewis, John G. Lewis Jr., and Dr. E. A. Johnson. The three Masons resisted pressure from white planters to use their influence against the union. They allowed Clark to rent the Masonic Hall for his mass meetings. Going from plantation to plantation, Clark founded about fifteen locals in Natchitoches and Red River Parishes. The membership consisted mostly of sharecroppers and laborers, but it also included teachers, ministers, spouses, and sympathizers. When the sheriff imprisoned Clark in July 1940, the Masons interceded to secure his release.[22]

In 1943, when the NAACP perfected a statewide structure, the Prince Hall Masons—along with labor unions, beauticians' associations, and other fraternal organizations such as the Elks and the Odd Fellows—provided vital support. Masons constituted a formidable leadership cadre. Former insurance agent Daniel E. Byrd, for example, revitalized the New Orleans branch and organized the State Conference of Branches, serving as its first president. In Natchitoches, the prime mover in organizing a parish-wide branch was Dr. Johnson, who edited *The Plumb Line* and held the office of senior grand warden in Eureka Grand Lodge. In 1948 Natchitoches showed the largest membership increase of any branch: from 51 to 765. That performance paved the way for Johnson's election as president of the State Conference of Branches in 1950, a position he held until his death four years later. Under Johnson's leadership the NAACP attacked racial segregation on multiple fronts, chalking up several victories, and opened the registration rolls to black voters in numerous parishes. By 1952 about one-third of the black adults in Natchitoches Parish had registered to vote—a far higher percentage than in Caddo, De Soto, and Rapides.[23]

The relocation of the Grand Lodge from Natchitoches to Baton Rouge in 1948 strengthened the alliance between the Masons and the NAACP. Grand Master John G. Lewis Jr. served on the boards of both state and national organizations. In 1951 the Masons created a legal research fund through which state grand lodges funneled money to the NAACP Legal Defense and Education Fund, headed by Thurgood Marshall. The sums were substantial and proved crucial to the NAACP's litigation, especially *Brown* and other school and university integration cases. The total in 1958 from all the grand lodges came to an impressive $142,000, including $24,000 from Louisiana. After accepting membership in the order, Marshall expressed his gratitude by representing the Prince Hall Masons when they took "illegitimate" rivals to court.[24]

During the weeklong Baton Rouge bus boycott in 1953, Masons helped raise thousands of dollars to fund an improvised transportation system composed of taxis, private cars, and black-owned gas stations. "I have never seen Negroes demonstrate so fully and completely that they are tired of being pushed around," wrote John G. Lewis Jr. This "Operation Free Lift" provided a model for the longer, better-known bus boycott in Montgomery, Alabama, the seminal event of the civil rights movement.[25]

What did the civil rights movement owe to the legacy of Reconstruction? It has become commonplace among historians to argue that Reconstruction was a partial success that laid the foundations for a "second Reconstruction" in the 1950s and 1960s. As Eric Foner put it, Reconstruction was not a failed revolution but an unfinished one. A recent college textbook stated it like this: "Reconstruction was not so much a promise betrayed as a promise waiting to be fulfilled."[26]

The problem with this "success delayed" or "promise fulfilled" argument is that by the time the federal government took serious steps to enforce the Fourteenth and Fifteenth Amendments—when the civil rights movement, backed by the moral zeitgeist, forced its hand—blacks had already been pushed off the land, virtually eliminated from the professions, shut out of government, confined to the margins of the industrial economy, and victimized by race riots, lynchings, and police brutality. After decades of systematic, structural, legal discrimination, relatively few had prospered. Meanwhile, during that near-century of oppression, generations of immigrants from Europe had enjoyed opportunities denied to African Americans, many of them rising to the uppermost rungs of business, politics, and the professions. Moreover, by the time blacks began to vote again in substantial numbers, migration had given whites a clear majority in both Natchitoches Parish and Louisiana as a whole. The potential for black political representation and influence was far smaller than in 1865. The promise of Reconstruction, therefore, can never be fulfilled. The adage "justice delayed is justice denied" is a more fitting verdict.

That is certainly how some blacks who lived through Reconstruction felt. Deprived of the comfort that a powerful civil rights movement would eventually destroy the Jim Crow system, they had no doubt that Reconstruction had failed. And many felt betrayed. Looking back upon of emancipation and Reconstruction, John G. Lewis Sr. found it hard to credit the Republican Party with nobility of purpose. The Lincoln administration had resorted to emancipation, he told a congressional committee in 1880, because it needed to recruit black soldiers; it had attacked slavery as a means of undermining the Confederacy. "I can illustrate it in this way: Two white men got fighting once over a coop of chickens, and in their quarrel they upset the coop and the chickens got out. And that is how they got free." P. B. S. Pinchback was hardly less disillusioned. Philanthropy did not explain emancipation and black suffrage, he told the Republican National Committee in 1876. "The first was a war measure, the latter grew out of the necessity of a loyal element in the South, and both were more in the interest of the Union, than the colored people." The Republican state governments elected by black voters "were controlled by white men and run in the interests of white men."[27]

In one sense, Reconstruction can be judged a success, albeit a messy one. As Mark W. Summers has argued, whites in the North, including most Republicans, were more concerned with restoring the Union and abolishing slavery than about guaranteeing equal rights for the South's black population. They wanted to "bring the nation back together and this time for good, to banish the prospect of future war, to break the power of the former slave states to menace or overawe the majority, [and] to end slavery and give that freedom more than a nominal meaning—and all this without sacrificing the basic political framework that had made the Union special." Reconstruction achieved these goals. That achievement, however, came at the expense of the freedpeople. And also, it could be argued, at the expense of America's democracy, for the South became a gigantic "rotten borough," a semi-dictatorship that distorted the nation's priorities and commitments. Moreover, the repeal of the Enforcement Acts in 1894 opened the door wide to electoral fraud, not only in the South but in New York and Chicago as well.[28]

When a bipartisan consensus in favor of making overt racial discrimination illegal emerged in 1964–65, it did so under radically different circumstances. By then, the federal government had vastly extended its powers and was no longer a honeypot of party patronage. The southern economy no longer depended upon black agricultural labor. A powerful labor movement, which included a million black workers, had forced the federal government to give more protection to civil liberties and civil rights. World War II had exposed the full horror of racism when taken to its logical conclusion, genocide, so when the United Nations adopted a Universal Declaration of Human Rights in 1948 it included a forthright proclamation of racial equality. The European colonial empires were crumbling; India had become an independent state, the most populous democracy in the world. Racial segregation was not only intellectually discredited but had become a serious embarrassment for the United States in the context of the Cold War. Blacks had more political influence and greater social capital. As Justice Robert H. Jackson put it in 1954, "present-day conditions" made a Supreme Court decision overturning *Plessy v. Ferguson* unavoidable. Capitalizing on these new circumstances, a well-organized, highly disciplined, broadly based, and brilliantly led civil rights movement made the demand for change irresistible.[29]

Historians and political scientists have sometimes called the civil rights movement a "Second Reconstruction." Activists in the movement, however, rarely invoked Reconstruction as either a model or an inspiration. Folk memories of that era were virtually extinct by the 1950s, and the activists of SNCC, CORE, and SCLC made little attempt to revive them. "After his emancipation in 1863," noted King, in one of his rare references to the period, "the Negro still confronted oppression and inequality. It is true that for a time, while the Army of Occupation remained in the South and Reconstruction ruled, the Negro had a brief period of eminence and political power. But he was quickly overwhelmed by the white majority." King's "I Have a Dream" speech, the most famous public statement of the civil rights movement, cited the Declaration of Independence and the Emancipation Proclamation but not the Constitution.[30]

There was another reason why civil rights leaders rarely mentioned Reconstruction: to do so would have hurt their cause rather than helped it. As Justice Jackson noted in weighing the *Brown* cases, the memory of Reconstruction had sustained segregation by emphasizing, for whites, "the deep humiliation of carpetbag government imposed by conquest." Reconstruction's failure had also fostered a tenacious belief that the prejudices of whites in the South were immutable. "Legislation is powerless to eradicate racial instincts," the Supreme Court declared in 1896, "and the attempt to do so can only result in accentuating the difficulties of the present situation." The conviction that race relations could not be changed by statute became a new orthodoxy that discouraged federal intervention for decades to come. As sociologist William Graham Sumner put it in 1906, "It is not at all what the humanitarian hoped and expected," but "legislation cannot make mores." Finally, Reconstruction convinced presidents that the use of military force in the South would always backfire and must be resolutely avoided.[31]

Consciously or instinctively, the civil rights movement that took shape after the Montgomery bus boycott of 1955–56 avoided the pitfalls that had bedeviled Reconstruction. Presenting itself as an indigenous, black-led southern movement, it inoculated itself against white segregationists' allegations that "outside agitators"—latter-day "carpetbaggers"—controlled it. Claiming to be nonpartisan, it sought and received support from both Democrats and Republicans. Although it understood the importance of power, the civil rights movement stressed moral and religious arguments rather than political ones. It resolutely avoided any hint of corruption; its leaders were selfless. By utilizing nonviolence, the civil rights movement retained the initiative, placed its white opponents on the defensive, and presented a courageous face to the world.

Despite an enormous scholarly literature on Reconstruction, very little of that knowledge has percolated down. The most violent political conflict in U.S. history outside time of war, the topic excites little popular interest. Hollywood, having served up two racist blockbusters in the shape of *Birth of a Nation* (1915) and *Gone with the Wind* (1939), shows little to no interest in Reconstruction's dramatic potential. Louisiana's tourist industry draws countless visitors to plantation homes along the Mississippi River, including one that highlights the sufferings of the slaves themselves. But a visitor to Louisiana—or a native of the state for that matter—cannot find a museum, a historical building, or even a historical marker devoted to the struggles of black and white Republicans during Reconstruction. The only memorials are ones that celebrate white Democrats who violently opposed the Republican Party. In 1891 the City of New Orleans erected the "Liberty Monument," which commemorated the White League uprising of September 4, 1874. In 1921 whites in Colfax unveiled a marble obelisk that paid tributes to the "heroes . . . who fell . . . fighting for white supremacy" on Easter Sunday 1873. Thirty years later, the state erected a marker describing the "Colfax Riot" as the end of "carpetbag misrule in the South."

In Natchitoches, the few traces of Reconstruction are hard to find. The courthouse, the scene of so many political meetings and confrontations, was replaced by a new building in 1896. Tucked behind a railroad track one can find Blount Street, the truncated remnant of what used to be a longer street. Where shotgun houses once stood, weeds now grow. Blunt was probably buried in the black Baptist cemetery nearby, but visible traces of his grave have disappeared. In American Cemetery, one of the oldest in the South, political enemies of Reconstruction lie cheek by jowl in death. The grave of E. L. Pierson, shot dead by J. H. Cosgrove on Christmas Day

1875, and the tomb of John G. Lewis, exiled from Natchitoches in 1878, are a stone's throw from the burial places of David Pierson and Milton J. Cunningham, the Democrats who waged war upon, and ultimately destroyed, the Republican Party. An impressive obelisk marks the resting place of Christopher Columbus Nash, who led the Democratic assault upon the Grant Parish Courthouse known to history as the Colfax Massacre.

The "Good Darky" statue long ago vanished from downtown Natchitoches. In 1968, when the KKK vandalized it and black militants threatened to blow it up, the city removed the statue in the dead of night. But taking monuments down is easier than putting them up. Historical markers note the founding of the first black churches, Asbury Methodist and First Baptist. Nothing, however, commemorates the election of the first black legislator in 1868 or the first black senator in 1870—nothing, in fact, to remind people of Reconstruction. It is as if a political struggle of forty years duration had never happened. The verdict of journalist and historian Lerone Bennett Jr., stated in 1967, may have been too pessimistic, but it is worth pondering: "The violent counterrevolution which overthrew Black Reconstruction in the South . . . dealt American democracy a blow from which it may never recover." Without an appreciation of what Reconstruction attempted, and how badly it failed, we shall be ill-equipped to understand the racial fault lines in present-day America. And the legacy of Reconstruction's failed revolution helps to explain why the democratic model of free and fair elections based upon universal suffrage has yet to be achieved.[32]

NOTES

Abbreviations

BFP   J. P. Breda Family Papers, Special Collections, Hill Memorial Library, Louisiana State University, Baton Rouge

DOJ   U.S. Department of Justice, General Records, RG 60, NARA

FB   U.S. Bureau of Refugees, Freedmen, and Abandoned Lands, RG 105, NARA

NARA   National Archives and Records Administration, Washington, D.C.

OR   *The War of the Rebellion: A Compilation of the Official Records of the Union and Confederate Armies.* 70 vols. Washington, D.C., 1880–1901. All references are to series 1 unless otherwise noted.

PHMP   Prince Hall Masons Papers, Eureka Grand Lodge of Louisiana, Amistad Research Center, Tulane University

RG   Record Group

SCC   U.S. Southern Claims Commission, Approved Claims, 1871–1880, https://www.fold3.com/documents/115166833/southern_claims_commission_approved_claims

USACC   Records of the United States Army Continental Commands, 1821–1928, RG 393, NARA

Introduction

1. Burton and Smith, *Colonial Natchitoches,* ix–xi, 37–50.

2. *Inventory of the Parish Archives of Louisiana: No. 25: Natchitoches Parish* (Baton Rouge: Louisiana State University, 1938), 3–9; Forstall, *Population of States and Counties,* 71.

3. Dollar, "'Black, White, or Indifferent,'" 68–78; Burton and Smith, *Colonial Natchi-toches,* 99–102; Mills and Mills, *Forgotten People,* xxi–xxviii, 15–76; McTigue, "Forms of

Racial Interaction," 166. In 1860 Natchitoches Parish had 959 free people of color; St. Landry Parish, with 956, had virtually the same number.

4. Mills and Mills, *Forgotten People*, 227–49; Dollar, "'Black, White, or Indifferent,'" 9–19, 103–9.

5. Tunnell, *Carpetbagger from Vermont*, 93; Lennon and Mills, "Mother, Thy Name Is *Mystery!*" 210.

6. Brasseaux, *Acadian to Cajun*, 93; *Natchitoches Union*, January 9, 1862; Dollar, "'Black, White, or Indifferent,'" 132–33.

7. *Natchitoches Union*, November 28, 1861.

8. Dollar, "'Black, White, or Indifferent,'" 102–3.

9. "Trinity Episcopal Church," http://trinityparish.info (accessed July 18, 2016); Dollar, "'Black, White, or Indifferent,'" 158–59.

10. Burton and Smith, *Colonial Natchitoches*, xi, 56–67; Olmsted, *Journey in the Seaboard Slave States*, 283–84.

11. Burton and Smith, *Colonial Natchitoches*, 84; Olmsted, *Journey in the Seaboard Slave States*, 283–84.

12. U.S. Congress, Senate Report 855, *Alleged Frauds and Violence in Election of 1878, part 1: Louisiana in 1878*, 519. "Much of the South" because in parts of the region, including parts of southern Louisiana, blacks continued to vote and elect Republicans until the end of the nineteenth century.

Chapter 1. Reconstruction in History

1. *New York Times*, January 20, 1879.

2. U.S. Congress, Senate Report 855, *Louisiana in 1878*, 485–87, 491–93, 513, 517.

3. Ibid., 489.

4. *People's Vindicator*, May 8, 1875.

5. U.S. Congress, Senate Report 855, *Louisiana in 1878*, 489; *People's Vindicator*, November 11, 1876.

6. U.S. Congress, House Report 261, *Condition of the South*, 3:550; U.S. Congress, Senate Report 855, *Louisiana in 1878*, 489, 524.

7. *People's Vindicator*, September 2, 1876.

8. Du Bois, *Black Reconstruction in America*, 631. For a good discussion of older interpretations of Reconstruction that highlighted black incapacity and Republican misgovernment, see Smith and Lowery, *The Dunning School*.

9. E. H. Durell to Dear Sisters, December 22, 1872, Durell Papers.

10. Stephen A. Hackworth to Thomas J. Durant, June 30, 1879, Durant Papers.

11. McPherson, *Battle Cry of Freedom*; McPherson, "Introduction"; Foner, "The Civil War and the Idea of Freedom," 8; Foner, "American Freedom in a Global Age," 4–6; Foner, "American Freedom in the Age of Emancipation," 436; Foner, *Reconstruction*, xxvii; Fogel, *Without Consent or Contract*, 413–17; Doyle, *The Cause of All Nations*, 7–11, 308–13.

12. Foner, *Reconstruction*, xxvii; Smith and Lowery, *The Dunning School*, xii.

13. Thomas J. Durant to Henry C. Warmoth, March 28, 1868, reel 1, Warmoth Papers.

14. Foner, "American Freedom in the Age of Emancipation," 436; Foner, "American Freedom in a Global Age," 4–6; Joseph Logsdon and Caryn Cossé Bell, "The Americanization of Black New Orleans, 1850–1900," in Hirsch and Logsdon, *Creole New Orleans*, 209.

15. Woodward, *The Future of the Past*, 22–23.

16. Escott, *Uncommonly Savage*, 35; Woodward, *The Future of the Past*, 23. Foner is curiously ambivalent about the outcome of Reconstruction. In 1988 he concluded that "what remains certain is that Reconstruction failed, and that for blacks its failure was a disaster whose magnitude cannot be obscured by the genuine accomplishments that did endure" (*Reconstruction*, 604). In 2013 he wrote that "Scholars now . . . emphasize its accomplishments as much as its failings" (Smith and Lowery, *The Dunning School*, xiii).

17. Du Bois, *Black Reconstruction*, 694.

18. Skowronek, *Building a New American State*. See also Fukuyama, *Political Order and Political Decay*.

19. Schurz, *Speeches*, 2:4.

20. Fitzgerald, *Splendid Failure*, 27; Fredrickson, *The Arrogance of Race*, 99–101.

21. Amos T. Akerman to Charles Prossner, November 9, 1871, reel 14, M699, DOJ.

22. U.S. Congress, Senate Report 695, *Removal of the Negroes from the Southern States to the Northern States*, 2:452.

23. William T. Sherman to John Sherman, September 21, 1865, in W. T. Sherman, *The Sherman Letters*, 256; Schurz, *Speeches*, 2:278–80.

24. Dawkins, *A Devil's Chaplain*, 66.

25. Gerstle, *Liberty and Coercion*, 2–3.

Chapter 2. The Collapse of Confederate Louisiana

1. C. T. Christensen to Captain Fitzhugh, May 27, 1865, F. J. Herron to Nathaniel P. Banks, June 3, 8, 1865, Philip H. Sheridan to U. S. Grant, June 8, 1865, and Report of Philip H. Sheridan, November 11, 1866, all in *OR*, 34, pt. 2:620–21, 748, 816–17, 749, 300.

2. Davis, *Inhuman Bondage*, 299.

3. McKitrick, *Andrew Johnson and Reconstruction*, 53–66.

4. Robinson, *Bitter Fruits of Bondage*, 220–22; Tunnard, *A Southern Record*, 281, 315–17.

5. "Thomas S. Bacon," folder 4041, approved claims, 1871–1880, SCC; James Cromie to L. O. Parker, September 5, 1867, reel 91, M1905, FB; *Christian Recorder*, June 29, 1867; Joseph Martin, "A Card to the Public," *Natchitoches Union*, June 26, 1862; "Thomas T. Wall, citizen, Springville, Natchitoches Parish," July 13, 28, 1865, Register of Letters Received, July–November 1865, vol. 170/324DG, E. 1945, Part II, USACC.

6. "Marco Givanovic," folder 17673, approved claims, 1871–1880, SCC.

7. Deposition of Samuel O. Scruggs, March 3, 1875, folder 18534, SCC; "Edward Rogeson Brownell," folder 17654, approved claims, 1871–1880, SCC.

8. Deposition of Emile Rost, "Marco Givanonic," folder 17673, SCC.

9. Banks to Edwin Stanton, April 6, 1865, *OR*, 34, pt. 1:212; Alstyne, *Diary of an Enlisted Man*, 294; Preston Pond Jr. to Henry W. Allen, May 8, 1864, *OR*, 34, pt. 3:962; Southern Claims Commission, *Summary Reports of the Commissioners of Claims: 5th and 6th General Reports*, 173–74.

10. Matthew Ussery et al., Resolutions, September 3, 1863, *OR*, 30, pt. 3:732–33.

11. J. G. Walker to W. R. Boggs, June 21, 1864, *OR*, 34, pt. 4:688; Frazier, "'Out of Stinking Distance,'" 165.

12. E. Surget to R. E. Wythe, February 4, 1864, A. H. May to Reives, February 19, 1864, H. C. Monnell to Richard Taylor, February 13, 1864, Taylor to Gen. Boggs, February 21, 1864, and Richard Taylor to John G. Walker, February 8, 1864, all in *OR*, 34, pt. 2:944, 965–66, 976–78.

13. Edward Dillon to S. D. Lee, January 29, 1864, C. Le de Elzac to Gen. Polignac, February 8, 1864, and M. L. Lyons to Richard Taylor, February 13, 1864, all in *OR*, 34, pt. 2:923, 952–53, 966–67; Haynes, *Thrilling Narrative*, 11, 46–47, 615–66; Brasseaux, *Acadian to Cajun*, 66–67, 124–27.

14. Richard Taylor to S. S. Anderson, April 24, 1864, *OR*, 34, pt. 1:581; Jones and Keuchel, *Civil War Marine*, 39, 56. U. S. Grant, the newly appointed commander in chief of the Union armies, instructed Banks to supply his army "as far as possible from the country occupied." His troops should confiscate "mules, horses, forage, and provisions" from rebel civilians. Grant to Banks, March 15, 1864, box 32, folder 2, Banks Papers; A. H. May to S. S. Anderson, March 24, 1864, *OR*, 34, pt. 1:509.

15. Bragg, *Louisiana in the Confederacy*, 172–74; unidentified planter to Arthemase, [April 1864], folder 8A, box 22, J. H. Williams Collection; Dorsey, *Recollections of Henry Watkins Allen*, 279–80.

16. Richard Taylor to Henry W. Allen, February 1, 1864, and Thomas E. Adams to S. Cooper, January 29, 1864, both in *OR*, 34, pt. 2:934, 921, Dorsey, *Recollections of Henry Watkins Allen*, 282; *Natchitoches Times*, July 2, 1864.

17. David F. Boyd to L. A. Bringier, May 17, 1865, Henry W. Allen to E. Kirby Smith, May 13, 1865, and Kirby Smith to Colonel Sprague, May 15, 30, 1865, all in *OR*, 48, pt. 1:190–99, 1310; Tunnard, *A Southern Record*, 337.

18. W. B. Franklin to A. L. Lee, October 23, 1863, *OR*, 26, pt. 1:775; Ripley, *Slaves and Freedmen*, 16–18.

19. Bragg, *Louisiana in the Confederacy*, 214–16.

20. Federal Writers' Project: Slave Narrative Project, Vol. 16, Texas, Part 2, Easter-King 1936, 153–56, https://www.loc.gov/item/mesn162, and Part 4, Sanco-Young, 131–32, Manuscript/Mixed Material, https://www.loc.gov/item/mesn164 (accessed July 20, 2017).

21. William, "Muskets and Magnolias," 194; Bragg, *Louisiana in the Confederacy*, 217; Thomas E. Anderson to S. S. Cooper, January 22, 1864, *OR*, 34, pt. 2:922.

22. Unidentified planter to Arthemase, [April 1864], box 22, J. H. Williams Collection; Blake, *Succinct History of the 28th Iowa Volunteer Infantry*, 31–32.

23. Ibid., 38–39; Gould, *History of the First-Tenth-Twenty-Ninth Maine Regiment*, 434; Flinn, *Campaigning with Banks in Louisiana*, 145.

24. Oakes, *Freedom National*, 416–21; J. Downs, *Sick from Freedom*, 22–28; Mills and Mills, *Forgotten People*, 264–65; Shadrack Aaron, John Baptiste, Andrew J. Baptiste, Moses Blacnchard, Milton Brack, Charles Caesar, Rafael Collins, John Denis, Henry Hall, Philip Hamilton, James Henry, William Jackson, Henry Jackson, Thomas Johnson, Providence Johnson, John Juplex [Dupleix], Robert Metoyer, Mason Mithchell, Zango Moore, Caesar Prudhomme, Alexander Prudhomme, Elijah Rachal, Joseph Valse, Polly Watch, Joseph Anastrap, Samuel Simon, James Ellis, Richard Gaskins, Calvin Harris, Thomas Levier, Thomas McCall, William Picton, Manuel Turner, all in *U.S. Colored Troops Military Service Records, 1861–1865*, reels 1817–1818, NARA, electronic version, ancestry.com; U.S. Congress, Senate Report 855, *Louisiana in 1878*, 145.

25. Whittington, "Concerning the Loyalty of Slaves in North Louisiana"; T. N. Waul to Jefferson Davis, November 18, 1863, *OR*, 26, pt. 1:425; William B. Franklin to Nathaniel P. Banks, December 21, 1863, box 30, Banks Papers; U.S. Congress, House Report 30, *Report of the Joint Committee on Reconstruction*, 4:77; Bragg, *Louisiana in the Confederacy*, 215.

26. Whittington, "Concerning the Loyalty of Slaves in North Louisiana," 494–95; Bragg,

Louisiana in the Confederacy, 215; Charles D. Elzee to S. R. Lidell, February 8, 1864, *OR,* 41, pt. 2:955.

27. For quotations from Homer and Washington, see note 20 above; Levissee Diary, 132–33, Levissee Papers.

28. Bergeron, "Free Men of Color in Grey"; Dorsey, *Recollections of Henry Watkins Allen,* 382. According to James H. Cosgrove, some "served in white Confederate regiments, in the ranks, and in the musical and hospital corps." See *Natchitoches Enterprise,* August 21, 1913.

29. Mills and Mills, *Forgotten People,* 258–75.

30. "John Carroll Jones House," https://www.nps.gov/nr/travel/caneriver/car.htm (accessed July 20, 2016); Mills, *Forgotten People; Summary Reports of the Commissioners of Claims: 5th and 6th General Reports,* 171; "Carroll Jones," U.S. Census 1850, 1860, 1870, ancestry.com; *Biographical and Historical Memoirs of Northwest Louisiana.*

31. John S. Sherman to William T. Sherman, May 16, November 10, 1865, April 23, May 12, July 8, 1866, November 1, 1867, in W. T. Sherman, *Sherman Letters,* 251, 259, 270–71, 276, 299; Trefousse, *Andrew Johnson,* 197–98.

32. Studies of Lincoln's policy regarding the restoration of Louisiana include Caskey, *Secession and Restoration of Louisiana;* J. G. Taylor, *Louisiana Reconstructed;* McCrary, *Abraham Lincoln and Reconstruction;* Tunnell, *Crucible of Reconstruction;* Rodrigue, *Lincoln and Reconstruction;* Hollandsworth, *An Absolute Massacre.*

33. Thomas J. Durant to Lincoln, February 10, 1864, and Lincoln to Hahn, March 13, 1864, Abraham Lincoln Papers at the Library of Congress, Manuscript Division (Washington, D.C.: American Memory Project, [2000–02]), http://memory.loc.gov/ammem/alhtml/alhome.html, accessed November 29, 2016 (hereinafter cited as Lincoln Papers); Banks to Lincoln, July 25, 1864, folder 34, Banks Papers; *Debates in the Convention for the Revision and Amendment of the Constitution of the State of Louisiana,* 633.

34. U.S. Congress, House Doc. 461, *Annual Report of the American Historical Association for the Year 1902,* 57th Cong., 2d sess., 1903, 452; Escott, *Lincoln's Dilemma,* 196–97.

35. Thomas J. Durant to George S. Boutwell, February 25, 1864, Durant to Thaddeus Stevens, February 29, 1864, Durant to John S. Blatchford, March 5, 1864, and Durant to Henry W. Davis, March 31, November 18, 1864, Durant Papers; Thomas J. Durant to Andrew Johnson, May 1, 1865, in Johnson, *Papers,* 8:6–8.

36. Michael Hahn to Lincoln, October 24, 1865, December 2, 1864, Lincoln to Stephen Hurlbut, November 14, 1864, Hurlbut to Lincoln, November 14, 1864, Memorial of Loyal Citizens of Louisiana to Lincoln, December 1, 1864, and Hurlbut to Lincoln, March 15, 1865, Lincoln Papers.

37. McCarthy, *Lincoln's Plan of Reconstruction,* 342, 381–82; W. C. Harris, *With Charity for All,* 245.

38. Works that underline an alleged evolution in Lincoln's views on race and argue that black suffrage was very much part of his thinking by 1865 include McCrary, *Abraham Lincoln and Reconstruction;* Belz, *A New Birth of Freedom;* L. Cox, *Lincoln and Black Freedom;* Foner, *This Fiery Trial;* and Rodrigue, *Lincoln and Reconstruction.* Studies that emphasize Lincoln's conception of the United States as a white republic include W. C. Harris, *With Charity for All;* Bennett, *Forced into Glory;* Lind, *What Lincoln Believed;* Escott, *"What Shall We Do with the Negro?"* On the question of Lincoln's policy on colonization, see Paludan, "Lincoln and Colonization"; Sebastian Page, "Lincoln, Colonization and the Sound of Silence," *New York Times,* December 4, 2012.

39. Aaron Walker to H. R. Pease, October 31, 1865, and Charles A. Meyers, "Report of the Red River Parishes," March 6, 1866, reel 1, M1026, FB. Charles Miller, Tri-Monthly Report, January 20, 1868, reel 91, M1905, FB.

Chapter 3. Freedom and Survival

1. Knox, *Camp-Fire and Cotton Field,* 449; *New York Times,* February 25, 1866.
2. *Natchitoches Times,* April 26, 1873; "Report of Indigent and Helpless Freedpeople," January 31, 1868, reel 92, M1905, FB.
3. Menn, *Large Slaveholders of Louisiana,* 296; William H. Henderson, Tri-Monthly Report, March 31, 1866, reel 5, M1027, FB.
4. Kilbourne, *Debt, Investment, Slaves; Natchitoches Times,* June 20, 1866.
5. Downs, *Sick from Freedom,* 7–8; William H. Henderson, Report, February 11, 1866, reel 5, M1027, FB.
6. May, "Medical Care of Blacks," 18–19, 52, 56; Carrigan, "The Saffron Scourge," 157–63, 169–75, 178.
7. Indentures of minor freedmen, January, 19, March 3, 1866, reel 92, M1905, FB; W. C. McElvoy to James Cromie, January 24, 1866, reel 91, M1027, FB; McTigue, "Forms of Racial Interaction," 122–23.
8. *Natchitoches Times,* January 5, 1866.
9. William H. Henderson, Monthly Report: Sabine and Natchitoches Parishes, March 31, 1866, and James Cromie, Monthly Report, May 4, 1866, reel 28, M1027, FB; J. W. Harris, "Plantations and Power"; Shlomowitz, "The Squad System on Post-Bellum Cotton Plantations"; Shlomowitz, "Transition from Slave to Freedman Labor"; Shlomowitz, "'Bound or Free?'"
10. *Natchitoches Semi-Weekly Times,* May 26, 1866, January 2, 1867; U.S. Congress, Senate Ex. Doc. 6, *Freedmen's Affairs,* 70; "Pests of Cotton," http://ipm.ncsu.edu/AG271/cotton/cotton.html (accessed July 9, 2016).
11. James Cromie, Endorsements and Memorandums, February 9, 1868, reel 90, M1905, FB. See also William H. Henderson, Tri-Monthly Report, March 31, April 20, 1866, reel 5, M1027, FB; James Cromie, Tri-Monthly Report, January 20, February 16, 1867, G. S. Williams, Tri-Monthly Report, January 20, 31, 1867, and J. A. Mower, Annual Report on the Condition and Operations of the Bureau, September 1867, all in reel 27, M1027, FB.
12. Cromie to Parker, September 30, 1867, and G. A. Hewlett to F. S. Lattier, October 23, 1868, reel 90, M1905, FB; James De Grey to A. F. Hayden, September 20, 1866, box 15, Letters Received, 1866, Dept. of the Gulf, USACC.
13. J. A. Mower to O. O. Howard, Annual Report, October 1866, reel 27, M1026, and Cromie, Monthly Report, July 1, 1866, reel 91, M1905, FB; Receipts from Freedmen, folder 385A, J. H. Williams Collection. Natchitoches Parish accounted for 40 percent of all the contracts in Louisiana recorded by the Freedmen's Bureau in 1866.
14. *Natchitoches Semi-Weekly Times,* February 13, 1867; S. M. Hyams to Cromie, July 25, 1867, L. H. Rushing to Cromie, March 20, 1867, and H. M. McLemore to Cromie, May 25, 1867, reel 91, M1905, FB.
15. Cromie to J. M. Lee, November 30, 1867, W. A. Tharp to Cromie, July 23, 1867, and G. S. Walmsley to Cromie, March 28, May 6, 25, 1867, reel 91, M1905, FB.
16. J. W. Butler to Cromie, July 18, 1867, reel 91, M1905, FB; *Shreveport Southwestern,* September 15, 1869.

17. Martin Flood, Tri-Monthly Report, January 27, 1867, reel 27, M1027, FB; *Natchitoches Times*, October 17, 1867; Highsmith, "Louisiana during Reconstruction," 194.

18. E. Rost to Cromie, March 11, 1867, Gabriel Prudhomme to Cromie, January 8, 1867, and B. J. Chapman to Cromie, May 14, 1867, reel 91, M1905, FB.

19. Charles W. Gardiner, Monthly Report, Plaquemines, January 31, 1866, reel 28, M1027, FB; Cromie to J. M. Lee, November 30, 1867, reel 91, M1905, FB.

20. Cromie to L. O. Parker, July 2, 31, August 19, September 5, 1867, Charles Miller, Tri-Monthly Report, December 10, 1867, February 10, 1868, and L. H. Warren to Miller, April 1, 1868, reel 91, M1905, FB; David H. Boullt Jr., Affidavit, February 10, 1868, reel 90, M1905, FB; Register of Supplies and Clothing Issued to Destitutes, July 1867–July 1868, reel 92, M1905, FB.

21. Howard, *Autobiograhy*, 2:228–35.

22. Ibid., 244.

23. *New York Times*, May 29, 1865; Rhodes, *History*, 5:381.

24. Oberholtzer, *History of the United States*, 1:21; Castel, *Presidency of Andrew Johnson*, 31.

25. Ripley, *Slaves and Freedmen*, 195; see the following items in Johnson's *Papers*: Reply to Delegation of Black Ministers, May 1, 1865, 8:62; Johnson to George H. Thomas, September 4, 8, 1865, 9:36–37, 43; Interview with George L. Stearns, October 3, 1865, 9:180; Speech to First Regiment, U.S. Colored Troops, October 10, 1865, 9:221–23; Interview with Alexander K. McClure, October 3, 1865, 9:311; Interview with James Dixon, January 28, 1866, 9:646; Interview with a Delegation of Blacks, February 7, 1866, 10:43–47; Benjamin B. French to Johnson, February 8, 1866, 10:57.

26. Perman, *Reunion without Compromise*, 15–20; Trefousse, *Andrew Johnson*, 215, 232–33; Carl Schurz to Johnson, June 6, 1865, Johnson, *Papers*, 8:191–92; Schurz, "The Logical Results of the War," September 8, 1866, in *Speeches*, 1:380–81.

27. F. L. Claiborne to Johnson, May 10, 22, 1865, *OR*, 48, pt. 1:537–38; H. A. M. Henderson to M. L. Smith, May 8, 1865, *OR*, series 2, vol. 8:541; S. S. Fairfield to Johnson, May 26, 1865, and A. J. Hamilton to Johnson, July 22, 1865, Johnson, *Papers*, 8:111–12, 459–60.

28. *Natchitoches Times*, June 7, 1865.

29. DiMarco, *Anatomy of a Failed Occupation*, 5; W. C. Harris, *With Charity for All*, 241–43; McCarthy, *Lincoln's Plan of Reconstruction*, 289–313, 494.

30. W. C. Harris, *With Charity for All*, 260; Welles, *Diary*, 2:279–80.

31. Denison to Chase, March 21, 1865, in American Historical Association, *Sixth Report of Historical Manuscripts Division*, 2:456; S. W. Behrman to Banks, April 23, 1865, Thomas W. Conway to Banks, March 21, 1865, Benjamin R. Plumly to Lincoln, March 23, 1865, and S. W. Behrman to Banks, April 23, 1865, all in box 35, Banks Papers; R. L. Banks to Andrew Johnson, May 3, 1865, and David Christie to Johnson, May 7, 1865, Johnson, *Papers*, 8:30, 43; Ripley, *Slaves and Freedmen*, 182; W. C. Harris, *With Charity for All*, 260–61, 272.

32. Hay, *Letters*, 250–51; Burgess, *Reconstruction and the Constitution*, 12.

33. Banks to M. D. Kavanagh, May 1, 1865, Kavanagh to Banks, May 3, 1865, and Banks to Hugh Kennedy, May 5, 1865, all in box 36, Banks Papers; McCrary, *Abraham Lincoln and Reconstruction*, 311–12; W. C. Harris, *With Charity for All*, 261, 272.

34. Trefousse, *Andrew Johnson*, 197–98; McKitrick, *Andrew Johnson and Reconstruction*, 279–318; McCarthy, *Lincoln's Plan of Reconstruction*, 488–90.

35. Caskey, *Secession and Restoration of Louisiana*, 165–70; Lowry, "Political Career of James Madison Wells," 1032–38; S. M. Quincy to Banks, June 1, 1865, box 36, Banks Papers;

"Interview with John A. Logan," May 31, 1865, and Wells to Johnson, July 3, 1865, both in Johnson, *Papers*, 8:154, 341–42.

36. McCrary, *Abraham Lincoln and Reconstruction*, 312–15; Wells to Johnson, July 3, 1865, and Lewis Texada to Johnson, June 26, 1865, Johnson, *Papers*, 8:341–42, 299.

37. Wells et al. to Johnson, May 26, 1865, Johnson, *Papers*, 8:154; *Louisiana Democrat*, June 28, 1865; *New York Times*, July 20, 1865; Lowry, "Political Career of James Madison Wells," 1038–43.

38. W. T. Sherman to J. Sherman, September 21, 1865, in W. T. Sherman, *Sherman Letters*, 256; Sheridan to Johnson, November 26, 1865, Johnson, *Papers*, 8:433.

39. Wells to Johnson, May 26, 1865, Johnson, *Papers*, 8:114.

40. Wells to Johnson, July 3, 29, 1865, William L. Sharkey to Johnson, August 20, 25, 1865, and Benjamin F. Perry to Johnson, August 25, 1865, all in Johnson, *Papers*, 8:342–42, 503, 627–28, 651–53.

41. Wells to Johnson, July 29, 1865, Johnson, *Papers*, 8:503.

42. Maj. Hiram Scofield to Maj. Gen. Lowell, December 7, 1865, and Judge Michael Ryan to Sheriff C. V. Ledour, n.d., box 2, Letters Received, Dept. of Louisiana, USACC.

43. Petition of White Citizens, Lafourche and Terrebonne Parishes to Wells, July 28, 1865, box 1, Letters Received, Dept. of the Gulf, USACC; Police Jury of East Feliciana Parish to Gen. E. R. S. Canby, July 13, 1865, and Citizens of Catahoula Parish to Canby, November 7, 1865, box 2, Letters Received, Dept. of the Gulf, USACC; [White citizens of Shreveport] to Canby, August 18, 1865, box 4, Letters Received, Dept. of the Gulf, USACC; and Brig. Gen. J. A. Sheets to Hoffman, tel., January 31, 1866, box 5, Letters Received, Dept. of the Gulf, USACC; Carter, *When the War Was Over*, 193–201.

44. *Louisiana Democrat*, October 11, 1865; Lowry, "Political Career of James Madison Wells," 1053–61; Caskey, *Secession and Restoration of Louisiana*, 173–79; J. G. Taylor, *Louisiana Reconstructed*, 70–73.

45. *Louisiana Democrat*, November 15, December 27, 28, 1865; Caskey, *Secession and Restoration of Louisiana*, 187–91.

46. See the following in Johnson's *Papers*: Francis P. Blair Sr. to Johnson, August 1, 1865, 8:516–20; Reply to Delegation of Black Ministers, May 1, 1865, 8:62; Johnson to George H. Thomas, September 4, 8, 1865, 9:36–37, 43; Interview with George L. Stearns, October 3, 1865, 9:180; Speech to First Regiment, U.S. Colored Troops, October 10, 1865, 9:221–23; Interview with Alexander K. McClure, October 3, 1865, 9:311; Interview with James Dixon, January 28, 1866, 9:646; Interview with a Delegation of Blacks, February 7, 1866, 10:43–47; Benjamin B. French to Johnson, February 8, 1866, 10:57.

47. George H. Thomas to Johnson, September 9, 1865, Johnson, *Papers*, 8:57.

48. F. M. Crandall to H. Hoffman, November 6, 1865, box 1, Letters Received, Dept. of Louisiana, USACC; James Harrison to J. S. Crosby, October 12, 1866, box 15, Letters Received, 1866, Dept. of the Gulf, USACC.

49. J. A. Sheets to Hoffman, January 31, 1866, and E. R. S. Canby to J. Madison Wells, January 31, 1866, both in box 5, Letters Received, 1866, Dept. of the Gulf, USACC.

50. E. Boedicker to G. K. Wood, January 12, 1866, box 5, Letters Received, 1866, Dept. of the Gulf, USACC; James Cromie, Monthly Report, February 20, 1866, reel 5, M1027, FB; Cromie to J. H. Markham, April 30, 1866, reel 28, M1027, FB.

51. C. C. Clay to Andrew Johnson, November 23, 1865, *OR*, 2:8, 812–15; Interview with Paschal B. Randolph, July 21, 1866, Johnson, *Papers*, 9:711; R. Taylor, *Destruction and Reconstruction*, 249.

52. Benjamin C. Turner to Johnson, April 9, 1866, Johnson, *Papers*, 10:375–91; Charles W. Gardiner, Monthly Report, January 31, 1866, reel 27, Records of the Assistant Commissioner for the State of Louisiana, M1027, FB; U.S. Congress, House Report 30, *Report of the Joint Committee on Reconstruction*, 4:83.

53. Taylor to J. G. Walker, February 8, 1864, *OR*, 34, pt. 2:951; Truman to Johnson, April 9, 1866, Johnson, *Papers*, 10:389.

54. Vandal, *Rethinking Southern Violence*, 23, 33, 46–47; [Report on Murders and Outrages in Louisiana, July 1865–February 1867], Miscellaneous Reports and Lists Relating to Murders and Outrages, March 1865–November 1868, reel 34, M1027, FB.

55. Carter, *When the War Was Over*, 221–25.

56. John L. Helm to Andrew Johnson, February 17, 1866, *Johnson Papers*, 111–13.

57. McFadden to Burbank, June 16, 1866, Letters Received, 1866, Dept. of the Gulf, US-ACC.

58. *Louisiana Democrat*, March 28, 1866; Lt. James De Grey to C. R. Stickney, August 31, 1866, and Capt. N. B. Blanton, Report, August 31, 1866, Letters Received, Dept. of the Gulf, USACC.

59. U.S. Congress, House Ex. Doc. 70, *Freedmen's Bureau*, 393–402; McFeely, *Yankee Stepfather*, 176–80.

60. Caskey, *Secession and Restoration of Louisiana*, 195; White, "Freedmen's Bureau in Louisiana," 24–25; *Louisiana Democrat*, December 27, 1865; A. S. Baird to E. R. S. Canby, February 6, 1866, Letters Received, Dept. of the Gulf, USACC.

61. The crucial role of the U.S. Army in enforcing emancipation, protecting the freedpeople, and nullifying the Black Codes is explored at length in G. P. Downs, *After Appomattox*.

62. Conway, *Freedmen of Louisiana*, 6, 15–16; Dept. of the Gulf, Special Orders No. 12, August 1, 1865, reel 7, M1027, FB; Thomas Callahan to John Pickett, October 28, 1865, box 2, Letters Received, Dept. of Louisiana, 1865, USACC; U.S. Congress, House, *Freedmen's Bureau*, 1866, 30–33.

63. Records of Freedmen's Court, 1865–68, reel 7, M1027, FB; Complaints book, Natchitoches Parish, 1866–67, reel 92, M1905, FB.

64. DiMarco, *Anatomy of a Failed Occupation*, 4.

65. *Natchitoches Times*, June 7, 1865.

Chapter 4. The Lost Cause and the Politics of Loyalty

1. *Natchitoches Semi-Weekly Times*, April 25, May 2, 1866.

2. Norrell, *The House I Live In*, xiv–xv.

3. S. S. Fairfield to Johnson, May 26, 1865, Johnson, *Papers*, 8:111–12.

4. Pollard, *The Lost Cause*; Tunnard, *A Southern Record*, xi.

5. Dorsey, *Recollections of Henry Watkins Allen*, 1, 257.

6. James H. Howry to Johnson, November 8, 1865, Johnson, *Papers*, 9:358.

7. C. E. Lipincott to Lyman Trumbull, August 29, 1865, reel 17, Trumbull Papers; *Natchitoches Semi-Weekly Times*, April 11, 1866.

8. Rable, *Civil Wars*; Gardner, *Blood and Irony*; Janney, *Burying the Dead*; *Natchitoches Semi-Weekly Times*, December 8, 1866.

9. *Natchitoches Semi-Weekly Times*, July 4, 1866, January 19, 1867.

10. Davidson, *Living Writers of the South*, 71–76; Raymond, *Southland Writers*, 645–53;

Mary E. Bryan, "Rights of Southern Women—Women and Work," *Natchitoches Semi-Weekly Times*, February 27, 1867. Twenty-five years old when the Civil War ended, Bryan had eloped at age fourteen, given birth to a son at fifteen, and published her first magazine article at sixteen. During a remarkably productive career that ended with her death in 1913, she worked as a highly paid editor, wrote countless essays and poems, and published twenty novels. Her marriage to Iredell Bryan produced five children and endured for fifty years, but "endure" is the right word: the union brought Mary little happiness.

11. Patty, "A Woman Journalist"; *Natchitoches Semi-Weekly Times,* February 13, April 6, 1867.

12. Stannie Lee [Laura S. Webb], "The Dream of Life," *Natchitoches Semi-Weekly Times*, October 24, 1866; Bryan, "The Planters of Louisiana," *Natchitoches Semi-Weekly Times*, January 30, 1867. Webb was the widow of a Confederate soldier and surgeon who had served in a Mississippi regiment and died of tuberculosis shortly after the war. Left with three young children, she became a schoolteacher while continuing to write poetry and fiction. See Raymond, *Southland Writers*, 527.

13. *Natchitoches Semi-Weekly Times,* January 19, 1867, December 19, 1866.

14. Pollard, *The Lost Cause Regained,* 13, 154–68.

15. Truman to Johnson, April 9, 1866, Johnson, *Papers*, 10:376.

16. Escott, *Uncommonly Savage*, 51.

17. Grant to Canby, February 17, July 24, 1866, box 15, Letters Received, 1866, Dept. of the Gulf, USACC; Joseph Holt to Andrew Johnson, December 27, 1865, January 5, 1866, Johnson, *Papers*, 9:435, 573; Johnson to Grant, February 17, 1866, Johnson to Gen. Daniel Sickles, April 23, 1866, ibid., 10:110, 442. For typical complaints about Johnson's pardons policy, see Joseph C. Bradley to Johnson, November 15, 1865, Alexander N. Wilson to Johnson, November 25, 1865, Finley Y. Clark to Johnson, December 4, 1865, and W. W. Holden to Johnson, December 6, 1865, ibid., 9:383–36, 431, 463, 407; and J. C. Colbrook to Lyman Trumbull, December 3, 1865, and J. W. Shaffer to Trumbull, December 28, 1865, reels 17–18, Trumbull Papers.

18. Brodie, *Thaddeus Stevens,* 214; Blair, *With Malice toward Some,* 256–57.

19. Varon, *Appomattox,* 62, 86–88, 121–25, 151–53.

20. Ibid., 200–202, 229–30; Bradley, *Bluecoats and Tar Heels,* 111–13; Sheridan to Johnson, November 26, 1865, Johnson, *Papers,* 9:433.

21. Interview with Alexander McClure, October 31, 1865, Johnson, *Papers,* 9:310; A. J. Hamilton to Johnson, July 22, 1865, Johnson, *Papers,* 8:459.

22. U.S. Congress, House Misc. Doc. 154, *Louisiana Contested Elections,* 2:107–8, 189.

23. Interview with Alexander K. McClure, October 31, 1865; "Fanatical Hate," *Louisiana Democrat,* December 27, 1865; Alcibiades De Blanc to Johnson, October 20, 1865, Johnson, *Papers,* 9:259.

24. Truman to Johnson, April 9, 1866, Johnson, *Papers,* 10:379; Carter, *When the War Was Over,* 229–30.

25. Sheridan to George H. Williams, March 27, 1866, reel 2, Sheridan Papers; A. Vallas to Carl Schurz, September 7, 1865, Letters Received, Dept. of Louisiana, USACC.

26. Blair, *With Malice toward Some,* 137–47.

27. Banks to Stanton, June 8, 1864, box 33, Banks Papers; E. D. Townsend, General Orders No. 42, August 28, 1864, *OR,* 26, pt. 1:917; Pope to Lincoln, April 10, 1865, *OR,* 34, pt. 1:131.

28. McCarthy, *Lincoln's Plan of Reconstruction,* 494.

29. Mackenzie, *Lincolnites and Rebels,* 179–80; Goodrich and Goodrich, *The Day Dixie Died,* 137–42; Rable, *Civil Wars,* 232.

30. Clemenceau, *American Reconstruction,* 84–85; S. S. Cox, *Three Decades of Federal Legislation,* 605.

31. W. G. Wyly to Johnson, August 10, 1865, *Johnson Papers,* 8:564; Wade H. Hough to Johnson, July 24, 1866, ibid., 10:723–24.

32. Stephens, *Recollections,* 147–48, 174–75, 188–207.

33. *Natchitoches Semi-Weekly Times,* January 10, 1866.

34. *Natchitoches Semi-Weekly Times,* January 5, 1866; *Louisiana Democrat,* August 15, 1866.

35. C. E. Lipincott to Trumbull, August 29, 1865, reel 17, Trumbull Papers; S. S. Fairfield to Johnson, May 26, 1865, Johnson, *Papers,* 8:111–12.

36. A. J. Edgerton to Sheridan, April 30, 1866, reel 2, Sheridan Papers; Ross A. Webb, "Kentucky: Pariah among the Elect," in Curry, *Radicalism, Racism, and Party Realignment;* 105–25; Marshall, *Creating a Confederate Kentucky.*

37. B. F. Perry to Johnson, August 29, 1865, Johnson, *Papers,* 8:870; *Louisiana Democrat,* October 18, 1865.

38. *Louisiana Democrat,* November 15, 1865; Ficklen, *History of Reconstruction in Louisiana,* 111–12.

39. Carter, *When the War Was Over,* 57; *Louisiana Democrat,* November 15, December 13, 1865.

40. Undentified writer to Washburne, [November–December 1865], letterbook 47, Elihu B. Washburne Papers; Field to Trumbull, May 19, 1866, Trumbull Papers; Newsham to Warmoth, April 5, 1866, all in Warmoth Papers; F. M. Crandall to H. Hoffman, November 6, 1865, O. McFadden to N. Burbank, July 13, 1866, Emil Boedicker to G. K. Wand, January 12, 1866, J. W. McDermid to C. G. Savolette, July 13, 1866, and Papers in the Case of John Miller, July 14, 1866, all in Letters Received, Dept. of the Gulf, USACC; *Louisiana Democrat,* July 4, 1866; D. E. Haynes to Canby, November 17, 1865, and Hiram Sheffield to Maj. Gen. Lowell, December 7, 1865, box 5, Letters Received, 1865, Dept. of Louisiana, 1865, USACC.

41. Carter, *When the War Was Over,* 37–40; Vandal, *Rethinking Southern Violence,* 124; U.S. Congress, House Misc. Doc. 154, *Louisiana Contested Elections,* 2:53.

42. *Natchitoches Semi-Weekly Times,* May 12, 1866, June 12, 1867.

43. *Natchitoches Semi-Weekly Times,* February 28, 1866.

44. Hugh J. Kennedy to Johnson, November 23, 1865, and Madison Wells to Johnson, January 30, 1866, Johnson, *Papers,* 9:426, 651; Thomas Cottman to Johnson, March 15, 1866, Wells to Johnson, March 15, 1866, Johnson to Kennedy, March 16, 1866, and Kennedy to Johnson, March 17, 1866, ibid., 10:256–64; R. King Cutler to Lyman Trumbull, August 29, December 6, 1865, and J. W. Shaffer to Trumbull, December 28, 1865, reel 17, Trumbull Papers; Paul Selby to Trumbull, February 24, 1866, reel 18, Trumbull Papers.

45. U.S. Congress, House Report 30, *Report of the Joint Committee on Reconstruction,* 4:81; Orin McFadden to Lt. Nathaniel Burbank, July 17, 1866, and Capt. P. Armin to Hayden, July 14, 1866, Letters Received, 1866, Dept. of the Gulf, USACC.

46. J. W. McDermid to Col. C. G. Savolette, July 13, 1866, P. Wiley to E. Washburn, n.d., N. B. Blanton, to A. F. Hayden, August 31, 1866, William H. Webster to C. R. Stickney, August 31, 1866, and Lt. James D. Grey to C. R. Stickney, August 31, 1866, all in Letters Received, Dept. of the Gulf, USACC.

47. Sheridan to George H. Williams, March 27, 1866, and E. D. Townsend to Sheridan, April 9, 1866, reel 2, Sheridan Papers; George L. Hartsuff to E. R. S. Canby, April 16, 1866, and Sheridan to Canby, January 19, 1866, Letters Received, Dept. of the Gulf, USACC.

48. Oberholtzer, *History of the United States*, 1:382.

49. Burgess, *Reconstruction and the Constitution*, 97–98; Houzeau, *My Passage at the New Orleans Tribune*, digital version, location 1766.

50. Carter, *When the War Was Over*, 252; *Louisiana Democrat*, August 8, 1866; *Natchitoches Semi-Weekly Times*, August 8, 1866; Burgess, *Reconstruction and the Constitution*, 102.

51. Sheridan to John Rawlins, June 5, 1866, reel 2, Sheridan Papers; Hollandsworth, *An Absolute Massacre*, 74; Hogue, *Uncivil War*, 49–51.

Chapter 5. Organizing the Republican Party

1. U.S. Congress, House Misc. Doc. 34, *Recent Election in Louisiana. Testimony*, 1.144.

2. Dollar, "'Black, White, or Indifferent,'" 159–62.

3. U.S. Congress, House Report 261, *Condition of the South*, 2:214; U.S. Congress, Senate Report 855, *Louisiana in 1878*, 145.

4. "A History of Hardy Bryan," http://www.thomasvillelandmarks.org/2012/01/25/a-history-of-hardy-bryan (June 12, 2013); "Hardy Bryan," "J. E. W. Bryan," ancestry.com, *1860 U.S. Federal Census* (June 11, 2013).

5. Manifest of Slaves, *Chipola*, March 12, 1853, reel 14, Slave Manifests of Coastwise Vessels filed at New Orleans, 1807–1860, M1895, National Archives. Blunt's twenty-five-year-old brother, Miles, who adopted the family name Martin after emancipation, was also in this group of imported slaves. In 1860 Maria owned 173 slaves; she operated the plantation with her son, Hardy Bryan.

6. In later life, he adopted the more "correct" spelling of "Blount."

7. *New Orleans Daily Picayune*, February 29, 1879; U.S. Congress, Senate Report 855, *Louisiana in 1878*, 557; McDonald, "Independent Economic Production," 492–93.

8. "History of Evergreen Baptist Church," c. 1914, http://files.usgwarchives.net/la/winn/churches/evergreen18gbb.txt (accessed July 8, 2015).

9. Robert Sheppard v. H. B. N. Brown, District Court, Natchitoches Parish, Opinion, January 20, 1908, and Raford Blunt to First Baptist Church, Natchitoches, Deed of Donation, book B, donation folios 52 and 53, December 2, 1870, Natchitoches Genealogical Society Archives, Old Court House, Natchitoches.

10. U.S. Congress, Senate Report 855, *Louisiana in 1878*, 137, 139.

11. J. J. A. Martin et al. to Benjamin F. Flanders, June 10, 1867, U.S. Congress, House Ex. Doc. 20, *Reconstruction*, 105; *People's Vindicator*, June 19, 1875; *New Orleans Republican*, June 18, 1868; *Bossier Banner*, February 1, 1868, quoting *Natchitoches Times*.

12. *Christian Recorder*, June 8, 1867.

13. *New Orleans Tribune*, April 28, 1867; *Christian Recorder*, June 8, 29, 1867; *Natchitoches Semi-Weekly Times*, May 22, 1867; Ficklen, *History of Reconstruction in Louisiana*, 96.

14. "Natchitoches Parish Slaveholders in 1862," http://files.usgwarchives.net/la/natchitoches/history/hist1890.txt (accessed September 10, 2013); "Robert Byron Jones," ancestry.com, *1860 U.S. Federal Census*.

15. *People's Vindicator*, March 22, 1879; "Henry Roby [sic]," ancestry.com, *1870 U.S. Federal Census* (accessed November 14, 2010).

16. "Prince Hall Grand Lodge of Ohio: Grand Lodge History," http://www.phaohio.org/mwphgloh/histfile.html (accessed July 21, 2015).

17. *Proceedings of the Thirty-First Annual Convocation of the Most Worshipful Eureka Grand Lodge, February 6–10, 1894* (New Orleans: Paragon Printing Co., 1894), 8, box 70, PHMP.

18. *People's Vindicator*, June 3, 1876; 1861 Census of Canada, record for John Lewis, ancestry.com; *Cincinnati City Directory for the Year 1842* (Cincinnati: E. Morgan & Co., 1842), 444; Cheek and Cheek, "John Mercer Langston," 34. Whether Lewis was born free, bought his freedom, was freed by his master, or escaped to freedom is impossible to establish.

19. Cheek and Cheek, "John Mercer Langston," 46–49; Middleton, *The Black Laws*, 40–49, 69–70, 74, 129.

20. McLaren, "'We had no desire to be set apart.'"

21. Entries for John G. Lewis and Toussaint L'Ouverture Delaney, 1870 U.S. Census: *Natchitoches, Louisiana*, ancestry.com (accessed July 20, 2017).

22. Charles A. Meyers, "Report of the Red River Parishes," March 6, 1866, reel 3, M1026, FB; Natchitoches Parish marriage records, http://genealogytrails.com/lou/natchitoches/marriage_records__natchitoches_JKL.html (accessed July 23, 2015).

23. "John G. Lewis," *Louisiana, Naturalization Records, 1836–2001*, ancestry.com (accessed July 23, 2015).

24. McCrary, *Abraham Lincoln and Reconstruction*, 252, 261; Hollandsworth, *An Absolute Massacre*, 23, 106; *Natchitoches Semi-Weekly Times*, October 13, 24, 1866, May 22, 1867.

25. *Christian Recorder*, June 29, August 31, 1867; *Natchitoches Semi-Weekly Times*, June 5, 12, 1867; *Chicago Tribune*, June 11, 1867; *Ouchita Telegraph*, June 13, 1867; U.S. Congress, House Ex. Doc. 20, *Reconstruction*, 104–7; *New York Times*, August 17, 1867.

26. *New York Times*, August 22, 1867.

27. "Ezra Hiestand," 1850 U.S. Federal Census, ancestry.com; U.S. Congress, House Ex. Doc. 68, *New Orleans Riots*, 21, 43; Richter, *Overreached on All Sides*, 178; *Natchitoches Spectator*, April 25, May 21, 1868.

28. Dawson, *Army Generals and Reconstruction*, 46–55; U.S. Congress, House Ex. Doc. 20, *Reconstruction*, 2–3, 5–11, 68–71, 79.

29. U.S. Congress, House Ex. Doc. 20, *Reconstruction*, 79–85, 93–94. The best summary of registration in Louisiana and elsewhere can be found in Sefton, *The United States Army and Reconstruction*, 128–43.

30. *Natchitoches Semi-Weekly Times*, May 8, June 5, 1867; Notice of Registration, Natchitoches Parish, May 15, 1867, Miscellaneous Records Relating to Voter Registration, 1867–68, Dept. of the Gulf, 1865–70, USACC.

31. U.S. Congress, House Ex. Doc. 20, *Reconstruction*, 80–85; G. A. Forsyth to Major O. D. Greene, May 3, 1867, Misc. Records Relating to Voter Registration, USACC.

32. J. F. Smith to C. Chaplin, May 10, 1867, folder 2, box 2, Chaplin, Breazeale, and Chaplin Papers.

33. Hyman, *Era of the Oath*, 125–26; U.S. Congress, House Ex. Doc. 20, *Reconstruction*, 92–94.

34. Dawson, *Army Generals and Reconstruction*, 55; U.S. Congress, House Ex. Doc. 20, *Reconstruction*, 74–76, 93–95; *Natchitoches Semi-Weekly Times*, May 8, 1867.

35. "Tabular Statement of Registration in the State of Louisiana," [1867], Miscellaneous Records Relating to Voter Registration, USACC; J. G. Taylor, *Louisiana Reconstructed*, 143–44.

36. Lt. William McGee, Statement, July 22, 1868, F. J. D'Avy and Emerson Bentley to W. SA. Hancock, February 16, 1868, Statement of F. J. D'Avy, February 26, 1868, and Statement of Kinzie Bates, February 26, 1868, all in box 3, Letters Received, Fifth Military District, USACC; U.S. Congress, House Ex. Doc. 20, *Reconstruction*, 95–99.

37. James Cromie to L. A. Parker, September 30, 1867, reel 90, M1905, FB; Delos White to L. H. Parker, July 21, 1867, reel 89, M1905, FB.

38. William H. Sterling, Circular, June 3, 1867, reel 91, M1905, FB.

39. Cromie to J. M. Lee, October 31, 1867, reel 91, M1905, FB.

40. U.S. Congress, House Misc. Doc. 154, *Louisiana Contested Elections*, 2:165.

41. R. C. Buchanan, Monthly Report, January 31, 1868, reel 27, M1027, FB; Fitzgerald, *Union League Movement*, 117–26; Hahn, *Nation under Our Feet*, 129–35; *Official Journal of the Proceedings of the Constitutional Convention*, 217; Oubre, "'Forty Acres and a Mule'"; Lanza, *Agrarianism and Reconstruction Politics*, 11–22.

42. *Louisiana Contested Elections*, 2:162.

43. *Constitution Adopted by the State Constitutional Convention of the State of Louisiana, March 7, 1868*, 3–4, 14–15, 17–18.

44. *Natchitoches Spectator*, July 7, 1868; *New Orleans Republican*, July 14, 1868; U.S. Congress, Senate Report 855, *Louisiana in 1878*, 509, 557; U.S. Congress, House Misc. Doc. 34, *The Recent Election in Louisiana: Testimony*, 1:190.

Chapter 6. Louisiana Democrats and the 1868 Elections

1. Sumner to Theodore Tilton, April 18, 1867, Sumner, *Selected Letters*, 2:394.

2. *Natchitoches Spectator*, December 7, 1867, January 23, 1868.

3. Varon, *Appomattox*, 239–40; Pryor, *Reading the Man*, 449–52.

4. Pollard, *The Lost Cause Regained*, 152–53.

5. *Natchitoches Spectator*, April 1, 1868; W. S. Mudgett to Warmoth, April 27, 1868, W. R. Meador to Warmoth, April 8, 1868, and Ku Klux Klan to Warmoth, April 27, 1868, reel 1, Warmoth Papers; Binning, "Henry Clay Warmoth," 117–20; U.S. Congress, House Misc. Doc. 154, *Louisiana Contested Elections*, 1:71, 212–16, 481–83; 2:68, 157–61.

6. J. M. Schofield, "Report of the Secretary of War," November 20, 1868, in *Message of the President of the United States*, 310; Robert C. Buchanan, Report of Military Operations, October 11, 1868, box 2, Letters Received, Dept. of the Gulf, USACC.

7. Binning, "Henry Clay Warmoth," 144–51; William P. Kellogg to Warmoth, July 30, 1868, John F. Deane to Warmoth, August 5, 9, 1868, and John Lynch to Warmoth, September 28, 1868, reel 1,Warmoth Papers; Dunning, *Essays on the Civil War and Reconstruction*, 228.

8. U.S. Congress, House Misc. Doc. 154, *Louisiana Contested Elections*, 1:285; U.S. Congress, House Misc. Doc. 34, *Recent Election in Louisiana: Testimony*, 4:160–61; *People's Vindicator*, October 23, 1875.

9. J. G. Taylor, *Louisiana Reconstructed*, 162–63; copy of KWC oath, May 22, 1867, reel 2, BFP.

10. In attempting to create white political unity, opponents of Congressional Reconstruction often used the label "Conservative," partly in deference to former Whigs, many of whom found the term "Democratic" objectionable.

11. U.S. Congress, House Misc. Doc. 154, *Louisiana Contested Elections*, 1:285, 2:3, 15–16, 33–38, 102, 146; U.S. Congress, House Misc. Doc. 34, *Recent Election in Louisiana: Testimony*, 4:123, 127; U.S. Congress, Senate Report 855, *Louisiana in 1878*, 120.

12. J. G. Taylor, *Louisiana Reconstructed*, 161–62; *Natchitoches Spectator*, July 28, 1868.

13. J. G. Taylor, *Louisiana Reconstructed*, 167–71; Dawson, *Army Generals and Reconstruction*, 86–87; Tunnell, *Crucible of Reconstruction*, 154–57; *Supplemental Report of the General Assembly of Louisiana on the Conduct of the Late Elections* (New Orleans: A. L. Lee, 1869), 59–60; U.S. Congress, House Misc. Doc. 154, *Louisiana Contested Elections*, 2:105, 116.

14. U.S. Congress, House Misc. Doc. 154, *Louisiana Contested Elections*, 1:32; G. M. Wickliffe to Rousseau, October 31, 1868, box 2, Letters Received, Dept. of the Gulf, 1865–70, Part 1, USACC; Lovell H. Rousseau, Report, in *Message of the President of the United States*, 414–15.

15. J. G. Taylor, *Louisiana Reconstructed*, 163.

16. *Supplemental Report*, 101; U.S. Congress, House Misc. Doc. 154, *Louisiana Contested Elections*, 2:122–23; *People's Vindicator*, July 11, 1874.

17. U.S. Congress, House Report 261, *Condition of the South*, 2:218; U.S. Congress, House Misc. Doc. 154, *Louisiana Contested Elections*, 1:477, 2:180.

18. U.S. Congress, House Misc. Doc. 154, *Louisiana Contested Elections*, 1:116–17, 521–22; Capt. N. B. McLaughlin to George A. Baldry, November 7, 1868, box 1, Letters Received, August 1868–April 1870, Dept. of the Gulf, USACC; E. H. Hosmer to J. M. Lee, November 12, 1868, reel 90, M1905, FB.

19. Hosmer to Lee, November 18, 1868, reel 90, M1905, FB.

20. U.S. Congress, House Misc. Doc. 154, *Louisiana Contested Elections*, 1:521–27; U.S. Congress, House Misc. Doc. 34, *Recent Election in Louisiana: Testimony*, 4:118.

21. *New Orleans Republican*, November 14, 17, 1868, January 17, 1877.

22. *Louisiana Democrat*, November 11, 1868; U.S. Congress, House Misc. Doc. 154, *Louisiana Contested Elections*, 1:117, 283.

23. U.S. Congress, House Misc. Doc. 154, *Louisiana Contested Elections*, 1:653; *Supplementary Report*, xxix.

24. See, for example, David Pierson testimony, U.S. Congress, House Report 261, *Condition of the South*, 2:547; W. H. Jack testimony, U.S. Congress, House Misc. Doc. 34, *Recent Election in Louisiana: Testimony*, 4:121.

25. *Christian Recorder*, June 8, 1867; James H. Cromie to L. A. Parker, Report for June 1867, and Charles Miller, Tri-Monthly Report, September 10, 1867, reel 91, M1905, FB. By July 1866 the Freedmen's Bureau was supporting thirteen schools in Natchitoches Parish.

26. Vandal, *Rethinking Southern Violence*, 7; U.S. Congress, House Report 261, *Condition of the South*, 3:543.

27. McTigue, "Forms of Racial Interaction," 293–98.

28. Ibid., 173–75; Brasseaux, *Acadian to Cajun*, 115–24.

29. McTigue, "Forms of Racial Interaction," 173–75; Dollar, "'Black, White, or Indifferent,'" 136–40; Mills, *Forgotten People*, 230–46.

30. *Natchitoches Semi-Weekly Times*, December 29, 1866.

31. Petition of Citizens of Natchitoches Parish, May 1, 1868, Miscellaneous Records Relating to Voter Registration, 1867–68, Dept. of the Gulf, 1865–70, Part 1, USACC; *Natchitoches Spectator*, December 5, 1867; June 16, 1868.

32. *Natchitoches Semi-Weekly Times*, February 13, March 2, 6, April 4, 1867.

33. *Natchitoches Semi-Weekly Times*, April 6, 10, 13, 1867.

34. *Natchitoches Semi-Weekly Times*, October 20, November 14, 1866, December 29, March 30, 1867.

35. *Natchitoches Semi-Weekly Times*, May 22, 1867; *Natchitoches Spectator*, May 21, June 8, July 14, August 18, 1868.

36. U.S. Congress, House Misc. Doc. 154, *Louisiana Contested Elections*, 1:271, 524.

37. Lonn, *Reconstruction in Louisiana after 1868*, 15; U.S. Congress, House Misc. Doc. 154, *Louisiana Contested Elections*, 2:522–23, 524. In his letter to Broadhead (June 30, 1868), Blair referred to black voters as "political vagabonds" who were committing "outrages upon the Ballot," and he called for a Democratic president-elect to declare Congressional Reconstruction "null and void" and "compel the army to . . . disperse the carpet bag State Governments [and] allow the white people to reorganize their own governments and elect Senators and Representatives." For the text of the letter, see *New York Times*, July 3, 1868.

38. C. Chaplin to J. G. White, August 29, 1872, folder 5, box 4, Chaplin, Breazeale, and Chaplin Papers.

39. Keith, *The Colfax Massacre*, 67–68; U.S. Congress, House Report 61, *Newsham vs. Ryan*, 1–8; J. Madison Wells testimony, U.S. Congress, House Misc. Doc. 154, *Louisiana Contested Elections*, 1:578–84.

40. Lonn, *Reconstruction in Louisiana after 1868*, 60–65; J. G. Taylor, *Louisiana Reconstructed*, 177–81; Tunnell, *Crucible of Reconstruction*, 157–60.

41. Lonn, *Reconstruction in Louisiana after 1868*, 38–39, 45–47; Tunnell, *Crucible of Reconstruction*, 158–59; Powell, "Centralization and Its Discontents," 110–15.

42. Lonn, *Reconstruction in Louisiana after 1868*, 87; Abbott, *For Free Press and Equal Rights*; U.S. Congress, House Misc. Doc. 211, *Political Troubles in Louisiana*, 368–69.

43. Tunnell, *Crucible of Reconstruction*, 148–49; J. G. Taylor, *Louisiana Reconstructed*, 186.

44. U.S. Congress, House Misc. Doc. 154, *Louisiana Contested Elections*, 1:274, 2:19, 199.

45. McTigue, "Forms of Racial Interraction," 80; U.S. Congress, House Misc. Doc. 211, *Political Troubles in Louisiana*, 283.

46. U.S. Congress, House Misc. Doc. 154, *Louisiana Contested Elections*, 2:57, 91–94; R. Taylor, *Destruction and Reconstruction*, 250.

47. U.S. Congress, House Misc. Doc. 154, *Louisiana Contested Elections*, 2:3, 50–51, 56, 99, 190.

48. Ibid., 63, 164.

Chapter 7. Republicans in Power

1. Foner, *Reconstruction*, 346.

2. Richardson, *The Death of Reconstruction*, 32–38, 63, 85–86.

3. DeSantis, *Republicans Face the Southern Question*, 35; Peskin, *Garfield*, 253.

4. "Consolidated Report of Election," Parish of Natchitoches, 17–18 April, 1868, Fifth Military District, 1867–68, USACC; *Natchitoches Spectator*, April 25, 1868.

5. "Consolidated Report of Election"; Tunnell, *Edge of the Sword*, 145.

6. *Weekly Louisianan*, February 5, 1871; Ward, "French Language in Louisiana Law." A parish-wide ban on hunting with firearms on the Sabbath, enacted by the police jury in 1872, also testified to the political dominance of black Protestants over Catholic Creoles; see *Ouchita Telegraph*, August 17, 1872.

7. Wartime Unionists: William H. Hiestand, Sam Parsons, Joseph Martin. Confederate veterans: N. A. Robinson, Virgil A. Barron. Northerners: James Cromie (Freedmen's Bureau), Charles F. Christy, and James Parker (teachers in freedmen's schools). Free men of

color: Charles Leroy, Richard L. Faulkner, Felix Meziere, Frank B. Vienne, Charles Dupre, Emile Silvie, Tranquillin Metoyer. Former slaves: Henry Dallas (police juror); Israel Jenkins, Henry Burns, Washington Breda (town council); Alex Thomas, E. Lavasin, C. Bush, J. A. Hart (constables).

8. *Opelousas Journal*, March 23, 1872; *Weekly Louisianan*, June 14, 1879; "Speech on Constitutional Amendment," n.d., box 2, Pinchback Papers.The U.S. Senate refused to seat Pinchback on the grounds that the disputed state election of 1872 made his title unclear. Yet the Senate seated William P. Kellogg in 1877 despite the fact that the disputed state election of 1876 made Kellogg's even more dubious.

9. McTigue, "Forms of Racial Interaction," 125–26; *People's Vindicator*, May 8, 1875; U.S. Congress, Senate Report 855, *Louisiana in 1878*, 489; U.S. Congress, House Report 261, *Condition of the South*, 3:214, 226, 229.

10. James Cromie, "Endorsements and Memorandums," February 1, 1868, reel 90, M1905, FB.

11. Agreement [labor contract], 1868–1869, box 3, folder 1, Chaplin, Breazeale, and Chaplin Papers.

12. John S. Levy to James Cromie, April 2, 1867, and Marco Givanovich to Cromie, March 10, 1867, reel 91, M1905, FB.

13. Gabriel Prudhomme to Cromie, January 8, 1867, and B. J. Orphan to Cromie, May 14, 1867, reel 91, M1905, FB.

14. Charles Roubieu to Charles Miller, June 8, 1867, and Charles Miller, Tri-Monthly Report, September 20, 1867, reel 91, M1905, FB; U.S. Congress, House Misc. Doc. 154, *Louisiana Contested Elections*, 2:62; Delos White to L. H. Wilson, July 21, 1867, reel 89, M1905, FB. See also Fitzgerald, *Union League Movement*, 141–60; and Rodrigue, *Reconstruction in the Cane Fields*, 81.

15. *Shreveport Southwestern*, March 30, 1870; William Payne to Eliza Payne, January 10, 1870, folder 14, box 1, J. H. Williams Collection.

16. Jaynes, *Branches without Roots*, 159–62, 167–73, 185–87; Hayden et al., *Freedom*, 37–39, 554.

17. Brown and Rivers, *Mary Edwards Bryan*, 242; U.S. Congress, Senate Report 695, *Removal of the Negroes from the Southern States to the Northern States*, 2:440; *New Orleans Crescent* (quoting *Natchitoches Times*), January 23, 1869; *Bossier Banner*, December 31, 1870; *New Orleans Republican*, January 19, 1872.

18. Robert M. Lusher to Sir (circular), June 20, July 7, 1866, folder 2, box 1, Chaplin, Breazeale, and Chaplin Papers; Monthly School Report, July 1866, and Charles Miller, Tri-Monthly Report, May 31, 1868, reel 91, M1905, FB; P. W. Holmes to G. A. Hewlett, September 11, 1868, reel 90, M1905, FB.

19. *Constitution of Louisiana*, 15; *Annual Report of the State Superintendent of Public Education for the Year 1871* (New Orleans: Republican, 1872), 14, 22, 425, 448.

20. U.S. Congress, House Report 261, *Condition of the South*, 3:292; William H. Redman [Redmond], *1870*; Census Place: *Ward 4, Natchitoches, Louisiana*; reel: *M593_518*; Page: *371B*; Image: *144*; Family History Library, ancestry.com; George W. Green, *1880*; Census Place: *4th Ward, Natchitoches, Louisiana*; reel: *457*; Family History Film: *1254457*; Page: *612A*; Enumeration District: *032*; Image: 0466, ancestry.com; Hicks, *History of Louisiana Negro Baptists*, 98–99; Bellamy, "Education of Blacks in Missouri."

21. James Cromie, Endorsements and Memorandums, October 8, 1868, reel 90, M1905, FB; *People's Vindicator*, July 25, 1874.

22. U.S. Congress, House Report 261, *Condition of the South,* 3:927–29. I have been unable to locate any biographical information about van Deusen (or Duzen).

23. *New York Times,* October 24, 1874; J. G. Taylor, *Louisiana Reconstructed,* 311; U.S. Congress, Senate Report 855, *Louisiana in 1878,* 489, 537–8; McAfee, *Religion, Race, and Reconstruction,* 97. For evidence of Blunt's literacy, see Raford Blunt to J. Ernest Breda, January 9, 1877, folder 13, reel 1, BFP. Blunt admitted the charge regarding his teacher's pay in testimony to a congressional committee; see U.S. Congress, House Report 261, *Condition of the South,* 3:224.

24. *People's Vindicator,* July 3, 1875, June 10, 1876; *Natchitoches Weekly Republican,* November 20, 1875.

25. *New Orleans Republican,* May 1, 1870; L. George to Warmoth, May 2, 1870, and James Cromie to Warmoth, May 5, 1870, both in reel 2, Warmoth Papers; Vandal, "Property Offenses," 139–41; Vandal, "Regulating Louisiana's Rural Areas," 86–88.

26. See the testimony of parish coroner A. P. Breda in U.S. Cong., House Misc. Doc. 34, *Recent Election in Louisiana: Testimony,* 4:156–63. On the difficulty of convicting the perpetrators of homicides in the South, see also Ayers, *Vengeance and Justice,* 17–32.

27. *People's Vindicator,* June 3, 17, 1876.

28. Brown and Rivers, *Mary Edward Bryan,* 242.

29. Cromie to Parker, Report for June 1867; Cromie to Parker, July 31, 1867, August 19, 1867; Cromie to J. M. Lee, October 31, 1867; U.S. Congress, Senate Report 695, *Removal of the Negroes from the Southern States to the Northern States,* 2:114.

30. Vandal, "Property Offenses," 127–43 (quotation on 133).

31. De Vries, "Between Equal Justice and Racial Terror."

32. Cromie to Delos H. White, August 10, 1867, Cromie to White, August 18, 1867, Charles Miller, Tri-Monthly Reports, September 10, 20, 1867, February 19, 1868, and Miller to L. O. Parker, September 5, 1867, reel 27, M1026, FB; *Natchitoches Spectator,* December 5, 31, 1867.

33. R. C. Buchanan to E. Whittesley, Monthly Report, January 31, 1868, reel 27, M1027, FB; Monthly Report of Supplies Issued to Planters, May and August 1868, reel 92, M1905, FB; G. A. Hewlett to L. H. Warren, September 9, 1868, reel 90, M1905, FB.

34. Vincent, *Black Legislators,* 99–100; Jaynes, *Branches without Roots,* 296; Woodman, *New South—New Law,* 68–78.

35. U.S. Congress, Senate Report 695, *Removal of the Negroes from the Southern States to the Northern States,* 3:475–76.

36. U.S. Congress, Senate Report 695, *Removal of the Negroes from the Southern States to the Northern States,* 2:143; U.S. Congress, House Report 261, *Condition of the South,* 3:223; Martin Flood, Tri-Monthly Report, January 27, 1867, reel 27, M1027, FB.

37. Higgs, *Competition and Coercion,* 55–57; Ransom and Sutch, *One Kind of Freedom,* 12, 238–43; U.S. Congress, House Report 261, *Condition of the South,* 2:223.

38. Louis Dupleix v. Elie Durand, No. 7485, October 22, 1868, District Court Record 18, Clerk of Court's Office, Natchitoches Parish Court House. The plaintiff was undoubtedly Louis Dupleix, former editor of the *Natchitoches Union* and *Natchitoches Semi-Weekly Times.*

39. Judge Osborn, Order, December 4, 1868, Dupleix v. Durand.

40. Jaynes, *Branches without Roots,* 298–300; Curtin, "'Negro Thieves' or 'Enterprising Farmers'?" 30; James D. Grey to A. F. Hayden, September 20, 1866, box 15, Dept. of the Gulf, Letters Received, USACC; U.S. Congress, Senate Report 695, *Removal of the Negroes from the Southern States to the Northern States,* 2:469; *People's Vindicator,* August 29, 1874.

41. Woodman, *New South—New Law*, 65, 68–70; U.S. Congress, House Report 261, *Condition of the South*, 2:223; U.S. Congress, Senate Report 695, *Removal of the Negroes from the Southern States to the Northern States*, 2:440.

42. *People's Vindicator*, September 4, 1875.

43. Ross, "Obstructing Reconstruction."

44. U.S. Congress, House Report 261, *Condition of the South*, 3:539–40, 914–20; *People's Vindicator*, August 1, 1874, September 30, 1876.

45. U.S. Congress, House Report 261, *Condition of the South*, 3:296.

46. Simmons and Leroy v. Boullt, in *Louisiana Reports* (New Orleans: Republican, 1874), 278–91.

47. U.S. Congress, House Report 261, *Condition of the South*, 3:287–89; Ball, Lyons and Co. vs. Boullt, No. 7901, District Court Record Book 19, Clerk of Court's Office, Natchtitoches Parish Court House; Simmons et al. v. Boullt, No 7907, District Court Record 19, 49–55, Clerk of Court's Office, Natchitoches Parish Court House. A modern-day parallel would be Republican charges that the Obama administration had "exploded the deficit" when most of the deficit in question had been created by the preceding Bush administration.

48. *People's Vindicator*, September 12, 1874; *Biographical and Historical Memoirs of Northwest Louisiana*, 310.

49. Act No. 93, in *New Orleans Republican*, July 9, 1872.

50. *Natchitoches Times*, April 26, 1873; *Mayor and City Council of Natchitoches vs. W. H. Redmond*, plaintiff's brief, March 25, 1875, box 2, Lewis Family Papers; *New Orleans Republican*, May 23, 1874.

51. Richard Kilbourne, review of *New Orleans after the Civil War: Race, Politics, and a New Birth of Freedom*, by Justin A. Nystrom, H-Net Reviews, May 2011, http://www.h-net. org/reviews/showrev.php?id=31788; Highsmith, "Louisiana during Reconstruction," 295.

Chapter 8. Unprincipled Politics

1. Thomas J. Durant to Banks, December 14, 1863, box 30, Banks Papers; U.S. Congress, *House Executive Documents*, 44th Cong., 1st sess., 1867, 65; Powell, "Centralization and Its Discontents," 113.

2. Powell, "Centralization and Its Discontents," 107.

3. U.S. Congress, House Report 261, *Condition of the South*, 2:973; U.S. Congress, House Misc. Doc. 211, *Political Troubles in Louisiana*, 38.

4. Campbell, "Political Life of Louisiana Negroes," 164.

5. *Constitution Adopted by the State Constitutional Convention* (New Orleans: Republican, 1868) 14.

6. Binning, "Henry Clay Warmoth," 122–23; U.S. Congress, House Misc. Doc. 154, *Louisiana Contested Elections*, 1:706; Robert C. Buchanan, Report, October 1, 1867, to October 1, 1868, October 11, 1868, box 2, Letters Received, Dept. of the Gulf, USACC.

7. Binning, "Henry Clay Warmoth," 123–24; Hahn to Warmoth, May 5, 1868, reel 1, Warmoth Papers.

8. James O. Fuqua to Warmoth, July 9, 1868, reel 1, Warmoth Papers.

9. Hyman, *Era of the Oath*, 131–34, 150–55.

10. *Constitution*, 14.

11. J. G. Taylor, *Louisiana Reconstructed*, 153; Frank Morey to Warmoth, December 4, 1872, reel, Warmoth Papers.

12. U.S. Congress, House Misc. Doc. 211, *Political Troubles in Louisiana*, 125, 268, 446.

13. Lincoln to George F. Shepley, November 21, 1862, Lincoln Papers; U.S. Congress, House Misc. Doc. 211, *Political Troubles in Louisiana*, 224, 438–39, 448.

14. William P. Kellogg to Stephen B. Packard, January 23, 1872, reel 3, Warmoth Papers. The most extensive discussion of corruption can be found in Binning, "Henry Clay Warmoth," 153–65, 185–89.

15. U.S. Congress, House Misc. Doc. 211, *Political Troubles in Louisiana*, 542; Sypher to Warmoth, July 13, 1871, Warmoth Papers. Carter knew whereof he spoke. According to Warmoth, he had a financial interest in "almost every measure that passed the legislature." Carter's attempted rebuttal did him little good. He admitted to signing a bill favoring the Chattanooga Railroad Company two days after the company offered him a position as attorney. He confessed to receiving 10,000 shares of the company's stock, "which I sold . . . and realized $5,000." Warmoth himself was no stranger to insider deals. In 1867 he received 100 shares in the Mississippi and Mexico Gulf Canal Company with a face value of $100,000, for which he paid nothing. Two years later he signed a bill furnishing the company state aid.

16. U.S. Congress, House Misc. Doc. 211, *Political Troubles in Louisiana*, 228, 257, 434–35.

17. Ibid., 11, 38, 263, 308; Binning, "Henry Clay Warmoth," 266–70.

18. U.S. Congress, House Misc. Doc. 211, *Political Troubles in Louisiana*, 141, 274–75, 375.

19. Du Bois, *Black Reconstruction in America*, 478. The factionalism within the Republican Party is detailed in Lonn, *Reconstruction in Louisiana after 1868*, 73–165; J. G. Taylor, *Louisiana Reconstructed*, 209–27; and Tunnell, *Crucible of Reconstruction*, 164–70.

20. U.S. Congress, House Misc. Doc. 211, *Political Troubles in Louisiana*, 379.

21. Republican Party of Louisiana, *Report of the Committee on Address*, 6–12; *Weekly Louisianan*, August 31, 1871, January 25, 1872.

22. *New Orleans Semi-Weekly Louisianan*, June 10, 1871; *Donaldsonville Chief*, May 25, 1872; U.S. Congress, House Misc. Doc. 211, *Political Troubles in Louisiana*, 123, 241; State of Louisiana ex rel. N. A. Robinson v. Charles F. Dranguet, in *Reports of Cases Argued and Determined in the Supreme Court of Louisiana*, 23:784–85. James Cromie, the first publisher of the *Red River News*, died of a heart attack while attending the Republican state convention in August 1870.

23. *Semi-Weekly Louisianan*, May 18, 1871; *Louisiana Democrat*, June 14, 1871; *People's Vindicator*, June 20, 1874. When Burdick quit the Republican Party in 1874 he sold the *Red River News* printing press to James Cosgrove, who used it to publish the virulently anti-Republican *People's Vindicator*.

24. Mitchell, "Oscar James Dunn," 277; *Opelousas Journal*, March 23, 1872.

25. U.S. Congress, House Misc. Doc. 211, *Political Troubles in Louisiana*, 38, 172, 454; Binning, "Henry Clay Warmoth," 136.

26. U.S. Congress, House Misc. Doc. 211, *Political Troubles in Louisiana*, 18, 120–23, 142, 245, 380–81, 394, 438; Republican Party of Louisiana, *Report of the Committee on Address*, 10–12.

27. U.S. Congress, House Misc. Doc. 211, *Political Troubles in Louisiana*, 298.

28. Ibid., 143, 221, 277, 281; Stephen B. Packard to Amos Akerman, July 27, 1871, and Oscar J. Dunn to U. S. Grant, July 28, 1871, Kellogg Papers; Dawson, *Army Generals and Reconstruction*, 110–11, 116–27; Powell, "Centralization and Its Discontents," 128–29.

29. Peskin, *Garfield*, 409; U.S. Congress, House Report 140, *Presidential Election Investigation*, 103.

30. U.S. Congress, House Misc. Doc. 31, *Presidential Election Investigation*, 1:87. Until 2006 Louisiana had no law against bribery.

31. Schurz, *Speeches*, 2:57, 322–23; *Ouchita Telegraph*, July 1, 1871.

32. U.S. Congress, House Misc. Doc. 211, *Political Troubles in Louisiana*, 50, 253–54, 295, 306–7, 384–86; J. C. Moncure et al., "Understanding between the Democratic members of the Louisiana House of Representatives and Gov. H. C. Warmoth," February 9, 1871, reel 2, Warmoth Papers; Tunnell, *Crucible of Reconstruction*, 150; Powell, "Centralization and Its Discontents," 117–23; J. G. Taylor, *Louisiana Reconstructed*, 231.

33. P. A. Morse and William M. Levy to Thomas J. Semmes, November 15, 1871, reel 2, Warmoth Papers.

34. Levy had fought in the Second Louisiana Infantry and served on General Richard Taylor's staff. Morse, an older man, had served as provost marshal, in charge of, among other things, enforcing conscription and suppressing disloyalty.

35. U.S. Congress, House Misc. Doc. 211, *Political Troubles in Louisiana*, 519; W. W. Farmer to Warmoth, May 15, 1872, reel 3, Warmoth Papers.

36. Lonn, *Reconstruction in Louisiana after 1868*, 140–62; J. G. Taylor, *Louisiana Reconstructed*, 227–36; Binning, "Henry Clay Warmoth," 296–310.

37. *Louisiana Democrat*, August 28, 1872.

38. Lonn, *Reconstruction in Louisiana after 1868*, 139–43; J. G. Taylor, *Louisiana Reconstructed*, 227–29; *Louisiana Democrat*, August 28, 1872; *Weekly Louisianan*, June 15, 1872; Morse to Warmoth, July 16, 1872, reel 3, Warmoth Papers.

39. Warmoth, *War, Politics, and Reconstruction*, 199–201.

40. Ibid., 200; Emerson Bentley to Warmoth, [July 1872?], and Thomas C. Durant to Warmoth, September 1872, both in reel 3, Warmoth Papers.

41. Tunnell, *Crucible of Reconstruction*, 170; Warmoth, *War, Politics, and Reconstruction*, 201.

42. U.S. Congress, House Report 597, *Sheridan vs. Pinchback*, 12, 18.

43. Ibid., 18–20; U.S. Congress, House Misc. Doc. 25, *Papers in the Case of George A. Sheridan vs. P.B.S. Pinchback*, 10–12.

44. U.S. Congress, House Ex. Doc. 91, *Condition of Affairs in Louisiana*, 115–16.

45. U.S. Congress, House Misc. Doc. 25, *Papers in the Case of George A. Sheridan vs. P.B.S. Pinchback*, 9–17; U.S. Congress, House Ex. Doc. 91, *Condition of Affairs in Louisiana*, 116–18.

46. U.S. Congress, House Ex. Doc. 91, *Condition of Affairs in Louisiana*, 51.

47. William M. Levy to Warmoth, November 8, 14, 1872, reel 3, Warmoth Papers.

48. Dawson, *Army Generals and Reconstruction*, 134–39; Lonn, *Reconstruction in Louisiana after 1868*, 181–205; J. G. Taylor, *Louisiana Reconstructed*, 241–49; Binning, "Henry Clay Warmoth," 323–32; U.S. Congress, Senate Report 457, *Louisiana Investigation*, 155, 195, 249, 405, 914.

49. J. G. Taylor, *Louisiana Reconstructed*, 241.

Chapter 9. The Natchitoches "Scalawags"

1. Statements of A. H. Leconte (first quotation), Leon Greneaux (second quotation), David H. Boullt Jr. (third quotation), in State v. J. E. Breda [1872], reel 2, J. Ernest Breda Papers.

2. Elcey Hertzog to Ernest Breda, April 13, 1873, reel 1, J. Ernest Breda Papers.

3. Lanza, *Agrarianism and Reconstruction Politics*, 33–34, 50–51.

4. *Shreveport Southwestern*, April 6, May 11, 1870; *Natchitoches Union Daily*, April 2, 1864; *Natchitoches Times*, March 20, 1869; *Red River News*, January 14, 1871; *Biographical and Historical Memoirs of Northwest Louisiana*, 342; *New Orleans Republican*, April 9, 1875.

5. The extent to which amnesty acts helped the Republican Party to recruit ex-Confederates is unclear. In 1870 Congress granted partial amnesty to 1,431 southern whites, restoring their right to vote while barring them from federal office unless they could take the "iron-clad oath." Blackstone was among those relieved. In 1872 Congress granted full amnesty to all but a handful of individuals. In practice, however, former Confederates who joined the Republican Party before the state and federal amnesties of 1870 had had no difficulty in voting and holding office; indeed, the state constitution of 1868 provided that ex-rebels "who favored the execution of the . . . Reconstruction Acts of Congress" (i.e., supported the Republican Party) could be relieved of their political disabilities. Hence Myers, Bossier, and Blackstone had all been able to vote and hold office *before* the amnesties of 1870. See Abbot, *Republican Party and the South*, 170; Foner, *Reconstruction*, 504; *Constitution Adopted by the State Constitutional Convention of the State of Louisiana*, 14; *New Orleans Republican*, May 4, June 26, 1870.

6. *New Orleans Republican*, March 3, 1870; Current, *Those Terrible Carpetbaggers*, 246–47.

7. Ernest Breda to Elcey Hertzog, November 18, 1874, reel 1, J. Ernest Breda Papers. Breda's uncle, C. F. Dranguet, stopped speaking to his Republican nephews. They deeply resented the slight.

8. U.S. Congress, House Report 261, *Condition of the South*, 3:205, 547; *People's Vindicator*, May 1, September 11, 1875. See also Baggett, *Scalawags*, 1–3.

9. Wyatt-Brown, *Southern Honor*, 22, 360. On the propensity of southerners to resort to personal violence in the name of honor, see also Franklin, *The Militant South*, 34–58; Ayers, *Vengeance and Justice*, 9–20, 99–100; Greenberg, *Honor and Slavery*, 53–62; Waldrep, *Roots of Disorder*, 27–29, 60–61; Hyde, *Pistols and Politics*, 13–14, 207, 260–61; Hamm, *Murder, Honor, and Law*, 7–10; Klotter, *Kentucky Justice*, 43–56; Carter, *When the War Was Over*, 18–19; and Vandal, *Rethinking Southern Violence*, 29–32.

10. J. E. Breda to James H. Cosgrove, July 15, 1874, reel 2, BFP.

11. U.S. Congress, House Misc. Doc. 34, *Recent Election in Louisiana: Testimony*, 2:314; Brundage, *Lynching in the New South*, 51.

12. Puckette's course can be traced in the *Bossier Banner*, April 13, June 8, June 29, August 3, 1872.

13. *Bossier Banner*, March 29, 1873, quoting *Natchitoches Times*.

14. *Rapides Gazette*, April 12, May 3, 1873; *New Orleans Republican*, April 27, 1873; M. J. Cunningham to J. E. Breda, June 4, 1873, reel 1, BFP; Minutes of Natchitoches Parish Republican Club, June 14, 1873, box 3, Lewis Family Papers; David Pierson testimony, U.S. Congress, House Report 261, *Condition of the South*, 3:551. In lengthy negotiations conducted through William M. Levy and Ross E. Burke (Democrats) and John G. Lewis, M. P. Blackstone, and L. H. Burdick (Republicans), N. A. Robinson had been the Republican candidate for district attorney, but when he died shortly after the 1872 election, Governor Kellogg appointed Ernest Breda to the position.

15. Lane, *The Day Freedom Died*, 90–91; Keith, *The Colfax Massacre*, 88–110; *Louisiana Democrat*, April 30, 1873.

16. *Louisiana Democrat*, April 16, May 14, 1873.

17. U.S. Congress, House Ex. Doc. 30, *Use of the Army in Certain Southern States*, 287–88; Kellogg to Williams, August 26, 1874, reel 2, M940, DOJ.

18. Elcey Hertzog to Ernest Breda, April 13, 1873, reel 1, BFP; Breda to George H. Williams, August 11, 1873, J. Erenest Breda Papers.

19. W. H. McCoy to Charles Christian, April 29, 1873, Kellogg Papers; U.S. Congress, House Ex. Doc. 30, *Use of the Army in Certain Southern States*, 287–88, 399–401.

20. Breda to Stephen B. Packard, August 11, 1873, J. Ernest Breda Papers; U.S. Congress, House Ex. Doc. 30, *Use of the Army in Certain Southern States*, 287–88, 401.

21. Lane, *The Day Freedom Died*, 141; Stephen B. Packard to George H. Williams, September 6, 1873, reel 1, M940, DOJ; J. R. Beckwith to George H. Williams, June 17, 1873, Kellogg Papers.

22. Lane, *The Day Freedom Died*, 143–53.

23. United States vs. Cruikshank, 92 U.S. 542 (1876); Goldman, *Reconstruction and Black Suffrage*, 88–106; Lane, *The Day Freedom Died*, 121–22, 244–46.

24. Ernest Breda to George H. Williams, August 11, 1873, J. Ernest Breda Papers.

25. P. A. Simmons, President Police Jury, and Charles Leroy, Treasurer, Natchitoches Parish vs. D. H. Boullt, Tax Collector, No. 5030; 26 La. Ann. 0277, Louisiana Supreme Court Case Files, UNO Historical Archives of the Supreme Court of Louisiana, D-Space at the University of New Orleans, http://libweb.uno.edu/jspui/handle/123456789/20664; Sections 2628, 2629, 2630, *Revised Statute Laws of the State of Louisiana* (New Orleans: B. Bloomfield, 1876), 682.

26. Leroy's support for the prosecution indicated his abandonment of the Republican Party. In 1874 he was serving as a policeman under the Democratic-controlled Natchitoches city council. Oddly enough—but indicative of how party allegiances shifted in unpredictable ways—the other plaintiff, P. A. Simmons, later joined the Republicans.

27. Simmons and Leroy vs. Boullt; *Rapides Gazette*, September 27, 1873; *Louisiana Reports* (1874), 277–79; U.S. Congress, House Report 261, *Condition of the South*, 3:914.

28. *People's Vindicator*, August 1, 1874.

29. Powell, "Centralization and Its Discontents," 110; *People's Vindicator*, March 25, 1875; "J. Jules Bossier," No. 1767, Succession Records, Clerk of Court's Office, Natchtitoches Parish Court House; George A. Kearney to John G. Lewis, September 7, 1882, and Raford Blount to Lewis, September 21, 1882, both in box 2, Lewis Family Papers.

30. *People's Vindicator*, February 20, 1875.

31. *People's Vindicator*, June 20, December 26, 1874; U.S. Congress, House Report 261, *Condition of the South*, 3:1038.

32. *People's Vindicator*, June 20, July 4, 25, 1874.

33. *New Orleans Bulletin*, July 11, 1874; *New National Era*, July 23, 1874; U.S. Congress, House Report 261, *Condition of the South*, 3:214.

34. *People's Vindicator*, June 20, July 18, August 29, 1874; *New Orleans Republican*, August 2, 1874; U.S. Congress, House Report 261, *Condition of the South*, 3:538, 553, 928. In August, however, Kellogg filled the vacancy, giving the Republicans a three-to-two majority.

35. *People's Vindicator*, June 27, July 11, 18, August 1, 1874, February 13, 1875.

36. U.S. Congress, House Report 261, *Condition of the South*, 3:216.

37. Ibid., 215–16; U.S. Congress, House Report 101, *Condition of the South*, 2:106, 143–44.

38. *New Orleans Republican*, January 29, 1875; U.S. Congress, House Report 261, *Condition of the South*, 3:215–16, 225, 229.

39. U.S. Congress, House Report 261, *Condition of the South*, 3:540–41, 544.

40. Tunnell, *Edge of the Sword*, 184; *People's Vindicator*, July 25, August 1, 1874; May 1, 1875.

41. U.S. Congress, House Report 261, *Condition of the South*, 3:155, 290, 540, 547; *People's Vindicator*, August 1, 8, 1874. The Republican officials whom the Tax Reform Association permitted to remain in office included police jury president V. A. Barron and clerk of court H. P. Mezière, the latter a freeborn African American.

42. Foner, *Reconstruction*, 376, 415–16; Wiener, "Planter Persistence and Social Change," 255–57. For Natchitoches, see the testimony of tax collector D. H. Boullt in Simmons and Leroy vs. Boullt.

43. Thornton, "Fiscal Policy," 349–71; Summers, *Ordeal of the Reunion*, 350–51; Fitzgerald, *Splendid Failure*, 154–55.

44. William H. Jack to George H. Williams, May 21, 1874, reel 1, M940, DOJ.

45. Powell, "The Politics of Livelihood," 315–37; Summers, *Ordeal of the Reunion*, 351–52.

46. U.S. Congress, House Report 261, *Condition of the South*, 3:280–82, 548–50; *People's Vindicator*, August 1, 1874; *New Orleans Republican*, August 7, 1874.

47. Henry C. Dibble to Charles Foster, letter, January 8, 1875, *New York Times*, January 9, 1875; Tunnell, *Carpetbagger from Vermont*, 139–40.

48. U.S. Congress, House Report 261, *Condition of the South*, 3:133.

49. Ibid., 307, 279–81, 291.

50. J. G. Taylor, *Louisiana Reconstructed*, 285–86; Dawson, *Army Generals and Reconstruction*, 150–60.

51. J. G. Taylor, *Louisiana Reconstructed*. 287–90; Tunnell, *Edge of the Sword*, 199–207; Brown and Rivers, *Mary Edwards Bryan*, 233.

52. U.S. Congress, House Report 261, *Condition of the South*, 3:136; Tunnell, *Edge of the Sword*, 194; *People's Vindicator*, September 12, 1874.

53. *Red River News*, June 28, 1873; U.S. Congress, House Report 261, *Condition of the South*, 3:132–33, 216–17.

54. *People's Vindicator*, August 29, 1874; U.S. Congress, House Report 261, *Condition of the South*, 3:217, 228; U.S. Congress, House Misc. Doc. 34, *Recent Election in Louisiana: Testimony*, 4:127.

55. U.S. Congress, House Report 261, *Condition of the South*, 3:218–19, 551.

56. Ibid., 219.

57. Ibid., 218–19, 546–47, 789; U.S. Congress, House Ex. Doc. 30, *Use of the Army in Certain Southern States*, 287–88, 200.

Chapter 10. The White League Insurrection

1. Summers, *Ordeal of the Reunion*, 345.

2. Kellogg to George H. Williams, November 11, 1873, reel 1, M940, DOJ; Kellogg to Grant, August 19, 1874, Kellogg to Williams, August 26, 1874, and J. R. Beckwith to Williams, June 25, July 9, September 5, October 7, 10, 17, 21, 1874, all in reel 2, M940, DOJ; Gillette, *Retreat from Reconstruction*, 136–52.

3. A. P. Field to George H. Williams, September 1, 1874, reel 2, M940, DOJ; U.S. Congress, House Report 261, *Condition of the South*, 3:250.

4. Reed, "David Boyd," 338; T. H. Williams, *Romance and Realism*, 38–41; Perman, *Road to Redemption*, 154–55; Warmoth to Lewis Texada, March 11, 1873, reel 3, Warmoth Papers; *Ouchita Telegraph*, June 21, 1873.

5. Jack Wharton to Henry Clay Warmoth, August 8, 1874, reel 3, Warmoth Papers; Ella Lonn, *Reconstruction in Louisiana after 1868,* 269–74; E. R. Williams, "Florida Parish Ellises," 136.

6. J. G. Taylor, *Louisiana Reconstructed,* 291–96; Dawson, *Army Generals and Reconstruction,* 169–73.

7. *People's Vindicator,* September 26, October 3, 1874; U.S. Congress, House Report 261, *Condition of the South,* 3:138.

8. *People's Vindicator,* July 18, 1874; U.S. Congress, House Ex. Doc. 30, *Use of the Army in Certain Southern States,* 200.

9. Dawson, *Army Generals and Reconstruction,* 172–78.

10. U.S. Congress, House Report 101, *Condition of the South,* 2:70–72; *People's Vindicator,* October 24, 1874; U.S. Congress, House Ex. Doc. 30, *Use of the Army in Certain Southern States,* 360–61.

11. *People's Vindicator,* November 14, December 12, 1874; U.S. Congress, House Report 261, *Condition of the South,* 3:164; Beckwith to Williams, October 12, 21, 1874, reel 2, M940, DOJ.

12. U.S. Congress, House Report 261, *Condition of the South,* 3:72, 922–23; unidentified clipping, "Louisiana's First Agricultural College," n.d., folder 1435, Melrose Collection; *New Orleans Bulletin,* November 11, 1874.

13. S. B. Packard to George H. Williams, November 1, 1874, reel 7, M940, DOJ; Dawson, *Army Generals and Reconstruction,* 195.

14. *People's Vindicator,* July 4, August 15, 29, 1874.

15. U.S. Congress, House Report 261, *Condition of the South,* 3:43, 444, 1038.

16. Lonn, *Reconstruction in Louisiana after 1868,* 283–86; U.S. Congress, House Report 261, *Condition of the South,* 3:472–73, 648–49, 1012–15; Rodrigue, *Reconstruction in the Cane Fields,* 167; E. R. Williams, "Florida Parish Ellises," 148–49. In return for promising to eschew violence and intimidation, Democrats gained representation on the Returning Board and a share of the local election officials. The two parties also formed an advisory committee that dealt with problems arising from the election campaign, but this cooperation quickly broke down.

17. *People's Vindicator,* October 10, 1874.

18. U.S. Congress, House Report 261, *Condition of the South,* 3:155, 760.

19. A. B. Levissee to George H. Williams, December 16, 1874, reel 2, M940, DOJ; U.S. Congress, House Report 101, *Condition of the South,* 2:106; U.S. Congress, House Report 261, *Condition of the South,* 3:20, 34.

20. *People's Vindicator,* October 31, 1874; U.S. Congress, House Report 101, *Condition of the South,* 2:71–72; U.S. Congress, House Report 261, *Condition of the South,* 3:220, 282.

21. *People's Vindicator,* January 30, 1875; U.S. Congress, House Report 261, *Condition of the South,* 3:132–33.

22. U.S. Congress, House Report 261, *Condition of the South,* 3:133, 219; *People's Vindicator,* January 9, 1875. Republican claims that about five hundred were turned away are plausible but unverifiable.

23. U.S. Congress, House Report 261, *Condition of the South,* 3:133, 226, 277–78.

24. *People's Vindicator,* November 7, 14, 1874; J. E. Breda to Elcey Breda, November 18, 1874, reel 1, BFP; U.S. Congress, House Report 261, *Condition of the South,* 3:134, 712–17.

25. U.S. Congress, House Report 261, *Condition of the South,* 3:133–34; *People's Vindicator,* November 21, 1874.

26. J. E. Breda to Elcey Breda, November 27, 28, 1874, folder 11, reel 1, BFP.

27. Jack Wharton to Henry C. Warmoth, October 8, 1874, reel 4, Warmoth Papers.

28. *New Orleans Republican*, December 6, 25, 1874; U.S. Congress, House Report 261, *Condition of the South*, 3:37, 89, 93.

29. *People's Vindicator*, December 26, 1874; U.S. Congress, House Report 261, *Condition of the South*, 3:20–21, 91–92; Lonn, *Reconstruction in Louisiana after 1868*, 287–90; J. G. Taylor, *Louisiana Reconstructed*, 303–4; Gillette, *Retreat from Reconstruction*, 121–22; Tunnell, *Edge of the Sword*, 226–29; U.S. Congress, Senate Misc. Doc. 14, *Electoral Vote of Louisiana,* 334–36.

30. Jack Wharton to Warmoth, October 8, 1874, and B. B. Jenning to Warmoth, September 29, 1874, both in reel 3, Warmoth Papers; U.S. Congress, House Report 101, *Condition of the South*, 2:80–81; Dawson, *Army Generals and Reconstruction*, 196.

31. Hogue, *Uncivil War,* 146–47; *Chicago Tribune*, January 2, 1875; Hugh J. Campbell, "The White League Conspiracy against Free Government," p. 8, January 11, 1875, box 3, Lewis Family Papers.

32. U. S. Grant, Message to Senate, January 13, 1875, and William W. Belknap to Sheridan, December 24, 1874, both in Grant, *Papers*, 16:13.

33. Philip H. Sheridan to William W. Belknap, January 7, 1875, reel 3, Sheridan Papers; Dawson, *Army Generals and Reconstruction*, 202–6.

34. Simpson, *The Reconstruction Presidents*, 172; Jennings to Warmoth, September 29, 1874, reel 3, Warmoth Papers.

35. Perman, *Pursuit of Unity,* 139–40; U.S. Congress, House Report 101, *Condition of the South*, 2:81–83; Grant, *Papers,* 26:261; U.S. Congress, House Report 261, *Condition of the South*, 3:179; *People's Vindicator*, December 26, 1874, January 16, 23, 1875.

36. J. G. Taylor, *Louisiana Reconstructed*, 304; *Shreveport Times* quoted in Lonn, *Reconstruction in Louisiana after 1868*, 293; *People's Vindicator*, December 16, 1875.

37. J. P. Breda to Ernest Breda, December 3, 6, 1874, and Ernest Breda to Elcey Breda, November 28, 1874, all in reel 2, BFP.

38. Sheridan to Belknap, January 6, 9, 10, 1875, reel 3, Sheridan Papers.

39. "Message to the Senate," January 13, 1875, Grant, *Papers*, 26:7; Levissee Diary, 23–28, Levissee Papers.

40. *Congressional Record*, Senate, 43d Cong., 2d sess. (1875), 367–70.

41. Simpson, *The Reconstruction Presidents*, 149–50; Garfield Diary, January 6, 7, 1875, reel 1, Garfield Papers.

42. "Message to the Senate," January 13, 1875, Grant, *Papers,* 26:3–16.

43. M. A. Southworth to Grant, telegram, January 10, 1875, Grant, *Papers,* 26:16.

44. Simpson, *The Reconstruction Presidents*, 172, 176.

45. B. B. Jenning to Warmoth, September 29, 1874; Hogue, *Uncivil War,* 138; Amos T. Akerman to Charles Prosser, November 11, 1871, reel 14, M699, DOJ; U.S. Congress, House Ex. Doc. 30, *Use of the Army in Certain Southern States*, 353.

46. U.S. Congress, House Misc. Doc. 154, *Louisiana Contested Elections*, 1:644–45.

47. Pinchback, "Speech to Republican National Committee," [1876], Pinchback Papers.

48. U.S. Congress, Senate Report 695, *Removal of the Negroes from the Southern States to the Northern States,* 2:451–52; Vandal, *Rethinking Southern Violence*, 80.

49. Sheridan to W. W. Belknap, January 5, 1875, reel 3, Sheridan Papers; O. P. Morton, *The President's Southern Policy* [1877], Pinchback Papers; Gillette, *Retreat from Reconstruction*, 125–26.

Chapter 11. The Politics of Murder

1. *New York Times*, October 24, 1874; Nordhoff, *Cotton States*, 54–55; *New York Tribune*, January 16, 1875. Recycled by historians: see, for example, J. G. Taylor, *Louisiana Reconstructed*, 465.

2. U.S. Congress, House Report 101, *Condition of the South*, 1:4–6.

3. Mosby to Grant, January 23, 1875, Grant, *Papers*, 26:29.

4. U.S. Congress, House Report 101, *Condition of the South*, 1:7; Lonn, *Reconstruction in Louisiana after 1868*, 323.

5. Lonn, *Reconstruction in Louisiana after 1868*, 323–34; U.S. Congress, House Report 261, *Condition of the South*, 1:10–19.

6. U.S. Congress, House Report 261, *Condition of the South*, 1:7–8, 23.

7. Ibid., 26.

8. Lonn, *Reconstruction in Louisiana after 1868*, 358–62; "The Agreement" [draft of Wheeler Compromise], January 18[?], 1875, Sheridan Papers; *The Louisiana Adjustment* (New Orleans: Republican Office, 1875), 30–37.

9. U.S. Congress, House Report 261, *Condition of the South*, 3:134; *People's Vindicator*, December 26, 1874, February 13, 1875.

10. U.S. Congress, House Report 816, *Conduct of Federal Officers in Louisiana*, 656; U.S. Congress, House Report 261, *Condition of the South*, 3:133, 571; *People's Vindicator*, February 6, 13, 1875.

11. U.S. Congress, House Ex. Doc. 30, *Use of the Army in Certain Southern States*, 201–4; Vandal, "Albert H. Leonard's Road," 63–69.

12. Perman, *Road to Redemption*, 160; *People's Vindicator*, April 4, 1875.

13. Hogue, *Uncivil War*, 137–44; W. H. Emory to George H. Williams, September 30, 1874, reel 2, M940, DOJ; Levissee Diary, p. 37, Levissee Papers.

14. A. B. Levissee to George H. Williams, December 16, 1874, reel 2, M940, DOJ.

15. George A. Forsyth to Sheridan, March 28, 1875, reel 3, Sheridan Papers; U.S. Congress, House Ex. Doc. 30, *Use of the Army in Certain Southern States*, 409–50; U.S. Congress, Senate Report 695, *Removal of the Negroes from the Southern States to the Northern States*, 2:128, 192–214.

16. Nordhoff, *Cotton States*, 18, 55; U.S. Congress, House Report 261, *Condition of the South*, 3:37, 448, 491; *New York Times*, October 17, 1874.

17. U.S. Congress, House Report 101, *Condition of the South*, 2:251; U.S. Congress, House Report 261, *Condition of the South*, 3:447, 516; *New York Times*, October 23, 1874.

18. U.S. Congress, House Report 261, *Condition of the South*, 3:532, 903–5, 2:11; Wilmer, *Defense of Louisiana*, 7.

19. U.S. Congress, House Report 261, *Condition of the South*, 3:454–55.

20. Ibid., 3:543, 2:7; Nordhoff, *Cotton States*, 54.

21. *Congressional Record*, 43rd Cong., 2d sess. (1875), 82.

22. Ibid., 45–54.

23. Dawson, *Army Generals and Reconstruction*, 220–22.

24. Ibid., 190; U.S. Congress, House Report 101, *Condition of the South*, 2:63, 72.

25. *Weekly Louisianan*, December 7, 1872; Hahn, *Nation under Our Feet*, 343.

26. Unsigned letter of blacks in Webster Parish to Grant, September 26, 1874, reel 2, M940, DOJ.

27. Petition of colored citizens for protection of their rights to Grant, May 1, 1875, reel 2, M940, DOJ.

28. Hicks, *History of Louisiana Negro Baptists,* 54; U.S. Congress, House Report 261, *Condition of the South,* 3:220; Hahn, *Nation under Our Feet,* 329.

29. *Weekly Louisianan,* July 17, 1875; *People's Vindicator,* July 3, 1875; Hahn, *Nation under Our Feet,* 359.

30. *People's Vindicator,* May 1, 8, June 19, 1875.

31. Powell, "Politics of Livelihood," 330; U.S. Congress, House Report 101, *Condition of the South,* 2:108–9; *People's Vindicator,* September 5, 1874.

32. *People's Vindicator,* April 1, 10, 1875; *New Orleans Republican,* April 9, 1875; *Richland Beacon,* April 24, 1875.

33. *Shreveport Southwestern,* May 19, 1869; U.S. Congress, House Misc. Doc. 34, *Recent Election in Louisiana: Testimony,* 4:124, 128–29.

34. *People's Vindicator,* May 1, 8, 15, 1875; U.S. Congress, House Misc. Doc. 34, *Recent Election in Louisiana: Testimony,* 4:109. The "People's Ticket" included one freeborn black, George Duncan, a barber. In 1876 Simmons was elected parish judge on the Republican ticket.

35. Powell, "Centralization and Its Discontents," 108; Act No. 29, "To Amend Act of July 5, 1872, to Incorporate the City of Natchitoches," April 25, 1875, in Louisiana Supreme Court, State of Louisiana ex rel. Simmons v. De Vargas, No. 5897, Lewis Family Papers.

36. Papers filed in Louisiana ex rel. Simmons v. De Vargas, Lewis Family Papers. Democrats contended that the state legislature that amended the city charter had not been lawfully elected (i.e., they were still disputing the outcome of the 1872 election).

37. *People's Vindicator,* July 8, 1876; U.S. Congress, House Misc. Doc. 34, *Recent Election in Louisiana: Testimony,* 4:104, 107–8.

38. *People's Vindicator,* November 7, 21, 1874, May 8, June 12, September 4, 11, October 23, 1875.

39. *People's Vindicator,* October 9, 16, 1875, April 22, May 13, 1876.

40. J. G. Taylor, *Louisiana Reconstructed,* 309–10; U.S. Congress, House Report 101, *Condition of the South,* 2:109–10; U.S. Congress, House Report 261, *Condition of the South,* 3:145, 975–76; *People's Vindicator,* August 15, 1874.

41. *People's Vindicator,* May 15, 1875.

42. J. E. Breda to James H. Cosgrove, July 15, 1874, reel 2, BFP.

43. *New Orleans Bulletin,* February 16, 1875; William H. Jack, "Et Tu Brute!" *People's Vindicator,* July 11, 1874; William Levy and David Pierson to William H. Jack and E. L. Pierson, July 15, 1874, and Pierson to Levy and Pierson, July 15, 1874, both in *People's Vindicator,* July 18, 1874.

44. *People's Vindicator,* July 11, 1874; Breda to Cosgrove, July 15, 1874, reel 2, BFP.

45. *People's Vindicator,* November 7, 20, 1875.

46. *New Orleans Republican,* December 29, 1875; *Atlanta Constitution,* December 31, 1875; *People's Vindicator,* December 4, 1875.

47. U.S. Congress, House Misc. Doc. 34, *Recent Election in Louisiana: Testimony,* 4:157, 162–165; *New Orleans Democrat,* January 2, 1875; *Shreveport Times,* December 28, 31, 1875, January 4, 1876; *New Orleans Republican,* December 31, 1875, January 1, 8, 1876; *Louisiana Democrat,* January 5, 1876; *New Orleans Bulletin,* January 18, 1876. Pierson's brother Horace fired back at Cosgrove when the latter approached the Pierson house.

48. Franklin, *The Militant South,* 55; J. G. Taylor, *Louisiana Reconstructed,* 419. Writes

Taylor: "in the main . . . the shoot-out replaced the duel. . . . Usually no call preceded the shooting on sight." See also Ayers, *Vengeance and Justice*, 268.

49. *New Orleans Democrat*, December 29, 1875, quoted in *New Orleans Republican*, December 31, 1875; *Shreveport Times*, January 4, 1876.

50. *New Orleans Republican*, January 8, 1876.

51. U.S. Congress, House Misc. Doc. 34, *Recent Election in Louisiana: Testimony*, 4:164; *New Orleans Republican*, December 29, 31, 1875.

52. Receipt, Folsom Bros. [gun shop], February 5, 1876, reel 1, and inventory of weapons, February 13, 1877, reel 3, both in BFP; U.S. Congress, Senate Report 855, *Louisiana in 1878*, 126; Breda family genealogy, Melrose Collection.

53. *People's Vindicator*, March 25, July 15, September 16, 1876.

54. Capt. J. A. Snyder to Assistant Adjutant General, September 6, 1875, Letters Sent, E1, vol. 2, Post of Natchitoches, vol. 5, USACC; U.S. Congress, Senate Report 701, *Louisiana in 1876*, 1:xxxv.

55. H. Langford to E. H. Durrell, October 22, 1875, Durell Papers; U.S. Congress, House Misc. Doc. 34, *Recent Election in Louisiana: Testimony*, 3:234–40, 276–83, 384–94, 432–33; U.S. Congress, Senate Report 701, *Louisiana in 1876*, 1:xxxiii–xxxviii, civ–cvi; *West Feliciana Sentinel*, February 3, 10, 1877.

56. Tunnell, *Edge of the Sword*, 242–43; *Louisiana Democrat*, May 10, June 28, 1876; Dawson, *Army Generals and Reconstruction*, 223–24.

57. U.S. Congress, Senate Report 701, *Louisiana in 1876*, 1:cxxxiii; U.S. Congress, House Misc. Doc. 31, *Presidential Election Investigation*, 3:364; Dawson, *Army Generals and Reconstruction*, 224–27, 232.

58. Lemann, *Redemption*, 121–24; Edwards Pierrepont to Adelbert Ames, September 14, 1875, reel 16, M699, DOJ; Perman, *Road to Redemption*, 161.

Chapter 12. The Election of 1876

1. Grant, *Papers*, 26:xii.

2. Hamilton, *The Full Monty*, 139; DiMarco, *Anatomy of a Failed Occupation*, 8.

3. Alphonso Taft to Richardson H. Baird, January 24, 1877, reel 16, M699, DOJ.

4. Perman, *Road to Redemption*, 160.

5. U.S. Congress, Senate Report 701, *Louisiana in 1876*, 1:264–66; Lonn, *Reconstruction in Louisiana after 1868*, 410–11; J. G. Taylor, *Louisiana Reconstructed*, 483.

6. U.S. Congress, House Misc. Doc. 34, *Recent Election in Louisiana: Testimony*, 2:156.

7. U.S. Congress, Senate Report 701, *Louisiana in 1876*, 1:163–64, 193–95, 229, 410, 628–30.

8. Ibid., xiii–xv; Perman, "Counter-Reconstruction."

9. J. G. Taylor, *Louisiana Reconstructed*, 487; Haworth, *Hayes-Tilden Disputed Presidential Election*, 89–90.

10. *People's Vindicator*, August 12, September 2, 9, October 7, 1876.

11. Lane, *The Day Freedom Died*, 37, 45, 50–52, 257; U.S. Congress, House Misc. Doc. 34, *Recent Election in Louisiana: Testimony*, 1:106–9; U.S. Congress, House Ex. Doc. 30, *Use of the Army in Certain Southern States*, 402–3.

12. U.S. Congress, House Report 261, *Condition of the South*, 2:12–13; U.S. Congress, Senate Ex. Doc. 17, *Affairs in Louisiana*, 21–22; U.S. Congress, House Misc. Doc. 34, *Recent Election in Louisiana: Testimony*, 1:115–20, 2:676–78.

13. U.S. Congress, House Misc. Doc. 34, *Recent Election in Louisiana: Testimony*, 1:142–

45, 189–92; Vincent, *Black Legislators,* 228; "Jerry Hall," 4th Ward, Natchitoches, Louisiana, reel 457, 1880 U.S. Census, ancestry.com. Hall was born in New York.

14. U.S. Congress, House Misc. Doc. 34, *Recent Election in Louisiana: Testimony,* 1:118, 147, 175, 189–91; U.S. Congress, House Misc. Doc. 31, *Presidential Election Investigation,* 3:548; J. G. Taylor, *Louisiana Reconstructed,* 360.

15. U.S. Congress, House Misc. Doc. 34, *Recent Election in Louisiana: Testimony,* 1:189, 195, 203.

16. U.S. Congress, House Misc. Doc. 31, *Presidential Election Investigation,* 3:548, 555; *People's Vindicator,* July 1, November 4, 1876.

17. J. G. Taylor, *Louisiana Reconstructed,* 481–82; Lonn, *Reconstruction in Louisiana after 1868,* 403–6.

18. Republican campaign committee minutes, July 26, 31, August 15, 23, 28, September 18, 1876, reel 3, BFP; *People's Vindicator,* September 23, 1876.

19. *People's Vindicator,* August 19, 26, 1876.

20. U.S. Congress, House Misc. Doc. 34, *Recent Election in Louisiana: Testimony,* 2:301–14, 633–34; U.S. Congress, House Misc. Doc. 31, *Presidential Election Investigation,* 3:142.

21. U.S. Congress, House Misc. Doc. 34, *Recent Election in Louisiana: Testimony,* 4:105–6. On October 7 the *Vindicator* reported the formation of a Natchitoches "Home Guard," with the ostensible aim of preventing interference with voting. The mounted patrol bore little resemblance to the rifle clubs of Ouchita Parish or the "Regulators" of the Felicianas. Its main function seems to have been stiffening the backbones of black Democrats rather than coercing black Republicans.

22. Capt. Charles Albert to Ernest Breda, November 6, 1876, and Albert to Assistant Adjutant General, November 28, 1876, vol. 5, Post of Natchitoches, USACC.

23. Dawson, *Army Generals and Reconstruction,* 230; Lonn, *Reconstruction in Louisiana after 1868,* 437.

24. Even the Democrats' own returns conceded Natchitoches Parish to the Republicans, confirming the election to the lower house of Henry Raby, John Lewis, and L. G. Barron. See U.S. Congress, House Misc. Doc. 34, *Recent Election in Louisiana: Testimony,* 3:19.

25. Holt, *By One Vote,* 172–74.

26. Assistant Adjutant General to Albert, November 11, 1876, Post of Natchitoches, US-ACC; *People's Vindicator,* November 18, 1876.

27. *People's Vindicator,* November 18, 1876; Ernest Breda to Elcey Breda, November 28, 1876, reel 1, BFP.

28. U.S. Congress, Senate Misc. Doc. 14, *Electoral Vote of Louisiana,* 757, 761–62; Pierson to Father, January 14, 1877, Pierson Family Papers; Tunnard to Breda, November 27, 1877, reel 1, BFP.

29. U.S. Congress, House Misc. Doc. 31, *Presidential Election Investigation,* 3:560.

30. Ibid., 2:771–72.

31. U.S. Congress, House Misc. Doc. 42, *Counting the Vote for President,* 180.

32. *New Orleans Republican,* November 24, 1876; U.S. Congress, Senate Ex. Doc. 2, *Vote for Electors in Louisiana,* 39–43; U.S. Congress, Senate Misc. Doc. 14, *Electoral Vote of Louisiana,* 7–9; U.S. Congress, House Misc. Doc. 31, *Presidential Election Investigation,* 1:407–8, 436, 1442; Lonn, *Reconstruction in Louisiana after 1868,* 445–450.

33. U.S. Congress, House Misc. Doc. 31, *Presidential Election Investigation,* 1:1452.

34. U.S. Congress, Senate Ex. Doc. 2, *Vote for Electors in Louisiana,* 8, 116.

35. *New Orleans Republican,* November 25, 1876; U.S. Congress, House Misc. Doc. 31,

Presidential Election Investigation, 1:771–72, 1441; U.S. Congress, House Report 140, *Presidential Election Investigation,* 97–98.

36. *New Orleans Republican,* November 25, 1876; U.S. Congress, Senate Ex. Doc. 2, *Vote for Electors in Louisiana,* 61–62; U.S. Congress, Senate Misc. Doc. 14, *Electoral Vote of Louisiana,* 47–48.

37. U.S. Congress, House Misc. Doc. 31, *Presidential Election Investigation,* 1:771–72.

38. U.S. Congress, Senate Misc. Doc. 14, *Electoral Vote of Louisiana,* 21–22, 47–48.

39. Ibid., 47–48; *New Orleans Republican,* November 25, 1876.

40. U.S. Congress, House Misc. Doc. 31, *Presidential Election Investigation,* 1:953–55.

41. *New Orleans Republican,* December 1, 3, 1876; *Electoral Vote of Louisiana,* 147; U.S. Congress, Senate Ex. Doc. 2, *Vote for Electors in Louisiana,* 556–63.

42. U.S. Congress, Senate Misc. Doc. 14, *Electoral Vote of Louisiana,* 757–61.

43. Pierson to Father, January 14, 1877, Pierson Family Papers; U.S. Congress, House Misc. Doc. 31, *Presidential Election Investigation,* 1:924.

44. U.S. Congress, House Misc. Doc. 42, *Counting the Vote for President,* 131–40, 144–59, 175–76, 202; U.S. Congress, House Misc. Doc. 31, *Presidential Election Investigation,* 1:80–91, 1411–20, 1438.

45. Tunnard to Breda, December 1, 1876, reel 1, BFP; *People's Vindicator,* December 16, 1876.

46. U.S. Congress, House Misc. Doc. 31, *Presidential Election Investigation,* 3:11, 1:644; McGinty, *Louisiana Redeemed,* 91–98; Dawson, *Army Generals and Reconstruction,* 244–46.

47. Grant to Kellogg, January 7, 1877, Grant, *Papers,* 28:106–7.

48. Beckwith and Pitkin to Taft and Grant, January 9, Packard to Grant, January 9, Campbell to Sherman, January 9, Cameron to Augur, January 9, Augur to Cameron, January 9, 10, Pitkin to Taft, January 10, and Grant to Augur, January 14, 1877, all in reel 3, M940, DOJ.

49. U.S. Congress, House Report 156, *Recent Election in Louisiana;* U.S. Congress, Senate Report 701, *Louisiana in 1876.*

50. Grant, *Papers,* 28:116, 165; Garfield Diary, January 19, 20, 1877, Garfield Papers.

Chapter 13. The Compromise of 1877

1. U.S. Congress, House Misc. Doc. 31, *Presidential Election Investigation,* 1:959, 3:604.

2. Ibid., 3:606; Packard to Taft, January 22, 1877, reel 3, M940, DOJ. "Every hour's delay," Packard wired U.S. Attorney General Alonzo Taft, "gives our opponents a stronger hold, weakens our forces, and renders my task more difficult."

3. H. L. Briggs to Ernest Breda, November 29, 1876, reel 1, BFP; *People's Vindicator,* December 2, 1876; U.S. Congress, House Misc. Doc. 34, *Recent Election in Louisiana: Testimony,* 4:158–69.

4. William H. Tunnard to Ernest Breda, December 1, 1876, reel 2, BFP; *People's Vindicator,* December 30, 1876; U.S. Congress, House Misc. Doc. 34, *Recent Election in Louisiana: Testimony,* 4:128–29. This story took root in popular memory and, as such stories often do, became embellished in the telling. A parish history written in 1956 turned Horton into famed outlaw John Wesley Hardin and had him "sent into this section for the purpose of disposing of the leaders of the Breda Faction." See "The Parish of Natchitoches, the City of Natchitoches, Their History, Officers, and Education," folder 23, Judge Jones Collection.

5. *People's Vindicator*, December 2, 30, 1876; U.S. Congress, House Misc. Doc. 34, *Recent Election in Louisiana: Testimony,* 4:128–29, 91–98, 112–14, 118–20, 129–33, 138–53.

6. *People's Vindicator*, February 24, 1877; U.S. Congress, House Misc. Doc. 31, *Presidential Election Investigation,* 3:607–9; Pierson to father, March 9, 1877, Pierson Papers.

7. Pierson to V. A. Barron, January 27, 1877, Breda to Barron, January 29, 1877, and Blunt to Breda, February 9, 1877, all in reel 1, BFP.

8. Thomas P. Chaplin to Dear Friend, February 3, 1877, folder 1, box 5, Chaplin, Breazeale, and Chaplin Papers; U.S. Congress, House Misc. Doc. 31, *Presidential Election Investigation,* 1:1431; E. H. Durell to Friend, November 26, 1879, Durell Papers.

9. Holt, *By One Vote,* 226–35.

10. *People's Vindicator*, February 24, 1877; Lewis to Breda, February 9, 1877, reel 1, J. Ernest Breda Papers; U.S. Congress, House Misc. Doc. 31, *Presidential Election Investigation,* 1:951–52.

11. Pierson to Father, January 14, 1877, Pierson Papers; Chaplin to Dear Friend, February 3, 1877, folder 2, box 5, Chaplin, Breazeale, and Chaplin Papers.

12. Dawson, *Army Generals and Reconstruction,* 236–37; Assistant Adjutant General to Albert, November 11, 1876, Post of Natchitoches, USACC; *People's Vindicator*, November 18, 1876.

13. Simpson, *The Reconstruction Presidents,* 295; U.S. Congress, House Misc. Doc. 31, *Presidential Election Investigation,* 1:961, 972–73, 3:595–616.

14. U.S. Congress, House Misc. Doc. 31, *Presidential Election Investigation,* 3:598, 616.

15. Pitkin to Department of Justice, December 14, 1876, and Packard to Alphonso Taft, January 22, 1877, both in reel 2, M940, DOJ.

16. *New Orleans Daily Picayune*, January 21, 1877; *People's Vindicator*, January 27, 1877; *New Orleans Republican*, January 24, April 7, 1877; U.S. Congress, House Misc. Doc. 31, *Presidential Election Investigation,* 3:605.

17. U.S. Congress, House Misc. Doc. 31, *Presidential Election Investigation,* 1:1457; Nystrom, *New Orleans after the Civil War,* 181–82; Lonn, *Reconstruction in Louisiana after 1868,* 489–90.

18. *New Orleans Republican*, January 11, 1877; Warmoth, *War, Politics, and Reconstruction,* 239.

19. Grant, *Papers,* 28:116; Packard to Taft, January 22, 1877, and N. B. Ross to Taft, January 22, 1877, reel 3, M940, DOJ.

20. U.S. Congress, House Misc. Doc. 31, *Presidential Election Investigation,* 1:466, 3:34; Dibble to Taft, March 7, 1877, reel 3, M940, DOJ.

21. U.S. Congress, House Misc. Doc. 31, *Presidential Election Investigation,* 3:618, 623–25.

22. Haworth, *Hayes-Tilden Disputed Presidential Election,* 257.

23. Garfield Diary, February 26, 1877, Garfield Papers; U.S. Congress, House Misc. Doc. 31, *Presidential Election Investigation,* 1:978–90; Woodward, *Reunion and Reaction,* 206–14; Polakoff, *Politics of Inertia,* 301–12.

24. U.S. Congress, House Misc. Doc. 31, *Presidential Election Investigation,* 3:33.

25. Woodward, *Reunion and Reaction,* 214, 221–22; Haworth, *Hayes-Tilden Disputed Presidential Election,* 270; U.S. Congress, House Misc. Doc. 31, U.S. Congress, House Misc. Doc. 31, *Presidential Election Investigation,* 1:990, 3:33, 624. See also Lonn, *Reconstruction in Louisiana after 1868,* 502–12.

26. Simpson, *The Reconstruction Presidents,* 209–10.

27. U.S. Congress, House Misc. Doc. 31, U.S. Congress, House Misc. Doc. 31, *Presidential Election Investigation*, 1:461, 3:11, 27; *People's Vindicator*, March 17, 1877.

28. Hayes, *Diary and Letters*, 3:428; Hayes, *Letters and Messages*, 19–22.

29. U.S. Congress, House Misc. Doc. 31, *Presidential Election Investigation*, 1:832–34; Hayes, *Diary and Letters*, 3:428–29.

30. U.S. Congress, House Misc. Doc. 31, *Presidential Election Investigation*, 3:9–11, 1:459; Lonn, *Reconstruction in Louisiana after 1868*, 522–23; Warmoth, *War, Politics, and Reconstruction*, 239.

31. Benedict, *The Fruits of Victory*, 65.

32. *New Orleans Republican*, May 16, 1877.

33. U.S. Congress, House Misc. Doc. 31, *Presidential Election Investigation*, 48–49.

34. Simpson, *The Reconstruction Presidents*, 215; Hair, *Bourbonism and Agrarian Protest*, 20.

35. *People's Vindicator*, March 17, 1877; U.S. Congress, House Misc. Doc. 31, *Presidential Election Investigation*, 1:807; *New Orleans Republican*, April 28, May 2, 9, 16, 1877.

36. *New Orleans Daily Democrat*, June 11, 20, 1877.

37. U.S. Congress, House Misc. Doc. 31, *Presidential Election Investigation*, 1:915.

38. E. H. Durell to Friend, February 8, 1878, Durell Papers.

39. Lane, *The Day Freedom Died*, 255; Vandal, "Albert H. Leonard's Road," 59–69.

40. U.S. Congress, House Misc. Doc. 31, *Presidential Election Investigation*, 1:937.

41. Ibid., 85–89, 1438.

42. Ibid., 921. The lengthy Potter Committee hearings of 1878, held in Washington and New Orleans under the official title of the House Select Committee on Alleged Frauds in the Presidential Election of 1876, were devoted in large part to Anderson's false allegations.

43. *New Orleans Daily Democrat*, April 8, May 2, 1877; *New Orleans Republican*, May 19, 1877.

44. *New Orleans Daily Democrat*, April 11, 1877; *People's Vindicator*, June 2, 1877.

45. U.S. Congress, House Misc. Doc. 31, *Presidential Election Investigation*, 1:598; *Donaldsonville Chief*, March 10, 1877; *New Orleans Republican*, June 2, 1877.

46. *West Feliciana Sentinel*, March 10, 1877; *New Orleans Daily Democrat*, May 29, 1877; U.S. Congress, House Misc. Doc. 31, *Presidential Election Investigation*, 3:559.

47. *People's Vindicator*, June 2, 1877.

48. *New Orleans Daily Democrat*, May 8, 26, 27, 29, June 4, 23, 1877. Former Republican congressman Joseph Newsham, a planter and merchant, also received a coffin threat. His note warned that he might meet "the same accident" that felled Weber. Newsham was the dead man's brother-in-law.

49. Pitkin to Alphonso Taft, November 1876, reel 3, M940, DOJ; Benedict, *The Fruits of Victory*, 65.

50. U.S. Congress, Senate Report 701, *Louisiana in 1876*, 3:2371, 2385, 2584; U.S. Congress, House Misc. Doc. 31, *Presidential Election Investigation*, 1:945.

51. Hayes, *Diary and Letters*, 3:429–30; U.S. Congress, House Misc. Doc. 31, *Presidential Election Investigation*, 1:849.

Chapter 14. Endgame in Natchitoches

1. *New York Tribune*, February 10, 1877; *New Orleans Daily Democrat*, April 25, 1877; "Legislative Caucus, 1877," box 2, Lewis Family Papers.

2. McGinty, *Louisiana Redeemed*, 217; *Weekly Louisianan*, September 29, 1877; *New Orleans Republican*, May 19, 1877.

3. Hair, *Bourbonism and Agrarian Protest*, 20–21; Nystrom, *New Orleans after the Civil War*, 192–94

4. *New Orleans Daily Democrat*, April 11, 1877; *People's Vindicator*, June 2, 30, 1877; *People's Vindicator*, June 2, 30, 1877; N. B. Ripley to Francis T. Nicholls, February 8, 1878; Madison Wells to John Sherman, February 11, 1878, both in letterbook 153, John Sherman Papers, Library of Congress.

5. John Sherman to Rutherford B. Hayes, February 9, 1878, and W. L. McMillen to Hayes, February 14, 1878, both in letterbook 153, Sherman Papers; George S. Lacey to Department of Justice, March 8, 18, 1878, reel 4, M940, DOJ.

6. *People's Vindicator*, November 11, 1876.

7. Ibid.

8. Ibid.; U.S. Congress, House Misc. Doc. 31, *Presidential Election Investigation*, 4:88, 113–14, 124.

9. *People's Vindicator*, November 11, 1876; U.S. Congress, House Misc. Doc. 34, *Recent Election in Louisiana: Testimony*, 4:100, 124.

10. U.S. Congress, House Misc. Doc. 34, *Recent Election in Louisiana: Testimony*, 1:313.

11. Ibid., 144, 148. "Turned out" by congregation: see, for example, the tribulations of Democratic-leaning Rev. Hardy Mobley in Iberia Parish recounted in Laura F. Mobley to E. M. Cravath, December 3, 8, 1874, Samuel Keller to Cravath, February 12, 1875, and Hardy Mobley to Cravath, February 22, 1875, all in box 57, American Missionary Association, Amistad Research Center, Tulane University.

12. Du Bois, *Black Reconstruction in America*, 451–53.

13. U.S. Congress, House Misc. Doc. 34, *Recent Election in Louisiana: Testimony*, 2:135, 1:116–17, 195.

14. Ibid., 4:96–97, 114, 118, 138, 142.

15. *People's Vindicator*, November 11, 1876.

16. *People's Vindicator*, August 24, 31, September 7, 1878.

17. John G. Lewis to Ernest Breda, June 29, 1878, reel 1, BFP.

18. U.S. Congress, Senate Report 855, *Louisiana in 1878*, 125, 131–32; "Natchitoches Case," handwritten statement, [1878/9], reel 1, BFP.

19. U.S. Congress, Senate Report 855, *Louisiana in 1878*, 115, 125–26; *People's Vindicator*, January 18, 1879.

20. U.S. Congress, Senate Report 855, *Louisiana in 1878*, 132; *New Orleans Republican*, October 5, 1878.

21. U.S. Congress, Senate Report 855, *Louisiana in 1878*, 485–86; *People's Vindicator*, February 1, 1879.

22. U.S. Congress, Senate Report 855, *Louisiana in 1878*, 133–34, 159–61, 487–88; *People's Vindicator*, March 22, 1879.

23. *People's Vindicator*, November 23, 1878, February 1, 1879; *New Orleans Daily Democrat*, February 26, 1879; *New Orleans Daily Picayune*, March 2, 1879; U.S. Congress, Senate Report 855, *Louisiana in 1878*, 488.

24. U.S. Congress, Senate Report 855, *Louisiana in 1878*, 505.

25. Ibid., 145.

26. Ibid., 543; *New Orleans Daily Picayune*, March 2, 3, 1879.

27. U.S. Congress, Senate Report 855, *Louisiana in 1878*, 135, 159–60, 505, 530; *New Orleans Daily Picayune*, March 2, 3, 1879; *People's Vindicator*, November 23, 1878, March 22, 1879.

28. U.S. Congress, Senate Report 855, *Louisiana in 1878*, 142, 488; *People's Vindicator*, November 16, 1878.

29. U.S. Congress, Senate Report 855, *Louisiana in 1878*, 493, 558–59.

30. *New Orleans Daily Picayune*, February 27, 1879; *People's Vindicator*, March 15, 1879; U.S. Congress, Senate Report 855, *Louisiana in 1878*, 154–56.

31. U.S. Congress, Senate Report 855, *Louisiana in 1878*, 116–17, 126–27, 493.

32. Ibid., 553; *New Orleans Daily Picayune*, February 9, 1879.

33. *New Orleans Daily Picayune*, March 22, 1879; U.S. Congress, Senate Report 855, *Louisiana in 1878*, 493.

34. U.S. Congress, Senate Report 855, *Louisiana in 1878*, 149, 494.

35. Ibid., 161–65; *People's Vindicator*, December 7, 1878.

36. *New Orleans Daily Democrat*, September 23, 24, 1878; *New York Times*, September 23, 1878.

37. *New Orleans Republican*, September 28, October 5, 1878.

38. *New Orleans Republican*, September 28, 1878; *New Orleans Daily Democrat*, September 29, 1878.

39. Elcey Breda to Jack Wharton, September 30, 1878, reel 4, M940, DOJ.

40. J. W. Gurley to Devens, October 10, 1878, Wharton to Devens, October 10, 28, 1878, and Leonard to Devens, October 12, 1878, all in reel 4, M940, DOJ; Goldman, "A Free Ballot and a Fair Count," 62–63.

41. *People's Vindicator*, November 9, 1878; *New Orleans Daily Democrat*, November 5, 1878; Hair, *Bourbonism and Agrarian Protest*, 78–81.

42. *New Orleans Daily Democrat*, November 8, 1878; *People's Vindicator*, November 9, 1878.

43. *People's Vindicator*, March 15, 1879.

44. Ibid.

45. Hayes, *Diary and Letters*, 3:510; Wang, *Trial of Democracy*, 162.

46. Wharton to Devens, November 20, 1878, and Leonard to Devens, December 1, 1878, reel 4, M940, DOJ; Devens to A. B. Newcomb, December 2, 1878, reel 14, M699, DOJ. Devens sent his own investigator to Louisiana, instructing him to not only gather evidence but also keep an eye on Jack Wharton, whose free-spending ways had aroused suspicion.

47. U.S. Congress, Senate Report 855, *Louisiana in 1878*, 489, 523, 526, 537–38,

48. *People's Vindicator*, November 16, 1878.

49. U.S. Congress, Senate Report 855, *Louisiana in 1878*, 18–19; J. P. Breda to Ernest Breda, January 14, 1879, reel 1, BFP.

50. Ernest Breda to Elcey Breda, November 25, 1878, folder 808, Melrose Collection.

51. Leonard to Devens, December 21, 25, 1878, reel 4, M940, DOJ; J. P. Breda to Ernest and Philippe Breda, January 14, 1879, and Emile Breda to Ernest and Philippe Breda, January 21, 1879, both in reel 1, BFP.

52. *New Orleans Daily Democrat*, January 30, 1879; *New Orleans Daily Picayune*, February 1, 1879; Leonard to Devens, February 17, 1879, reel 4, M940, DOJ.

53. Leonard to Devens, February 8, 1879, reel 4, M940, DOJ.

Chapter 15. The Slow Death of the Republican Party

1. *New Orleans Daily Picayune*, February 26, 1879; Nystrom, *New Orleans after the Civil War*, 115–17.

2. *New Orleans Daily Democrat*, March 3, 1879; C. C. Chaplin to Thomas P. Chaplin, March 5, 1879, folder 2, box 5, Chaplin, Breazeale, and Chaplin Papers.

3. *New Orleans Daily Picayune*, March 7, 1879; Wang, *Trial of Democracy*, 208–11.

4. Fleming, "A Ku Klux Klan Document"; U.S. Congress, Senate Report 855, *Louisiana in 1878*, 130–31, 138, 503, 507–8.

5. *New Orleans Daily Picayune*, March 7, 1879; *New Orleans Daily Democrat*, March 7, 1879.

6. *New Orleans Daily Picayune*, March 1, 2, 3, 1879; *New Orleans Daily Democrat*, March 3, 4, 5, 1879.

7. C. C. Chaplin to T. P. Chaplin, February 28, 1879, folder 2, box 5, Chaplin, Breazeale, and Chaplin Papers.

8. *New Orleans Daily Picayune*, March 7, 1879.

9. *New Orleans Daily Democrat*, March 7, 1879.

10. *New Orleans Daily Democrat*, February 25, 1879; *People's Vindicator*, March 15, 1879; C. C. Chaplin to T. P. Chaplin, March 1, 1879, folder 2, box 5, Chaplin, Breazeale, and Chaplin Papers.

11. *People's Vindicator*, March 15, 1879; *New York Times*, March 17, 1879.

12. Ernest Breda to Elcey Breda, May 14, 1879, J. P. Breda to Philippe and Ernest, January 14, April 7, 1879, and Emile Breda to Philippe and Ernest Breda, January 21, 1879, all in reel 2, BFP.

13. *New York Times*, March 31, 1879.

14. Devens to G. K. Chase, March 12, 1879, reel 14, Leonard to Devens, April 9, 1879, reel 4, and Leonard to Benjamin H. Brewster, January 25, 1883, reel 5, all in M940, DOJ; *New York Times*, March 17, 1879; Goldman, *"A Free Ballot and a Fair Count,"* 64–74, 93–94, 107–16, 135–38, 148–63; Wang, *Trial of Democracy*, 199–200, 216–17, 300.

15. *New York Times*, January 12, 1879; *New Orleans Daily Democrat*, May 23, 1879. The phrase "the law and the prophets" is from Matthew 7:12.

16. *New York Times*, January 20, 1879; *Colfax Chronicle*, November 16, 1878.

17. Hair, *Bourbonism and Agrarian Protest*, 85; U.S. Congress, Senate Report 695, *Removal of the Negroes from the Southern States to the Northern States*, 2:75–80.

18. Hirshon, *Farewell to the Bloody Shirt*, 64; *New Orleans Daily Democrat*, April 22, 1879.

19. U.S. Congress, Senate Report 695, *Removal of the Negroes from the Southern States to the Northern States*, 2:39, 101–8, 126–28, 155–59; Hahn, *Nation under Our Feet*, 317–30.

20. *New Orleans Daily Democrat*, April 20, 1879; U.S. Congress, Senate Report 695, *Removal of the Negroes from the Southern States to the Northern States*, 2:75–80.

21. *Weekly Louisianan*, April 26, 1879.

22. *New Orleans Daily Democrat*, April 18, 20, 1879.

23. *New Orleans Daily Democrat*, April 20, 1879; *Weekly Louisianan*, February 15, March 13, 1879.

24. *People's Vindicator*, October 11, 1878, April 5, 19, 1879; *New Orleans Daily Democrat*, October 3, 1878, April 13, 1879. Two blacks signed affidavits confessing to involvement in such a plot. The confessions may have been coerced, the reports exaggerated or fictitious, but they testified to white anxieties.

25. Nystrom, *New Orleans after the Civil War*, 201–2.

26. Ernest Breda to Elcey Breda, April 12, 1879, reel 2, BFP; "J. E. Breda," 1880 U.S. Census, Natchitoches Parish, ancestry.com; *People's Vindicator*, March 13, 1880; U.S. Congress, Senate Report 695, *Removal of the Negroes from the Southern States to the Northern States*, 2:46.

27. "A. R. Blunt," 1880 U.S. Census, Orleans Parish; "L. A. J. Blount," 1880 U.S. Census, Natchitoches Parish, ancestry.com; Blunt to Lewis, September 21, 1882, box 2, Lewis Family Papers; *New York Times*, August 30, December 6, 1884.

28. Campbell, "Political Life of Louisiana Negroes," 214; paper reorganizing "Attucks Guards," March 19, 1881, box 1, H. J. Rudisill to Lewis, July 13, 1883, box 2, and Sterling Barrow to Lewis, December 22, 1883, box 1, all in Lewis Family Papers; *Proceedings of the Eureka Grand Lodge of Ancient and Accepted Masons of Louisiana, 1878–79* (New Orleans: T. H. Thomason, 1880) and *Proceedings of the Twenty-First Annual Convention of the Eureka Grand Lodge of Ancient and Accepted Masons of Louisiana, 1884* (New Orleans: Henry Powers, 1884), 31, both in box 70, PHMP.

29. *People's Vindicator*, July 4, 1874; U.S. Congress, Senate Report 695, *Removal of the Negroes from the Southern States to the Northern States*, 2:442.

30. Campbell, "Political Life of Louisiana Negroes," 205; *Weekly Louisianan*, March 13, 1880.

31. List of Votes Polled in the Parish of Natchitoches, November 2, 1880, reel 2, BFP; Hair, *Bourbonism and Agrarian Protest*, 113–15.

32. Executive Committee minutes, October 11, 1883, January 7, March 19, April 5, 1884, reel 3, BFP.

33. Warmoth, *War, Politics, and Reconstruction*, 248–59; Uzee, "Republican Politics in Louisiana," 82–87; Nystrom, *New Orleans after the Civil War*, 217–19.

34. C. F. Ladd to Lewis, April 26, June 27, 1884, box 1, PHMP; Uzee, "Republican Politics in Louisiana," 97.

35. Executive Committee minutes, September 25, 1889, reel 3, BFP.

36. Executive Committee minutes, April 5, May 2, 1884, September 25, 1889, reel 3, BFP; *Louisiana Populist*, March 13, 1896.

37. Uzee, "Republican Politics in Louisiana," 143; Rodrigue, *Reconstruction in the Cane Fields*, 134–35.

38. Hair, *Bourbonism and Agrarian Protest*, 176–85; Rodrigue, *Reconstruction in the Cane Fields*, 181–91; Scott, *Degrees of Freedom*, 77–88; Hahn, *Nation under Our Feet*, 419–21; *Proceedings of the Twenty-Fifth and Twenty-Sixth Annual Convocation of the Eureka Grand Lodge, 1888–89* (New Orleans: Henry Powers, 1889), 8–10, box 70, PHMP.

39. Uzee, "Republican Politics in Louisiana," 122–23; Hirshon, *Farewell to the Bloody Shirt*, 182; Campbell, "Political Life of Louisiana Negroes," 236–37.

40. Hair, *Bourbonism and Agrarian Protest*, 61–72, 142–56, 194–97; *Natchitoches Enterprise*, August 8, 1889.

41. Hair, *Bourbonism and Agrarian Protest*, 211–33; Gaither, *Blacks and the Populist Movement*, 170–72.

42. Prather, *Resurgent Politics and Educational Progressivism*, 98–100; Anderson, *Race and Politics in North Carolina*, 227; Hair, *Bourbonism and Agrarian Protest*, 248–52.

43. Gaither, *Blacks and the Populist Movement*, 172–76.

44. *Louisiana Populist*, April 17, October 26, November 1, 1895, March 13, 1896.

45. Uzee, "Republican Politics in Louisiana," 152–59; Webb, "History of Negro Voting in Louisiana," 205–20; *Louisiana Populist*, March 27, April 10, 1896,

46. *Louisiana Populist*, April 10, 1896.

47. Uzee, "Republican Politics in Louisiana," 160; *Louisiana Populist*, March 13, 20, 1896.

48. *Louisiana Populist*, March 27, 1896; Uzee, "Republican Politics in Louisiana,"154; Executive Committee minutes, April 15, 1896, reel 2, BFP.

49. Hair, *Bourbonism and Agrarian Protest*, 262–64; *Louisiana Populist*, May 1, 1896; *Hearings before the Committee on Elections No 1, April 14, 1910, in the Case of Henry C. Warmoth v. Albert Estopinal* (Washington D.C., 1910), 42.

50. *Louisiana Populist*, May 1, July 10, 1896; *Natchitoches Enterprise*, June 11, 1896.

51. Perman, *Struggle for Mastery*, 38–41; Hirshon, *Farewell to the Bloody Shirt*, 200–233; Gaither, *Blacks and the Populist Movement*, 60–61; Wang, *Trial of Democracy*, 232–49

52. Perman, *Struggle for Mastery*, 136–37.

53. Hair, *Bourbonism and Agrarian Protest*, 277–78; Webb, "History of Negro Voting in Louisiana," 240–45.

54. *Natchitoches Populist*, February 3, 1899; *Natchitoches Enterprise*, March 2, 1899.

55. Booker T. Washington to Charles W. Chesnutt, July 7, 1903, Washington, *Papers*, 196–97.

56. *Natchitoches Enterprise*, June 26, 1902.

Chapter 16. Reconstruction's Legacy and the Civil Rights Movement

1. Because Blunt died intestate, a legal dispute ensued over the administration of his estate and the care of his minor children. America Starks, the mother of Florence Varner, contested the appointment of their elder half brother Richard Blount, partly on the grounds that Blount had been involved in a homicide in 1903, a crime for which he was acquitted by turning state's evidence. However, Judge Charles V. Porter dismissed Starks's suit, noting that the children lived in a "comfortable home, where they are under the care of their brothers and sister, and surrounded by the friends of their late father, who was . . . the 'idol' of the negroes in the parish." In 1908 Judge Sam J. Henry appointed Blount the children's tutor, a responsibility that he faithfully discharged until 1924, when the youngest child, Raford, reached the age of majority. See "Raford Blount," No. 2590, Succession Records, Clerk of Court's Office, Natchitoches Parish Court House.

2. Robert Sheppard et al. v. H. B. B. Brown et al., case files, 1907–09, District Court, Natchitoches Parish, Natchitoches Genealogical Society.

3. *Natchitoches Enterprise*, January 7, 1915, March 23, 1916, January 15, 1920.

4. *Natchitoches Enterprise*, February 22, 1922.

5. G. B. Bryan to Jackson L. Bryan, June 15, 1926, J. A. Ducournau Collection.

6. J. A. Ducournau to Mayor Roy Scott, November 8, 1968, Ducournau Collection.

7. "The Historical Marker Database," http://www.hmdb.org/Marker.asp?Marker=42188. Dedicated in 1895, the monument stood in a county that had been a stronghold of the Ku Klux Klan during Reconstruction.

8. In the first three decades of the twentieth century there was much discussion among white women's groups, especially the United Daughters of the Confederacy, about honoring the "Black Mammy." In 1923 the Senate approved a bill that authorized the placement of a statue on the Mall "in memory of the faithful slave mammies of the South." Black newspapers, the NAACP, and the women's auxiliary of the Grand Army of the Republic protested against the proposal, and the bill failed in the House. Although the Confederate Memorial in Arlington National Cemetery has a frieze that includes a "Black Mammy,"

no statue or monument devoted to that legendary figure ever got built. See Tony Horwitz, "The Mammy Washington Almost Had," *Atlantic*, May 31, 2013, http://www.theatlantic.com/national/archive/2013/05/the-mammy-washington-almost-had/276431.

9. J. H. Cosgrove to Milton Dunn, January 19, 1914, folder 1415, Melrose Collection.

10. *Bossier Banner*, February 3, 1887, March 19, 1891, February 2, 1901, August 31, 1911; *Natchitoches Enterprise*, November 17, 1898.

11. *New Orleans Republican*, April 24, 1874; *Louisiana Populist*, July 26, 1895.

12. "Notes on Breda Family" and "Breda Cemetery," folder 1-A-4, Powell Collection; *Natchitoches Times*, August 13, 1937.

13. *Natchitoches Times*, May 22, 1931.

14. O. C. W. Taylor, "Retires from White Firm after 55 Years," *Crisis*, October 1941, 334; "James Lewis, Jr.," *Sepia Socialite*, January 1942; Theodoulu, "Minority Status," 6; Cripps, "The Lily White Republicans," 40, 245; Heersink and Jenkins, "Southern Delegates and Republican National Convention Politics"; R. B. Sherman, *The Republican Party*, 135–37, 153–54, 237–38; DeVore, "Rise from the Nadir," 18–19, 27–33.

15. Lanza, *Agrarianism and Reconstruction Politics*, 18–24, 30, 38–52, 122–24; Oubre, "Forty Acres and a Mule"; Schweninger, "A Vanishing Breed," 48–49; "U.S. Census Historical Data, County-Level Results for 1900," http://mapserver.lib.virginia.edu (accessed November 20, 2015).

16. Rable, *But There Was No Peace*, 185; Perman, *Road to Redemption*, 260–62; Rodrigue, *Reconstruction in the Cane Fields*, 190; J. G. Taylor, "Louisiana: An Impossible Task," 215; Ransom and Sutch, "One Kind of Freedom: Reconsidered"; Foner, *Nothing but Freedom*, 72; Foner, *Reconstruction*, 597; Tolnay, *The Bottom Rung*, 12; Hilgard, *Report on Cotton Production*, 70, 94–96. See also Daniel, *The Shadow of Slavery*; Cohen, *At Freedom's Edge*; Blackmon, *Slavery by Another Name*; Kerr-Ritchie, *Freedpeople in the Tobacco South*; Curtin, *Black Prisoners and Their World*.

17. Margery Dallet, "Case of Clinton Clark, Natchitoches, La.," August 17, 1940, folder 19, box 3, Harold N. Lee Papers, Special Collections, Howard-Tilton Memorial Library, Tulane University.

18. Pfeifer, *Rough Justice*, 161–78; *Bryan Morning Eagle*, April 13, 1902; *Natchitoches Enterprise*, June 24, 1897; Davey and Clark, *Remember My Sacrifice*, 61–65, 78–87.

19. Fairclough, *Race and Democracy*, 42–43.

20. John G. Lewis to Rev. Cortez Thompson, September 9, 1884, box 2, PHMP.

21. C. F. Ladd to Lewis, March 13, 1884, Israel Thomas to Lewis, July 2, 1884, and Lewis to Blunt, September 15, 1884, all in box 2, PHMP. See also *Proceedings of the Twentieth Annual Convention of the Most Worshipful Eureka Grand Lodge* (New Orleans: Henry Powers, 1883), 8, 19; *Proceedings of the Twenty-First Convention* (New Orleans: Henry Powers, 1884), 31; *Proceedings of the Twenty-Second Conventions* (New Orleans: Henry Powers, 1885), 9, 18, 41; *Proceedings of the Twenty-Fifth and Twenty-Sixth Conventions* (New Orleans: Henry Powers, 1889), 14–15; and *Proceedings of the Thirty-First Convention* (New Orleans: Paragon Printing Co., 1894), 49–52, all in box 70, PHMP; *Louisiana Populist*, March 20, 1896. The fact that both men, as fathers, suffered grievous bereavements during these years may also have helped sour their relationship. In 1897 one of Lewis's sons was beaten to death by a group of blacks, Six years later, one of Blunt's sons was implicated in the gang murder of a black youth. He saved himself by turning state's evidence.

22. Davey and Clark, *Remember My Sacrifice*, 69–84; Dallet, "Case of Clinton Clark."

23. Lucille Black to Gloster Current, June 21, 1949, box 70, Branch Files, 1940–1955,

Part 2, Group C, National Association for the Advancement of Colored People Papers, Library of Congress; Fairclough, *Race and Democracy*, 68–73; *Sepia Socialite*, June 1942, 97; Walkes, *Jno. G. Lewis, Jr.*, 185; Southern Regional Council, *Negro Voter Registration in Southern States*.

24. http://www.creolegen.org/2013/04/01/baton-rouges-odd-fellows-temple-1925-bev-erly-victor-baranco-sr-1869–1933 (accessed April 24, 2016); *Crisis*, March 1954, 175; Muraskin, *Middle-Class Blacks*, 230–31. The Grand Lodge bought the Odd Fellows building, erected in 1925.

25. John G. Lewis Jr. to Julian A. Thomas, June 23, 1953, http://www.amistadresearch-center.org/single-post/2016/10/31/Defenders-of-Social-Justice-The-Prince-Hall-Masons-of-Louisiana (accessed July 22, 2017).

26. Oakes et al., *Of the People*, 479.

27. *Negro Exodus*, 2:452; Pinchback, Speech to Republican National Committee, [1876], Pinchback Papers; *Weekly Louisianan*, June 14, 1879.

28. Summers, *Ordeal of the Reunion*, 395–96.

29. "Memorandum by Mr. Justice Jackson," March 15, 1954, copy courtesy of Professor Michael J. Klarman. As Michael Lind has put it, the civil rights movement "was part of a global process of overturning white supremacy that occurred simultaneously throughout the world in the decades following World War II" (*What Lincoln Believed*, 251).

30. M. L. King, *Papers*, 323.

31. "Memorandum by Mr. Justice Jackson," p. 3; Plessy v. Ferguson, 163 U.S. 557 (1896), at 251, http://www.law.cornell.edu/supct/html/historics/USSC_CR_0163_0537_ZO.html; W. G. Sumner, *Folkways*, 78–79. On the influence of Sumner on American social science, see Myrdal, *An American Dilemma*, 1048–57; Prothro, "Stateways v. Folkways Revisited," 352–53.

32. Klobucar, "Thinking outside the (Wooden) Box," 9–10; Bennett, *Black Power U.S.A.*, 360. The statue stands in the Museum of Rural Life outside Baton Rouge. In 1989 a state legislator complained that the plaque was offensive, and museum staff covered it up.

BIBLIOGRAPHY

Primary Sources

Alstyne, Lawrence van. *Diary of an Enlisted Man*. New Haven, Conn.: Tuttle, Morehouse and Taylor, 1910.

American Historical Association. *Sixth Report of Historical Manuscripts Division, With Diary and Correspondence of Salmon P. Chase*. Washington, D.C.: Government Printing Office, 1903.

Banks, Nathaniel P. Papers. Library of Congress, Manuscripts Division, Washington, D.C.

Biographical and Historical Memoirs of Northwest Louisiana. Chicago: Southern Publishing Co., 1890.

Blaine, James G. *Twenty Years of Congress: From Lincoln to Garfield*. Norwich, Conn.: Henry Bill, 1884.

Blake, E. E. *A Succinct History of the 28th Iowa Volunteer Infantry*. Belle Plaine, Iowa: Union Press, 1896.

Breda, J. Ernest. Papers. Special Collections, Tulane University, New Orleans, Louisiana.

Breda, J. P., and Family. Papers. Special Collections, Hill Memorial Library, Louisiana State University, Baton Rouge (microfilm).

Bruce, Blanche K. Papers. Moorland-Spingarn Research Center, Howard University, Washington, D.C.

Burke, Edward A. *Statement of Facts Relating to Election in Louisiana. November 7th, 1876*. Washington, D.C., 1877.

Butler, Benjamin F. *Private and Official Correspondence of Gen. Benjamin F. Butler during the Period of the Civil War*. 5 vols. Norwood, Mass., 1917.

Chandler, William E. Papers. Library of Congress, Manuscripts Division, Washington, D.C.

Chaplin, Breazeale, and Chaplin. Papers. Special Collections, Hill Memorial Library, Louisiana State University, Baton Rouge.

Chase, Salmon P. *The Salmon P. Chase Papers*. Vol. 5. Ed. John R. Niven. Kent, Ohio: Kent State University Press, 1998.

Chronicling America: Historic American Newspapers. http://chroniclingamerica.loc.gov/newspapers.

Clemenceau, Georges. *American Reconstruction, 1865–1870*. 1928; New York: Da Capo, 1969.

Conway, Thomas W. *The Freedmen of Louisiana: Final Report of the Bureau of Free Labor, Department of the Gulf*. New Orleans: New Orleans Times Book and Job Office, 1865.

Constitution Adopted by the State Constitutional Convention of the State of Louisiana, March 7, 1868. New Orleans: New Orleans Republican, 1867.

Cox, S. S. *Three Decades of Federal Legislation*. Washington, D.C.: J. M. Stoddart, 1885.

Davey, Elizabeth, and Rodney Clark, eds. *Remember My Sacrifice: The Autobiography of Clinton Clark, Tenant Farm Organizer and Early Civil Rights Activist*. Baton Rouge: Louisiana State University Press, 2007.

Debates in the Convention for the Revision and Amendment of the Constitution of the State of Louisiana. New Orleans: W. R. Fish, 1864.

Denison, George S. Papers. Library of Congress, Manuscripts Division, Washington, D.C.

Dorsey, Sarah A., ed. *Recollections of Henry Watkins Allen*. New York: M. Doolady, 1866.

Ducournau, J. A. Collection. Cammie G. Henry Research Center, Watson Memorial Library, Northwestern State University of Louisiana, Natchitoches.

Durant, Thomas J. Papers. New-York Historical Society, New York City.

Durell, E. H. Papers. New-York Historical Society, New York City.

Fleming, Walter L. "A Ku Klux Klan Document." *Mississippi Valley Historical Review* 1, no. 4 (1915): 575–78.

Flinn, Frank M. *Campaigning with Banks in Louisiana, '63 and '64, and with Sheridan in the Shenandoah Valley in '64 and '65*. Lynn, Mass.: Thomas P. Nichols, 1887.

Garfield, James A. Papers. Library of Congress, Manuscripts Division, Washington, D.C. (microfilm).

Gould, John M. *History of the First-Tenth-Twenty-Ninth Maine Regiment*. Portland: Stephen Berry, 1871.

Grant, Ulysses S. *The Papers of Ulysses S. Grant*. Ed. John Y. Simon. Vols. 19–28. Carbondale: Southern Illinois University Press, 1991–2005.

Greeley, Horace. Papers. Library of Congress, Manuscripts Division, Washington, D.C.

Hay, John. *Letters of John Hay*. Washington, D.C.: Printed but not published, 1908.

Hayes, Rutherford B. *Diary and Letters of Rutherford Birchard Hayes*. Ed. Charles Richard Williams. 5 vols. Columbus: Ohio State Archaeological and Historical Society, 1922.

———. *Letters and Messages of Rutherford B. Hayes*. Washington, D.C.: Government Printing Office, 1881.

Haynes, Dennis E. *A Thrilling Narrative of the Suffering of the Union Refugees*. Washington, D.C.: McGill and Witherow, 1866.

Hilgard, Eugene W. *Report on Cotton Production of the State of Louisiana*. Washington, D.C.: Government Printing Office, 1881.

Hills, Alfred C. *Emancipation in Louisiana*. New Orleans: The Era, 1864.

Hoar, George F. *Autobiography of Seventy Years*. New York: Scribner, 1906.

Houzeau, Jean-Charles. *My Passage at the New Orleans Tribune: A Memoir of the Civil War Era*. Ed. David C. Rankin. Baton Rouge: Louisiana State University Press, 2001.

Howard, O. O. *Autobiography of Oliver Otis Howard*. 2 vols. New York: Baker and Taylor, 1907.

Howe, Timothy O. *Speech of Timothy O. Howe, February 17, 1875*. Washington, D.C.: Government Printing Office, 1875.

Johnson, Andrew. *The Papers of Andrew Johnson*. Ed. Paul H. Bergeron. Vols. 8–11. Knoxville: University of Tennessee Press, 1989–94.

Jones, James P., and Edward F. Keuchel, eds. *Civil War Marine: A Diary of the Red River Expedition, 1864*. Washington, D.C.: Museums Division, Headquarters, U.S. Marine Corps, 1975.

Judge Jones Collection. Miscellaneous. Cammie G. Henry Research Center, Watson Memorial Library, Northwestern State University of Louisiana, Natchitoches.

Julian, George W. *Political Recollections, 1840 to 1872.* 1883. Reprint, Miami: Mnemosyne Publishing, 1968.

Kellogg, William P. Papers. Special Collections, Hill Memorial Library, Louisiana State University, Baton Rouge.

King, Martin Luther, Jr. *The Papers of Martin Luther King, Jr.* Vol. 3, *Birth of a New Age.* Ed. Clayborne Carson et al. Berkeley: University of California Press, 1997.

King, Wilma, ed. *A Northern Woman in the Plantation South: Letters of Tryphena Blanche Holder-Fox, 1856–1876.* Columbia: University of South Carolina Press, 1993.

Knox, Thomas W. *Camp-Fire and Cotton Field: Southern Adventure in Time of War.* New York: Blelock, 1865.

Lee, Harold N. Papers. Special Collections, Tulane University, New Orleans, Louisiana.

Levissee, Aaron B. Papers. Library of Congress, Manuscripts Division, Washington, D.C.

Lewis, John G., and Family. Papers. Amistad Research Center, Tulane University, New Orleans, Louisiana.

Lincoln, Abraham. *Abraham Lincoln Papers at the Library of Congress.* Manuscript Division (Washington, D.C.: American Memory Project, 2000–2002), http://memory.loc.gov/ammem/alhtml/alhome.html.

Louisiana, General Assembly. *Supplemental Report of Joint Committee on the Conduct of the Late Elections.* New Orleans: A. L. Lee, 1869.

Melrose Collection. Miscellaneous. Cammie G. Henry Research Center, Watson Memorial Library, Northwestern State University of Louisiana, Natchitoches.

Message of the President of the United States. Washington, D.C.: Government Printing Office, 1868.

National Association for the Advancement of Colored People. Papers. Library of Congress, Manuscripts Division, Washington, D.C.

Nordhoff, Charles. *The Cotton States in the Spring and Summer of 1875.* 1876. Reprint, New York: Burt Franklin, n.d.

Official Journal of the Proceedings of the Constitutional Convention. New Orleans: J. B. Roudanez, 1868.

Olmsted, Frederick Law. *A Journey in the Seaboard Slave States in the Years 1853–1854.* 1856. Reprint, New York: Putnam, 1904.

Pierson Family Papers. Special Collections, Tulane University, New Orleans, Louisiana.

Pinchback, P. B. S. Papers. Moorland-Spingarn Research Center, Howard University, Washington, D.C.

Pollard, Edward A. *The Lost Cause: A New Southern History of the War of the Confederates.* New York: E. B. Treat, 1866.

——. *The Lost Cause Regained.* New York: G. W. Carleton, 1868.

Powell, Myrtle Blanchard. Collection. Cammie G. Henry Research Center, Watson Memorial Library, Northwestern State University of Louisiana, Natchitoches.

Prince Hall Masons, Eureka Grand Lodge of Louisiana. Papers. Amistad Research Center, Tulane University, New Orleans, Louisiana.

Raymond, Ida, ed. *Southland Writers: Biographical and Critical Sketches of Living Female Writers of the South.* Philadelphia: Claxton, Remsen and Haffelfinger, 1870.

Reid, Whitelaw. *After the War: A Tour of the Southern States, 1865–1866.* Ed. C. Vann Woodward. 1866. Reprint, Harper & Row, 1965.

Reports of Cases Argued and Determined in the Supreme Court of Louisiana. Vols. 23, 26. New Orleans: Republican, 1871, 1874.

Republican Party of Louisiana. *Address of the State Campaign Committee.* New Orleans: J. K. Stephens, 1868.

———. *Proceedings of the Convention of the Republican Party of Louisiana.* New Orleans: Tribune, 1865.

———. *Report of the Committee on Address.* New Orleans: Citizens' Guard, 1871.

———. *State Reforms in Louisiana.* New Orleans, 1875.

Schurz, Carl. *The Reminiscences of Carl Schurz.* 3 vols. New York: McClure, 1907.

———. *Speeches, Correspondence and Political Papers of Carl Schurz.* Ed. Frederic Bancroft. Vols. 1–2. New York: Putnam, 1913.

Sheridan, Phillip H. Papers. Library of Congress, Manuscripts Division, Washington, D.C. (microfilm).

Sherman, John. *John Sherman's Recollections of Forty Years in the House, Senate and Cabinet: An Autobiography.* New York: Warner, 1895.

———. Papers. Library of Congress, Manuscripts Division, Washington, D.C.

Sherman, W. T. *The Sherman Letters. Correspondence between General and Senator Sherman from 1837 to 1891.* Ed. Rachel Sherman Thorndike. New York: Scribner, 1894.

Southern Loyalists' Convention. New Orleans: Tribune, 1866.

Stephens, Alexander H. *Recollections of Alexander H. Stephens.* Ed. Myrta Lockett Avary. New York: Da Capo Press, 1971.

Summary Reports of the Commissioners of Claims: 5th and 6th General Reports. Washington, D.C.: Government Printing Office, 1877.

Sumner, Charles. *Selected Letters of Charles Sumner.* Ed. Beverly Wilson Palmer. 2 vols. Boston: Northeastern University Press, 1990.

Supreme Court of Louisiana. Historical Archives. D-Space at the University of New Orleans, Earl K. Long Library. http://libweb.uno.edu/jspui.

Taylor, Richard. *Destruction and Reconstruction: Personal Experiences of the Late War.* New York: D. Appleton, 1879.

Tourgee, Albion W. *An Appeal to Caesar.* New York: Ford, Howard and Hulbert, 1884.

———. *A Fool's Errand, and Part II, The Invisible Empire.* New York: Ford, Howard and Hulbert, 1880.

Trowbridge, J. T. *A Picture of the Desolated States; and the Work of Restoration, 1865–1868.* Hartford, Conn.: Stebbins, 1868.

Trumbull, Lyman. Papers. Library of Congress, Manuscripts Division, Washington, D.C. (microfilm).

Tunnard, William H. *A Southern Record: The History of the Third Regiment Louisiana Infantry.* Baton Rouge, 1866.

U.S. Army. Records of the United States Army Continental Commands, 1821–1928. Record Group 393, National Archives and Records Administration, Washington, D.C.

U.S. Bureau of Refugees, Freedmen, and Abandoned Lands. Records of the Assistant Commissioner for the State of Louisiana. M1027, Record Group 105, National Archives and Records Administration, Washington, D.C.

———. Records of the Field Offices for the State of Louisiana. M1905, Record Group 105, National Archives and Records Administration, Washington, D.C.

———. Records of the Superintendent of Education and the Division of Education. M1026, Record Group 105, National Archives and Records Administration, Washington, D.C.

U.S. Congress. House Ex. Doc. 1. *Report of the Secretary of War.* 40th Cong., 3d sess., 1868.

———. House Ex. Doc. 20. *Reconstruction.* 40th Cong., 1st sess., 1867.

———. House Ex. Doc. 30. *Use of the Army in Certain Southern States.* 44th Cong., 2d sess., 1877.

———. House Ex. Doc. 68. *New Orleans Riots.* 39th Cong., 2d sess., 1867.

———. House Ex. Doc. 70. *Freedmen's Bureau.* 39th Cong., 1st sess., 1866.

———. House Ex. Doc. 91. *Condition of Affairs in Louisiana.* 42d Cong., 3d sess., 1873.

———. House Ex. Doc. 102. *Property Seized in Louisiana.* 40th Cong., 2d sess., 1868.

———. House Ex. Doc. 209, vol. 10. *Letter on Correspondence of Colonel Emory.* 42d Cong., 2d sess., 1872.

———. House Ex. Doc. 209, vol. 15. *Letter on Affairs in New Orleans.* 40th Cong., 2d sess., 1868.

———. House Ex. Doc. 291. *Elections in Southern States.* 41st Cong., 1st sess., 1869.

———. House Ex. Doc. 342. *Letter on Execution of the Reconstruction.* 40th Cong., 2d sess., 1868.

———. House Misc. Doc. 25. *Papers in the Case of George A. Sheridan vs. P.B.S. Pinchback.* 43d Cong., 2d sess., 1874.

———. House Misc. Doc. 31. *Presidential Election Investigation: Testimony Taken by the Select Committee on Alleged Frauds in the Presidential Election of 1876.* 4 parts. 45th Cong., 3d sess., 1879.

———. House Misc. Doc. 32. *Papers in the Contested Election Case of Newsham v. Ryan.* 41st Cong., 1st sess., 1869.

———. House Misc. Doc. 34. *The Recent Election in Louisiana: Testimony Taken by the Select Committee on the Recent Election in Louisiana.* 6 parts. 44th Cong., 2d sess., 1877.

———. House Misc. Doc. 42. *Counting the Electoral Vote: Testimony before the Select Committee on the Privileges, Powers, and Duties of the House of Representatives in Counting the Vote for President and Vice-President of the United States.* 44th Cong., 2d sess., 1877.

———. House Misc. Doc. 43. *Petition for Removal of General Hancock.* 40th Cong., 2d sess., 1868.

———. House Misc. Doc. 54. *Papers in the Case of W. B. Spencer vs. Frank Morey.* 44th Cong., 1st sess., 1876.

———. House Misc. Doc. 154. *Papers on Louisiana Contested Elections.* 2 parts. 41st Cong., 2d sess., 1869.

———. House Misc. Doc. 211. *Political Troubles in Louisiana.* 42d Cong., 2d sess., 1872.

———. House Report 16. *New Orleans Riots.* 39th Cong., 2d sess., 1867.

———. House Report 25. *New Orleans Custom-House.* 39th Cong., 2d sess., 1867.

———. House Report 30. *Report of the Joint Committee on Reconstruction.* 4 parts. 39th Cong., 1st sess., 1866.

———. House Report 61. *Newsham vs. Ryan.* 41st Cong., 2d sess., 1870.

———. House Report 92. *Affairs in Louisiana.* 42d Cong., 2d sess., 1872.

———. House Report 101. *Condition of the South.* 2 parts. 43d Cong., 2d sess., 1875.

———. House Report 140. *Presidential Election Investigation: Investigation of Alleged Electoral Frauds in the Late Presidential Election.* 45th Cong., 3d sess., 1879.

———. House Report 156. *The Recent Election in Louisiana.* 2 parts. 44th Cong., 2d sess., 1877.

———. House Report 261. *Condition of the South.* 3 parts. 43d Cong., 2d sess., 1875.

———. House Report 597. *Sheridan vs. Pinchback.* 43rd Cong., 1st sess., 1874.

———. House Report 816. *Conduct of Federal Officers at New Orleans.* 44th Cong., 1st sess., 1876.

U.S. Congress. Senate. Senate Ex. Doc. 2. *Vote for Electors in Louisiana: A Message from the President of the United States transmitting a letter, accompanied by testimony. Addressed to him by Hon. John Sherman and others, in relation to the canvass of the vote for electors in the State of Louisiana.* 44th Cong., 2d sess., 1876.

———. Senate Ex. Doc. 6. *Freedmen's Affairs.* 39th Cong., 2d sess., 1867.

———. Senate Ex. Doc. 14. *President's Brief of Message on Reconstruction.* 40th Cong., 1st sess., 1867.

———. Senate Ex. Doc. 15. *Reports on Recent Disturbances in Louisiana.* 40th Cong., 3d sess., 1869.

———. Senate Ex. Doc. 16. *President's Message on Outrages Committed by Disloyal Persons.* 41st Cong., 3rd sess., 1871.

———. Senate Ex. Doc. 17. *Affairs in Louisiana.* 43d Cong., 2d sess., 1875.

———. Senate Ex. Doc. 23. *Seizure of Cotton.* 42d Cong., 2d sess., 1872.

———. Senate Ex. Doc. 53. *Registered Voters in Rebel States.* 40th Cong., 2d sess., 1868.

———. Senate Misc. Doc. 14. *Memorium of Hon. J. E. McDonald, Hon. Lewis V. Bogy, and Hon. John W. Stevenson in relation to the counting by the returning board of the State of Louisiana for the appointment of presidential electors November 7, 1876.* 44th Cong., 2d sess., 1877.

———. Senate Misc. Doc. 44. *Electoral Vote of Certain Southern States: Testimony taken before the sub-committee of the Committee on Privileges and Elections.* 44th Cong., 2d sess., 1877.

———. Senate Misc. Doc. 46. *Communication from Hon. Michael Hahn.* 43d Cong., 2d sess., 1875.

———. Senate Misc. Doc. 50. *Testimony of James E. Anderson.* 45th Cong., 3d sess., 1879.

———. Senate Misc. Doc. 79. *Proceedings of the Committee on Privileges and Elections on the Contested Cases of William P. Kellogg and Henry M. Spofford as Senators from the State of Louisiana.* 46th Cong., 2d sess., 1880.

———. Senate Report 1. *Alleged Outrages in Southern States.* 42d Cong., 1st sess., 1871.

———. Senate Report 41. *Report on Condition of Affairs in the Late Insurrectionary States.* 42d Cong., 2d sess., 1872.

———. Senate Report 457. *Louisiana Investigation.* 42d Cong., 3d sess., 1873.

———. Senate Report 626. *P.B.S. Pinchback.* 43d Cong., 2d sess., 1875.

———. Senate Report 695. *Removal of the Negroes from the Southern States to the Northern States.* 3 parts. 46th Cong., 2d sess., 1880.

———. Senate Report 701. *Louisiana in 1876.* 3 parts. 44th Cong., 2d sess., 1877.

———. Senate Report 855. *Alleged Frauds and Violence in Election of 1878.* 2 parts. Part 1: *Louisiana in 1878.* 45th Cong., 3d sess., 1879.

———. Senate Report 867. *Presidential Election in Louisiana.* 45th Cong., 3d sess., 1879.

U.S. Department of Justice. General Records, Record Group 60, National Archives and Records Administration, Washington, D.C. (microfilm).

U.S. Southern Claims Commission. Approved Claims, 1871–1880. www.fold3.com.

Warmoth, Henry Clay. Papers. Southern Historical Collection, University of North Carolina, Chapel Hill (microfilm).

———. *War, Politics, and Reconstruction: Stormy Days in Louisiana.* 1930. Reprint, New York: Negro Universities Press, 1970.

Washburne, Elihu B. Papers. Library of Congress, Manuscripts Division, Washington, D.C.

Washington, Booker T. *The Booker T. Washington Papers.* Vol. 7, *1903–4.* Ed. Louis R. Harlan and Raymond W. Smock. Urbana: University of Illinois Press, 1977.

Wells, J. Madison. *Message of the Governor of Louisiana.* New Orleans, 1867.

Williams, J. H. Collection. Cammie G. Henry Research Center, Watson Memorial Library, Northwestern Louisiana State University, Natchitoches.

Wilmer, J. P. B. *Defense of Louisiana.* New Orleans, 1874.

Wiltz, L. A. *Argument, with Statement of Facts.* New Orleans: Clark & Hofeline, 1875.

Secondary Sources

Abbott, Richard H. *For Free Press and Equal Rights: Republican Newspapers in the Reconstruction South.* Ed. John W. Quist. Athens: University of Georgia Press, 2004.

———. *The Republican Party and the South, 1855–1867.* Chapel Hill: University of North Carolina Press, 1986.

Abzug, Robert H., and Stephen E. Maizlish, eds. *New Perspectives on Race and Slavery in America: Essays in Honor of Kenneth M. Stampp.* Lexington: University Press of Kentucky, 1986.

Allen, James S. *Reconstruction: The Battle for Democracy, 1865–1876.* New York: International Publishers, 1937.

Anderson, Eric. *Race and Politics in North Carolina, 1872–1901: The Black Second.* Baton Rouge: Louisiana State University Press, 1981.

Anderson, Eric, and Alfred A. Moss, eds. *The Facts of Reconstruction: Essays in Honor of John Hope Franklin.* Baton Rouge: Louisiana State University Press, 1991.

Andrew, Rod, Jr. *Wade Hampton: Confederate Warrior to Southern Redeemer.* Chapel Hill: University of North Carolina Press, 2008.

Andrews, E. Benjamin. "A History of the Last Quarter-Century in the United States." *Scribner's Magazine,* May 1895, 566–86.

Ayers, Edward L. Ayers. *Vengeance and Justice: Crime and Punishment in the 19th-Century American South.* New York: Oxford University Press, 1984.

Baggett, James Alex. *The Scalawags: Southern Dissenters in the Civil War and Reconstruction.* Baton Rouge: Louisiana State University Press, 2002.

Baker, Bruce. *What Reconstruction Meant: Historical Memory in the American South.* Charlottesville: University of Virginia Press, 2007.

Barnes, Donna A., and Catherine Connolly. "Repression, the Judicial System, and Political Opportunities for Civil Rights Advocacy during Reconstruction." *Sociological Quarterly* 40, no. 2 (1999): 327–45.

Behrend, Justin J. "Freedpeople's Democracy: African-American Politics and Community in the Postemancipation Natchez District." Ph.D. diss., Northwestern University, 2006.

Bellamy, Donnie D. "The Education of Blacks in Missouri Prior to 1861." *Journal of Negro History* 59, no. 2 (1974): 143–57.

Belz, Herman. *A New Birth of Freedom: The Republican Party and Freedmen's Rights, 1861 to 1866.* Westport, Conn.: Greenwood Press, 1976.

Benedict, Michael Les. *A Compromise of Principle: Congressional Republicans and Reconstruction, 1863–1869.* New York: Norton, 1974.

———. *The Fruits of Victory: Alternatives in Restoring the Union, 1865–1877.* Philadelphia: Lippincott, 1975.

Bennett, Lerone, Jr. *Black Power U.S.A.: The Human Side of Reconstruction 1867–1877.* Baltimore: Penguin Books, 1969.

———. *Forced into Glory: Abraham Lincoln's White Dream.* Chicago: Johnson Publishing Company, 2000.

Bergeron, Arthur W., Jr. "Free Men of Color in Grey." *Civil War History* 32, no. 3 (1986): 247–55.

———. *Guide to Louisiana Confederate Military Units, 1861–1865.* Baton Rouge: Louisiana State University Press, 1989.

Berman, Ari. *Give Us the Ballot: The Modern Struggle for Voting Rights in America.* New York: Picador, 2015.

Binning, Francis W. "Henry Clay Warmoth and Louisiana Reconstruction." Ph.D. diss., University of North Carolina at Chapel Hill, 1969.

Blackmon, Douglas A. *Slavery by Another Name: The Re-enslavement of Black Americans from the Civil War to World War II.* New York: Doubleday, 2008.

Blair, William A. *With Malice toward Some: Treason and Loyalty in the Civil War Era.* Chapel Hill: University of North Carolina Press, 2014.

Blight, David W. *Race and Reunion: The Civil War in American Memory.* Cambridge: Belknap Press, 2002.

Bowers, Claude G. *The Tragic Era: The Revolution after Lincoln.* New York: Blue Ribbon Books, 1929.

Bradley, Mark L. *Bluecoats and Tar Heels: Soldiers and Civilians in Reconstruction North Carolina.* Lexington: University Press of Kentucky, 2009.

Bragg, Jefferson Davis. *Louisiana in the Confederacy.* 1941. Reprint, Baton Rouge: Louisiana State University Press, 1969.

Brasseaux, Carl A. *Acadian to Cajun: Transformation of a People, 1803–1877.* Jackson: University Press of Mississippi, 1992.

Breaux, Peter J. "William G. Brown and the Development of Education: A Retrospective on the Career of a State Superintendent of Education of African Descent in Louisiana." Ph.D. diss., Florida State University, 2006.

Brock, W. R. *An American Crisis: Congress and Reconstruction, 1865–1867.* New York: Harper Torchbooks, 1963.

Brodie, Fawn. *Thaddeus Stevens: Scourge of the South.* New York: Norton, 1966.

Brooksher, William Riley. *War along the Bayous: The 1864 Red River Campaign in Louisiana.* Dulles, Virginia: Brassey's, 1998.

Brown, Canter, Jr., and Larry Eugene Rivers. *Mary Edwards Bryan: Her Early Life and Works.* Gainesville: University Press of Florida, 2015.

Brundate, W. Fitzhugh. *Lynching in the New South: Georgia and Virginia, 1880–1930.* Urbana: University of Illinois Press, 1993.

Buck, Paul H. *The Road to Reunion, 1865–1900.* New York: Vintage, 1959.

Burgess, John W. *Reconstruction and the Constitution, 1866–1876.* New York: Scribner, 1902.

Burton, H. Sophie, and F. Todd Smith. *Colonial Natchitoches: A Creole Community in the Louisiana-Texas Frontier.* College Station: Texas A&M, 2008.

Burton, Orville Vernon, and Robert C. McMath, eds. *Toward a New South? Studies in Post–Civil War Southern Communities.* Westport, Conn.: Greenwood Press, 1982.

Campbell, Clara L. "The Political Life of Louisiana Negroes, 1865–1890." Ph.D. diss., Tulane University, 1971.

Carrigan, Jo Ann. "The Saffron Scourge: A History of Yellow Fever in Louisiana, 1786–1905." Ph.D. diss., Louisiana State University, 1961.

Carter, Dan T. *When the War Was Over: The Failure of Self-Reconstruction in the South, 1865–1867*. Baton Rouge: Louisiana State University Press, 1985.

Caskey, William M. *Secession and Restoration of Louisiana*. 1938. Reprint, New York: Da Capo, 1970.

Castel, Albert. *The Presidency of Andrew Johnson*. Lawrence: Regent's Press of Kansas, 1979.

Censer, Jane Turner. *The Reconstruction of White Southern Womanhood, 1865–1895*. Baton Rouge: Louisiana State University Press, 2003.

Cheek, William, and Aimee Lee Cheek. "John Mercer Langston and the Cincinnati Riot of 1841." In *Race and the City: Work, Community, and Protest in Cincinnati, 1820–1970*, ed. Henry Louis Taylor, 29–59. Urbana: University of Illinois Press, 2013.

Cimbala, Paul A. *Under the Guardianship of the Nation: The Freedmen's Bureau and the Reconstruction of Georgia, 1865–1870*. Athens: University of Georgia Press, 1997.

Cobb, James C. "Beyond Planters and Industrialists: A New Perspective on the New South." *Journal of Southern History* 54, no. 1 (1988): 45–68.

Cohen, William. *At Freedom's Edge: Black Mobility and the Southern Quest for Racial Control, 1861–1915*. Baton Rouge: Louisiana State University Press, 1991.

Coulter, E. Merton. *William G. Brownlow: Fighting Parson of the Southern Highlands*. Chapel Hill: University of North Carolina Press, 1937.

Cox, LaWanda. *Lincoln and Black Freedom: A Study in Presidential Leadership*. Columbia: University of South Carolina Press, 1981.

Cox, LaWanda, and John H. Cox. *Politics, Principle, and Prejudice, 1865–1866: Dilemma of Reconstruction America*. New York: Atheneum, 1969.

Cripps, Thomas R. "The Lily White Republicans: The Negro, the Party, and the South in the Progressive Era." Ph.D. diss., University of Maryland, 1967.

Crouch, Barry A. *The Dance of Freedom: Texas African Americans during Reconstruction*. Austin: University of Texas Press, 2007.

Current, Richard N. *Lincoln's Loyalists: Union Soldiers from the Confederacy*. Oxford: Oxford University Press, 1992.

———. *Those Terrible Carpetbaggers: A Reinterpretation*. New York: Oxford University Press, 1988.

Curry, Richard O., ed. *Radicalism, Racism, and Party Realignment: The Border States during Reconstruction*. Baltimore: Johns Hopkins University Press, 1969.

Curtin, Mary Ellen. *Black Prisoners and Their World: Alabama, 1865–1900*. Charlottesville: University of Virginia Press, 2000.

———. "'Negro Thieves' or 'Enterprising Farmers'?: Markets, the Law, and African American Community Regulation in Alabama, 1866–1877." *Agricultural History* 74, no. 1 (Winter 2000): 19–38.

Cutrer, Thomas W., and T. Michael Parish, eds. *Brothers in Gray: The Civil War Letters of the Pierson Family*. Baton Rouge: Louisiana State University Press, 1997.

Daniel, Pete. *The Shadow of Slavery: Peonage in the South, 1901–1969*. Urbana: University of Illinois Press, 1990.

Davidson, James W. *The Living Writers of the South*. New York: Carleton, 1869.

Davis, David Brion. *Inhuman Bondage: The Rise and Fall of Slavery in the New World*. Oxford: Oxford University Press, 2006.

Dawkins, Richard. *A Devil's Chaplain: Reflections on Hope, Lies, Science, and Love.* Boston: Houghton Mifflin, 2003.

Dawson, Joseph G., III. *Army Generals and Reconstruction: Louisiana, 1862–1877.* Baton Rouge: Louisiana State University Press, 1982.

Degler, Carl N. *The Other South: Southern Dissenters in the Nineteenth Century.* New York: Harper & Row, 1974.

DeSantis, Vincent P. *Republicans Face the Southern Question: The New Departure Years, 1877–1897.* Baltimore: Johns Hopkins University Press, 1959.

DeVore, Donald E. "The Rise from the Nadir: Black New Orleans between the Wars, 1920–1940." M.A. thesis, University of New Orleans, 1982.

de Vries, Mark Leon. "Between Equal Justice and Racial Terror: Freedpeople and the District Court of De Soto Parish during Reconstruction." *Louisiana History* 66, no. 3 (Summer 2015): 261–93.

DiMarco, Louis A. *Anatomy of a Failed Occupation: The U.S. Army in the Former Confederate States, 1865 to 1877.* Arlington, Va.: Institute of Land Warfare of the United States Army, 2007.

Dollar, Susan E. "'Black, White, or Indifferent': Race, Identity, and Americanization in Creole Louisiana." Ph.D. diss., University of Arkansas, 2004.

———. "The Freedmen's Bureau Schools of Natchitoches Parish, 1865–1868." M.A. thesis, Northwestern State University of Louisiana. 1994.

Downing, David C. *A South Divided: Portraits of Dissent in the Confederacy.* Nashville: Cumberland House, 2007.

Downs, Gregory P. *After Appomattox: Military Occupation and the Ends of War.* Cambridge: Harvard University Press, 2015.

Downs, Jim. *Sick from Freedom: African-Americans and Suffering during the Civil War and Reconstruction.* Oxford: Oxford University Press, 2012.

Doyle, Don H. *The Cause of All Nations: An International History of the American Civil War.* New York: Basic Books, 2015.

Du Bois, W. E. B. *Black Reconstruction in America.* 1935. Reprint, New York: Touchstone, 1995.

Dunning, William A. *Essays on the Civil War and Reconstruction.* New York: Macmillan, 1904.

Emberton, Carole. *Beyond Redemption: Race, Violence, and the American South after the Civil War.* Chicago: University of Chicago Press, 2013.

Escott, Paul D. *Lincoln's Dilemma: Blair, Sumner, and the Republican Struggle over Racism and Equality in the Civil War.* Charlottesville: University Press of Virginia, 2014.

———. *Uncommonly Savage: Civil War Remembrance in Spain and the United States.* Gainesville: University Press of Florida, 2014.

———. *"What Shall We Do with the Negro?" Lincoln, White Racism, and Civil War America.* Charlottesville: University Press of Virginia, 2009.

Fairclough, Adam. *Race and Democracy: The Civil Rights Struggle in Louisiana, 1915–1972.* Athens: University of Georgia Press, 1995.

Ficklen, John R. *History of Reconstruction in Louisiana through 1868.* Baltimore: Johns Hopkins University Press, 1910.

Fitzgerald, Michael W. *Splendid Failure: Postwar Reconstruction in the American South.* Chicago: Ivan R. Dee, 2007.

———. *The Union League Movement in the Deep South: Politics and Agricultural Change during Reconstruction.* Baton Rouge: Louisiana State University Press, 1989.

———. *Urban Emancipation: Popular Politics in Reconstruction Mobile, 1860–1890.* Baton Rouge: Louisiana State University Press, 2002.

Fleming, Walter L. *The Sequel of Appomattox.* New Haven: Yale University Press, 1919.

Fogel, Robert W. *Without Consent or Contract: The Rise and Fall of American Slavery.* New York: Norton, 1989.

Foner, Eric. "American Freedom in a Global Age." *American Historical Review* 106, no. 1 (2001): 1–16.

———. "American Freedom in the Age of Emancipation." *Journal of American History* 81, no. 2 (1994): 435–60.

———. "The Civil War and the Idea of Freedom." *Art Institute of Chicago Museum Studies* 27, no. 1 (2001): 8–25.

———. Foreword. In *The Dunning School: Historians, Race, and the Meaning of Reconstruction,* ed. John David Smith and J. Vincent Lowery, ix–xii. Lexington: University Press of Kentucky, 2013.

———. *Freedom's Lawmakers: A Directory of Black Officeholders during Reconstruction.* Baton Rouge: Louisiana State University Press, 1996.

———. *Nothing but Freedom: Emancipation and Its Legacy.* Baton Rouge: Louisiana State University Press, 1983.

———. *Reconstruction: America's Unfinished Revolution, 1863–1877.* New York: Harper & Row, 1988.

———. "Reconstruction Revisited." *Reviews in American History* 10, no. 4 (Dec. 1982): 62–100.

———. *This Fiery Trial: Abraham Lincoln and American Slavery.* New York. Norton, 2010.

Ford, Lacy K. *Deliver Us from Evil: The Slavery Question in the Old South.* Oxford: Oxford University Press, 2009.

Forstall, Richard L., ed. *Population of States and Counties of the United States: 1790–1990.* Washington, D.C.: U.S. Department of Commerce, Bureau of the Census, 1996.

Foster, Gaines M. *Ghosts of the Confederacy: Defeat, The Lost Cause, and the Emergence of the New South.* New York: OUP, 1987.

Franklin, John Hope. *The Militant South, 1800–1861.* Cambridge: Belknap Press, 1956.

———. *Reconstruction: After the Civil War.* Chicago: University of Chicago Press, 1961.

Frazier, Donald S. "'Out of Stinking Distance': The Guerilla War in Louisiana." In *Guerillas, Unionists, and Violence on the Confederate Home Front,* ed. Daniel Sutherland, 151–70. Fayetteville: University of Arkansas Press, 1999.

Fredrickson, George. *The Arrogance of Race: Historical Perspectives on Slavery, Racism, and Social Inequality.* Middletown, Conn.: Wesleyan University Press, 1988.

Freehling, William W. *The South vs. The South: How Anti-Confederate Southerners Shaped the Course of the Civil War.* Oxford: Oxford University Press, 2001.

Fukuyama, Francis. *Political Order and Political Decay: From the Industrial Revolution to the Globalization of Democracy.* London: Profile Books, 2014.

Gaither, Gerald H. *Blacks and the Populist Movement: Ballots and Bigotry in the New South.* Tuscaloosa: University of Alabama Press, 2005.

Gallagher, Gary W., and Alan T. Nolan, eds. *The Myth of the Lost Cause and Civil War History.* Bloomington: Indiana University Press, 2000.

Gardner, Sarah E. *Blood and Irony: Southern White Women's Narratives of the Civil War, 1861–1837.* Chapel Hill: University of North Carolina Press, 2004.

Genovese, Eugene D. *A Consuming Fire: The Fall of the Confederacy and in the Mind of the White Christian South.* Athens: University of Georgia Press, 1998.

Gerstle, Gary. *Liberty and Coercion: The Paradox of American Government.* Princeton: Princeton University Press, 2015.

Gillette, William. *Retreat from Reconstruction, 1869–1879.* Baton Rouge: Louisiana State University Press, 1979.

Glymph, Thavolia. *Out of the House of Bondage: The Transformation of the Plantation Household.* Cambridge: Cambridge University Press, 2008.

Goldman, Robert M. *"A Free Ballot and a Fair Count": The Department of Justice and the Enforcement of Voting Rights in the South, 1877–1893.* New York: Fordham University Press, 2001.

———. *Reconstruction and Black Suffrage: Losing the Vote in Reese v Cruikshank.* Lawrence: University Press of Kansas, 2001.

Goodrich, Thomas, and Debra Goodrich. *The Day Dixie Died: Southern Occupation, 1865–1866.* Mechanicsville, Pa.: Stackpole Books, 2001.

Greenberg, Kenneth S. *Honor and Slavery: Lies, Duels, Noses, Masks, Dressing as a Woman, Gifts, Strangers, Humanitarianism, Death, Slave Rebellions, the Proslavery Argument, Baseball, Hunting, and Gambling in the Old South.* Princeton: Princeton University Press, 1996.

Hahn, Steven. *A Nation under Our Feet: Black Political Struggles in the Rural South from Slavery to the Great Migration.* Cambridge: Belknap Press, 2003.

Hair, William Ivy. *Bourbonism and Agrarian Protest: Louisiana Politics, 1877–1900.* Baton Rouge: Louisiana State University Press, 1969.

Hamilton, Nigel. *The Full Monty: Montgomery of Alamein, 1887–1942.* London: Penguin, 2001.

Hamm, Richard L. *Murder, Honor, and Law: Four Virginia Homicides from Reconstruction to the Great Depression.* Charlottesville: University Press of Virginia, 2003.

Harris, J. William. "Plantations and Power: Emancipation on the David Barrow Plantation." In *Toward a New South? Studies in Post–Civil War Southern Communities,* ed. Orville Vernon Burton and Robert C. McMath, 246–64. Westport, Conn.: Greenwood Press, 1982.

Harris, Williams C. *With Charity for All: Lincoln and the Reconstruction of the Union.* Lexington: University Press of Kentucky, 1997.

Haworth, Paul L. *The Hayes-Tilden Disputed Presidential Election of 1876.* Cleveland: Burrow Brothers, 1906.

Hayden, Renée, Anthony E. Kaye, Kate Masur, et al. *Freedom: A Documentary History of Emancipation, 1861–1867,* series 3, vol. 2, *Land and Labor, 1866–1867.* Chapel Hill: University of North Carolina Press, 2013.

Hebert, Jacquelyne Mary. "Beyond Black and White: The Civil Rights Movement in Baton Rouge, Louisiana, 1945–1972." Ph.D. diss., Louisiana State University, 1999.

Heersink, Boris, and Jeffery A. Jenkins. "Southern Delegates and Republican National Convention Politics, 1880–1928." *Studies in American Political Development* 29 (April 2015): 72–86.

Hicks, William. *History of Louisiana Negro Baptists from 1804 to 1914.* Nashville: National Baptist Publishing Board, 1915.

Higgs, Robert. *Competition and Coercion: Blacks in the American Economy, 1865–1914.* Chicago: University of Chicago Press, 1997.

Highsmith, William E. "Louisiana during Reconstruction." Ph.D. diss., Louisiana State University, 1954.

———. "Some Aspects of Reconstruction in the Heart of Louisiana." *Journal of Southern History* 13, no. 4 (1947): 460–91.

Hirsch, Arnold R., and Joseph Logsdon, eds. *Creole New Orleans: Race and Americanization.* Baton Rouge: Louisiana State University Press, 1992.

Hirshon, Stanley P. *Farewell to the Bloody Shirt: Northern Republicans and the Southern Negro, 1877–1893.* Chicago: Quadrangle, 1968.

Hogue, James K. *Uncivil War: Five New Orleans Street Battles and the Rise and Fall of Radical Reconstruction.* Baton Rouge: Louisiana State University Press, 2006.

Hollandsworth, James G., Jr. *An Absolute Massacre: The New Orleans Race Riot of July 30, 1866.* Baton Rouge: Louisiana State University Press, 2001.

———. *The Louisiana Native Guards: The Black Military Experience during the Civil War.* Baton Rouge: Louisiana State University Press, 1993.

Holt, Michael F. *By One Vote: The Disputed Presidential Election of 1876.* Lawrence: University Press of Kansas, 2008.

Hyde, Samuel C., Jr. *Pistols and Politics: The Dilemma of Democracy in Louisiana's Florida Parishes, 1810–1899.* Baton Rouge: Louisiana State University Press, 1996

Hyman, Harold M. *The Era of the Oath: Northern Loyalty Tests during the Civil War and Reconstruction.* Philadelphia: University of Pennsylvania Press, 1954.

———, ed. *New Frontiers of the American Reconstruction.* Chicago: University of Chicago Press, 1966.

Hyman, Harold M., and William M. Wieck. *Equal Justice under Law: Constitutional Development, 1835–1875.* New York: Harper and Row, 1982.

Janney, Caroline E. *Burying the Dead but Not the Past: Ladies' Memorials Associations and the Lost Cause.* Chapel Hill: University of North Carolina Press, 2008.

———. *Remembering the Civil War: Reunion and the Limits of Reconciliation.* Chapel Hill: University of North Carolina Press, 2013.

Jaynes, Gerald D. *Branches without Roots: Genesis of the Black Working Class in the American South, 1862–1882.* New York: Oxford University Press, 1986.

Johnson, Ludwell H. *Red River Campaign: Politics and Cotton in the Civil War.* Kent, Ohio: Kent State University Press, 1993.

Joiner, Gary D. *Through the Howling Wilderness: The 1864 Red River Campaign and Union Failure in the West.* Knoxville: University of Tennessee Press, 2006.

Keith, LeeAnna. *The Colfax Massacre: The Untold Story of Black Power, White Terror, and the Death of Reconstruction.* Oxford: Oxford University Press, 2008.

Kerr-Ritchie, Jeffrey R. *Freedpeople in the Tobacco South: Virginia, 1860–1900.* Chapel Hill: University of North Carolina Press, 1989.

Kilbourne, Richard H. *Debt, Investment, Slaves: Credit Relations in East Feliciana Parish, Louisiana, 1825–1885.* Tuscaloosa: University of Alabama Press, 1995.

Klobucar, Gretchen V. "Thinking outside the (Wooden) Box: A Rhetorical Analysis of the Ethical Complexity of the Uncle Jack Statue." M.A. thesis, University of of North Carolina at Chapel Hill, 2011.

Klotter, James C. *Kentucky Justice, Southern Honor, and American Manhood: Understanding the Life and Death if Richard Reid.* Baton Rouge: Louisiana State University Press, 2003.

Kornowski, Sister Mary S. "Natchitoches during the Civil War and Reconstruction." M.A. thesis, Catholic University of America, 1949.

Kousser, J. Morgan, and James M. McPherson, eds. *Region, Race, and Reconstruction: Essays in Honor of C. Vann Woodward*. New York: Oxford University Press, 1982.

Lane, Charles. *The Day Freedom Died: The Colfax Massacre, the Supreme Court, and the Betrayal of Reconstruction*. New York: Henry Holt, 2008.

Lanza, Michael L. *Agrarianism and Reconstruction Politics: The Southern Homestead Act*. Baton Rouge: Louisiana State University Press, 1990.

Lathrop, Barnes F. "Disaffection in Confederate Louisiana: The Case of William Hyman." *Journal of Southern History* 24, no. 3 (1958): 308–18.

Lemann, Nicholas. *Redemption: The Last Battle of the Civil War*. New York: Farrar, Straus and Giroux, 2006.

Lennon, Rachel Mills, and Elizabeth Shown Mills. "Mother, Thy Name Is *Mystery!* Finding the Slave Who Bore Philomène Daurat." *National Genealogical Society Quarterly* 88 (September 2000): 201–24.

Lestage, H. Oscar. "The White League n Louisiana and its Participation in Reconstruction Riots." *Louisiana Historical Quarterly* 18 (July 1935): 617–95.

Lind, Michael Lind. *What Lincoln Believed: The Values and Convictions of America's Greatest President*. New York: Anchor, 2006.

Litwack, Leon F. *Been in the Storm So Long: The Aftermath of Slavery*. New York: Vintage, 1979.

Logan, Rayford W. *The Betrayal of the Negro: From Rutherford B. Hayes to Woodrow Wilson*. New York: Collier Books, 1965.

Lonn, Ella. *Desertion during the Civil War*. 1928. Reprint, Lincoln: University of Nebraska Press, 1998.

———. *Reconstruction in Louisiana after 1868*. New York: Russell and Russell, 1918.

Lowry, Walter M. "The Political Career of James Madison Wells." *Louisiana Historical Quarterly* 31 (October 1948): 995–1123.

Mackenzie, Robert Tracy. *Lincolnites and Rebels: A Divided Town in the Civil War*. New York: Oxford University Press, 2009.

Marler, Scott P. "'A Monument to Commercial Isolation': Merchants and the Economic Decline of Post–Civil War New Orleans." *Journal of Urban History* 36, no. 4 (2010): 507–27.

Marshall, Anne E. *Creating a Confederate Kentucky: The Lost Cause and Civil War Memory in a Border State*. Chapel Hill: University of North Carolina Press, 2010.

Martin, Bessie. "*A Rich Man's War, A Poor Man's Fight*" *Desertion of Alabama Troops from the Confederate Army*. 1932. Reprint, Tuscaloosa: University of Alabama Press, 2003.

Martinez, J. Michael. *Carpetbaggers, Cavalry, and the Ku Klux Klan: Exposing the Invisible Empire during Reconstruction*. Lanham, Md.: Rowman and Littlefield, 2007.

Maxwell, David B. "James Hugh Cosgrove, Louisiana Newspaper Editor, 1842–1914." M.A. thesis, Northwestern State University of Louisiana, 1973.

May, John Thomas. "The Medical Care of Blacks in Louisiana during Occupation and Reconstruction." Ph.D. diss., Tulane University, 1971.

McAfee, Ward M. *Religion, Race, and Reconstruction: The Public Schools in the Politics of the 1870s*. Albany: State University of New York, 1998.

McCarthy, Charles H. *Lincoln's Plan of Reconstruction*. New York: McClure, Phillips, 1901.

McClain, Charles. "California Carpetbagger: The Career of Henry Dibble." *Quinnipiac*

Law Review 28 (2009): 885–967. Available at http://scholarship.law.berkeley.edu/fac-pubs/660.

McCrary, Peyton. *Abraham Lincoln and Reconstruction: The Louisiana Experiment.* Princeton: Princeton University Press, 1978.

McCurry, Stephanie. *Confederate Reckoning: Power and Politics in the Civil War South.* Cambridge and London: Harvard University Press, 2010.

McDonald, Roderick A. "Independent Economic Production by Slaves on Antebellum Louisiana Sugar Plantations." In *The Slavery Reader,* ed. Gad Heuman and James Walvin, 486–506. London: Routledge, 2003.

McFeely, William S. *Yankee Stepfather: General O. O. Howard and the Freedmen.* New York: Norton, 1994.

McGinty, Garnie W. *Louisiana Redeemed: The Overthrow of Carpet-Bag Rule, 1876–1880.* 1941. Reprint, Gretna, La.: Pelican, 1998.

McKitrick, Eric. *Andrew Johnson and Reconstruction.* Chicago: University of Chicago Press, 1960.

McLaren, Kristin. "'We had no desire to be set apart': Forced Segregation of Black Students in Canada West Public Schools and Myths of British Egalitarianism." *Histoire Sociale/ Social History* 37 (2004): 33–34.

McPherson, James M. *Battle Cry of Freedom: The Civil War Era.* New York: Oxford University Press, 1988.

———. "Introduction: Last Best Hope for What?" In *We Cannot Escape History: Lincoln and the Last Best Hope of Earth,* ed. McPherson, 1–16. Urbana: University of Illinois Press, 1995.

McTigue, Geraldine M. "Forms of Racial Interaction in Louisiana, 1860–1880." Ph.D. diss., Yale University, 1975.

Menn, Joseph Karl. *The Large Slaveholders of Louisiana, 1860.* New Orleans: Pelican, 1998.

Middleton, Stephen. *The Black Laws: Race and Legal Process in Early Ohio.* Athens, Ohio: Ohio University Press, 2005.

Mills, Gary B. *The Forgotten People: Cane River's Creoles of Color.* Baton Rouge: Louisiana State University Press, 1977.

Mills, Gary B., and Elizabeth Shown Mills. *The Forgotten People: Cane River's Creoles of Color.* Rev. ed. Baton Rouge: Louisiana State University Press, 2013.

Mitchell, Brian Keith. "Oscar James Dunn: A Case Study in Race and Politics in Reconstruction Louisiana." Ph.D. diss., University of New Orleans, 2011.

Moore, Waldo W. "The Defense of Shreveport: The Confederacy's Last Redoubt." *Military Affairs* 17, no. 2 (Summer 1953): 72–82.

Morris, Roy, Jr. *Sheridan: The Life and Wars of General Phil Sheridan.* New York: Crown Publishers, 1992.

Mountcastle, Clay. *Punitive War: Confederate Guerillas and Union Reprisals.* Lawrence: University Press of Kansas, 2009.

Muraskin, William A. *Middle-Class Blacks in a White Society: Prince Hall Masonry in America.* Berkeley: University of California Press, 1975.

Myrdal, Gunnar. *An American Dilemma: The Negro Problem and Modern Democracy.* New York: Harper & Bros., 1944.

Nelson, Scott R. *Iron Confederacies: Southern Railways, Klan Violence, and Reconstruction.* Chapel Hill: University of North Carolina Press, 1999.

Nieman, Donald G. "Andrew Johnson, the Freedmen's Bureau, and the Problem of Equal Rights, 1865–1866." *Journal of Southern History* 44, no. 3 (Aug. 1978): 399–420.

Norrell, Robert J. *The House I Live In: Race in the American Century.* New York: Oxford University Press, 2005.

Nystrom, Justin A. *New Orleans after the Civil War: Race, Politics, and a New Birth of Freedom.* Baltimore: Johns Hopkins University Press, 2010.

Oakes, James. *Freedom National: The Destruction of Slavery in the United States, 1861–1865.* New York: Norton, 2013.

Oakes, James, et al. *Of the People: A History of the United States since 1865.* New York: Oxford University Press, 2011.

Oberholtzer, Ellis P. *History of the United States since the Civil War.* 5 vols. New York: Macmillan, 1917.

Olsen, Otto H. *Carpetbagger's Crusade: The Life of Albion Winegar Tourgee.* Baltimore: Johns Hopkins University Press, 1965.

Oubre, Claude. "'Forty Acres and a Mule': Louisiana and the Southern Homestead Act." *Louisiana History* 17, no. 2 (Spring 1976): 143–57.

Paludan, Phillip Shaw. "Lincoln and Colonization: Policy or Propaganda?" *Journal of the Abraham Lincoln Association* 25, no. 1 (2009): 23–37.

Patty, James S. "A Woman Journalist in Reconstruction Louisiana: Mrs. Mary E. Bryan." *Louisiana Studies* 3, no. 1 (1964): 77–104.

Perkins, A. E. "Some Negro Offices and Legislators in Louisiana." *Journal of Negro History* 14, no. 4 (1929): 523–28.

Perman, Michael. "Counter-Reconstruction: The Role of Violence in Southern Redemption." In *The Facts of Reconstruction: Essays in Honor of John Hope Franklin,* ed. Eric Anderson and Alfred Moss, 130–34. Baton Rouge: Louisiana State University Press, 1991.

———. *Pursuit of Unity: A Political History of the American South.* Chapel Hill: University of North Carolina Press, 2009.

———. *Reunion without Compromise: The South and Reconstruction, 1865–1868.* Cambridge: University Press, 1973.

———. *The Road to Redemption: Southern Politics, 1869–1879.* Chapel Hill: University of North Carolina Press, 1984.

———. *Struggle for Mastery: Disfranchisement in the South, 1888–1908.* Chapel Hill: University of North Carolina Press, 2001.

Peskin, Allan. *Garfield.* Kent, Ohio: Kent State University Press, 1978.

Pfeifer, Michael J. *Rough Justice: Lynching and American Society, 1874–1947.* Chicago: University of Illinois Press, 2004.

Polakoff, Keith Ian. *The Politics of Inertia: The Election of 1876 and the End of Reconstruction.* Baton Rouge: Louisiana State University Press, 1973.

Poole, W. Scott. *Never Surrender: Confederate Memory and Conservatism in the South Carolina Upcountry.* Athens: University of Georgia Press, 2004.

Powell, Lawrence N. "Centralization and Its Discontents in Reconstruction Louisiana." *Studies in American Political Development* 20 (Fall 2006): 105–31.

———, ed. *The Louisiana Purchase Bicentennial Series in Louisiana History.* Vol. 7, *Reconstructing Louisiana.* Lafayette: Center for Louisiana Studies, University of Louisiana at Lafayette, 2001.

———. *New Masters: Northern Planters during the Civil War and Reconstruction.* New Haven: Yale University Press, 1980.

———. "The Politics of Livelihood: Carpetbaggers in the Deep South." In *Region, Race, and Reconstruction: Essays in Honor of C. Vann Woodward*, ed. J. Morgan Kousser and James M. McPherson, 315–47. New York: Oxford University Press, 1982.

Prather, H. Leon. *Resurgent Politics and Educational Progressivism in the New South: North Carolina, 1890–1913*. Cranbury, N.J.: Associated University Presses, 1979.

Prothro, James W. "Stateways v. Folkways Revisited: An Error in Prediction." *Journal of Politics* 34, no. 2 (May 1972): 352–64.

Pryor, Elizabeth Brown. *Reading the Man: A Portrait of Robert E. Lee through His Private Letters*. New York: Viking, 2007.

Rable, George C. *But There Was No Peace: The Role of Violence in the Politics of Reconstruction*. Athens: University of Georgia Press, 2007.

———. *Civil Wars: Women and the Crisis of Southern Nationalism*. Urbana: University of Illinois Press, 1991.

Ransom, Roger L., and Richard Sutch. "One Kind of Freedom: Reconsidered (and Turbo-Charged)." Historical Paper 129, *National Bureau of Economic Research*, September 2000, 11–17.

———. *One Kind of Freedom: The Economic Consequences of Emancipation*. Cambridge: Cambridge University Press, 1977.

Reed, Germaine M. "David Boyd: Southern Educator." Ph.D. diss., Louisiana State University, 1970.

Rhodes, James Ford. *History of the United States since the Compromise of 1850 to the Final Restoration of Home Rule at the South in 1877*. 7 vols. New York: Macmillan, 1904.

Richard, Allan C., Jr., and Mary M. H. Richard. *The Defense of Vicksburg: A Louisiana Chronicle*. College Station: Texas A&M University Press, 2004.

Richardson, Heather Cox. *The Death of Reconstruction: Race, Labor, and Politics in the Post–Civil War North, 1865–1901*. Cambridge: Harvard University Press, 2001.

Richter, William Lee. *Overreached on All Sides: The Freedmen's Bureau Administrators in Texas, 1865–1868*. College Station: Texas A&M University Press, 1991.

Ripley, Peter C. *Slaves and Freedmen in Civil War Louisiana*. Baton Rouge: Louisiana State University Press, 1976.

Robinson, Armstead L. *Bitter Fruits of Bondage: The Demise of Slavery and the Collapse of the Confederacy, 1861–1865*. Charlottesville: University of Virginia Press, 2005.

Rodrigue, John C. *Lincoln and Reconstruction*. Carbondale: Southern Illinois University Press, 2013.

———. *Reconstruction in the Cane Fields: From Slavery to Free Labor in Louisiana's Sugar Parishes, 1862–1880*. Baton Rouge: Louisiana State University Press, 2001.

Rogers, William Warren, Jr. *Black Belt Scalawag: Charles Hays and the Southern Republicans in the Era of Reconstruction*. Athens: University of Georgia Press, 1993.

Ross, Michael A. "Obstructing Reconstruction: John Archibald Campbell and the Legal Campaign against Louisiana's Republican Government, 1868–1873." *Civil War History* 49, no. 3 (2003): 235–53.

Rubin, Anne Sarah. *A Shattered Nation: The Rise and Fall of the Confederacy, 1861–1868*. Chapel Hill: University of North Carolina Press, 2005.

Rushing, Toni Galliano. "The Memoirs and Reminiscences of Albert H. Leonard." M.A. thesis, Northwestern State University of Louisiana, 1972.

Russ, William A. "Registration and Disfranchisement under Radical Reconstruction." *Mississippi Valley Historical Review* 21, no. 2 (Sept. 1934): 163–80.

Schweninger, Loren. "A Vanishing Breed: Black Farm Owners in the South, 1631–1982." *Agricultural History* 63 (Summer 1989): 41–60.

Scott, Rebecca J. *Degrees of Freedom: Louisiana and Cuba after Slavery.* Cambridge: Belknap Press, 2005.

Sefton, James E. *The United States Army and Reconstruction, 1865–1877.* Baton Rouge: Louisiana State University Press, 1967.

Sherman, Richard B. *The Republican Party and Black Americans from McKinley to Hoover, 1896–1933.* Charlottesville: University Press of Virginia, 1973.

Shlomowitz, Ralph. "'Bound or Free?': Black Labor in Cotton and Sugarcane Farming, 1865–1880." *Journal of Southern History* 50, no. 4 (1984): 569–96.

———. "The Squad System on Post-Bellum Cotton Plantations." In *Toward a New South? Studies in Post–Civil War Southern Communities*, ed. Orville Vernon Burton and Robert C. McMath, 265–80. Westport, Conn.: Greenwood Press, 1982.

———. "The Transition from Slave to Freedman Labor Arrangements in Southern Agriculture, 1865–1870." *Journal of Economic History* 39, no. 1 (March 1979): 333–36.

Simkins, Francis Butler. *The Everlasting South.* Baton Rouge: Louisiana State University Press, 1963.

Simpson, Brooks D. *The Reconstruction Presidents.* Lawrence: University Press of Kansas, 1998.

Singletary, Otis A. "The Election of 1878 in Louisiana." *Louisiana Historical Quarterly* 40, no. 1 (Jan. 1957): 46–53.

———. *Negro Militia and Reconstruction.* Austin: University of Texas Press, 1957.

Skowronek, Stephen. *Building a New American State: The Expansion of National Administrative Capacities, 1877–1920.* Cambridge: Cambridge University Press, 1982.

Smith, John David, and J. Vincent Lowery, eds. *The Dunning School: Historians, Race, and the Meaning of Reconstruction.* Lexington: University Press of Kentucky, 2013.

Snyder, Perry Anderson. "Shreveport, Louisiana, during the Civil War and Reconstruction." Ph.D. diss., Florida State University, 1979.

Southern Regional Council. *Negro Voter Registration in Southern States.* Atlanta: Southern Regional Council, June 7, 1957.

Stampp, Kenneth P. *The Era of Reconstruction, 1865–1867.* New York: Vintage, 1965.

Stampp, Kenneth P., and Leon F. Litwack, eds. *Reconstruction: An Anthology of Revisionist Writings.* Baton Rouge: Louisiana State University Press, 1969.

Stanley, Amy Dru. *From Bondage to Contract: Wage Labor, Marriage, and the Market in the Age of Slave Emancipation.* Cambridge: Cambridge University Press, 1997.

Steedman, Mark D. "Resistance, Rebirth, and Redemption: The Rhetoric of White Supremacy in Post–Civil War Louisiana." *Historical Reflections* 35, no. 1 (2009): 97–113.

Summers, Mark W. *A Dangerous Stir: Fear, Paranoia, and the Making of Reconstruction.* Chapel Hill: University of North Carolina Press, 2009.

———. *The Ordeal of the Reunion: A New History of Reconstruction.* Chapel Hill: University of North Carolina Press, 2014.

Sumner, William Graham. *Folkways: A Study of the Sociological Importance of Usages, Manners, Customs, Mores, and Morals.* Boston: Ginn & Company, 1906.

Sutherland, Daniel E., ed. *Guerillas, Unionists, and Violence on the Confederate Home Front.* Fayetteville: University of Arkansas Press, 1999.

———. *A Savage Conflict: The Decisive Role of Guerillas in the American Civil War.* Chapel Hill: University of North Carolina Press, 2009.

Tatum, Georgia Lee. *Disloyalty in the Confederacy.* 1934. Reprint, Lincoln: University of Nebraska Press, 2000.

Taylor, Joe Gray. "Louisiana: An Impossible Task." In *Reconstruction and Redemption in the South,* ed. Otto H. Olsen, 202–35. Baton Rouge: Louisiana State University Press, 1980.

———. *Louisiana Reconstructed, 1863–1877.* Baton Rouge: Louisiana State University Press, 1974.

Theodoulu, Stella Z. "Minority Status to Serious Partisan Alternative? The Case of the Louisiana Republican Party, 1948–1983." Ph.D. diss., Tulane University, 1984.

Thompson, Elizabeth Lee. *The Reconstruction of Southern Debtors: Bankruptcy after the Civil War.* Athens: University of Georgia Press, 2004.

Thompson, Virginia Elaine. "Southern Small Towns: Society, Politics and Race Relations in Clinton, Louisiana, 1824–1880." Ph.D. diss., Rice University, 2003.

Thornton, J. Mills, III. "Fiscal Policy and the Failure of Radical Reconstruction in the Lower South." In *Region, Race, and Reconstruction: Essays in Honor of C. Vann Woodward,* ed. J. Morgan Kousser and James M. McPherson, 349–94. New York: Oxford University Press, 1982.

Tolnay, Stewart E. *The Bottom Rung: African American Family Life on Southern Farms.* Urbana: University of Illinois Press, 1999.

Tolnay, Stewart E., and E. M. Beck. *A Festival of Violence: An Analysis of Southern Lynchings, 1882–1930.* Urbana: University of Illinois Press, 1995.

Trefousse, Hans L. *Andrew Johnson: A Biography.* New York: Norton, 1989.

———. *Thaddeus Stevens: Nineteenth-Century Egalitarian.* Chapel Hill: University of North Carolina Press, 1997.

Tregle, Joseph G. "Thomas J. Durant, Utopian Socialism, and the Failure of Presidential Reconstruction in Louisiana." *Journal of Southern History* 45, no. 4 (Nov. 1979): 485–512.

Tunnell, Ted, ed. *Carpetbagger from Vermont: The Autobiography of Marshall Harvey Twitchell.* Baton Rouge: Louisiana State University Press, 1989.

———. *Crucible of Reconstruction: War, Radicalism, and Race in Louisiana, 1862–1877.* Baton Rouge: Louisiana State University Press, 1984.

———. *Edge of the Sword: The Ordeal of Carpetbagger Marshall H. Twitchell in the Civil War and Reconstruction.* Baton Rouge: Louisiana State University Press, 2001.

Uzee, Philip D. "Republican Politics in Louisiana, 1877–1900." Ph.D. diss., Louisiana State University, 1950.

Valelly, Richard M. *The Two Reconstructions: The Struggle for Black Enfranchisement.* Chicago: University of Chicago Press, 2004.

Vandal, Gilles. "Albert H. Leonard's Road from the White League to the Republican Party: A Political Enigma." *Louisiana History* 36 (Winter 1995): 55–76.

———. "Black Violence in Post–Civil War Louisiana." *Journal of Interdisciplinary History* 25, no. 1 (Summer 1994): 45–64.

———. "'Bloody Caddo': White Violence against Blacks in a Louisiana Parish." *Louisiana History* 25, no. 2 (1991): 373–88.

———. "Property Offenses, Social Tensions, and Racial Antagonism in Post–Civil War Louisiana." *Journal of Social History* 31, no. 1 (Fall 1997): 127–53.

———. "Regulating Louisiana's Rural Areas: The Function of Parish Jails, 1840–1885." *Louisiana History* 42, no. 1 (Winter 2001): 59–92.

———. *Rethinking Southern Violence: Homicides in Post–Civil War Louisiana, 1866–1884.* Columbus: Ohio State University Press, 2000.

Varon, Elizabeth H. *Appomattox: Victory, Defeat, and Freedom at the End of the Civil War.* New York: Oxford University Press, 2014.

Vincent, Charles. *Black Legislators in Louisiana during Reconstruction.* Baton Rouge: Louisiana State University Press, 1976.

Waldman, Michael. *The Fight to Vote.* New York: Simon and Schuster, 2016.

Waldrep, Christopher. *Roots of Disorder: Race and Criminal Justice in the American South, 1817-80.* Urbana: University of Illinois Press, 1998.

Walkes, Joseph A., Jr. *Jno G. Lewis, Jr.—End of an Era: The History of the Prince Hall Grand Lodge of Louisiana, 1842-1979.* Leavenworth, Kans.: J. A. Walkes, Jr., 1986.

Wang, Xi. *The Trial of Democracy: Black Suffrage and Northern Republicans, 1860-1910.* Athens: University of Georgia Press, 1997.

Ward, Roger K. "The French Language in Louisiana Law and Legal Education: A Requiem." *Louisiana Law Review* 57, no. 4 (Summer 1997): 1296-98.

Waugh, Joan. *U.S. Grant: American Hero, American Myth.* Chapel Hill: University of North Carolina Press, 2009.

Webb, Addie B. W. "A History of Negro Voting in Louisiana, 1877-1906." Ph.D. diss., Louisiana State University, 1962.

Weiner, Marli F. *Mistresses and Slaves: Plantation Women in South Carolina, 1830-1880.* Urbana: University of Illinois Press, 1998.

Weitz, Mark A. *More Damning than Slaughter: Desertion in the Confederate Army.* Lincoln: University of Nebraska Press, 2005.

Welles, Gideon. *The Diary of Gideon Welles.* 3 vols. Boston: Houghton Mifflin, 1911.

Wells, Carol, ed. *War, Reconstruction and Redemption on Red River: The Memoirs of Dosia Williams Moore.* Ruston, La.: McGinty Publications, 1990.

Wetta, Frank J. "'Bulldozing the Scalawags': Some Examples of the Persecution of Southern White Republicans in Louisiana during Reconstruction." *Louisiana History* 21 (Winter 1980): 43-58.

White, Howard A. "The Freedmen's Bureau in Louisiana." Ph.D. diss., Tulane University, 1959.

Whittington, G. P. "Concerning the Loyalty of Slaves in North Louisiana in 1863: Letters from John H. Ransdell to Governor Thomas O. Moore." *Louisiana Historical Quarterly* 14 (1931): 491-97.

Wiener, Jonathan M. "Planter Persistence and Social Change: Alabama, 1850-1870." *Journal of Interdisciplinary History* 7, no. 2 (Autumn 1976): 235-60.

Wiggins, Sarah Woolfolk. *The Scalawag in Alabama Politics, 1865-1881.* Tuscaloosa: University of Alabama Press, 1991.

William, Ora G. "Muskets and Magnolias: Four Civil War Diaries by Louisiana Girls." *Louisiana Studies* 3 (1965): 187-99.

Williams, David. *Bitterly Divided: The South's Inner Civil War.* New York: New Press, 2008.

Williams, Ernest Russ. "The Florida Parish Ellises and Louisiana Politics, 1820-1918." Ph.D. diss., University of Southern Mississippi, 1969.

Williams, T. Harry. *Romance and Realism in Southern Politics.* Athens: University of Georgia Press, 1961.

Wilson, Charles Reagan. *Baptized in Blood: The Religion of the Lost Cause, 1865-1920.* Athens: University of Georgia Press, 1980.

Winters, John D. *The Civil War in Louisiana.* Baton Rouge: Louisiana State University Press, 1963, 1991.

Woodman, Harold. *New South—New Law: The Legal Foundations of Credit and Labor Relations in the Postbellum Agricultural South.* Baton Rouge: Louisiana State University Press, 1995.

Woodward. C. Vann. *American Counterpoint: Slavery and Racism in the North-South Dialogue.* Boston: Little Brown, 1971.

———. *The Burden of Southern History.* New York: New American Library, 1968.

———. *The Future of the Past.* New York: Oxford University Press, 1989.

———. *Reunion and Reaction: The Compromise of 1877 and the End of Reconstruction.* Garden City, N.Y.: Doubleday Anchor, 1956.

———. *Thinking Back: The Perils of Writing History.* Baton Rouge: Louisiana State University Press, 1986.

Wright, Gavin. *Old South, New South: Revolutions in the Southern Economy since the Civil War.* Baton Rouge: Louisiana State University Press, 1986.

Wright, George C. *Racial Violence in Kentucky, 1865–1940: Lynchings, Mob Rule, and "Legal Lynchings."* Baton Rouge: Louisiana State University Press, 1990.

Wyatt-Brown, Bertram. *Southern Honor: Ethics and Behavior in the Old South.* Oxford: Oxford University Press, 1982.

Zuczek, Richard. *State of Rebellion: Reconstruction in South Carolina.* Columbia: University of South Carolina Press, 1996.

INDEX

Page numbers in *italics* refer to illustrations.

Bryan, Maria, 88, 342n5
Bryan, Mary Edwards, 45, 63, 88, 339–40n10; on Coushatta murders, 190; on freed people, 119, 138–39; Lost Cause and, 67–69; patriarchy and, 68; political moderation of, 118–19; on sharecropping, 134
Buard, Ida, 297
Buchanan, Robert C., 101, 110, 151
Bullard, Charles, 80, 91–92, 289
"Bulldozing," 184, 188–90, 214, 219, 231–32, 238, 247, 268–72, 276, 295
Burch, J. Henri, 324
Burdick, Lucius H.: Custom House faction and, 157–58; *Red River News* and, 158, 350n23; Tax Payers Association and, 184
Bureau of Refugees, Freedmen, and Abandoned Lands, 9, 18, 25, 60, 107, 139; black political participation and, 101–103; crops seized by, 139, 142; Johnson's hostility to, 102; labor contracts and, 43–45, 61, 139–41; political activity of, 102–3; public schools and, 134–35; violence against blacks and, 59, 81, 110; vulnerability of agents, 82. *See also* Army, U.S.
Burgess, John W., 51, 83
Burke, E. A., 275; Compromise of 1877 and, 253–54, 256, 258–59, 261–62
Burke, Ross E., 113, 119, 170, 201, 244; elected sheriff, 175
Butler, Benjamin F.: on Louisiana politics, 160
Butler, J. W., 46
Byerly, D. C., 204
Byrd, S. M., 318

Caddo Parish, 55, 82, 109, 112, 115–16, 200; emigration from, 300; Enforcement Acts and, 299; lawlessness of, 116; planters in, 141
Caldwell Parish, 59
Cameron Parish, 159
Campbell, Hugh J., 204, 265
Campbell, John A., 257
Campti, 30, 88, 135, 184, 247, 249
Canby, E. R. S., 55, 61, 82
Carnival, 294
"Carpetbaggers:" departure from Louisiana of, 265; stereotype of, 158–59.

See also Republican Party: northern migrants in
Carr, Mortimer, 153–54, 160; Crescent City Gas Company and, 155
Carrière, Ozémé, 29, 117
Carter, Andrew, 90
Carter, Dan, 83
Carter, George W., 158–59, 160, 350n15; on corruption, 150
Carter, Gilbert, 232
Carver, Marshall H., 280
Casey, Mary, 136
Catholic Church, 7–8
Chandler, Zachariah, 243
Chaplin, Chichester C., 100, 226, 256, 281, 296–97
Chaplin, Thomas, 257–58
Chapman, Sam, 270
Chase, Salmon P., 36, 39
Chase, Valentine, 112
Chesnutt, Charles W., 314
Cincinnati: free blacks in, 93–94; race riots in, 94
Citizens Party (New Orleans), 306
Civil Rights Act (1866), 60, 133
Civil rights movement, 14–15, 326–29, 370n29
Civil War: destruction wrought by, 30, 41; historical significance of, 14–15; Natchitoches and, 6, 25–27, 30
Claiborne Parish, 109
Clark, Clinton, 322, 324–25
Clemenceau, Georges, 75–76
Cleveland, Grover, 305–6
Cloutierville, 184
Coleman, H. Dudley, 308
Colfax, Schuyler, 208
Colfax Chronicle, 299
Colfax massacre, 115, 175–76, 210–11, 219; impact on Republican Party, 176–80; monument to, 329
Colonization movement. *See* Blacks: emigration movement and
Colored Farmers Alliance, 308
Compromise of 1877: E. A. Burke and, 253–54, 256, 258–59, 261–62; characterized, 253; Electoral Commission, 257; Grant, status quo order of, 254–58; Hayes and, 261–69; Republican Party, consequences for, 264–66; Wormley House hotel conference, 262; Vietnam quagmire, parallel with, 272–73

Confederates, former: Amnesty Acts and, 352n5; arrogance of, 49–50, 73; disfranchisement of, 99–101; excuses for secession of, 76–77; lack of penitence of, 72–74; militias formed by, 55, 110; New Orleans riot and, 84; pride in war service of, 73–74. *See also* "Lost Cause"

Confederate Memorial (Arlington National Cemetery), 318

Confederate States of America: declining support for, 28–31; repression of dissent in, 29–31

Congress, U.S.: black enfranchisement and, 1, 84, 98; Louisiana and, 208–9, 216–17, 220–21. *See also* Louisiana, Congressional investigations

Congressional Reconstruction: American exceptionalism and, 17–18; black suffrage and, 98; "carpet-bag rule," alleged horrors of, 315–17; civil rights movement and, 326–29; failure of, 1, 15, 18–24; historical significance of, 14–15, 326–30; idealism and, 15–18; international context of, 18; Vietnam quagmire, compared with, 272–73

Conner, John, 91

Constitution, Louisiana (1868), 105

Constitutional convention: of 1864, 38–39; of 1867–68, 90, 97, 104–5, 107; of 1898, 313

Conway, Thomas, 58, 60, 81, 135

Cosgrove, James Hugh, 145, 171, 213, 264, 269, 295, 303, 318–19; abuse of Republicans by, 185, 215; arrest of, 197–98; black office-holding, opposition to, 276; on Raford Blunt, 12–13, 90, 223–24, 277–79, 302; Coushatta murders and, 190, 197; death of, 319; election of 1874 and, 200–201; election of 1876 and, 238–39, 277; election of 1878 and, 287–89; E. L. Pierson, quarrel with, 216, 228–31, 358n47; reform and, 226–27; threats by, 205, 224, 227–28, 231, 279, 291; Wheeler Compromise and, 216–17, 224

Cosgrove, John, 169–71

Cosgrove's Weekly, 319

Coupland, T. V., 155

Coushatta murders, 115, 190, 195, 219

Cox, Jacob D., 128

Cox, S. S., 76

Crawford, Thomas S., 177

Criminal justice, 137–38

Cromie, James, 45–48, 57, 102–3, 113, 115, 129, 132–33; death of, 350n22; *Red River News* and, 122, 171

Cunningham, J. H., 36, 201, 291

Cunningham, Milton Joseph, 8, 10–12, 106, 201; on Raford Blunt, 290; death of, 319; elected district attorney, 244; election of 1872 and, 175; election of 1874 and, 185–86; election of 1876 and, 242, 245, 248; election of 1878 and, 281–86; *Plessy v. Ferguson* and, 319; Tax Reform Association and, 184–86; Teller Committee and, 290; *United States v. Cunningham* and, 295–96

Custer, George Armstrong, 34

Dallas, Henry, 129

Davis, David Brion, 25

Davis, James J., 298

Davis, Jefferson, 71

Davis, Lucy, 137

De Blanc, Alcibiades, 23, 111

De Klyne, Thomas, 178

Delany, Martin R., 93, 95

Delany, Toussaint L'Ouverture, 95, 135

Democratic Party, 19; black suffrage and, 125, 313–14; "Bourbons," 272–73, 276, 305, 309; defense of violence by, 123–24, 218–21, 238; election of April 1866 and, 79–80; election of 1872 and, 164; election of 1874 and, 195, 198–200, 207; election of 1876 and, 235–40; election of 1888 and, 305–6; electoral fraud and, 304–6, 312; Greeley, endorsement of, 164; intimidation by, 8, 237–38; "mixed tickets" and, 307; nomenclature of, 344n10; state lower house, attempted seizure of, 204–5; Warmoth and, 162–65. *See also* Knights of the White Camelia

—Democratic Party (Natchitoches Parish): appeals to black voters by, 119–21, 239–40, 279; black support for, 279; city council and, 226–27; coercive tactics of, 1–3; compromise of 1873 and, 176, 353n14; 1868 election and, 114–20; 1870 election and, 174; 1872 election and, 162–63, 165–67, 174–75; 1874 election and, 198, 201–2, 355n16; 1876 election and, 238–40, 255–56, 360nn21,24; 1878 election and, 8, 10–13, 279–89; electoral fraud and, 304–5; exiled Republicans and, 303–4; factionalism and, 305; *New York Times*, described by, 299; police jury and, 226; Republican factionalism and, 162–63; Tax Reform Association and, 182–90; violence and, 189–90. *See also* Cosgrove, James Hugh; Cunningham, Milton Joseph; Levy, William M.; Pierson, David; *United States v. Cunningham*

Denison, George S., 39

De Soto Parish, 82, 109, 115–16, 153, 200, 202–3; courts in, 139; election of 1876 and, 243, 247, 249; election of 1896 and, 311; Ku Klux Klan and, 113–14

De Trobriand, Regis, 205

Deusen (Duzen), S. van, 136

De Vargas, J. D., 201, 225–26: elected mayor of Natchitoches, 146

Devens, Charles S., 288, 290, 298, 365n46

De Vries, Mark, 139

Dibble, Henry C., 15, 153, 155–56, 260, 265; on corruption, 154; on dueling, 174; election of 1872 and, 167; election of 1876 and, 249; on taxation, 227; Warmoth and, 160; on White League, 188

Dinkgrave, B. F., 238

Disfranchisement: black voters and, 313–14, 323, 332n12; ex-Confederates and, 99–101

Donaldsonville, 80

Dorsey, Sarah A., 65

Dostie, A. P., 83

Dranguet, C. L., 202, 257, 268, 285, 291, 296

Du Bois, W. E. B., 14, 18, 313; on Louisiana politics, 156

Dubuclet, Antoine, 203

Dula, John S., 270

Duncan, George, 279, 358n34

Dunn, Fabius McKay, 204

Dunn, Oscar J., 93, 130, 151, 324; break with Warmoth and, 156; Custom House faction and, 156–58; death of, 158

Dunning, William A., 110

Dupleix, Louis, 63, 118–19, 141–42, 171, 183; bridge contract and, 144; White League and, 184

Dupré, Charles, 90, 129

Durand, Victor, 91, 141–42

Durant, Thomas J., 16, 39, 165

Durell, Edward H., 14, 257, 266

East Feliciana Parish, 45, 270–71; political murders in, 231–32

Elam, J. B., 202

Elks, 324–25

Ellis, E. John, 253, 259, 261

Ellis, Thomas C., 73

Emigration. *See* Blacks: emigration movement and

Emory, William H., 196–97, 204; on Wheeler Compromise, 217

Enforcement Acts, 22, 121, 195, 207, 286, 294, 298–99; repeal of, 313. *See also United States v. Cruikshank*; *United States v. Cunningham*

English Civil War, 70

Escott, Paul D., 18, 70

Evarts, William, 263

Evergreen Baptist Church, 89

Ezernack, Edward, 166, 201, 257, 304

Ezernack, Joseph, 92, 226

Fairfax, Alfred, 299

Farmers and Laborers Mutual Union (Natchitoches Parish), 308

Faulkner, Richard, 37, 113–14, 120, 129, 279; Tax Reform Association and, 186

Field, A. P., 40, 80, 195

Fifteenth Amendment, 121

First Baptist Church (Natchitoches), 42, 89, 135; schism in, 315

Fish, Hamilton, 252

Flanders, Benjamin F., 89

Fleming, Walter L., 295

Fletcher, A. J., 97

Flood, Martin, 141

Flowers, Eli H., 239–40

Foner, Eric, 14–15, 18, 127, 326, 333n16

Forsyth, George A., 218

Foster, Murphy J., 311–12

Franklin, John Hope, 229

Franklin Parish, 82, 177

Free blacks, 5–6, 35–36, 116–17, 331–32n3; in New Orleans, 93, 95; in Ohio, 93–95; in Ontario, 93–95; in Toronto, 94–95

Freedmen's Bureau. *See* Bureau of Refugees, Freedmen, and Abandoned Lands

Frisbee, H. N., 209

Fugitive Slave Act (1793), 94

Fullerton, J. Scott, 60

Gair, John, 231, 272

Garfield, James A., 128–29, 208–9, 212, 252, 257; on Louisiana politics, 160

Garza [Garcia], Alex, 255

Gens de couleur. See Free blacks

Gerstle, Gary, 25

Gibson, Randall L., 253, 261

Givanovich, Marco, 6, 27–28, 92, 99, 130, 132

Gleaves, Richard H., 93

Goldstein, Gabriel, 282–83

Gone with the Wind (film, 1939), 103, 329

"Good Darky" statue. *See* "Uncle Jack" statue

Grant, Ulysses S., 1, 21, 23, 71–72; election of 1876 and, 244, 251, 253–54, 256, 258–62; Louisiana and, 204–8, 216, 233, 254–57, 259–66; unpopularity of, 208; use of troops and, 193, 195–97, 207, 232–34, 244, 251, 258

Grant Parish, 239, 247; disputed election in, 175. *See also* Colfax massacre

Gray, Robert, 112, 220

Greeley, Horace, 71; on carpetbaggers, 161; runs for president, 164

Green, George W., 135–36

Greenback-Labor Party, 308

Greneaux, Leon, 226

Guillory, Martin, 29

Hager, John S., 221

Hahn, Michael, 38–39, 51, 83, 96, 151

Haines, Lewis, 141–42

Hall, Françoise, 132

Hall, Jerry, 239–40, 278

Hall, W. P., 275

Hancock, Winfield Scott, 110

Harris, Arthur H., 177

Harris, J. P., 242, 278

Harrison, Benjamin, 306

Hartman, John, 283

Hatch, Edward, 112

Hayes, Rutherford B., 1, 234, 276, 300; conciliation policy of, 265–66, 272–73; election of 1876 and, 243–45, 249–52, 263; election of 1878 and, 289–90

Hays, Harry, 84

Hayward, Ebenezer, 90, 119

Hazen, Alfred, 114, 189

Hearsey, H. J., 275, 288

Henderson, Hamp: lynching of, 219

Henderson, William, 43

Henry, Joseph, 186

Henry, Samuel J., 310–11, 368n1

Hertzog, Cecile, 298

Hertzog, Elcey, 171

Herwig, P. F.: Levee Bill and, 155

Hiestand, Ezra, 97

Hiestand, William H., 97–96, 105, 129

Hoar, George F., 214–15

Hoar Committee, 214–16, 218–20, 223, 227, 229, 290

Hogue, James K, 209

Holmes, P. W., 135, 201

Holt, Joseph, 71

Homer, Bill, 34

Homestead Act (1862), 104

Honor: culture of, 21, 209; oath of allegiance and, 77; "scalawags" and, 173–74, 228

Hornsby, J. R., 286, 290

Horton, "Scabby Face Bill," 255, 361n4

Hosmer, E. H., 114

Houzeau, Jean-Charles, 83

Howard, Charles T., 275

Howard, Oliver, Otis, 48

Howe, Timothy O., 251, 270

Hughes, John C., 97

Hunter, Robert A., 219

Hunter, Thomas, 136

Hurlbut, Stephen A., 39

Hyman, Harold, 152

Hynes, Samuel "Curley-Headed," 191, 249

Insurrection scares, 56–57, 219–30, 282–83, 287

Irish Troubles, 235

Iron-clad oath, 121, 151, 352n5

Isabelle, Robert H., 151

Isle Brevelle, 5–6, 33–36, 117, 120, 129

Israel, Jacob, 91

Jack, William H., 119, 121, 144, 190, 225–26, 228, 268, 277, 283; death of, 318; on taxation, 187

Jackson, Robert H., 328

"Jayhawkers," 29, 55, 80, 117

Jewell, E. L., 205

Johnson, Andrew, 24; Black Codes and, 56; black suffrage and, 52; Civil Rights Bill and Freedmen's Bureau Bill and, 81; compared with Lincoln, 50–52; 1868 election and, 110; Freedmen's Bureau and, 49, 102; initial popularity of, 49; leniency toward ex-Confederates, 71–73,

81, 340n17; Proclamation of Amnesty and Reconstruction of, 48–49; racial attitudes of, 49; Reconstruction Acts and, 100–101; Republican Party and, 52; U.S. Army and, 82

Johnson, E. A., 324–25

Johnson, J. P., 255, 284

Johnson, King, 120

Johnston, Joseph, 72

Jones, Carroll, 36–37, 226, 276

Jones, John, 96–97

Jones, Richard, 96–97

Jones, Robert B., 91–92, 96–97

Joubert, B. F.: on carpetbaggers, 159

"Kansas Fever." *See* Blacks: emigration movement and

Kearney, R. M., 144

Kelley, William D., 40

Kellogg, William P., 168, 174–75, 182, 184–85, 208–9; "bulldozers," appointments of, 271–72; Colfax massacre and, 176; elected Senator, 260; election of 1874 and, 194–95; election of 1876 and, 241, 250, 258; law enforcement and, 271–72; Republican factionalism and, 306, 308; Wheeler Compromise and, 215–17; White League and, 183

Kemp, John, 112

Kennedy, Hugh, 80

Kilbourne, Richard H., 147

King, George, 232

King, Martin Luther, Jr., 328

Kinston, North Carolina, 72

Kissinger, Henry, 273

Knights of Labor: sugar strike of 1887, 307–8

Knights of the White Camelia, 109–13

Ku Klux Klan, 22–23, 109, 113–14, 197, 207, 330

Lacey, George S., 276

Lacour, Coralie, 219

Ladd, C. F., 306–7

Lafayette Parish, 247

Lafourche Parish, 102, 307–8

Lake Providence, 82

Lamar, L. Q. C., 221

Langston, Isaac T., 89

Laws, John, 269

Lee, A. L., 159

Lee, Robert E., 108

Lee, Stannie. *See* Webb, Laura S.

Leet, John E., 266

Leonard, Albert H., 205, 216–17, 266, 288; Natchitoches investigation and, 290, 292, 298–99. *See also United States v. Cunningham*

Leroy, Charles, 36, 90, 129, 279; bridge contract and, 144; Custom House faction and, 158; John G. Lewis and, 95; Republican Party, alienation from, 180, 182, 353n26; Tax Reform Association and, 186

Levisee, Aaron B.: bribery and, 267; Compromise of 1877 and, 253, 261; on Louisiana politics, 160–61; on Wheeler Compromise, 217; on White League, 200

Levy, William M., 88, 106, 119–20, 165, 167, 174, 205, 319, 351n34; David H. Boullt Sr. and, 181; Compromise of 1877 and, 253, 261–62; death of, 318; election of 1878 and, 284; E. L. Pierson and, 216; on Republican factionalism, 162–63

Lewis, Alice, 95

Lewis, James, 324

Lewis, John G., Jr., 321, 323–26

Lewis, John G., Sr., 21–22, 182–83, 272, 314; background of, 92–95; Baptist church and, 213; on blacks' vulnerability, 210; Raford Blunt and, 95, 324, 369n21; on Congressional Reconstruction, 326–27; death of, 320; election of 1872 and, 166–67; election of 1874 and, 200; election of 1876 and, 241–42, 248; election of 1878 and, 280, 284–85; election of 1896 and, 311; emigration movement and, 300; exile from Natchitoches and, 303; Prince Hall Masons and, 303, 323–24; Republican Party and, 95–96; as schoolteacher, 136; threats against, 314, 317; Warmoth faction and, 157

Lewis, Joseph Collins, 93–94, 434n18

Lewis, Scott, 323–24

Lewis, Virginia, 320

Lewis, W. B., 118

Liberal Party, 163–65

Lincoln, Abraham: colonization of blacks and, 335n38; Reconstruction policy of, 26, 36–40, 51, 153; magnanimity of, 71. *See also* Black suffrage

Lodge, Henry Cabot, 312

Longstreet, James, 108, 121, 239

185, 189; Warmoth faction and, 157–58, 164–65

NAACP. *See* National Association for the Advancement of Colored People
Nash, Christopher Columbus, 178, 330
Natchitoches, Parish of: Baptist churches in, 87; black farmers in, 321; black voter registration in (1867), 99–101; Catholic Church and, 7–8; character of, 127–31, 322; Civil War and, 35–36; Congressional Reconstruction and, 1–3, 99; cotton cultivation, 5; criminal justice system and, 137–39; election of April 1868 and, 109; election of November 1868 and, 113–15; election of 1872 and, 165–67, 182; election of 1874 and, 198–203; election of 1876 and, 243–45, 247–50, 256; election of 1878 and, 10–13; election of 1880 and, 304; election of 1888 and, 306; free blacks in, 5–6, 35–37, 332n3; Freedmen's Bureau in, 95, 114, 116, 345n25; French culture of, 3, 5–7, 116–17; history, 3–8; immigration to, 4–5; Jones-Stauffer affair, 96–97; Knights of the White Camelia and, 110–13; NAACP and, 332, 325; native white population in 1860, 4; police jury of, 129, 180, 182, 184, 226, 268, 353n34; public schools in, 134–37, 268; school board of, 135; slavery in, 5, 7–8; special taxes in, 144–46; compared with St. Landry Parish, 116–17; taxes in, 187, 227; violence, relative absence of, 3, 8, 40, 115–19, 255–56, 322; warrants, speculation in, 145–46, 180–81. *See also* Civil War; Democratic Party; Planters; Republican Party; Sharecropping; Tax Reform Association; Unionists, southern; White League
—Natchitoches, town of, 4, 7, 41; city charter of (1872), 146; election of November 1868, 115, 146; election of 1870, 146; election of 1874, 146; election of 1875, 225–26; indebtedness of, 146; parades in, 132; Red River and, 4; school board of, 135
Natchitoches Enterprise, 310–12, 314; racism of, 316–17
Natchitoches People's Vindicator, 12–13, 90, 132, 138, 183, 202, 244, 256, 265, 275; White League and, 186, 196, 205, 295
Natchitoches Republican, 158, 201, 228, 265
Natchitoches Spectator, 105, 107, 113, 120, 122

Natchitoches Times, 40, 45–46, 80, 99, 174, 224; on death of Alfred Hazen, 114–15; black suffrage and, 119; on freedpeople, 62; on Andrew Johnson, 81; on New Orleans riot, 84; on oath of allegiance, 77; on planters, 118; political moderation of, 119
National Association for the Advancement of Colored People, 323–25
National Colored Colonization Society, 300
National Republicans (Louisiana), 308, 310
New Orleans, 3–6, 10, 26, 33, 35, 38–39, 41, 43, 46, 51; Citizens Party, 306; city charter of 1872, 122; city charter of 1875; 1868 election and, 112; Knights of the White Camelia in, 111; police force of, 52, 61, 83–84, 112, 121; Prince Hall Masons in, 93, 95; riot of 1866, 82–84, 119
New Orleans Custom House, 123
New Orleans Daily Democrat, 275, 287–88, 292, 297, 302
New Orleans Daily Picayune, 293
New Orleans Democrat, 230
New Orleans Republican, 230, 265
New Orleans Tribune, 83
Newsham, Joseph P., 80, 121, 363n48
New York Herald, 212
New York Times, 287, 298–99
New York Tribune, 211
Nicholls, Francis T.: conciliation policy, 272–76; denunciation of violence, 237, 269; election of 1876 and, 243–50; election of 1878 and, 287, 299; election of 1888 and, 305–6; Grant and, 254–57; inaugurated as governor, 250–51; nominated by Democrats (1876), 237; Tensas report of, 305
Nixon, Richard M., 273
Nordhoff, Charles, 212, 220
Norrell, Robert J., 65
Norwood, T. M., 220–21
Nystrom, Justin A., 302

Oath of allegiance: during Civil War, 74–75, 81; coercive nature of, 75; false swearing and, 76–77; "honor" and, 77; unreliability of, 75–77
Odd Fellows, 324–25
Ohio: Black Laws of, 94
Opelousas, 56, 101
Osborn, John, 129–30, 142, 144, 180–82

Ouchita Parish, 109, 238, 247
"Ouchita Plan," 304
Ouchita Telegraph, 196

Packard, Stephen B., 155, 257, 265; election
of 1876 and, 241–42, 244–47, 250–52;
Grant and, 254, 258–61; Hayes and,
261–64
Palmer, John, 247
Panic of 1873, 187, 193
Panic of 1893, 309
Parker, James, 105
Parker, John M., 316
Parson(s), Samuel, 27, 91, 129, 186
Patton, Isaac W., 237
Payne, Charles, 283
Payne, William, 45, 134, 226
People's Party. *See* Populists
Perman, Michael, 205, 235, 312
Perrow, Benjamin, 314
Pharr, John N., 310, 312
Phillips, Edward, 91
Phillips, Wendell, 71
Phillips, William B., 177, 239–40
Pickett, George, 72
Pierrepont, Edwards, 232–33
Pierson, Aaron H., 115
Pierson, David, 12, *108*, 144, 174, 197–98,
226, 272, 318–19; Raford Blunt and,
191–92; death of, 319; election of 1872
and, 175; election of 1876 and, 243–44,
249–50, 256, 258, 262; election of 1878
and, 284; Hoar Committee and, 215, 220;
Tax Reform Association and, 184, 186,
188
Pierson, Edward L., 140, 184, 190–91, 225,
227; character of, 215–16, 228; death of,
230, 358n47; elected mayor of Natchitoches, 146; election of 1872 and, 165–67;
election of 1874 and, 200–201; Hoar
Committee and, 215–16; quarrel with
Cosgrove, 228–30
Pierson, Joseph, 186
Pinchback, Pinkney Benton Stewart, 15,
130–31, 155, 260, 272; on blacks' vulnerability, 210; on Congressional Reconstruction, 327; emigration movement
and, 301; Republican factionalism and,
158, 162, 306; U.S. Senate, rejection by,
209
Pinkston, Eliza, 247

Pitcher, Maru, 318
Pitkin, J. R. G., 246, 249, 259, 261, 266, 270
Plaisance, C., 45–46
Plaisance, J. B., 226
Planters, 41–42; cheating by, 44–46, 139–42;
Chinese immigrants and, 46–47; debts
of, 44–45, 140; emigration movement
and, 302; labor contracts and, 43–44,
132–34, 140; political pressure on em-
ployees by, 277; sharecropping and, 134,
140–43
Plaquemines Parish, 312
Plessy v. Ferguson, 328
Pollard, Edward A., 65, 69, 109
Ponder, W. A., 191
Pope, Henry, 112
Pope, John, 75
Populists, 309–13; black officeholding and,
310; black voters and, 309–11; in Loui-
siana, 309–12; in Natchitoches Parish,
310–12; in North Carolina, 309
Porter, Charles, 282
Powell, Lawrence N., 122, 224
Powers, Frank, 271
Presidential Reconstruction. *See* Johnson,
Andrew; Lincoln, Abraham
Prince Hall Masons, 93–96, 307–8; Corin-
thian Lodge No. 17 (Cincinnati), 9; Co-
rinthian Lodge No. 19 (Natchitoches);
Dawn of Light No. 22 (Natchitoches),
Dawn of Light Printing Company, 324;
Eureka Grand Lodge (Louisiana), 93,
303, 320, 323; Grand Lodge of Ohio,
93; Louisiana Farmers Union and, 324;
NAACP and, 324–25; in Ontario, 93, 95;
Parsons Lodge No. 5 (New Orleans),
303; Reconstruction and, 324; Rich-
mond Lodge No. 4 (New Orleans), 93;
Shreveport lodge, 324
Prudhomme, Gabriel, 47, 133
Puckette, C. J. C., 171; 1872 election and,
174–75; Republican Party and, 224, 227
Pugh, Mary, 307

Raby, Henry, 92, 182–83, 241, 319–20; death
of, 320; emigration movement and, 300;
Warmoth faction and, 157, 164–65
Racism, 23–24, 107–8, 123–25, 221, 299,
316–17, 326; decline of, 327–28
Radical Republicans, 19–20, 26, 39–40,
49–50, 52–54

Raines, Sam, 281–82
Rapides Parish, 28–29, 59, 74; Knights of the White Camelia and, 113
Rapides Tribune, 113
Reconstruction. *See* Congressional Reconstruction; Johnson, Andrew; Lincoln, Abraham
Reconstruction Acts (1867), 98; black voter registration and, 98–101; white voter registration and, 99–101
Redmond, William H., 135, 166; defalcation of, 146–47, 182–83
Red River News, 111, 113, 122, 350n23
Red River Parish: political violence in, 232
Reform Party, 163–64
Register, R. C., 177
Rehn, George, 91
Reid, Joe, 289
Republican Party, 15–16, 264–66, 349n47; "black-and-tan" faction, 308; black laborers and, 139–43; black ministers and, 278–79; black suffrage and, 36–49, 84, 107–8; Compromise of 1877; consequences of, 264–66; corruption issue and, 151–62, 213, 350n15; Custom House faction, 154, 156–62, 241; election of 1874 and, 193–95, 214, 355n16; election of 1876 and, 240–43; election of 1878 and, 288; factionalism in, 19–20, 149, 154–62, 260, 306; federalism and, 22, 25, 179, 235; Freedmen's Bureau agents in, 153; freedpeople and, 127–28; French language and, 129–30; Hoar Committee and, 214–16; idealism and, 150, 161; land question and, 103–4, 107; law enforcement and, 271–22; "lily-white" faction, 308, 310, 313; loss of state power, 193; "mixed tickets" and, 307, 311; northern migrants in, 14, 149–54, 172, 265; political manipulations of, 151; political patronage and, 122–23, 305–6, 308; Populists and, 309–12; reform and, 226–27; reputation of, 161; split in party, 157; state militia and, 121, 160, 176, 178, 184, 195–96, 205, 209, 217, 239, 260–62; sugar planters and, 307, 310; taxation and, 187–88; in twentieth century, 321; vulnerability of, 19–22, 109–10, 205, 209–11, 260; white southerners in, 14, 177–78, 265–66
—Republican Party, Natchitoches Parish:

armed self-defense and, 230; black officeholding and, 129–31, 346–47n7; black support for, 127; "bulldozing," effects on, 272; compromise of 1873 and, 176, 352n14; constitutional convention (1867–68) and, 97; corruption issue and, 143–47, 212; death of E. L. Pierson and, 230; election of 1872 and, 157–58, 164–67; election of 1874 and, 200–203; election of 1876 and, 241–43; election of 1878 and, 288–89; election of 1880 and, 304; election of 1884 and, 307, 309; election of 1888 and, 305–6; election of 1896 and, 309–12; ex-slaveholders and, 91–92; Freedmen's Bureau and, 130; freedom of movement and, 131–33; French language and, 129–30; *gens de couleur* and, 129–30; immigrants in, 91; Independence Day rally (1868), 105–6; intimidation of voters by, 278–79; murder of Stauffer and, 96–97; organization of, 90–98; patronage and, 157; police jury and, 226; Populists and, 309–12; public schools and, 134–37; after Reconstruction, 304–13; siege mentality of, 230; split in party and, 157–58, 164; Unionists in, 91, 97, 346n7; white southerners in, 91–92, 129–31, 171–72, 224–25, 289, 346–47n7; white support, lack of, 127
Returning Board, 122, 216, 236, 268, 313; election of 1872 and, 165, 167–68, 226; election of 1874 and, 202, 214, 355n16; election of 1876 and, 244–50, 256
Robinson, Navile A., 92, 105, 129, 172; Custom House faction and, 158
Rodrigue, John C., 322
Rost, Emile, 28, 47
Roudanez, Jean Baptiste, 38
Rousseau, Lovell, 112
Russell, W. E., 189
Ryan, Michael P., 121

Sabine Parish, 115, 200, 202, 243
"Scalawags," 123, 320; definition of, 173; honor and, 173–74, 228; ostracism of, 173. *See also* Republican Party: white southerners in
Scanland, J. M., 113, 120
Schools. *See* Natchitoches, Parish of: public schools in
Schuler, Hans, 317

264; attempted murder of, 232; on E. L. Pierson, 215–16
"298," 295, 298

"Uncle Jack" statue, *316*, 317–18, 330, 370n32
Unification Movement, 195–96
Unionists, southern, 78–79, 121; black suffrage and, 81, 83; hostility toward, 79–81; in Natchitoches Parish, 27–28, 80, 289, 346–47n7; in Rapides Parish, 28–29; small numbers of, 78; in Winn Parish, 29
Union Parish, 123
United Confederate Veterans, 319
United Daughters of the Confederacy, 318, 368–69n8
United States v. Cruikshank, 178–80, 194–95, 235
United States v. Cunningham, 293–99; jury in, 297
Universal Declaration of Human Rights, 327

Vandal, Gilles, 80, 139
Varner, Florence, 315, 368n1
Vienne, Frank, 132
Vienne, John B., 90, 129, 289
Violence: banditry and, 80, 117, 138; against blacks, 57–58; against black soldiers, 58; Cincinnati riots, 94; Colfax massacre, 175–76; Coushatta murders, 190; defense of by Democrats, 218–21, 268; dueling, 174, 229–39; 1868 elections and, 106–10; homicides, 136–38; incitements to, 109; Jones-Stauffer affair, 96–97; lynching and, 219, 322; New Orleans riot (1866), 82–84; personal quarrels and, 97, 138, 169–71, 204, 224, 358–59n48; by planters, 45; political murders and, 112, 177, 190, 206–7, 211, 217–18, 231–32, 238, 269; in Red River valley, 3, 40, 58–59, 82, 194, 218, 210, 220, 232; "Regulators," 232; Republican factionalism and, 159–60; St. Landry Parish and, 116–17; Texas and, 219, 255

Wade, Benjamin F., 40
Wall, Thomas W., 27
Wallace, Ambrose, 298, 300
Walmsley, G. S., 46

Walsh, J. J., 153
Walsh, John A., 155
Ward, William, 239–40, 278–79
Warmoth, Henry Clay, 16, 109, 126, *149*, 260, 267; black support of, 164; black voters and, 156, 154; on corruption, 150; Democratic Party and, 156, 161–62; election of November 1868 and, 110, 112; election of 1872 and, 163–65, 167; election of 1888 and, 305–6; election of 1896 and, 312; election laws and, 121–22, 157, 159, 165; Grant and, 164; Kellogg and, 195; killing of D. C. Byerly and, 204; patronage and, 156–57; political behavior characterized, 146–47, 152; state militia and, 121, 160; strong-arm tactics of, 160
Washburn, W. W., 278
Washington, Booker T., 314
Washington, Ella, 35
Washington, George, 154
Watson, James, 207, 220
Webb, Laura S., 68, 340n12
Weber, D. A., 246; murder of, 269
Webster Parish, 247
Welles, Gideon, 51
Wells, James Madison, 96, 121; bribery and, 267; candidate for Congress, in 1878, 294–95; 1866 New Orleans election and, 81; election of 1876 and, 245–46, 248–50, 256; election as governor, 79–80; former Confederates and, 51–54, 81; Johnson and, 53–55; oath of allegiance and, 77; political shifts of, 148; prosecution of, 276; removal from office, 99. *See also* Returning Board
West, J. R., 246, 249, 265
West Feliciana Parish, 246, 269–70, 276
West Feliciana Sentinel, 268
West-Kimball gang, 138
Wharton, Jack, 202, 257, 266, 287–88, 365n48; on White League, 196
Wheeler Compromise, 216–17, 221, 223–24, 227
Wheyland, Walter R.: death of, 160
White, Delos C., 102, 239
White, Edward D., 305
White League, 203–4, 208–9, 221, 238; in Caddo Parish, 205; in Natchitoches, 184–90, 205; in New Orleans, 183–84, 196–97, 205–7; in Red River Parish, 186, 190

White primary, 310
Whites. *See* Democratic Party; Planters; Racism; Republican Party; Unionists, southern; Violence
Wickliffe, George M., 112
Wickliffe, Robert C., 238
Williams, George H., 176–77, 194, 197, 217
Williams, John R., 191
Williams, Rachel, 290
Wilmer, J. P. B., 218–19

Wiltz, Louis, 275
Windom, William, 300
Winn Parish, 29, 92, 102, 109, 115, 203, 226; banditry in, 138
Woods, William W., 178, 293, 296–97
Woodward, C. Vann, 18, 261–62
Woodward, Alfred, 184
Wyatt-Brown, Bertram, 173

Yellow fever: epidemic of 1878, 280, 285, 287, 293

ADAM FAIRCLOUGH is professor emeritus at Leiden University, where he held the Raymond and Beverly Sackler Chair of American History and Culture from 2005 until 2016. He studied modern history at Oxford University (B.A., 1974) and received his Ph.D. in American studies from Keele University in 1977. He is the author of seven other books, including *To Redeem the Soul of America: The Southern Christian Leadership Conference and Martin Luther King, Jr.*; *Race and Democracy: The Civil Rights Struggle in Louisiana, 1915–1972*; *Better Day Coming: Blacks and Equality, 1890–1970*; and *A Class of Their Own: Black Teachers in the Segregated South*.

Printed in the United States
By Bookmasters